HUNGER AND POVERTY IN SOUTH ASIA

HUNGER AND POVERTY IN SOUTH ASIA

J. ALBERT RORABACHER

GYAN

Hunger and Poverty in South Asia

Rs. 980

ISBN: 978-81-212-1027-0

Published in 2010 in India by
Gyan Publishing House
23, Main Ansari Road, Darya Ganj,
New Delhi-110002
Phones : 23282060, 23261060
Fax : 011-23285914
E-mail: books@gyanbooks.com
Website: www.gyanbooks.com

Lasser Type Setting by: Rudra Computer Graphics, Delhi
Printed at : GIAN RIDHI OFFSET PRINTERS

Dedication

To Hava, my friend, my guide, and my guardian; and without whom this book could never have been realized

Contents

List of Boxes

List of Figures

List of Illustrations

List of Maps

List of Tables

Abbreviations, Acronyms, and Glossary

ABPSD	AgriBusiness Promotion and Statistics, Division Statistical (Nepal)
ABSP	Agricultural Biotechnology Support Project
Africa	Sub-Saharan Africa
AGRA	Alliance for a Green Revolution in Africa
AU	African Union
BHC	Alpha-hexachlorohexane
BIS	Bureau of Indian Standards
BP	Best Practices
BTRC	Bangladesh Telecommunication Regulatory Commission
CABIO	Collaborative Agriculture Biotechnology Initiative
CAF	Corporate Agriculture Farming
CBS	Central Bureau of Statistics (Nepal)
CGIAR	Consultative Group on International Agricultural Research
CIMMYT	The International Maize and Wheat Improvement Center – better known by its Spanish-language acronym CIMMYT, from *Centro Internacional de Mejoramiento de Maíz y Trigo*
CIS	Countries of the Commonwealth of Independent States, formerly the USSR
CPI	FAO Cereal Price Index
CPN(M)	Communist Party of Nepal, Maists
Cr. (Crore)	Equals 10,000,000

CRED	Center for Research on the Epidemiology of Disasters
CSE	Centre for Science and Environment
D&PLC	Delta and Pine Land Company
DAC	Development Assistance Committee
DDA	Doha Development Agenda
EFTA	European Free Trade Agreement
FAO	Food and Agriculture Organization of the United Nations
FAP	Flood Action Plan (Bangladesh)
FTA	Free Trade Agreement
GDP	Gross Domestic Product
GE	Genetic Engineering
GHI	Global Hunger Index
GM	Genetic Modification
GMO	Genetically modified organism or Genetic modification organizations
GNP	Gross National Product
GoB	Government of Bangladesh
GoI	Government of India
GoN	Government of Nepal
GoP	Government of Pakistan
GURT	Genetic Use Restriction Technologies
HCH	Synonym for BHC
HDI	Human Development Index
HDR	Human Development Report
HPI	Human Poverty Index
HYV	High Yielding Variety
IDRC	International Development Research Centre
IFFCO	Indian Farmers Fertilizer Cooperative, Ltd.
IFPRI	International Food Policy Research Institute
IGKV	Indira Gandhi Krishi Vidyalaya
IITA	International Institute of Tropical Agriculture
IK	Indigenous Knowledge
IPGRI	The International Plant Genetic Resources Institute
IPR	Intellectual Property Rights
IRRI	International Rice Research Institute
ISAAA	International Service for the Acquisition of Agri-biotech Applications

ISDR	International Strategy for Disaster Reduction
ISPs	Internet Service Providers
IUCN	International Union for the Conservation of Nature
Kharif	Summer cropping season. Planting, March to May; harvest June to October
Lakh	Equals 100,000
LMOs	Living modified organisms
MOAC	Ministry of Agriculture and Cooperatives (Nepal)
MSP&PP	Minimum Support Price and Procurement Price
Mt	Metric tonnes, 1,000 kg or 2,200 lbs.
NAP	National Agricultural Policy of 1999, Bangladesh
NARC	Nepal Agricultural Research Council
NEPAD	New Partnership for Africa's Development
NGO	Non-Government Organization
NREGS	National Rural Employment Guarantee Scheme
OCHA	United Nations Office for the Coordination of Humanitarian Affairs
OECD	Organization for Economic Co-operation and Development
OFDA	Office of Foreign Disaster Assistance of the USAID
POPs	Persistent Organic Pollutants
PSTN	*Public Switched Telephone Network*
Quintal	100 kg
Rabi	Winter cropping season. Planting, November to February; harvest, March to June
RNA	Royal Nepal Army
RNF	Rural Non-Farm
SACU	Southern Africa Customs Union
SAWTEE	South Asian Watch on Trade, Economics, and Environment
SSA	Sub-Saharan Africa
Taka	*Basic unit of Bangladesh currency*
T-GURT	Genetic Trait Control
TRIPS	Trade-related aspects of intellectual property rights
UN	United Nations
UNCTAD	*United Nations Conference on Trade and Development*
UNDP	United Nations Development Programme
UNWFP	*United Nations World Food Programme*

UPOV	International Union for the Protection of New Varieties of Plants
USAID	United States Agency for International Development
USDA	United States Department of Agriculture
VDC	Village Development Committee, Nepal
WHO	World Health Organization
WIPO	World Intellectual Property Organization

Preface

This book is the result of a challenge leveled at the author by the Gyan Publishing House. An earlier volume, that could easily have been and was characterized as being esoteric, prompted the challenge. The test was to both expand the book's scope, geographically, and, at the same time, reduce its esoteric character. As the editing process began, an entirely new topic seemed to emerge. It was geographically much broader and, more importantly, it was much more relevant, regarding the human condition in the modern world. *Hunger and Poverty in South Asia* is the product of that challenge.

The endnotes list most of the works used in the course of the book's compilation but represent only the tip of the iceberg, so to speak, with regard to the works consulted during its preparation. From these other books, articles, and websites, ideas were gleaned and subsequently germinated into new ideas. For those of you that have gone unacknowledged, I apologize.

I hope that this volume stimulates the reader to explore much more deeply the problems that are discussed herein, with each justifiably representing a book in itself. An effort has been made to provide an overview of the problems and the interconnectedness of hunger and poverty. It also attempts to underscore the fact that a broad range of factors contribute to each of these problems – historical, cultural, political, economic, and environmental. There is no one simple cause or solution. Within each village, state, nation, and region, the problems of hunger and poverty manifest themselves in very different ways but there are also unifying themes. It is these themes that we have sought to uncover here, even if only to scratch the surface.

In one respect or another, everyone I have ever met, as well as all I have ever read contributed to this book. No book is ever solely the work of the author. Much of the matrix of this book was passed on to me by my mentor, Joseph E. Schwartzberg, many years ago. I am only sorry that it took me so long to realize just how much he had so freely given me. His consummate humanitarianism and concern for his fellow man are legion, especially toward the people of South Asia. With the publication of this volume, I hope to bridge a portion of the gap that time and distance have created.

No literary effort, no matter what its genre, is created in a vacuum. There are always those unsung heroes that frequently toil and receive little or no recognition. First among those on this list is Hava Rorabacher, my wife. Many is the night she went to bed alone while I 'worked' on. I owe her a great debt of gratitude. Her support, although often given by default, was nonetheless indispensible. Ilona 'Nona' Gardner was an indefatigable ally in the current effort, as she has been with all my writings. While I toiled with the words and ideas, she helped me transform them into something that was both informative and readable. Without her, this book would never have come to fruition. It would have remained random thoughts and mental ramblings, without form or style. Finally, I want to thank Amit Garg for setting me, unknowingly, on the current journey.

John A. Rorabacher

Barrie, Ontario, Canada

1

The Problem

Map 1-1: Global Hunger in Sub-Saharan Africa and South Asia

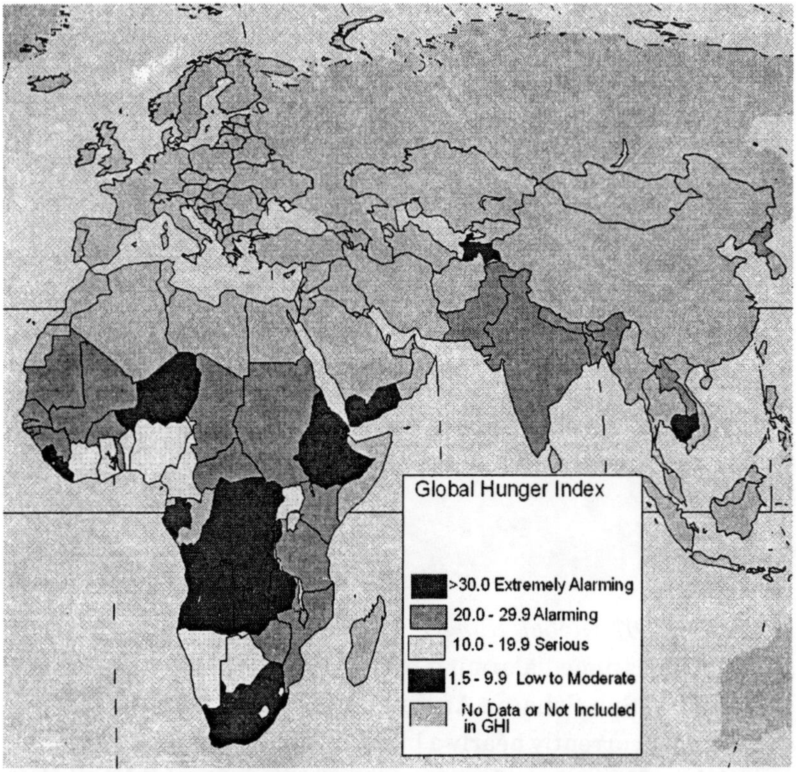

Source: Modified from (Wiesmann, Doris, et. al., October 2007)

Introduction

Until recently, one in seven people went to bed hungry every night. Consequently, hunger is possibly one of the world's preeminent problems. In 2009, it became one in six. There are those that would argue that global warming, air pollution, water pollution, population growth, or AIDS are more important concerns. However, it is difficult for someone suffering from the effects of malnutrition, the mother of a child suffering from *Kwashiorkor*, or some one who has been reduced to skin and bone, to have much interest in whether or not the polar ice caps are melting. Starvation changes one's priorities, perceptions, and perspectives. It is difficult to be concerned with abstract world problems when your stomach is empty.

Illustration 1-1: Mother and Child: Victims of Famine, Ethiopia

The *2007 Global Hunger Index Report* tells us that world hunger has assumed alarming proportions in 36 countries – 25 of which are in Sub-Saharan Africa and 9 in Asia.[1] Recent estimates suggest that currently nearly a billion people suffer, and 30 million people die of hunger each year, most of whom are children.[2] How do we reconcile these numbers? How do we put them in perspective?

One billion people represents approximately $1/7^{th}$ of the world's total population. Thirty million deaths each year means that, of the 221 recognized countries in the world, only 39 have populations larger than the number of people who die of starvation each year. In other words, 82.3 percent of all the countries in the world have smaller populations than die due to malnutrition each year!

Nearly half of the world's hungry live in India, an estimated 350-plus million, and that number may have increased by more than 50 million due to increases in world food prices just during the period 2008-09. World Bank Group President Robert B. Zoellick recently commented:

For 2 billion people, high food prices are now a matter of daily struggle, sacrifice and for too many, even survival. We estimate that already some 100 million people may have been pushed into poverty as a result of high prices over the last 2 years. This is not a natural disaster. Make no mistake, there is nothing natural about this. But for millions of people it is a disaster.[3]

Most of the other half of the world's chronically hungry live in Sub-Saharan Africa (hereafter, simply Africa). The people of Africa are the poorest and most food insecure people in the world, and from all indications, their condition is worsening. Many of the causes of hunger and poverty in Africa are similar to those in South Asia but some are quite unique to Africa.

Food and Famine

In terms of absolute food production, the world currently produces enough food to feed everyone. World agriculture produces roughly 17 percent more calories per person today, more than it did 30 years ago, and this was accomplished at the same time the world's population grew nearly 70 percent. There is sufficient food produced to provide every person with at least 2,720 kilocalories per day.[4]

If surplus of calories are being produced, why do we still have world hunger? The problem is not production but rather:

(1) Food is unevenly distributed throughout the world;
(2) Existing food is not readily redistributed;
(3) Like any other commodity, food is not available cost free, and most importantly,
(4) Many people are too poor to purchase the food that is available.

Famines occur when available food is not redistributed for economic or political reasons. It is not caused solely by a decline in production. During famine, food frequently remains either on shop shelves or in storage facilities, where it oftentimes spoils, rots, or is consumed by vermin. During drought or periods of flooding, cultivators frequently lose their crops. Crops, for many cultivators, represent the food they eat. These are subsistence cultivators. For others, there are no crops to sell. Neither group has the money necessary to purchase the food they need. Likewise, small artisans and craftsmen either have no raw materials or customers. Without the income that comes from farming and related activities, entire communities can collapse economically. Food may be available in the market but with no income, it cannot be obtained. In areas where food is, in fact, scarce, demand causes prices to rise, placing the poor at an even greater economic disadvantage.

In a normal, competitive supply and demand market situation, food will be removed from any area where there are few or no legitimate buyers to areas where there are buyers. As a consequence, the food needed in famine-struck areas is frequently removed to other markets for purely economic reasons. Unless governments step in, and stabilize prices and supplies of food, hunger can quickly turn into starvation and death.

If we are to address world hunger, we must also address world poverty. It does not matter if we increase food production a thousand-fold. If we do not address world poverty, hunger will continue because people will still not be able to purchase the food they need.[5] The solution, then, is to enable the poor to either produce more food or empower them to buy it.

Local situations are made all the more difficult by market prices that are frequently controlled, not by local supply and demand, but by large multinational food corporations. Oxfam Canada states, categorically:

Today, six or fewer companies control around 70 percent of the world's agricultural commodity trade. More and more of the food we eat is owned and controlled by food multinational corporations who dominate every sector from seed to transportation to processed [foods]. Multinational companies make money at every step in the food production chain – at the expense of the small farmers who produce the food and people who pay more money each year to eat a less diverse and more processed diets.[6]

If we accept the principle that poverty is the foremost cause of hunger, what problems contribute to impoverishment? Among the most 'visible' causes are:

- War and armed conflict;[7]
- The vagaries of nature that result in famine;[8]
- Environmental degradation;[9]
- Low *per capita* agricultural productivity;[10]
- Land rights;[11] and
- Changes in plant/crop bio-diversity.[12]

The question is how did we get to the position where the world produces sufficient foodstuffs for every man, woman and child and, yet, one in six people still goes to bed hungry every night. Equally important is the question of why so many poor and hungry people are concentrated in Africa and South Asia?

Part of the answer to both of these questions lies in the respective histories of these regions. According to the Nobel Prize-winner, Amartya Sen, governance plays an important role in the pattern of poverty and hunger. Sen suggests that:

In the terrible history of famines in the world, there is hardly any case in which a famine has occurred in a country that is independent and democratic with an uncensored press . ...The persistence of severe famines in many of the sub-Saharan African countries – both with 'left-wing' and 'right-wing' governments – relates closely to the lack of democratic political systems and practice.[13]

In countries where there are regular and free elections, public action has much to do with the prevention of famine and starvation. Since government policy and action has a direct impact on the mobilization of food resources, free elections serve to reward or penalize politicians and makes them accountable. Therefore, the practice of democracy seems to ensure that people have the power to affect change, and this plays an important part in preventing hunger; although it may not, necessarily, end poverty. However, the effectiveness of government does have an impact on the delivery of socio-economic outcomes for the poor. Sen further points out that, before India became a free nation, famines were commonplace.

In fact, one of the worst famines in Indian history – the Bengal Famine of 1943, which killed approximately 1.9 million people – was the last catastrophic famine in India. Thereafter, there have been famines but they have always been limited in their effects and duration. The decline in the number and duration of famines in India, Sen attributes to India's democratic system of governance, not to increased food production.

Food is almost always available. The worst effects of famine result when food stocks are not mobilized and redistributed among the needy. When it is not mobilized, people suffer, go hungry, and even starve to death. The failure of governments to mobilize and respond to crop and economic failure is ultimately the root cause of long-term human suffering in famine areas.

Governance also involves the efficient and equitable management of resources and revenues. It involves the provision

Map 1-2: Extreme Poverty Map

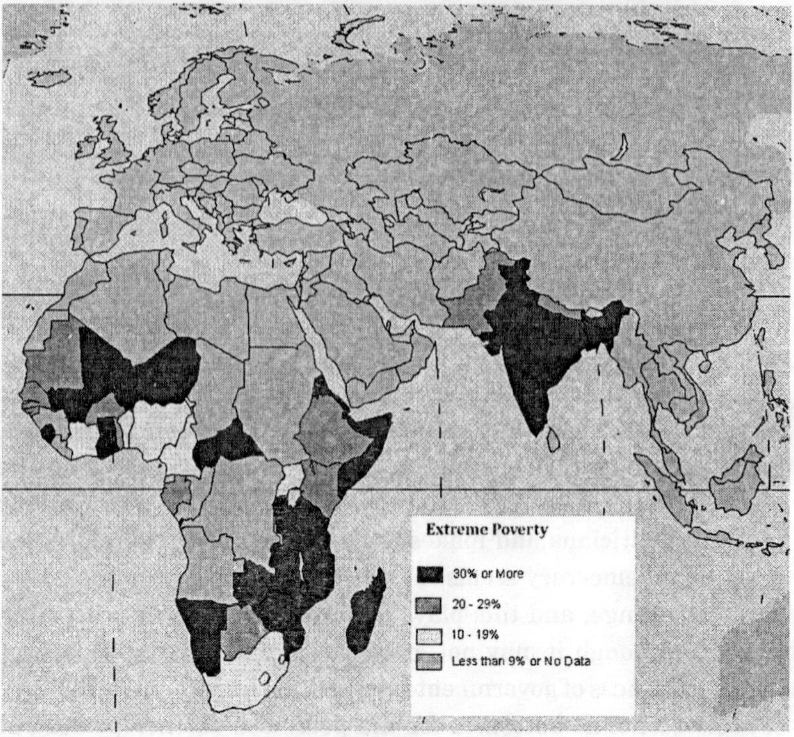

Source: Adapted and modified from FAO Poverty Map.

of essential infrastructures. Failure to provide or maintain adequate infrastructures, generally exacerbates poverty.[14] Likewise, the government's ability to provide educational opportunities, especially as regards literacy, tends to either perpetuate or reduce the cycle of poverty. Finally, governmental corruption can effectively undermine all efforts to eliminate national poverty. Either the squandering or the theft of national treasuries have both short- and long-term consequences for nation-building and the elimination of poverty and hunger.[15]

Some Background

Immediately following World War II, the world was beset by a series of monumental problems, including:

- Decolonization and post-colonial nation-building.
- Rapidly growing population.
- Growing food shortages.

Decolonization

In 1945, many Western European nations maintained colonial possessions, primarily in Africa and Asia. Among these were Great Britain (the United Kingdom), France, Portugal, Spain, the Netherlands, and Belgium. Although the process of decolonization continues today, within less than twenty years, most of the colonial possessions of these European colonial powers had become free and independent nations. Currently only France and Great Britain continue to retain possession of colonies, primarily in the Caribbean, South America and the southwest Pacific.

If one compares Map 1-1, 1-2, and 1-3, it becomes clear that, at least on the surface, a pattern exists between current levels of poverty and hunger and colonialism, especially as it reflects on British and French colonialism.

Post-Colonial Nation Building

Among the first nations granted independence following WW II was India. India was almost immediately faced with the task of building a nation and, at the same time, it was beset with the problems of food shortages, the result of a rapidly growing population and low agricultural productivity. For reasons of political economy, the founding fathers of Indian democracy had to immediately address

Map 1-3: Colonialism, 1945

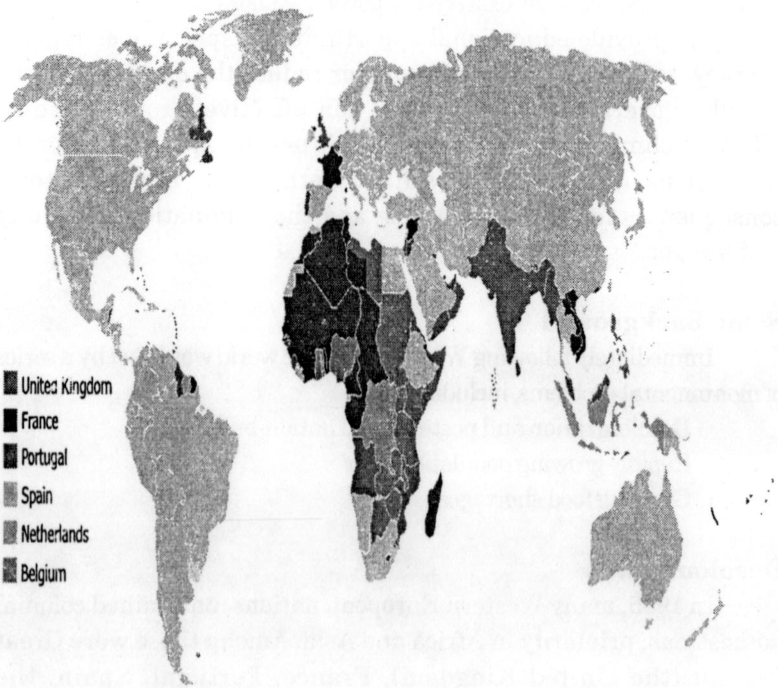

Source: (Katsaris, 2005).

the consequences of persistent famine, near famine, and hunger. Failure to feed the population would only lead to political unrest – protests, riots, outright rebellion and the real possibility that the newly integrated nation would disintegrate into a number of ethno-linguistic states.[16]

In the absence of a modern, highly productive agricultural sector, the Indian government was forced to import massive quantities of the essential foodgrains, wheat and rice. Through the United States' PL-480 program, millions of tonnes of grain were imported and paid for using Rupees. This strategy served as a food palliative for India's immediate food needs and reduced the threat to the nation's nascent democracy.

Similar problems were faced by almost every nation following independence. The first order of business for each nation was to simultaneously build a functioning nation state and, at the same time, feed its people. Some nations were politically and economically more successful than others. In some cases, the legacy or failure of the newly free nations to politically stabilize themselves has led to a legacy of political unrest and unending civil war.

Food Shortages

The Green Revolution was a technological response to growing world-wide food shortages that resulted as a consequence of the widespread introduction and use of modern medical practices after WW II. Modern medical practices, while not necessarily preventing diseases, served to reduce the death rates and insured that children lived to adulthood. Life expectancy began to increase; and with it more adults lived to reproduce. Although death rates declined, the crude birthrate remained unchanged.

History has conditioned most peasant societies to believe that it is necessary to have many children in the hopes that enough would survive to adulthood to insure the family's well-being. Even though medicine had extended life expectancies, it did not change the peasantry's belief in having large families. The end result was a rapid growth in world population. Population growth rates would not stabilize in many countries until the peasantry genuinely realized that it was possible to have fewer children and still meet the family's social and economic needs.

In many newly created, post-war countries, like India, population growth rates surged beyond the land's carrying capacity in the 1950s. The inability of India's cultivators to increase gross production or *per capita* productivity, combined with droughts in the mid-1960s, and threatened widespread famine.[17]

It was recognized that there needed to be a massive increase in agricultural production and productivity but neither the technology nor infrastructures existed that would permit these increases. The Green Revolution served to relieve the immediate specter of famine through a systematic implementation of a program that focused on a 'package of practices,' which included mechanization, the increased use of pesticides, herbicides and fertilizers, the use of hybridized plant types, and the application of irrigation.[18]

While the increases in production and *per capita* productivity were nothing short of miraculous, they were not realized without trade-offs. Over the last quarter century, we have seen a marked decrease in the number of plant varieties available to agriculture. Roughly 8 percent of all know plant food varieties are currently being utilized; and only 12 plant species and 5 animal species account for 75 percent of the world's food supply!

Dependence on a narrow genetic plant base makes the world's food supply vulnerable to both disease and climatic change.[19] Man's food supply, like no time before in human history, is dependent upon an agricultural base that has shrunken in terms of its diversity. If ever there were a sword of Damocles hanging over mankind's head, it would be our dependence on an ever-shrinking genetic agricultural base.

Production Increases

Due to their ability to respond to the application of high dosages of fertilizer, when combined with reliable sources of water, and their ability to produce two, and sometimes three crops a year, high-yielding seed varieties increased overall agricultural production. The production of rice and wheat in many developing countries increased by 75 percent between 1965 and 1980, with only a 20 percent increase in the area planted in these crops. The ability to harvest two crops a year with the new seeds contributed to these increases.[20] In India, production more than doubled between 1960 and 1993.

HYVs spread rapidly. By the mid-1980s, roughly 50 percent of the wheat and nearly 60 percent of the rice sown in developing countries were improved strains. In India, with less than 100 hectares sown in HYVs in 1965, over 50 million hectares were sown in HYVs by 1980; and in Punjab, the proportion of wheat and rice sown in HYVs was 96 percent and 95 percent, respectively, in 1978-79.[21]

Additionally, there were few improved seed varieties for most other crops until the 1980s. Included in this latter group were pulses, *jowar, bajra, ragi*, small millets, barley, cotton, oilseeds, jute, *mesta*, and tobacco. Today improved seed varieties have become entrenched and represent the backbone of many developing nations' agricultural successes *and* failures.

In 1985, Michael Lipton wrote:

If the farmers of the third world today used the same cereal varieties as in 1963-64, and everything else remained unchanged, then tens of millions of people would this year die of hunger.[22]

Population Growth

When population growth exceeds the carrying capacity of the land, or an environment, the result is overpopulation. Famine has traditionally been the primary indicator that the equilibrium between human numbers and the carrying capacity of the land has become unbalanced. Such is the case in much of South Asia and Africa.

World population growth, between 1950 and 2005, represents a period unprecedented in human history. During this period, world population grew 156.2 percent. Much of this growth occurred in Asia. Population grew at a much slower rate in Africa, Europe, Latin America, North America, and Oceania, during the same period. See Figure 1-1, below.

Figure 1-1: World Population Growth, 1950- 2005

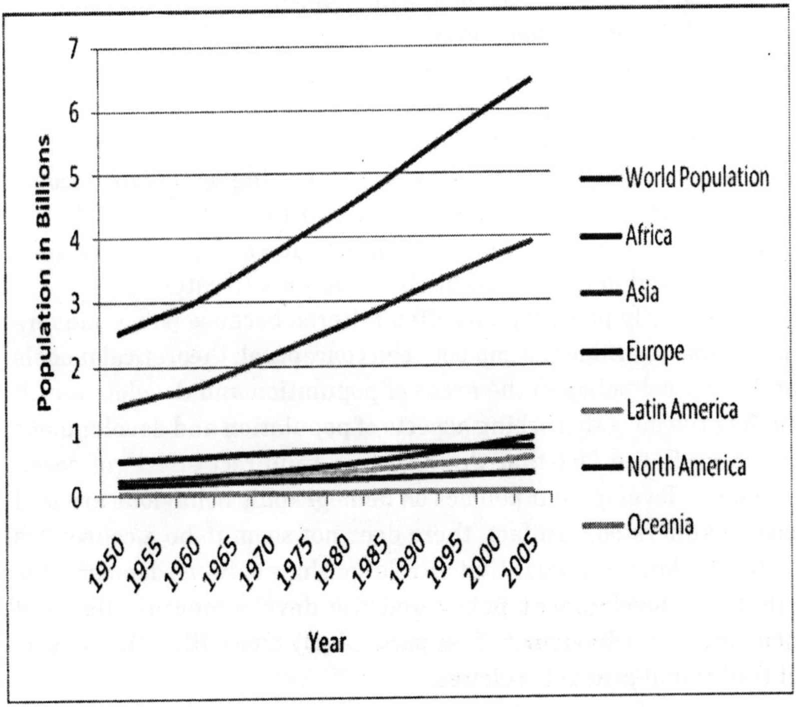

Population Growth and Development

Population growth can be viewed as a boon or the bane of economic development, depending on whether it is seen as the motive force behind the development process or as an impediment.[23] These polarized assessments of population growth's effects have evolved from a recent propensity of academics and planners to reconsider the very meaning of the term "development." Not until the early 1970s was the term "development" detached from the concept that it is solely a function of aggregate economic growth. More recently, development has taken on a much broader interpretation. Now, most discussions of development include questions of absolute poverty, growing inequality, and rising under- and unemployment, as well as aggregate growth in gross national product (GNP), but more commonly gross domestic product (GDP).

Most economists and planners see rapid population growth as an impediment to development. Uncontrolled population growth generally slows economic growth in the following ways:

- By outpacing food production capabilities and increasing the dependency-ratio.
- By increasing under- and unemployment.
- By lowering income levels.
- By reducing savings and investments.
- By undermining human efficiency and productivity.

Many planners and economists seem to be agreed that one way to accelerate economic growth, i.e., raising *per capita* income and productivity, is to reduce the birth rate, or to stimulate the adoption of a fertility pattern similar to that which prevails in most industrialized nations – low birth *and* low death rates.

Family planning has often faltered because policy-makers are unable to bridge the gap between conceptual, theoretical models and practical policy in the areas of population and development.[24] Among the most disturbing aspects of population and development planning is the fact that the direct and indirect effects of socio-economic development policies on demographic behaviour are still poorly understood. In fact, there does not seem to be a consensus on the qualitative or quantitative relationships between demographic effects of development policy and the developmental effects of demographic behaviour.[25] This particularly true within the context of traditional peasant societies.

Our Goal

Looking at maps of world hunger and poverty, two regions of the world stand out – Sub-Saharan Africa, and South Asia. See Figure 1-1 and Figure 1-2. Both regions exhibit 'extremely alarming' to 'alarming' levels of hunger and poverty. Part of the poverty-stricken nature of Africa can be attributed to the dislocations caused by incessant war and civil strife, the ravages of such diseases as malaria and AIDS, weather, famine, and the failure of the Green Revolution to take root. In South Asia, the Green Revolution found a home. The so-called 'package of practices' that characterizes the Green Revolution were accepted eagerly by cultivators and agricultural productivity, both on a national and *per capita* basis, increased markedly. India became the demonstration plot for the Green Revolution. Nowhere else has the Green Revolution been so completely and so thoroughly implemented. As a consequence, India is often perceived as the archetype for other adopting nations.

The Green Revolution in India, by most measures, has been a success. However, those successes were achieved at a cost. Part of that cost reflects its regional and social development. Spatially, the Green Revolution was unevenly implemented in and between the states, regions, and areas. Likewise, its economic benefits have been uneven and, oftentimes, have led to an increased gap between the successful and marginal cultivators and has resulted in an increasing number of landless laborers. Despite its success, India still remains the home to almost half of the world's hungry and poor. If the Green Revolution was such a success, why are so many Indians hungry and poor?

Although there is no way to deny that hunger is a direct function of poverty, the causes of poverty differ from country to country. There are similarities but every poor country has its own unique set of social, economic, political, and environmental problems to contend with. Within the context of hunger, poverty, and the Green Revolution, we will explore some of the root causes of hunger and poverty in South Asia and Sub-Saharan Africa.

References

1. (Wiesmann, Doris, et. al., October 2007), p. 4, in the Forward by Prof. Joachim von Braun. Only two countries fall outside Asia and

Sub-Saharan Africa, Haiti in the Western Hemisphere and Yemen in the Middle East.

2. (Ramonet, 1998).
3. (The World Bank, 2008).
4. (FAO, Reducing Poverty and Hunger, the Critical Role of Financing for Food, Agriculture, and Rural Development, 2002), p. 9.
5. (Shah, 2008).
6. (Oxfam Canada, 2008).
7. The UN reports that as many as 32.9 million people have been displaced, of which 9.9 million are refugees, as of December 2006. See (UNHCR, 2007), p. 7. Conflict and war is less important to the issue of poverty but is monumental as a cause of hunger. In combination, famine and war cause less than 10 percent of hunger deaths. See (The Hunger Site, 2008).
8. The vagaries of nature include: climate and weather changes, drought, and flooding.
9. Environmental factors include: soil erosion and exhaustion, desertification, water depletion and contamination.
10. *Per capita* productivity falls when cultivable land is lost to desertification or flooding, or exhaustion, and cannot be compensated for with new technology. Inefficient agricultural practices contribute to *per capita* productivity's decline.
11. How land is owned and the owner's relationship with the state contributes to the enhancement or reduction in productivity, especially as it relates to taxation or rents and contributes to the diversion of land to non-productive uses.
12. The Green Revolution can be characterized by the large scale loss of plant genetic diversity and the erosion of biodiversity. See (Shiva, 1992), p. 81.
13. (Sen, Amartya, 1997).
14. See, (Jalilian, Hossein and John Weiss, November 2004); and (Singh, 2001).
15. For example, "Mallam Nuhu Ribadu, the chairman of Nigeria's Economic and Financial Crimes Commission, said $400 billion was squandered between independence from Britain in 1960 and the return of civilian rule in 1999, reported the Daily Telegraph Saturday" (Malaysia Today, 2005). See also (Neumann, 2007).

16. The irony is that, since Independence, India has slowly subdivided the nation's original states into a series of smaller ethnic and linguistic states; and in so doing, has undermined economic viability and squandered an opportunity to benefit from the resolution of socio-economic problems through social and economic integration. Likewise, such subdivision does nothing to aid much needed nation-building.
17. (Parayil, 1992), pp. 738-739.
18. (Dahlberg, 1979), p. 67; and (Freebairn, 1995), p. 277.
19. See (FAO) and (IDRC-CRDI, Facts and Figures on Food and Biodiversity, 2008).
20. (Wolf, October 1986), p. 15.
21. (Dogra, 1984), p. 171
22. (Lipton, Michael and Richard Longhurst, 1985), p. 1. Also referenced in (Wolf, October 1986), p. 15.
23. On the one hand, there is the classical-traditional Malthusian school of economists who see population as an obstacle for impediment to rapid economic growth. The opposing school sees population growth as the pressure-stimulus that serves as the catalyst for the improvement of the economic systems and forces increased production, especially in agriculture. See (Boserup, 1965).
24. See (Todaro, 1977), pp. 24-44.
25. *Ibid.*, p. 31. For a comprehensive survey of some recent materials dealing with the interrelationships between population and development, see (Cassen, 1976), pp. 785-830.

2

The Green Revolution Finds a Home

Introduction

The history of agriculture is the history of intensification. Agricultural systems have been modified, time and again, to increase output per acre or the productivity of the individual cultivator. With each new agricultural breakthrough, *per capita* productivity has increased.

With the alarming increase in world population following WW II, food shortages were becoming a reality, both as a practical and a political concern. For many of the newly freed colonial possessions, the necessities of political and social nation building were threatened by inadequate food supplies. The solution to the worldwide threat of food shortages came in the form of the Green Revolution.

The Green Revolution

It is frequently suggested that the Green Revolution started in the United States, but this is historically and geographically incorrect. The concepts behind the Green Revolution were, indeed, initiated in the U. S., but it was in central and northern Mexico that those ideas became a reality. At the International Maize and Wheat Improvement Center, better known by its Spanish acronym, CIMMYT, the Green Revolution was born.[1]

The most groundbreaking work of the CIMMYT resulted in the development of dwarf wheat varieties that produced a heavy head of grain on a strengthened stalk that was highly responsive to large doses of chemical fertilizer and water. This was accomplished using traditional agronomic, strain and seed selection (hybridization techniques) and not, as is so commonly believed, by genetic bio-engineering or genetic modification. Genetic modification (GM) came much later.

The problem facing Norman Borlaug and his team at CIMMYT was how to create a wheat strain that was responsive to high doses of fertilizer without becoming 'leggy.' Very early on, Borlaug had identified more than 100 wheat varieties that were responsive to chemical fertilizers but each genetically directed the additional nutrients to stem growth (becoming leggy) and not to grain head development. Tannahill writes:

One of the great barriers to increased [wheat] . . . production in hot countries is that when traditional plants are heavily fertilized, they shoot up to an unnatural height and then collapse. If they are grown closely enough together to prevent this, one plant shades the other and the yield is reduced.[2] *During the Mexican experiments, however, and after tests involving 40,000 crossbreeds of plant, it was found that if a short stemmed grain were thickly sown at the right depth and adequately irrigated, it could take massive doses of fertilizer without becoming lanky and give spectacularly high yields.*

In 1962 the International Rice Research Institute [IRRI] was set up in the Philippines to find a rice as miraculous as the Pitic 62 and Penjamo 62 wheats, rice being at the time the main item of diet for six out of every ten people in the world. Success came quickly although it was to prove a qualified success. By 1968 a new crossbred variety. IR8, was being grown on millions of acres in eight countries, yielding on average three times as much grain as traditional varieties and sometimes considerably more.[3]

The successes with wheat and rice were followed by the development of hybrid maize (corn). The wheat, maize, and rice hybrids produced by the CIMMYT and IRRI served as the basis for the Green Revolution. These high yielding varieties were developed in semi-arid Mexico and the tropical wetlands the Philippines. It is within these same types of environments that the Green Revolution was to have its greatest successes. Of all the nations that sought to implement and benefit from the Green Revolution, nowhere has it been as well implemented, accepted, and beneficial as in India. In India, the Green Revolution truly found a home.

Although the term 'Green Revolution' can be ascribed to any new agricultural technology that has the effect of increasing food production, the Green Revolution has come and gone. The most profound changes in worldwide agriculture occurred between 1965 and 1985. Since then, there have been production-improving advances made in the area of agronomy but none as impressive as those pioneering changes that occurred in world agriculture, in general, and in Indian agriculture, in particular, (between 1965 and 1985) in those 20 years.

Many observers believe that it is time for a Second Green Revolution. The benefits of genetic modification (GM) may represent the next great technological leap in agriculture. However, except for the qualified adoption of a handful of genetically modified crops, GM has not received unequivocal acceptance. Part of GM's acceptance problems may well be the result of experiences with the Green Revolution, or simply greater public awareness. The GM issue will be addressed subsequently.

In Africa, in 1980, 20 countries were on the urgent list of the FAO's countries needing food. The people in these countries were eating 10 percent less than they had a decade earlier.[4] In the intervening 29 years, the number of countries urgently needing food has increased to at least 25 and possibly more. Although some countries in Africa have made progress in the fight to curb hunger, they are in the minority. In the period 1981 – 2003, collectively, the countries of Africa have lowered their Global Hunger Indices by 2.7 points, while South Asia has lowered its collective score by 15.1 points.[5]

Africa has among the highest Global Hunger Index (GHI) scores in the world. It is estimated that there are nearly a billion hungry people in the world, distributed nearly equally between Africa and South Asia.[6] While the number of hungry may be nearly the same, Africa's population is only 80 percent of that of India, 800 million versus 1.028 billion. More importantly, Sub-Saharan Africa's total land area is 7 times larger than that of India.[7] While the number

Figure 2-1: Worldwide Foodgrain Production and Demand, 1960 – 2006

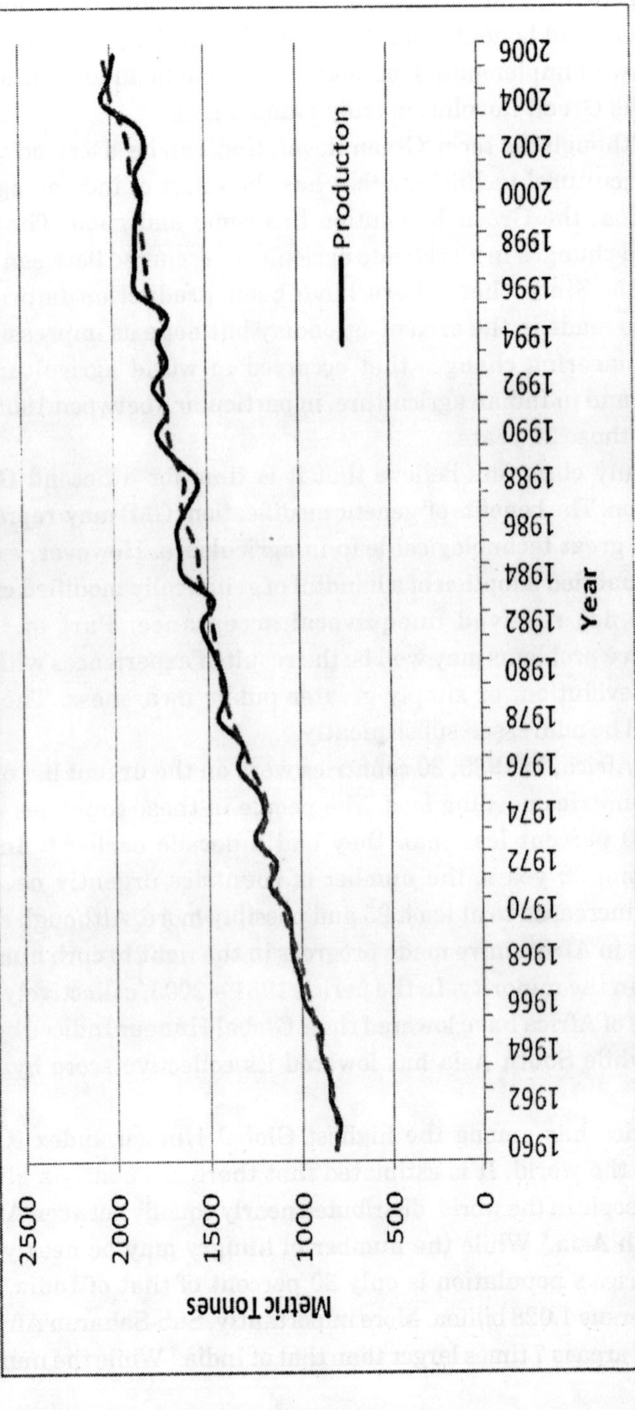

Note: The green line in Figure 2-1 represents worldwide foodgrain demand. It fluctuates much less than production and has increased steadily since 1960.

Source: Compiled by Earth Policy Institute from USDA, Production, Supply and electronic database, www.fas.usda.gov, updated 12 June 2006.

of hungry people is slowly declining in South Asia, in Africa, their number is on the rise according to the FAO.[8]

Genetic Modification

Agronomists now argue that the next cycle of significant increases in crop productivity can only be ensured by either resorting to agro-biotechnology or another round of agricultural intensification. Agro-biotechnology is generally defined by agronomists as the genetic modification (GM) of existing plants. Genetic modification involves technologies that will allow selected genetic material to be transferred into other plants, including the possibility of transferring genetic material from unrelated species.[9] (Unlike the hybridization work done by Borlaug and others, using traditional cross-breeding techniques to achieve their goal, GM should be capable of creating genetically new plant species and plant types.)

A number of world organizations and various United Nations institutions believe that one of the major constraints to increasing crop yields is the lack of improved seeds. They believe that agro-biotechnology is the only way to resolve this problem.[10] For the cultivator in the field, how the seed he plants is produced is probably much less important than other considerations, like yield rates, access to useable agricultural information, access to adequate amounts of fertilizer, pesticides, or herbicides, the maintenance of soil fertility, and adequate rainfall. However, even peasant cultivators, especially in Africa, have shown genuine concern over GM plants that the large multinational seed producers wish to introduce into their countries.

The Example of Bt Cotton

In India at least one GM crop has been gaining acceptance, despite environmental concerns. The crop is called Bt Cotton, Bt standing for *Bacillus thuringiensis*. *Bacillus thuringiensis* is a bacterium that produces a crystalline protein that is toxic to the American boll weevil – the larva of a moth that consumes cotton bolls, destroying them. In the past, Bt was sprayed on the cotton plants to fight the larvae. With GM technology, the Bt protein is produced by the cotton plant itself.

Recently, three problems have emerged regarding Bt cotton. First, there seems to be a growing belief that the boll weevil is developing a resistance to Bt toxin. Second, the use of the improved cotton has lead to a decrease in the use of other pesticides. As a consequence, other cotton pests have begun to reassert themselves. Finally, crop yields seem to be declining. Whether these declines are problems associated with the plants, themselves, soil deficiencies, or just the resurgence of other yield-robbing pests, will have to be determined through research.

Anecdotally, there are those who have attributed the increase in Indian farmer suicides with the cultivation of Bt cotton, or any of the other HYVs, for that matter. In most cases, the suicides have been directly linked to increased indebtedness – a growing consequence of having to purchase the non-renewable components of the package of practices associated with the cultivation of improved seed varieties.[11]

Sustainable Growth

Achieving sustainable growth in farm production is a very complex problem, and needs an integrated holistic approach. Agricultural technology is only one piece of the puzzle. With all the problems facing cultivators in developing countries, no one can possibly believe that agricultural technology will solve all of them. It may improve productivity but it will not, in and of itself, solve the multitude of problems every cultivator must wrestle with on a daily basis.

The question of whether or not there will be sufficient food in almost every nation in Sub-Saharan Africa and South Asia is taking on increasing importance, as populations continue to grow, but with no comparable increases in food production. In South Asia, there has been a small increase in production. In Sub-Saharan Africa, 16 of 26 countries have *not shown an increase in agricultural production*. In fact, Africa has shown an overall decline in production. In other areas, where the Green Revolution has been implemented, a pattern of production leveling off is clearly observable.[12]

The decline in food production does not necessarily mean that there is less food to eat. There is still surplus production. Even so, many people go hungry each day. The decline in agriculture is more evident in terms of agricultural income.

The Green Revolution in India

The Green Revolution, in its various permutations, spread throughout much of India; however, this spread was not uniform. It was a process that needed to adapt to India's varied phisography, weather patterns, agricultural technologies and socio-economic institutions; hence, it became a part of the Indian economic fabric in some states and made little impact in others. Eventually, however, the effects of the Green Revolution were felt in every state, although its impact varies markedly.

Punjab, Haryana and parts of Uttar Pradesh were among the initial and biggest beneficiaries of the Green Revolution.[13] This group of northern and north-western states stood out largely because they were perceived as the granaries of northern India, even before the Green Revolution. During colonial times, the agricultural diligence of the cultivators and the innate fertility of the land in the Northwest were well documented by the British.[14] The British had invested heavily in the area's agricultural infrastructure, especially with investments in canal irrigation systems, roads, and railways. Their faith in the cultivators and their investments in large-scale irrigation systems were rewarded handsomely, even in the absence of improved seed varieties. Additional lands came under cultivation and agricultural production and revenues increased.[15]

When the Green Revolution was initiated in India, wheat and rice were given the highest priority since they were the staples of the Indian diet, and as the Government sought to stave off mass starvation, which seemed a real possibility in the mid-1960s. By the mid-1990s, the Green Revolution had ushered in an era of foodgrain surpluses, permitting export opportunities.

High Yielding Varieties - Wheat

High yielding varieties of wheat were the first improved seed varieties to receive widespread attention and acceptance among Indian cultivators. In general, the cultivation of the new wheats required little change in the then current agricultural technologies. The most significant change in traditional cultivation practices was the introduction and use of chemical fertilizers. Later, pesticides and herbicides were introduced, along with the rapid expansion of tubewell and pumpset technologies for irrigation. The expansion of irrigation technology contributed significantly to overall agricultural productivity. More land was being cultivated with better producing seed varieties. With the addition of each of the new agricultural inputs, per hectare and *per capita* productivity increased. Along with increased productivity came increased income.

By 1999, seventeen (17) of the largest states in India were devoting over 50 percent of their agricultural area to the cultivation of HYV wheat, with Kerala and Manipur cultivating 100 percent of their wheat area with improved seed, while Haryana, Punjab, Gujarat, Tamil Nadu, Arunachal Pradesh, and Meghalaya cultivated 80 percent or more of their cultivable land in HYV wheats.[16]

High Yielding Varieties - Rice

The earliest rice varieties were not, initially, as readily adaptable to India's climate and phisography. Further, the new varieties of rice required significant changes in traditional planting and cultivation practices. Wheat required much less training to be successful and almost no changes in traditional cultivation techniques. As a consequence, the adoption of HYV rice was a much slower process. Once cultivators had seen the successes that were possible with the cultivation of the improved varieties of wheat, the adoption of improved varieties of rice quickly followed.

Surprisingly, in some areas that had adopted the earliest HYV rice varieties, cultivators began to abandon their use. It was discovered that many of the earliest varieties were neither well suited to areas that were overcast during much of the *kharif* season, especially in areas heavily influenced by the monsoons, nor in areas that were prone to protracted flooding.[17] Where the varieties were not well adapted to the local environmental conditions, the cultivators, wisely, reverted to the time-tested local varieties. As better, acclimatized varieties were introduced, cultivators, again, returned to the use of the new varieties. Only recently, however, have the rice breeders been able to create varieties that are tolerant of long periods without direct sunlight and long periods of submergence.[18]

Since their initial introduction, India has released more than 640 improved rice varieties – 64 percent of them for irrigated areas, 27 percent for the rain-fed lowlands, and 19 percent for upland areas.[19] The coverage of modern high yielding rice varieties reached 51 percent for *kharif* and 66 percent for *rabi* paddy in India by 1999.[20]

However, the rate of adoption varies significantly from state to state. For *kharif* paddy, the adoption rate is only 4 percent in Nagaland but 90 percent in Punjab. During the *rabi* season, Nagaland cultivates, again, only 2 percent of its area in HYVs, while Jammu and Kashmir cultivates 92 percent.[21]

At one time, Punjab and Haryana, both well-irrigated areas, cultivated almost no rice, except small areas devoted to the cultivation of Basmati rice as a cash crop. More recently, with the advent of improved, less water-demanding varieties, these traditionally wheat-producing states have become the largest commercial producers of rice in India.

Achieving self-sufficiency in rice production and maintaining price stability are important objectives in low-income countries, where rice is the staple food and is the basis for national food security, generating employment and income for poor people. Asia produces and consumes 90% of the world's rice. Most rice-growing countries in Asia, particularly India, have done remarkably well in meeting their rice needs over the past three decades using Green Revolution technologies. The future, however, poses a major challenge. Recently, the IRRI noted:

By 2030, the world must produce 70% more rice than it produced in 1995 to meet demand created by increasing populations and rising incomes. This production increase must be achieved on less land, with less labor, less water, and less pesticide, and it must be sustainable. Increasing the yield potential of rice varieties is considered an important strategy for meeting this challenge.[22]

The question, then, is, can agriculture meet the challenge?

A Lag in Adoption

The Government of India (GoI) used the same logic for the distribution of the earliest improved seeds that it had used for the selection of the districts for the Intensive Agricultural Districts

Programme (1960-75).[23] It restricted the availability of many of the high yielding varieties of wheat, rice and some improved varieties of maize to those areas that had the greatest probability of ". . . achiev[ing] early grain production increases."[24]

Consequently, the introduction of many HYVs was restricted to limited areas for nearly a decade by the Government's own account.[25] This fact, at least in part, explains the lag between the earliest availability of the HYV seeds and their widespread adoption and use.

By implementing a variety of rural and community development programs, the GoI gave the impression that every effort was being made to push rural and agricultural development everywhere. However, the full weight of the resources needed for such an undertaking were simply unavailable. Recognizing that universal coverage was impossible, the Government concentrated its scarce resources in areas where they would provide the quickest and greatest return on the government's limited investment resources. This pattern of preferential investment continues to be observed. One need only compare the HDIs and poverty rates for India's states to see the consequences of public policy and investments. The pattern also seems to correspond to irrigation rates. Arid and semi-arid, irrigated areas have fared far better than unirrigated, rain-fed areas. See Maps 2-1 through 2-3, below.

Consequences of HYV Adoption

Biological Entropy

High yielding variety seed is the cornerstone of the Green Revolution. Unlike earlier (local or *desi*) seed varieties that could be used year after year with no appreciable change in yield, HYVs have to be replaced regularly. This is mandatory to maintain its built-in productivity. Due to biological entropy, improved seed varieties lose their ability to perform as HYVs, if used as seed over successive years. This requires the purchase of new seed, as well as the application of chemical fertilizers, pesticides, and irrigation water. Cultivators are forced to become part of the larger socio-economic marketplace. Further, they are forced into assuming a financial risk that was not necessary using traditional seed types and agricultural methods. All these influences have had a direct impact on traditional values, traditions, and economic linkages.

Map 2-1: Human Development Indices by State, India, 2001

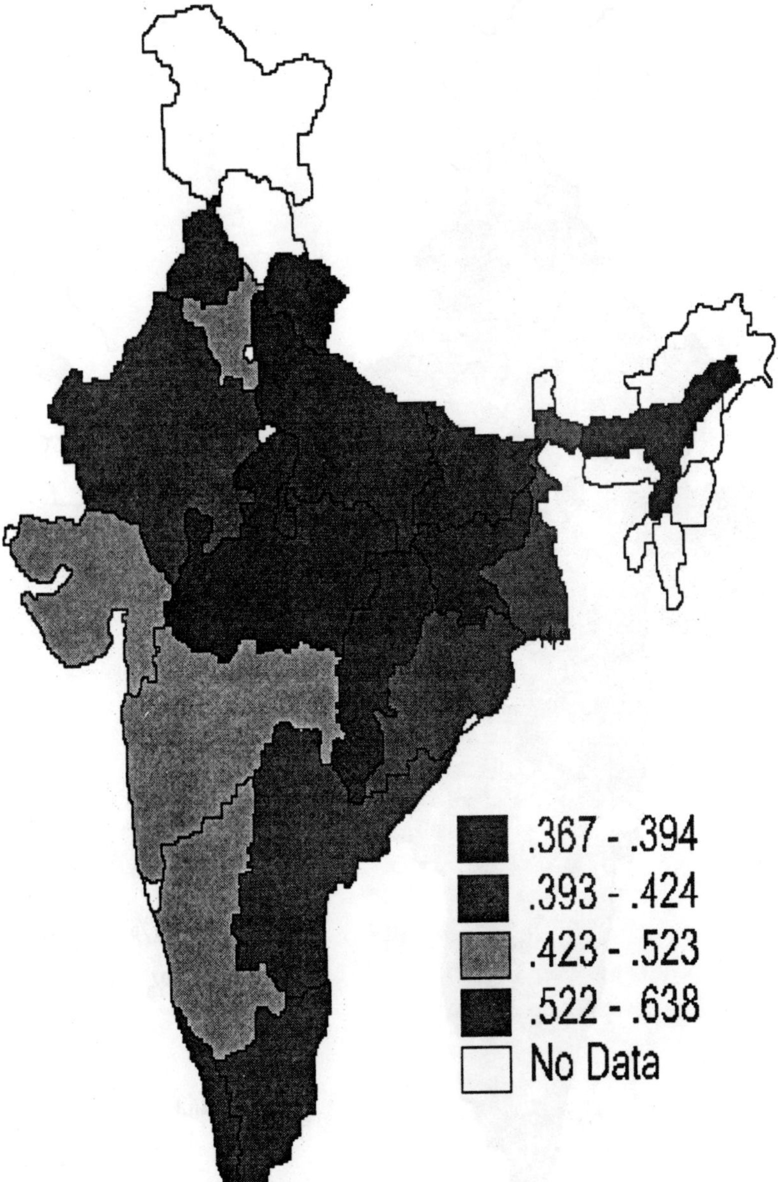

Source: Modified from HDI 2001 Report

Map 2-2: Human Poverty Rates by State, India, 2000

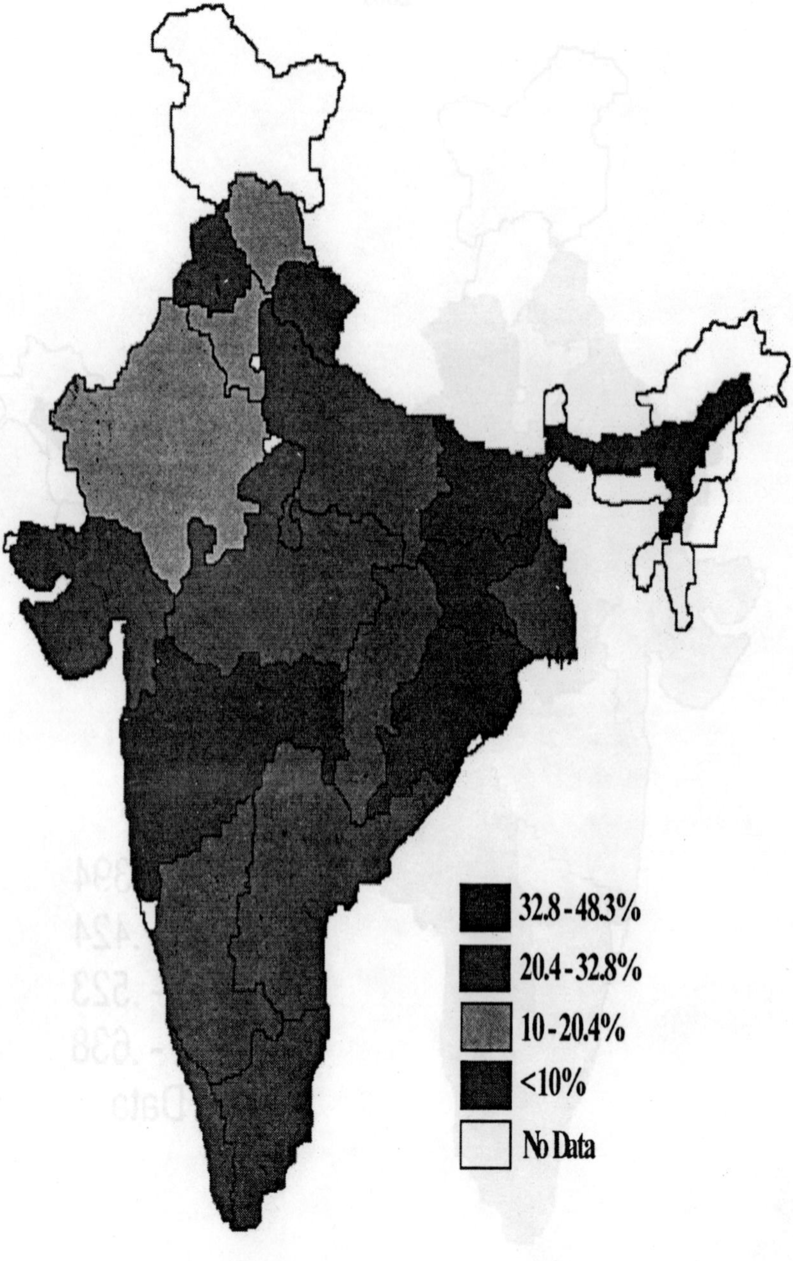

Source: Modified from (Kijima, Yoko; and Peter Lanjouw, September 2003)

Map 2-3: Irrigated Area as Percentage by State

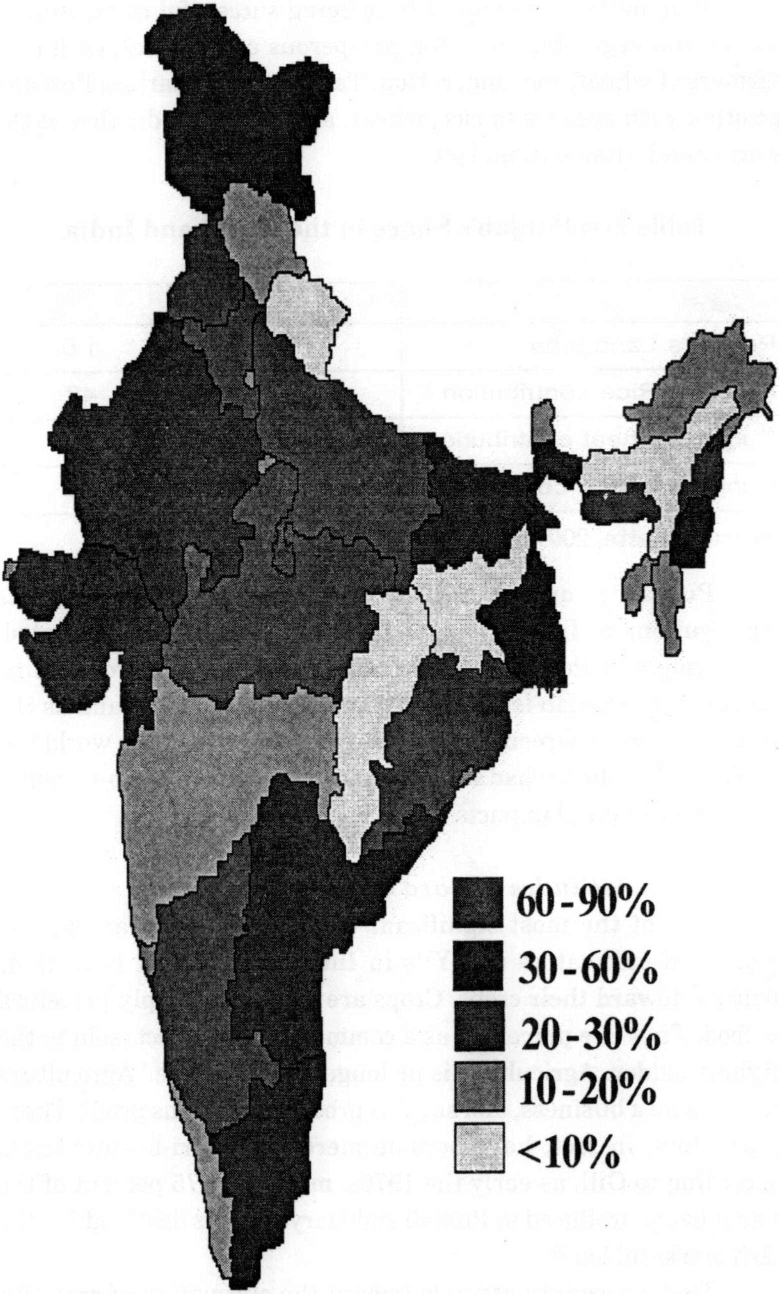

Source: Adapted and modified from (MapsofIndia.com, 2006)

Punjab as the Green Revolution Model

Punjabi farmers moved from being successful cultivators of wheat and vegetables to being prosperous commercial, cash crop farmers of wheat, rice and, cotton. Table 2-1 summarizes Punjab's position with regards to rice, wheat, and cotton production at the world and Indian national level.

Table 2-1: Punjab's Share in the World and India

Particulars	World's (%)	India (%)
Punjab's Land area	0.33	1.6
Punjab's Rice contribution	1	42
Punjab's wheat contribution	2	55
Punjab's cotton contribution	2	24

Source: (Batta, 2007).

Punjab is one of India's smallest states, however, its contributions to India's food security cannot be underestimated. The farmers of Punjab are world-class by any standard. It is no wonder that Punjab is considered India's breadbasket and as the prototype for the Green Revolution. Nowhere else in the world has the Green Revolution had such positive, and negative, socio-economic and environmental impacts.

Changes in Attitudes Toward Crops

One of the most significant changes observed among the successful cultivators of HYVs in India's Northwest is in their attitude toward their crops. Crops are no longer simply perceived as food. They are perceived as a commodity, a product sold to the highest bidder. Agriculture is no longer 'a way of life.' Agriculture has become a business, and surplus production means profit. These cultivators, in fact, have become mercenary agri-businessmen. According to Gill, as early the 1970s, more than 75 percent of the wheat being produced in Punjab and Haryana was destined for the cash marketplace.[26]

This mercenary attitude toward the cultivation of crops for the sole purpose of profit becomes part of the explanation for the willingness of ardent wheat farmers of Punjab and Haryana to substitute rice cultivation for maize. While maize had been the predominant *kharif* food crop, rice cultivation has replaced it almost completely. The reasons are given by the cultivators themselves: there is much more profit to be had cultivating rice, the demand for rice seems to be increasing year after year, and the government's Minimum Support Prices and Procurement Prices (MSP&PP) are much less volatile for rice, than they are for wheat.[27] Both the production and the demand for wheat has peaked. Economically, it only makes sense to find a more readily marketable product. Rice is that product.

Thus, a wheat-rice cropping pattern emerged in areas like Punjab, Haryana, and western U.P. Gradually, the cultivators in these states became unusually successful, producing significant surpluses year after year. By the mid-1990s, their surpluses permitted foodgrain exports for the first time in modern history. These surpluses meant food security for the country and ever-increasing incomes for the cultivators. However, as production rates began to stagnate, so did the farmers' incomes. At the same time, some of the long-term effects of wheat-rice cultivation were beginning to be recognized. Among the most important of which was groundwater depletion in many parts of Punjab and Haryana, as well as soil degradation, erosion, water contamination and depletion, and access to markets and infrastructure. At this point, the Government of Punjab and the GoI became concerned with excessive foodgrain production and environmental damage.

It is common to hear about the crisis in agriculture in Punjab, and elsewhere. However, the crisis is different, depending on the audience. For the farmers, it is an economic crisis, with incomes stagnating or even beginning to decline. For the governments involved, the crisis relates to food security and environmental problems. Among the farmers, when it was announced that India would join the WTO in 1995, there was a serious concern that India's WTO membership would jeopardize Indian agricultural incomes, especially in terms of the government's MSP&PP.

In response to the foodgrain surpluses and the real possibility that Punjab's groundwater resources could become depleted, the Government of Punjab has proposed a reduction of wheat and rice production, by reducing the acreage under these crops by 30 percent and forcing farmers to diversify their cropping patterns.[28] The cultivators have steadfastly refused to comply. Bureaucratic confusion exists between the Government of Punjab and the GoI. The GoI would also like to see a reduction in wheat-rice production and agricultural diversification but not if it were to jeopardize national food security. As a consequence, the farmers of Punjab are receiving mixed messages from their governments.

The 2006 Wheat Crisis[29]

The GoI had decided, as early as 2001, that the cropping patterns of Punjab and Haryana had to change. The then Prime Minister Vajpayee, in comments to farmers in Punjab and Haryana, suggested that they should:

Look beyond wheat and paddy and switch to horticulture, floriculture, oilseeds and vegetable production and have a good export potential.[30]

Vijpayee's comments were echoed, again, in February 2005. This time, however, they were no longer simply suggestions. The Food and Agriculture Minister, Sharad Pawar, stated, unequivocally:

Punjab, Haryana and parts of U.P. are satisfying the country's hunger. I want Punjab and Haryana to reduce their production of wheat and rice, which is in abundance. [31]

The GoI realized that the grain cultivators of India were not going to heed its suggestion to reduce wheat and paddy production and diversify. The time for saber rattling was over and Government implemented a plan that gave their wishes teeth. They all but froze the minimum support prices and procurement prices (MSP&PP). The Government's actions and the cultivators' response resulted in the so-called 'Foodgrain Crisis of 2006.' The farmers withheld their harvest, refusing to sell it to the Government at prices that, for some, were less than the costs of production. When the Government was forced to purchase approximately 2 million tonnes of foodgrain on the world market, the cultivators felt they had made their point – they would not sell their produce if they could not make a reasonable profit. Little did they realize that they had fallen prey to the Government's calculated plan.

The Government realized that it was cheaper to purchase foodgrains on the world market than produce them domestically. The time for domestic production at all costs was over. It was time to move India's commercial agriculturalists into the world marketplace and become less dependent on domestic price supports. The world demand for fruits and vegetables was expanding rapidly, and the Government had made the decision that it would stake a claim to part of that global market. It only had to *persuade* its farmers to become part of that process.

Although the Government was forced to return to the world market to insure adequate stockpiles of foodgrain, it did so willingly. The decision to purchase foodgrains on the world market was a pragmatic one. In the end, the Government's point had been made – diversify or suffer.

The commercial farmers of India obviously have the ability to become successful in the production of other crops, but during the changeover from wheat-rice cultivation to any of a number of other cash crops, they want the Government to shoulder part of the burden such a move would entail. One Punjabi farmer commented:

Give the farmers a little and we, in return, are willing to give our lives. When we were told to grow dwarf wheat and paddy, we did so. When we were told to grow eucalyptus and poplar, we did so. We would be happy to switch over to pulses and oilseeds, but for that the government has to offer us a minimum purchase price.[32]

Unfortunately, the Government wants the farmers to make the necessary changeovers without any assistance, simply for fiscal reasons. In the absence of any kind of crop insurance programs, either public or private, the changeover, at least for the first few years, is a risky undertaking for the unsupported farmer. However, crop diversification, if history is a witness, is necessary for any sustainable agricultural economy and the long-term economic development of a nation.[33]

Beant Singh reduced the issue of diversification to its essentials, as regards the farmers' position, when he said:

Changing to an alternative cropping pattern is a major decision. Wheat and paddy are strong survival crops. They almost never fail. None of the alternative crops can ensure us even half the income being earned from wheat and paddy. Why should we allow our incomes to drop while incomes in other sectors continue to go up?[34]

Diversification does have its benefits; although Shergill is quick to point out that the cultivators of Punjab are unlikely to return to diversified agriculture, with each cultivator producing a variety of crops each season. These cultivators have become fully commercialized modern farmers.[35] They have become agro-businessmen, concerned with little more than profit maximization and agricultural specialization. There is no room for general, diversified agricultural production because diversified agriculture is neither efficient nor as economically productive. For the Indian commercial farmer, diversified agriculture represents subsistence agriculture.

If, however, diversification means the exchange of one cash crop for another, then, diversification would fit into the commercial Indian farmer's mindset. At the moment, there are few, if any, alternatives to wheat-rice cultivation in terms of income production. If, however, the governments (Indian national government and the Government of Punjab) were to assist cultivators in making the changeover, they would be much more receptive to their wishes.

If the authorities are correct in their assessment of the urgency of crop diversification and the governments are not willing to assist the farmers in making the changeover from wheat-rice cultivation to oilseeds and pulses, the farmers are likely to continue their current agricultural practices until there is no more water to be pumped and Punjab becomes a veritable desert. In that case everyone loses.

More recently, the governments have begun exploring various other crop alternatives to pulses and oilseeds, which have been the most discussed alternative crops for the purposes of diversification. Olive cultivation is now considered a *bona fide* substitute crop.[36] Olives have the potential to produce 3 times the income per hectare when compared to wheat or rice – as much as Rs. 300,000 per hectare.[37] The only obstacle to the adoption of olive cultivation is the time required between adoption and the realization of acceptable levels of income. Fruiting would not begin until the third year after planting, and it would take six years before full production would be achieved. The farmers feel the need for assistance during the period between planting and the realization of reasonable incomes. Without government subsidies or other assistance, voluntary participation in agricultural diversification, no matter how lucrative it might be in the end, is unlikely. The cultivators live in the here and now, not the future.

Increased Risk-Taking

Since the HYV package is costly and represents a financial risk to traditional farmers, proponents of the Green Revolution targeted a specific client base they called 'progressive farmers.' These cultivators were deemed to be the only ones in a position to take the risks involved. As a result, the poor cultivators have not been the main beneficiary of the Green Revolution. The 'progressive farmer,' the agricultural equivalent of an entrepreneur, is predisposed to embrace outside economic linkages, while the 'traditional' cultivator is skeptical of the whole HYV package and sees little advantage. For many of the small cultivators, the large investments of time and labor without a commensurate return was sufficient reason not to adopt. As it turns out, prudence on the part of the less progressive cultivators was, at least financially speaking, a wise decision. In the beginning, the cost of the package of practices was expensive and oftentimes unreliable. Without all its constituent parts, the full benefit of the HYVs could not be realized.

Initial Adopters

The first adopters were those able to make the investment necessary to gain access to the Green Revolution's package of practices. Leddy calls this the 'capital entry barrier' – a useful term for characterizing the progressive cultivators' financial ability to acquire the Green Revolution's requisite inputs.[38] For the Green Revolution to assert itself, the full complement of the 'package of inputs' – improved seeds, water, chemical fertilizers, pesticides, and enough land for the economy of scale to work – must be adopted. Therefore, credit availability, irrigation, marketing boards and government extension agencies also become integral parts of the Green Revolution.

The net effect of targeting progressive cultivators was to promote the Green Revolution in areas most likely to immediately benefit from it. This decision to focus on these progressive concentrated money, staff, and inputs in already well endowed agricultural areas. Production was the goal: Equity was not a major consideration.[39] The unfortunate consequence of this initial decision to concentrate the requite resources needed for the implementation of the Green Revolution was that the initial regional and economic patterns that resulted have remained, largely, unchanged. Although the concept of the Green Revolution is widespread, its effects have remained very insular.

Thus, the agricultural benefits of the Green Revolution have been regionally constrained, and along with it, its socio-economic benefits. Some areas have witnessed a nearly complete revitalization of their overall economy. Other areas have experienced an overall decline in general well-being, as evidenced by the escalation or continuation of persistent poverty.

While the benefits of the Green Revolution have been felt in every state in India, its true successes were felt most profoundly in Punjab, Haryana, and Kerala. Later, Himachal Pradesh, portions of western Uttar Pradesh, Gujarat. and Rajasthan would benefit. For the remainder of the nation, the Green Revolution has been either poorly received or implemented.

High Yielding Variety Seed Adoption Patterns

Even though the concept of using HYV seed is almost universally accepted throughout India, according to a recent National Sample Survey Organization (better known as the NSSO) report, only 59 percent of the total area planted, for both food and cash crops, is planted using improved seed.[40]

This adoption rate varies significantly from state to state and from crop to crop. See Table 2-1 and Figure 2-2, below. The suitability of the improved wheat seed to the environment of Northwest India and its almost universal acceptance is witnessed by just how quickly the area under cultivation increased.

Although Punjab and Haryana are consistently viewed as among the most progressive agricultural states, Gujarat tops all the other states in 3 crop areas and overall average for all crops. Kerala, recognized as predominantly a rice-producing area, tops the list of wheat producers with 100 percent of its wheat area sown in improved varieties. Sikkim is consistently at the bottom of the

Table 2-2: Rank Oder of the Major States of India by Percentage of Area under Improved Seed Varieties and Crop-Group

State	*Paddy kharif*	*Paddy rabi*	*Wheat*	*Other Cereals*	*Pulses*	*Oil Seeds*	*Fodder*	*Other*	*All Crops*
Gujarat	77	79	90	86	81	71	50	95	84
Haryana	87	76	84	82	27	80	52	82	78
Punjab	90	51	87	54	43	73	71	79	84
West Bengal	73	72	70	81	69	68	2	71	72
Maharashtra	39	82	60	72	50	60	43	88	69
Rajasthan	31	85	78	67	62	76	52	61	68
Tamil Nadu	72	70	89	64	73	71	38	64	68
Andhra Pradesh	79	75	66	69	71	40	46	59	65
Karnataka	76	67	43	68	51	69	39	60	65
Uttar Pradesh	51	64	58	44	34	47	63	52	52
Bihar	43	72	62	46	33	38	27	50	49
Mizoram	41	38	80	50	25	34	40	52	43
Madhya Pradesh	21	69	46	51	31	52	26	49	40
Orissa	36	55	54	38	59	33	0	60	40
Kerala	77	72	100	23	29	14	0	28	37
Himachal Pradesh	36	31	33	27	26	8	27	42	32
Sikkim	14	4	18	3	0	0	0	0	4
All India	51	66	63	64	47	59	56	65	59

Note: The orange highlighted numbers represent the highest percentage of adoption for that crop-group by state. The yellow highlighted numbers represent the lowest percentage of adoption for that crop-group by state.

Source: Adapted from (NSSO, 1999), Table T15, p. 31.

improved variety adoption list. Although considered a wheat-producing state, Punjab is the leader in *kharif* paddy plantings.

The Other Components of the 'Package of Practices'

Chemical Fertilizer

Of all modern inputs, except water, the use of chemical fertilizers is by far the single most important input. In general, the use of chemical fertilizers increases yields for both improved seed varieties and local (*desi*) seed varieties, but to obtain peak production with the improved seed varieties fertilizer use is essential.

The use of chemical fertilizers is now almost universally accepted by cultivators in every state. There are a few holdouts, like Nagaland and Mizoram, with usage at only 6 percent and 3 percent, respectively, but most states are now posting 70 to 99 percent use rates.[41] Punjab leads the nation in chemical fertilizer use.[42]

In comparative and absolute terms, India has gone from one of the lowest consumers of chemical fertilizers per hectare of arable land to one of the largest. As early as 1998, India became the third largest consumer of chemical fertilizers in the world after China and the United States. It has been suggested that one-half of all the increases in grain production during the 1970s and 1980s – the primary period for the Green Revolution in India—was the result of increased use of fertilizers.

Until 2004, fertilizer consumption outstripped domestic production, and India was forced to import chemical fertilizers, much of it coming from the United States. See Table 6, below. Gradually, under pressure and support from the central government, domestic production of fertilizers increased rapidly. This production began to reduce India's dependence upon foreign imports. Each year the gap between production and consumption grows smaller.

In December 2006, the Government of India announced that fertilizer production had finally exceeded consumption. According to data supplied by India's Ministry of Chemicals and Fertilizers:

Production during December is estimated at 1.766 million metric tons (MT) of urea and 481,000 MT of DAP, for an overall increase against targets of 1.733 million MT and 482,000 MT respectively. In fact, during December, 2003, 1.807 million MT urea was dispatched to the States against the target of 1.76 million MT. Cumulative availability of urea during the current Rabi season by the end of December, 2003 has been 6.641 million MT and this level of availability was satisfactory in all the States.

A Government analyst said there have been no reports of fertilizer shortages so far during the rabi season. Further, the sale of urea during Rabi 2003-04 up to 31.12.2003 was 6.272 million MT which was higher by about 9% as compared to the corresponding period of the previous year.[43]

One side effect of increased fertilizer usage is the increasing amounts of fertilizer that do not reach crops. Substantial quantities of fertilizers are leached out of the soil, contaminating groundwater supplies, as well as run-off from the fields, ending up in rivers, creeks, streams, lakes, ponds and tanks. These, in turn, serve to feed algal and weed growth. The growth of algae results in significant decreases in soluble oxygen. In especially severe circumstances, fish and other fresh water animal life can suffocate and die off, producing an environmental hazard for humans and animal life, alike.

Agricultural development in India is no longer simply a matter of surrendering traditional farming methods. Cultivators no longer base their agricultural decisions on what tradition has taught them, generation after generation.[44] In the mid-1970s, it might have been said that Indian cultivators had some understanding of the basic principles and advantages of chemical fertilizer application, along with the benefits of other agricultural inputs and improved practices. This is no longer the case. Today's cultivator has become increasingly knowledgeable about the cultivation process, from planting through marketing.

The Indian cultivator is no longer constrained by tradition, and it is unwise for Westerners to perceive Indian cultivators, even in comparatively isolated villages, as "out of touch." It is easy, or even enticing, to conceive of cultivators as being largely village-bound. Nothing could be further from the truth. Indians have had, for generations, a custom very similar to the Australian "walk about." Using every means of conveyance, or just walking, it is not uncommon for a cultivator from one region of India to be found hundreds of miles from home, just for the sake of the experience.

Figure 2-2 : Level of Electrification by State, India, 2005

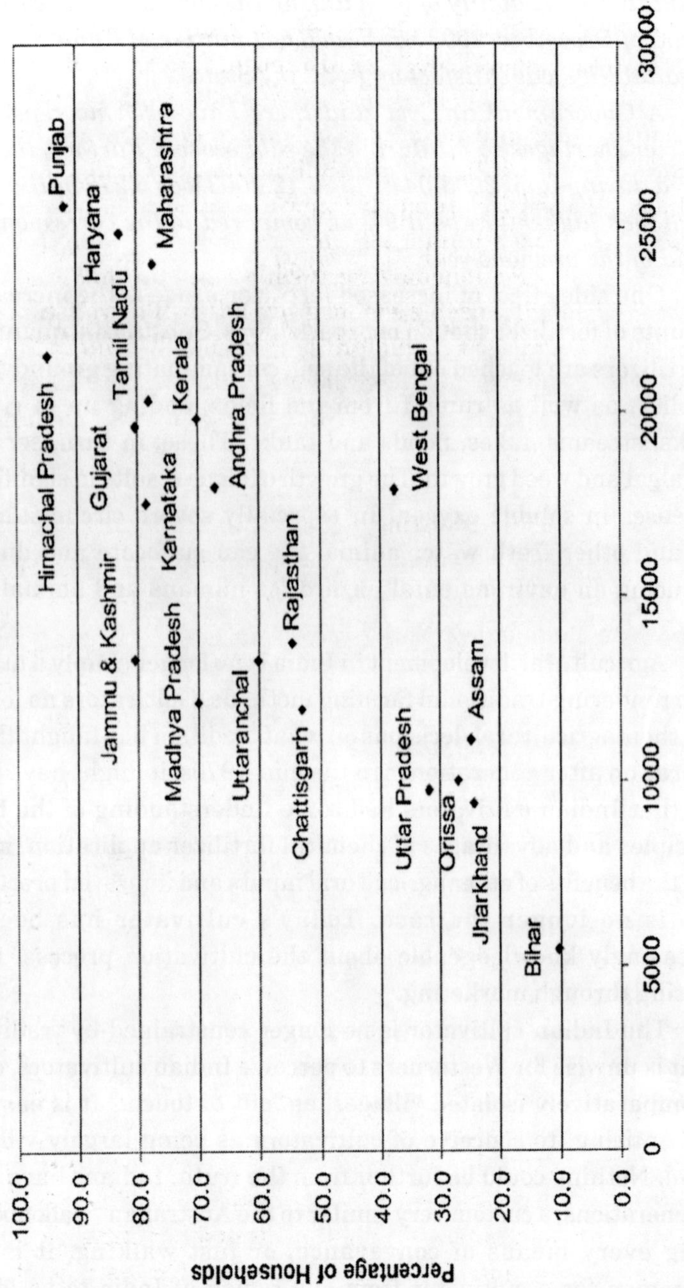

Source: (Modi, Vijay, December 2005) citing Census of India, 2001

These journeys expose them to new ideas and methods, and upon coming home they share their adventures, tales, and information about what other cultivators are doing. Indian cultivators are no longer quaint, uninitiated farmers. No matter their land ownership status, they have grown into savvy tillers of the soil. Agriculture may not be a business for them, at least not in the sense of the agri-businesses in many Western societies. They are not that detached from the soil, since their very day-to-day existence depends on what they grow on their plots of land. For this reason, their decisions must be even more precise. There is no local safety net on which to fall back.

Some new advances in communication systems have enlarged the average cultivator's world view.[45] Tradition plays a part in the cultivator's world view, but that view grows larger every day. Radios, televisions, computers with Internet access, and even individually owned, handheld Simputers are becoming surprisingly commonplace in many villages with electricity. The Ministry of Power contends that 87% of villages are electrified, while only 42-44% of rural households are electrified, with Himachal Pradesh most completely electrified, and Bihar the least electrified.[46] All the 'progressive' states – Punjab, Gujarat, and Haryana are clearly near the top of the electrified list. The one exception is Rajasthan, which falls in the middle area. See Figure 2-3.

However, all other inputs aside, it is the use of fertilizers that will carry them to the next level of collective production and increased *per capita* productivity. They demand information on how to procure and use improved agricultural inputs, and chemical fertilizers are but one of these inputs.

Chemical Pesticides

Chemical pesticides are used as a prophylactic, i.e., with the intent to protect crops against a broad range of insect infestations. In and of themselves, they do not increase yields. However, without their prophylactic properties, improved yields would surely decline. The use of pesticides varies markedly among the states, with the percentage of areas reporting their use ranging from as little as 2 percent, for Mizoram, to as high as 88 percent for Punjab.[47]

Although not as widely accepted as HYV usage, pesticide use is widely recognized as a necessary part of the modern inputs package, since these HYVs are much more pest sensitive than many *desi* varieties, which were acclimatized to specific areas over generations and much more resistant to local pests.

The high-yielding varieties introduced and later modified in India are susceptible to a variety of diseases, blights, and pests. Chemical pesticides represent the most efficient, versatile, and effective method for the control of these pests and insect infestations.

Chemical control of agricultural pests was virtually unknown in India until the mid-1960s, although the use of DDT, as part of India's extensive anti-malaria program, was common as early as the mid-1940s. Widespread use of DDT in India, and in most developing countries, was because of its comparatively low cost, ease of use and ease of storage and transportation. In addition, there were no equally effective, economical substitutes of DDT at the time.

Other pesticides, like BHC (Benzene Hexachloride) powder, Eldrin, Aldrin, Parathion, Malathion, Lindane, Chlordane (to mention but a few of literally hundreds) are generally more expensive to produce, more difficult to store and transport, and more difficult to use than DDT. Nevertheless over time DDT was discovered to have an ecological downside, and its use declined gradually. Other pesticides came to replace DDT for many purposes, but these pesticides, too, had their shortcomings. The new pesticides are the Indian cultivators' only defense against certain pests. Without these pesticides, they would not be capable of protecting their crops or increasing productivity.

Realizing the fundamental importance of pesticides, as well as the benefits derived from producing them domestically, the Indian government responded by sponsoring the construction of production facilities in many parts of the country. Of the more than twenty pesticides commonly used throughout India, at least sixteen are now manufactured almost exclusively domestically. While the government has been instrumental in the establishment of production facilities, it has seen fit to allow questions of production and marketing to be answered by the private manufacturers and to allow a modified free enterprise approach to marketing.

As the cropping patterns became more intensive, the use of pesticides also increased. Consumption of all pesticides between

Figure 2-3: Chemical Inputs by Type[20]

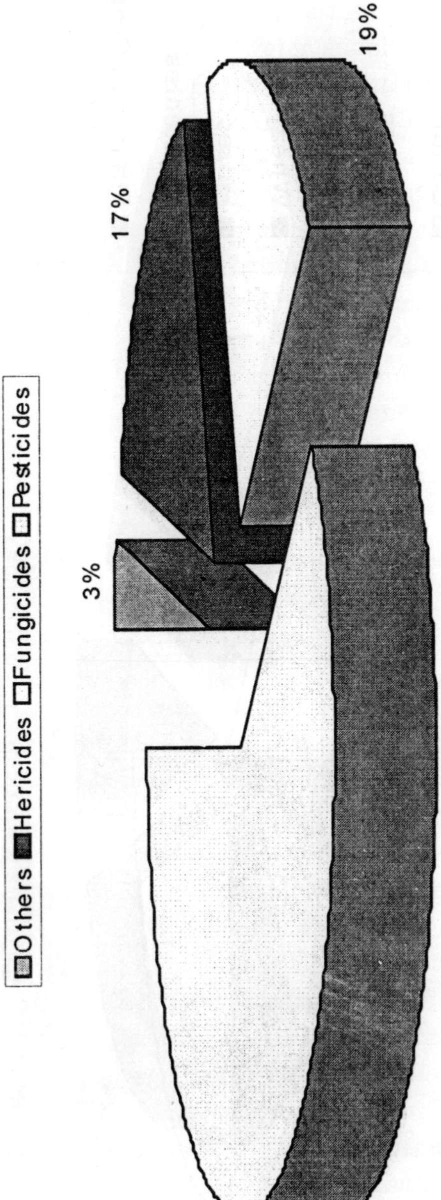

Figure 2-4: Pesticide Use by Crop Type

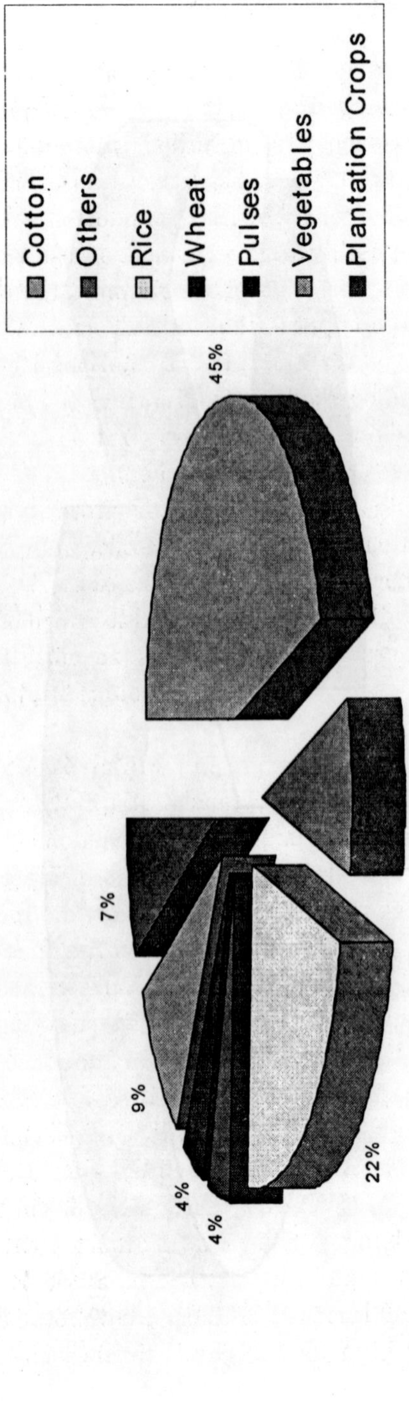

1971 and 1996 increased more than two hundred percent — from 24,306 tones to 61,367 tones.[48]

Despite their recognized beneficial aspects, pesticides also represent significant ecological and biological dangers. These dangers are magnified by the fact that the majority of cultivators using these pesticides do so without the counsel of agricultural extension officers and without the knowledge of the potential hazards associated with their use.

Many cultivators cannot conceive of the potential environmental and health problems that may result from the use of these chemicals. The control of pesticides would, at best, be extremely difficult and, at worst, impossible without curtailing their useful qualities. In the short run, the Indian government chose to place a higher priority on the need for increased food production than on the 'potential' dangers imposed by the widespread use of these toxic chemicals. It was held that "when" domestic food production met domestic food requirements, then the environmental and biological implications of chemical pesticides could be reexamined.

While there are no real substitutes for synthetic pesticides, their consumption began to decrease in the mid-1990s. This decrease stemmed from the feeling that there were environmental problems associated with their use and misuse by cultivators, issues and concerns surrounding the safe storage of these products and the emergence of definable ecological impacts.

As evidenced by Illustration 8-1, the safe handling and storage of pesticides is a serious concern. Not only do cultivators frequently not protect themselves from exposure to these potentially harmful products such storage begs the escape of these products into the environment. They can enter the bio-sphere either as air-borne particulates, as residue on the users clothing, which falls to the ground, as spillage, when the products are transported into and out of the storage facility and in the field prior to or following application. The mishandling and storage of such products provides ample opportunity for these products to get into the environment.

Herbicides

Of the modern agricultural technologies, herbicide use rates, in general, are well below those posted for improved seeds, fertilizers, and pesticides. The All-India herbicide rate is only 22 percent of area cropped. Punjab uses more pesticides than any other state, with nearly 80 percent of area cropped receiving herbicidal treatment. Haryana, with 61 percent, followed by Tamil Nadu, with 51 percent usage, have adoption rates that are nearly double that of any other state.[49]

Although the use of herbicides has the potential of reducing the amount of human labor required during weeding operations, the cash outlay, often exceeds the cost of comparable amounts of human labor. Therefore, cultivators are much more prone to substitute cheap human labor for expensive chemical herbicides. Further, recent environmental problems – soil and groundwater contamination – coupled with widespread formal and informal warnings, have served to curtail herbicide usage.

Irrigation

Irrigation is not a modern agricultural input. It is potentially more important than chemical fertilizer use in terms of importance. Irrigation increases yields with either improved seed varieties or *desi* seeds. The use of assured irrigation, while not quite as important in areas of adequate rainfall during the cropping seasons, is exceedingly important in arid and semi-arid areas. However, even in areas that suffer from annual flooding, e.g., Bihar, drought to near-drought conditions often prevail soon after the end of the monsoons. Therefore, it is entirely possible for Bihar to suffer both flooding and drought in the same year. In fact, Bihar has suffered from famine and near-famine more frequently than any other state.[50] Consequently, even in apparently well-watered areas, irrigation plays an important part, ensuring against the vagaries of the monsoons or nature.

It is for this reason that irrigation is considered an indispensible part of the modern agricultural inputs package. Although canal irrigation has been the backbone of irrigation systems in India beginning under the British, the advent of tubewells and pumpsets has served to significantly broaden the area available for year round cultivation. These two systems fall into two broad categories – public canals and private tubewells and pumpsets. The former exploits water runoff, rivers and public-built canal systems. The latter exploits groundwater reserves.

Punjab and Haryana are the beneficiaries of the largest public irrigation systems, largely constructed by the British before Independence. Similar, widespread systems do not exist in most other states, although Tamil Nadu and Andhra Pradesh possess comparable public systems.

In every successful agricultural area, it is the use of private tubewells and pumpsets that irrigates the largest portion of cultivable area. The reason for this is that the public irrigation systems suffer from age and are dependent upon gravity for the distribution of water. Pumpsets and tubewells overcome the effects of gravity on water and open far larger areas to the potential of irrigation.

Groundwater supplies approximately 27 million hectares of farmland. This means it services almost 60% of the country's total irrigated land area. The change from surface to groundwater usage has been extremely rapid since the 1970s. In just two decades, groundwater irrigated lands have increased by 105 percent. In contrast, the areas of surface-water irrigated land rose by only 28% over the same period (1970-1994). This change was most striking in northern India -- the heart of the Green Revolution.[51]

A count of mechanized wells and tube wells also illustrates how quickly groundwater irrigation has spread. Numbers of wells have rocketed in the last 40 years, from less than one million in 1960 to more than 19 million in the year 2000.[52]

Conclusions

Although the Green Revolution was born in the plant breeding laboratories of Mexico and the Philippines, it was in India that it became fully articulated. Here the primary components of the Green Revolution – high yielding seed varieties, chemical fertilizer use, pesticide and herbicide use, and reliable irrigation – were brought together with life-saving consequences. Famine became a thing of the past but it did not eliminate persistent hunger.

No modern agricultural input can be considered a panacea for India's agricultural problems. Technological innovations alone are not the solutions to India's food problems. Each modern input carries with it new problems. Each calls for its own unique support system which, in turn, calls for another support system. It is the

Map 2-4: Increases in Groundwater-Irrigated Area As A Percentage Of Net Cropped Area, 1970-94

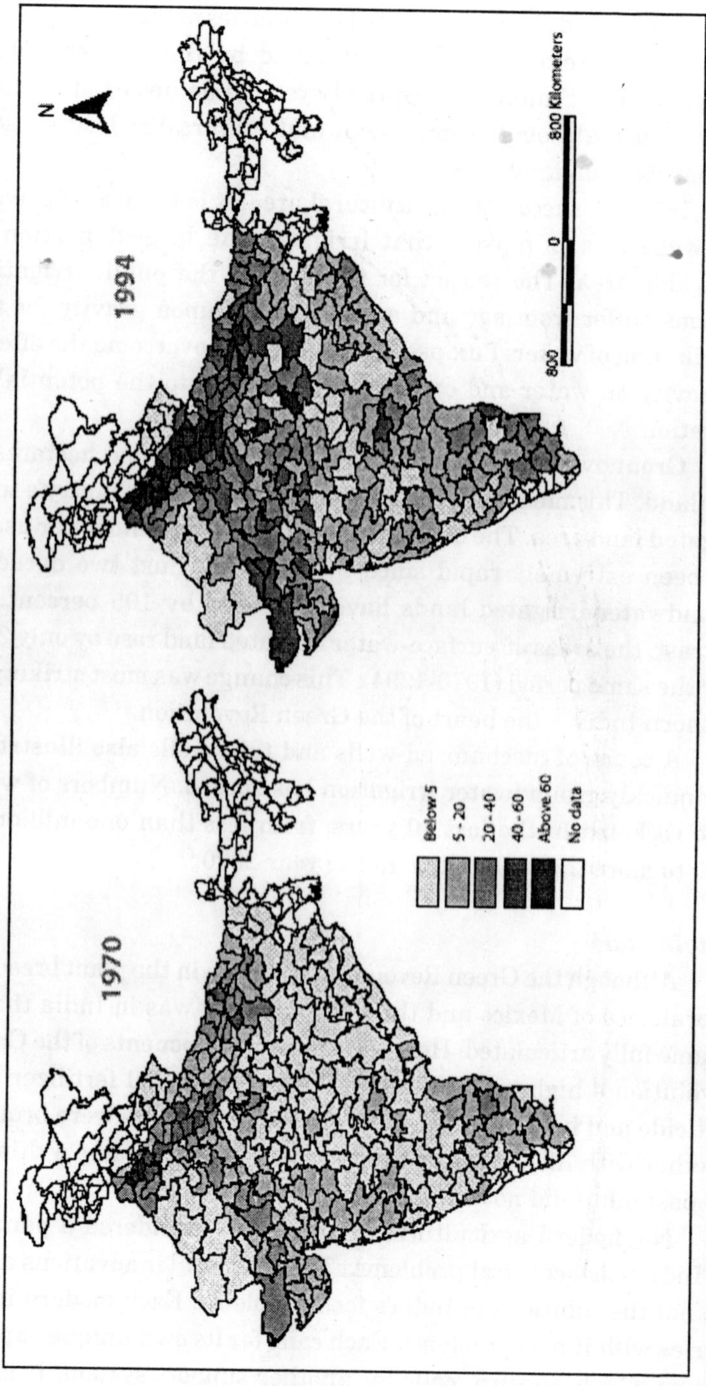

Source: (IWMI, No Date), Figure 2.

essential complementarities of these modern innovations that will, ultimately alter and sustain the economic structure of rural India.

Each innovation will increase the *per capita* productivity of cultivators, but as a package of practices, complementarities are more fully realized. For example, in 1956-66, the New Agricultural Strategy (NAS) was adopted and put into action. It consisted of a package of measures designed to get the quickest possible increase in food grain production, and consisted of incentive prices for cultivators, and concentration of the use of new high-yielding varieties, fertilizers, and plant protection measures on an estimated 13 million hectares of land which had an 'assured' supply of water.[53] Alone, any one of these measures would probably have stimulated or resulted in increased food grain production, but as a package the individual components would more readily remedy the existing agricultural stagnation.

Of the new inputs, however, the adoption of high-yielding varieties would, in the absence of any of the other modern inputs, probably assure the cultivator greater returns on his investment. The application of fertilizers or pesticides to *desi* varieties would have increased yields but not as dramatically as the simple adoption of the high-yielding plant varieties. The contributory effect of assured water, however, cannot be underestimated.

Additionally, modern inputs will undoubtedly modify the social fabric of rural India, whether adopted singly or as a package. While their introduction has increased *per capita* productivity over much of India, they have also produced certain socio-economic and political problems. Some of these issues will be addressed later.

While the new technologies have improved the lot of many cultivators, it has done little for those cultivators unable to afford their use. As a consequence, there is an uneven distribution of the benefits of the Green Revolution among cultivators. Those with the financial ability and capital have been able to invest in the package of improved agricultural practices and have realized varying rates of return on those investments. Yet, despite their investments, many adopters have not reported optimal increases in productivity, nor have they achieved the improved standard of living that was supposed to have accompanied the adoption of the new technologies.

Consequently, non-adopters observe the adopters with varying degrees of envy or relief. Some witness considerable investments in time, effort, and money, which do not appear to provide commensurate returns in the form of yields.[54] Others see only the social and political prestige and power that have accrued to their high-yielding-using neighbors, and wish they too could share in them. This latter view has tended to factionalize rural India even further between the prosperous "Haves" and the indigent "Have Nots." The difference between these 'classes' of cultivators is largely a matter of perception on the part of individual cultivators and does not necessarily follow traditional communal or caste lines.

Often the cultivators who extract the greatest benefits from the new inputs are those who possess a keener capacity for the management of their resources. This is particularly important in scarce-resource situations and relates to both the management of agricultural inputs and the ability to deal effectively with administrative and political environments, through which access to resources are frequently controlled. Those most able to 'cultivate' relations with the local and district development officials tend to acquire the inputs necessary for greater productivity.

The dissatisfaction that exists between the agricultural winners and losers in the race for the benefits of modern technologies has not been transformed into massive political unrest and confrontations. Whether or not this differential will flare into serious confrontations will depend on how the administrative officers at each level of the development hierarchy deal with the problems of rural equity and social justice among small and large cultivators. It may be that the disparities between the large and small cultivators will prove much less of a factor in the political stability of rural India than the disparities that exist between the rapidly growing landless population and the landed cultivators.

References

1. CIMMYT is the Spanish acronym for Centro Internacional de Mejoramiento de Maíz y Trigo at El Batán near Texcoco in México state.

2. This is still a 'problem' with high yielding varieties of wheat and rice. This problem is called photosensitivity. Most HYVs of wheat and rice require significant amounts of direct sunlight to produce. This photosensitivity becomes a problem in areas where during the peak growing period the sky is continuously overcast, for example, in summer monsoon areas.
3. (Tannahill, 1988), pp. 336-337.
4. *Ibid.*, p. 338.
5. (Weisman, Doris, Lioba Schoninger, and Iris Weingartner, October 2006) p. 15.
6. (IDRC-CRDI, 2008).
7. It must be noted that the term 'South Asia' and India are not interchangeable nor synonymous. South Asia, or the 'subcontinent,' includes the countries of India, Pakistan, Bangladesh, Bhutan, Nepal, and Sri Lanka. For out purposes, however, the terms South Asia and the subcontinent will exclude Bhutan and Sri Lanka.
8. (FAO, State of Food Insecurity in the World, 2006) and (USDA, June 2007), p. 14.
9. (Indira, A.; M. R. Bhagavan; and I. Virgin, 2005), pp. 9-10.
10. Among these are: Rockefeller Foundation, World Bank, Asian Development Bank, Nuffield Council on Bioethics, the International Agricultural Research Centers (IARCs) of the CGIAR system, the IFPRI, IFAD, FAO, and UNDP.
11. See, for example, (Mishra, 2005); (Navdanya, 2004); (Long, Jessica, 2007); (Sainath, 2007); and (Sengupta, 2006).
12. See (FAO, The State of Food and Agricultue, 2007), p. 120.
13. Later Gujarat and Rajasthan were added to the list of states that benefitted profoundly from the Green Revolution.
14. There is a whole literature devoted to the lionization of the Punjabi Jat cultivators and their contributions to the welfare of the British Raj. It was also recognized that the lands of East and West Punjab (now Punjab in India and in Pakistan) were among the most fertile in all colonial India. All that was needed was water. This the British provided in the form of monumental earthworks and an elaborate canal system. For example, see (Cunningham, 1853) and (Darling, 1931).
15. See, (Banerjee, Abhijit and Lakshmi Iyer, 2005), (Kapur, Shilpi and Sukkoo Kim, 2006), and (Islam, 1997).

16. (NSSO, 1999), Table T15, p. 31.
17. The author, during fieldwork conducted in Darbhanga District, Bihar, discovered that by 1974-75, many cultivators had abandoned the use of HYV rice varieties because large portions of the district flooded to a depth sufficient to submerge the dwarf rice plants, just as they were 'heading out.' As a consequence, the plants rotted and the entire crop was lost. After repeating this scenario for several seasons, the cultivators returned to the use of local, or *desi* varieties, that were taller and did not get submerged.
18. See (Bangladesh News, 2008); (Ronald Laboratory, 2006); and (Sarkar, R. K., J. N. Reddy, S. G. Sharma and Abdelbagi M. Ismail, 2006).
19. IRRI, McLean, (August 2002)p. 91.
20. (NSSO, 1999),Table T15, p. 31. India's own data on the area currently cultivated in improved rice varieties is at variance with those of the IRRI. The IRRI estimates the area to be 78 percent of the rice harvested area in the same year, 1999. See (IRRI, J. L. McLean, 2002), p. 91. Here we are taking the more conservative figure of 51 percent.
21. (NSSO, 1999).
22. (Rothschild, G.H.L., 1998).
23. See (Staples, 1992) for an insightful review of the Ford Foundation's participation in Indian agricultural development from 1951 through 1992.
24. *Ibid.*, p. 16.
25. (NSSO, 1999), pp. 27-28.
26. (Gill, 1972).
27. See (Shergill, H. S., 2005), p. 239.
28. (Shergill, H. S., 2005), p. 239.
29. Much of this section is based on: (RUPE, 2006a) and (RUPE, 2006b).
30. *Ibid.*
31. (RUPE, 2006b).
32. (Sehgal, 2005).
33. (Jones, E. L.; and S. L. Woolf (eds), 1969).
34. *Ibid.*
35. (Shergill, H. S., 2005), p. 241.
36. (Tiwari, 2007).
37. See (States Bureau, 2008); (Jolly, 2008); and (ThaindianNews.Com, 2008).

38. The idea of the 'capital entry barrier' of the 'first innovator' was first observed in an anonymous on-line paper. Web reference: www.cnr.berkeley.edu/classes/espm-165/lectures/greenrev.htm. Possible author – George Leddy, instructor, for a course called Comparative International Rural Development, U.C. Berkeley, Spring, 2002, aka Environmental Science Policy and Management 165.
39. (Staples, 1992), p. 16.
40. (NSSO, 1999), Table T16, p.33.
41. NSSO (August 1999), *op. cit.*, Table T 17, p. 35-36.
42. *Ibid.*
43. See, Statpub.com (2004).
44. (Schultz, 1964 and 1971), p. 3.
45. New communication issues will be dealt with in a later section.
46. (MoP, 2005), as cited in (Modi, Vijay, December 2005), p. 20. The author will admit that the 87 percent rural electrification rate seems high. A more modest figure would be somewhere around 50 percent for both villages and households.
47. (NSSO, June 2005).
48. <www.indiastat.com> is an excellent source for information on a variety of subjects relating to India and her various economic sectors.
49. *Ibid.*
50. (Government of Bihar, 1973).
51. (IWMI, No Date)
52. *Ibid.*
53. (Abel, Martin E., 1971), p. 4.
54. See, for example, (Nijhawan, Inder P., 1975)

3

Sub-Saharan Africa: Poverty, Colonialism, Geography, and Disease

Map 3-1: Gross National Income Per Capita

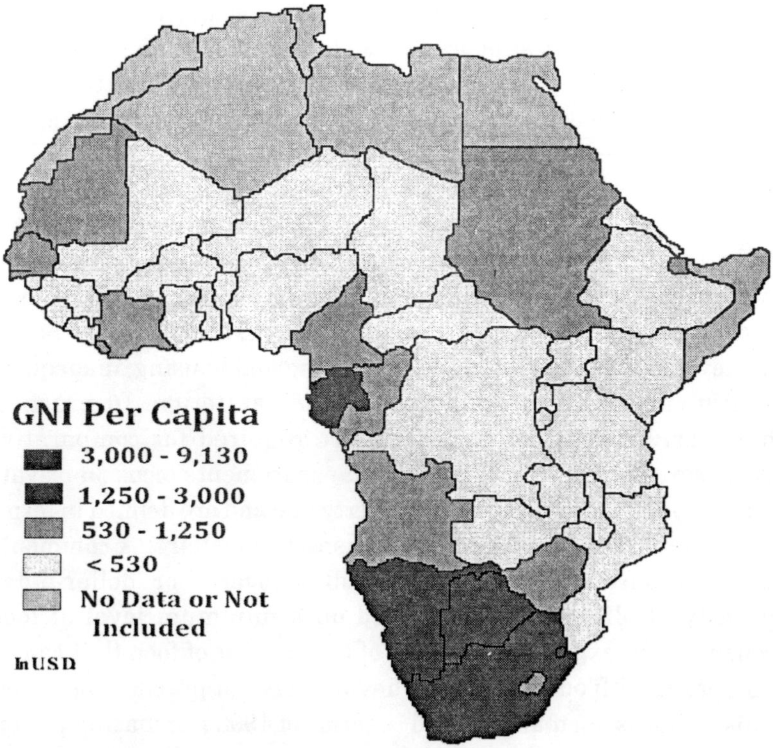

Source: (Rural Poverty Portal, 2008).

Introduction

Sub-Saharan Africa is composed of 47 nation states, having a total estimated population of approximately 788 million.[1] Together these nation states represent, possibly, the largest concentration of poor in the world and their numbers are growing rapidly, by an estimated 2.3 percent per annum.[2] All one need do is examine any Human Development Index map or any map showing comparative levels of poverty or hunger to see the extent and scope of poverty in the region.

Africa is unique among the developing regions of the world. Not only is it the poorest but it is the only region having a *negative* per capita economic growth rate.[3] Essentially, this means that the region is dependent upon foreign aid and relief for its very survival.

Africa is the economic equivalent of astronomy's Black Hole. It sucks in everything of economic value without any appreciable response in the form of economic equivalency or a demonstrable improvement in hunger and poverty levels. If current food production trends continue, with no ameliorative changes in sight, can or will the world be able to support Africa? In the short term, the answer is obviously, yes, but for how long? There is a lot written about How to End Poverty in Africa and South Asia but is it working?

What is Poverty and How do We Define It?

Poverty is a multidimensional condition and is variable over time and by perception. Therefore it comprises both physical as well as psychological components. Most poor people define their condition largely in terms of material deprivation — not enough money; lack of employment, food, clothing and housing; inadequate health care, clean drinking water and sanitation. In practice, however, less subjective criteria are required for comparative purposes. Generally, most poverty measurements focus on private consumption below an objective poverty line and are defined in terms of an absolute norm for a narrow aspect of welfare. A commonly used measure is what is called 'dollar poverty' or 'dollar-a-day poverty.' Dollar poverty is based on a minimum level of food consumption expressed in terms of the amount of food that can be purchased with one U.S. Dollar having constant purchasing power. This Dollar is normally pegged in terms of 1993 purchasing power, making time series comparisons possible.

People deemed poor in terms of income are generally poor with regard to other objective measures. Those below the dollar-a-day poverty line typically spend at least 70 – 80 percent of their disposable income on food, most of it on basic food staples, and risk consuming too few calories for health maintenance. Likewise, people this poor are usually unable to afford adequate clothing, housing, schooling, or health care. Without access to education the children of poor parents doom themselves to much lower earning potential.

Measures of Poverty

Human Development Index (HDI)

Among the many measures of poverty, one that has been deemed most popular and useful is the Human Development Index or HDI. It is a multidimensional-indexed basic needs measure, developed in 1990 by Mahbub ul Haq, Sir Richard Jolly, with help from Gustav Ranis and Lord Meghnad Desai. It has been used since then by the UNDP in its annual Human Development Reports (HDRs). It is claimed that ideas of the Nobel Prize winning welfare economist, Amartya Sen, were influential in the development of the HDI. The HDI is a weighted index of life expectancy at birth; a weighted average of over-15 literacy and primary, secondary and tertiary enrollment rates; and per capita purchasing-power-parity (PPP) GDP.

While it has its detractors, it is currently the most recognized and accepted tool for evaluating and tracking human development. The HDI, essentially, has replaced the use of various GDP derived measures of human well-being.

The HDI is rationalized on the grounds that human beings endeavor to lead long healthy lives, to have a decent standard of living, and to acquire knowledge in which case the focus of development policy should be to expand the choices and capabilities of people in these areas.[4] While various GDP-based measurements can be utilized to evaluate the human condition, the HDI approach consolidates the data in ways GDP statistics cannot.

The HDI has a range from zero (0) to one (1), with one representing the highest level of human development. Annually, the UNDP publishes a world report, in which all participating nations are rank ordered.

In the most recent HDR – 2007/2008 – the highest ranked country was Iceland (1), with a score of 0.968, and the lowest ranked country was Sierra Leone (177), with a score of 0.336.[5]

Human Poverty Index (HPI)

The HPI is an indication of the standard of living in a country developed by the United Nations. If human development is about enlarging choices, poverty means that opportunities and choices most basic to human development are denied. From a human development perspective, poverty means more than the lack of what is necessary for material well-being. It is a measure of the extent to which people in a country are not benefitting from development. HPI is a measure of deprivation whereas HDI is a measure of development, the two often being used in conjunction to establish a country's level of development and standard of living. For policy-makers, the poverty of choices and opportunities is often more relevant than the poverty of income. The poverty of choices focuses on the causes of poverty and leads directly to strategies of empowerment and other actions to enhance opportunities for everyone. Recognizing the poverty of choices and opportunities implies that poverty must be addressed in all its dimensions, not income alone.

Rather than measure poverty by income, the HPI uses indicators of the most basic dimensions of deprivation: a short life, lack of basic education and lack of access to public and private resources. The HPI concentrates on the deprivation in the three essential elements of human life already reflected in the HDI: longevity, knowledge and a decent standard of living. The HPI is derived separately for developing countries (HPI-1) and a group of select high-income OECD countries (HPI-2) to better reflect socio-economic differences and also the widely different measures of deprivation in the two groups.[6]

HDI consists of three main components, longevity, knowledge and standard of living, and assesses these components as development. HPI assesses the same three components from an opposite point of view to take into account factors that HDI does not include.

Global Hunger Index (GHI)

Unlike the HDI and HPI, the GHI has the advantage of going beyond dietary energy availability, which is the focus of the Food and Agriculture Organization of the United Nations' (FAO's) measure of undernourishment. The GHI's broader conceptual basis better reflects the multidimensional causes and manifestations of hunger. The index takes into consideration inequitable resource allocations both between households and within households, since the latter also affect the physical well-being of children. Sufficient food availability at the household level does not guarantee that all members benefit from it in equal measure.

All three index components are expressed as percentages and are equally weighted. The GHI score varies between the best possible score of 0 and the worst possible score of 100. Higher scores indicate greater hunger; the lower the score, the better the country's situation. GHI scores above 10 are considered serious, scores greater than 20 are alarming, and scores exceeding 30 are extremely alarming.

Who Are the Poor?

When we speak of the poor, we must first ask ourselves, exactly who are the poor and how do we define poverty? In general, the poor belong to one of several groups:

- Wage laborers and the landless
- Small-scale farmers
- Households headed by women
- Rain-fed farmers and those living on marginal lands
- Indigenous people – Scheduled castes and tribes
- Nomads and herders
- Displaced persons.[7]

These categories are not necessarily applicable everywhere. There are regional variations but, in general, most of the world's one billion poor fall within one or more of these groups. Almost universally, wage laborers, especially landless agriculturalists, are poor, except in Africa, where the number of agricultural laborers is comparatively small by comparison with other regions of the world. In Africa, landed small small-scale farmers make up the largest number of the poor.

Households headed by women are almost synonymous with poverty throughout the world, but in much of Sub-Saharan Africa, household headed by women are nearly as likely to be poor as those headed by men.

Agriculturalists living in areas where irrigation is readily available are much less likely to face the prospect of poverty, when compared to those agriculturalists who practice rain-fed agriculture.[8] In most cases, rain-fed agriculture is practiced on degraded and marginal lands. Nearly two-thirds of the world's poor live on marginal lands.[9] Likewise, most small-scale landholders tend to live in dryland areas almost everywhere throughout the world.

In parts of the world, indigenous populations are almost always subject to economic and social discrimination, resulting in their inability to secure credit and gainful employment. This is especially true in South Asia. Nomads and non-commercial pastoralists seldom achieve livelihoods much above subsistence due to the very nature of their nomadic lifestyle and the occupation of severely marginal lands.

Figure 3-1: Global Distribution of Rural Poverty

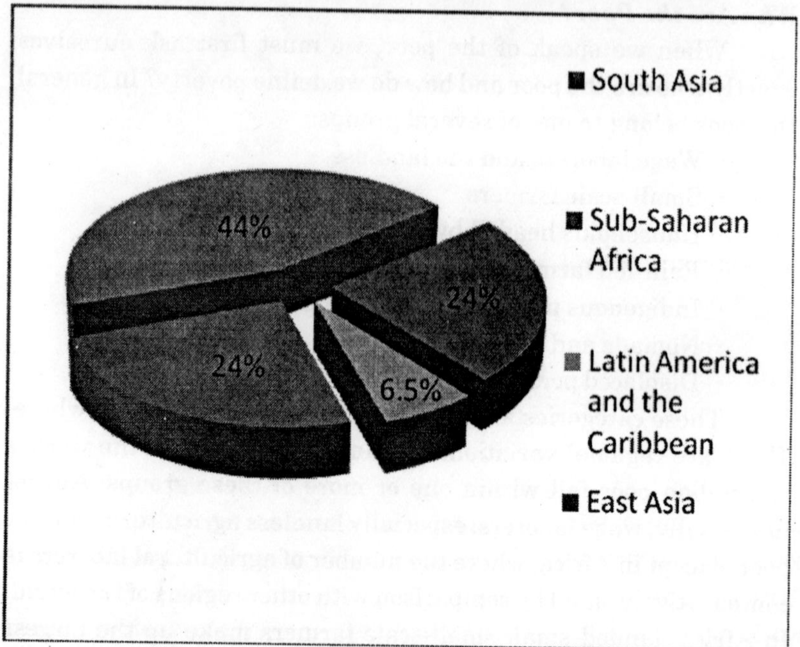

Source: After (IFAD, 2001), p. 16.

Figure 3-2: Global Distribution of Poverty

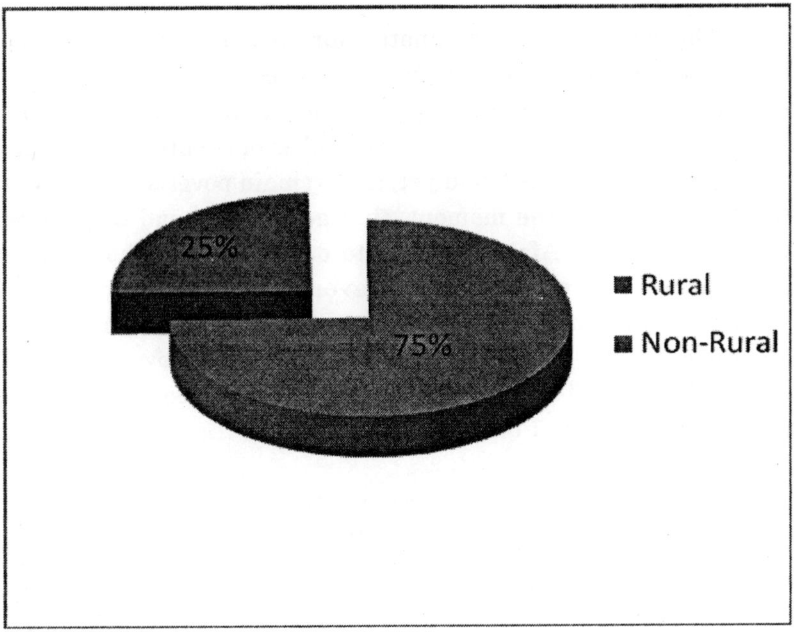

Source: After (IFAD, 2001), p. 16.

Finally, people displaced by civil war and unrest have been forced to abandon their belongings and lands in an effort to achieve safety. As a consequence, they leave behind the only assets that provides them with any hope of survival. As refugees, they generally become wards of adjacent states or world relief organizations.

The poor of the world are also characterized by being predominantly rural, they have very little land, and the land they own is typically marginal in character. Their livelihood is dominated by agriculture, either as a small-scale cultivator or as a wage-earning landless laborer. What little income they earn is spent on essential foodstuffs. They are illiterate. They are typically unhealthy, for lack of food and medical care.

Some 1.2 billion people worldwide earn less than a dollar-a-day; they are in what is commonly termed 'dollar poverty.' Forty-four per cent are in South Asia, about 24 percent in Sub-Saharan Africa.[10] Currently, 70 percent of the 'dollar a day' poor live and work in rural areas; and if projections are correct, their number will decline by only 10 percentage points by 2025.

The Roots of Sub-Saharan Poverty

Governance

The most frequent explanation for Africa's poor performance is that the region suffers from poor governance, especially as reflected in political unrest, war and armed conflict, and corruption. While governance is an issue for a number of countries in Africa, many are well governed, and yet, they remain poverty-stricken. If we do assume, for the moment, that governance and corruption were the cause of Africa's failure to develop, there should be a correlation between them. However, if we simply compare Transparency International's perceived corruption ratings with economic growth, African countries with high and low corruption ratings lag behind their Asian counterparts with equal or higher ratings. See Table 3-1 below.

Table 3-1: Corruption Perception Rank versus GDP Growth Rate, 1980-2000[11]

	Corruption Perception Rank	*Average Yearly GDP per Capita Growth*
Sub-Saharan Africa		
Ghana	70	0.3
Senegal	76	0.5
Mali	78	0.5
Malawi	83	0.2
Asia		
India	83	3.5
Pakistan	92	2.4
Indonesia	122	3.5
Bangladesh	133	2.0

Source: (Sachs, 2005), p. 191.

Obviously, governance and corruption alone do not explain Africa's poverty.

This is not to say that the issue of governance should be ignored but, within the overall context of the region's problems, it would appear that it is subordinate to other problems facing the region. Poor governance is comparatively easy to identify and, therefore, easy to vilify. There are numerous other problems that are potentially more significant.

Sachs' group writes:

. . . *tropical Africa, even in well-governed parts, is stuck in a poverty trap, too poor to achieve robust, high levels of economic growth (and in many places, simply too poor to grow at all). More policy or governance reform, by itself, is not sufficient to overcome this trap. Specifically, Africa's extreme poverty leads to low national saving rates, which in turn lead to low or negative economic growth rates. Low domestic saving is not offset by high inflows of private foreign capital, for example foreign direct investment, since Africa's poor infrastructure and weak human capital discourage private capital inflows. With very low domestic saving and low rates of market-based foreign capital inflows, there is little in Africa's current* dynamics that promotes an escape from poverty.[12]

Putting aside traditional economic explanations for persistent poverty – the failure to accumulate capital and its interaction with labor, impoverished people unable save, and rapid population (consumption) growth – we need to find less theoretical and more practical explanations. Admittedly, the theoretical interplay of capital, labor, savings, and population growth generally explains how a group of people, a nation, or a region becomes stuck in a cycle of unending poverty, the poverty trap, but it does not truly explain why or how Africa got into its current situation — the largest concentration of poverty stricken people in the world.

Africa's current socio-economic problems are not new nor a recent phenomenon. They have been a long time in the making. At almost every stage in the history of the region, a new nail has been driven into the coffin of the region. The following factors have contributed to the current state of the region:

- Unrepentant colonialism and tribalism
- Geography
- A very high disease burden
- The low productivity of agriculture and the absence of an African Green Revolution.[13]

Colonialism

Colonial domination is generally seen as abhorrent and justifiably maligned, but if colonies do not or cannot sustain themselves, they are abandoned. The African colonies, traditionally supplied agricultural products and mineral wealth, all of which went to the colonial homeland for consumption, processing, or conversion through manufacture. In return, the colonies were given the opportunity to purchase back their resources as manufactured goods.

Colonialism in Africa may have been more predatory than anywhere else in the world. Africa's people and resources were egregiously exploited. When the colonial powers did abandon Africa in the mid-20th Century, they left behind shell nations that had been environmentally, economically, politically, and socially exploited, nay, raped.

African colonialism may have resulted in the preeminent example of cultural, political, and economic devolution. Even so, there are those who believe that Africa's colonialism had some beneficial consequences. Some suggest that the continent would have been completely unprepared for the modern era had colonialism not established the concept of political states and introduced modern market concepts and economics.[14] The counter argument suggests that Africa was so devastated by colonialism that it was even less prepared for the modern era and independence than if it had simply been left on its own. To expect the new nations of Africa to repair over 400 years of socio-economic and political predation by European powers, and build democratic institutions, organize a functioning educational system, implement a system of indigenous and foreign commerce and trade, and all the other forms of modern development, in a single generation, is simply unrealistic. The current state of the African nations, it would seem, militates against any suggestion that colonialism had any beneficial consequences.

The Root Causes of Colonialism

Although there are a multitude of potential explanations for the colonial expansion of Western European nation states, beginning in the 15th Century the driving forces behind European colonialism were political and economic competiveness and religion. Overseas expansion enhanced how each nation perceived itself and how it was perceived by its competitors. Trade was considered a form of war, and trading stations were often referred to as forts, with good reason.

The search for new products to trade drove the Europeans' explorations. The Portuguese were the first to establish trading centers, first in West Africa, then beyond. From these African outposts, they established a trade in precious metals, especially gold, and slaves. Somewhat later, the lure of spices took them around the Cape of Good Hope and into the Indian and Pacific oceans. Trading directly with the sources of exotic spices eliminated competition, reduced the costs of overland transport and, until piracy became an institutionalized and often nation-sanctioned form of covert warfare, sea transport was comparatively fast and reliable. Adam Smith, in his *The Wealth of Nations*, spoke of the advantages of sea transport, saying:

There could be little or no commerce of any kind between the distant parts of the world. What goods could bear the expence of land-carriage [to the far corners of the Earth]? Or, if there were any so precious as to be able to support this expence, with what safety could they be transported through the territories of so many barbarous nations?[15]

Much of the cost associated with long, overland transport was a function of tariffs, duties, and taxes extorted by the rulers of the kingdoms through which the spices had to travel on their way to Europe. Water transport of such valuable goods made them less expensive and more readily available to a larger market population.

Equally important was the felt need of the Portuguese and Spanish to convert non-believers to Christianity in the form of Catholicism. In fact, the Spanish incorporated the need to press for the conversion of native populations as the primary tenet of and reason for exploration. Thus, missionaries accompanied almost every team of Portuguese and Spanish explorers and traders to the New World, Africa, South Asia, and the East.

The Evolution of Colonialism in Sub-Saharan Africa

By the end of the 16th Century, Portuguese naval supremacy began to give way to other, larger European powers, especially the Dutch, English, and French; and by the early 19th Century, Great

Britain was the dominant economic, political, and naval power in the world. For reasons of political economy, the British did not establish many formal colonies, but they controlled other nations in order to increase their economic power. They often were able to extend their power without asserting formal political control. Political control would have added administrative and defensive costs and responsibilities. One major exception to this policy was the situation in India, which became the crown jewel in Great Britain's overseas Empire, with its beginnings in the 17th Century with the East India Company.

Although the colonization of Africa was initiated in the 15th Century by the Portuguese, it was not until the resurgence of Germany and France that the colonization was pursued in earnest. Each of the European nations began vying for overseas possessions. The competing nations began to formally colonize territories, especially in Africa. In the 'Scramble for Africa,' European nations partitioned Africa among themselves at the Berlin West Africa Conference (1884-1885). Ironically, not a single African was invited to or participated in the conference.

The Germans were granted southwestern Africa, along with Tanganyika in East Africa. The Portuguese received Mozambique and Angola, in southern Africa. Belgium took the Congo, and France took possession of Senegal, the Cameroons, and several other colonies in western Sudan and Central Africa. The British claimed the rest of the continent. The result was that almost every part of the Africa was a colony of some European power.

Following WW I, Britain and France took over the colonial possessions of Germany and the Ottoman Empire in Africa and the Middle East. They managed these areas, called mandates, as trustees under direction of the League of Nations. Mandated territories were supposed to be managed in the interests of the indigenous peoples, as well as in the interests of the world at large. Following World War II, the United Nations (UN) replaced the Mandates Commission with the Trusteeship Council, and the areas that had been known as mandates were relabeled as trusts. Under the old Mandate Commission, the European powers had assumed that a mandate would remain dependent on the administering nation, without ever becoming an independent state. The charter for the Trusteeship

Council, however, required the administering nations to set a target date for the trusts' independence.

Map 3-2: Colonial Africa, circa 1916

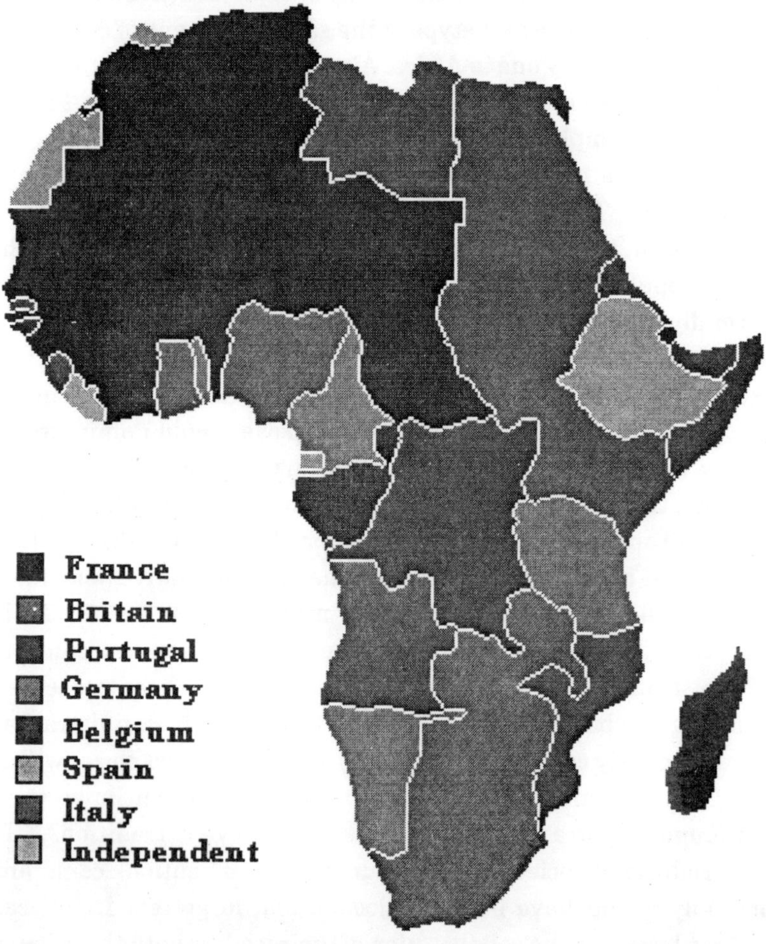

Source: (Swedish fusilier, 2008)

Several Asian colonies, India, Ceylon, and Burma, stepped-up their struggle to end colonial domination. After achieving independence and becoming members of the UN General Assembly, several of these former colonies led a campaign against colonialism, pointing to the provisions of the Trusteeship Council charter. In this way, trusteeship served to accelerate the movement toward decolonization throughout the world.

Types of Colonies

Although there are essentially two types of colonial types – colonies of settlement and colonies of exploitation – in Africa, by far the most common form was the colony of exploitation. South Africa was the not only the archetype of the settlement type of colony but it was also the only one in Africa. Algeria might be added to the list of African settlement colonies but, in reality, it was the French intention to simply annex it as a new province.

Colonies of exploitation differed greatly from colonies of settlement. The primary difference was that in colonies of exploitation, the colonial rulers were grossly outnumbered by the native population. In Africa, as in British India, the colonial powers normally allied themselves with the powerful native elites; and it was through these alliances that political and economic control was exerted. As long as the powerful native classes had a stake in the success of the colonialists, the colonial power could dominate the colony with minimal economic or military expense. For example, in India, the British colonial service seldom exceeded 1,200 British personnel and yet dominated a population of several hundred million. Yet, almost all the day-to-day functionaries were native personnel.

In the absence of sufficient manpower or resources to effectively and directly administer their colonies, colonial administrations had to rely on local powerbrokers. These local elites, realizing the benefit of working with the colonial administration, were effectively co-opted; at the same time, they gained power within their own communities and were rewarded. To legitimize their newfound importance petty leaders would invent traditions.[16] In less traditional societies and cultures, these inventions could and probably would have been overlooked and forgotten. In African society, however, the collaboration of their leaders with the colonial powers and the invention of traditions only served to destabilize the long-established social structures of the colonies.

Once the colonial powers lost the support of the native power brokers, they found themselves in a difficult position. They could either invest large sums to buy power and maintain a strong military presence, or they could relinquish power to native leaders. Both strategies were tried but, in the end, local resistance resulted in the disengagement of the colonial powers from their colonies.

Colonies of exploitation were simply not economically or politically tenable in the absence of native cooperation.

Part of the success of the native elites was also based on a tradition of bribery and nepotism. Following independence, bribery evolved into wholesale corruption and the financial resources of many nations were plundered for the sole benefit of native political and economic leaders. In Nigeria alone, it is estimated that not less than 400 billion dollars was either squandered or embezzled by the nation's leaders between 1960 and 1999.[17] To put this amount in some kind of perspective, 400 billion dollars is larger than the total amount of foreign aid provided to all of Africa during the same period![18]

Political Practice in the Colonies

By its very nature, colonialism is inherently un-democratic. Colonial governments seldom permitted native participation in governance. Political decisions were made without the benefit of input from the indigenous people. Consequently, the native populations were never given the opportunity to practice self-governance until the colonial powers abandoned them. As a consequence, most of the newly emerging colonies had little or no concept regarding the day-to-day workings of self-rule or governance.

The establishment of law and order was one of the primary objectives of every colonial regime, and considerably more money went into the creation and maintenance of policing authorities, than went into social or infrastructural development spending. Little to no home funding was available to most colonial administrators. Each colony was required to be self-sufficient, even in the face of the rapacious removal of the colony's mineral and economic assets.

The lack of funding to implement genuine social and economic change meant that the colonial officers were forced to follow a policy of divide and conquer. By implementing policies that intentionally weakened indigenous power networks and institutions, the colonial powers were able to maintain their power and influence. Many of Africa's current political problems can be traced back to colonial policies that sought to exploit linguistic, religious, and ethnic differences. In so doing, instead of building a nation, the colonialists sought to weaken local groups by implementing policies that would tear at the very social fabric of an already tribal environment.

Also, in their haste to colonize Africa, the colonial powers divided the continent into spheres of influence, giving no consideration to traditional boundaries, history, or cultural or ethnic diversity. As a consequence, traditionally antagonistic groups found themselves thrown together with one another. Only colonial domination contained these traditional animosities. Following independence, many of these same boundaries defined the new African states, without addressing the smoldering cultural and ethnic differences of the population. Even today, these differences have not been adequately addressed, except in the form of civil wars, conflicts, and rebellion, which, in some cases have resulted in the

Map 3- 3: Traditional African Tribal and Modern National Boundaries

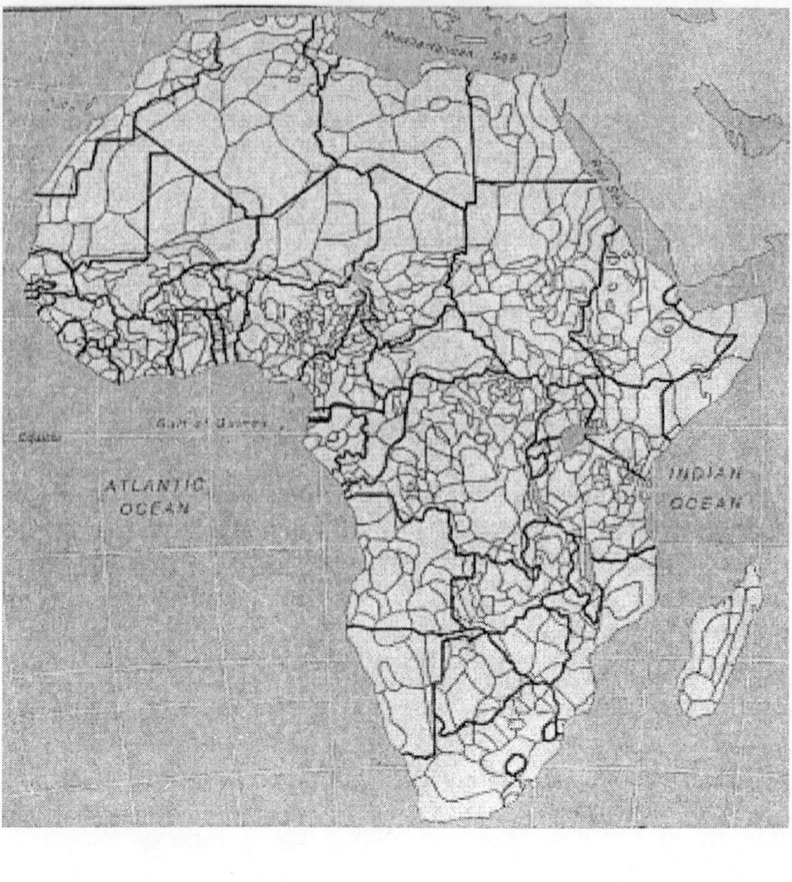

creation of still more political units, for example, Eritrea was separated from Ethiopia in 1993, after more than 30 years of ethnic civil war.[19]

One need only look at a map depicting traditional tribal and modern African national boundaries to begin to grasp the difficulty that colonial administrators and modern political leaders faced in their efforts to maintain law and order, and peace. Africa is a veritable quilt work of ethnic, cultural, economic, religious and linguistic differences; and many of these differences had coalesced into institutionalized antagonism well before the arrival of the Europeans. See Map 3-3.

Economic Practices in the Colonies

Two types of colonial economies prevailed in Africa. The first was based solely on the extraction of the colony's mineral resources. This required that the colonials focused their attentions on the discovery, exploitation, and export of the colony's most profitable resources. In these colonies the emphasis was on the development of mining operations, especially gold, silver, and precious stones, like diamonds.

The second type of economy was based on the identification and export of agricultural products, especially those that could be used at home for food or as raw materials for manufactures. Little or no attention was given to local needs, uses, or consumption.

All the profits from the export of minerals and agricultural products were sent to home. The small tariffs, duties, and taxes placed on exports were retained in the colony for the financial and operating requirements of the colonial regime. As a consequence, the in-country colonial regimes were almost continuously on the verge of financial collapse.

Whether for mining operations or farming, inexpensive labor was required. When adequate numbers of laborers could not be recruited to work in the mines or the fields, the colonial regimes, often resorted to schemes based on forced labor. In either case, the laborers were poorly paid, worked in unsafe conditions, survived in unsanitary and deplorable housing, and often were separated from their families for long periods. These long term separations posed both social and economic hardships on the families. Wives and children were often left to fend for themselves with little or no financial support since the wage paid to the conscripted or volunteer laborer was, at best, grossly inadequate. However, to have paid the workers more or improved working or living conditions would have reduced profits.

Undoubtedly, one of the most significant consequences of colonialism is the alienation of the indigenous people from their land with the arrival of European colonists. The best agricultural lands were appropriated by the colonists and the less desirable, less productive lands were left to the indigenous population. On the best, well-watered agricultural lands, European colonists built their plantations, while the local people were forced to survive on agriculturally marginal land in areas of low rainfall.

The return of the appropriated lands, even today, years after independence, is a genuine legal and political issue for many. In the absence of reliable, historical documentation, it becomes increasingly difficult to restore legitimate land rights to the descendants of those people who were originally alienated from their land.

Social Implications of Colonialism

To supply the labor requirements of the mines and plantations, large numbers of people were uprooted from areas that were not involved in colonial production to areas that were. Often these large-scale movements of people left families stranded and alone in villages, while the family's head was far away working in a mine or on a plantation. This frequently resulted in both men and women having to cope with spousal absences. These movements had a number of consequences for traditional African societies. Social and cultural beliefs and practices were affected by contacts with peoples with differing social organizations and beliefs. Included in these changes were such simple but important habits as the type of food eaten or how it was prepared. They also, over time, altered the traditional family structures in parts of Africa. Where once the extended family arrangement was the dominant form, the nuclear family structure was becoming much more prevalent. Such processes caused further change and stress within the context of traditional African social structures, and they never recovered, even after the close of the colonial period.

Early colonialist encountered people with myriad religious beliefs alongside the practice of Islam, which was the largest formal religion in Africa . With colonialism came Christian missionaries. Today, nearly half of the people in former colonies refer to themselves as Christians. British and French colonials actively discouraged Christian missionary work in Muslim areas, unlike the Portuguese and Spanish. Even so, indigenous religions and religious beliefs have survived alongside mainstream Christianity and Islam.

Many Muslims in colonial Africa had access to Koranic education, even before the onset of the colonial period. However, this form of education was restricted to the learning and understanding of the Koran, and did not necessarily include general educational skills, for example, numeracy, economics, or critical thinking. Also, the Koran is written in Arabic, and many Muslims were given no formal instruction in their native, local languages.

Although the colonial authorities believed that it was important to 'enlighten' and 'civilize' the indigenous population, no effort seems to have been made to provide the children of the colonies with formal, general educational opportunities. What educational opportunities that were made available were primarily through the work of missionaries, not the colonial regime. However, the missions could only do so much. As a consequence, throughout the colonial period, most African children did not receive formal educational training. In fact, no colony could boast that even half of their children were functionally literate. Almost all the native leaders of modern African independence movements and post-colonial leaders were the product of missionary education.

Despite the legitimate belief that colonial domination left in its wake a legacy of social, economic, and political destitution, it does not explain Africa's failure to thrive during the post-colonial independence period. Other areas of colonial domination are experiencing rapid economic development. Undoubtedly, the premier example of this process is India. There is little difference between the implementation of British colonialism in Africa or India; yet, today India is the second fastest growing economy in the world, with an annual growth rate of around 8 percent, and creating more new billionaires in a year than other countries have done in hundreds of years.[20] Obviously, colonialism in Africa, in spite of all its bad press, cannot adequately explain the region's inability to mount a sustainable drive toward economic growth.

Alex Perry of *Time* suggests that India has to one "indispensible asset" that serves to explain much of its political and economic success: "the ingenuity of its citizens."[21] As a consequence of sheer human effort and creativity, economic progress is achieved in spite of poor infrastructure, weak government, searing inequality, corruption and crime, poor sanitation, inadequate and outdated transport, inadequate medical care, and abject poverty. If British colonialism did not suck the life out of India and render it a seething socio-economic morass, why did it in Africa? Clearly, there must have been other factors at work that produced the situation we see today in Africa.

Geography

W. Gorden East wrote, concerning how the physical environment affects historical events:

The geographical elements which are compounded in any area of land, which can be analysed separately but are in fact interdependent, range from climate, position, structure, land forms (including relief and drainage), soils, and vegetation, to human societies themselves and all that they engrave upon the soil. . . .

All of these and other interconnected factors condition, though they do not determine, the activities of man, who is himself no mean agent of geographical change.[22]

If ever there was a case, where one could invoke the possibility of geographical determinism, Africa might well be a suitable example. The geography of Africa simply may represent one of the leading causes of the region's socio-economic difficulties. First, it is an immense area occupied by comparatively few people, there are virtually no navigable rivers, and as a consequence, they are isolated from one another and the world. Second, it consists of large areas of highlands and basins that are covered by a range of vegetation types but tends to be dominated by savannahs, or grasslands, and semi-arid brushy woodlands. Third, the weather ranges from hot and humid (rain forest to savannah) to hot and dry (steppe to desert conditions), yet there is sufficient moisture almost everywhere to permit the breeding of disease-carrying mosquitoes. Finally, the soils of Africa have been depleted of their fertility by both nature, in the form of rainfall, which leaches out nutrients, and man, who has cropped the land mercilessly without the benefit of modern chemical or organic fertilization. As Sach's so succinctly put it:

. . . geography has conspired with economics to give Africa a particularly weak hand.[23]

Africa is plagued by problems of distance, disease, drought, and a difficult ecology. Even with all our scientific resources, technology, and mobility, we cannot evade or control all the dangers and difficulties that are simply a part of our environment. For less technologically advanced societies, both past and present, we can only imagine how severe and foreboding the physical setting of Africa must have seemed. In the absence of suitable technology, technology that would permit people to alter their environment or better adapt to it, history may well be all geography.

Population Distribution and Market Isolation

Africa represents a large land mass occupied by comparatively few people, who have been, either because of culture, ecology, or economy, concentrated in the interior of the continent. See Map 3-4.

This pattern is somewhat surprising, since almost everywhere else in the world, people have tended to live – near the coasts, near supplies of fresh water, in temperate climates, in flat terrain, and where the soils are most fertile. In general, the distribution of people in Africa does not comply with most of these general human tendencies. The people of Africa do not live along the coasts, they are distributed throughout areas of moderate-to-severe water shortages, very little of Africa is temperate, and the soils tend to be poor. It does have, however, immense areas of flat grasslands but in these areas there is little rainfall and the soils tend to be lacking in fertility without major inputs of human technology. One could say that Africa has everything going against it.

As a consequence of the population's concentration in the interior, combined with relatively low population densities and a large landmass, the transportation of goods and raw materials mandates transport over great distances. During colonial times, with the emphasis on the out-shipping of raw materials –

Map 3-4: Population Densities in Africa

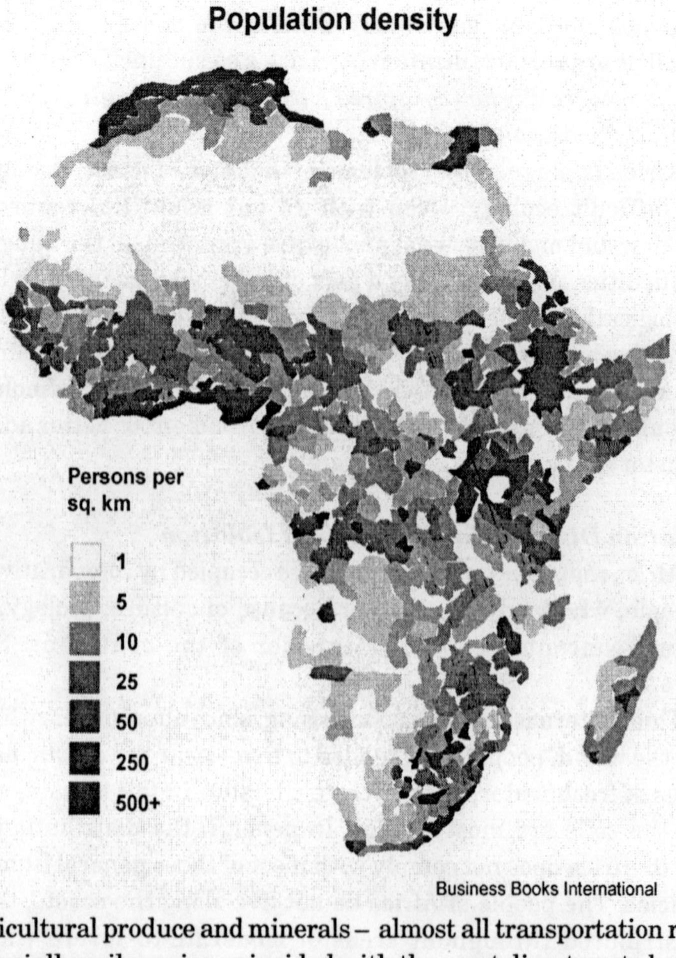

agricultural produce and minerals – almost all transportation routes, especially rail service, coincided with the most direct route between mines and transshipment points, ports. Moreover, Africa is effectively cut-off from the more populated and more highly developed nations or markets of Europe and the Mediterranean. By land, they are cut-off by the Sahara Desert; and sea transport, especially for those countries accessing the sea routes from the eastern side of the continent, must either 'sail around the Cape' or utilize the Suez Canal. Both of which result in added distance and expense.

Further, one need only look at a topographic map of Africa to see that there are few natural harbors along the thousands of miles of coastline. Normally, populations cluster around harbors but with no deepwater harbors, there was no advantage to living along the coasts; and malaria was much more prevalent along the coasts than in the higher elevations of the interior. Furthermore, the slave trade, for centuries, made those living along the coasts much more vulnerable. Living in the interior made it more difficult for slave traders to capture and transport their captives back to their waiting ships, since numerous rapids in nearly every major river in makes it impossible for ships and boats to run upriver any appreciable distance, thereby accessing the African interior.

Drawing from Torero and Chowdhury:

Unlike Asia and Latin America, Africa inherited a highly dispersed and unevenly distributed infrastructure from its colonial past. There was little, if any, improvement of infrastructure during the colonial era, and, according to Platteau (1996), 'in some important respects, it can even be said that colonial policy reinforced the handicaps of AFRICA' (p. 200). The limited infrastructure that was built during that era was driven by the objective of connecting natural resources to export markets. For example, Platteau noted that 'two-thirds of the African railways built in the colonial period connected mines to a coastal harbor.' (p. 200). The rest of the continent was virtually ignored and, according to Boserup (1981), 'only the Union of South Africa with mass immigration of Europeans had more than six meters of railways per square kilometer in 1970 and six countries had no railways at all.' (p. 148).[24]

Equally important is the general absence of any extensive road system from the coast to the interior, or within the interior. Outside the major urban centers, paved roads are the exception, rather than the rule. In large measure, this is simply a function of the high costs associated with road construction and maintenance.

Johnson has gone so far as to say:

Perhaps the lack of roads is the greatest handicap to a productive economy, because physical isolation means not only an inability to sell produce and to buy necessary consumer goods but involves an intellectual separation of the roadless villages from currents of thought and action in urban areas and from information and ideas in those rural areas that are in better contact with towns and cities.[25]

The low population densities are also reflected in very few towns and cities, which further exacerbates both transport, trade, and general communication and the diffusion of ideas. The villages of Africa are frequently little more than the a clustering of a few huts that enclose an area used to protect chickens and other livestock and some firewood. Most have no electricity, no sanitation, no telecommunications, and virtually no motorized vehicles, and many do not even have animal-drawn, transport. In effect, the hinterlands of the existing markets, towns, or cities are significantly larger than one finds elsewhere, and they are much more dispersed.

In the absence of well integrated water or road transport infrastructure, the costs of accessing either internal or world markets are extremely high and is exacerbated by long distances between the markets and the widely distributed, rural population. The effect of high transportation costs in Africa was examined by Limao and Venables. They concluded that if transportation costs could be halved, it could increase the volume of transport nine-fold.[26] For example, between 1986 and 1988 long-distance freight tariffs in French West Africa were over five times higher than comparable tariffs in India, Pakistan and Vietnam.[27] More recent studies suggest that long distance freight rates in Tanzania are three times higher than in Indonesia.[28] At present, if Africa transport costs could be brought into line with other developing nations of South, East and Southeast Asia, it would go a long way toward freeing it from the poverty trap it finds itself in.

High Disease Burden

Disease has always been seen as a consequence of poverty, not as a cause. In the case of malaria and HIV/AIDS an argument can be made that together these diseases do, in fact, contribute to the poverty of Africa. The relationship has been anecdotally observed but, until recently, either the data were unavailable, or no one pursued and tested the observations. They were simply assumed to be true. Now, a number of eminent scholars have endeavored to establish the link between disease and national impoverishment.

When one compares maps of HDI or poverty with malaria incidence maps, almost immediately one can see that the patterns are nearly congruent. Gallup, Snow, Kiszewski, and Sachs all have come to nearly the same conclusion – there is a strong correlation between the incidence of malaria and slow economic development.[29] This is particularly true in Africa. Virtually all efforts to eradicate the disease in tropical countries have been unsuccessful. Those countries that have eliminated malaria have all been either subtropical or islands.[30] The only parts of Africa free of malaria are the northern and southern extremes, which have the richest countries on the continent.

Malaria

Of the 150 countries with populations greater than 1 million in 1995, which accounted for more than 99% of the world's population, 44 face chronic problems with malaria. Thirty-five (35) of these 44 countries are in Africa. Of the 119 poorest countries, all but 12 have some incidence of malaria.[31] Of the Earth's 6+ billion people, 3.2 billion are at risk of malaria transmission. Between 350 and 500 million cases of clinical malaria are reported annually. Of those afflicted, about one million die; 90 percent of those that die live in Africa and most are children![32]

Malaria is a vector driven infectious disease caused by protozoan parasites of the genus *Plasmodium*. Only four types of the plasmodium parasite can infect humans; the most serious forms of the disease are caused by *Plasmodium falciparum* and *Plasmodium vivax*, but other related species (*P. ovale*, *P. malariae*) can also affect humans. Malaria parasites are transmitted only by the female mosquito of the genus *Anopheles*. There are approximately 400 *Anopheles* species, of which 30-40 transmit all four parasites of the genus *Plasmodium* that cause malaria.

Four factors contribute to the incidence of malaria:

- Climate
- The distribution of the *Anopheles* mosquito
- The particular species of the *Anopheles*
- The distribution of the four *Plasmodium* species.

The generally held belief that malaria is only a danger in tropical and subtropical climatic zones is incorrect. The transmission of malaria can occur anywhere that the *Anopheles* mosquito or the *Plasmodium* parasite are able to survive. Map 3-5, below, shows just how widely distributed the *Anopheles* mosquito species is.

Map 3-5: Distribution of the Genus Anopheles

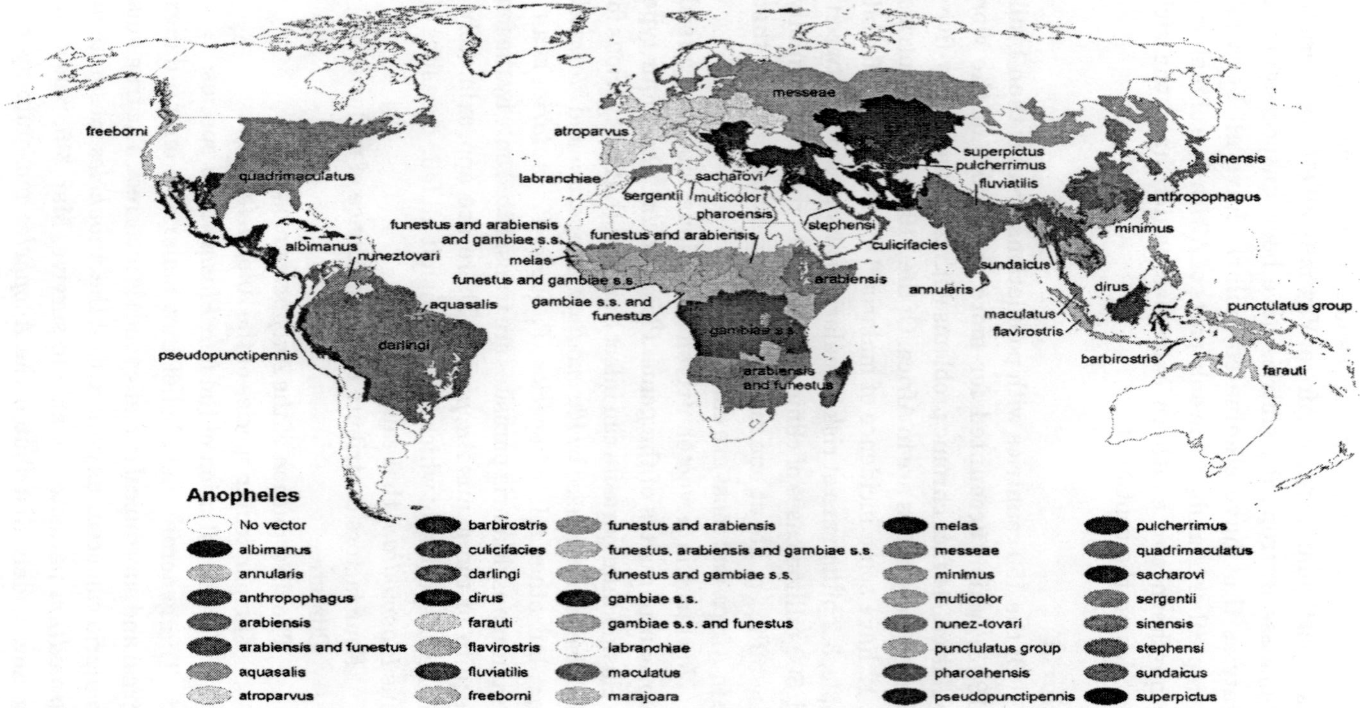

Source: (Kiszewski, Anthony, et. al., 2004)

Malaria can be transmitted year round but factors affecting its transmission include: high altitudes, during cooler seasons in some areas, and in deserts. The most important factor is the vector, or the *Anopheles* mosquito. Without the *Anopheles*, there would be no mechanism for the transmission of the parasite, since the *Plasmodium* parasite is dependent upon the *Anopheles* for the completion of its life cycle, a process known as sporogony, and the reintroduction to a new human or animal host. The process of sporogony normally takes two weeks, depending upon the ambient temperature; and two weeks is about the life span of the mosquito. The warmer the temperature, the faster the process of sporogony, and the greater the likelihood that the mosquito will bite a second host, transferring the newly gestated *Plasmodium* parasite to a new host.

In Africa a number of *Anopheles* mosquito species are common. Of the African species, some are indiscriminate in their choice of hosts. Some feed on animals, some feed on man, and some feed on both. The transfer of malaria requires the mosquito to bite a host twice, once to infect itself with the *Plasmodium* parasite and a second bite to transfer the parasite to a new host.

In much of Africa, the *Anophelese gambiase s.s.* species prefers to bite only humans. In addition, the *A. gambiase s.s.* and the deadliest genus of *Plasmodium*, *P. falciparum* often team up, making a formidable combination – a mosquito almost exclusively dependent on human blood and the most lethal form of malaria for humans. In addition, these two species have one of the largest distributions in Africa.

If a *gambiase* bites an infected host and becomes infected, in all likelihood it will bite a second human, thereby transferring the malaria parasite to the new host and the parasite's life cycle begins anew. In Africa and India, alike, there are species that will more frequently feed on cattle, two out of three times. When they feed on cattle, the odds of infecting a new human host declines.

Mathematically, the chance that an Indian mosquito will feed off two humans in a row is about one out of nine, whereas in Africa it's about one out of one, or nearly certain. The force of transmission of malaria in Africa is therefore roughly nine times that of India because of the difference of mosquito species.[33]

Map 3-6: Malaria Ecology Index

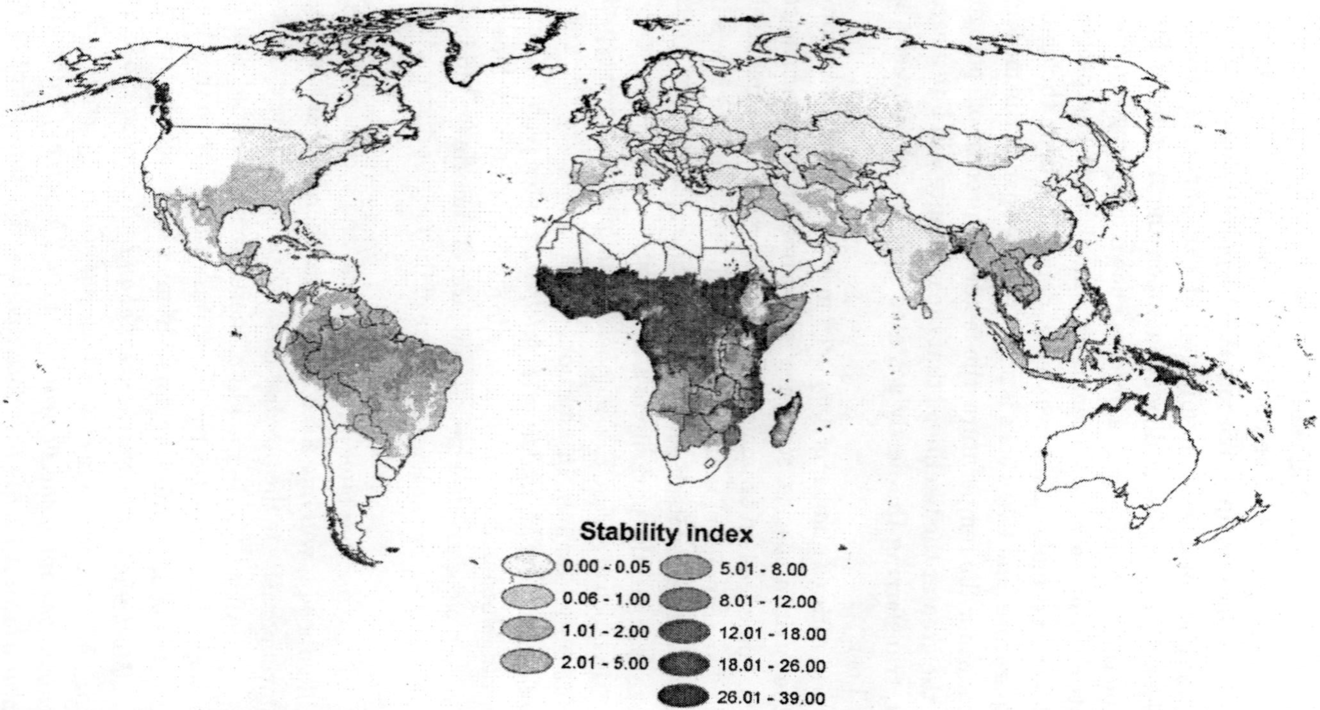

Source: (Kiszewski, Anthony, et. al., 2004)

Furthermore, two of the four species of malarial parasite that infect man exist in Africa. The species known as *P. falciparum* is the most deadly and is responsible for the largest number of human deaths in Africa. The second variant, *P. viavax*, is widespread in the tropics and subtropics but is much less lethal.One could not ask for a more suitable ecology than that of Africa for malaria. It has high temperatures, almost limitless breeding places, and mosquitoes that prefer to feed on humans, rather than cattle. There are very few other locations in the world that share similar ecologies. Within this ecological context, it is much easier to appreciate the underlying malaria burden that is imposed on Africa's population.

Malaria is treatable. In many areas that were once infected by the malaria parasite, it has been eradicated, through the elimination of breeding grounds or breaking the life cycle of the parasite. In sub-tropical and temperate climatic zones, the process of eradication is much simpler than in tropical areas. Malaria has been eradicated in North America, most of Europe, Asia north of the Himalayas, China, North Africa, the Middle East, Australia, and the southern half of South America. See the areas of malarial persistence, Figure 3-7, below.

In Africa, malaria eradication programs have proven largely ineffective. As a consequence, virtually everyone in Africa contracts the disease at least once a year, requiring medical attention. Others live with the disease year-round, without clinical symptoms.

Forty (40) percent of the world's population, 2.6 billion people, is at risk of malaria, which killed at least a million people in 2004. Ninety (90) percent of those that died were children, and 90 percent lived in Africa. The number of malaria related deaths is on the rise, with some experts suggesting that the number of malaria deaths may be as high as three million every year.[39] In part, this is the result of the failure of malaria eradication programs, failure to institute or perpetuate such programs, and the encroachment of malaria on areas that had been malaria free or areas that had been brought under control. In some areas, the *Anopheles* has become immune to many of the current insecticides used in their control.

Map 3-7: Malarial Persistence[34]

Source: Map Modified from (Hay, S. I., et. al., 2004)***HIV/AIDS***

The Impact of Malaria and HIV/AIDS

According to the Global Fund's Disease Report, 2005, the incidence of HIV and AIDS reached its highest level in 2004, with an estimated 39.4 million people living with the infection or disease. At the same time, the disease killed an estimated 3.1 million people, worldwide.[35] Of all the world's regions, Africa has the largest share of HIV and AIDS victims, an estimated 25.4 million, or 64.5 percent of the world total; and of the 3.1 million who died of the disease, Africa accounted for nearly 75 percent of those deaths.[36]

By comparison, in South and Southeast Asia, the incidence of HIV and AIDS is estimated to be 6.4 million in 2004.[37] India, in particular, has among developing nations, an exceedingly low incidence level, 1 percent, but with a population in excess of 1 billion, that level if incidence represents nearly 80 percent of South and Southeast Asia's total number of victims. India was hit early by the disease. Only recently has the disease become a source of concern in Nepal, while, in Pakistan and Bangladesh, the incidence level is extremely low, among the lowest in the region.[38]

Recently, the number of HIV and AIDS cases has been on the rise, although the pattern of new cases varies from country to country and region to region. Nevertheless, nearly 40 million people have the infection or disease, and that number is increasing. AIDS kills approximately 3 million people each year.

Together, malaria and HIV/AIDS affects nearly half of the world's total population! Half of the world's population has been, in all likelihood, condemned to premature death, and many of these deaths will be our next generation, our children. This is, a startling statistic. With these facts, what does it portend for Africa, where the bulk of the world's malaria and HIV/AIDS victims live? Basically, at least on the surface, things are likely to get worse long before they get better.

Sachs and others have repeatedly demonstrated the causal relationship between disease and poverty. The relationship between the two, however, is not linear, i.e., disease causes poverty and poverty increases the incidence of disease. There is a reciprocal relationship between them.

HIV/AIDS and malaria play a significant role in slowing and even reversing current economic growth and development progress for entire countries and regions. Low-income households have less access to resources, information and products to protect them from disease. When they are ill, the poor in most countries also have limited access to adequate health services and may lose badly needed income because they are too sick to work. The direct costs of illness (i.e. treatment and care) to households in the poorest countries and the indirect costs of lost earnings and other opportunity costs escalate according to the severity and duration of the disease:

Each episode of malaria may cost up to 3% of a household's annual income – and a household may experience many episodes per year; the average annual loss of income in the poorest households in Malawi is 20%.[40] Terminal AIDS disease costs from 8 to 100% of household income.[41] The burden of these diseases at the individual and community level leads to a significant macroeconomic impact:

- The per capita GDP of malaria-affected countries is less than one-fifth of the GDP of non-affected countries.
- The countries hardest hit by HIV/AIDS in Africa are losing 1 to 2% in economic growth every year.[42]

In the long term, AIDS has the potential to cause the collapse of entire economies as it dramatically weakens human capital from generation to generation.

All disease imposes a significant burden on the health care systems of every nation but it is more deeply felt in already poor developing nations. Up to 70% of hospital beds are allocated to AIDS-related diseases in Africa.[43] Malaria accounts for up to 40% of outpatient visits and up to 50% of all hospital admissions in Africa.[44] Overcrowding in hospitals in parts of Asia and Africa commonly result in two patients per hospital bed, putting patients with depressed immune systems at further risk while in hospital.

In some countries, health workers are at greater risk of contracting HIV simply due to inadequate supplies of basic commodities such as latex gloves. The continuing devastation of health sector capacity through the deaths of trained staff has prompted some countries to give treatment priority to doctors, nurses and others who work in the health sector, in order to keep them alive to care for others.

In Botswana, up to one-third of health workers are HIV-positive, and the figure is expected to rise to 40% by 2005.[45] In Lusaka, the capital of Zambia, 39% of midwives and 44% of nurses are estimated to be living with HIV.[46]

With these truths firmly fixed in our minds, the question is why? Why are the people of Africa being devastated by the malaria and HIV/AIDS epidemics? In part, the First World, the developed nations of the world, have tacitly given up on Africa. This resignation may not appear in official statements or policy announcements but, nevertheless, the sentiment exists. On the positive side, however, there are a plethora of non-governmental organizations (NGOs) working alone or in concert to address the issues of HIV/AIDS and malaria. The only drawback to these NGOs is funding. They simply do not have or have access to the resources necessary to adequately combat either disease. The governments of the world do.

In the case of malaria, the World Health Organization, World Bank, USAID, and International Monetary Fund are providing little to no support for malaria eradication or treatment. Instead of grants or projects in each country of malaria-infested Africa, there is only the occasional and albeit nominal effort. Instead of billions of dollars devoted to research and eradication programs, the grants are in the tens of millions of dollars.[47] Such small amounts are a disgrace, especially in light of the scope and magnitude of the problem and its direct impact on peoples' lives and the economies of their countries.

The situation of HIV/AIDS is similar but different. It is similar to the extent that the developed nations of the world have made few, if any, concessions with regard to the provision of medications that might, even if they won't cure the disease, at least prolong the lives of those already infected. Between 1990 and 1998, on average only $74 million was allocated to all programs for HIV and AIDS control efforts from all sources of funding.[48]

Additionally, based on an analysis of the amounts provided over the years, it is apparent that the grants or loans were sporadic year to year. Likewise, the agencies and organizations which should have had the highest profiles often were absent from the field for years on end. For example, the World Bank provided only three dedicated loans for the control of AIDS between 1990 and 1998 in Africa. Equally shocking is the fact that AIDS funding declined by as much as 50 percent between 1988 and 1997, to less than $10 per HIV infected person, and this estimate is believed to be overestimated.[49] Since then, the number of infected has grown almost exponentially.

Why has the epidemic of HIV and AIDS in Africa, apparently gone unaddressed? The history of the pandemic suggests that donor nations' priorities and financial stringency, and issues within recipient countries, brought about the past and present levels of aid funding. The consequence of this neglect has been that what started out as an epidemic, is now a pandemic, with millions of people being infected each year and an equal number dying, many of which live in Africa. The inattention of the developing nations was exacerbated by their inaction or gross underfunding of AIDS prevention programming. As a consequence, the original outbreak, which might have been contained, just as Ebola outbreaks have been, is now a resident evil in almost every country of the world.

There is also the built-in inertia of government and aid agencies. Even as the numbers of AIDS victims increased, domestically and internationally, and medical progress was being made in the treatment of the AIDS retroviruses, government agencies and aid organizations were exceedingly slow to respond. By the time they had begun to respond, it was too late and too little. The world was already faced with a pandemic.

In addition, the all-omniscient developed countries 'decided' what the developing nations needed. As a consequence, instead of the donor countries listening to the specific needs and requests of the receiving nations, the donors fabricated the type and form of assistance the receiving nations would receive. Failing to listen to the receiving nations resulted in inefficiency, assumptions based on the lack of in-the-field knowledge, and the belief that the donor nations were better prepared to make judgment calls that receiving nations were not prepared to make. This decision-making, from the top down, effectively permitted an epidemic to evolve into a worldwide catastrophe. Once the genie was out of the box, no amount of money could put it back. Since the beginning, the developing countries, which had all the answers, underestimated the magnitude of the problem, and ethnocentrism prevented taking action in time to stop the spread of a catastrophic killer. Now, that killer is sapping the very life out of Africa.

Together, AIDS and malaria are literally sapping the strength of the people, killing them, consuming the individual and collective resources of the people and their governments, hindering every effort to stimulate economic development, and even driving the economies of some of these Sub-Saharan nations backward.

Observations

Since the first colony was established in the region, the resources of each colony have been plundered for economic reasons and colonial aggrandizement, not for the benefit of those colonized. Even with the decolonization of the region, little changed. Self-rule, while heady stuff after years of colonial domination, carried with it burdens and responsibilities that the native populations did not have to address as long as they were dependencies. More importantly, colonialism deprived the people of both the right and the ability to be self-governing. They had absolutely no experience in self-governance; and yet, independence thrust this responsibility on the ill-prepared people, with, oftentimes, disastrous consequences, economically and in terms of human lives.

Combined with the lack of experience in the area of self-governance, the independent countries of Africa had to deal with the absence of a developed infrastructure, an ecology that, if not preventing social and economic uplift, at least slowed it, and the burden of a persistent, endemic disease, malaria. Added to this was the emergence of HIV and AIDS. Historically, economically, politically, and environmentally, Africa was dealt an exceedingly poor hand, and nothing seems to have changed the region's run of bad luck. In fact, it just seems to get worse, with no observable end in sight, because of the lackluster efforts of the developed nations of the world. At every turn, the nations of Africa have been thwarted at self-improvement and have been unable to take advantage of the nominal assistance of the donor nations of the world. To characterize Africa as a quagmire is almost too generous a label. Saying that Africa is caught in a poverty trap is like saying to a man under water for an hour, "You're drowning."

References

1. (PRB, August 2007), p. 7. Typically, the number of nations included in Sub-Saharan Africa is 53; however, for our purposes some island natons have been excluded from our list and consideration, for

example, Madagascar, São Tomé and Príncipe, Comoros, Mauritius, Seychelles, as well as South Africa.

2. UN Report, 12/98.
3. (Sachs, Jeffrey D., et. al., April 29, 2004 Version), p. 2.
4. (Ogwang, 2001), p. 3. See also, (Engineer, February 22, 2008).
5. (UNDP, 2007), Table 2, p. 234-237.
6. See Technical Note 1, pp. 355-361, (Watkins, Kevin, et. al., 2007)
7. (Rural Poverty Portal, 2008); and (IFAD, 2001), p. 22.
8. (Rao, C. H. H.; S. K. Ray; and K. Subbarao, 1988).
9. (Nelson, M.; R. Dudal; H. Gregersen; N. Jodha; D. Nyamai; J. Groenewol; F. Torres; and A. Kassam, 1997).
10. (IFAD, 2001), p. 15.
11. A higher corruption rating indicates greater perceived corruption.
12. (Sachs, Jeffrey D., et. al., April 29, 2004 Version), p. 3.
13. This list of causes for Africa's current situation is based, in part, on (Sachs, Jeffrey D., et. al., April 29, 2004 Version).
14. See, for example, (Rodney, 1973); (Geyer, 2006); (Organski, 1968 (Digitized version May 2007); and (Doro, Marion E. and Newell Maynard Stultz , 1970).
15. (Smith, 1937), Book I, Chapter III, p. 19.
16. (Hobsbawm, Eric. J. and Terence O. Ranger, 1983).
17. (Malaysia Today, 2005)
18. *Ibid*. See also, (Mbeki, 2005)
19. See (Iyob, 1997) and (Kendie, 2005).
20. See (Elliot, Michael, et. al., 2006).
21. *Ibid.*, p. 27.
22. (East, 1965), p. 6.
23. (Sachs, 2005), p. 208,
24. (Torero, Maximo and Shyamal Chowdhury, April 2004), p. 2.
25. (Johnson, 1970), p. 196.
26. (Limao, N. and A.J. Venables, 1999).
27. (Rizet C. and J. Hine, 1993).
28. (Hine, J.L. and S.D. Ellis, 2001).
29. (Gallup, John Luke and Jeffrey D. Sachs, 2001); (Kiszewski, Anthony, et. al., 2004); (Snow, R. W., et. al, 2005); and (Sachs, 2005). See also, (Carter, Richard and Kamini N. Mendis, 2002); (Hay, S. I., et. al., 2004); and (Murray, C. J. L., and A. D. Lopez, 1997).
30. (Gallup, John Luke and Jeffrey D. Sachs, 2001), p. 85.

31. *Ibid.*
32. (WHO, 2005), p. xvii.
33. (Sachs, 2005), p. 199.
34. Map modified from (Hay, S. I., et. al., 2004), p. 328.
35. (The Global Fund, 2005), p. 10.
36. *Ibid.*, p. 14.
37. (The Global Fund, 2005), p. 20.
38. *Ibid.*
39. *Ibid*, p. 6.
40. (The Global Fund, 2005), p. 7.
41. (Russell, Steven, 2004b), see Table 4; see also, (Russell, Steven, 2004a).
42. (The Global Fund, 2005), p. 7.
43. *Ibid.*
44. *Ibid.*
45. *Ibid.*
46. *Ibid.*
47. (Sachs, 2005), p. 200.
48. (Attaran, Amir and Jeffrey Sachs, 2001), p.59.
49. *Ibid.*

Postscript

Recently, in *Popular Science* magazine (March 2009) and its website, PopSci.Com, an article appeared announcing the preliminary results of field trials conducted in Afria for an anti-milarial vaccination. The drug was prepared for the U. S. military by GlaxoSmithKline. For Corey Binns complete website posting -- *Knocking our Malaria*, See Appendix C.

4

Sub-Saharan Africa: Ecological and Agricultural Problems

Map 4-1: Farming Complexes of Sub-Saharan Africa

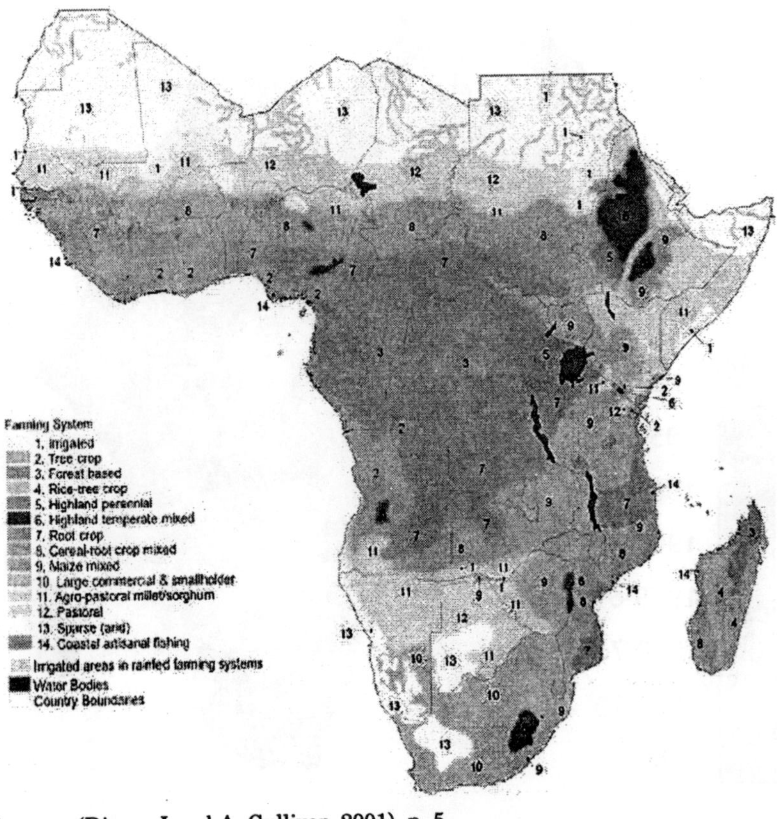

Source: (Dixon, J and A. Gulliver, 2001), p. 5.

Introduction

Sub-Saharan Africa is the only region in the world that over the last four decades has not increased its overall or *per capita* agricultural food production. Food production has not kept pace with the continent's basic food or industrial raw material needs.[1] While the number of malnourished was halved in Asia and Latin America between 1960 and 2000, it fell by only 2 percent in Africa. Agricultural productivity grew at an average annual rate of approximately 3 percent outside Africa, while in Africa it grew by only 0.6 percent until very recently.[2]

Sub-Saharan agriculture, with very few exceptions, has been in trouble since the first nations gained independence in the late 1950s. See Map 4-2, below. Countries that, before independence,

Map 4-2: Independence Dates for African Nations

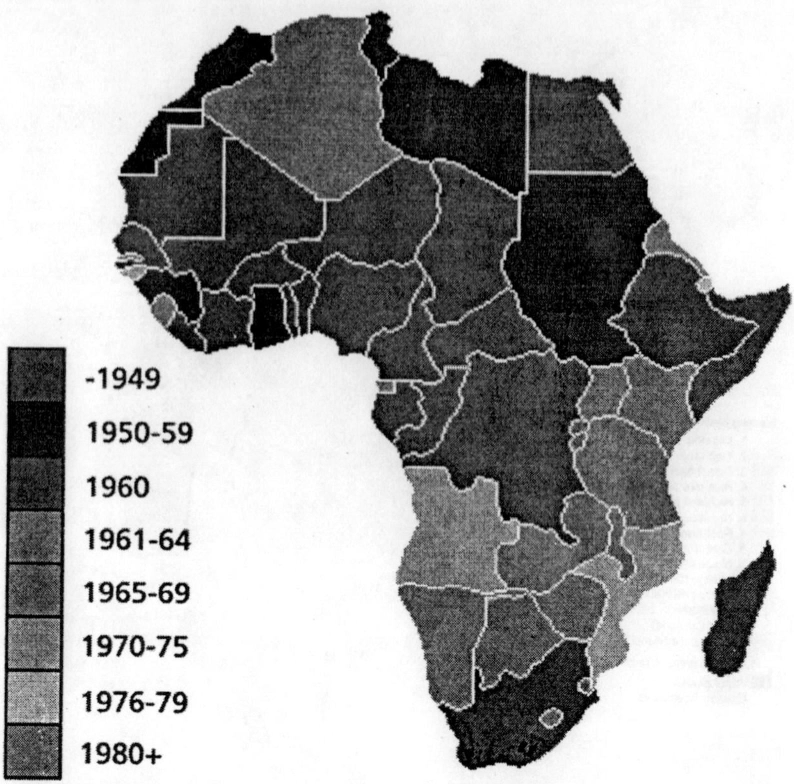

Source: (Roke, 2006)

had been self-sufficient in food and even exported agricultural produce and agricultural raw materials, have all become net food importers. Explanations for the current situation range from agriculture's inability to keep pace with population increases, the peoples' inability to cope with environmental insufficiencies, changes is consumption patterns, the non-availability of new agricultural technologies, infrastructural failures, and political neglect.[3] Civil wars and armed conflicts must also be added to this list. These conflicts disrupt agricultural pursuits, as well as interfering with the transport of produce to and between markets.

The decline in African agriculture, however, cannot be explained by population growth. *Actual production fell.* As a consequence, food insecurity has increased at the national and individual level, and with it, a decline in caloric intake. Now, the caloric intake in Africa is the lowest in the world and it is the only region where the number of malnourished is higher than it was 40 years earlier.

Africa and the Green Revolution

Everyone is waiting for Africa's Green Revolution, but there is very little indication that it is even on the way. Admittedly, there have been improvements in the agricultural sector but it is obvious that these changes have neither had the long-term effects that the planners and politicians had thought nor were they sufficiently persistent. More importantly, due to the inability of either the multinational corporations, who are pushing for modern agricultural research and development, or the African nations, individually and collectively, to come to a final agreement on the issues surrounding research, development, marketing, and agricultural trade, agricultural development has all but stagnated. This is especially true in the area of genetic engineering (GE) or genetic modification (GM), which nearly all development agencies see as the most promising area for agronomic research and food production within the context of Africa.

Africa is the only major region of the world that has yet to benefit from its own Green Revolution.[4] Africa has absorbed portions of Asia's model of the Green Revolution but with disappointing results. Many experts believe that an African version of the Green

Revolution is essential if it is to achieve food security. At present, approximately one-quarter of the total potentially arable land in of Sub-Saharan Africa is being utilized.[5] In the absence of monumental capital investments, it may not be possible to expand the agricultural land base. Normally, the utilization of existing arable land is the least expensive method for increasing agricultural production. This is not the case in Africa, however. To compensate for the inability to expand Africa's cultivable land area, agricultural intensification is essential. Food yields in Africa are the lowest in the world.[6] Improving its agricultural production and productivity is the key to combating hunger and stimulating the region's overall economic development.

Obstacles to an African Green Revolution

Differences in Ecologies

It has been suggested that the agronomic breakthroughs that resulted in South Asia's Green Revolution may not be directly transferrable within the context of Africa.Until the 1980s in India, the primary improved seed varieties were limited to wheat and rice. Other crops were developed later.

In Africa, the farmers cultivate a broad range of food crops that reflect Africa's more diverse agro-ecological zones. In general, their agricultural systems do not revolve around wheat and rice cultivation. The African dietary staples emphasize vegetables.The primary staple crops include: yams, plantains, green bananas, and cassava. Maize is only a secondary staple in the African diet.

Also, they depend largely on rain-fed cropping, rather than irrigation. Only 4 percent of Africa's arable land is irrigated. Although much of Africa has abundant water supplies, the region uses less than 3 per cent of its water resources, the lowest percentage in the developing world.[7] Reliance on rainfall makes the cultivators and their crops vulnerable to climatic or weather changes.

Within Sub-Saharan Africa, there are at least 12 recognized, major farming complexes.[8] The region is home to a wealth of ecological niches and bio-diversity. See the Map 4-1 at the beginning of the chapter and Table 4-1, below. Diversity is the norm in African farming. At the level of the individual farmer, there is further diversification. Typically, an individual farmer will grow 10 or more

Table 4-1: Major Farming Systems of Sub-Saharan Africa

Farming System	*Region*	*Agricultural Population as % f Region*	*Principal Crops or Livelihoods, in order of importance*
Irrigated	1	2	Rice, cotton, vegetables, rain fed crops, cattle, and poultry
Tree Crops	3	6	Cocoa, coffee, oil palm, rubber, yams, maize, and off-farm work
Forest Based	11	7	Cassava, maize, beans, and cocoyam
Rice-Tree Crops	1	2	Rice, banana, coffee, maize, cassava, legumes, livestock, and off-farm work
Highland Perennial	1	8	Banana, plantain, enset, coffee, cassava, sweet potato, beams, cereals, livestock, poultry, and off-farm work
Highland Temperate Mixed	2	7	Wheat, barley, tef, peas, lentils, broad beans, rape, potato, sheep, goats, livestock, poultry, and off-farm work
Root Crops	11	11	Yams, cassava, legumes, and off-farm work
Cereal-Root Crops Mixed	13	15	Maize, sorghum, millet, cassava, yams, legumes, and cattle

(Contd.)

(Contd. Table 4.1)

Farming System	*Region*	*Agricultural Population as % f Region*	*Principal Crops or Livelihoods, in order of importance*
Maize Mixed	10	15	Maize, tobacco, cotton, cattle, goats, poultry, and off-farm work
Large Commercial & Smallholder	5	4	Maize, pulses, sunflowers, cattle, sheep, goats, and remittances
Agro-Pastoral Millet/Sorghum	8	8	Sorghum, pearl millet, pulses, sesame, cattle, sheep, goats, poultry, and off-farm work
Pastoral	14	7	Cattle, camels, sheep, goats, remittances
Sparse (Arid)	17	1	Irrigated maize, vegetables, date palms, cattle, and off-farm work
Coastal Artisanal Fishing	2	3	Marine fish, coconuts, cashew, banana, yams, fruit, goats, poultry, and off-farm work
Urban Based	<1	3	Fruit vegetables, dairy, cattle, goats, poultry, and off-farm work

Source: (Dixon, J and A. Gulliver, 2001),

different crops in a season. The multiple cropping tradition among cultivators is both the boon and bane of African agriculture.

On the positive side, multiple cropping enhances the individual cultivator's chances of ameliorating the vagaries of nature. In essence, multiple cropping is traditional agriculture's equivalent of the statistician's game theory. Through years of experience, agriculturalists have developed cropping strategies that, under a broad range of potential weather outcomes, will either insure or maximize survivability.

The only drawback to this strategy is that multiple cropping reduces overall agricultural output since there are no economies of scale associated with any one crop and, therefore, there is only a limited likelihood of a marketable surplus. While this traditionally insured the probability of the cultivator's survival, it did not permit him to become involved in the much larger economic market system, especially the cash based economy of modern societies. Any surpluses realized were simply bartered for other foodstuffs required for subsistence. Thus, diversity locks cultivators into a perpetual cycle of minimal subsistence and precludes the ability to invest in technologies that would increase production. It also precludes the advantages of specialization.

African farming complexes are characterized by soils that have been leached to the point of near sterility and are, therefore, fragile. Continued use has only contributed to the soil's declining fertility. In the absence of broad spectrum solutions to the problems associated with multiple cropping, it must become more productive on a *per capita* basis, if Africa is to produce sufficient food to feed its people. This is obviously a simplistic assessment of a very complex problem but in the end, increased agricultural productivity is absolutely essential. Until the problems of Africa's existing agricultural complexes can be either streamlined or improved piecemeal, food security will remain an ever present problem.

The InterAcademy Council (IAC) examined the current farming systems of Africa in an effort to determine which of these agricultural complexes are most likely to contribute to Africa's overall agricultural production and would most effectively resolve the region's food insecurity problems. It selected:

- **The maize-mixed system**, based primarily on maize, cotton, cattle, goats, poultry and off-farm work;
- **The cereal/root crop-mixed system**, based primarily on maize, sorghum, millets, cassava, yams, legumes, and cattle;
- **The irrigated system**, base primarily on rice, cotton, vegetables, rain fed crops, cattle and poultry; and
- **The tree crop-based system**, based primarily on cocoa, coffee, oil palm, rubber, yams, maize, and off-farm work. (In Table 4-1, these farming systems have been highlighted in yellow.)

Focusing research on these four agricultural complexes should provide scientists with an opportunity to explore solutions to problems and anticipate potential constraints that new technologies will entail. Within each of these complexes certain problems must be addressed:

(1) The development of crops that are ecologically consistent with Africa's diverse micro-ecologies.
(2) The development of technologies that are compatible with the region's depleted soil types.
(3) The implementation of irrigation systems based on individual cultivators not large-scale networks.
(4) The reduction of post-harvest food losses, which currently range from 10 to 100 percent, especially perishable fruits and vegetables.[9]

In Asia, irrigated rice-wheat systems predominate and, as a consequence, the introduction of improved rice and wheat varieties quickly made a profound impact on the food systems of that region. Africa's diverse agricultural systems means that no single improvement in agricultural production will be equally profound. A much more comprehensive set of strategies will be necessary to overcome its ecological and crop diversities. This situation increases the complexity and funding necessary to achieve the same kinds of results as seen in India and other Asian nations. More investment in a broader range of agricultural research and development will be required in Africa. In all likelihood, there will not be a single Green Revolution in Africa. Instead, there will numerous small green <u>*revolutions*</u>, each tied to a particular crop or cropping system; and for this reason, the evolution of Africa's Green Revolutions will take much longer than the Asian antecedents.

Even though the Asian Green Revolution seemed to appear 'unexpectedly' in the mid-1960s and early 1970s, it had begun nearly twenty years earlier in Mexico and the Philippines.[10] Agronomic research is time consuming, and in light of this, one cannot expect overnight results in Africa. The start-up of such research in Africa, and elsewhere, has been delayed by under-investment at both the national and international levels, and a growing resistance to the latest 'silver bullet' — genetic engineering. The delay in obtaining adequate research funding for both crops and techniques, has meant the loss of extremely valuable time. The consequence of this loss is the continuous growth of undernourishment, malnutrition, and outright starvation among the most vulnerable people in Sub-Saharan Africa.

Indigenous Knowledge (IK) and Best Practices

As complicated as the physical geography and cropping patterns of Africa are, they pale in comparison to Africa's cultural diversity. India is always used as a prime example of cultural diversity, with a population of over one billion, speaking more than 1,000 separate languages and dialects. In Africa, there are approximately 800 million people speaking 2,000 distinct languages and dialects.

Some linguists suggest that the language of a people reflects, to a degree, their physical surroundings. Africa embodies a veritable multitude of physical environments and each cultural group has adapted itself to that tiny part of the physical landscape.[11] The list of major farming systems or livelihoods would seem to give credence to this concept.

In all likelihood, a component-by-component transfer of India's Green Revolution to Africa would be disastrous. What Africa requires is a Green Revolution that is indigenously crafted or tailored to the specifics of Africa's traditions and environments. At the heart of India's successes was, for lack of better terminology, a mind-set that was compatible with Western approaches to agriculture, especially in the agricultural heartland of India — Punjab, Haryana, Uttar Pradesh, Gujarat, and Rajasthan. Here the Green Revolution established its deepest roots. Africa cultivators do not share such a mindset.

Despite the slavish manner in which western agronomic knowledge has been accepted and implemented throughout the world, western-based formal knowledge remains but one of many knowledge systems.[12] Acknowledging that there are 'other ways of knowing' should lead us to reevaluate many of our fundamental notions about development, environmental conservation, heritage protection, and access to information and education. Indigenous or local knowledge (IK) refers to a complete body of knowledge, know-how and practices maintained and developed by peoples, generally in rural areas, who have histories stemming from long time intimate interaction with their natural environment.

These sets of understandings, interpretations and meanings are part of a cultural complex that encompasses language, naming and classification systems, practices for using resources, ritual, spirituality and worldview. It provides the basis for local-level decision-making about many fundamental aspects of day-to-day life, for example, hunting, fishing, gathering, agriculture and husbandry, food production, water, health, and adaptation to environmental or social change. Non-formal knowledge — in contrast to formal knowledge — is transferred orally, from generation to generation, and is therefore seldom documented.

IK is defined by the following:

- Locally bound and indigenous to a specific area
- Culture- and context-specific
- Non-formal knowledge
- Orally transmitted, and generally not documented
- Dynamic and adaptive
- Holistic in nature
- Closely related to survival and subsistence for many people.[13]

Amid the complexities of Africa's tribal setting, the importance of indigenous knowledge cannot and should not be overlooked. Success of an African Green Revolution, or some variant of it, will depend on adaptation, and much of that adaptation may have as much to do with the acknowledgement of local lore and knowledge as it does ecological expertise. It is much like folk medicine. It works without having modern science behind it.

IK is based on experience, often tested over centuries of use, adapted to local culture and environment. It is dynamic and changing.[14] IK may be related to a common practice seen in communities that are indigenous to a specific area. Often IK is simply referred to as 'traditional knowledge'. Traditional or local knowledge, refers to the large body of knowledge and skills that have been generally developed outside the formal educational system, and is independent of what might be called modern scientific methods. IK is embedded in culture and is unique to a given location or society. IK is an important part of the lives of the poor; because it is the basis for decision-making of communities in terms of food security, human and animal health, education and natural resource management, each of which is critical to the success of Africa's Green Revolution.[15]

The Debate on How to Approach Africa's Green Revolution

An ideological battle is raging in- and outside Africa over the best way to address the continent's low agricultural productivity and assure long-term food security for its people. In light of the ongoing concern and rhetoric over chronic hunger, it would be natural to assume that everyone would welcome every effort offered to boost Africa's lagging agricultural production. However, this is not necessarily the case, since the conflict between the two camps is based on the merits and demerits of two fundamentally different approaches to agriculture.

The first camp advocates the implementation of already proven Green Revolution technologies – the same technologies that were so successful in Asia and Latin America in the 1960s and 1970s. This camp recommends the use of hybrid, high yielding commercial seed varieties. It is suggested that these commercially produced seed types would replace farmer-saved seed, which is the current method for obtaining seed in virtually all of Africa. This changeover would require capital outlays for new seed every season or two, and would thrust cultivators into modern, currency based markets. In addition to commercial seed, cultivators would be expected to begin using chemical fertilizers, chemical pesticides, and chemical herbicides, each of which is a cash exchange input. In general, this group embraces any technology-based innovation that will improve agricultural production, including the newest agronomic technology, gene modification, or GM.

The second group believes that the Green Revolution approach is not only inappropriate within the African context but has the potential to do more harm than good, both environmentally and socio-economically. While their objections to biotechnology are broad, they are most strident in their opposition to the introduction of GM seed types within the African environment, whether domestically or foreign developed or produced.

Even though both groups recognize that most farming in Africa is based on independent small landholders, with an emphasis on self-sufficiency and a long history of traditional farming practices, they cannot agree on how or where changes should be made. Both camps have their local political, economic, and scientific supporters, as well as an international cadre of aid, science, and development advisers. Within the agricultural milieu of Africa, these smallholders generally only incorporate selective modern methods, those that fit within their existing agricultural traditions.

In the past, as the fertility of the soil was exhausted through repeated use, the traditional practice of shifting cultivation was used to compensate for declining fertility and production. This practice is no longer practical. Population growth has almost completely curtailed its practice. There simply is not sufficient land to permit the continuation of slash-and-burn agriculture. This means that the soils are worked almost continuously without fallowing. At least by practicing shifting cultivation, the land left behind was given an opportunity to reclaim some of its natural fertility, being allowed to fallow. Now, with the soil in almost continuous use, there is no opportunity for it to rejuvenate and, as a consequence, there is an even more rapid decline in fertility. The application of chemical fertilizers does not replace the organic component of the soil, nor does it replace necessary micronutrients and trace elements required by both local and high yielding crop types.

Furthermore, chemical fertilizer is an expensive input. In most cases, it is not locally or domestically produced and, therefore, must be imported, thus increasing its base cost. Added to an already high cost must be added transportation costs. Together, the cost of fertilizer and its transport, puts fertilizer beyond the purchasing capabilities of most small holder cultivators.

Traditional methods of soil rehabilitation, the use of manures, ash, and compost, are used inconsistently and unevenly throughout Africa. Essentially, there is no tradition of fertilization that the soil scientists can use to build upon. The introduction and use of the new fertilizer-based technologies will necessitate the development of new fertilization traditions, and this will entail the development of a system of agricultural extension agents.

Much of the agriculture of Africa is based on rain-fed cultivation methods. If irrigation is to become more widespread, it must first be recognized as a new 'best practice' and this requires the development of yet another cultivation tradition.[16]

The issues of seed type, fertilizer, pesticide, and herbicide use have been considered and, in some instances, implemented, and have failed. The sheer size of the African continent is an obstacle. There has been a genuine lack of sufficient and sustained funding, political will, and political stability. In addition, infrastructural insufficiencies have played a part in the failure of many input-related distribution programs. Above all, in the case of fertilizer subsidy programs, they have proven expensive and difficult to maintain. In large measure, these subsidy programs have failed, not for lack of interest on the part of the cultivators, but for lack of fiscal support by the national leaders and depleted treasuries.

Two recent initiatives – the New Partnership for Africa's Development (NEPAD) and the Alliance for a Green Revolution in Africa (AGRA) – have sought to address the full range of Africa's agricultural development problems. AGRA, in particular, is a most ambitious effort. It places a considerable emphasis on biotechnology and intends to address the issues of high yielding seed varieties and distribution, access to fertilizer, the training of African agronomists, soil scientists, and extension workers. This is one of the first 'shotgun' approaches to the agricultural problems of Africa.

Both the NEPAD and AGRA initiatives are opposed by a network of African farmer and environmental groups. Opposition is focused on the heavy use of chemical fertilizers and other agro-chemicals. These groups object to petrochemicals being used because they pollute the environment. Furthermore, they are too expensive for most small cultivators and, therefore, their use militates against sustainability. Maybe more importantly, it is their belief that to repeat the Asian Green Revolution scenario would make African cultivators dependent on commercial, agri-business suppliers of modern inputs.

Although these arguments are based on examples coming out of Asia, one of the most cogent arguments has to do with the tendency of modern agriculture's mono-cropping, or monoculture. Modern agricultural paradigms inherently push cultivators toward agricultural specialization and the commercialization of agriculture. Monocultures lead to the loss of biodiversity and, oftentimes, the loss of traditional seed varieties. They also argue that, basing an entire continent's future on a few seed types is an invitation to disaster, especially if an unknown blight or disease should develop, it could virtually destroy the monoculture varieties. Agricultural diversity has a long tradition in Africa, and the opponents of monoculture cultivation find solace in that diversity. Somewhere between these two extremes lies a middle ground that both groups will eventually find.

As the debate continues, each side must keep in mind that any delay in making either side's agenda national policy, or some compromise position, people continue to go hungry and even die. The debate cannot go on indefinitely for the peoples' sake.

Arguments Against AGRA

The Alliance for a Green Revolution in Africa (AGRA) is a $150 million joint venture between the Rockefeller Foundation and the Bill & Melinda Gates Foundation. With its backing and successes in the original Green Revolution, one would think the Rockefeller Foundation would know what it was doing. No one could possibly find fault with the Foundation's desire to push for an African equivalent of the Asian Green Revolution. However, almost immediately after the announcement that the joint venture had been organized, it was met with criticism. The overriding criticism of the initiative suggests that 'as proposed, it does not take into consideration the failures of the original Green Revolution.'[17]

Also, the critics of the alliance question why is it necessary. According to the World Bank, the Consultative Group on International Agricultural Research (CGIAR) has invested a substantial portion of its $350 million annual budget in Africa.[18]

CGIAR's contributions to Green Revolution projects in Africa seem to have resulted in, at best, only a nominal improvement in meeting its goals. If the Green Revolution approach has not been productive, as witnessed by only limited agricultural gains, maybe it is time we accept one of the following propositions:

[1] It simply does not work within the context of Africa. Either it failed to adapt to Africa, or the people failed to adapt to the demands of the original version of the Green Revolution.

[2] It 'passed over' Africa for whatever reason. Or the timing was not right.

The idea that it simply 'passed over' Africa, although an outside possibility, is difficult to fathom. Likewise, 'the timing was not right' is also a possibility. Of these two explanations, the first can be rejected because Africa was surrounded by the Green Revolution and it was, at least at the governmental and scientific levels well known and understood. For whatever reasons, neither the governments nor the agronomists of Africa took a genuine interest in it, but if it was a well recognized agronomic strategy, other factors must have been at work. Within this context, it did pass over Africa simply because the national leaders and agronomists were preoccupied with other matters.

The idea that the timing was not right may be a much better explanation. The Green Revolution in South Asia was being implemented at about the same time as the nations of Africa were beginning to realize independence. In the midst of the social, political, and economic turmoil that followed independence in almost every new African nation, the political leadership was, in fact, preoccupied with the problems of nation-building and national unification. From this standpoint, their neglect of agriculture is theoretically understandable. In their minds, they had bigger problems to be concerned with. The people in the hinterlands would take care of themselves. They had taken care of themselves for millennia, a few more years would not make much of a difference. They would address agricultural problems once the problems of state had been resolved.

In most cases, the problems of state were addressed fairly quickly, although quickly may be relative – 15 to 20 years. Since then, however, the needs of the agriculturalists continued to go unresolved. One would think that the agricultural problems of the individual nations would have been recognized and attended to over at least the last 20-plus years but they were not.

Neither the environment nor the people of Africa have changed appreciably over the last 40 years. Nor has their agricultural way of life. If anything, their plight has worsened significantly. It is entirely possible that the introduction or reintroduction of the Green Revolution to Africa may have missed its time, since the problems facing Africa are now substantially larger and even more urgent. More and more poor people are starving and malnourished than they were 40 years ago. The old technologies may be passé within the context of modern Africa and its immediate need for food.

The opponents of the AGRA suggest there are numerous reasons why it is a waste of resources.[19] Among their arguments are:

(1) A Western agricultural paradigm of agriculture was imposed on India's cultivators, and while it worked in selective areas, in others it did not, and often caused social and economic dislocations.

(2) By their very nature, the Green Revolution technologies degrade the physical environment, degrading the soil and depleting scarce water resources.

(3) Almost inevitably, the Green Revolution leads to a reduction in the biodiversity in the areas where it has been implemented.

(4) The introduction of genetic engineering (GE) – the driving force behind the AGRA initiative – will make African agriculture much more vulnerable.

For the major players in the GE controversy, it is especially important to the long-term success of their overall strategy to insure that they can sustain customers' dependence on them. Monsanto, already a major player in GE technologies, now possesses the ability to guarantee repeat business. Monsanto, together with the United States Government, holds the world patent rights to the so-called 'Terminator' – Genetic Use Restriction Technology, or GURT. GURT is a technology that permits seed providers to 'engineer in' a trait that will cause the seed to commit 'suicide' after one harvest, thus giving the seed provider total control over the seed they produce. No longer will the seed user – the cultivator – be able to save seed from one harvest and plant them for the next season. The harvested grain or produce will be genetically sterile. This kind of control over plants and seed users has never existed before in the history of mankind.

This genetic trait will force farmers return to Monsanto's seed vendors year after year, or any of the other seed companies to whom Monsanto licenses its terminator trait. As Engdahl commented:

If broadly introduced around the world, it could within perhaps a decade or so make the world's majority of food producers new feudal serfs in bondage to three or four giant seed companies such as Monsanto or DuPont or Dow Chemical.[20]

The possibility of three or four large multinationals controlling much of the world's food production is almost unfathomable and unthinkable. More importantly, there is the question of ethics. Should any for-profit company be permitted to exert such control over the world and over essential food grains, or any other food crop for that matter? Such technology, if broadly implemented, could result in the world becoming hostage to a corporation. It is both unthinkable and unacceptable. The world must take a very serious look at this technology and develop some kind of assurance that it is not and will not evolve into a form of worldwide economic oppression or used for political domination.

The push for GE crop types is largely in the hands of powerful multinational corporations, who are desperately looking to expand their markets and market shares. Furthermore, large multinationals will endeavor to control and profit from virtually every step in the agricultural cycle, from the provision of seed and other manufactured inputs to the sale of the end product.

Since each producing company will have proprietary rights over their seed type, the smallholder will have to abide by the information and practices of the seed producer to obtain optimal production. The smallholder assumes all risk in the event of crop loss, while the suppliers of the seed and inputs realize their profits and have no liability. They will have made their profits before the first seed has germinated. For the multinationals, it is a win-win situation.

The seeds will be proprietary and there is always the possibility that GE seed from one producer could contaminate that of another, with unknown consequences. Therefore, it will become necessary for seed producers to observe exclusive cropping territories. In effect, this will give the multinationals virtual monopolies within given areas. In effect, the process could be viewed as a new form of micro-colonization. The nations of Africa will simply be carved into exclusive opportunity zones, analogous to free trade zones but for the benefit of a single multinational.

The truly unfathomable aspect of the AGRA initiative is the fact that it has consulted with the largest multinationals involved in seed and fertilizer production, with other philanthropic organizations, a broad range of multinational development agencies but has not consulted with the end users of the technological strategies being proposed. Like much of the aid packages being offered to Africa, at every level, it is foreign nationals who are making all the decisions concerning 'how things should be.' Little to no input is being received or provided by the local peasant cultivator groups. Again, AGRA appears to be just another example of a top-down decision-making process, one that potentially could do more environmental and economic harm, than good, and may not necessarily have a beneficial impact on Africa's food needs.

The Genetic Engineering (GE) Controversy

The *raison d'être* for the multitude of African aid organizations is the belief that the nations of Africa are incapable of solving their own problems. On the surface, this may be true. Every aid organization, whether they are concerned with economic, social, or agricultural development – which are all intimately interrelated – suffers from the innate belief that they somehow have the answer to Africa's problems or, more importantly, they somehow feel it is their responsibility to correct the problems they perceive. Despite the massive amounts of money and manpower that are being consumed in Africa, only a modicum of progress has been made over the last forty years, especially in the realm of food production and food security.

Behind every development effort are the donors – governments, non-governmental organizations, public and private foundations, and corporations or multinationals. Each one of these donors has an agenda, and while some may be truly altruistic, for the majority, there is some kind of gain or advantage being sought. Such is the case with the multinational, agricultural corporations. Globalization of the world economy necessitates that every business look beyond its domestic boundaries for new markets and market shares. Africa is, for all intents and purposes, a large untapped market. Nearly a sixth of the world's population lives in Africa, and these people, if their economic condition can be improved, constitute a potentially large market for goods and services. Realizing this, multinationals are able and willing to make token investments for the opportunity to reap profits in the future. A dollar invested today could easily represent millions of dollars in future business. This may seem to be a mercenary point of view but it is also good business planning. At every stage of development, there are opportunities for the multinationals to make a profit.

All one need do is look at the flow of aid funding throughout Africa. For every dollar of aid that is provided to the governments of Africa, the largest portion of that dollar finds its way back to one or more of the more highly developed donor nations. Whether right or wrong, aid providers believe that the recipient countries simply do not have the technological base nor the personnel to tackle their problems in-country. Even with the development of in-country facilities, monies still flow out to the donor nations for equipment and personnel. Aid is simply very self-serving for the donor nations. It generates business opportunities 'back home' and, at the same time, builds future markets 'out there.' Such is the case with genetic or bio-engineering.

Raymond Bokor writes:

Many corporations — particularly the agribusiness giants — think Africa lacks technological expertise in meeting its food needs and therefore have lured governments to adopt genetic engineering technology as a panacea to end hunger as well as to bring economic and social relief to the masses.[21]

Genetic engineering or Genetic Modification (GM) of crops will not, by itself, accomplish any of these laudable ends.

The Problems with Genetic Engineering

Within the context of African agriculture and government, there are three overlapping areas of concern:

- The fear that large multinationals will dominate and control African agriculture
- Issues surrounding the regulation of multinationals and the control of biotechnology as it relates to genetic crop contamination
- The lack of knowledge concerning the technology and compliance with the African Model Law on Biosafety, especially as it applies to input in the decision-making process.

In part, the controversy surrounding the use of genetically modified crops stems from a lack of knowledge. The opposition to GM seems tied to those speaking the loudest, those who attempt to perpetuate irrational, unnecessary ignorance — the myth-spreading activists. Opposition also has a lot to do with the public's general hostility toward unaccountable corporations and nameless and faceless scientists who we believe do not entirely know what they are doing, and an attachment to an idea of 'nature' that is emotional, sentimental and irrational. In addition, it would seem that too many scientists have become confused about the difference between science and the practical applications of science. Scientists today need to realize that public opinion is often nearly as powerful as science itself; and that how they apply their science is important. In other words, corporations and scientists need to evaluate how their products will be used, by whom, and for what purpose. If they are unable to communicate their vision to the public effectively, and not in terms of quarterly profit projections or learned journal articles, they face inevitable public castigation. Presently, corporations and scientist are their own worst enemies. This is particularly so with regard to genetic engineering or the process of genetic modification.[22]

As Pinstrup-Anderson and Schioler suggest, with proper biosafety procedures plant modifications derived from genetic research need not be riskier than those derived from traditional plant breeding. Genetic engineering has advantages over traditional plant breeding methods. Through genetic re-engineering desired characteristics can be produced much more rapidly and can extend well beyond the plant's own gene pool. Therefore, the possibilities for combining genes, within and across species, makes it possible to increase food production almost endlessly.[23]

It can be argued that hunger is a myth in Africa. This does not mean that hunger does not exist but that the hunger that does exist is not entirely a problem of production. It is more a problem of economics. There are many reasons for the current and projected food shortages. Among the most important is the lack of income to buy food, a lack of infrastructure (roads or adequate transport to get products to market), inadequate post-harvest storage, domestic and international trade policies, lack of inputs, lack of information, and unsustainable farming practices. All the production in the world will do little to alleviate hunger if these problems are not addressed, or if food is permitted to sit in warehouses to rot or to be consumed by vermin. If these problems are not resolved, people will continue to starve.

Amartya Sen and others have routinely suggested that famine is more often a function of people lacking the ability to buy food than the absence of food.[24] All we need to do is look at Africa's hunger in terms of geography. Hunger is unevenly distributed. There are pockets of abject hunger and there are pockets of plenty. Economics – inadequate incomes and access to land and agricultural inputs – explains much of the existing pattern of hunger.

Furthermore, despite food surpluses in other parts of the world, the realities are that these surpluses cannot and will not be redistributed; because large-scale transfers of food are logistically difficult, time-consuming, and very costly – there is no one able or willing to pay for it. Globally, food grains are simply a commodity, and as such, they come at a cost that must be borne by someone. Relief agencies, public and private, must contend with limited budgets, and they simply do not have sufficient funding to accommodate all the poor of the world. Therefore, the essential albeit surplus foodgrains sit untouched in grain silos and *godowns* throughout the world.

Multinationals have had a difficult time selling the idea of GE and GM crops to consumers in the United States and Europe. They have not, however, lacked governmental support. In fact, USAID is one of the multinationals most earnest salesmen and devotees. As the door seemed to be closing on the widespread use of GE in the production of domestic food crops in the U.S., USAID began pressing for its introduction to Africa. After all, it was a virtually untapped market and the public there did not know much about GE and GM. Maybe that market could be tapped without all the cumbersome requirements of transparency and public involvement in the decision-making process.

Multinational Domination

Africa's free political leaders are justifiably concerned that the major players in the of GE and GM movement will come to dominate the development, supply, and trade in the grains and other products that will come out of GE research and distribution. One need only look at the list of the sponsors for many of the largest agricultural and GE initiatives over the last few years. In 2002, USAID announced the launch of a 10 year $100 million program for the developing world, the Collaborative Agriculture Biotechnology Initiative (CABIO).[25] The purpose of CABIO is to assist developing countries develop access to and manage the tools of modern biotechnology. Part of CABIO's role is to lobby for stricter intellectual property rights legislation and plant variety protection in developing countries, all of which is necessary to protect companies like Monsanto and Pioneer Hi-Bred, who are already heavily involved in African agricultural development and supporters of USAID projects, while Alcon/Cargill helps sponsor the U.N. World Food Programme along with Archer Daniels Midland.[26] Further, CABIO will carry on the work of the Agricultural Biotechnology Support Project (ABSP), which was set up and funded by USAID. USAID effectively admits it acts as a marketing arm of the US GM industry when it states on its website:

The training and awareness raised by ABSP... has given the private sector a better assurance allowing some companies such DNA Plant Technology, ICI Seeds (Syngenta), Pioneer Hi-Bred and Monsanto to agree on technology transfer projects...An interesting feature of the programme, uncommon in donor funded projects, is the fact that ABSP has supported the filing of two patents during the development of research agreements.[27]

USAID funds the International Service for the Acquisition of Agri-biotech Applications (ISAAA), an organization that promotes the growth of GM in the developing world.[28] The ISAAA actively supports various GM projects in Africa to develop GM bananas, sweet potatoes and maize. ISAAA is also funded by Bayer, CropScience, Monsanto, Pioneer Hi-Bred, Syngenta, Alcon/Cargill, Dow AgroSciences, KWS SAAT AG and the USDA.

F. William Engdahl, in his book *Seeds of Destruction*, offers the following facts:

3 companies control 71 percent of all soybean crushing.

5 companies control 90 percent of all global grain trading.

4 agro-chemical / seed giants control 75 percent of all improved seed production.

4 companies control the agricultural chemicals market.

6 companies control 75 percent of the global pesticides market.[29]

In light of these figures, is there any wonder why the leaders of any developing nation would be suspicious with regard to their dealings with any of the large multinational agro-inputs corporations? When these types of companies come calling, bearing gifts, the leaders have to know they are expected to give up something; and that is control over the agricultural system of the country. The corporations will protect their vested interests at all costs. If the local population gains something in return, that is simply a bonus. Therefore, both government officials and the cultivators in the field are justified in their concern over multinational domination of the marketing, supply, and distribution of agricultural inputs, and the trade in agricultural outputs.

If the multinationals succeed in obtaining proprietary rights in the agriculture of a nation, by offering inexpensive agricultural research, in the end, the multinationals will be little different than the European colonialists earlier in the 20th century. The African leaders should view the multinationals as they would "Greeks bearing gifts." They should be very circumspect about entering into any arrangement that could jeopardize their political and economic independence and food sovereignty and security.

The Regulation of BioTechnology

The regulation of biotechnology centers on three areas:

- The regulation of the companies providing biotechnical products in the country.
- The regulation and enforcement of intellectual property rights.
- The regulation or enforcement of biosafety laws.

In November 2005 the Cairo Declaration was created, endorsing the report of the High-Level Panel which committed the members of the African Ministerial Council to work together to develop a 20-year African biotechnology strategy.[30] A number of policy statements were proffered.

Where possible and practical, the African nations have elected to regulate biotechnology and biosafety at the global level through different multilateral instruments and processes, from binding rules to flexible guidelines and financing. The main processes address the following aspects: transnational movement of living modified organisms (the Cartagena Protocol on Biosafety); access to genetic resources and sharing of benefits arising from their utilization (the Convention on Biological Diversity); finance for biosafety capacity-building activities (the GEF); access to plant genetic resources for food and agriculture (the FAO International Treaty on plant genetic resources for food and agriculture); trade in biotech products including agricultural commodities (the World Trade Organization (WTO) including its agreements on the application of sanitary and phytosanitary measures and on technical barriers to trade; standard-setting organizations related to international trade of plants, animals and food (International Plant Protection Convention, the World Organization for Animal Health and CODEX *Alimentarius*); and intellectual property rights over biotech products (the WTO Agreement on trade-related aspects of intellectual property rights (TRIPS) and the World Intellectual Property Organization (WIPO).[31]

One of the most important agreements in the long list of documents governing biosafety in Africa is the Cartagena Protocol on Biodiversity, which came into force in 2002. This agreement regulates the trans-boundary movement of living modified organisms (LMOs) resulting from modern biotechnology and ensuring their safe transfer, handling and use. It thus establishes rules and procedures for allowing the import of LMOs and requirements for documentation for LMO exports. In 2007, the main issue that was addressed by negotiators within the Cartagena Protocol was liability and redress for the harm caused by LMOs. In May 2008, a meeting was held to allow African countries to evaluate the first five years of the Protocol's implementation.

Following the adoption of Africa's Science and Technology Consolidated Plan of Action in August 2005[32] by the African Ministerial Council on Science and Technology, and the African Union (AU), a High-Level African Panel on Modern Biotechnology was established to facilitate regional dialogues on policies for biotechnology. Their report was presented in July 2006.[33]

As we have already seen, for the large multinationals – those providing the seed and other manufactured inputs – it is in their best interests to control competition, with the best case scenario being a monopoly, which reduces competition and permits the imposition of arbitrary product pricing. In most instances, governments discourage or have outlawed the creation of monopolies, which are not in the public's best interests. In the case of biotechnology, however, it has been argued that due to the high level of investment in research and development prior to marketing, competition would make it difficult for the corporations to recoup their substantial investments, as well as current production costs. In the short term, this may be an accurate assessment. However, assuming these corporations are going to be 'in the game' for a long time to come, it will only mean that the amortization of their start-up expenses will be longer. What, then, should the amortization period be, 5, 10, 20, or 40 years? The corporation should not be permitted to make that decision. That responsibility should rest with the host nation and after careful consideration rules and regulations and public comment, the rules should become law.

Secondly, the host nation must consider the issue of liability. African nations, however, seem split regarding this issue. On one hand, are those countries who expect to be large biotechnology exporters, and their traditional allies, such as the US, Canada, Australia, Argentina and New Zealand, who do not favor a tough liability instrument, and question its usefulness or need within the Biosafety Protocol's context, cautioning on the effects of such a regime on agricultural exports and biotech research. On the other hand, are those countries that will most likely be net importers of biotech products. They are requesting the strictest biosafety liability rules, including the responsibility of exporting states and a broad consideration of damages.[34]

While the issues associated with GE's potential for the contamination of nearby traditional crop types or cross species contamination, especially between animals and humans, is still unsettled, host governments must anticipate such possibilities, in the event the scientists on either side of the argument are wrong. The host nations must provide for monitoring and the enforcement of biosafety violations and their consequences. Failure to anticipate the unthinkable is not an option. Anticipate the worst and hope for the best.

One of the basic principles of a fair and transparent marketplace is for producers to benefit from their innovations and products when they deliver, or bear responsibility when those same products fail to deliver or cause harm to a third party. It is only fair that the burden should be put on the developer of the technology. The multinational corporations must be held responsible in the event their GM crops contaminate organic or other non-GM varieties, or human beings.

Even though policy makers, GM corporations, farmers and consumers have yet to get to a conclusive agreement on the issue of liability, both sides of the argument have polar opposite points of view. The corporations are concerned with liability resulting from the potential infringement on their intellectual property rights, while the other side is concerned with the issue of liability from the point of view of the environment and the people.

The corporations wish to protect their intellectual property rights vis-à-vis farmers' rights, especially as regards the farmers' right to save seeds, a time worn tradition everywhere in Africa. The European Free Trade Commission has sought to negotiate a bilateral free-trade agreement (FTA) with the Southern Africa Customs Union (SACU) that would require members to allow patents on biotechnological inventions. Since this term is not defined, that would mean that potentially, patents on both plants and animals could be granted. Furthermore, the free trade agreement would ask SACU members to join the International Union for the Protection of New Varieties of Plants (UPOV convention), which is a specific form of intellectual property protection for plants.

New signatories to the UPOV convention would have to sign on to the 1991 version, which forbids farmers from exchanging seeds of protected varieties and also severely curtails or eliminates farmers ability to save seed. Such IPR provisions — especially the one restricting farmers' right to save seed— would be very anti-farmer and very anti-sustainable agriculture, as up to 90% of seeds planted in SACU countries are farm-saved seed and also raise serious ethical concerns.

According to Amadou C. Kanoute,

. . . the IPR provisions in the EFTA FTA with SACU clearly contradict the position taken by the African Group at the June 2003 TRIPS Council meeting: "Patents on life forms are unethical and the TRIPS Agreement should prohibit them." The IPR provisions associated with "genetic engineering" are very problematical for farmers, for consumers and the overall socio-economic developmental needs of our countries.

For all these reasons, it might make more sense to put scarce money in other technologies that are more ecologically and socially rational or in the development of other alternative cropping systems or pest control mechanisms that may yield the same goals as the GE / GM approach.

Rather than ask how "green genetic engineering" can fit it in with environmental protection, health and poverty alleviation, I think the more important point is to define the problem that needs solving and then talk about the various different ways –and biotechnology or "green genetic engineering" may be one way out of numerous ways to solve the said problem.

I'd argue that "genetic engineering" is not the ideal solution to agricultural problems, especially in developing countries. I'd argue that a more holistic, agro ecological, participatory approach is more appropriate. And I'd argue for an approach that is more knowledge-intensive rather than capital intensive.[35]

Other issues aside, the primary concern for the public is the coexistence of the different types of agricultures. This is turning into a nightmare for everyone. If there were no validity in the preservation of biodiversity, there would be little or no debate. However, the loss of native species may represent a significant loss if someday a truly fundamental problem should arise as a result or consequence of GE. Native species could then provide for a proven fallback position. In their absence, there would be no fallback position to begin building from. In essence, we would beginning from scratch, or 10,000± years ago.

The issues of corporate and public liability are difficult. Eventually, some middle-ground resolution will be hammered out, with neither side absolutely satisfied. However, it is the responsibility of the government to insure the welfare of its people in the absence of no other alternative, especially in those areas where market forces cannot or do not apply. Such is the case with liability. Both sides have rights and responsibilities; it is defining them that poses the problem for politicians and the lawyers.

The most practical approach to the issue of liability will be for that group of African nations that are adamant about their desire for strict liability laws to step back and assess what their expectations are regarding the value of biotechnology and the potential for environmental harm. Likewise, the multinationals will need to take a step back and assess their current position of limited or no liability. They must also assess the long-term benefit from their liaison with a these newly opening markets. Somewhere between their current positions is a compromise position that both can hopefully live with. They both must act before the opportunity for both evaporates.

Knowledge and Information Communication

The concept of GE and GM, and their relationship and efficacy in Africa have been debated for more than a decade, and it is still on-going. In general, African nations have been slow to incorporate and develop many of the newest technologies available to African agriculture. Part of the cause for the delays in acceptance and implementation of these new technologies, forgetting about the debate over whether or not they should even be part of the African agricultural scene, is the failure of the political leaders and the aid organizations, donor nations, and the scientists to adequately explain both the benefits and drawbacks of GE/GM to the people of Africa. While GE and GM are in fact akin to rocket science, the proponents of these technologies have failed to communicate with the populations they purport to serve. At the level of molecular biology and genetics, the topic is difficult to understand by the layman. However, humans have an amazing ability to demystify and 'dumb-down' complex concepts and make them intelligible to non-experts.

For example, Stephen Hawking, an intellectual icon, a wheelchair bound theoretical physicist, is part of that small community of scholars who are seeking to uncover the fundamental laws of the universe. He is searching for the elusive *Theory of Everything*. In his everyday life he deals with such concepts as black holes, supergravity, supersymmetry, quantum theory, M-theory, superstring theory and p-branes, concepts 'beyond most people's comprehension.' However, in his *The Universe in a Nutshell*, he makes these almost science-fictionesque concepts comprehensible for most layman.[36]

This is what political leaders, aid organizations, donor nations, and scientists have failed to do. In response to their failings, these proponents become defensive and further isolate themselves from the people, who could, or would support their activities, if they were made to understand what the debate is all about. As a consequence, the public becomes suspicious and resentful. All the suspicion and resentment could be eliminated through straight-forward communication. The on-going debate suggests that the message has not been heard or understood.

The proponents of GE and GM need to talk to the public in a language they can understand. Most people will never comprehend the real science behind genetic engineering but they do not need to. They need to understand what the science can and cannot do for them. Susanna Horning Priest in her book, *Grain of Truth*, uses the example of DNA. Just because people cannot, necessarily, give a reasonable definition of DNA or do not know how DNA works, does not mean they should not have a voice in arguments about biotechnology or cloning.[37]

Summing Up

Technological solutions, as advocated by those in favor of the implementation of a second generation of the Green Revolution, will not eliminate Africa's food shortages.It is not simply an issue of production. Other fundamental changes are needed, especially those that will integrate cultivators economically and geographically.

The consequences of colonialism, tribalism, disease, and religious differences, while important issues, are not the causes of the current situation in Sub-Saharan Africa. The more important issues may be economic and geographical isolation, and the inability of national governments to integrate their populations into a functioning and functional market network. Historic adaptations to the highly varied ecology of Africa has set the pattern for the people and has caused African agriculture to be highly dispersed and adapted to the local eco-niches in which the people live. These adaptations have fractionalized African agriculture, producing numerous agricultural complexes that exploit Africa's environmental diversity.

In most areas of the world, agricultural patterns have developed around the cultivation of certain cereal crops – usually wheat and rice. In Africa, this type of cultivation never emerged. Therefore, improvements in Africa's agriculture are not as simple as the application of new agricultural technologies to one or two key crops. Diversification of Africa's agriculture, while historically protecting cultivators against the vagaries of nature, now complicates agronomists' efforts to move Africa to its next production plateau. Unless the people are able to consolidate or narrow their forms of agriculture, agronomists will be faced with the task of addressing technologies that will fit a broad range of crops and environments. This will, obviously, increase the time it takes to develop satisfactory crop varieties.

In much of the developed world, either due to history or environment, the rise of the wheat-rice complexes simplified the agronomist's task. They could focus on two primary staple crop types. At present, this is not the situation in Africa. Changing dietary traditions are difficult since it involves cultural, as well as economic changes. Attempts at fostering changes in cultural heritages and traditions is about as easy as the alchemist's task of changing base metals into gold.

References

1. (FAO, 2006) and (FAO, September 2005).
2. (Moussa, Sami Zaki, March 2002), p. 9.
3. (Simms, July 2005). See also, (Magrath, John (ed), October 2006).
4. (Lobe, Kenton, February 2007), p. 2.
5. (Molua, Ernest L. and Mummy W. Rajab, March 2002)

6. (Stronach, 2006). Member of Parliament, Canada, and heavily involved in Canada's African development programs.
7. According to UN Food and Agriculture Organization Director-General Jacques Diouf.
8. (Dixon, J and A. Gulliver, 2001).
9. (IAC, 2004), p. xx.
10. See the brief discussion and history of the wheat and rice projects in Mexico and the Philippines in Chapter 3.
11. The Sapir–Whorf hypothesis, also known as the "linguistic relativity hypothesis," postulates a systematic relationship between the grammatical categories of the language a person speaks and how that person both understands the world and behaves in it. The hypothesis postulates that a particular language's nature influences the habitual thought of its speakers: that different language patterns yield different patterns of thought. See, (Brown, 2005) for a discussion of this linguistic theory and some alternatives to the issue of environmental impacts on language and thought.
12. See (Nakashima, 2000) and (Kothari, 2007).
13. (Boven, Karin; and Jun Morohashi. (eds), 2002), p. 13.
14. (IRRI, 1996).
15. See, (Nwokeabia, January 2006); (The World Bank, 2004); and (Boven, Karin; and Jun Morohashi. (eds), 2002).
16. The concept of Best Practice is not reserved for "ultimate truths" or "gold standards." Best Practice means accumulating and applying knowledge about what is working and not working in different situations and contexts. In other words, it is both the lessons learned *and* the continuing process of learning, feedback, reflection, and analysis (what works, how and why, and so forth).

    At its most basic, Best Practice suggests a simple maxim: Don't reinvent the wheel; learn in order to improve it, and adapt it to your terrain to make it work better.

    The process of Best Practice is manifested in three ways:

    - The exchange of experience, including sharing between individual experts and Technical Resource Networks (TRNs)
    - Pilot testing, operations research, and other projects and programs
    - Documentation including formats such as audiovisual cassettes, CDs, and presentation graphics (however, it is

important to remember that Best Practice is not simply documentation, but an approach to sharing and using knowledge).

Adapted from (UNAIDS, September 2000), p. 3.

17. See, (Rosset, 2006); (GRAIN, September 2006); (Heim, Krisiti and Sandi Doughton, 2006); and (Holt-Gimenez, Miguel A, Altieri, and Peter Rosset, October 2006).
18. (The World Bank, May 9, 2003), Volume 1, Overview Report, p. 5. CGIAR is a strategic alliance of members, partners and international agricultural centers that mobilizes science to benefit the poor.
19. (Holt-Gimenez, Miguel A, Altieri, and Peter Rosset, October 2006).1
20. (Engdahl, Doomsday Seed Vault" in the Arctic, 2007b)
21. (Bokor, Spring 2004).
22. See, (Meek, 2002).
23. (Pinstrup-Anderson, Seeds of Contention, October 2001b). See also (Pinstrup-Anderson, Seeds of Contention, 2001a).
24. See (Shah, 2008), especially the section on world hunger and poverty.
25. (Avery, August 2002).
26. (USAID, March 2002).
27. *Ibid.*
28. (ISAAA, January 2008), last page of brochure, p. 5.
29. (Engdahl, Seeds of Destruction: The Hidden Agenda of Genetic Manipulation, 2007a).
30. (AMCOST, November 2006).
31. (IISD, Wednesday, February 7, 2007).
32. (AU/NEPAD, Africa's Science and Technology Consolidated Plan of Action, August 2005)
33. (AU/NEPAD, Freedom to Innovate: Biotechnology in Africa's Development. Draft Report of the High Level African Panel on Modern Biotechnology, July 2006).
34. (CBD, Decembeer 7, 2006).
35. (Kanoute, November 2004), p. 4.
36. (Hawking, 2001).
37. (Priest, 2001).

5

Pakistan

Box 5-1: Pakistan Comparative Data

HDI/Rank/Year: 0.552/136/2005
Per Capita GDP: 2,370 USD
Population: 167.762 million (July 2008 est.)
Labor Force in: Agriculture: 42% (19.6%)*
Industry: 20% (26.8%)*
Services: 38% (53.7%)*
* Percent of GDP

Population Below the Poverty Line: 24.0%
Population Density: 215.4 people/sq.km.
Land Area: 778,720 sq km.
Arable Land: 190,319.2 sq. km.
Arable Land Per Person: 0.1 Ha/person
Irrigated Area: 182,300 sq km (2003)
Irrigated Area as % of Arable Land: 95.8%

Introduction

Inevitably, in large measure due to differences in the size of the countries surrounding India, the countries of Pakistan, Nepal, and Bangladesh are often overlooked when the Green Revolution is discussed. However, each is unique because of its physical geography, population, cultural heritage, and agricultural needs. As a function of these differences, the Green Revolution, when it was implemented, displayed its own distinctive adoption patterns.

In 1964 Pakistan began importing and testing improved wheat seeds developed by Borlaug and his team in Mexico at the CIMMYT. The results of these tests proved promising, and in 1965 Pakistan and India agreed to purchase 450 tons of the improved seed. Both orders were placed too late to ship them from the CIMMYT's normal transshipment port in Mexico. Borlaug, personally, arranged to have the shipments transported overland from Mexico to Los Angeles, where they were placed on ships, heading to Pakistan and India. Within a day of the shipments arriving in Los Angeles, war broke out between India and Pakistan. The war delayed the arrival of the seed until after the normal October planting time. Nonetheless, Borlaug instructed the governments to plant the seeds anyway. Despite the delay and other technical problems, the seeds grew.

In the spring of 1966, the crop was larger than anything the Pakistani agronomists had ever seen, in spite of the fact that it was planted late and it had been a dry winter. In fact, yields rose by 70 percent that first year.[1] For the next planting, the governments ordered 18,000 tons of the new seeds. With normal rainfall, the harvest resulted in so much grain that there were not enough people to harvest it. The harvest overwhelmed the people and the system.

There weren't enough bullock carts to haul the wheat to threshing floors. There weren't enough jute bags, trucks, rail cars or grain storage facilities. Some towns closed schools temporarily to house the grain. And millions were no longer hungry.[2]

Table 5-1: Pakistan's Productivity Improvements, 1950-2007

Crops	*1950*	*2007*	*2007 Increase in Production in Times*
	Production Millions of Tonnes		
Wheat	3.9	23.7	6
Rice	0.8	5	6
Maize	4	9.8	24
Sugarcane	7.8	47.2	56
Cotton (Bales)	1.3	14.3	11

Source: (PARC, 2007).

Within three years of the introduction of the improved seeds, (West) Pakistan became self-sufficient in terms of wheat production. Wheat yields nearly doubled from 4.6 million tons in 1965 to 7.3 million tons by 1970. By 2007, Pakistan's wheat production exceeded 23.7 million tonnes. Since the late 1960s, food production has increased faster than the rate of population growth.[3]

Much of Pakistan's success with the Green Revolution stems from a unique combination of assets. Unlike all the other nations of South Asia, Pakistan enjoyed the benefits of:

- Large landholdings
- A well-developed irrigation network
- A small agricultural laborer workforce, requiring mechanization
- A historical precedent of agricultural commercialization
- A reasonably well developed market, road, and railway infrastructure.

Nowhere else in colonial India had the British invested as much time, effort, and money as they had in West Punjab. The preconditions for the Green Revolutions were already in place by the time Borlaug introduced his CIMMYT wheat.

Initially, as a research agronomist, Borlaug had believed that the development of the new high yielding seed varieties would be his most challenging task. When he became involved in the process of introducing his creations in India and Pakistan, he quickly realized that the development of the new seed technology may have been groundbreaking but it was not the biggest obstacle he had to overcome.

Once the cultivators had been shown the merits of his new agricultural technologies, the only obstacle to the widespread adoption of the technologies was the peasants' ability to obtain them. Almost all the new technologies required that they be purchased. There was no more saving seed for the next planting; and fertilizer, pesticides, and herbicides were non-renewable. The cultivators needed credit or the financial resources to permit them to purchase the inputs and obtain reliable irrigation water. The research scientist found himself in the position of having to become an agricultural statesman. Dealing with people and bureaucracies was much more difficult than dealing with plants.

Government participation was oftentimes insufficient or outright obstructive, and the goals of Borlaug and the government often seemed to be at cross-purposes. For example, fertilizer use was regulated by the Pakistani government. It was not a free market commodity. In the beginning, Borlaug's new wheats were starving because fertilizer use was restricted.[4] After repeated meetings with Pakistan's political leadership, the fertilizer regulations were modified, resulting in broader availability and distribution.

Since governments in most developing countries control the domestic price of foodgrains, they can either support or undermine cultivators' efforts. In the beginning, the governments of Pakistan and India kept the price of wheat artificially low, well below the price on the world market. On the one hand, the governments' strategy has to be commended. With so many hungry people, it was believed that keeping foodgrain prices low would make it easier for them to obtain the food they needed. With little or no profit to be realized from the sale of their surpluses, however, cultivators simply cut back on production, which undermined the poor once again. Borlaug lobbied the governments, making his case for increasing market support pricing for foodgrains. As prices improved, production increased. Borlaug had been right.

At this stage in the Green Revolution, the governments of South Asia were desperate for increased food production. It was literally a matter of life and death. Consequently, the governments adopted an agricultural development strategy that could be characterized as 'production at any cost.' Realizing that Borlaug had been right in his assessment of the role of foodgrain price supports, they became artificially high, which tended to push foodgrain production from being a subsistence activity into a commercial venture. Over time, as foodgrain production met, then exceeded domestic requirements, the governments independently reversed their price support policies. The time for production at any cost was over. There were other pressing agricultural concerns, and only by decreasing support prices could the cultivators be gently coerced to comply with the new paths the governments had elected to follow in the wake of the globalization of agriculture in the 21st Century.

Other areas Borlaug felt were in need of attention were infrastructure (including roads, transportation, electricity, irrigation, and petrochemicals), the development of national research organizations, and subsidies for inputs. Eventually, he obtained tacit government support for his seeds and input needs.

Some Consequences of the Green Revolution in Pakistan

Ultimately, the Green Revolution in Pakistan was executed much as it would be in most of the Third World. The component parts of the Green Revolution were almost mindlessly accepted by village cultivators. They proved enthusiastic about the prospect of improving their economic situation. The transfer of the technologies and the subsequent changes in traditional agricultural methods proved to be comparatively easy.

The Pakistani cultivators were culturally and psychologically ready for any change that would lead them out of long-standing poverty and hunger. Consequently, it was not the desire to adopt that caused the lag between introduction and adoption.The delaying factors effecting the immediate adoption of the Green Revolution lay in the areas of rural capital availability, water control, and land reforms. In parts of India, the actual inputs were in short supply. In Pakistan, however, input non-availability was not so much from a lack of supply but due to lack of suitable transport and all-weather roads.

In Pakistan the key factor slowing the implementation of the Green Revolution had little or nothing to do with the ultimate end users or the new technologies. In large measure, it was a problem of Pakistani politics failing to keep pace with the technologies. In the early years, the transfer of the new technologies was limited largely to irrigated, well capitalized areas. In the end, it was the larger, wealthier cultivators who reaped the benefits of the Green Revolution, a situation that prevails today. The espoused goals of social and economic improvement for the poor were not realized. Pakistan has yet to find the perfect balance between the principles of equity and efficiency in agriculture. As a consequence, the existing inequalities between the better capitalized, larger cultivators and the under- or un-capitalized smaller cultivators, have been exacerbated. For many observers, it became apparent that major transfers of technology without social leveling was potentially explosive, and where it was not explosive, it often resulted in political unrest, a problem that has faced many developing nations and Pakistan in particular.[5]

While Western development agencies have been concerned with social and economic benefits for all, these concerns have often not been shared by the political leadership. Political and economic elitism has been a longstanding tradition in Pakistan and there are many that have resisted the tenets of equality and social justice. Fear of losing power, as a result of large scale adoption of the Green Revolution, was a genuine concern for the political and economic elites. Further, democracy, in its broadest context, was not a central theme in Pakistani society, politics, or economics. Almost without a break, the imperatives of authoritarian central government have ridden rough shod over provincial rights and regional autonomy. Punjabi interests have all but eclipsed those of other ethnic groups. Further, government elites have reaped the benefits of agricultural successes, with little concern for society at large. As a consequence, political tension has long been a part of the political landscape of Pakistan. Regional, ethnic, and class conflicts continue unabated. Within this politically charged environment, with each group attempting to carve out its own sphere of influence, agricultural development, equity, and social justice all take a back seat.

Observers of the Green Revolution began criticizing its inherent inequalities. In many countries the rich benefitted far more from the new technologies than did the poorer, smaller landholders. Taking a very myopic view, some critics even suggested that traditional farming, where everyone was comparatively miserable, was morally superior to increasing the gap between the rich and poor.[6] Borlaug made no apologies for the Green Revolution. In response to the criticism that it was not fair and equitable, he replied:

Whcat isn't political. It doesn't know that it's supposed to be producing more for poor farmers than for rich farmers. When you produce something that's good for the small farmer, the big farmer can use it too . . . .

Inequalities have been present since the day mankind was kicked out of the Garden of Eden . . . .[7]

There is no denying that the Green Revolution does cause change in rural societies. The most immediate consequence was, in fact, the widening of the gap between the rich and poor, between the large and small landholders, and between the landed and the landless. It also accentuated the differences between regions within countries, especially between the well-watered and poorly watered regions. Possibly more so in Pakistan, than for any other nation, the adoption of the component parts of the Green Revolution, and their cumulative consequences, resulted in economic changes that had significant consequences for Pakistan's national politics.

It has been argued that the breakup of Pakistan into Pakistan and Bangladesh was at least, in part, the result of the differential between the two states and the implementation of the Green Revolution. West Pakistan benefitted immeasurably from the introduction of the improved wheats. Wheat production rose rapidly and self-sufficiency was quickly achieved but not so in East Pakistan. East Pakistan continued to be a net food importer.

East Pakistan was the Pakistani version of the Green Revolution's stepchild. While the benefits of the improved rice varieties were well recognized, annual flooding, the absence of flood controls, inadequate road and rail infrastructure, and rice varieties that were not resistant to long periods of submergence, pre-doomed the early adoption of the first miracle rices. Thus, the benefits of the Green Revolution seemed to fully accrue to West Pakistan and by-passed East Pakistan. West Pakistan's political domination and the economic exploitation of East Pakistan, as well as cultural differences, caused irreparable problems between the states. Not even the bond of Islam was able to bridge the growing differences and disparities between the two parts of the nation. As a consequence, the separate states of Pakistan and Bangladesh were born.

Pakistan's Variant of the Indian Green Revolution

While the Green Revolution progressed along lines similar to those in India, in Pakistan two important, albeit slight, variations emerged. First, tubewell use increased much more rapidly in Pakistan, and second, tractor usage and technology increased far more quickly in Pakistan.[8]

Canal Colonies

Pakistan's climatic regime is largely arid to semi-arid. With more than 85 percent of the country suffering from unreliable and inadequate rainfall, irrigation is the mainstay of agriculture. This was recognized by the British during the colonial period. The British readily recognized the potential fertility of the soils of Punjab and the industriousness of the Jat cultivators that inhabited the area. The expansion of agricultural production was only limited by the availability of water.[9]

Cultivation had been long established along the Indus and its various tributaries, but due to local relief, the irrigation systems were limited to inundated lands immediately adjacent to the rivers. If production were to be increased, the irrigation system had to be expanded. This the British did. In East and West Punjab, the British invested billions of rupees in large-scale canal irrigation systems, and the development of roads, railroads, and towns and markets, with a large portion of that investment being made in West Punjab. Between 1873 and 1903, the Punjab rail system increased from 400 miles to over 3,000, and irrigation increased from 2,744 to 16,983 miles of canals.[10]

Table 5-2: Distribution of Climatic Types by Province in Pakistan

Province	*Arid*	*Semi-Arid*	*Sub-Tropical*	*Other*	*Total*
Punjab	15.0%	7.5%	2.1%	1.3%	25.9%
Sindh	16.9%	0.8%	0.0%	0.0%	17.7%
Baluchistan	18.8%	24.8%	0.0%	0.0%	43.6%
N.W.F.P.	0.8%	2.1%	1.9%	4.6%	9.4%
FATA	0.0%	1.7%	1.4%	0.3%	2.2%
Total	51.5%	36.9%	5.5%	6.2%	100.0%

Source: (GoP, Chapter-1 Introduction — PDF File)

Within a very few years, Punjab was regarded as British India's model agricultural province.[11] Over a period of 25 years, the British put in place the largest network of canals the world has ever seen. In the end, nearly 23,000 miles of canals were constructed in Punjab, and an additional 6,000 miles of canals were constructed in Sindh. By 1921, more than 11 million acres were irrigated by the canals in

Map 5-1: Aridity Map of Pakistan

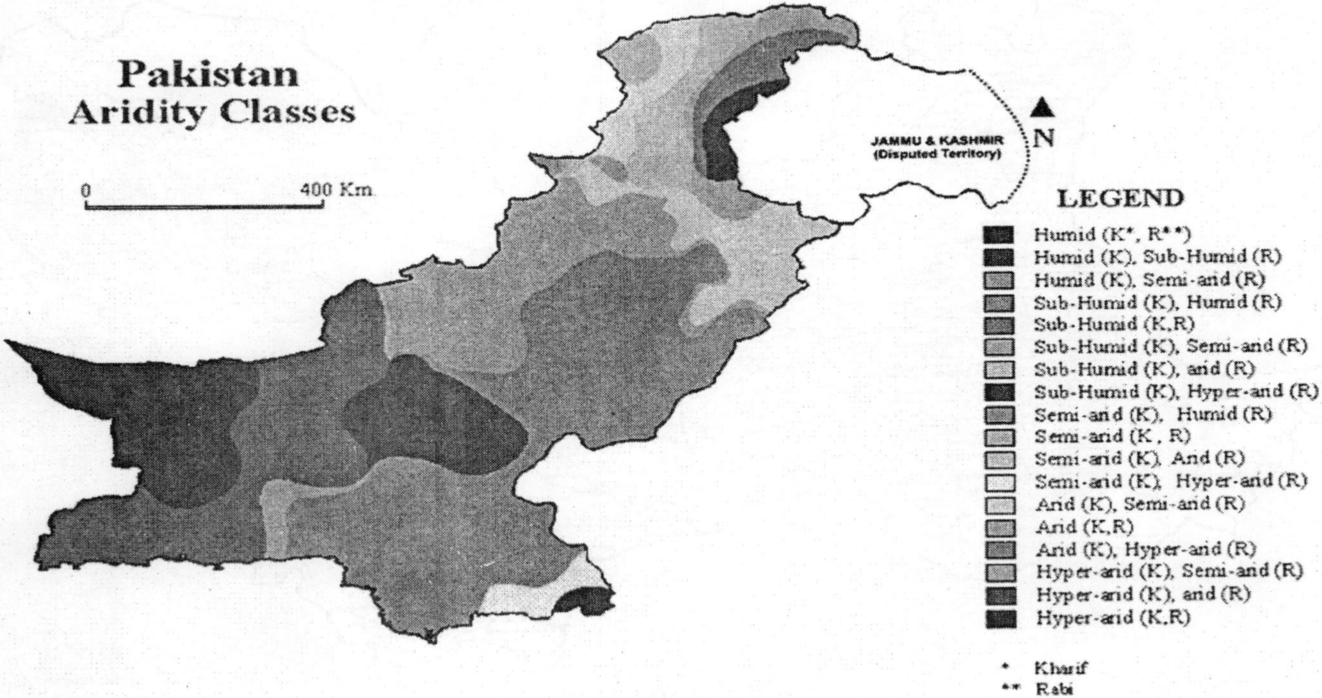

Source: Meteorology Department and WRRI, NARC/PARC

Map 5-2: Approximate Division Line Between British East (India) and West Punjab (Pakistan) Prior to Partition

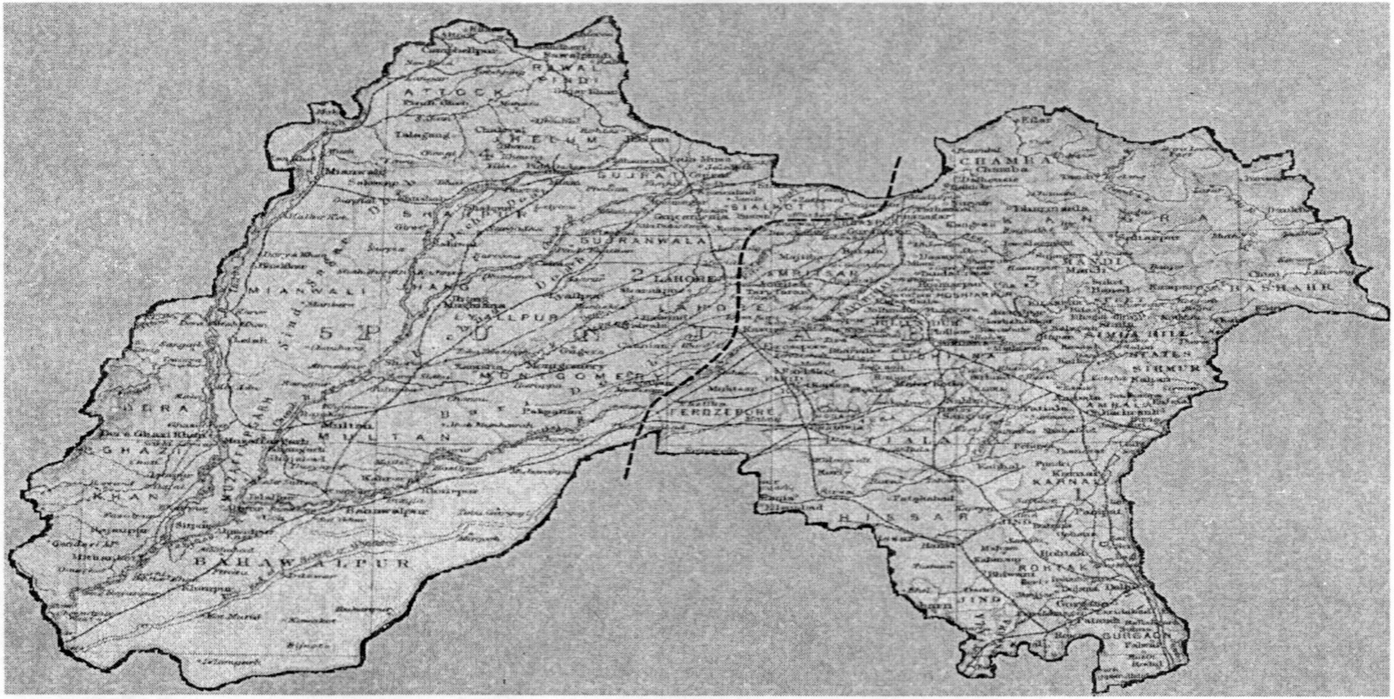

Note: Dashed line represents approximate divisional boundary[17]

Punjab and Sindh.[12] Along with the increase in canals came increased agricultural production, which set off a chain reaction in the form of social, economic, political, and infrastructural development.[13]

British involvement in Punjab provided an opportunity to achieve a number of goals. First, in East Punjab population growth was causing land fragmentation and agricultural overcrowding, and when the canal colonies were opened to settlement, a preference was given to Punjabis rather than people from other provinces.[14] Second, the British wished to reward the Sikhs and Muslims who had remained loyal to the Crown during the Sepoy Mutiny of 1857.[15] Third, through the selection of loyal Muslims and Sikhs, a yeoman class of farmers stood between British India and potential invaders from the northwest.[16] Finally, the canal colonies provided much needed foodgrain production, cotton, and cattle and horse breeding on a commercial scale, as well as an additional source of much needed revenue.

The land grants to the canal colonists were in units of 50 acres, with the largest being 2,500 acres. Many landowners supplemented their grants through purchase.[18] The large land grants, along with the British push for the production of commercial crops – wheat, cotton, and sugarcane – instilled a commercial attitude among the canal colonists. Later, at the time of Partition, many of these successful, commercial farmers, especially the Sikhs and Hindus, returned to their home districts and cities and instilled a new vitality in the otherwise staid villages and towns of central East Punjab. The return of the canal colonists, together with their experiences and commercial agricultural skills, prepared Punjab for success once the Green Revolution's package of practices were introduced. It was the heritage of agricultural commercialism in the canal colonies that permitted the Punjabis, in Pakistan and India, to become successful commercial farmers.

The canal colony experience contributed significantly to the willingness and the ability of the Punjabi farmers to invest in the Green Revolution's new technologies. In Pakistan the landholdings were already much larger than those in East Punjab, giving the Pakistani farmers an even larger economic base, or ability to adopt the required inputs. In East Punjab the landholdings were substantially smaller as a result of the implementation of strict land reforms. Credit for purchases was available through longstanding village cooperative societies and moneylenders. Although canal irrigation gave West Punjab a slight edge over East Punjab, it was the emergence of the use of tubewells and pumpsets that allowed Pakistan's cultivators to surge ahead and become self-sufficient in wheat more quickly.

Tubewells

Before the Green Revolution, the canal irrigation system constructed by the British was the principle means of irrigation. Canal irrigation covered an estimated 7.7 million hectares, and represented 81 percent of Pakistan's total irrigated area. At this time, tubewell irrigation was insignificant, with only 30,000 hectares irrigated. Today, canal irrigation still represents over 78 percent of irrigation coverage. However, between 1950 and 2005, the total area under irrigation nearly doubled, from 9.61 to 18.34 million hectares. See Table 5-3, below. A significant part of that increase has come from tubewell use. The increase in the area irrigated by tubewells coincides with the implementation of the Green Revolution, as seen in the jump in area irrigated between 1960-65 and 1965-70. Since 1965-70, the area irrigated by tubewells has increased steadily.

Each new well, however, tapped the groundwater reserves of the nation. At first the demand was meager but with each new year, more and more demands were made on the water tables. Because of the aridity of the climate, recharge of the aquifers was slow and, in many areas, incapable of keeping pace with the rate of draw-down. The net result was that the groundwater reserves were being depleted at an alarming rate.

Today, Pakistan continues to rapidly deplete its underground water resources. Observation wells near the twin cities of Islamabad and Rawalpindi in the fertile Punjab plain show a fall in the water table between 1982 and 2000 that ranges from 1 to nearly 2 meters a year. In the province of Balochistan . . . water tables around the capital, Quetta, are falling by 3.5 meters per year. Throughout the province, six basins have exhausted their groundwater supplies, leaving their irrigated lands barren. Sardar Riaz A. Khan, former director of Pakistan's Arid Zone Research Institute, expects that within 10–15 years virtually all the basins outside the canal-irrigated areas will have depleted their groundwater supplies, depriving the province of much of its grain harvest.[19]

Under these circumstances, Pakistan's agricultural survivability, at least based on groundwater irrigation, is in jeopardy. In time, Pakistan's agriculture will have to retreat to canal irrigated areas and no-till approaches. What happens then?

Table 5-3: Area (ha) Irrigated by Source, 1950-2005

Year	*Canals*	*Tubewells*	*Other*	*Total*
1950-55	7.77	0.03	1.81	9.61
1955-60	9.64	0.09	1.51	11.24
1960-65	9.03	0.39	1.63	11.05
1965-70	8.92	1.02	2.31	12.25
1970-75	9.24	2.27	1.22	12.73
1975-80	10.29	2.28	1.08	13.65
1980-85	11.42	3.07	0.96	15.45
1985-90	11.48	3.88	0.82	16.18
1990-95	12.05	3.88	0.56	16.49
1995-00	14.43	2.97	0.26	18.29
2000-05	14.38	3.39	0.23	18.34

Source: (GoP, Pakistan Economic Survey, 1994-95, 1995), p. 58; and (GoP, Economic Survey of Pakistan, 2005-06, 2006), Table 2.11, Area Irrigated by Different Sources.

Figure 5-1: Changes Area Irrigated by Source, 1950-2005

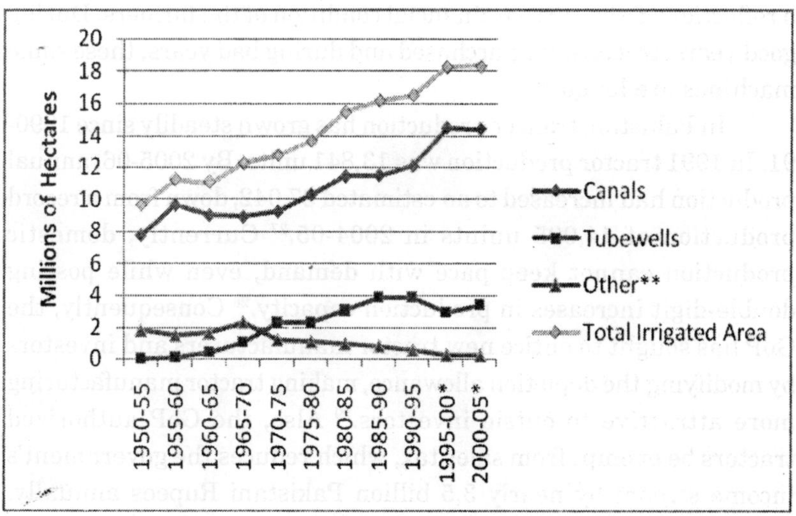

Mechanization: Tractors

Tractors were introduced almst simultaneusly with tubewells. In 1960, there were only 1,665 tractors in all Pakistan. Eight years later, there were approximately 19,000 and by 1984, their number had increased nerly tenfold to 187,255.[20] While the increased number of tractors is impressive, it must be understood that the Pakistani use of tractors differs from those used in Indian East Punjab, where the tractors tend to be smaller. The difference in size reflects the differences in scales of operations between the two Punjabs. For example, in 1982, 84 percent of the tractors used on Pakistani holdings were above 35 horsepower.[21] Pakistan's current demand for tractors has outstripped domestic production capacity. At present product falls short by 15,000 to 20,000 units annually, with the greatest demand for tractors over 50 horsepower.[22]

In East Punjab, tractors are common, however, due to smaller average size of holdings, tractor size is generally smaller.[23] The 4 to 10 hectare landowners are the most frequent tractor purchasers in East Punjab and account for over half of all tractors purchased. Since tractor use on smaller sized holdings is problematic, these middle-sized landowners are also the most susceptible to financiel overextension and indebtedness. As a consequence, in many parts of East Punjab, weekly 'tractor bazaars' are held, where farmers attempt to sell their tractors for the purposes of debt relief.[24] Each week 500-600 tractors are for sale.[25] The sell-off of tractors is typlically a reflection of the current financial condition of the farmers. During good years, tractors are purchased and during bad years, these same machines are let go.[26]

In Pakistan, trancor production has grown steadily since 1990-91. In 1991 tractor production was 13,841 units. By 2005-06, annual production had increased to an estimated 37,042, down from a record production of 44,095 unints in 2004-05.[27] Currently, domestic production cannot keep pace with demand, even while posting double-digit increases in production capacity.[28] Consequently, the GoP has sought to entice new tractor manufacturers and investors by modifying the depletion allowance, making tractor manufacturing more attractive to outsie investors.[29] Also, the GoP authorized tractors be exempt from sales tax, which reduces the government's income stream by nearly 3.5 billion Pakistani Rupees annually.

Further, to make importation easier, import duties on tractors have been lifted.[30]

The GoP, has recognized the need for agricultural mechanization and is making every effort to promote domestic machinery manufacture, as well as streamlining the process of machinery importation. The type and quantity of machinery required is based on the larger average size of holdings and an acute shortage of skilled agricultural labor. In many respects, Pakistan's style of agriculture has become a mirror of many commercialized agricultural systems around the world. It is not following the Indian model because of differences in the way the Green Revolution manifested itself. In India there is a surplus of agricultural laborers. In Pakistan, there is a distinct shortage of qualified laborers.

Issues and Challenges

Declining Agricultural Production

Although Pakistan has undergone considerable industrial growth over the last twenty years, agriculture remains an important part of the Pakistani economy. It employs approximately half of the labor force, and contributes nearly a quarter of the state's GDP. Agricultural production has exceeded population growth rates since the inception of the Green Revolution. However now there are indications that production and productivity are beginning to wane, as the resource base upon which the Green Revolution in Pakistan was built is declining. This is nowhere more evident than in the area of irrigation. Water resources have become uncertain and variable, and these have a direct impact on agricultural production. Over time, irrigation results in one of two conditions, unless steps are taken to counteract them before they become serious and production-robbing problems. These are waterlogging and soil salinity. Since the beginning of the Green Revolution, nearly third of Pakistan's 22 million hectares of agricultural land has become affected by soil salinity, and may have lowered agricultural production by as much as 25 percent.[31] Equally destructive is waterlogging, which affects nearly 38 percent of Pakistan's gross irrigable area.[32.]

Food production has increased by more than 50 percent over the last twenty years, while the area under cultivation has risen by less than 10 percent. This difference represents an increase in agricultural intensification, and with it agricultural productivity. Much like portions of India, where crop yields are exceedingly low, yields in Pakistan are below their potential. See Figure 5-4, below. While the seed varieties available to Pakistani cultivators have an average yield *potential* of 10 metric tons per hectare, the average yield is only 2.6 m/t and for the most progressive farmers, it is half the yield potential, with no appreciable gains having been made in the last decade.

Since the early 1990s, yields have improved but there remains room for improvement.[33] As a result of low yields, Pakistan's food supply remains dependent upon good harvests year after year, which increases its agricultural vulnerability and food insecurity. Therefore, climatic changes or changes in the availability of either rainfall or irrigation water could very quickly undermine the agricultural progress that the country has experienced since the Green Revolution.

Figure 5-4: Yield Gaps for Wheat

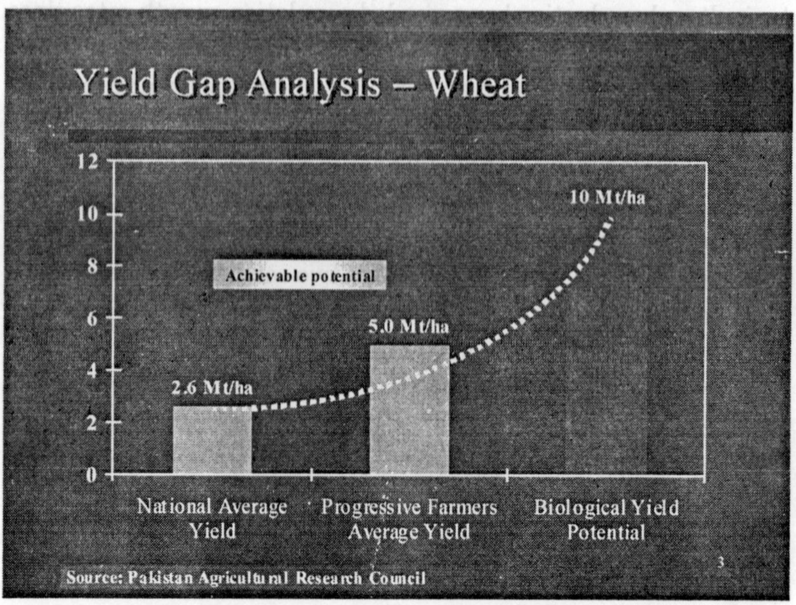

Table 5-4: Yield Gap for Selected Crops in Pakistan

Selected Crop	*World Average Yield kg/Ha*	*Average Yield Kg/Ha*	*Yield Gap Kg/Ha*	*Unachieved Potential As a Percent*
Wheat	2,720	2,262	458	16.8
Rice	3,916	2,882	1,034	26.4
Maize	4,343	1,768	2,575	59.3
Sugarcane	127,400	100,000	27,400	21.5
Rape & Mustard	2,743	641	2,102	76.6
Cotton	1,576	1,602	-26	-1.6

Source: Wheat, Rice, and Maize (Business Recorder, 2007), Sugarcane (Bahada, Khan, Muhammad Jama, and Hamdullah Azim, 2004), Rape and Mustard (Sandhu, G.R., 1993), and Cotton (UNCTAD, 2008)

Figure 5-4 provides information on world average yields, Pakistan's average yields and the gap between the two figures. For every crop type, Pakistan's yield rates are well below world averages. Compare these figures with Table 5-1, above. Although impressive yield increases have been achieved, the world averages have increased even faster.

At the beginning of the 1990s, there were indications that per capita agricultural production had begun to stagnate. The same pattern has emerged in parts of India. Additional inputs or seed improvement may compensate for the deteriorating effects of commercialized agriculture on soil but declining returns are generally unavoidable. In the absence of major changes in Pakistan's agricultural patterns and resource consumption, there is a very real possibility that production will suffer, ending in food deficits, as land is either put out of production or cannot be irrigated.

Changing Rural Credit Systems

Like most developing nations, a large percentage of the population lives in rural areas. However, unlike most South Asian nations, in Pakistan more than 60 percent of poor rural household ***are not*** farming households.[34] Many of the rural population are involved in direct non-farm activities, such as product processing, trade and transport, and these activities account for over half of total rural incomes. For this reason, it is becoming imperative that, in addition to traditional farm-related production credit, farm-related non-production credit systems need to be developed. For the remaining agricultural poor population, 38 percent are of small landowners, with almost no access to commercial credit. They must rely almost exclusively on moneylenders for the needs.

The Consequences of Larger Landholdings

Landholdings still remain concentrated in the hands of the few. It has been estimated that 45 percent of the land area of Pakistan is controlled by only 2 percent of the households.[35] Their land ownership has given these households a stranglehold on and control over water and agricultural subsidies and, therefore, the lion's share of the benefits resulting from increased agricultural growth and production. Likewise, agricultural credit programs have ostensibly accrued to these larger farmers, as well. As a consequence, they have been able to capitalize on agricultural subsidy programs, increase their landholdings through purchase, and have substituted comparatively more expensive human labor with access to cheaper farm machinery. This pattern is quite in opposition to the machinery-human pattern observed in many places in India or Bangladesh, where cheap supplies of landless laborers abound.

India's commercial wheat farmers of Punjab and Haryana are credited, or chided, for becoming Asia's equivalents of America's agro-businessmen — agricultural capitalists. However, Pakistan's farmers, especially those in Punjab are possibly even more like their Western counterparts, with a rising dependency on mechanization over human labor.

Changes Needed for Sustained Agricultural Growth

The adoption of many Green Revolution technologies, as well as the extension of irrigation, seem to have reached a point where there simply is nowhere left to go. The practical limit of most current improved seeds has been reached. Part of the reason for the plateauing of agricultural production lies in the fact that agricultural research and development have been declining over the last ten years or so. Almost all past research was focused on irrigated agriculture, while rain-fed and arid agriculture were largely ignored.

No-Till Agriculture[36]

Although no single change in the agricultural repertory of cultivators will alleviate all the problems associated with current agricultural production, options are becoming available, especially for countries and areas limited by inadequate rainfall or little or unreliable irrigation. Among these are no-tillage techniques, which have grown in popularity, for they promise to improve cultivator incomes and are consistent with the development of sustainable agriculture. At one time, no-till agriculture was associated with slash and burn cultivation. Traditionally, this form of agriculture degraded the soil rapidly, resulted in soil erosion, and famine. As such, it was an unsustainable agricultural system alternative.

As used herein, no-till is the planting of crops in previously unprepared soil by opening a minimal hole or slot of sufficient size and depth to permit seeding. At least 30% of the soil surface remains covered with residues of cover crops. The maximum benefits of no-till are obtained only if the package follows three simple principles:

- The soil is disturbed as little as possible.
- The soil is covered by plants or plant residues.
- Crops must be rotated.

As simple as the no-till system appears, due to technical and economic constraints, it is used in only a few locations as it is difficult to adhere to the underlying principle practices noted above. Further, the development of sustainable no-till packages requires a strong research effort and such teams are oftentimes difficult, expensive, and time-consuming to assemble.

No-till is comparatively easy to adapt to existing wheat-rice rotation systems, like those found in the Indo-Gangetic Plain. In South America and Sub-Saharan Africa, the system has been difficult to implement, largely due to the need to adapt it to local environmental and cultural differences. In the irrigated areas of the Indo-Gangetic Plain, the development of no-till practices has been impeded by the lack of locally adapted seed drills (planters) and water management techniques.

Permanent no-till cannot be used for crops that require massive soil disturbance for planting or their harvest, for example potatoes or groundnuts. In arid areas, where the main objective is water conservation, the soils are disturbed only to meet this objective.

Advantages of No-Till

Compared to conventional tillage, no-till has numerous agronomic advantages.[37] When combined with residue management, no-till limits soil erosion. It improves water conservation by increasing infiltration and reducing evaporation. It improves the condition of the soil by increasing organic matter content, improving soil structure, and preventing the formation of a plow-pan. Because there is no plow-pan, root systems develop better.[38] The availability of nutrients in the soil also improves. No-till increases flexibility in the timing of crop operations. The turnaround time between crops is reduced, so crops can be planted closer to the optimal dates. Crops can be planted in soils with higher moisture levels. Farmers do not have to wait as long to plant after a rain, or in dry soils before the rains begin.

There are also economic advantages to no-till. It reduces costs, even for small-scale farmers who buy herbicides, because expensive hand-weeding can be eliminated by using herbicides. It requires fewer implements as well as less tractor power, reducing investment in agricultural machinery and extending the life of tractors. It reduces labor requirements and simplifies labor management.[39] Reduced labor requirements enable small-scale farmers to undertake other income-generating activities, such as growing horticultural crops or dairying, provided that they can access the markets.

The physical work involved in no-till is less demanding compared to conventional tillage. Larger areas can be planted with the same amount of machinery and labor. In some instances, yields increase with no-till. In certain areas, three harvests per year become feasible. Production risks fall.

Production in marginal areas of low moisture levels or steep slopes becomes possible. In several counties, small-scale farmers themselves have mentioned that with no-till they get a larger and steadier income; the need for family labor falls, allowing children to attend school. The increased income resulting from no-till often permits families to pay for their children's education. Increased income has enabled families to improve their quality of life.

Finally, no-till has several important environmental benefits. The soil cover reduces erosion and favors water infiltration, diminishing the probability of mudslides in hilly areas and reducing the pollution of waterways with agrochemicals. Pollution may also be reduced as fewer and less toxic agrochemicals are used. Reductions in agrochemicals, combined with the non-disturbance of the soil, favor the development of beneficial insects. Greenhouse gas emissions are greatly reduced by lower consumption of fossil fuels, the smaller amount of organic matter that is transformed into carbon dioxide, and lower methane emissions. Increased fertilizer efficiency reduces the formation of nitrous oxides, and due to reduced fertilizer consumption, less energy is used in their production. Taken together, these benefits give a good indication of how no-till contributes to the agronomic, economic, and ecological sustainability of cropping systems.

Several characteristics of no-till facilitate its adoption. First, the economic benefits often become evident in the first year, whereas problems generally do not arise until the third year, when crop rotation becomes mandatory and additional investments in land and implements may become necessary.

Second, the start-up costs associated with no-till are small. The only specialized components of no-till are a planter and knowledge. Since no-till planters can also be used for conventional tillage, the only start-up cost would be the small cost of converting a conventional planter into a no-till planter. If a no-till planter replaces a conventional planter, there is a cost only if the conventional planter is replaced before it is completely amortized.

The other specialized inputs are the farmer's investments in learning about the technology, which include the farmer's time, the costs of acquiring information, mainly through buying specialized literature and participating in special events and field trials. None of these costs, however, is substantial when compared with the variable costs invested every year by a commercial farmer. For the smallest cultivators, these start-up costs may be initially significant. Large-scale farmers, either individually or collectively, often generate their own information about no-till; whereas small-scale farmers often must rely on no-till projects organized and funded by development agencies.

A third characteristic of no-till that encourages adoption is that investment indivisibilities are small. The latest generation of no-till planters may be expensive, but many countries have active markets for second-hand equipment. The technology for converting conventional planters into no-till planters is well known and relatively inexpensive. Even though the transformed planter may not be as effective as a new one, it will normally perform satisfactorily.

A fourth advantage is that no-till can be adopted partially or in stages. In many cases, farmers have tried no-till on small areas until they have a good command of the package of practices. Then, they can expand the technique to other parts of their landholdings over time.

Finally, although the principles behind no-till are complex, the immediate economic consequences of small departures from the optimal package of recommended practices are usually minimal. Farmers can learn about the technology over time. If a farmer does not use the best rotation, the consequences are not felt completely in the first year but increase gradually over time, as soils can begin to deteriorate. This phenomenon typically becomes apparent, especially in the third and subsequent years after to-till has been implemented.

Restrictions on No-Till Adoption

One of the most difficult restrictions to overcome is that no-till requires a complete departure from conventional farming practices. In switching from conventional tillage to no-till, the farmer must learn about the dynamics of a system that is out of equilibrium and usually takes up to five years to reach a steady state. In the first two years, the farmer obtains benefits from the new technology. The transition to no-till reaches a critical point in the third year, when factors particular to each farm, especially the evolution of pest and weed populations, need to be addressed. Farmers can, and often do, revert to conventional tillage when they are faced with problems that they cannot solve without outside intervention.

No-till requires substantial adaptation to local conditions. In areas with weak research systems, researchers may develop packages for some regions but not for others. In semi-arid environments, it is difficult to produce enough biomass (sufficient plant residue) to provide a proper soil cover.

In many developing countries, residues are used to feed animals. Since plant residues are low quality feed, this demand reflects low-productivity livestock enterprises. To date, farmers have not adopted no-till with mulch in areas where residues are used as feed. It has been suggested that farmers may solve this problem by replacing draft animals with tractors or the development of formal pastures. Since no-till involves a transition from a low biomass producing system to a high biomass system, in some cases the additional biomass may sustain both no-till and livestock. It is possible, however, that farmers will prefer to use the additional biomass to expand their herds. Short-term economic considerations may induce farmers not to use adequate rotations, reducing the system's long-term sustainability. The incidence of weeds, pests, and diseases may increase, especially when rotations are not used.

Plant varieties adapted to no-till agriculture may not be available. Often seed companies and national breeding programs develop plant varieties for traditional production systems and more productive cropping environments. Areas considered to have low potential for agriculture under conventional tillage may become high potential areas under no-till, but generally new varieties are not developed for these areas until they have consolidated as major agricultural regions. Very few public research institutions breed plant varieties specifically for no-till conditions, although specially adapted varieties may perform better. For example, wheat varieties perform very differently when planted in beds or in the traditional manner, but breeders have started to develop wheat varieties for bed planting only recently.

In the climatic transition zones in Pakistan, no-till may well be, in the absence of reliable surface or groundwater irrigation, or electrical power for pumpsets, a workable agricultural alternative on lands that might otherwise be left to grazing or go unused. Therefore, it represents a means of further expanding cultivable land and agricultural production.

Irrigation

Irrigation is the single most important component of Pakistan's agricultural sector. Without irrigation, much of Pakistan is too arid to support modern agricultural regimens. Although recognized for its importance, it has been neglected. There are growing signs of inefficiency and system maintenance failures. It has been estimated that the system's overall conveyance efficiency stands at 45 percent.[40] In addition, water losses have increased over the years due to improper canal maintenance. Seepage results in water losses to the aquifer and contributes to problems of soil salinity and waterlogging under certain circumstances. The barrages have been neglected, reducing their effectiveness during peak water periods.

Illegal pumping from canals has altered the availability of water, especially to the so-called 'tail-enders,' those farthest from the main canals. Often, these tail-enders have little or no irrigation water available to them. As a consequence, if more expensive tubewell irrigation is not available, their crops succumb to the ravages of the arid environment. In either case, the farmers' investments are either severely curtailed or completely lost. The repair and maintenance of the canals, while not countering the water thefts caused by illegal pumping, would conserve more water and possibly improve the plight of the tail-enders.

The supply of irrigation water on a year-round basis is emerging as an obstacle to year-round agricultural production. An improved system of water storage and management could improve water shortages during the winter, and take advantage of oversupply during the summer, when the rivers and canals are at their highest levels.

The failure to maintain the canal system is almost always the consequence of government finance. Governments always find 'other needs' more pressing than routine maintenance. However, it is the tedious day-to-day maintenance that keeps the physical machinery of the state running and working smoothly.

Further, the GoP has failed to implement and enforce existing cost recovery programs. The Irrigation Department must become more accountable, and its bureaucratic structure needs to become more efficient, which would result in increased revenues for system maintenance, as well as increased general-purpose funds.

Finally, problems associated with waterlogging, soil salinity, surface and groundwater contamination, and land degradation are rapidly becoming serious concerns. Waterlogging and salinity are allied problems, both resulting from inadequate drainage accompanied by unrelenting, year-round irrigation. These two problems may well be potentially the most difficult to resolve because, once they are recognized, remedial action is often prohibitively expensive to implement and the land becomes unusable. In many areas, more land is lost to waterlogging and salinity than over-cultivation.

Land

Pakistan has, as a result of its climate and history, a tradition of large landholdings. This has resulted in high levels of inequality between the various socio-economic groups. There are two opposing arguments involved in the land issue. On the one hand is the argument that, those with the necessary resources should be in control of productive resources. On the other hand, however, is issue of justice and equity. The current regimen in land does not satisfy the principles of justice and equity.

Land reform – both tenancy reform and redistribution - is conceptually important to poverty alleviation. In addition to production benefits, land reform helps to change the local political structure by giving more voice to the poor. Re-distributive land reform, whether through market-assisted land reform programs or otherwise, continue to remain a substantive policy issue for poverty reduction. The efficacy of such reforms, however, are debatable.

In general, land reforms are based on the proposition that owner-operated family farms are generally more efficient in the use of land and other inputs than large farms operated with supervised wage labour; and secure property rights promote long term investment in productivity enhancing technologies and conservation.[41] Land reforms not only directly benefit tenants, they also benefit agricultural laborers.[42]

These types of land reform are generally of two types: First, tenancy reform, including the enhancement of tenurial security as an intermediate or second-best step as well as ownership by the tenants as the best option.

Second, redistribution of landholdings above a certain ceiling to the landless.

Even before the introduction of improved seed varieties in the late 1960s, observational data seemed to suggest that small farms had higher yields per unit area than large farms. It was believed that land reforms were advisable on the grounds that they would reduce the inequality of rural incomes and improve efficiency. When the Green Revolution technologies were introduced, however, a new era in agricultural thinking seemed to evolve. The new technologies were perfectly adapted to the already existing 'elite-farmer' style of agriculture in Pakistan. The application of increasing amounts of human labor to increase productivity was negated by the application of technology and increased use of improved seeds, water, and fertilizer. The larger farmers, with their greater financial power, had no difficulty in acquiring the necessary inputs. In Pakistan, it was possible to increase agricultural production and growth without the application of large amounts of limited and expensive human labor and without making real changes in the rural power structure.

Land plays an important role in reducing poverty and empowering the poor. In Pakistan the power of the landed class is really a monopoly that has served as a barrier to social and economic progress for the poor. Through land reforms, landlords' far-reaching political and economic power is reduced and more power can be given to the poorer workers on the land. At least on three occasions, Pakistan has attempted to implement land reforms designed to limit land holdings and redistribute the land among the smaller landholders or landless.[43] All three attempts have failed. Despite these documentable failures, the IFAD has repeatedly called for land reforms in Pakistan, particularly in Sind and Punjab provinces.[44]

According to the *Pakistan Census of Agriculture 2000*, farms below 25 acres constituted roughly 95 percent of the total number of farms in Pakistan, and represent 63 percent of total farm area. It is on these smaller farms that the land reformers believe the fate and future of Pakistan's agriculture rest.[45]

Now that large-scale farms are approaching the upper limit of yield per acre, using existing technologies, the question becomes how do we increase production from here on? In Pakistan, the primary emphasis has been on commercial agriculture and large-scale operations. It has become a tradition, a national way of thinking. History has also shown that large-scale agricultural specialization tends to be the most productive, at least on a *per capita* basis. The smaller cultivators, by and large, have been overlooked. Yields on the small landholdings have not kept pace with those on the larger farms, at least in terms of *per capita* yields and productivity, largely due to the small-holders' lack of economic access to yield-increasing technologies. If land reforms are deemed necessary within the context of Pakistan, they might be better called agrarian reforms – reforms that promote and assist the small landholders improve their productivity. Land reforms have not worked in Pakistan, and they have had little real, long-term effect in most other countries.

Land Reforms

In India, following Independence, attempts were made to impose land reforms. Although the legislation was passed, it was never fully implemented nor enforced. Only in Punjab, with the return and resettlement of the Canal Colonists, were tenurial and redistribution land reforms fully implemented, followed shortly thereafter by the Green Revolution.

After more than half a century, many have begun to argue that the time, effort, and resources spent on land reforms did little to accelerate or impede the Green Revolution. An unanticipated outcome of the Green Revolution is that there is no evidence to suggest that the formulation, legislation, and implementation of land reforms were necessary prerequisites for success. Years of debate, preparation, passage of legislation, and attempts to implement and enforce reforms seem to have been unnecessary. For the purposes of political-economy, however, they do serve an important purpose.

Reforms in India did remove parasitic *zamindars* and other intermediaries, but little was achieved in the areas of tenancy and land consolidation; and only slight improvements were made in terms of rural social justice, equality, and equity. Each of these areas of reform was thought to be necessary for the improvement of agricultural productivity. History played a gigantic trick on all the players in the agricultural development process. Nothing more than making improved technologies available to farmers able to use them was necessary. With or without government intervention, had the modern inputs been made available to most cultivators, they would have adopted them.

Further, as enacted, the effects of land reforms in India devolved over time, returning the land to nearly the same conditions as prevailed prior to the land reforms. Tenancies increased; and due to the continued adherence to traditional land inheritance laws, the landholdings became smaller and smaller and fragmented.

The Next Revolution

Now that the First Green Revolution is quickly fading, it may be time to review what alterations may be deemed necessary for the next generation Green Revolution. The rules of the Next Green Revolution, if there is indeed one coming, may well be different from those of the past. The last Green Revolution was felt most intensely by those able to invest in the new, modern agricultural technologies – mostly the larger landholders. If Ahmad Sultan is correct the Second Revolution may well benefit cultivators at all levels.[46] The next revolution may be an outgrowth of communications technology as much as it will be agricultural. The *e-Choupal* system in India may represent the first of many farm to market and supermarket sales initiatives.[47] *E-Choupal* has already circumvented the traditional *mandi* system of marketing produce, by linking cultivators directly to a large scale marketing organization. In effect, *e-Choupal* has eliminated many of the barriers that have stood between the producers in the field and the end market consumers. Under the old *mandi* system, several layers of middlemen, government officials, and moneylenders intervene between the producer and the end-users of products. The next Revolution in agriculture may be the commercialization of all levels of agriculture, eliminating traditional profit-sapping intermediaries, and the consolidation of produce for shipment to consumers, either domestically or internationally.

Recent developments in the area of agricultural integration – the so-called 'field to fork' approach to agricultural development –

portend a new era in Pakistan's agriculture. This approach to agriculture entails the vertical integration of agriculture and a shift away from traditional ideas of both production and marketing, especially in terms of reducing the abuses resulting from market middlemen and local markets.

Vertical integration tends to push cultivators toward higher-value-added crops and activities, and this will have a profound impact on the small-scale farmer. They will be forced to participate in the cash-based marketplace and this will increase their direct involvement in the marketing of their produce. It is hoped that the vertical integration of Pakistan's agricultural sector will have long-term benefits for the small, poor cultivators by increasing incomes and promoting equity.

Toward this end, a number of large foreign investors have entered into agreements with domestic Indian service providers to coordinate, consolidate, process, and export produce to Europe and the Middle East. Other similar partnerships are being negotiated, and like the *e-Choupal* system, they are all dependent upon telecommunication beginning at the field level and all the way to world markets. These organizations, if they follow *e-Choupal's* model, will provide access to information, group purchasing opportunities for inputs, as well as consumer goods, the handling and marketing of cultivators' produce. [48]

For some time now, Pakistan has been in talks with German retailers, with an eye to the creation of a cost-cutting chain of grocery supermarkets. These chains would purchase farm products from the farmers at fair prices and sell them to consumers through their own retail outlets.[49] Such chains may well accomplish what formal land reforms could not. They would begin to equalize agricultural opportunities at all levels and for all landholders.

Further, with an emphasis on consumer pricing, i.e., reducing prices to their lowest possible level, exorbitant procurement prices will become a thing of the past and this will have a direct impact on Pakistan's largest landholders. The feudal power held by the large landholders is largely based on their ability to manipulate and take advantage of support prices. Under the current system, consumers at every level pay dearly and the middlemen fill their pockets. With the advent of the producer-to-retailer system, support prices will become a thing of the past and the number and role of agricultural intermediaries will cease to exist, thus improving competition and profitability, especially for the smallest producers.

Preparing for Corporate Agriculture Farming

Either due to economic realities or political pressures, in 2002, the GoP enacted a law that ostensibly removed the ceiling on land holdings, as well as lifting import duties on agricultural machinery and equipment.[50] The federal cabinet approved a Corporate Agriculture Farming (CAF) package aimed at luring foreign investors. The new policy includes a tax holiday of five years for irrigated agriculture, seven years for rain-fed land and 10 years for cultivable wasteland. The transfer of land for corporate agricultural farms would also be exempted from duties.

This change in direction flies in the face of traditional development wisdom and those international aid and development agencies that have pushed for so long for a more equitable distribution of the agricultural land base and, as an outcome, the increase in rural incomes, the reduction of poverty, and the reduction in the number of rural landless. The GoP seems to have decided that, for economic and political reasons, those best suited to own and manage Pakistan's agricultural land base are those with the assets to do so. Further, it is also a concession to the legitimacy of large-scale commercial agriculture within a South Asian setting. Either due to exigency or facing the realities of population numbers and available land, elsewhere in South Asia, farming is a small to micro-scale endeavor.

While it may be the government's acquiescence to the demands of the largest landholders that prompted its turnabout over the need for land reforms, it could well be seen as just another maneuver for reasons of political economy. However, if the concept of consumer pricing becomes a reality in Pakistan's agricultural production and marketing, all of the concessions being granted to the largest landholders may be of little value in the long run.

Animal Husbandry

A growing subsector of Pakistani agriculture has been in livestock and animal husbandry. In fact, this is currently the fastest

Figure 5-5: Changes in Dietary Energy Supply over Time

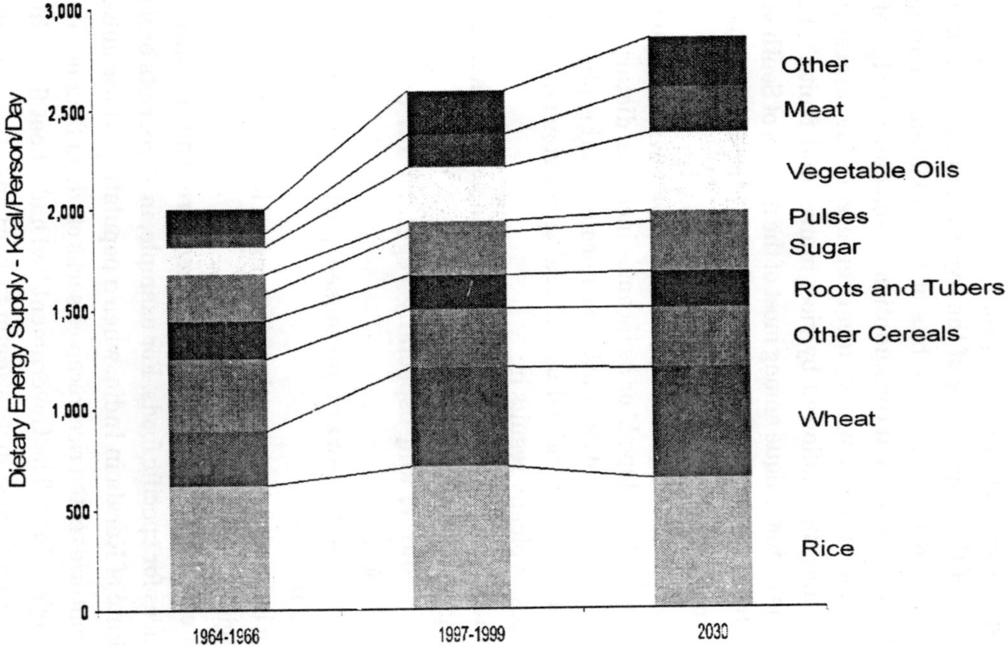

Source: Modified from (FAO, World agriculture: towards 2015/2030. Summary report, 2002), p. 18.

growing subsector in Pakistani agriculture. It now represents nearly half of Pakistan's agricultural GDP. Even so, this sector has been neglected by modern researchers. Its neglect is all the more incongruous in light of the fact that the British, more than a hundred years earlier, had promoted commercial horse and cattle breeding. In spite of researchers' disinterest, it has become an important part of Pakistan's agricultural strength.

Part of the importance of the livestock industry in Pakistan is the result of the dietary habits of the Pakistanis. Throughout most of South Asia, meat consumption is well down the list of main foods consumed. After wheat, meat represents the largest part of the Pakistani diet, followed by rice, maize, and fruits.[51] In fact, Pakistan is rather unique among most of the nations of Southwestern and Southern Asia, regarding the importance of meat and this cannot be explained simply as a function religion.

As countries move through the development continuum, from 'developing' to 'developed,' or as incomes increase, dietary changes or shifts in consumption patterns normally take place. These changes, unless constrained by cultural or religious inspired food avoidances, typically results in:

- Wheat and rice remain the dietary staples but their overall contribution to the daily diet lessens.
- Meat, dairy, and especially vegetable oil consumption increases.
- A movement toward increased portability and ease of preparation.
- An increased consumption of processed foods, especially those high in refined sugars.[52]

In certain areas of the world, there are long traditions and preferences for specific foods. For example, in 1966, riots broke out in the State of Kerala in India, when a population whose ancestors had for centuries eaten rice, received sacks of wheat flour originating in Borlaug's fields.[53] The Government had had wheat flour shipped to Kerala from Punjab in its attempt to avert an outbreak of famine. Instead, the people seemed to prefer starvation rather than eat wheat. Ultimately, they ate the wheat flour but the incident demonstrates just how recalcitrant people are to changes in their food habits.

The consumption of comparatively high levels of meat in Pakistan seems to fall in this category. Pakistan's achievement of food self-sufficiency, in general, improvement in the overall standard of living, and a long tradition of commercial livestock herding, in Sindh and Baluchistan, helps to explain the Pakistani preference for meat products. Further, improved inland transport of agricultural products improves producers' abilities to get their products to markets far from home.

In addition, Pakistan is ahead of most other South Asian nations in terms of urbanization. The level of urbanization in Pakistan is approximately 37 percent. This is not high by global standards but it is the highest rate among the South Asian countries. Urbanization contributes significantly to rapid change in dietary consumption, possibly due to increased exposure to alternative food choices afforded within the urban environment.

Observations

Although India is considered the prototype for the implementation of the Green Revolution, as it evolved in the late 1960s and 1970s, the evolution of the Green Revolution was equally spectacular in Pakistan, even though its evolution was different. In terms of realizing self-sufficiency in foodgrains, Pakistan took the lead, and after only three years, self-sufficiency was a reality for the first time.

Much of Pakistan's initial success with the Green Revolution was a function of environmental and socio-economic good fortune. The basic tenets of the new agricultural technologies fit perfectly within the setting as provided by Pakistan. The landholdings were large and amenable to mechanization. Although mostly arid, the British had provided an extensive system of canal irrigation, to which the Pakistanis supplemented with tubewell irrigation, bringing still more acreage under production. The British had also inculcated an entrepreneurial, commercial attitude among many of the farmers of Pakistan, beginning with the canal colonists in the late 19th century. Further, the British had fostered the integration of Pakistan's markets and agricultural producers through the development of an integrated road, rail, and market system. Although there were poor cultivators, small landholders, and landless laborers, the large landowners were not dependent upon them, as mechanization was the preferred substitute of human labor.

Agricultural production on these large holdings increased rapidly. The smaller landholders' productivity lagged well behind the large farming units until fairly recently, when the upper limits of productivity were reached using the existing Green Revolution technologies on the large farms. In addition, issues of water availability for irrigation has become a limiting factor. Other alternatives are needed. Part of the solution, now, may be to improve the small-holders' productivity and begin utilizing lands that have remained largely unproductive due to the lack of water. No-till techniques may represent a beneficial alternative to widespread and inefficient irrigation.

Today Pakistan is faced with the reality that, under current agricultural technology, agricultural yields have probably reached their peak, and unless there is a significant change in agricultural technology, there is nowhere to go from here. Yields have peaked and most of the easily accessible arable land has been exploited. Canal irrigation has been extended to nearly its greatest possible extent. Now, only groundwater resources remain, and even these have been under attack since early in the evolution of Pakistan's Green Revolution.

Without new agricultural technology, continued increases in agricultural productivity are becoming increasingly difficult to realize. No-till agricultural techniques portend greater productivity but, these too, will quickly reach their absolute extent, constrained by the aridity of the landscape.

Due to the nation's overall aridity, large landholdings have been a historical necessity. As a consequence, Pakistan's land remains largely in the hands of a few large landowners; and it is these landowners who have realized the greatest benefits of the Green Revolution. Land reforms have proven ineffective; and if history is any guide, they may have been a waste of time and effort in those areas where they have been enacted and implemented. In the end, social, economic, and political realities have served to negate the effects of such land reforms. Furthermore, there seems to have been no correlation between the adoption of the Green Revolution technologies and land reforms.

Land size, in fact, has proven to be a better gauge of agricultural success. Simply put, the larger landholders, due to their greater financial resources, have been quicker to adopt improved technologies and benefit from them. In large measure, this is a function of large landholdings are more in keeping with the agricultural paradigm upon which the Green Revolution was developed – modern commercial agriculture. This explains much of Pakistan's and India's Green Revolution successes, at least in terms of wheat and rice cultivation. Both East and West Punjab are at the center of Pakistan's and India's agricultural successes, and this is where the Western agricultural paradigm was most completely implemented and realized.

In addition, the British had fostered a stockbreeding tradition in the less well-watered portions of Pakistan. Commercial stockbreeding only served as an extension of an already existing practice among the tribal people of Sindh and Baluchistan, who today serve as the livestock breeders for Pakistan's growing meat market.

As a consequence of history and culture, the Pakistanis have progressed quickly and are well into the transition between being a developing nation and a developed nation. Already, the Pakistanis' food consumption patterns are showing signs of having made the transition to a diet similar to those observed in the West, and now there is a push toward the adoption of modern grocery supermarkets, with an increased emphasis on prepared and prepackaged foods.

Likewise, probably more so than any nation in South Asia or Africa, Pakistan is much more urbanized, and while the country is still considered poor, the largest portion of the poor are not rural agriculturalists. In most developing nations, the rural poor, whether small landowners or landless laborers, make up the bulk of each country's poor. Such is not the case in Pakistan.

Pakistan, for a variety of reasons, stands alone in South Asia.

References

1. (Easterbrook, 1997). Easterbrook's article first appeared in *The Atlantic Monthly*, in January 1997, Volume 279, No. 1, pages 75-82. The on-line version is used here.

2. (Ganzel, 2007).
3. *Ibid.*
4. The government restrictions that existed at the time, essentially channeled the available fertilizer stocks to the elite landowners, making their availability to the small cultivators almost impossible.
5. (Critchfield, 1971). See also (Shiva, 1992). Both anticipated increased violence stemming from the unequal benefits of the Green Revolution. While tensions surely increased, there seems to be little evidence of large-scale or broad based inter-class violence.
6. (College of Food, Agricultural and Natural Resource Sciences, Unknown).
7. *Ibid.*
8. Although tubewell and tractor use in Pakistan increased much more quickly initially. Over time, the use rate between India and Pakistan closed. Differences in tractor technology, however, did not change. Ultimately, the larger landholdings in Pakistan dictated the use of larger, more powerful tractors.
9. Canal irrigation projects in Punjab under the British started in East Punjab in the early 1880s. For example, the Sirhind Canal in Ludhiana District was completed in 1882. Inundation canals were used traditionally in West Pakistan but they were limited in range and were only seasonally useable. Perennial canal construction was initiated in West Punjab in 1885. The first project was the Sidhnai Canal in Multan District which was completed in 1886. In East and West Punjab, there were more than 38 major and minor irrigation projects undertaken, either by the indigenous population or the British, taking water from the Sutlej, Indus, and Chenab rivers. See (Headrick, 1988) p. 191, Figure 4, for the location of the primary West Punjab canal projects.
10. (Tatla, Darshan Singh, 1995), p. 69.
11. Talbot, British Rule in Punjab, 1849-1947: Characteristics and Consequences, 1991).
12. (Calvert, 1922), p. 121.
13. (Jaffrelot, Christophe (ed)., 2004), p.154; See (Ali, The Punjab Under Imperialism, 1885-1947, 1988)
14. (GoI (Raj), 1904), p. 29; and (GoI (Raj), 1915), paragraph 4. Nearly four-fifths of the colonists originated from the more densely inhabited districts of Amritsar, Gurdaspur, Jalandhar, Hoshiarpur,Ludhiana,

Ambala, and Sailkot; and two-thirds of them were Jat Sikhs, Mulsims, and Hindus (Krishan, 2004), p. 80. It is estimated than approximately a million Jat cultivators migrated from East Punjab to West Punjab to become either canal colonists or serve in a support position, See (Talbot, Khizr Tiwana, The Punjab Unionist Party and the Partition of India, 1996), p. 55.

15. Today the rebellion of 1857 is referred to by a variety of names – the Indian Rebellion of 1857, the Great Rebellion, the Indian Mutiny, the Revolt of 1857, and most recently the more politically correct terminology, India's First War of Independence, has become popular.
16. The British were especially fearful of Russian invasions through the Khyber and —Bolan Passes through the Hindu Kush Mountains. It was believed that the yeoman Sikhs and Muslims would afford the British a first line of defense against such incursions.
17. The boundaries of British East and West Punjab would be modified at the time of Partition in 1947 and subsequently, and East Punjab would be further subdivided into the states of Punjab, Haryana and Himachel Pradesh between 1966 and 1971. See (Schwartzberg, Joseph E. (ed), 1978), pp. 87 (Plate IX.C.2 a) and p. 78 (Plate IX.A.2 a).
18. See (Ali, Working Paper No. 94-04, March 1994).
19. (Brown, Lester R., 2008).
20. (Zaidi, 1999), p. 25.
21. (Gotsch, 1982).
22. (GoP, Economic Survey of Pakistan, 2005-06, 2006), pp. 17-18.
23. For example, the leading tractor producer in India, PTL, manufactures six models, ranging in size from 25-40 horsepower. Its PTL's Swaraj 735, a 39 hp model, makes up 60 percent of the company's annual sales.
24. Although the East Punjab farmers are perceived, as a group as prosperous, there has been an alarming increase in farmer suicides over the last decade. Agricultural debt has been gauged to be the primary cause for these suicides. Other problems, surely play a part, but indebtedness is the fundamental reason behind these deaths. Farmer suicides are not, however, unique to Punjab. They are becoming a problem throughout much of India. See, for example, (Newman, January 2007); (Frontline World, 2005); (Navdanya, 2004); (Sinha, 2006); (Mishra G. , 2005); and (Rajivlochan, 2006).

A 2006 on-line article in *Dawn*, suggests that there may have been more than 15,000 farmer suicides annually, over the last 5 years (Ahmad, Sultan, 2006).

25. (Singh, 1997). See pp. 80-81 and 158.
26. A possible alternative to the purchase of tractors might be the development of agricultural machinery leasing, which would have the benefit of tying up less capital up front and would permit farmers to return the equipment to the lessor at the end of the term of the lease.
27. *Ibid.*. See Table 2.1 (B), Basic Data on Agriculture.
28. *Ibid.*, p. 6.
29. *Ibid.*, p.17.
30. *Ibid.*, pp. 4 and 256.
31. (Hussain I. , May 2005),
32. *Ibid.*
33. For example, in the case of Bihar, yields are well below potential and average yields for every crop. See (Yadav, C.P., B.S. Gupta, and S. Kumar, 2000), pp. 113-119. Figures for yields have improved in Pakistan since (Sandhu, G.R., 1993).
34. (The World Bank, 2008a).
35. *Ibid.*
36. Much of this section is based on (Ekboir, 2002), pp. 2-8.
37. See, for example (Beck, D.L.; J.L. Miller; and M.P. Hagny, 1999); (Derpsch, 1999); (Sayre, 1998).
38. Plow-pans are the result of compaction. The plow-pan horizon becomes much densely compacted than the actively worked soils, the soils frequently plowed and cultivated. This compaction resists water pass-through and inhibits plant root development. When it occurs naturally, it is referred to as hard-pan.
39. See (Ekboir, J.M., K. Boa, A.A. Dankyi, 2001).
40. (The World Bank, 2008a).
41. (IFAD, 2002), p. 55.
42. *Ibid.*
43. In 1959 land ceilings were set. These were based on individual, not family holdings. Individuals simply divested their holdings to other family members, thus avoiding any real land losses. A second attempt was made in 1972. The ceilings were based on individual ownership, not families, and again, the reforms failed. In 1977

attempts were made to introduce and implement land reforms and these too had little effect.

44. (IFAD, 2002), p. 56.
45. (GoP, May 2003), Table 1.1, p. 2 of Tables.
46. (Ahmad, Sultan, 2006)
47. For a description of the *e-Choupal* gateway market system, see (Annamalai, Kuttayan and Sachin Rao, August 2003); (Anupindi, 2002-03); (Kumar, 2005); and (Ramamurthi, Bhaskar, 2002).
48. Ibid.
49. *Ibid.*
50. See, (Business Recorder, 2005).
51. (IRRI, J. L. McLean, 2002), p. 206. In Nepal, India, and Bangladesh, meat consumption is not even a part of the 'Main Food Consumed' list.
52. (FAO, World agriculture: towards 2015/2030. Summary report, 2002), p. 19.
53. (Easterbrook, 1997).

6

Nepal

Box 6-1: Nepal Comparative Data

HRI/Rank/Year: 0.534/142/2005
Per Capita GDP: 1,550 USD
Population: 29.519 million (July 2008)
Labor Force in: Agriculture: 76 % (38%)*
Industry: 6 % (20%)*
Services: 18 % (42%)*
* Percent of GDP

Population Below the Poverty Line: 30.9%
Land Area: 143,181 sq km.
Population Density: 206.2 people/sq. km,
Arable Land: 23,009.2 sq. km.
Arable Land Per Person: 0.08 Ha/person

Introduction

Food security and most of Nepal's development issues are inextricably tied to its extreme topographical variation, ecological complexity, agricultural and economic diversity, poor connectivity, and, most important of all, political unrest and insurgency. All of the nation's mountain districts are classified as food deficit areas, and most of those in the hill country also suffer from food deficits.

Rugged terrain, coupled with an inadequate all-weather roads system, makes it extremely difficult to communicate or transport agricultural inputs or produce to and from markets.

Ironically, in the early 1960s, Nepal had the highest agricultural productivity in South Asia and was a food exporter but by the early 1990s, its productivity had declined, until it became the least productive country within the subcontinent.[1] Nepal's agricultural sector simply ceased to grow, while the Green Revolution embedded itself in the rest of South Asia. At theroot of Nepal's agricultural stagnation is soil degradation following deforestation. The soils were fragile, and cultivation depleted it of its organic and micronutrient content. In the absence of either organic or chemical fertilization, the soils simply degenerated, becoming little more than inert mountain soils. As a consequence, agricultural production declined, while population growth increased. Nepal become a net food importer in the 1980s, a situation that continues today.[2]

Poverty, in both relative and absolute terms, is increasing. Nepal was 142nd among the 177 HDI nations reporting for the Human Development Report for 2007/2008, with an HDI of 0.534. Of the nations of South Asia, Nepal has the lowest ranking. Below Nepal in the HDI rankings are most of the countries of Sub-Saharan Africa.[3]

Table 6-1: Changes in Human Development Index, Nepal, 1975-2005

Year	*HDI*
1975	0.301
1980	0.338
1985	0.38
1990	0.427
1995	0.469
2000	0.502
2005	0.534

Source: (UNDP, 2007c), Table 2, p. 236.

Nepal's HDI has shown a 75 percent increase since 1975. It was not until 2000, however, that Nepal was able to extract itself from that group of countries labeled 'Low Human Development,' those countries with HDIs of 0.500 or less. Even so, poverty continues to represent a significant problem, despite the fact that, at least statistically, the number of people living below the poverty line (BPL) has shown improvement. Curiously, the BPL figures have shown improvement and then retreat numerous times over the last twenty years. In 1985 the population BPL was 42.5 percent. In 2000, it had declined to 40 percent.[4] Currently, the rate is 30.9 percent. See Box 6-1, above. Government programs for the alleviation of poverty seem to be working, although there is much debate regarding the impact of remittances on local poverty levels. It is estimated that there are over a million Nepalese who live abroad and send regular remittances to relatives in Nepal.[5] The importance of remittances to the Nepalese economy must be put in context. Nepal's GDP is 5.5 billion USD. Remittances during 2007 were estimated to be 1.6 billion USD.[6] This means a sum equal to nearly one-third of Nepal's GDP is gained through remittances from abroad.

Changes in the percentage of population below the poverty line may also reflect changes in the number of people actively involved in agriculture, since poverty is primarily a rural problem. Unlike the other countries of South Asia, Nepal has the lowest urbanization and the smallest industrial and services sectors in all of South Asia. The urbanization rate is currently less than 15 percent.[7] See Box 6-1, above. Surprisingly, the urban poverty rate is less than the rural rate, 10 versus 35 percent, respectively.[8] In most South Asian countries it is the cities that have the higher poverty rate, since the rural unemployed and disenfranchised often migrate there in hopes of gainful employment. There are few alternatives to rural employment in the absence of rapidly expanding industrial or service sectors in Nepal. Essentially, there is nowhere for the rural poor to go to receive relief.

In 1981, 91 percent of the population was engaged in agriculture. In 1991, the figure had dropped to 81 percent, and in 2001, it had dropped further to 66 percent.[9] Since 2001, that rate has risen 10 percentage points. See Box 6-1. In part, the rise is the result of increased opportunities in agriculture and the realization

Map 6-1: Nepal Poverty by Ilakas

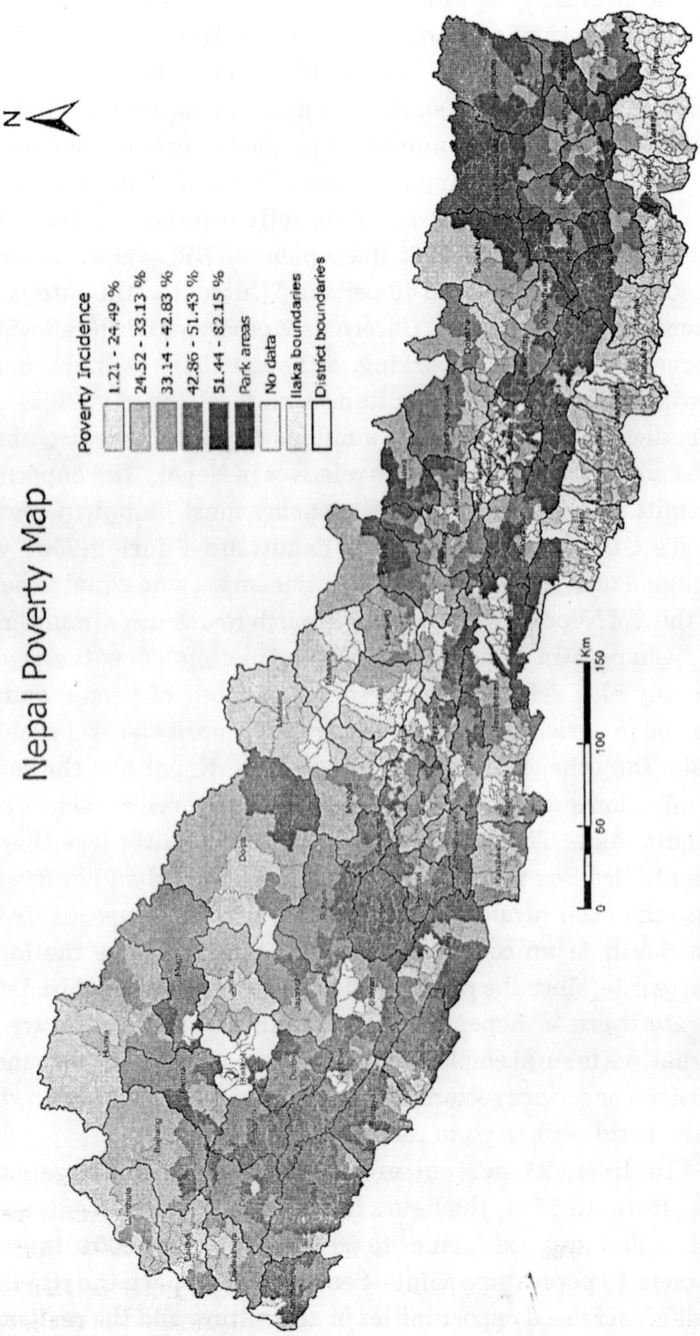

Source: CBS/Government of Nepal, UNWFP, and the World Bank

by many rural workers that things are not necessarily better in the cities.

Agricultural wages rose nearly 25 percent between 1995 and 2004. Non-agricultural wages increased 20 percent, and skilled wages more than doubled during the same period.[10] Out-migration siphoned off some the surplus labor and tightened local labor markets, thus forcing wages to increase, especially for agricultural laborers. While wages increased for non-agriculturalists and agricultural laborers, poor performance in the crop sector caused the incomes of farmers and landowners to stagnate. This represents one of the few times ever that agricultural laborers have improved their relative economic position vis-à-vis landowners.

Nepal faces a variety of challenges regarding agricultural and rural development. Agriculturally, Nepalese agriculture is faced with a pattern of subsistence cultivation in an environment that is hampered by pernicious insecurity, caused by violence, as well as a changing environment, the result of climatic change.

The improvements already made in poverty reduction are all the more significant since they were achieved in a politically difficult time. A multi-party democracy was established in the 199Os, and the country survived three general elections and fifteen changes in government — each of these governments lasting less than a year. Party ideologies were discarded in order to achieve coalition governments, which disintegrated due to vested political and personal interests. The Maoists, the Communist Party of Nepal, Maoists CPN(M), took-up arms in 1996 against the backdrop of internal political bickering and lack of political leadership. The conflict became a low-grade insurgency in 2002, when it escalated disrupting life, especially in the countryside, with attacks on government facilities and targeting political functionaries and public leaders. See the OCHA 'Politically Affectedness Map', Map 6-2, below.

In February 2005,King Gyanendra dismissed the coalition government (the third and most representative interim government since October 2002) and formed a new Council of Ministers under his own chairmanship. This polarized the political scene even further. If economic gains are to continue, Nepal will need to resolve its current political stalemate. Equally important is the need to eliminate or co-opt the Communist and other insurgents.

Map 6-2: Political Affectedness in Nepal, ending 30 April, 2008

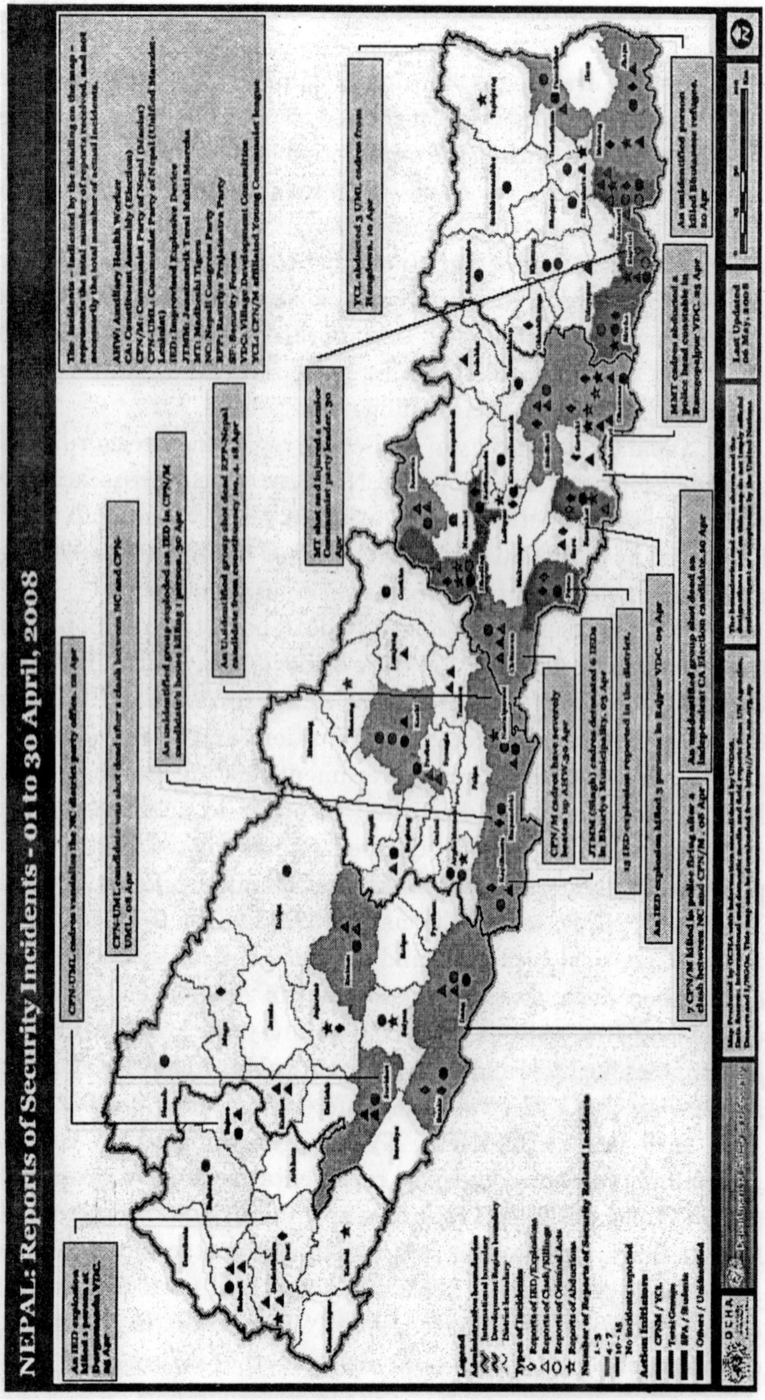

History has shown that insurgencies and armed conflict are generally incompatible with general economic development and rural development in particular. All one need do is look to the examples in Sub-Saharan Africa.

Figure 6-2, an OCHA map, provides a graphic summary of some recent insurgent activities for one month, April 2008. Insurgency threatens personal and institutional security and interferes with the process of poverty reduction and rural development. Maoist/Communist insurgents emerged in response to the unrelenting poverty that prevails throughout the country. The persistence of insurgent violence is at least in part the result of the government's inability to enforce the law, except in the largest villages and towns. Although now a recognized part of the government, the CPN(M), other political groups and simple bands of thugs continue to terrorize large areas throughout Nepal.[11]

Likewise, in recent years, violence between the ethnic Nepalese and those of Indian origin, known as *Madheshis,* has broken out. The *Madheshi* have been demanding more say and participation in local politics, a demand rejected by the native Nepalese.[12] Although their demands were initially a peaceful demand for political recognition, some among the *Madheshi* have organized themselves into a self-proclaimed insurgency, known as the Madeshi Tigers, reminiscent of the Tamil Tigers of Sri Lanka.

Government's inability to enforce the law reflects the inaccessibility of many areas due to inadequate infrastructure, especially all-weather roads. This protects the insurgents from the government but it also serves to isolate many rural communities from regular contact with the government and their integration into a broader national economy. Government assistance seldom makes it way into these isolated communities and this slows overall rural development.

Nepal's agriculture is characterized by subsistence cultivation of low-value crops, especially cereals. It has been estimated that less than 13 percent of all agricultural output is traded in market places.[13] The low level of agricultural commercialization is reflected in agriculture's low contribution to the national GDP – 40 percent. Although this figure is declining, there is ample room for increased crop and *per capita* productivity. Within the context of such a poor, highly dispersed, isolated and decentralized agricultural system, it would seem almost fanciful to talk about the agricultural commercialization. However, within the Nepalese context, commercialization may simply mean the adoption of such improved agricultural methods and inputs as will permit the cultivators to produce a meager marketable surplus above and beyond mere subsistence. Even these meager goals are thwarted by threats of violence, inadequate communication and transport networks, the unavailability of modern agricultural technologies, and the means to pay for them. Failure to integrate the far flung communities of Nepal into a national social, political, and economic network will only serve to perpetuate the status quo – rampant poverty.

The political condition of Nepal cannot, in itself, explain Nepal's current lack of development. Other factors are at work, as well. Unlike India and Pakistan, Nepal's lack of overall economic and agricultural development is largely the result of geography. Nepal, first and foremost, is a comparatively small nation with the smallest proportion of arable land to total land area among the nations of South Asia. See Figure 6-1.

Even in the Tarai Region, Nepal's primary agricultural region, severe and unreliable weather conditions have an impact on what would be normally classified as sub-tropical to tropical climatic conditions. In addition, the topography of the nation has had an adverse impact on the development of modern infrastructure. Building roads in mountainous areas, simply to link villages, is a tedious, dangerous, time-consuming, and an expensive proposition.

General Constraints on Agriculture

Topography

A variety of environmental and socio-economic problems plague Nepal's agricultural sector,none more important than environmental constraints. Environmentally, Nepal's problems can be broken down into topography, climate, water management and irrigation, and suitable crop types.

Nepal consists of three natural divisions, which appear as ribbon-like swaths across the length of the country, east-west. These are:

- Mountains
- Hills
- Tarai

The Himalayan range makes up the northern border of the country and represents 16 percent of the total area of Nepal. Within this region are found eight of the world's ten highest mountains, and is the home to less than 8 percent of the nation's population.

Hills comprise approximately 68 percent of the total area of the country. This region is covered with deep valleys and terraced ridges. About 45 percent of the country's population lives in the

Figure 6-1: Arable Land as Percentage of National Land Area

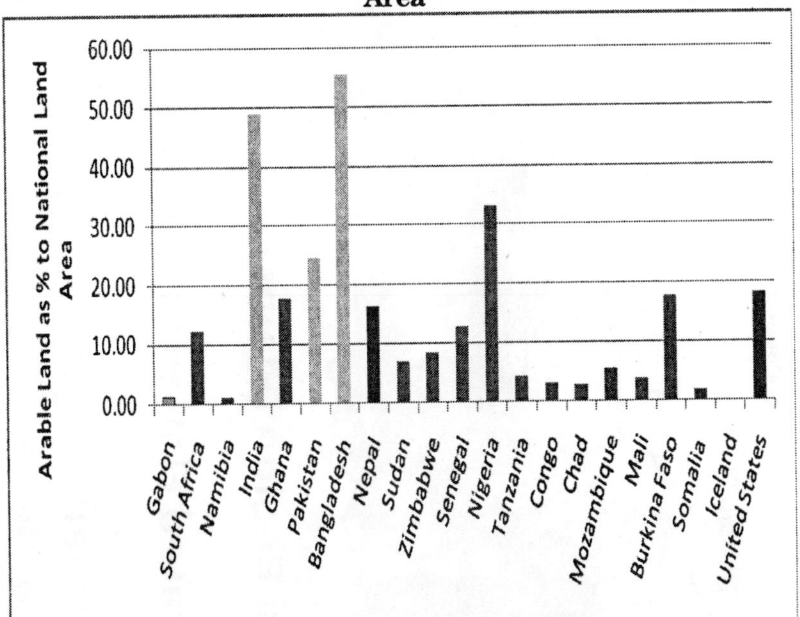

hills region. This area is very rugged with local relief averaging more than 2,500 meters from the valley floors to the hilltops.

The Tarai runs along the southern border. This narrow strip of land averages only 20 km in width. These lowlands cover approximately 16% of the total land area of Nepal. It provides excellent farming land and the average elevation of flatlands is 100 to 300 m. above sea level. About 48% of the country's population occupies this region, and contains the majority of the fertile farmland

Map 6-3: Natural Divisions of Nepal

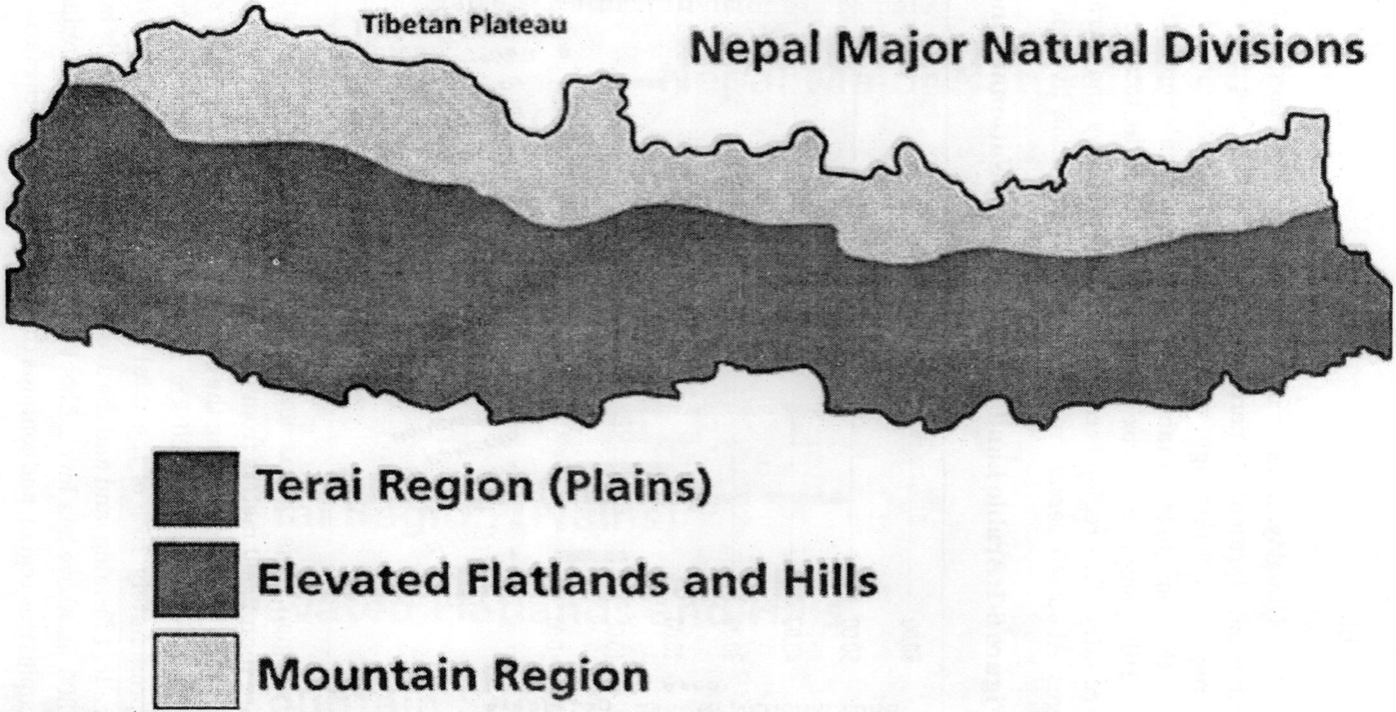

Source: Adapted and modified from (Acharya, Sanjaya, 2004), p. 201.

of the country. Over 60 percent of the grains grown in Nepal are grown in the Tarai and constitutes 70 percent of all the arable land in the country.

Topographically, the construction of modern infrastructure, i.e., roads and railways, is exceedingly difficult in Nepal's northernmost Mountain Region, and difficult in the less mountainous Hills Region. For example, in all of Nepal, there are no broad-gauge railroads and only 59 kms of narrow gauge railroad. There are only 17,280 kms of roadways in the entire country, and only 9,829 kms are paved.[14] One need only look at a transportation map to Nepal to see that there is almost no connectivity within the Mountain Region, and little in the Hills Region. Differences in local relief between hilltops, mountaintops, and plateau regions and valley floors are drastic, and the valleys are generally not contiguous or interconnected, even by passes.

Climate

Due to their exceptionally short growing seasons, the Mountain and Hills regions make only minor contributions to Nepal's agricultural production. At best they represent the lowest subsets of the nation's agricultural subsistence category.

Although the Tarai is the primary agricultural region of Nepal, the crops often succumb to blasts of cold air descending from the terrain farther north. In addition to cold damage, the Tarai suffers from strong winds and hailstorms, damaging crops as they stand in the fields. The bulk of precipitation—nearly 80 percent—occurs during the annual monsoon. The pre-monsoon season, from March to May, is hot and dry, the monsoon season (generally June to September) is hot, and the post-monsoon season typically lasts through mid-October. Mid-October through March is typically dry and cold.

The area is also prone to prolonged drought or rainfall that is often excessive, unpredictable or erratic. Although Nepal theoretically receives abundant rainfall, its distribution throughout the year causes concern because, with the monsoon rains come floods, landslides, and other extreme events. Most floods occur during the onset of the monsoon season when heavy precipitation coincides with snowmelt in the mountains. As a consequence of the broad range of weather conditions that prevail in the Tarai, agriculture is at best a gamble.

The Effects of Global Warming

Weather-related extremes, which are postulated by those concerned with the effects of Global Warming, could portend events like excessive rainfall, longer drought periods, landslides and floods. Currently these types of problems seem to be increasing both in terms of magnitude and frequency. More floods and glacial lake outbursts could destroy irrigation and water supply systems, roads, bridges, settlements and productive land. If floods continue to become either more frequent or more extensive, there is a real probability that the number of flood related deaths will increase.

Land degradation could reduce crop productivity and put more pressure on the existing land base of the nation. In the dry season, increased evaporation could lead to water scarcity. Soil moisture deficits, droughts, fire and possible pest outbreaks would, in all likelihood, decrease crop yields. It has been suggested that climate change could have major impacts on a variety of ecosystems, land and water resources, health, and major economic sectors, especially agriculture. Currently only anecdotal reports of climatic changes in Nepal are coming from cultivators. One report contends that the size of apples has increased due to increased temperatures. Likewise, some farmers are now able to grow crops they could not grow previously, e.g., cauliflower, cabbage, chili, tomato and cucumber, which used to need greenhouses to survive. Others believe that water intrusion into their homes is the result of changes in rainfall patterns.[15]

Some reports suggest that temperatures are increasing and thus far these have been favorably received by farmers. For example, recent studies suggest that the annual increase in temperature in the uplands of Nepal is approximately 0.04 to 0.060° C per year, or 0.4 to 0.6° *per decade*. In the Tarai, this warming is significantly lower or even lacking. These minute increases in temperature have led the study researchers to postulate that they have caused increased precipitation and accelerated glacial melt and retreat.[16]

There seem to be two groups involved in the Global Warming issue – the Believers and the Non-Believers. It is no longer a debate.

For many, the issue has been settled. After all, the United Nations, the United Nations Development Programme, and the signatories to the Kyoto Agreement have legitimized the Global Warming claims and have set forward programs to combat the growing greenhouse gases menace. In fact, the 2007/2008 Human Development Report was dedicated to and titled: *Fighting Climate Change: Human Solidarity in a Divided World*. The UNDP's HDR 2007/2008 website states:

Climate change is the defining human development challenge of the 21st Century. Failure to respond to that challenge will stall and then reverse international efforts to reduce poverty. The poorest countries and most vulnerable citizens will suffer the earliest and most damaging setbacks, even though they have contributed least to the problem. Looking to the future, no country—however wealthy or powerful—will be immune to the impact of global warming.

The Human Development Report 2007 / 2008 shows that climate change is not just a future scenario. Increased exposure to droughts, floods and storms is already destroying opportunity and reinforcing inequality. Meanwhile, there is now overwhelming scientific evidence that the world is moving towards the point at which irreversible ecological catastrophe becomes unavoidable. Business-as-usual climate change points in a clear direction: unprecedented reversal in human development in our lifetime, and acute risks for our children and their grandchildren.

There is a window of opportunity for avoiding the most damaging climate change impacts, but that window is closing: the world has less than a decade to change course. Actions taken—or not taken—in the years ahead will have a profound bearing on the future course of human development.[17]

There is no doubt that there is a causal relationship between temperature, rainfall, and crop yields. The current stocks of improved and local seed varieties were developed under certain environmental conditions and those conditions are now apparently changing. It is known that wheat and rice yields decline as temperatures increase or as water availability decreases. Assuming temperatures are increasing and rainfall is decreasing, as alleged by the Global Warming advocates, serious thought needs to be given to the development of more temperature and rainfall tolerant improved seed varieties of wheat and rice, since they are the two primary staples throughout much of the world. If we wait too long, believing we can miraculously slow Global Warming, we may be unprepared for what our environment is becoming.

Who Will be Most Vulnerable?

No one will be immune from the effects of Global Warming but some groups will be at greater risk than others. Three groups will feel the earliest and greatest impacts of climatic change. The first group will be those lacking ameliorative technologies, or the

Box 6-2: Is Global Warming Simply a Part of a Long Term Natural Process?

While Global Warming is the current buzz among scholars, the media, and among politicians, temperature changes of 0.4 and 0.6° C *per decade*, or 4 to 6° *in a century*, would hardly seem significant enough to warrant all the attention. A degree a year, now you're talking about something to be concerned about. It has been suggested that the Earth has undergone numerous cycles of climatic change and each has taken thousands of years to complete. There is probably no doubt that Mankind has contributed to, or has even accelerated the current cycle, but it is still simply part of a cycle. No matter how powerful we humans feel we are, we can neither prevent nor stop one of Earth's natural cycles. We can, however, learn and prepare for the change. We may well be placing too much emphasis on the wrong portion or segment of the cycle. Instead of being concerned with the beginning of the change, we should be much more concerned with its middle or end segments. Those are the periods during which real chaos will prevail, since desertification will be in full swing. That is when Mankind will be most environmentally helpless and vulnerable.

Mankind adapted to the last Ice Age. We are now beginning to experience the move into the next, new warmer phase of the Warm-Cold cycle. Since we cannot in all likelihood prevent the continuation of the cycle, we had better prepare for it. We should not waste our time debating what we can do to stop or reverse it. Instead, we should prepare for the inevitable.

least developed societies or nations of the world. The second group will be those most closely tied to the natural environment for their subsistence and livelihood, especially agriculturalists. Finally, those living in more remote and ecologically fragile environments will be at heightened risk.[18]

The people of Nepal fall within all of these groups. The ecology of the Himalayas is dependent upon the cold for the maintenance of its ice and snow. Changes in the mountains' ice and snow will have an impact on the lives and livelihoods of the local communities that survive there. For many of these mountain communities, which are already poor, climatic change will result in economic and agricultural dislocations. Thus, the most marginal and disadvantaged mountain people of Nepal are likely to be among the most vulnerable. The landless, those that depend on nature, and those who are most economically and technologically backward and isolated, will be among the most vulnerable. Their inability to trade, an ineffective infrastructure, and lack of communication will make it difficult for them to adapt to climate changes.

Most of Nepal's rural poor depend on the small scale exploitation of local resources and agriculture for their livelihood. As such, they have very few options available to them. They have no way to diversify or insulate themselves against calamitous changes in their physical environment. Part of their vulnerability stems from their inability to accumulate sufficient economic resources or assets with which to either rebuild their lives after catastrophic losses or obtain shelter elsewhere. Thus, the most vulnerable are also those with the least ability to adapt or recover.

Among the most catastrophic losses for the poorest segments of poor societies is the loss of crops and housing. For those living on fragile and isolated mountain slopes, among the list of potential disasters are droughts, landslides, erosion, and flash or sheet flooding. Climatic change has increased these threats. Rainfall is essential for mountain agriculture, in the absence of springs or streams. Rainfall patterns have begun to change in many areas already. The once reliable monsoon rains are now unreliable. Further, more recently, extreme rain events result in landslides, erosion, the destruction of homes, even the loss of human lives.

While too much water is a problem for those living in the mountains and hill regions, the lack of water is equally serious for the cultivators and residents of the Tarai. Much of the agriculture, as practiced in the Tarai Region, is based on river water and monsoon precipitation. The former is dependent upon snowfall in the mountains and glaciers. The runoff from the annual snow and ice melt accumulates in the major rivers that traverse Nepal, most of which originate in Tibet and flow into the Ganges and ultimately into the Bay of Bengal. See Map 6-4.

The time of the snow and glacial melt and runoff are crucial to the agriculturalists of the Tarai. In agriculture, timing is everything. There is a time to plant, a time to irrigate, and a time to harvest. For millennia, these activities varied very little from season to season. Now, there is more climatic variability. The agriculturalist must balance temperature, soil conditions, and water availability to determine the right time to plant. With increased temperatures, especially at the headwaters of the rivers, the annual runoff would begin sooner and would have a shorter duration. This means that the water needed at the time of planting would come earlier and, sometimes, before the soil conditions are optimal for planting and seed germination. Mean monthly discharges show that global warming would shift the peak discharge month from August to July, due to the fact that the snow cover on mountaintops would melt earlier. This could lead to increased flooding and more pronounced variations in water availability throughout the year. In some areas, drought could become a problem.

Rising mean temperatures would also influence the onset of the monsoons. It has already been observed that ,with the increased temperatures, the monsoons' arrival has changed and their intensity and amounts have increased. Increased temperatures seem to have had the effect of delaying the onset of the monsoons. The monsoons typically begin in June and continue into September. The effect of early winter runoff and the delay of the monsoons' arrival is to increase the chances of drought during a critical time in most crops' development – when the new plants are developing their root systems. The amount of soil moisture is critical at this stage of development. Likewise, the delayed arrival of the monsoons would

Map 6-4: The Rivers of Nepal

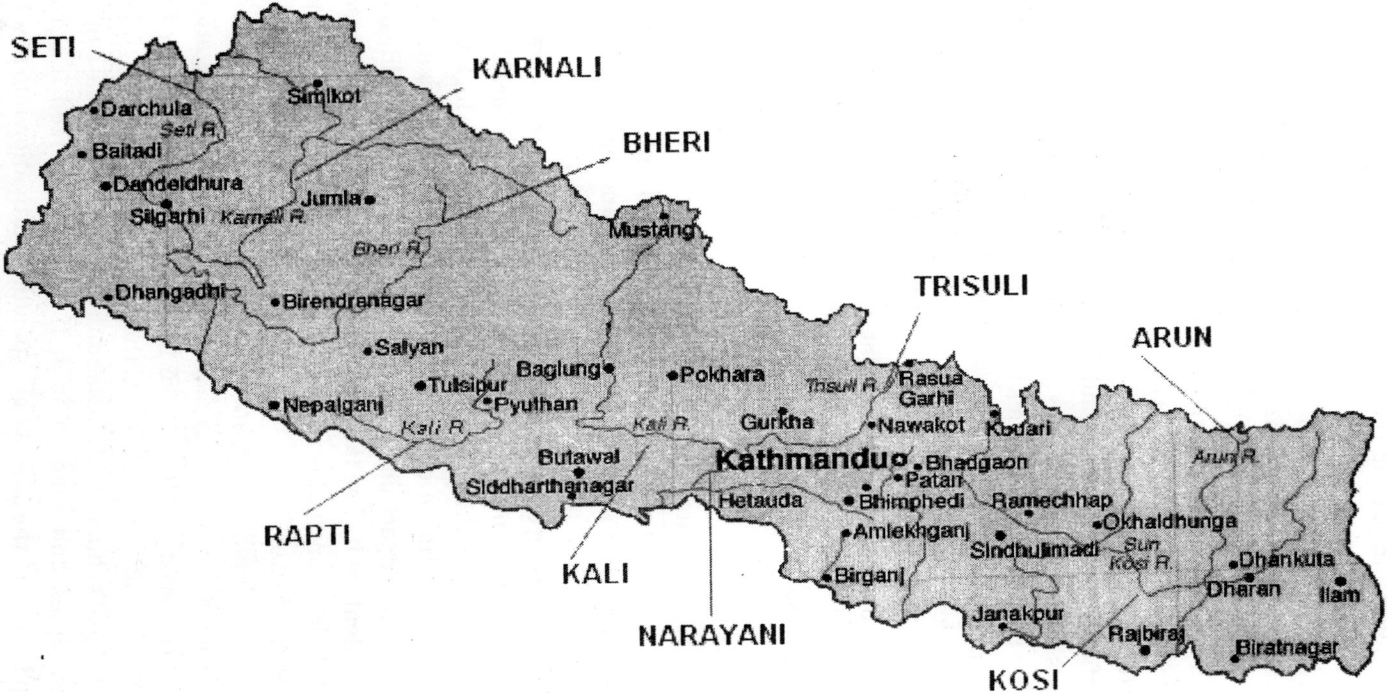

Source:< http://www.nepalvista.com/features/rivers-of-nepal.php#map>

also have an impact on the dry season, following the monsoons. It would begin later and extend further into the following spring.

Decreased precipitation from November to April would have an impact on the winter and spring crops. Rice yields would fall in the Western and Far Western Regions where a greater population of the poor live and threaten food security. Due to diverse topography, culture, and climatic conditions, different cropping patterns exist in many parts of Nepal. Extreme events such as rainfalls causing flooding and landslides, droughts, heat stress, hot winds, cold waves, hailstones and snowfalls are undesirable. In recent years, their frequency seems to have increased noticeably, and long dry spells and cold waves have had a negative impact on crop production. These could lead to crop failures and eventually to famine. Similarly, at the other end of the scale, high humidity creates a favorable environment for the growth of fungal and bacterial diseases. In addition, some insects and pests will become more active and damage crops.[19]

Irrigation

Approximately 80 percent of all the water in Nepal is used for agricultural purposes. Nearly 38 percent of agricultural land of Nepal, mostly in the Tarai, is irrigated and only 17 percent is irrigated year-round.[20]

Increasing temperatures will increase evapotranspiration and decrease winter precipitation, which could lead inexorably to more droughts in Nepal. In addition, many rivers could face highly variable flows with climate change. Increased variability would have a significant impact on irrigation and those whose livelihoods are dependent on it. The land that can be cultivated varies by season and its location, and is a function of the availability of dependable irrigation water.

As rainfall, runoff, and spring melt-water become increasingly variable, an even greater demand will be made on irrigation and irrigation systems to achieve food and financial security for the cultivators of Nepal. Based on the data already collected, it is clear that Nepal's climate is changing and threatens traditional cultivation techniques and seed choices. If Nepal is to feed its growing population, in the absence of expanding cultivation into new lands, agricultural productivity and *per capita* productivity must increase. Neither can be achieved without a major attempt at harnessing the water resources of Nepal and the adoption of improved agricultural techniques and inputs.

Wasted Water and Flooding

Currently too much water is wasted or underutilized, both for agricultural and power generation purposes. Much of the water wealth of Nepal simply flows away often with dire consequences for those living farther down stream. Nearly every river and stream that leaves Nepal flows into the states of Uttar Pradesh and Bihar in India. For centuries the Bagmati, Mahananda, and Kosi rivers, among others, have caused extensive flooding, particularly in eastern Bihar.

Of the 38 districts in modern Bihar State, as many as 24 have experienced reportable flooding over the last seven years, the worst occurring in 2002 and 2004, with no district claiming to be flood free. Flooding has become an annual event for many of these districts despite, or in spite of, an extensive embankment system. In some cases, 80 percent of some districts are flooded, with water up to 10 feet deep, for much of the monsoon season, June to September, with catastrophic economic and social consequences. Infrastructures are destroyed, as roads, bridges, and railroads are washed away. Homes are destroyed, and often, hundreds of lives are lost each year.

The dynamics surrounding these annual floods are quite simple. Most of the rivers of northern Bihar have their headwaters or catch basins in Nepal, and to a lesser degree, in Tibet. The flooding visited on Bihar is the result of problems of water management and control in Nepal, not in Bihar. Bihar is the hapless recipient of Nepal's water abundance.

Since India's Independence, India has sought to engage the Nepalese government in a joint venture, where the rivers that pour into Bihar would be dammed and flooding could be controlled, or at least managed, downstream. After 60 years of meetings with the Nepalese government, following a multitude of proposals for studies and investigations, nothing concrete has been negotiated between the two governments.

From a practical, political and economic perspective the Nepalese have nothing to gain from the construction of dams or barrages for the purposes of flood abatement in India. The only tangible benefit accruing to Nepal might be the electrical power the proposed dam(s) would generate. They would only inherit a massive maintenance obligation. Every river leaving Nepal carries with it a huge burden in the form of silt, sand, gravel, and stone. If a dam were constructed, the burden of the river would collect on the upstream side of the dam, requiring a massive maintenance effort. If this accumulation of waterborne sediment is not routinely disposed of, the functional life span of the dam is reduced markedly. This type of maintenance would be massive, never-ending and expensive for either or both governments. Under the circumstances, is it any wonder that neither government has truly championed the Herculean effort such a dam would entail? For purposes of political economy, however, the politicians on both sides of the border benefit from the appearance of concern. In the long run, delay and finger-pointing are their best strategies.[21]

Water and Irrigation Solutions

In light of the current concern over climatic change in Nepal, it is difficult to envision much action being taken to resolve Nepal's persistent water issues. If increasing agricultural production, through the commercialization of Nepal's agriculture, is the national goal, then, Nepal must:

- Begin to more efficiently organize and manage water resources, including the construction of barrages, dams, and irrigation canals.
- Promote surface and groundwater irrigation, especially for commercial and industrial crops in the Tarai.
- Develop year-round irrigation in perennial flow areas and irrigation water storage facilities in drought prone areas.
- Develop tube well extraction systems in areas where groundwater is deemed practical and accessible.
- Develop small scale hydro facilities foı the purposes of supporting lift irrigation in hilly areas.

Crop Types and Agricultural Commercialization

Most of the Nepalese population is dependent on a few crops — rice, maize, and wheat. Like many other parts of the world, these are among the principle food grain staples, and the existing inventory of improved seed types are probably adequate but only as they apply to the Tarai Region, with its tropical to sub-tropical climate regime. With improvements in local support structures – improved credit availability, inputs availability, better access to local, region, national, and international markets, and the dissemination of information, with regard to improved agricultural techniques and technologies and current market information – Nepal's subsistence cultivators can be drawn into the mainstream of modern agriculture, what the World Bank calls 'agricultural commercialization.'[22]

Assuming current climatic changes continue, even in the Tarai Region, the current inventory of seeds and techniques will no longer remain tenable. Climate change will necessitate changes in crops and crop varieties, improved water management and irrigation systems, the alteration of planting schedules and tillage practices, and land use planning. In addition, the Government must develop, implement, and maintain policies that will improve how production and distribution systems cope with fluctuations in yields, especially in regardto a system of agricultural price supports. In addition, government action must be taken to address a variety of other agriculture-related issues, including:

- Resource conservation for agricultural sustainability
- Development of genetically adaptive varieties
- The commercialization of hybrid maize production, especially as regards the conversion of *surplus* maize into biofuels
- Crop diversification programs should be encouraged
- A comprehensive land use policy, which would include some components of land reform, especially as regards tenancy restrictions, the reduction of land fragmentation, landlordism, and unequal land distribution problems.

The seed varieties currently in use in the Tarai are not necessarily well suited to the Hills or Mountain regions of the country. Therefore, agronomic research centers will need to be established, funded, and maintained with an emphasis on the development of crops and crop types that are suitable for cultivation in the Hills and Mountain regions of the country. The development of the new varieties, however, will not be enough. In addition, the Government will need to:

- Provide agricultural extension services to promote and educate cultivators in the use of the new varieties
- Strengthen transportation infrastructures, to ensure that cultivators become integrated into the national economy and are able to take advantage of off-season employment opportunities
- Identify market opportunities for new crops, especially those that can be commercially produced in an effort to relieve the financial insecurity of small land holders.
- Decentralize governmental decision-making processes, making government more responsive to the needs of the populations being served.

As a result of low agricultural growth rates and high population growth rates, Nepal has not been self-sufficient in food grain production since the 1980s. Low growth rates generally are seen as a result of limited use of agricultural technologies and declining landholding sizes. From 1962 to 2002, the total agricultural area increased about 57 percent, and the number of landholdings grew approximately 120 percent, but the population increased by 146 percent. In the same period, the amount of agricultural land declined from 0.18 to 0.13 hectares per person, and the average size of holdings has declined from 1.1 to 0.8 hectares. In 2002 nearly 60 percent of holdings did not produce sufficient food to feed a household, and almost 97 percent of these holdings were two hectares in size or smaller. Furthermore, tractors or threshers are used on less than 10 percent of total holdings, and approximately 65 percent of landholdings are rain-fed rather than irrigated.

The use of pesticides, fertilizers, high-yielding seeds, and irrigation has increased but mostly by owners of landholdings larger than two hectares. Cropping intensity has increased, with adverse environmental consequences, such as soil erosion. [23]

Much has already been accomplished in Nepal but there is much more that needs to be done, especially in response to what appears to be long term environmental and climatic changes, whose real consequences have only begun to be felt. Nepalese cultivators need to adopt new methods and crops if they are to adapt to this changing natural environment.

Issues and Challenges

Conflict Resolution

Currently, increased political and ethnic violence throughout Nepal has served to undermine many of the successes resulting from domestic and national development efforts and international aid programs. For national development to thrive, the people must trust that law and order will be maintained and provide an environment conducive to continued development. Failure to provide civil peace and, at the same time, provide for public discussion becomes a difficult balancing act for most governments. Nepal's is no different. Based on their espoused ideological demands, the Communists will not be satisfied with simple participation in the democratic government of Nepal. They continue to advocate sweeping clean the social, political, and economic slates of the country, and replacing them with a new Maoist forms of communist society. Inevitably, the Communists will either take over the government completely or they will have to be co-opted or eliminated. Until either is achieved, Nepal will remain a state under siege.

Agricultural Commercialization

In 1989, Nepal began the process to joint the WTO. In October 2004, it became the 147th member and only the second least developed nation to do so.[24] India had become a member 1995. Nepal and India have had a the long-term trade relationship; however, as both became WTO members, their trading relationship is now governed by international guidelines. Nepal and India immediately granted one another Most Favored Nation trading status. Historically, nearly two-thirds of the Nepal's trade relations has been with India. Now, however, Nepal finds itself trading at a disadvantage. First, India has traditionally heavily subsidized its agriculture through tariffs, while Nepal's agriculture remains unsubsidized.[25] Secondly, due to changes in consumption patterns and rising agricultural prices in India, India is no longer able to supply foodgrains or other foodstuffs to its traditional trading partners, like Nepal.[26]

Currently, India must endeavor to feed itself. This is quite a turnaround for India. Only a few years ago, she was a net food exporter. India's food surpluses are no longer what they were, due to the GoI's pressure on farmers to diversify production and reduce rice and wheat production in favor of other commercial crops. Apparently, Mamohan Singh's decision that, if fruits and vegetables grown in India can get good prices abroad, he does not want to grow food grains at any cost. He would rather use a part of the large export earnings to buy food grains from abroad. In mid-2008, India had no surpluses available for export. As a consequence,

the Government of India recently restricted the export of all staple food to maintain domestic supply. While the restriction may partly ameliorate the problems in India, it hurts the food situation in its South Asian neighbours due to their dependence on India for food. Thus, the food-related problems in India have a regional effect manifested in the form of rising regional food prices.[27]

Without India as a reliable source of food, starvation in Nepal is a real possibility, unless it can be obtained on the world market. However, since early 2008, food prices around the world have been rising significantly, which means that available food will come at a significant price. Nepal has no quick-fix to this turn of events. Nepal needs to produce more food now or produce more income with which it can purchase food.

Nepal's agriculture must be streamlined and productivity increased if it wishes to even feed its own people. To accomplish this goal, Nepal will need to reorganize its agricultural sector completely and immediately. To begin to increase production to meet even domestic needs alone, will mean the implementation of a program geared to extract every bit of agricultural production from the existing land base, and increase production through commercial agriculture, or expand the amount of land under cultivation, or both. The commercialization of Nepalese agriculture, however, is fraught with a number of problems.

First, land holdings are small, with the average landholding being 0.5 ha. Further, these holdings are frequently fragmented parcels that are scattered around the village. As a consequence, the prospects for commercializing Nepalese agriculture through any form of mechanization would seem difficult.[28]

Second, population pressure demands that productivity be increased on a *per capita* basis. This will require greater intensification, within the context of existing technology, or the implementation of suitable new technology. Failure to produce more agricultural products will mean ultimately that Nepal's current food shortages will worsen, and there is no guarantee that India will be able to assist any of its normal trading partners any time soon.

To accomplish the goals of increased food production for domestic purposes and trade, this country will require agricultural intensification on a major scale. The down side to intensification is that it will inevitably result in the misuse of the country's land resources, which are already degraded due to over exploitation.

Furthermore, Nepal's low rate of productivity stems from a relatively low use of production inputs as compared to the South Asian average. At current levels of fertilizer consumption, the soils of Nepal are being robbed of their nutrient content, year after year, with the consumption exceeding replacement by 93 percent.[29]

Ironically, despite being the second richest country in terms of water resources in the world, chronic shortages of water at various places in the country is a common problem. These resources simply have not been developed for the purposes of agricultural use. In the midst of plenty, there is scarcity. Of particular importance is the need to develop reliable, year-round irrigation.

Likewise, with great ecological diversity there are ample opportunities for producing agriculturally unique products that will permit Nepal to exploit international markets. It is only a matter of identifying these market-rich products and beginning the efficient cultivation of them. Unfortunately, Nepal's food needs are immediate. In the absence of an assured source of food grains from India, food scarcity is an inevitable reality.

Some commodities already have been identified that fulfill Nepal's need for export-oriented agricultural production. Among these are: honey, cardamom, tea, coffee, ginger vegetable seeds, off season fresh vegetables and citrus fruit (especially mandarin). One of the obstacles to the quick commercialization of Nepal's agriculture comes in the form of government finance or assistance. Although agriculture produces up to 40 percent of the nation's GDP, the government spends less than 4 percent of its budget on agricultural extension and research.[30] At no time during the period 2001 through 2007, has the government's agricultural extension and research budget exceeded 3.94 percent, and in most years the budgeted amount averaged 2.69 percent.[31] These kinds of investments are incompatible with the goal of rapidly improving Nepalese agriculture, in general, and the swift changeover from subsistence agricultural practices to commercialized agriculture, with surpluses intended for the export market, in particular.

Agricultural specialization, in the absence of its inability to produce sufficient basic amounts of food grains, becomes of paramount importance for the generation of national and individual income for the purpose of buying the food needed. Although remittances complement normal income sources, they already play too large a part in the peoples' survival strategies.They should be used to supplement incomes but not be part of the income necessary for simple survival. This places too many people at risk. A downturn in remittance receipts could be economically catastrophic for many, and could potentially lead to outright starvation.

The problems of Nepal are complicated by geography and a failure of the government to make timely and sufficient investments in the agricultural sector. Part of the problem stems from political instability accompanied by insurgency. The inability of the government to maintain political and security control over the country only exacerbates the plight of the general population and further fans the flames of the insurgents.

The inability to access large portions of the country, via a well-developed system of roadways, permits the insurgents to operate almost at will. Without peace, law and order, the people will not find themselves in a position where they feel confident that whatever investments they are able to make in their agricultural enterprises will result in an improvement in their life situation. It is, therefore, imperative that the government provide protection for cultivators. Failure of the cultivators to thrive only means that the rest of the population will find it increasingly difficult to *survive*. A safe environment can only come about through access: access for the purposes of law enforcement and access to markets for cultivators. Both are dependent upon improvement in basic infrastructure, especially roads and land based communication networks.

Although land reforms will not necessarily result in increases in agricultural productivity, they may be needed to redress problems of excessive fragmentation, which undermines cultivators' willingness to mechanize their agricultural operations. Mechanization will also need to be responsive to the realities of land use. Mechanization need not follow the pattern of Pakistan or India's Punjab. Within the context of Nepal, it may mean gas or diesel-operated tillers, which are small enough to transport easily between land parcels and terraced fields within difficult terrain.

Mechanization also has the benefit of reducing cultivators' dependence on increasingly expensive agricultural labor.If production can be increased and, at the same time, reducing labor costs, it will only mean increased income for the cultivators. The obvious downside to this changeover would be that increased numbers of agricultural laborers would be no longer required. It is a difficult tradeoff, at least on the larger scale. On the cultivator level, it may not appear such a big problem but as the number of unemployed laborers increases, they become a larger and larger problem for the state's welfare system. In large enough numbers, they become a political problem, either as the basis for a movement or the potential recruiting grounds for more insurgents.

With sufficient commercialization, many of the disenfranchised agricultural laborers might well find employment opportunities in agricultural processing, transport, marketing, or other allied industries. The transfer of laborers out of agricultural production and into non-agricultural occupations would serve three purposes. First, the dislocated laborers would not become a burden on the state, from a welfare standpoint. Second, employed by allied agricultural industries would mean they would have the income to become consumers, thereby serving to increase the demand for still more produce and products. Finally, they would no longer be available as fodder for politically motivated insurgencies.

At the root of Nepal's problems is poverty at both the individual and government levels. Agricultural production simply is not sufficient to feed the people and, at the same time, produce sufficient income to supplement the subsistence cultivators' meager living standard. Likewise, the government is hampered by inadequate revenue. Without necessary revenue, it cannot invest in agriculture, in extension services, research necessary for the adaptation of existing crop types or the development of new crops tailored to Nepalese ecologies, or provide for much needed infrastructure. It would seem that the government is little able to sustain itself much beyond the confines of its state houses. Government is little prepared to venture beyond the largest villages and the capital. Government is hemmed in on all sides, leaving the bulk of the country to the insurgents, which in many cases, are little more than armed gangs preying on the helpless. Many have no defined political agenda and as a consequence, one cannot classify them as political insurgents. They are, pure and simple, marauding, armed thugs.

Tourism

Tourism is touted as a major industry for Nepal. With the natural beauty of an almost untouched environment, especially in the mountain region and, to a certain degree, the hills region, Nepal would seem to be a tourists' paradise. However, reliance on tourism is, at best, a gamble, for two reasons. First, the insurgencies pose a potential threat to the lives of the tourists, whether for political reasons or as hapless victims for the purposes of ransom. Second, tourism is a fickle enterprise. It is best suited to income supplementation, rather than income dependency. Ttourism is largely a function of spendable income on the part of foreigners and the belief they will have a safe *and* enjoyable experience. Almost over night, if incomes change at home or fear for safety becomes an issue, tourists will simply stop coming. For this reason, it should not be relied upon as a major income-stream generator. Countries catering to tourist must be, first, self-sufficient and second, perceived as safe. At present, Nepal cannot meet either of these requirements.

The worldwide economic turnaround that burst on an unsuspecting public in late 2007 and exacerbated in 2008 and 2009 has had the effect of radically altering travel and tourism spending. Without tourist dollars coming from the affluent countries of North America and Europe, tourism in Nepal will, inevitably, suffer, and with it, Nepal's leading source of hard currency exchange.

References

1. (Tiwari, M. with Ojha, G., Upadhyay, S., Maharjan, K.H. and Huddleston, B., 2002)
2. (Koirala, G.P. and Thapa, G.B., 1997), as cited in (Gill, 2002), p. 3.
3. (UNDP, 2007c), Table 2, pp. 235-237.
4. (Acharya, Sanjaya, 2004), Table A2: Poverty Indices, p. 213.
5. See (Ratha, Dilip and Zhimei Xu, 2008). Between 2000 and 2007, remittances to Nepal increased from 111 million USD to 1.6 billion USD, a substantial and economy altering increase within the context of Nepal.
6. (Regmi, Bimal R. and A. Adhikari, 2007), p. 6.
7. (The World Bank, June 26, 2006), Table 2.8, p. 27.
8. *Ibid.*, p. iii.
9. *Ibid.*, Table 7, p. 204.
10. *Ibid.*, p. ii.
11. *Besides the CPN(M), there are numerous other insurgent groups. Among these are: the* (JTMM) Janatantrik Terai Mukti Morcha (Singh), (YCL: CPN/M) affiliated Young Communist league; (TWA: Tharu Welfare Association, CWP) Chure Bhawar Pradesh, (MT) Madheshi Tigers, (TA) Terai Army, Limbuwan, *other political parties, student groups, and criminal groups. These groups resort to extortion, 'donation demands,' murder, beatings, IEDs, bombings, and arson to terrorize the civilian population and achieve their political and economic agendas.*
12. (PatnaDaily.com, 2007).
13. World Bank estimate.
14. (CIA, 2008), Nepal, railway data, 2006; roadway data, 2004.
15. (Dahal, 2005).
16. See, (Shrestha, 1999); and (Dahal, 2005).
17. (UNDP, 2007c).
18. (UNFCCC, 2004).
19. (Regmi, Bimal R. and A. Adhikari, 2007), p. 13.
20. *Ibid.*, p. 16; and (The World Bank, 2008)
21. (Rorabacher, 2008), p. 49.
22. (The World Bank, 2008).
23. (Federal Research Division, November 2005), pp. 11-12.

24. The first least developed nation to join the WTO was Cambodia, April 2004.
25. (Matangi Maskay, Nephil and Rojan Bajracharya, 2008), p. 21.
26. See, (SAWTEE, 2008), p. 4; and *ibid.*
27. (Matangi Maskay, Nephil and Rojan Bajracharya, 2008), *p. 21*
28. (CBS, 2004)
29. (MOAC, 2007),
30. (Ghimire, 2008), p. 44.
31. *Ibid.*, p. 44, Annex 1.

7

Bangladesh

Box 7-1: Bangladesh Comparative Data

HRI/Rank/Year: 0.547/140/2005
Per Capita GDP: 2,053 USD
GDP Index: 0.504
Population: 153.547 million (July 2008)

Labor Force in:	Agriculture:	63 %	(19%)*
	Industry:	11 %	(28.7%)*
	Services:	26 %	(52.3%)*
		* Percent of GDP	

Population Below the Poverty Line: 45.0%
Land Area: 133,910 sq km.
Population Density: 1,146.6 people/sq. km.
Arable Land: 74,172.7 sq. km.
Arable Land Per Person: 0.048 Ha/person **Irrigated Area:** 47,250 sq km (2003)
Irrigated Land as % of Arable Land: 63.7%

Introduction

Bangladesh is generally perceived as one of the most impoverished countries in the world, and yet, it possesses the highest percentage of arable land to total area of any country in South Asia. See Box 7-1. Agriculture remains the primary source of employment for over 60 percent of the population yet generates only 19 percent of the nation's Gross Domestic Product.[1] The key to understanding Bangladesh's persistent poverty lies in understanding its environmental problems, its agricultural adaptations, and history.

Figure 7-1: Change in Share of GDP, Bangladesh, 1975-2004

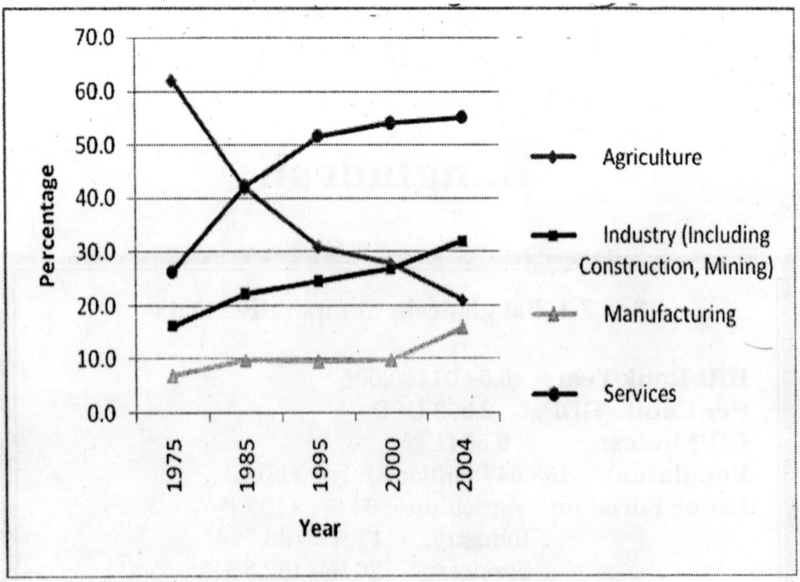

Source: (Ahmed, Raisuddin and Zahurui Karim, 2006), p. 130.

Figure 7-1 depicts the change in the percentage of the Gross Domestic Product (GDP) between the four main economic sectors of Bangladesh's economy. There has been a significant decline in agriculture's share of the nation's GDP since 1975. The contributions of the mining and industrial sector have been steady increases, albeit much less pronounced. There has been a pronounced increase, however,in the service sector's contribution, although the rate of increase began to slow after 1995. The figures clearly indicate that Bangladesh's economy is rapidly moving away from an agriculture-dominated economy, toward a more modern economic structure based on industrial production and the provision of services. Although the contribution of the services sector has shown an amazing increase, it has not had the effect of reducing the number of people still employed in agriculture. The growth of the services sector can be, at least in part, explained as a reclassification of workers, with much of the recent increase in this sector attributable to the marketing and processing of agricultural products. The rapid commercialization and diversification of Bangladesh's agriculture has necessitated a transfer of manpower from agricultural production to agricultural processing. However, the siphoning off of agricultural labor has not kept pace with the economic growth of the services sector. The people in the services sector simply are economically more productive than their agricultural counterparts.

While agriculture's contribution to the economy has declined since 1975, the number of people employed in agriculture has declined much less quickly. While 80 percent of Bangladesh's population lives in rural areas, at least 54 percent of them are dependent upon agriculture and the rest on rural non-farm (RNF) labor.[2] The question, then, is what part of the agricultural labor force is being transferred out of production and into agricultural processing – landless or the smallest landholders? If it is not the landless laborers, in all likelihood, little progress is being made in the reduction of the numbers of the most economically depressed segment of the population.

Recent estimates of poverty in Bangladesh suggest that the incidence of poverty and hunger has declined. It is suggested that the poverty rate dropped below 50 percent at the end of 2000 for the first time since Bangladesh's formation in 1971. The current poverty rate is believed to be declining by one percent per year.[3]

Agricultural production increased at a relatively steady rate in the years following Bangladesh's independence from Pakistan but not fast enough to close the gap caused by rapid population growth. Official statistics indicate that agricultural production rose every year during the 1980s, but the gains did not exceed 3.8 percent, and during three of those years, the growth rate was less than 1 percent.[4] Even so, agricultural foodgrain imports have continued unabated since Independence, although rice production is very close to meeting domestic needs.

Through the large-scale adoption of improved rice varieties, Bangladesh has improved its rice production over the last three decades. This growth has occurred despite the loss of arable land and the predomination of small farmers and a large landless workforce. Irrigation now serves over 50 percent of cultivated land and the adoption of improved varieties has increased to roughly 63 percent of the rice area. Rice production has increased from 17.6 million tons of paddy in 1975–76 to 37.6 million tons in 2000–01.[5]

Rice is central to Bangladesh's economy and agriculture, accounting for nearly 18 percent of the Gross Domestic Product (GDP) and providing about 70 percent of an average citizen's total caloric intake. The rice area totals approximately 10 million hectares and accounts for 75 percent of the total area of agricultural crops, and 93 percent of the total area planted to cereals.[6] Thus the rice sector is by far the most important provider of rural employment.

For several years, the political climate in Bangladesh has been, at best, uncertain, with no quieting effects visible on the political horizon. Even so, the nation's GDP grew at an impressive 6.6 percent in 2007, little changed from the year before. Part of the success of Bangladesh's growth was spurred by remittances from abroad. In 2007, remittances rose to nearly US $6 billion.[7]

Despite Bangladesh's economic progress, the country is dominated by poverty and a population tied to the land. However, the land is held, largely, in the hands of a few and the gap between the rich and poor seems to be widening, as the benefits accruing from agricultural production are increasingly concentrated in the hands of the largest landholders. The benefits of the Green Revolution has bypassed most of the smaller landholding cultivators.

Revitalizing Bangladesh's agriculture will require connecting the rural poor to markets by improving rural infrastructure, improving the availability and management of water, improving agricultural technology, increasing the capacity to adapt technologies, and speeding diversification and commercialization. In 1999, the GoB announced an aggressive policy statement, known as the National Agricultural Policy (NAP). While this policy statement mirrors the idealistic policy statements from most developing nations' governments, it contained at least a desire, if not a full-fledged commitment to transform subsistence agriculture into commercial farming through the exploitation of European markets. In 2006 the Bangladesh Government announced that it had *"already entered into the European Market for export of vegetables and other high value crops."*[8] These types of moves should help propel Bangladesh's agricultural sector into new areas and improve desperately needed rural incomes, much of which could accrue to the most vulnerable and needy, the small landholders for whom the cultivation of high value vegetables should put them on an equal footing with the much larger landholders for the first time.

Even so, Bangladesh remains a low-income, food-deficit country with annual average food grain imports of 2 million± metric tons. Approximately half of the population (63 million people) lives below the food poverty line, and spend 70 percent of their household income on food. These 28 million people, representing 20 percent of the total population, are considered 'ultra poor.'[9] Further, Bangladesh is subject to recurrent emergencies and natural disasters, which often deprive the poorest segments of the population of the few physical possessions and assets they have managed to accumulate.

Environmental Constraints

At the time of Bangladesh's initial partition from India, becoming East Pakistan, the Hindu Bengalis fled to India, leaving behind their land and the civil service positions they had dominated. Local Muslims confiscated the abandoned lands, simply replacing Hindu landlords with Muslim landlords, and landholdings continued to be concentrated in the hands of a comparative few.

Currently an estimated 53 percent of the land is under cultivation but this number is falling, causing a situation of growing land scarcity. Agricultural land is being lost and there is very little scope for bringing new land under cultivation. The main reasons for the scarcity of productive agricultural land are due to :

- rapid population growth,
- land degradation,
- unequal distribution of land, and
- land use conflicts.

Since 1951, Bangladesh's population has grown from 42.16 million people to an estimated 153.55 million, a net increase of 111.39 million people. Or, put another way, Bangladesh's population has more than tripled in 57 years. This has placed an increasing burden on the land resources of the country. The current man-land ratio has grown to a point where one can safely say that sustained agricultural development is in jeopardy. Simply put, population has grown to the point that the land is no longer able to support the population burden with current agricultural technologies.

Secondly, land degradation is taking land out of production, through erosion, soil depletion, salinity, and waterlogging. As a consequence, tracts of good land are being lost to agricultural production.

Thirdly, a small number of households own most of the land According to the National Agricultural Census, 24.14 per cent of farmers own 56.89 per cent and operate on 58.81 per cent of the land. On the other hand, landless and small farmers, each owning little over half a hectare, constitute 64 per cent of total households but own only 26.24 per cent and operate on 23.3 per cent of the land.[10]

Finally, the spread of cities and land requirements for infrastructural projects have placed a demand on land. It has been estimated that 1 percent of the cultivable land is being lost to urbanization and infrastructural improvements.[11]

The combination of land lost to environmental problems and changes in land use make it increasingly difficult for the people of Bangladesh to support themselves agriculturally. Were it only issues of population, land ownership, environmental degradation, and changes in land use, the people might be able to adapt. However, in addition to all these problems, they must contend with a growing incidence of natural hazards.

Natural Disasters

It is estimated that nearly half of the world's population – 3.4 billion people – live in areas where at least one environmental hazard could have an impact on them. These areas, the World Bank calls 'Hotspots.' See Map 7-1. Among the most pernicious of these hazards are:

- Cyclones (and wind-related storms)
- Floods
- Droughts
- Earthquakes.[12]

Bangladesh is vulnerable to each of these, *as well as* storm surges, tornadoes, hail and lightning, erosion, and land- and mudslides on a regular basis. Probably no other nation experiences more weather and geologic hazards than Bangladesh. Although it is included in the highly vulnerable category, Bangladesh should be in a category all its own – **Extremely Vulnerable**.

Each natural disaster takes a toll on human lives, destroying peoples' possessions, their homes, or the resources essential livelihood. Two factors contribute to Bangladesh's environmental vulnerability.First, Bangladesh is at the vertex of the land masses of India on the west and Myanmar on the east. These landmasses effectively funnel the monsoons, as well as storms originating in the Indian Ocean or the Bay of Bengal toward Bangladesh.

Map 7-1: Nations Most Vulnerable to Two or More Hazards

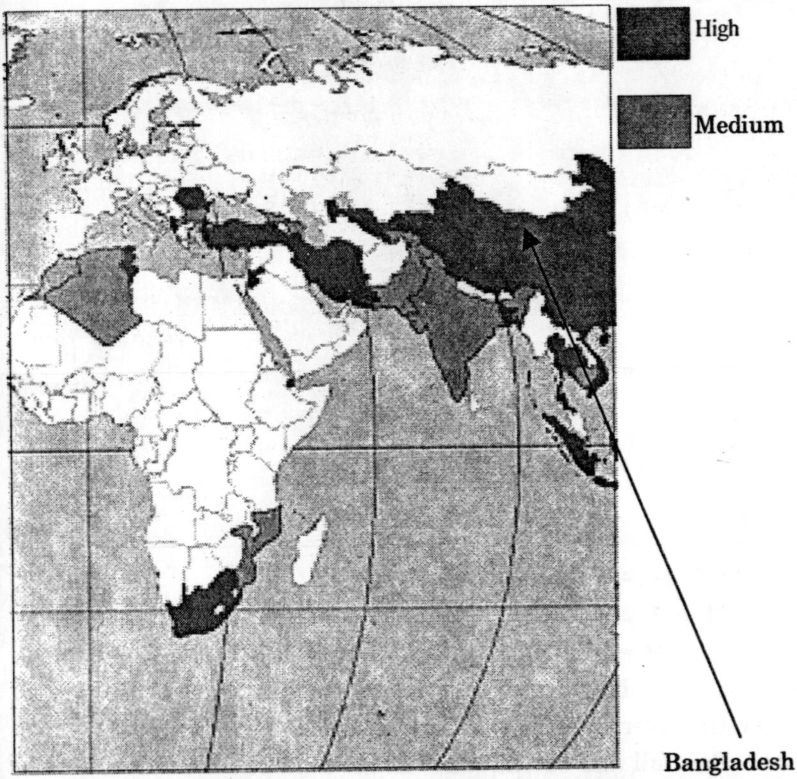

Source: Adapted from <http://www.worldbank.org/ieg/naturaldisasters/maps/>

Second, the physiography of Bangladesh and the morphology of the numerous rivers that transect the country contribute to recurring disasters. One need only look at a topographic map of Bangladesh to see that it is largely a gigantic, low lying river delta with almost no local relief. Therefore, it has virtually no defense against riverine flooding or tidal surges from the Bay of Bengal. Map 7-2, provides a shaded relief representation of the loof

Bangladesh. Virtually all of Bangladesh falls below 153 meters above sea level, and much of the southern half of the country is only a few meters above sea level.

Map 7-2: Relief Map of Bangladesh

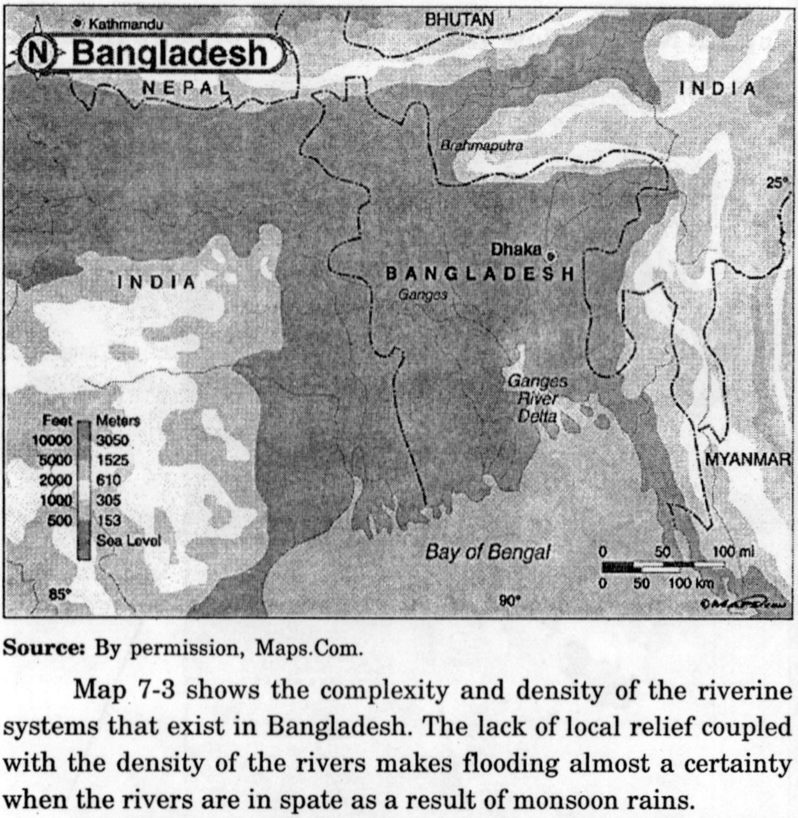

Source: By permission, Maps.Com.

Map 7-3 shows the complexity and density of the riverine systems that exist in Bangladesh. The lack of local relief coupled with the density of the rivers makes flooding almost a certainty when the rivers are in spate as a result of monsoon rains.

Rainfall and earthquakes in the adjacent mountains add to the disaster situation. The anticipated effects of climatic change will also have a significant impact on the future disaster scenarios for Bangladesh. If climatic change does result in increased rainfall, or modifies the timing of the rains, it will undoubtedly alter rain induced flooding. Flooding is such a common component of the Bangladeshis' lives that they have developed terminology to describe the character of flooding – *Bonna* or *Borsha*. When the floodwater damages resources, and disrupts communication and livelihoods, it is called *Bonna*. Normal, non-destructive flooding is called *Borsha*. The term *Borsha* is seldom used.

Map 7-3: River Systems of Bangladesh

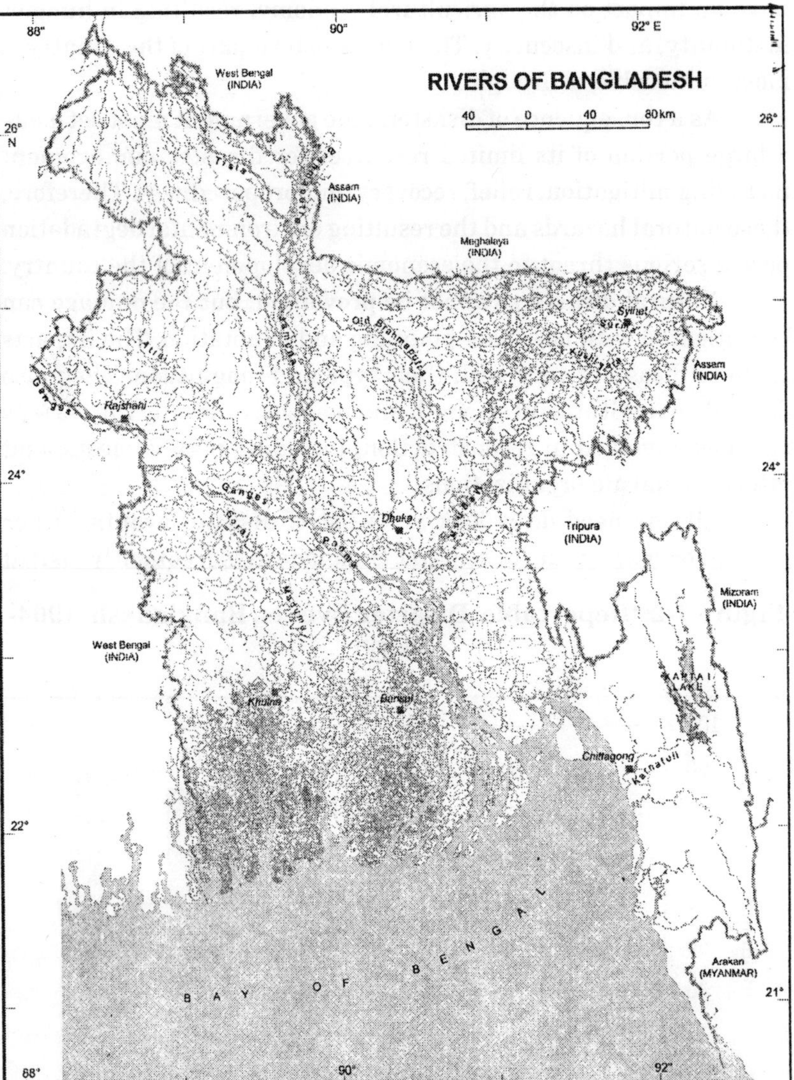

Cyclones and storm surges occur frequently and cause significant destruction in the coastal areas of the country. Tornadoes also frequently hit. Tropical cyclones and tornadoes uproot trees, telephone, telegraph and electric lines, destroy bridges, houses, kill people and domestic animals, all resulting in serious and adverse consequence for the economy and the environment.

Although the country has enough rain, droughts frequently have an impact on the agricultural economy, resulting in hunger, instability, and insecurity. The northwestern part of the country is most vulnerable to drought.

As a consequence of disasters, the government must set aside a large portion of its limited resources for disaster management including mitigation, relief, recovery and preparedness. Therefore, these natural hazards and the resulting environmental degradation pose a serious threat to the economic development of the country.

Natural disasters cannot be prevented, but the damage can be mitigated with adequate planning and adaptation. The impacts of these disasters vary with their type and magnitude. They also depend on institutional strength and responsiveness by the various agencies involved in reconstruction, including both domestic and international aid organizations.

All one need do is look at a list of disaster events, either natural or man-made, to see that Bangladesh is frequently visited

Figure 7-2: 'Reportable' Disaster Events, Bangladesh, 1904-2007[13]

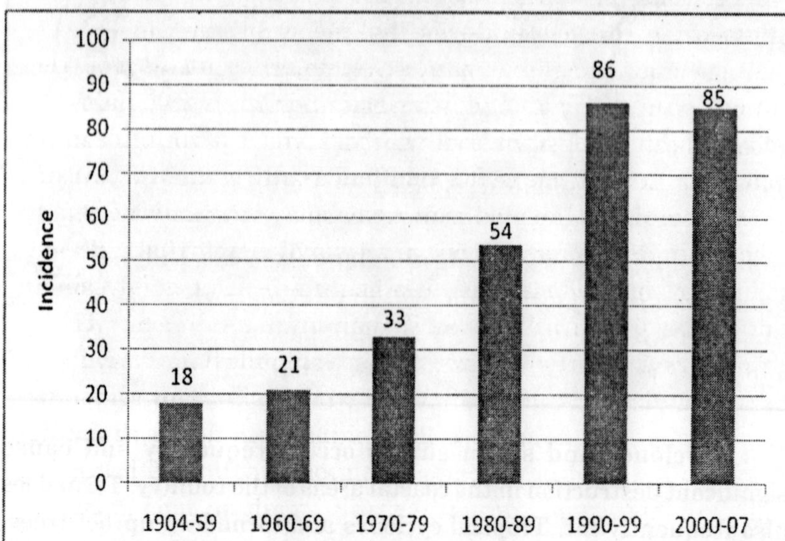

Source: (SNDP, 2008); USAID Disaster Reports; UNEP Disaster Reports; and EM-DAT: The OFDA/CRED International Disaster Database – www.emdat.be, Université Catholique de Louvain, Brussels (Belgium).

by a variety of disasters. These events seem to be increasing in their frequency. Between 1904 and 1960, there were only 18 'reportable' events. Thereafter, the incidence rate seems to climb rapidly. See Figure 7-2.

In all likelihood, one can discount the data for the period 1904-1959 as inadequate or incomplete. Thereafter, however, the reporting and data are probably more consistent and complete. Even discounting the earlier period, there is a definite and increasing trend in the number of 'reportable' incidents in Bangladesh.

The increase in natural disasters is not, however, limited only to Bangladesh. It would seem that over the last 100 years, the aggregate total of disaster events has been increasing on a worldwide basis. See Figure 7-3. Between 1976 and 1985, approximately 0.6 billion people were affected by natural disasters. Between 1986 and 1995, the number increased to 1.6 billion; and between 1996 and 2005, the number jumped to 2.3 billion. The vast majority of those affected were in developing countries like Bangladesh. Between 1991 and 2000, a staggering 211 million people were killed or affected by these disasters; and of these, 98 percent were from countries with low or medium HRIs. [14]

Causes of Natural Disasters

How do we explain the almost exponential increases in the incidence of natural disasters as witnessed by the graph in Figure 7-3? The answer has a number of components:

- Population increases
- Urbanization
- Changes is land use
- Coastal encroachment.

Population

Until the 1940s, the world's population growth rate was comparatively low. Thereafter, however, population increased rapidly, mostly in the developing nations of the world and especially in Africa and Asia. During this period, the world population increased from approximately 2.7 billion to roughly 6.5 billion.[15] This increase resulted in higher concentrations of people with more people to be affected.

Figure 7-3: Number of Worldwide Natural Disasters by Year, 1900-2007

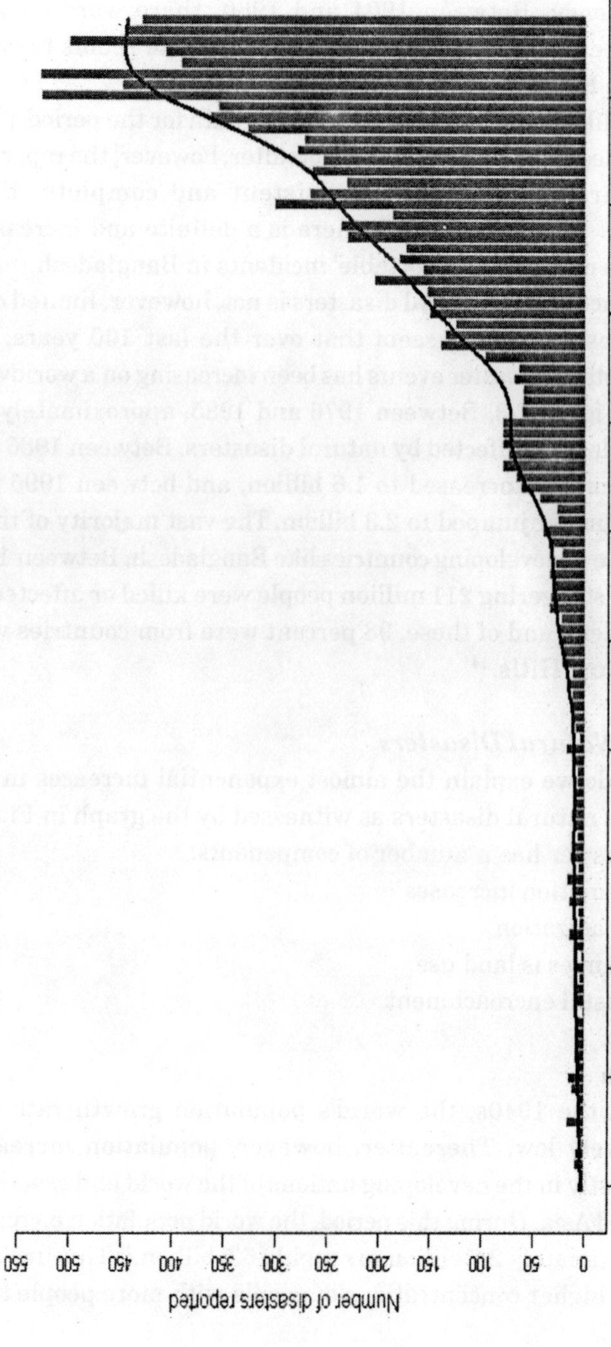

Source: EM-DAT: The OFDA/CRED International Disaster Database – www.emdat.be, Université Catholique de Louvain, Brussels (Belgium).

Just as populations increased, more and more people migrated from rural areas to cities.[16] In 1950, only a third of the world's population lived in cities. Today more than half of the world's population live in urban areas. In 1950, New York was the world's only megacity – a conurbation of 10 million people or more. In 2006, there were 25 megacities, 19 of these were in developing countries. Further, the majority of these megacities are located within easy reach of the nations' coasts, which are inherently more vulnerable than interior locations.

As the world's population migrated from rural areas into growing urbanized areas, population densities within and immediately outside the cities increased. At the same time, undeveloped buffer lands that once surrounded the cities gave way to human occupation. As the prime residential locations were occupied, less favorable areas became occupied, and in many cities, slums developed in these areas. Further, uncontrolled and unplanned urban development permitted the disruption of natural watershed dynamics and frequently contributes to flooding. The occupants of these secondary and tertiary residential areas are generally the poorer segments of the city's population and, therefore, they are also the most vulnerable to natural disasters.[17]

Added to these geographic and demographic factors is the fact that wind and flooding are the fastest growing types of natural disasters, making coastal locations all the more vulnerable and dangerous for people and economic activity. Flooding and wind go hand-in-hand. Tropical storms, as well as hurricanes, are accompanied by heavy rainfall. Together they represent a deadly combination.

Even though the incidence of wind and flooding disasters are on the increase, they do not currently account for the bulk of human misery associated with natural disasters. Together, extreme temperatures, drought, floods, mudslides, water surges, and windstorms affect more people than all other natural disasters combined. During 1972–2006, more than 5.25 billion people were affected by such disasters, compared with about 11.5 million for all other disasters combined (earthquakes, insect infestations, volcanoes, and wildfires). Storms and floods had an impact on about 67 percent of the individuals affected, or 3.5 billion people.[18]

Figure 7-3 leaves no doubt about the rapid increase in natural disasters occurring around the world. The question is why the rapid increase? We have already seen that there are more people living in potentially vulnerable areas. This pushes the number of people affected up but it does not explain why the disaster incidence, frequency, or severity is on the rise.

In the absence of an absolutely defensible hypothesis that meets our need to categorically explain the increased number and severity of weather-related hazards, the best current explanation has to do with Global Warming. As the Earth warms, it has an impact on ocean temperatures, rainfall, wind, tornadoes, droughts, windstorms and desertification on a global scale. Since it is the oceans that power our climates and weather, Global Warming must be given serious consideration. Until a better explanation emerges, all the current data supports the increases in natural hazards as a function of the planet's current increase is temperature and may well be the cause of so many natural disasters and human suffering.

Man-made Disasters

The list of natural problems that beset Bangladesh almost boggle the mind – droughts, cyclones, tornadoes, earthquakes, windstorms, hail, ocean surges, and coastal erosion. Little or nothing can be done to stop them. Then there are those tragedies that stem from human activities and human interactions with nature. Some of these interactions are unavoidable, as well. Some could be avoided if Man had the capacity to look beyond his present situation and project his actions into the future. Within the unavoidable category, is flooding.

Within the avoidable category we find:

- Surface and groundwater pollution (Arsenic)
- Air pollution
- Loss of Wetlands
- Soil degradation
- Global Warming.

Flooding

Although flooding is generally thought to be a natural disaster, it is oftentimes also the result of Man's attempt to alter his physical environment to his immediate needs, with no thought given to the long-term consequence of those actions. Floods, in the absence of human involvement, are just floods, part of a millennia old natural hydrologic process. Whenever humans become involved in floods, either as agents of change or as part of the natural landscape, floods become disasters, catastrophes, calamities, or tragedies and often people lose their lives, their possessions, their homes, and their means of livelihood.

Bangladesh, as we have already seen,is flat and low-lying. Fundamentally, Bangladesh, together with West Bengal, is a one-of-a-kind *delta*. Most other deltas are the creation of a single river, but the Bengal delta is the creation of three mighty rivers, the Ganges, the Brahmaputra, and Meghna. To place the delta and, therefore, Bangladesh's situation in the proper perspective, a few facts are in order. First, the catchment basin of the three rivers is 1.758 million square km, which is about *half the size* of the catchment basin for the Mississippi. Second, the catchment basin involved five different nations – Nepal, India, Bhutan, China, and Bangladesh. Third, the deltas of most other major rivers constitute a very small portion of the nation through which their rivers flow. In the case of Bangladesh, it is *all* delta. Fourth, the Ganges-Brahmaputra-Meghna basin receives *four times* the rainfall of the Mississippi. However, unlike most other river systems, those of the Bengal delta receive 85 percent of their rainfall, usually, within a 4-month rainy season. Thus, the floods are concentrated and there are extremes in the rivers' volumes and flows between peak and dry seasons. Fifth, annually, these three rivers carry approximately *two billion tons* of sediment, in the form of silt, sand, gravel, and stone – toward the sea. This is the highest sediment/burden level of any other river system in the world. Finally, the combined length of the Bengal delta system's river channels is about *three times* that of the Mississippi. Taken together, these facts can be distilled into one simple statement: Bangladesh is the product of one of the mightiest river systems in the world. The hydraulic and delta-forming processes at work in Bangladesh are gargantuan in their proportions, and associated with these proportions are equally large problems.

Over the millennia, sediments have accumulated, forming Bangladesh.Today, the Bengal delta is still growing. Little of the delta has reached a stage were much of the floodplain has been abandoned and where it is of sufficient height that it is seldom subject to inundation. See Figure 7-4. As a consequence, the Bengal delta continues to grow, and will continue do so for centuries to come, based on the fact that only two-thirds of the delta is still in the third phase of every delta's four-part growth cycle.[19]

Delta and floodplain building continues but at different times during the flood season. During the onset of floodwaters, the waters' velocity carries much of the river-borne burden out into the Bay of Bengal, where it is deposited, adding to the delta's under- and above-water dimensions. As the velocities decrease, toward the end of the wet season, the sediment that would normally have been discharged into the Bay begins to settle in the rivers' channels. Over time, the channels fill, pushing the mean level of the rivers higher.

This permits later floodwaters to crest even higher, and in time, the water either breaches the natural or man-made levees or

Figure 7-4: Typical River Morphology

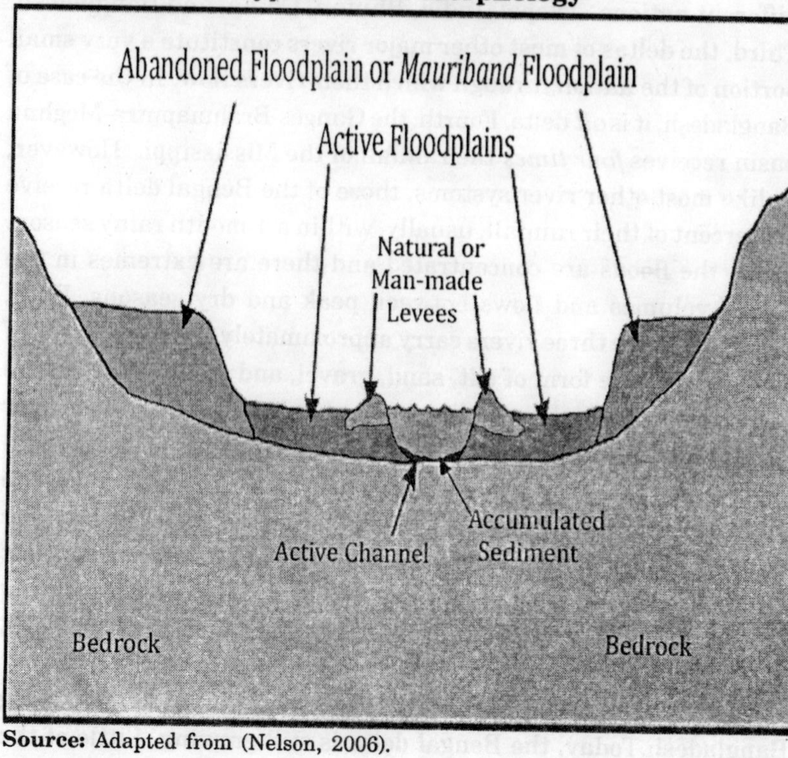

Source: Adapted from (Nelson, 2006).

simply flows over them, flooding the surrounding floodplain. With each successive cycle, the floodplain increases in height as sediment is deposited.

The process of delta and floodplain building is normally calculated in terms of centuries or thousands of years. Recent evidence suggests that these processes are quickening in the Bengal delta. Global Warming is causing the glaciers and snow in the Himalayas to melt more quickly and earlier. In addition, the warming is increasing the evaporation rate of ocean waters. With more moisture in the air, the rains become heavier and more intense. The increase in glacial melt, snow runoff, increased precipitation, along with changes in the timing of the burst of the monsoons results in changes in peak water flows in the rivers. It also means that more sediment can be carried downstream by a larger volume of faster moving water. More sediment is available to be transported by the rivers due to soil erosion, resulting from increased deforestation in Nepal and India. Global Warming is also causing sea levels to rise, as the glaciers and polar ice packs melt. Higher sea levels means that the recession of upstream flooding is delayed.

Levees and Embankments

When floods come, politicians begin devising means to either exploit them or defend against them, which in terms of political economy essentially means the same thing. Politicians are quick to curry the favor of their constituents, even as history has repeatedly proven that certain political options do nothing more than cause confusion and exacerbate already difficult situations. Such is the case with flooding in Bangladesh and in the adjoining states of India.

Most cultivators simply want to be "protected" from annual floods. It is more a knee-jerk response than a well formulated solution to a perceived problem. As long as population pressure on the land remains in equilibrium with the land's capacity to produce, the annual floods are welcomed events, even celebrated. Traditionally, cultivators understood the floods. They knew when they would arrive, how deep the flood waters would be, and how long their land would be inundated. They understood the fertilizing effects of the silt that would be deposited on their fields. When the floods came, they were prepared. As greater and greater demands were made of the land, and there were no new lands that could be brought under cultivation, the only way to increase production was to work the existing land more intensely. Once no more agricultural productivity could be exacted from the available land, no matter how intensely it was worked, the annual floods became a hindrance, for they kept the cultivators off the land for months on end. The benefits of silt-fertilization was forgotten. It was more important to be on the land, working it.

"Logic" tells cultivators and politicians that, if the waters can be contained, the cultivators will find the protection they require. Almost invariably, cultivators and politicians, alike, arrive at the same conclusion, if levees or embankments could be built, they would protect the farmers and their lands from the ravages of future floods.

Even before the British became involved in river management or control, the common people along flood-prone rivers would construct earthen *bundhs*, *bunds*, or embankments. They had to construct these structures themselves because local rulers, landlords, or *zamindars* rarely assisted in such enterprises. They would construct these earthworks either individually or through co-operative efforts, using the limited man-power and the primitive technology available to them. The people did not have the resources to efficiently maintain their creations. As a consequence, while they might repel moderate floods, during high floods, their embankments were often washed away or breached. Consequently, there was very little interference with the natural regimen of the river and the helpless people could do little to prevent the river from flowing freely and inundating extensive areas almost annually. They would attempt to mitigate the devastations by dispersing the flood waters as quickly as possible by diverting it through natural and man made channels, and back to the river's main channel.

William Willcocks speaks very highly of this system of irrigation.[20] Likewise, the old Imperial gazetteers of Bengal record that the lands of Bihar and Bengal were among the most prosperous due to the effects of the floods. Population pressure on land was not manageable and the people did not need to settle in low-lying flood prone areas, nor were they forced to use these lands for productive purposes. There remained inland water bodies like *bils* or marshes that acted as buffers, absorbing considerable quantities of flood water and thus mitigating the severity of high floods. As population pressures grew, however, the people found it necessary to occupy these much more hazardous and vulnerable landscapes, putting themselves in harm's way, putting themselves directly in the path of the annual floods.

The British interference with the rivers began, not so much to control the floods, but as augmentation and protection of land revenues and other interests they had developed, like the railways and the coal mines of Bihar and Bengal. Despite changes in its role in India, the East India Company was basically a commercial organization. Its chief obligation was to earn profits for its shareholders. Its chief source of income was land revenue. To avoid the need of the time-consuming process of repeatedly establishing new revenue settlements and to save on the cost of collection, in some areas it made permanent settlements. These settlements were not with the tillers of the soil but with a handful of *zamindars* who had become hereditary revenue collectors. The Company, confused by the bewildering complexity of the Indian land tenure systems, chose to reconstitute and redefine land rights and revenue obligations. It arbitrarily declared these revenue collectors as the 'actual proprietors' of the land, and it was these *zamindars* that became responsible to the Company for the payment of land revenues, and not the tillers of the soil.[21]

The Company did nothing more than what was absolutely necessary to secure their income and increase their profits. Together, the Company and the *zamindars* "operated as two grinding stones between which the poor peasants were mercilessly ground."[22] When the floods came, neither the Company nor the *zamindars* came to the aid of the hapless peasants under them. The peasants had to be self-reliant at every turn. Rescue and flood controls represented very heavy expenditures and guaranteed no return against huge expenditures. On the other hand, if schemes like the digging of canals for irrigation, or reclamation of lands by draining the *bils* or swamps, the construction of embankments or the clearing of jungle had the potential for the long term increase in income and profits, the Company could be persuaded to make the required investments. The permanent settlements also included a provision that the *zamindars* would maintain the existing embankments and improve their estates. In reality very few, if any, of them took good care of the embankments or fulfilled the expectations of their overlords.[23]

Thus the embankments, which were found to exist at the beginning of the British rule along the rivers of greater Bengal and Bihar, were initially built, not by the landlords nor the rulers, but by the villagers themselves. Against high floods they were useless. Had these local embankments not represented a potential threat to the Company's railways or the interests of the coal mine owners, the Company would not have become involved. However, when it became apparent that they posed a threat to the Company's vested interests, they assumed the responsibility for the embankments' maintenance.

Wherever the British assumed responsibility for embankment maintenance, it became apparent that their maintenance and reinforcement was followed by much more devastating floods. Where there were no embankments, the rivers, when they were in spate, would gently sweep across the landscape, depositing their burden of silt and would then recede. As the rivers became channelized by the better-engineered and maintained levees, their velocity increased, allowing the waters to carry, in addition to silt, sand, gravel and rocks. Initially, this burden was deposited in the river channels, as defined by the levees. This had two effects. First, the fertility-giving benefits of the silt were lost, and agricultural production fell. Second, the mean level of the rivers rose, as the original riverbed was filled with debris. Soon, the mean levels of the rivers were higher than the original floodplains. In some areas, the river levels increased to heights of three or four meters above the surrounding flood plain, requiring that the levees be further strengthened and elevated.

The increased river velocities also permitted the larger-sized burden to scour the face of the embankments. In time, this scouring action ate away at the embankments and, created holes or breaches. These breaches, in and of themselves, would not be catastrophic but the increased height of the mean river levels causes them to become catastrophic. Instead of simply spreading out over the flood

Figure 7- 5: Embanked Rivers, Levees, Scours and Breaches

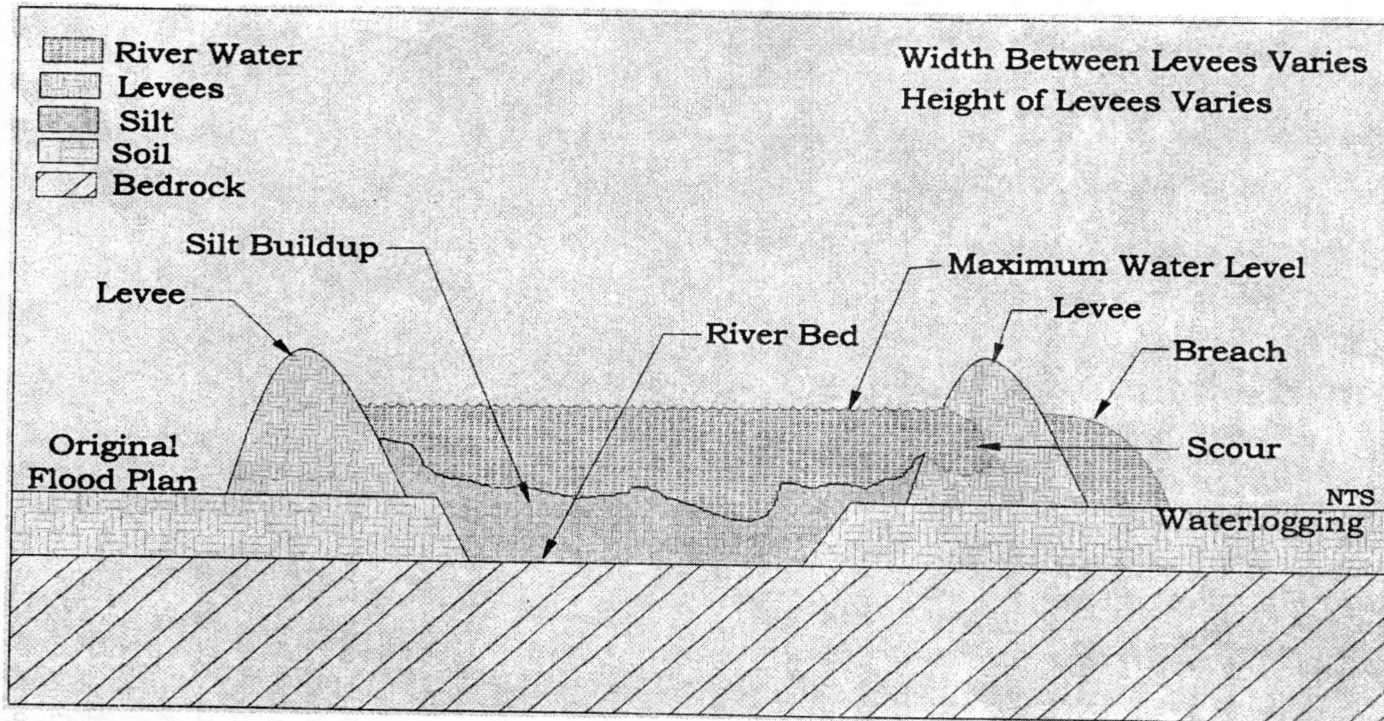

Source: Author

plain, the rivers would now cascade/crash down onto the lower floodplains. These cascades carry with them sand, gravel, and stone. These are then deposited on the surrounding landscape.

Further, once the water breached the levees, it often became trapped outside the levees and cut off from the river channel. The same is true of normal rain run-off. With no possibility of returning to the river, it accumulated in the soil, resulting in permanent or long-term waterlogging. In some areas, where there was no way to return the water to the river channel, people would wait for the water to evaporate, sometimes for more than a year. In some cases, previously reclaimed arable land became unusable swamplands.

The British, weighing the advantages and disadvantages of 'taming' the rivers of eastern India, after nearly 15 years of experimentation with the Damodar, abandoned the idea of state-sponsored embankment programs. By 1869, the British refused all demands to control the waters of numerous rivers using embankments. If flood control resulted from the construction of dams and barrages, all well and good, but embankments had proven to be worthless, or at least an overly expensive method of flood control. Even so, it was not until 1918, almost fifty years after the initial decision to stop building embankments, that the final order for the complete removal of the Raj's network of embankments was promulgated. A number of factors delayed the final implementation of the government's plan to remove all government-constructed embankment systems. First and foremost, the decisionmakers were concerned with the questions of cost. They feared that the removal of the embankments would require the payment of compensation for lands likely to be inundated. They were also concerned with the possibilities of adverse effects that might accrue to the rivers' courses. The fate of the embankments on the Damodar reflected the British concern over what might happen to the Hoogly River and eventually the impacts on the port of Calcutta (now Kolkata). In the end, the use of embankments as a safeguard against flooding has never proven a workable solution.

Much later, but this time in the state of Bihar in eastern India, a coalition of politicians and the state government developed a flood control plan based on the construction of thousands of kilometers of levees. Just as with the embankments in Bengal under the British, they failed to stem the tide of floods. However, the scale of the Bihar embankments was much, much greater. The levees were much higher and more extensive. As a consequence, the subsequent floods were more extensive and destructive. In fact, flooding has proven to be one of the most detrimental factors confronting cultivators. The same is true in West Bengal and Bangladesh.

In 1954, the embankments in Bihar began as 160 km of intermittent, poorly constructed *maharaji* and *zamindari* embankments. When completed the Bihar embankment system consisted of 3,430± km of embankments.[24] In 1952, it was estimated that 2.5 million hectares were flood prone. When the *bunds* were completed, the flood prone area had *increased* to 6.88 million hectares.[25] Looking at a topographic map of Bihar one very quickly observes that the flood prone area is now also the area the government claims is already protected.

In Bangladesh a total of 5,695 km of embankments, including 3,433 km in the coastal areas, 1,695 flood control/regulating structures, and 4,310 km of drainage canals have been constructed by the Bangladesh Water Development Board during the last several decades.[26] The success of these embankments have matched those in eastern India. See Map 7-4.

Following the 1988 flood the Government of Bangladesh (GoB) adopted a World Bank sponsored flood action plan (FAP) that calls for the additional construction of hundreds of kilometers of embankments along the great rivers of the Bangladesh delta, enormous drains, and compartments on the flood plains. The feasibility of the FAP has been criticized by numerous researchers on the basis of technical, economic, environmental, socio-political, and ecological grounds. The Dhaka Integrated Flood Protection Embankment aka Eastern Bypass Road Multipurpose Project, which is a part of the FAP, has a calculated initial coast of 24,758.21 million taka.[27]

History has repeatedly proven that the effectiveness of such embankments is debatable at best and foolhardy at worst, yet governments and international funding agencies continue to support their construction, ill advised as they may be. A number of studies have been undertaken. Each has concluded that the total amount of damage to the economy, crops, and infrastructures due to floods

Map 7-4: Embankments in Bangladesh

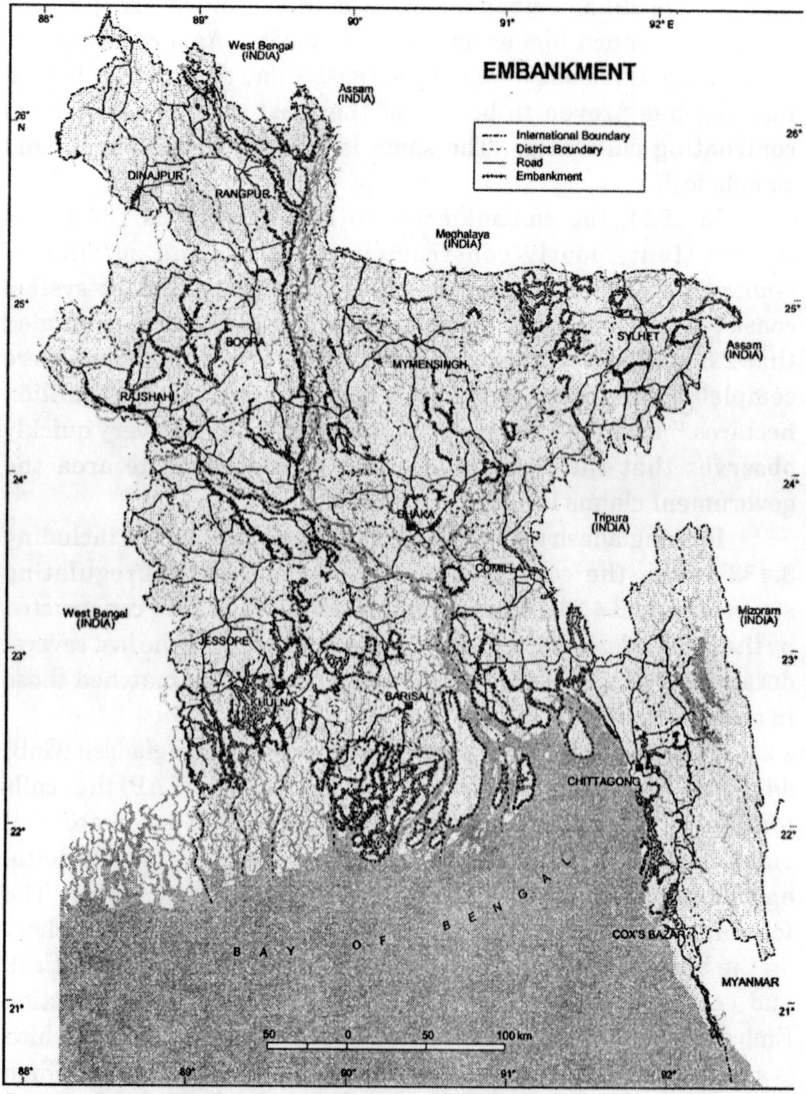

Source: (Islam, M. Aminul; and M. Fazlul Bari, 2006)

has steadily increased in spite of all efforts to control them in Bangladesh.[28]

The primary problems associated with embankments have been: (1) The rapid build-up of silt, sand, gravel and stone in the riverbeds, (2) the scouring of the embankments resulting in catastrophic breaches, (3) the increased height of the mean water level of the rivers and its role in exacerbating the damages resulting from inevitable levee breaches, and (4) increased water-logging outside the embankments.

To lesser or greater degrees, government and private embankments have been constructed throughout Bihar, West Bengal and much of Bangladesh. While the smaller, private embankments pose much less of a problem, government sponsored and maintained embankments are much more of a problem for cultivators. Almost inevitably, the floods that breach the government levees are more destructive and longer lived. After years of floods, villagers insist that they are prepared to deal with natural floods. "It is man-made floods that have wreaked havoc on them [farmers] all these years."[29] Floods that come through unrepaired breaches rise more slowly, not like bulldozers smashing everything in their path, as happens when the levees breach suddenly and without warning.

In addition, many farmers report production increases and improved yields once the floods are free to come and go, unobstructed by levees. They are reporting production statistics unlike anything many of them have seen in years. Many of the cultivators in the fields have come to recognize that the man-made floods are much worse than those before the advent of embankments. The waters once overwhelmed the people and the land, but it was nowhere as destructive as modern-day floods. The people understood the floods. They knew what to expect. They knew about the depths, duration and extent of the floods; and they would take reasonable precautions. Over time, the people have undergone what Karunakaran calls "a nomenclature change – from 'worshippers of floods' to 'victims of floods.'[30]

In the end, more land has been lost to embankment-related processes than were ever lost to over-cultivation. When the natural flow of rivers is modified, and they are not permitted to expand and contract with the seasons, the floodplain and the people suffer. In most cases, agricultural productivity declines.Today, cultivators must leverage their agricultural production. They cannot afford to waste even the slightest advantage. Man-made floods, it would seem, are working against the cultivators in the fields.

While the devastating effects of flooding are bad enough – loss of crops, livestock, homes, possessions, and human lives – there are costs associated with government relief efforts, both in India and Bangladesh. Each year governments at all levels must organize and implement a variety of relief plans. First they must save lives. Then they must provide food, water, shelter, and public health services to combat waterborne diseases and the effects of human waste in makeshift refugee camps. These efforts, while aided by international aid agencies and workers, represent a gigantic, repetitive drain on the scarce resources of India and Bangladesh.

Likewise, the government must repair or replace damaged infrastructures. Often, bridges, railways, roads, and overland communication systems are devastated by the floods. Years of work can be undermined and destroyed in a matter of hours. Due to the natural physiography of Bangladesh, transport infrastructure has always been expensive and difficult to construct. Thus, floods only serve to weaken an already enfeebled system.

Floods, then, may well be the one environmental problem that has an impact on the people of Bangladesh, across the board – economically, socially, and politically. Undoubtedly, one of the biggest problems facing the Bangladesh government involves disaster preparedness. The government seems to have no long-term plans in place with regard to disaster preparedness. Plans for dams, bridges, and drainage systems are poorly conceived and even more poorly implemented. Part of this problem stems from a lack of a system to oversee regional and even local coordination. Part of this lack of coordination extends to water control projects with other adjacent nations, in particular Nepal.

Arsenic

The GoB and international development agencies began digging hundreds of thousands of tubewells around the country in the 1970s. The water from these wells did not have to be boiled to kill bacteria. The wells had a significant impact on the health of everyone but especially the children. This saved the economically floundering government the cost of ever more expensive health care. As the incidence of chronic waterborne diseases plummeted, the new water system appeared to be a triumph of public health.

The clean water program led to one of the worst environmental disasters in the history of Bangladesh. Due to the geology of Bangladesh, the biologically uncontaminated water in the local aquifers is naturally laced with arsenic in concentrations up to 40 times over the declared safe level.[31]

Arsenic was first discovered in the water supplies of West Bengal in India in the 1990s, where people were developing symptoms of arsenicosis. Currently, about 1/3 of the tubewells in Bangladesh show signs of contamination. Most of these wells pump up water exceeding the arsenic standard of 50 ppb (parts per billion). In some areas arsenic levels are 2000 ppb, 40 times over the acceptable level for potable water. Most of the wells register 200 to 400 ppb of arsenic. It is estimated at over 55 million people are or have been exposed to arsenic poisoning.[32]

Current estimates suggest that 52 districts are affected, which encompasses approximately 80 percent of the country.[33] The long-term prognosis for the people afflicted is unclear but some have died, some have skin blisters and a variety of lesser symptoms. It may take decades before the real extent of arsenic poisoning is fully realized.[34]

In addition to the naturally occurring arsenic, it has been suggested that:

Apparently, some of the chemical fertilizers and pesticides used in Bangladesh contain high amounts of arsenic, which might have been introduced into groundwater. According to this study, there is no evidence that arsenic originated from any natural source in Bangladesh. It is also claimed that a large amount of arsenic trioxide is kept in stock at Ghorasal Fertilizer Factory in Bangladesh for use or disposal to unknown destinations. About 30% of the fertilizers used in Bangladesh are lost through surface run-off. It is also suggested that in some parts of Bangladesh there is an apparent correlation between the amount of fertilizers used in crops and the amount of arsenic present in groundwater.[35]

Arsenic contamination of groundwater is not unique to West Bengal and Bangladesh but they are among the worst known cases so far. A 2007 study suggests that over 140 million people in 70 countries may have varying levels of arsenic poisoning from their drinking water.[36] Further, it has been suggested that rice grown with arsenic contaminated water draws the arsenic up into the grain where it is concentrated. People eating these contaminated grains

Map 7-5: Extent of Arsenic Poisoning in Bangladesh and West Bengal

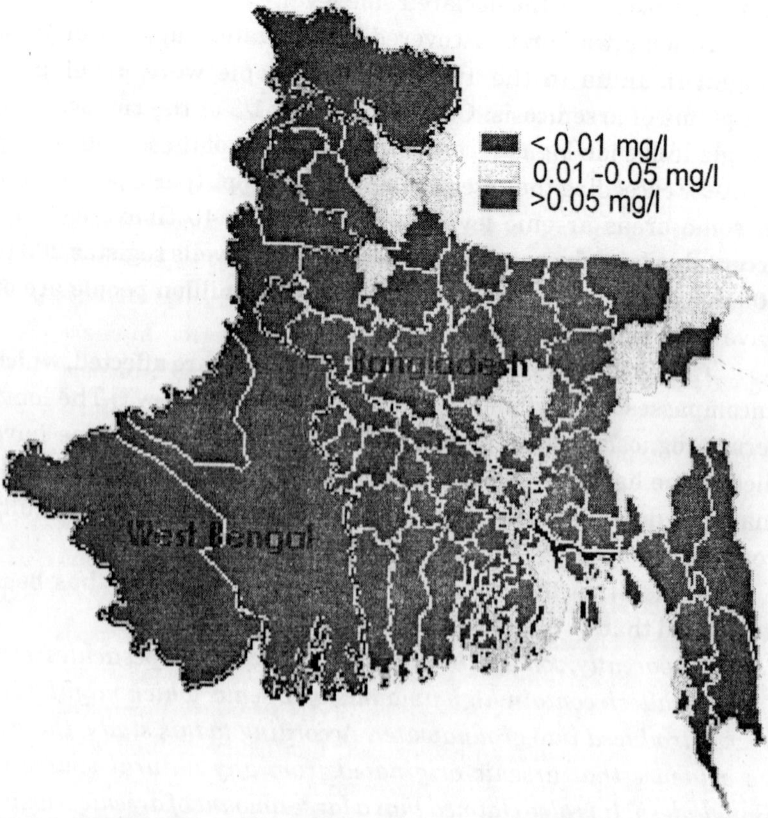

Source: (Khalequzzaman, Md., Fazlay S. Faruque, and Amal K. Mitra, 2005), p. 2, after (Chowdhury, U. K., et. al., 2000).

ingest the arsenic. Arsenic transfers from soil to rice is about 10 times more efficiently than in other grain crops.

It really matters little whether the source of arsenic in Bangladesh's water supply is naturally occurring or the result of fertilizer misuse or use, or pesticide and fertilizer run-off, or the result of mishandling industrial chemicals and waste products. Either way, Bangladesh must face yet another disaster, one that is just unfolding and may have long-term consequences. What is more important is to find a remedy to rectify the problem. At least one American chemistry professor has developed a dual parallel SONO filter that will filter out the arsenic in drinking water.[37]

The SONO filter works without electricity, using three stacked buckets. The top bucket is filled with coarse river sand and a composite iron matrix, which serves as the active arsenic removal component. The middle bucket contains coarse river sand and wood charcoal to remove organic impurities. The bottom bucket contains fine river sand and brick chips to remove fine particles and stabilize water flow. The SONO filter is manufactured in Bangladesh using local raw materials at a cost of $35-$40. It produces 20 liters of clean water per hour, requires little maintenance, and lasts a minimum of five years. It is also "green," in the sense that it does not produce any hazardous waste.

Hussam says he has distributed 32,500 of the filters in Bangladesh, including to more than 1,000 schools. "We are beginning to see the effect of drinking clean water on patients being cured of melanosis and keratosis [skin ailments], and most people feel better," he said. People are also more aware of the importance of clean, potable water.

"We have plans to distribute the filter in India and Nepal," Hussam said.[38]

Hussam's filter, however, does not have the capacity to provide irrigation water and, therefore, it will have no impact on the process of arsenic take-up by plants in the field. It is a simple and safe way for families to purify their drinking water. It may not help those already afflicted but it may save the next generation of Bangladeshis from similar pain and hardship.

Issues and Challenges for Bangladesh

Although all developing nations of South Asia are predominantly rural and dependent upon agriculture, the rural population in Bangladesh is the epitome of that statement. Nearly 80 percent of the population of Bangladesh's population lives in rural areas and 53 percent of them are poor. The rural poor constitute roughly 85 percent of the country's poor population.[39] To meet its overall economic development goals, agricultural production will need to increase at a compound rate of 4 percent per annum, and 7 percent per annum in its non-farm sectors. Considering Bangladesh's economic, political, and infrastructural realities, combined with its demographic and environmental challenges, the likelihood of it meeting its 2015 Millennium Development Goal (MDG) of halving its poverty.rate, is most unlikely.

Shrinking Land Base

Two-thirds of the nation's total land area is cultivated, roughly 9.3 million hectares. Of this cultivated area, 75 percent is planted in rice. There is no uncultivated arable land into which Bangladesh can expand. Thus the most intractable problem facing Bangladesh's agricultural productivity is its shrinking land base.

Despite the geologic, land-building resulting from riverine sedimentation, pressure on the land is intense and getting worse. Although the population growth rate is comparatively low – 1.6 percent – the number of people that are added to the total population is staggering. Already, Bangladesh has one of the highest population densities in the world, more than 1,445 people per sq. km.[40] As the population grows, each family's landholdings become smaller and smaller because of the observance of traditional inheritance practices.[41] Because of this, there is a need for the implementation of land reforms that focus on the consolidation of landholdings into economically productive units. Further, increased urbanization and changes in land use around cities reduces cultivable area. Currently, urban growth and sprawl consumes approximately 1 percent of the existing cultivable area of Bangladesh annually.[42] Simply put, Bangladesh's population is about to outgrow its country.

Cropping Patterns

Within the context of agricultural intensification, rice accounts for about 77% of the total cropped area and two-thirds of the value added in crop production; jute accounts for another 8 percent, and the remainder in tea, sugarcane, oil seeds, tobacco, gram and other pulses.[43] In 1999-2000, nearly 50% of the net cropped land was double cropped, and 13% triple cropped. The emphasis of government policy has been on achieving foodgrain production self-sufficiency with support systems in place to insure the efficient distribution of modern agricultural inputs such as chemical fertilizers and irrigation water. These support policies and major improvements in the public sector research and extension agencies have allowed the country to achieve a record 5% per year growth in cereal production from 1996 to 2000.

The current development strategy focuses on agricultural and crop diversification through reallocation of resources away from the production of rice, to be achieved through a continuous increase in the productivity of land and labor, and timely supply of high-quality seeds and fertilizer.

Fertilizer

Although the government, initially supported fertilizer use through subsidies, during the 1980s subsidies were removed. Nonetheless, the pattern of fertilizer use remained entrenched and demand and use increased nearly 100 percent between 1970 and 2000. However, with the removal of the subsidies, fertilizer use became unbalanced. Cheaper sources of fertilizer were sought. Due to price differences for the component parts of the blended fertilizers, formulas were altered and this affected the efficacy of the resulting fertilizers. This, in turn, had a negative impact on crop yields and the environment.

Rice

Currently, rice production appears to be sufficient. In fact, rice prices may be declining to the point where they are too low to provide cultivators with sufficient incentive to continue their current levels of production. As staple foodgrain production reaches self-sufficiency the price tends to decline precipitously. Bangladesh may be arriving at that threshold for rice. It is at this time that cultivators should be urged to diversify and, simultaneously, government should release and replenish national stores. The combination of these two market policies would result in diverting some agricultural lands to other high-value crops and non-crop production, while, at the same time, supporting rice prices during this transition period. The continued use of price supports would provide cultivators with an economic safety net during the risky period of transition.

Recent research has indicated that a wheat-rice system in Bangladesh has proven to be advantageous, but unlike their Punjabi counterparts, the cultivators of Bangladesh have become seasonally more diversified. Previously, it was believed that the rice-wheat cropping pattern was the major cereal production pattern throughout much of South Asia, thinking that growers were sowing cereals

Figure 7-6: Area (000s ha) Under Major Crops, 2002

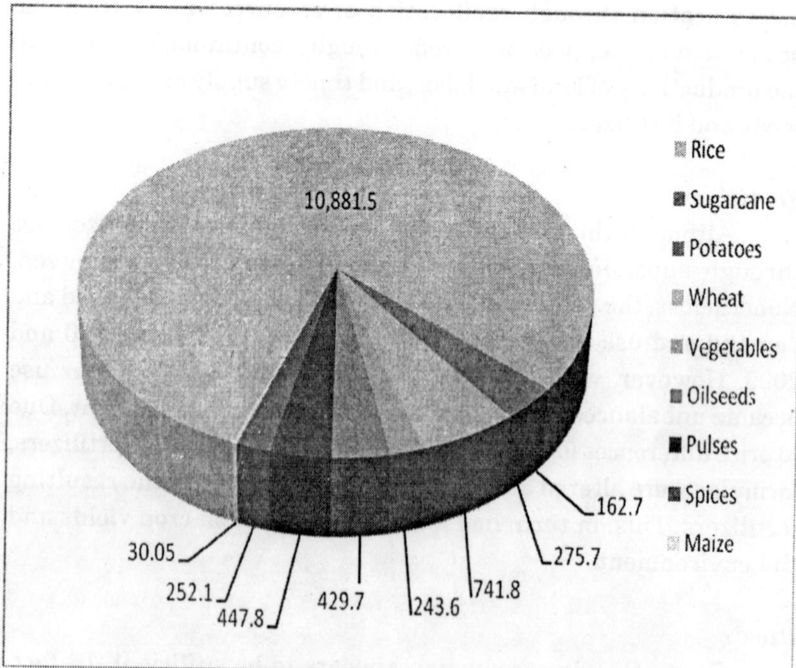

Source: After (Rahman, 2003), Slide 3.

continuously year after year, when in fact, they were actually becoming increasingly diversified in their planting practices. At least in Bangladesh, the cultivators are sowing what has been termed 'break crops.' They sow pulses, oilseeds, potatoes, vegetables, and sugarcane on the plots previously in rice-wheat.[44] See Figure 7-6.

Wheat

Improved varieties of wheat arrived comparatively late to Bangladesh. Introduced to consumers through food aid programs in the mid-1970s, and not through the CIMMYT, production expanded rapidly through the early 1980s in response to the newly created demand. Through most of the 1980s and early 1990s, however, production leveled off at around 1 million metric tons as productivity increases eased, although production surged in 1984-85 to 1.4 million metric tons, and nearly reached that level again in 1993-94 (1.3 million metric tons). The latest surge can be attributed principally to the shift of land from *boro* rice to wheat because of the strong dip in rice prices. Another dip in 1994 seems to have dampened the prospects of any further expansion of wheat production in a predominantly rice-eating population.[45]

According to a study by the CIMMYT and IFPRI, wheat can compete both financially and economically with other winter season crops under rainfed conditions, but it cannot compete with improved *boro* rice under irrigated conditions in most areas of the country.[46] Under circumstances in which rice becomes exportable, wheat could become an attractive alternative under irrigation in the central, north-central and southwest regions. These conclusions suggest that wheat will continue to be an important rainfed crop, but that *boro* rice will displace it as irrigation expands to meet domestic rice needs. On the other hand, *boro* would probably not displace wheat in order to export common rice.

Maize

Maize currently occupies only about 3,000 hectares, a level that has remained largely unchanged over the last two decades. Part of the problem with maize cultivation is that a significant market for the grain has yet to develop.[47] It is consumed principally as green cob, either roasted or boiled with some spices as a snack, and is considered an inferior grain. Most consumers are not aware of its potential use in domestic cooking. At present, food preference or avoidances are working against maize consumption. As a consequence, unless substantial efforts are made to promote its use as a foodgrain for humans, it is unlikely that public acceptance will change significantly. The use of maize in ration shops may influence its use among a wider population and, at the same time make it possible to target the poorest segments of society.[48]

Industrial uses of maize have not developed. However, with the emergence of a commercial poultry industry in Bangladesh, the market for maize has strengthened significantly. Throughout the world, maize is the preferred grain for commercialized poultry production because of its balance of energy, protein, fiber, and micronutrients. Typically it represents more then 60 per cent of most mixed feeds for poultry. The largest poultry producer in Bangladesh has been forced to import maize from India to meet his requirements.[49] Even as production has increased over the last decade and more improved varieties are being developed, most production is geared to foodgrain for animals and not for human consumption.

Disincentives to production are associated with poor productivity. In part, this is due to comparatively poor yields. Yields are lower than in the rest of South Asia – about half that of Pakistan and India – and much lower than in the West. Maize yields currently average only 0.8 metric tons per hectare. Lower use of inputs is largely responsible for these low yield rates. Results from farm demonstration plots, however, show that maize can be grown very successfully in Bangladesh in all seasons with the application of adequate amounts of fertilizer, water, and pesticides.[50] However, to make such an undertaking economically legitimate,a much larger market for maize must be cultivated, especially in the form of domestic food and feed markets.

According to economic analyses of intensive maize production, assuming use of improved composite varieties, maize can be sufficiently competitive and profitable to compete with irrigated *boro* rice. Survey data show that maize results in a stronger net financial return than rice or wheat in both summer and winter seasons, and financial returns are even greater under demonstration plot conditions, suggesting a very large potential for improving on-farm productivity. However, these results assume that maize is sold primarily as green cob rather than as a foodgrain.[51]

Infrastructural Weaknesses and Markets

Infrastructural weaknesses represent two interrelated problem areas for Bangladesh. First, input and output marketing must be strengthened. Second, there is a need for the development of a better functioning system of roadways and general information systems.

In general, cultivators have a difficult time obtaining requisite inputs due to complicity and price-setting amongst traders. Likewise, similar difficulties exist for the marketing of the meager surpluses that exist. As a consequence, the prices for inputs are high and the prices for produce is comparatively low. These high margins represent a disincentive for all cultivators but especially for the smallest. The use of quality inputs, like improved seeds, fertilizers, pesticides, machinery, and irrigation is critical if cultivators are to diversify and increase production.

Despite improvements, agricultural inputs continue to experience problems of timeliness, poor quality, and high prices. Although these problems are to be found everywhere, they are most pronounced in the more remote rural areas. Thus, these cultivators are tacitly removed from involvement in the larger national economy from beginning to end. More governmental control of agricultural marketing, with an increased emphasis on minimum price supports for produce and stronger 'watch dog' input pricing, is imperative. Marketing reforms must be explored.

Marketing infrastructures for rice are adequate but inadequate for other agricultural products, especially perishables. Of special importance is the need for agro-processing, including transport, storage, processing, and marketing. These activities are dependent upon the timely and reliable supply of agricultural inputs at reasonable prices.

Just as important is the provision of improved physical and social infrastructures. These include all-weather roads, electricity, communication and safe water supplies, as well as health and education programs. In its most elemental context, connectivity is productivity. Time wasted travelling to obtain inputs or sell produce is largely wasted time. Likewise, time spent travelling to obtain information is wasted time. Therefore, the agricultural productivity of cultivators would be improved simply by reducing time spent travelling to markets or in obtaining needed information. Communication, then, is extremely important to productivity. One researcher observed that: ". . . telecommunications investment made a bigger contribution to economic growth than almost anything else."[52] By the end of May 2008, the Bangladesh Telecommunication Regulatory Commission (BTRC) reported 1.271 million public switched phone network (PSPN) phone subscribers, out of a population of 153 million, or one subscriber for every 121 people in the country, with the rate significantly lower in rural areas.[53]

Although cell phone usage is increasing, it is primarily an urban phenomenon. The PSTN system also provides the primary internet service link between internet service providers (ISPs) and individual users. Assuming telecommunications is an integral part of modern commerce, there is much that needs to be done in Bangladesh to achieve communications between the people and much needed information sources, especially as it has an impact on overall and agricultural development.

The *e-Choupal* network in India has demonstrated the effectiveness of timely information availability. A similar farm-to-factory gateway system could easily resolve marketing, as well as input and other consumer goods purchases, as it would all be present in one simple computerized system. With the rapid increase in domestic, wireless telephone networks, an *e-Choupal*-type information and marketing system should be comparatively easy to implement.

While progress has been made in the area of improved roadways, improvements in the area of electrification has not made equally impressive headway. Currently, it is estimated that only 15 percent of villages have electrical service.[54]

Observations

Boro and Golden Rice – Time Consuming

For nearly 30 years, from independence in 1971, until 1998-99, the people of Bangladesh suffered from an almost chronic state of semi-starvation, due to political upheavals, droughts, floods, and an inability to produce adequate quantities of rice, the staple of Bangladesh's daily dietary regime. In 1998-99 *boro* rice was introduced. *Boro* rice is an irrigated, dry-season, high-yielding, photo-insensitive, bed-germinated, transplanted hybrid. With its introduction Bangladesh slowly began to harvest enough rice to claim near self-sufficiency for the first time since independence.

Over the last three decades, the area under *boro* rice has increased from 0.8 to 3.4 million hectares, at the expense of the very low-yielding and risky deepwater *aman* and upland *aus* rice crops, almost all of which have been planted in non-high yielding local varieties. Over this period, the area under *aus* rice has declined from 3.4 to 1.3 million hectares and that of deepwater *aman* rice from 2.1 to 0.7 million hectares. However, *aman* rice still covers 5.7 million hectares.[55] During the *aman* and *boro* seasons, alone, over 30 rice varieties are planted, either by transplanting or by broadcasting.

One of the most recent changes in Bangladesh's rice production has been the diversion of more and more *aus* land to the cultivation of high-value vegetable and fruit crops, as part of Bangladesh's overall agricultural diversification process. The goal of Bangladesh's agricultural diversification programs is to make it possible to participate more fully in the global agricultural produce market, which will make it fiscally easier to import essential foodstuffs at a cost less than domestic production.

Even though rice production is nearing self-sufficiency, rice research and development continues to improve on *boro* rice's high yielding characteristics, for example, one of the latest *boro* derivatives is Jagaron-1 (GB-4).[56] Successive introductions of still better acclimatized varieties has improved yields.

One of the long awaited varieties that will soon become available is Golden Rice, engineered by scientists working at the Swiss Federal Institute of Technology and the agribusiness company, Syngenta.[57] This new rice is eagerly anticipated because of its production as well as its ability to produce â-carotene, from which the human body can produce Vitamin A. No other rice variety contains â-carotene, which means that where rice is the predominant food source, VAD, or Vitamin A Deficiency will result. VAD causes blindness in children and other health problems in adults, such as immunodeficiencies. Vitamin A and zinc alone could save 25% of the 12 million children who die annually because of malnutrition worldwide.[58] Equally important, its yellow color does not seem to have met with market or consumer resistance, since the quality of grain and its ability to prevent health problems have overcome its color difference – yellow to orange. These qualities, however, could not have been achieved without genetic engineering.

The motivation behind the development of Golden Rice originated with Dr. Ingo Potrykus of the Swiss Federal Institute of Technology, as early as 1972, but it took 27 years before Golden Rice 1 (GR 1) became a reality in 1999. GR 1 was later improved and became known as Golden Rice 2 in 2004. Both were the result of the Golden Rice Project.[59] It was not until the Fall of 2004, however, that the first field trials were undertaken in Louisiana in the United States. The irony of the first field trials is that they were conducted so far from Golden Rice's intended final home – Asia – and after so many years. The reason they were not tested somewhere in Asia was that the target countries in Asia did not have suitable biosafety regulations in place for testing purposes. Following the successful field tests in the U.S., other field tests are anticipated before Golden Rice's scheduled 2011 release date.[60]

Altogether, more than a dozen years will have slipped by between the time the new rice was first developed and when it will become commercially available. Between inception and final release, nearly 40 years will have passed. For some countries, like Bangladesh, even twelve years to develop beneficial and more productive new rice varieties may mean that they will arrive too late for those that have starved or succumbed to preventable diseases.

In agriculture, almost every improvement is not measured from season to season but from decade to decade, and more often in terms of generations. The agricultural problems facing Bangladesh are conceptually quite simple. The country is small, most of its arable land is currently under cultivation, population growth and its consequences, are now competing with agriculture for land, and at the same time, the people are unable to produce all the food they require. Loss of cultivable land, even marginal lands, will have an impact on total agricultural production. Only recently has Bangladesh even approached food self-sufficiency under current land availability and agricultural technology. Loss of land, with no changes in agricultural technologies, will only mean that the progress made in food production will begin to reverse itself, and increasingly severe food shortages will be the consequence. Agricultural diversification and the commercialization of Bangladesh's agriculture, combined with participation in the global agricultural economy may be the only way to avoid mass starvation. Instead of producing all the food the nation requires, i.e., food security, Bangladesh will need to rearrange its economy to become food self-reliant – dependent upon the global food market for its staples. This position of self-reliance will depend on the provision of other goods and services on a global scale that will permit and guarantee the ability to import essential foodstuffs. In short, Bangladesh has few alternatives. It is obvious that its agricultural base is incapable of supporting its growing population. It has exploited virtually all the available arable land, most crops grown are the best available under current technology, and both are being worked intensively. There seems little room for improvement under current circumstances and conditions. In the absence of the ability to become food secure, Bangladesh has few alternatives but to strive for food self-reliance within the global economy.

Even the ability to become self-reliant will represent a major challenge, especially in light of the current state of Bangladesh's physical infrastructures, access to markets, and current educational situation. The world economy is replete with illiterate, untrained manual laborers. What is needed are world class skilled service providers. Currently, the adult literacy is 41 percent, secondary enrollment is 47 percent of the secondary age cohort, and only 6 percent of the college age cohort is enrolled in college-level institutions.[61] This, across the board lack of education makes it increasingly difficult for Bangladesh to achieve the status of a world class service provider.

Under the circumstances, while the future appears to be brightening for the population of Bangladesh, the reality seems to be that, in almost every sector of the Bangladeshi economy, there is nowhere to go. Agriculture is on the threshold of stagnation, having exploited virtually every available hectare, using the best available seed and technologies, and the manpower available. The people are wringing almost every available bit of production from the land. The industrial and manufacturing sectors are limited by the availability of raw materials and resources. The service sector is limited by trained and skilled personnel. All three economic sectors suffer from infrastructural and management inadequacies.

It would seem that, at every turn, the people are met with almost insurmountable obstacles, and one of the largest of these is the continued growth in the food-, good-, and services-demanding population. Even with a comparatively low rate of population growth – 1.6 percent per annum — more than 2.5 million new mouths must be fed, educated, and provided for each year, placing an ever-increasing burden on the Bangladeshi's already overtaxed and enfeebled system.

MDGs and Disasters

For most of the rural residents of Bangladesh, life in the village means limited travel opportunities, lack of access to input and output markets, limited (if any) telecommunications opportunities, no electricity, unsafe water supplies and waste disposal, limited educational opportunities, poverty and malnutrition. The strengthening of public services to the rural areas is, obviously, a must if Bangladesh is to come close to meeting its MDGs by 2015. As it stands now, the likelihood of achieving the goal of reducing its poverty level to 26.5 percent seems to be slipping further and further away.

Paper progress would appear impressive. Assets are committed, roads, bridges, drainage systems, telephone and electrical lines are being constructed, only to see much of that effort destroyed by natural disasters – floods, sheet rainfall, wind storms, storm surges, tornadoes, and mudslides. There is possibly no area on Earth that is so adversely affected by natural hazards as Bangladesh. The impact of these phenomena are compounded by the vulnerabilities resulting from existing population densities, too little protected land, and inadequate infrastructural systems and an impoverished government and people.

References

1. (Ahmed, Raisuddin and Zahurui Karim, 2006), p. 130.
2. (The World Bank, 2008c).
3. The rate of one-percentage point drop in poverty per year witnessed in Bangladesh—amounting to about a 10 percent decline in the poverty rate between 1991-92 and 2000—is often termed modest. However, it must be remembered that such a rate places Bangladesh among the leaders in terms of poverty reduction rates. (Binayak Sen and David Hulme, (eds), May 2004), p. 1.
4. (Binayak Sen and David Hulme, (eds), May 2004), See footnote 1, p. 1.
5. (Hossain, Mahabb, et. al., October 2003), p. 1.
6. (The World Bank, 1997).
7. (UNESCAP, 2008).
8. (Super Admin, 2006).
9. (UNWFP, 2008)
10. (Alam, 2003), pp. 426-427. See also, (Saha, Bimal Kumar, 2001).
11. (The World Bank, 2008c).

12. (Dilley, Maxx; et. al., 2005).
13. Data from the SNDP, USAID, UNEP, and EM-DAT were combined to obtain a total number number of events for the period 2000-2007. The total number of events, through 2007, numbered 85, with two more years left in the decade. Already the number of events was one less than in the period 1990-1999.
14. (IEG, June 2007), p. 2.
15. (UN Population Division, 2008).
16. Two-thirds of the world's population growth since 1950 has been absorbed by cities.
17. (Mellinger, A. D., J. D. Sachs, and J. L. Gallup., 1999). Mellinger suggests that the later arrivals in cities tend to occupy more dangerous locations than did their predecessors.
18. EM-DAT: The OFDA/CRED International Disaster Database <www.em-dat.net >
19. Typically, the four stages of a delta's development include:
    Stage I — Silt carried by the river is deposited at the mouth of the river below sea level. The undersea fan of sediment of the Bengal delta is 1000 km wide, over 12 km in depth, and 3000 km long, extending beyond Sri Lanka.
    Stage 2 — Portions of the sediment fan are periodically above sea level.
    Stage 3 — Continued silt deposits produce active floodplains that are only submerged during peak rain/flow periods.
    Stage 4 — Active floodplains rise until they are no longer inundated, except under the most extreme flood/flow conditions. See (Islam, ca. 1990).
20. (Willcocks, 1984).
21. There is a substantial literature surrounding the emergence and development of the *zamindari* class and efforts to remove them following the independence for Pakistan and India in 1947. To a lesser or greater degree, the effects of the *zamindari* system and the *zamindars* still remains in many parts of rural Bihar, West Bengal, and Bangladesh.
22. (Biswas, 2003).
23. *Ibid.*
24. (Krishnakumar, 1999).
25. (Prasad, 2003), Slide 28 of 29. See also, (Karunnakaran, 2004), pp. 1-2.

26. (Khalequzzaman, 2004)
27. The current exchange rate for the *taka* is 68.275 *taka* to the U.S. Dollar (September 12, 2008).
28. (Khalequzzaman, 2004).
29. (Karunnakaran, 2004), p. 3.
30. (Karunnakaran, 2004), p. 1.
31. (M IT, 2002).
32. *Ibid.* See also, (Khalequzzaman, Md., Fazlay S. Faruque, and Amal K. Mitra, 2005) and (Safiuddin, Md., and Md. Masud Karim, November 2001).
33. (Chowdhury, U. K., et. al., 2000).
34. (Khalequzzaman, Md., Fazlay S. Faruque, and Amal K. Mitra, 2005) provide an excellent discussion of the symptoms associated with arsenicosis.
35. (Khalequzzaman, Md., Fazlay S. Faruque, and Amal K. Mitra, 2005). See also, (Chakraborty, A. K.; Saha, K. C., 1987); and (Anwar, 2004).
36. (Black, 2007). See also (Associated Press, 2007).
37. (Thomas, 2007)
38. *Ibid.*
39. (The World Bank, 2008c).
40. See Box 7-1.
41. Land is traditionally held by the male head of the family and upon his death, it is divided equally among his sons. This results in both the dis-consolidation and fragmentation of landholdings.
42. (The World Bank, 2008c).
43. (IRRI, J. L. McLean, 2002), p. 99.
44. (Meisner, Craig; Michael Morris; and Nuimuddin Chowdhury, Unknown) and (Meisner, Craig; Michael Morris; and Nuimuddin Chowdhury, 1996).
45. (Ateng, 1996).
46. (Chowdhury, Morris, and Meisner, 1994).
47. (Karim, September 1992).
48. (Ateng, 1996).
49. (Ateng, 1996).
50. (The World Bank, June 30,1995), Appendix A, Table A.2.
51. (Karim, September 1992).
52. (Quadir, 2000). See, also (Khandker, Shahidur R.; Zaid Bakht; and Gayatri B. Koolwal, April 2006)

53. (BTRC, 2008). PSTN stands for 'public switched telephone network' and represents the world's collection of interconnected voice-oriented public telephone networks, both commercial and government-owned. It is also referred to as the Plain Old Telephone Service (POTS). Its the aggregation of circuit-switching telephone networks that has evolved from the days of Alexander Graham Bell. Today, it is almost entirely digital in technology except for the final link from the central (local) telephone office to the user.
54. (The World Bank, 2008c).
55. (IRRI, J. L. McLean, 2002), p. 101.
56. See, for example, (Hossain, Janaiah, & Husain, 2003).
57. On November 13, 2000 Novartis and AstraZeneca merged their agribusinesses to form Syngenta, the first global group focusing exclusively on agribusiness. It must be noted that, unlike many other large companies involved in GE/GM agribusiness activities, Syngenta transferred control of its proprietary rights in Golden Rice to a humanitarian foundation in 2004, commonly known as the Golden Rice Humanitarian Board, or HumBo. HumBo will make the Golden Rice available to "those who need it at no additional cost," according to HumBo's website: http://www.goldenrice.org/index.html.
58. (Golden Rice Humanitarian Board, 2007).
59. The Golden Rice Project was the result of an initiative by the Rockefeller Foundation, and is based on a widely recognized need for a sustainable bio-fortification approach to contribute to alleviating micronutrient deficiencies worldwide. See also, (Potrykus, 2000).
60. (Mayuga, 2007) and (Golden Rice Humanitarian Board, 2008).
61. (UNESCO, 2008). See also: http://www.ilo.org/public/english/region/asro/bangkok/skills-ap/skills/bangladesh_literacy.htm.

8

The Green Revolution – Environmental Consequences: The Indian Experience

Ecological Consequences of the Green Revolution

Agriculture is first and foremost a process set within a specific setting, an ecological niche. This niche may constitute a few hectares or millions of hectares. Within these niches there is normally a symbiosis between the agricultural activities of man and the medium within which it operates. The Green Revolution, unlike many other processes, has had a largely deleterious impact upon this environment. Almost everywhere the Green Revolution has been implemented, it has resulted in soil degradation, water overuse, environmental pollution, and the loss of biodiversity.

Soil Degradation

The Green Revolution, when fully articulated, is a form of commercial agriculture, and tends to be rapacious of soils. The normal organic and trace minerals to be found in undisturbed soils are quickly consumed by the nutrient-demanding, improved seeds. The soils are further destroyed by the application of large amounts of fertilizers, pesticides, and herbicides, as well as the continuous use of irrigation.

In the past, agriculture as practiced in most parts of the world and before the advent of commercial agriculture, tended to be symbiotic with the soil. Manure from livestock and straw and the non-edible portions of crops were plowed back into the soil, thereby replacing the organic matter that had been consumed by the crops. The micronutrients that were consumed were replaced through periods of fallowing, often as pasture for livestock.

Commercialized agriculture, on the other hand, especially in South Asia, where manure is often used for fuel and straw and the non-food portion of plants are used for fodder, does not permit the replacement of organic matter. Further, multiple cropping, accompanied by small landholdings, precludes the possibility of fallowing. Even before the arrival of improved seeds, the lands of South Asia, and especially those in India and Bangladesh, were used season after season and year after year without a break. The human response to increased population pressure is initially to intensify the exploitation of the soil, first with more labor inputs, and later, more yield-improving inputs.

In the areas of high humidity, high temperatures, and heavy rainfall, the soil is degraded by nature itself, through the process of leaching. The organic component of the soil breaks down more quickly and is washed away by heavy rainfall. The implementation of Green Revolution technologies only served to accelerate what nature had already begun.When nutrient-hungry and improved seeds, high humidity, high temperatures, and near-constant irrigation or long periods of flooding combine, the soil's organic and micronutrient content is very quickly depleted.

For the first few years after the introduction of the Green Revolution, most soils were 'fresh enough' to survive the demands of the new seeds, and much less chemical fertilizer was required to maintain expected yields. However, as the natural nutrients in the soil were depleted, it became necessary to apply increasing amounts of chemical fertilizers to provide the nutrients necessary for the new seeds, in soils that were becoming little more than sterile mediums, providing only root support for the plants.

One system for the determination of soil degradation is quite simple:

Sight Degradation – yields are reduced by < 10 percent
Moderate Degradation – yields are reduced by 10 – 50 percent
Severe Degradation – yields are reduced by > 50 percent.[1]

In general, this classification system would seem overly generous. For the observant cultivator, any reduction in yield would surely become noticeable even at a ten percent reduction level. Anything more than that and he would be in a panic, assuming normal weather conditions during the cropping season.

While chemical fertilizers may provide the basic nutrients for crops, they do not contain or replace essential trace elements. As a consequence of these diverse processes, basic soil fertility declines, and with it, crop productivity. For example, in Indian Punjab, agricultural production increased by nearly 5 percent per annum from 1965 to 1975. Thereafter, agricultural production began to decline; and it has not stopped. In 2005-06, Punjab's agricultural growth rate dropped below 2 percent per annum. See Figure 8-1. Similar patterns are emerging almost everywhere where the Green Revolution has followed the India model.

Figure 8-1: Change in Punjab's Agricultural Growth Rates, 1965-70 to 2006

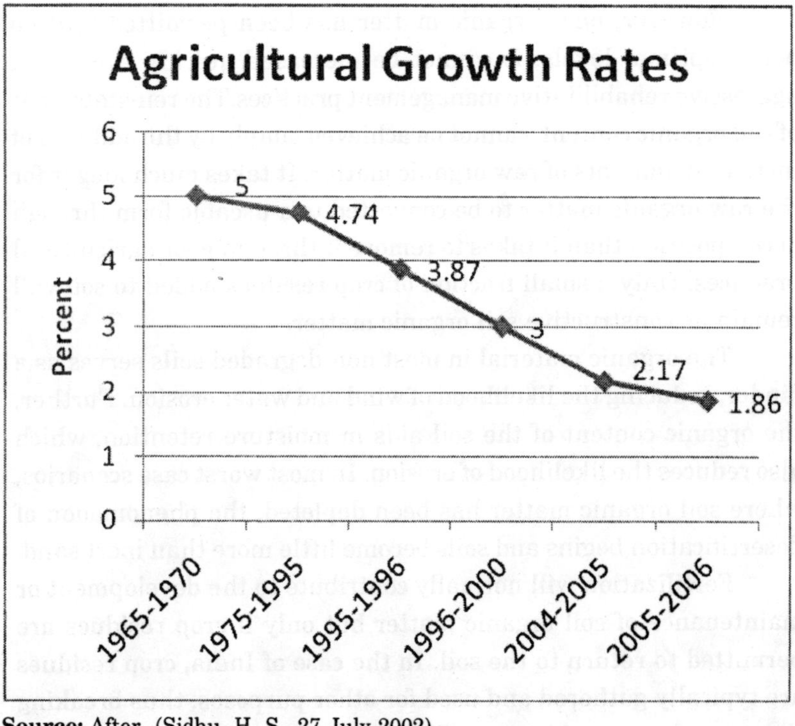

Source: After (Sidhu, H. S., 27 July 2002).

Soil Exhaustion and Organic Matter

The soils of Punjab have become exhausted by relentless use and constant year-round irrigation. In many respects the soils of Punjab, and in other areas where the Green Revolution was fully implemented, have become inert planting mediums for crops. Organic matter absorbs and hold nutrients in the soil in plant available forms.[2] Organic matter together with bacteria and fungi in the soil, aggregate the soil, promoting good soil structure, aeration, helps maintain tilth,[3] water infiltration, and resistance to erosion and crusting. The amount of organic matter in the soil contributes to productivity but there is "no direct quantitative relationship between soil productivity and total soil organic matter."[4] In fact, lowering the organic content of some soils actually improves the release of soil nutrients but only to a point. Too much organic matter traps nutrients. If too little organic matter is present nutrients disappear from the soil. Maintaining a proper balance is imperative to productivity.

However, once organic matter has been permitted to drop below optimal levels, it cannot be increased quickly even with aggressive rehabilitative management practices.The reinstatement of soil organic content cannot be achieved simply by the addition of increased amounts of raw organic matter. It takes much longer for the raw organic matter to be converted to a useable form through decomposition than it takes to remove it through poor agricultural practices. Only a small fraction of crop residues added to soil will remain as constructive soil organic matter.

The organic material in most non-degraded soils serves as a binder, reducing the likelihood of wind and water erosion. Further, the organic content of the soil aids in moisture retention, which also reduces the likelihood of erosion. In most worst case scenarios, where soil organic matter has been depleted, the phenomenon of desertification begins and soils become little more than inert sand.

Fertilization will normally contribute to the development or maintenance of soil organic matter but only if crop residues are permitted to return to the soil. In the case of India, crop residues are typically gathered and used for other purposes, thus breaking the normal crop residue-to-soil cycle.

Effects of Pesticides and Herbicides on Soil

The increased use of pesticides and herbicides also contributes to soil degradation. These toxic chemicals effectively sterilize the soil, killing off the bacteria and fungi that play an important part in the conversion of soil's organic matter into useable nutrients. They also kill earthworms that aerate the soil and provide for water infiltration. Bacteria and fungi also serve as a first line of defense against many plant diseases and diseases of the soil. Further, due to their persistence, the toxins in pesticides and herbicides remain active in the soil for long periods and prevent rehabilitative soil management efforts.

The toxic effects of pesticides and herbicides on bacteria, fungi, nematodes, and other soil dwelling life, could help explain the increased need for yet more pesticides to control pests. As one community of insects and animals is eliminated from the soil, others are able to take advantage of the newly created habitat, and these new arrivals may well be more harmful than the original inhabitants ever were.

Soil Salinity or Salinization and Waterlogging

Salinization and waterlogging of soils are the result of year-round agricultural irrigation and inadequate drainage. In Punjab these two processes have been accelerated with the advent of commercial wheat-rice cropping and near year-round irrigation. In the case of increased soil salinity, long periods of irrigation, followed by high temperatures, which dry the soil, will bring subsoil salts to the surface, where these accumulate as crystals in and on the surface. With adequate drainage, these salts would be washed out and would be carried away.

It has been estimated that human-induced soil salinity problems affect:

- 27 million hectares, in India.[5]
- 1.62 million hectares, in Pakistan[6]
- Nearly 1 million hectares, in Bangladesh.[7]

Rice is among the crops most affected by soil salinity, especially during the seedling and transplanting stages, and just before panicle initiation,and ends with flowering and pollination. Other crops are affected but only when soil salinity levels increase to much higher levels.

The counterpoint to soil salinity is waterlogging. Waterlogging is also caused by poor drainage, when water cannot escape or remains on the land indefinitely. In semi-arid areas, waterlogging is caused by heavy irrigation use; and canal seepage often contributes to the problem. In areas like northern Bihar, annual floodwaters that are caught outside river embankments cannot return to the river. They remain trapped until such time as the waters evaporate, which in some cases may be up to a year. In some areas, waterlogging has become a permanent condition and the land never dries out.

A development block known as Kusheshwar Asthan, in southeastern Darbhanga District, Bihar, has become permanently waterlogged as a direct consequence of the Kosi Embankment. At one time, this block was prone to severe flooding but the flood waters always receded. Now, they no longer recede. Recently the situation in Kusheshwar Asthan was described as a:

> *. . . block in Darbhanga, where the Kamla, Kosi and the Kareh converge, has . . . turned into a huge expanse of water that refuses to drain out. Boats ply in this area round the year and water hyacinth has replaced paddy. Landlords here have turned into waterlords. In keeping with the fast changing character of the land here, the government has been quick to declare the area as a bird sanctuary!* 8

Water builds up in the soil until the water table rises to the root zone. When this happens, the plants are no longer able to obtain oxygen, inhibiting plant growth or even resulting in the death of the plant. If the condition persists, and the land cannot be drained, the land must be abandoned, or designated as waterfowl preserves, for that is all they are good for.

Lester Brown reported that in the late 1980s, in a report had been prepared to ascertain the condition of India's lands. He suggested that over 39 percent of India's 329 million hectares could be classified as having been degraded.[9] Within less than 40 years, the landscape of India had changed appreciably. In 1949,

> *. . . field records of ten centuries prove that the land produces fair crops year after year without falling in fertility. A perfect balance has been reached between the manorial requirements of the corps harvested and the nature processes which recuperate fertility.*[10]

Somewhat later, G. Clarke commented:

When we examine the facts, we must put the Northern Indian cultivator down as the most economical farmer in the world as far as the utilization of the potent element of fertility, nitrogen, goes. . . . We need not concern ourselves with soil deterioration in these provinces. The present standard of fertility can be maintained indefinitely.[11]

Since the time of Howard and Clarke, much has changed, and the single most destructive change would seem to have been the adoption of the Green Revolution's improved agricultural technologies. Together, these inputs have degraded the Indian landscape to the point that Howard and Clarke would probably not recognize it. Indian cultivators have effectively sterilized their soils, robbing it of its nutrient content, subjected it to wind and water erosion, caused it to become salt-laden or waterlogged. They would be surprised at the increased levels of agricultural productivity, at least when compared with productivity at the time of Independence. Things have changed dramatically but not all for the better, especially not for the soils upon which the Indian cultivator must depend.

Overuse of Water

As a direct consequence of the Green Revolution, water has become, like most of the package of inputs, simply a commodity, one of the factors of production. When viewed as such, its overall importance in the life of Indian agriculturalists becomes debased. As a debased input, its other attributes and importance become less meaningful.

The Green Revolution has resulted in the depletion and pollution of water. Of the various inputs that make up the Green Revolution, water is potentially the most important single input. The expansion and intensification of irrigation alone would have improved agricultural production and yields, in the absence of improved seeds. With the improved seeds, however, production and yields increased even more. As a consequence, the water resources of India were exploited to their fullest and even over-exploited in many areas.

Tubewells and Pumpsets

When canal irrigation or surface water supplies were either unreliable, unavailable, or inadequate, tubewell and pumpset technologies permitted cultivators to tap groundwater reserves, resulting in groundwater supplies being drawn down. Normal recharge rates in many areas have not been sufficient to compensate for the amounts of water being withdrawn from the aquifers. This is especially true in the heartland of India's Green Revolution, Punjab.

Punjabi farmers have been sinking more and more tubewells, which has permitted them to effectively cultivate lands that would have been impossible using canal irrigation. As a function of the extensive and uncontrolled use of tubewells, in some areas, Punjab is rapidly depleting its groundwater resources. As an indicator of the demands being placed on Punjab's groundwater reserves, one need only look at the increase in the number of tubewells that have been drilled. In 1970-71, there were an estimated 128,000 tubewells in all Punjab. By 2004-05, that number had increased to well over 1.17 million, a 9-fold increase in a little over thirty years.[12]

The problem with groundwater depletion is that it is an invisible, technical problem. Unlike crops dying in the field for lack of rain, or forest or grass fires following spells of exceptionally dry weather, groundwater depletion is not immediately apparent. It is recognizable only when wells must be drilled deeper and deeper to maintain adequate water flows.

Groundwater depletion is a simple problem with a very difficult solution. It is simple in the sense that we know the cause: over exploitation and inadequate aquifer recharge rates. It has been suggested that the recharge rate in Punjab is running one-third behind the amount needed to maintain constant water levels, and as a consequence, over a third of Punjab groundwater levels are falling by over 18 to 30 cm a year.[13] In the remainder of the state, in those areas that are predominately irrigated by canal water, the water table is rising. See Map 8-1, below.

If the aquifers of central Punjab are not permitted to recharge, agriculture based on irrigation in Punjab will not be sustainable. It is a simplo equation – the amount of groundwater removed via tubewells must be balanced by an equal amount of recharge water.

Map 8-1: Changing Water Levels/Waterlogging and Salinization, Punjab

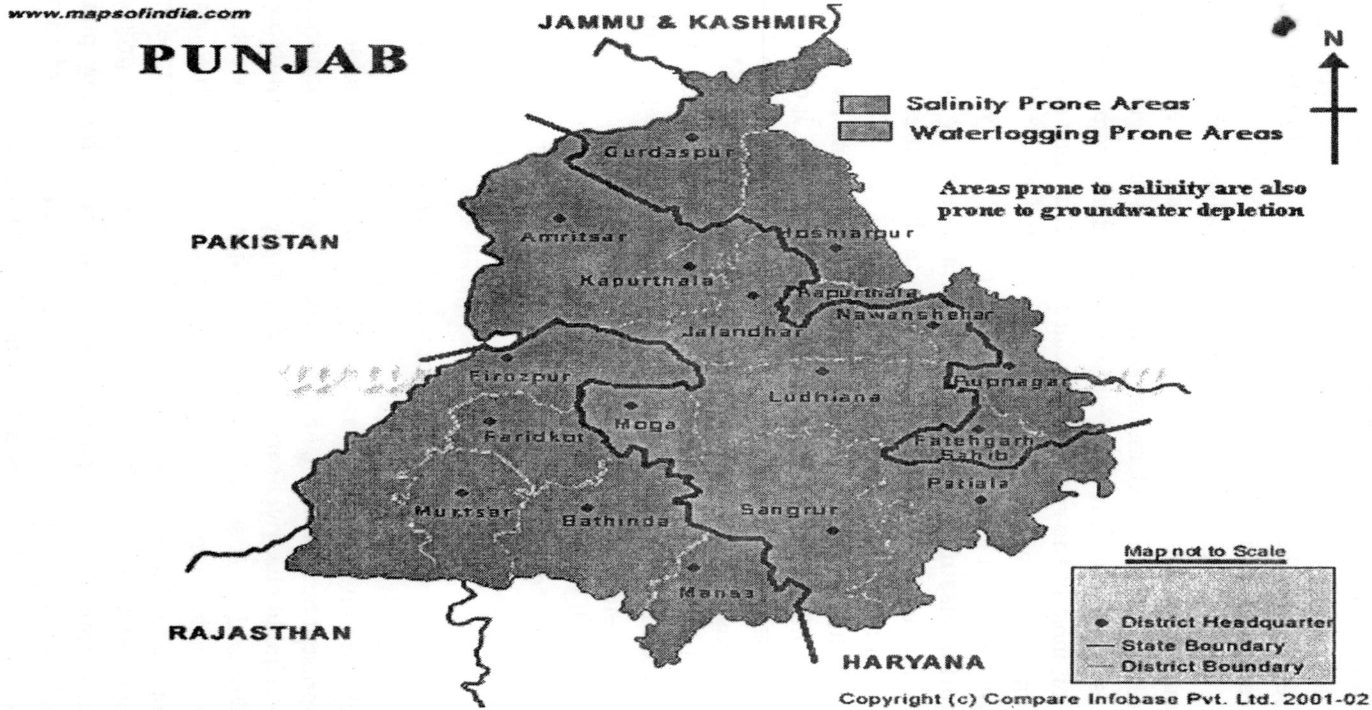

Source: After (Yadev, et. al., 2000c)

At the current rate of extraction, the aquifers under Punjab could be depleted by the year 2025, in which case Punjabi agriculture will essentially cease to exist, or will be so restricted that India's breadbasket could well become a food deficit area.

It has been suggested that surplus surface water be injection pumped into the aquifer to assist in the aquifer's recharge. There are two logistical problems associated with this proposal. First, where does one find surplus surface water in arid and semi-arid Punjab, when most of the rivers are so controlled that they are little more than streams of water in the center of what used to be bona fide river channels? Second, the injection of surface water into the aquifer, assuming that it had efficacy, simply represents a guaranteed way to further contaminate the aquifer with surface contaminants.

Further, with the control and pernicious misuse of surface water and the depletion of groundwater resources, it can only lead to the desertification of Punjab. Other areas, like Haryana, Gujarat, and Rajasthan are also observing similar water resource depletions. Likewise, Pakistan is finding its water resources are becoming depleted for the same reasons. In some areas, Pakistan's aquifers have subsided by a much as 3 meters a year.[14]

Each year tubewells must be driven further and further into the aquifer to sustain the need for irrigation water. As the wells are driven deeper, a change in pumping technology becomes necessary. Centrifugal pumpsets, that had worked so well for decades, are becoming useless. They are incapable of pumping water from depths that are now often greater than 125 feet (± 40 meters). Now, submersible pumps are required. The new submersible pumps represent an additional, high expense investment and require access to reliable electrical service. Together, these two requirements – increased expense and electric availability – place some cultivators in a disadvantageous position. They either do not have the resources to procure the new pumps or they do not have access to electrical power at their well sites. Again, only the larger, more prosperous cultivators are in a position to benefit from the new pumping technology, and it will permit them to continue cultivation, while the smaller cultivators will be unable to compete.

New pump technology will also permit the remaining farmers to draw down the water table even further. In time, it will be drawn down to the point where not even the larger cultivators will have access to groundwater for their crops. In which case, farmers will be forced to abandon tubewell irrigation all together. Current pumping and irrigation practices threaten the very existence and sustainability of agriculture.

Assured irrigation, first in the form of canal irrigation, then supplemented with pumpsets, and now complemented by tubewell irrigation, contributed heavily to the agricultural successes of the Green Revolution. Now, that very success threatens to destroy agriculture in many areas, for without water, the Green Revolution cannot continue, and there is the real possibility that no agriculture will be possible in some of the most productive areas. Therefore, success has been its own worst enemy.

India's grain harvest, squeezed both by water scarcity and the loss of cropland to non-farm uses, has plateaued since 2000. A 2005 World Bank study reports that 15 percent of India's food supply is produced by mining groundwater. Stated otherwise, 175 million Indians are fed with grain produced with water from irrigation wells that will soon go dry.[15]

The groundwater depletion problem was recognized, but in many areas it was almost too late. To avoid the total collapse of agriculture, the Government of India and the Government of Punjab have pressed for agricultural diversification – especially for the production of crops that require substantially less water than most current commercial crops, like wheat and rice. However, the economic success of many farmers has been a function of leaving traditional diversified cultivation behind and becoming agricultural specialists. As specialized farmers, commercial farmers, these cultivators' incomes increased markedly. Now the government wants them to return to essentially subsistence cultivation without the benefit of government support or assistance. The alternative is self-destructive, for both agriculture and the agriculturalists, but it is difficult for successful farmers to simply step back in time, to a simpler way of life, and find themselves facing the real possibility of poverty and hunger all over again. There are many cultivators, many retired now, that experienced life before the Green Revolution, benefited from it, and may now be forced to give it all up. Further, the size of one's landholdings may not give any cultivator an advantage, if a solution to the water problem does not materialize. Without reliable water supplies, the specter of famine may once again become a reality.

Environmental Contamination

In comparative and absolute terms, India has gone from one of the lowest consumers of chemical fertilizers per hectare of arable land to one of the largest. As early as 1998, India became the third largest consumer of chemical fertilizers in the world, after China and the United States. It has been suggested that one-half of all the increases in grain production during the 1970s and 1980s – the primary period for the Green Revolution — was the result of increased fertilizer use.

Until 2004,fertilizer consumption outstripped domestic production, and India was forced to import chemical fertilizers, much of it coming from the United States. Gradually, under pressure and

Figure 8-2: Fertilizer Use kg/ha, India, 1961- 1995

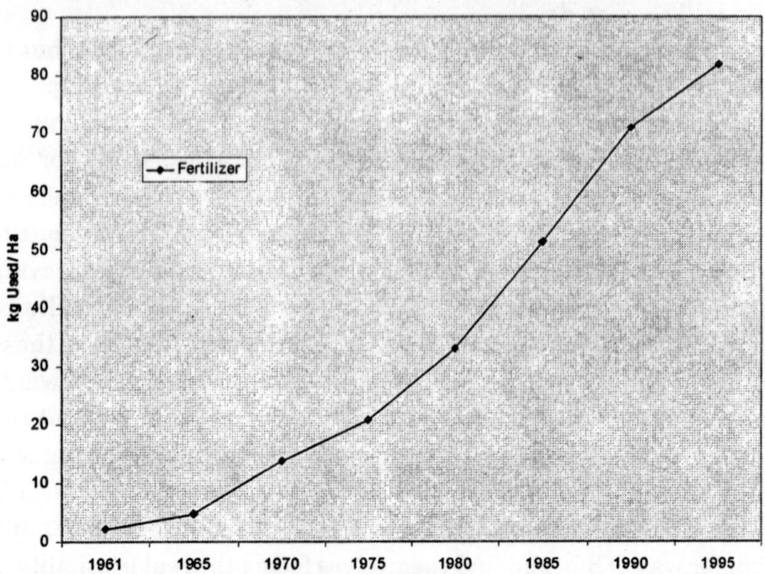

Source: (Food and Agricultural Organization of the United Nation (FAO), 2006)

support from the central government, domestic production of fertilizers increased rapidly. This production began to reduce India's dependence upon foreign imports. Each year the gap between production and consumption grew smaller and smaller. In December 2006, the Government of India announced that fertilizer production had exceeded consumption for the first time.[16]

Increased consumption was stimulated by a number of factors, most important of which were the Intensive Agricultural District Programme; the High-Yielding Varieties Programme; and the development of more and more high-yielding varieties of wheat and rice.

The primary thrust of most of these development programs' extension work has been directed toward the adoption of nitrogenous fertilizers because these have the greatest impact on yields for the investment costs. While both *desi* and high-yielding varieties responded to the application of fertilizer in the beginning, it was soon observed that yields were not keeping pace with increased fertilizer applications. Ultimately it was observed that yields were actually declining. The combined interplay of agricultural intensification, increased use of fertilizers, and highly demanding fertilizer-responsive, high-yielding varieties had depleted many of the micro-nutrients and trace elements, such as zinc, as well as

Table 8-1: Fertilizer Consumption versus Food grain Production, India, 1961-98

	Fertilizer Consumption		*Food grain Production*	
Year	*Tons (000,000)*	*kg/ha*	*Tons (000,000)*	*kg/ha*
1951-52	0.07	0.6	52	536
1961-62	0.34	2.2	82.7	705
1971-72	2.7	16.2	105.2	858
1981-82	6.1	34.3	133.3	1,032
1991-92	12.7	69.8	168.4	1,382
1995-96	13.9	74.4	185.1	1,499
1996-97	14.3	76.9	198.2	1,605
1997-98	15.	84.3	199.1	1,613

Source: Statpub.com (2004).

phosphorous and potash.[17] In response, phosphate and potash imports were increased. Gradually, the crops began to respond, with yields bouncing back and then again increasing.

One side effect of increased fertilizer usage is the increasing amounts of fertilizer that do not reach crops. Substantial quantities of fertilizers are leached out of the soil, contaminating ground water supplies, as well as run-off from the fields, ending up in rivers, creeks, streams, lakes, ponds and tanks. These, in turn, serve to feed algal and weed growth. The growth of algae, especially in lakes, ponds, and tanks, results in significant decreases in soluble oxygen. In especially severe circumstances, fish and other fresh water animal life can suffocate and die off, producing an environmental hazard for humans and animal life alike.

Agricultural development in India is no longer simply a matter of surrendering traditional farming methods. Cultivators no longer base their agricultural decisions on what tradition has taught them, generation after generation.[18] In the mid-1970s, it might have been said that Indian cultivators had some understanding of the basic principles and advantages of chemical fertilizer application, along with the benefits of other agricultural inputs and improved practices. This is no longer the case. Today's cultivator has become increasingly knowledgeable about the cultivation process, from planting through marketing.

For many, the only real obstacle to the adoption of fertilizers lies in their ability to obtain these inputs at reasonable prices. For the vast majority of cultivators, the application of fertilizer is no longer simply buying a sack of "ANS," "NPK," or Harabahar, and spreading it on their fields. It has become a science. In fact, knowledge of fertilizers, their characteristics, application rates, and benefits from one crop to another and from one piece of land to another, results in heated discussions among cultivators. It is not uncommon to hear cultivators discussing the relative merits of various nitrogen and phosphate mixtures, or various "brand name" fertilizers and their effects on yields.

The Indian cultivator is no longer constrained by tradition, and it is unwise for Westerners to perceive cultivators, even in comparatively isolated villages, as "out of touch." It is easy, or even enticing, to conceive of cultivators as being largely village-bound.

Nothing could be further from the truth. Indians have had, for generations, a custom very similar to the Australian "walk about." Using every means of conveyance, or just walking, it is not uncommon for a cultivator from one region of India to be found hundreds of miles from home, just for the sake of the experience. These journeys expose them to new ideas and ways of doing things, and upon coming home they share their adventures, tales, and information about "what other cultivators are doing." Indian cultivators are no longer quaint, uninitiated farmers. No matter their land ownership status, they have grown into savvy tillers of the soil. Agriculture may not be a business for them, at least not in the sense of the agri-businesses in many Western societies, but they are not that detached from the soil, since their very day-to-day existence depends on what they grow on their plots of land. For this reason, their decisions must be even more precise. There is no local safety net on which to fall back.

Chemical Pesticides

The high-yielding seed varieties introduced and later modified in India are susceptive to a variety of diseases, blights, and pests. Chemical pesticides represent the most efficient, versatile, and effective method for the control of these pests.

Chemical control of agricultural pests was virtually unknown in India until the mid-1960s, although the use of DDT, as part of India's extensive anti-malaria program, was common as early as the mid-1940s. Widespread use of DDT in India, and in most developing countries, was because of its comparatively low cost, ease of use and ease of storage and transportation. In addition, there were no equally effective, economical substitutes of DDT at the time.

Other pesticides, like BHC (Benzene Hexachloride) powder, Eldrin, Aldrin, Parathion, Malathion, Lindane, Chlordane (to mention but a few of literally hundreds) are generally more expensive to produce, more difficult to store and transport, and more difficult to use than DDT. Nevertheless over time DDT was discovered to have an ecological downside, and its use declined gradually. Other pesticides came to replace DDT for many purposes, but these pesticides, too, had their shortcomings. The new pesticides

Figure 8-3: Consumption of Pesticides, India, 1966 – 2001

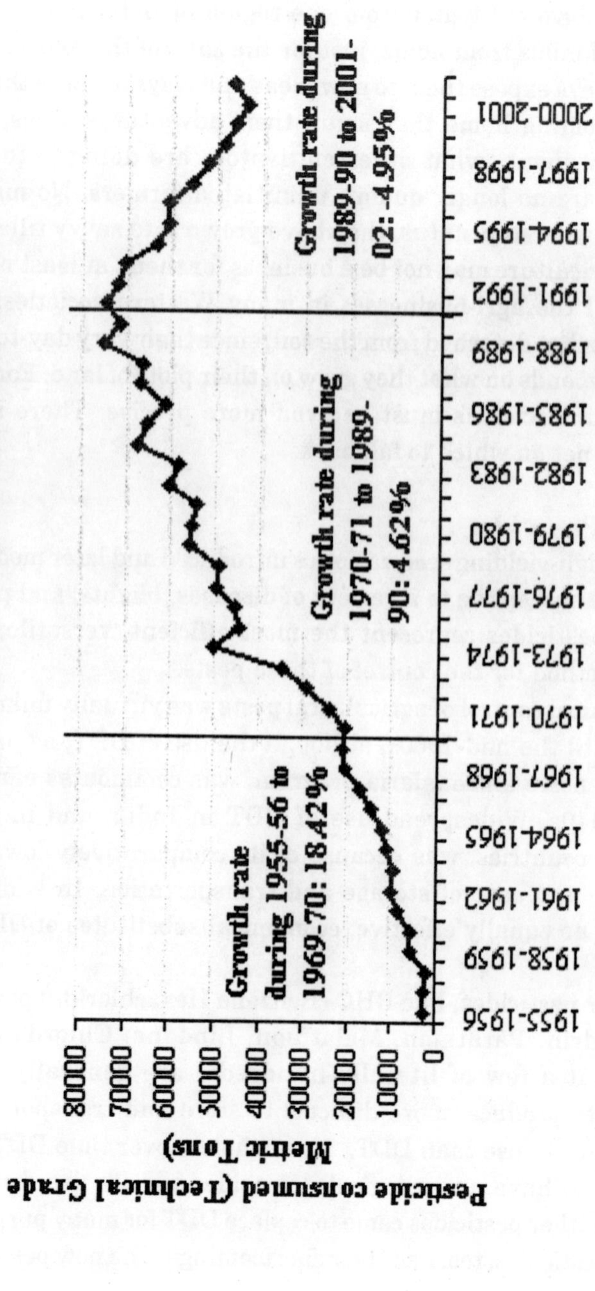

Source: (Krishna, Vijesh V., N.G. Byju , and S. Tamizheniyan, 2007).

are the Indian cultivators' only defense against certain pests. Without these pesticides, they would not be capable of protecting their crops or increasing productivity.

Realizing the fundamental importance of pesticides, as well as the benefits derived from producing them domestically, the Indian government responded by sponsoring the construction of production facilities in many parts of the country. Of the more than twenty pesticides commonly used throughout India, at least sixteen are now manufactured almost exclusively domestically. While the government has been instrumental in the establishment of production facilities, it has seen fit to allow questions of production and marketing to be answered by the private manufacturers and to allow a modified free enterprise approach to marketing.

As the cropping patterns became more intensive, the use of pesticides also increased. Consumption of insecticide in agriculture increased more than 100% from 1971 to 1994-96. Insecticide consumption in India, which was approximately 22,013 tonnes, increased to 61,766 tonnes by 1994-96. Consumption of all of these pesticides between 1971 and 1996 increased more than two hundred percent — from 24,306 tonnes to 61,367 tonnes.[19]

Despite their recognized beneficial aspects, pesticides also represent significant ecological and biological dangers. These dangers are magnified by the fact that the majority of cultivators using these pesticides do so without the counsel of agricultural extension officers and without the knowledge of the potential hazards associated with their use. Many of the cultivators cannot conceive of the potential environmental and health problems that may result from the use of these chemicals. The control of pesticides would, at best, be extremely difficult and, at worst, impossible without curtailing their useful qualities. In the short run, the Indian government chose to place a higher priority on the need for increased food production than on the "potential" dangers imposed by the widespread use of these toxic chemicals. It was held that "when" domestic food production met domestic food requirements, then the environmental and biological implications of chemical pesticides could be reexamined.

While there are no real substitutes for synthetic pesticides, their consumption began to decrease in the mid-1990s. This decrease stemmed from the feeling that there were environmental problems associated with their use and misuse by cultivators, issues and concerns surrounding the safe storage of these products and the emergence of definable human and ecological impacts.

As witnessed by Illustration 8-1, the safe handling and storage of pesticides is a serious concern. Not only do cultivators frequently not protect themselves from exposure to these potentially harmful products such storage provides, nay, begs for the escape of these products into the environment. They can enter the bio-sphere either as air-borne particulates, as residue on the users' clothing, which falls to the ground, as spillage, when the products are transported into and out of the storage facility and in the field prior to or following application. The mishandling and storage of such products provides ampleopportunity for these products to get into the environment.

Illustration 8-1: Pesticide Storage Somewhere in Punjab

Problems with Pesticides

By the time food sufficiency was achieved, much of the potential damage caused by pesticides had already been set in motion. Most pesticides belong to a group of synthetic chemicals, commonly referred to as POPs – Persistent Organic Pollutants. POPs release toxic substances into the environment. They are very stable and long-lived, and build up in the food chain. They are lipophilic — they accumulate in the fatty tissues of living things. Once they enter the body of an animal or human, they simply are never rejected or eliminated. As we age, the concentration of POPs in our bodies increases and, with the increased concentrations, their potential effects on health become potentially more serious. They are also semi-volatile, which means they can remain on or in the ground for years, and then end up in the food chain.

India is one of the largest users of pesticides, and currently has large stockpiles of many products that include POPs. It is one of only three remaining manufacturers of DDT.[20]

Additionally, India exports more than 800,000 kg of POP pesticides, including Aldrin, DDT, BHC and chlordane to many other countries. Despite the fact that many pesticides are banned from production in India, many are still being produced and exported. Some banned pesticides are still readily available in markets in both Pakistan and India.[21]

Concern over worldwide pesticide use prompted the United Nations Environmental Programme and the World Health Organization to publish their report entitled: *Public Health Impact of Pesticides Used in Agriculture*.[22] In 2003, it was estimated that 355,000 people, worldwide, died due to unintentional pesticide poisonings.[23] More recently, distraught cultivators, especially in India, have begun committing suicide using pesticides.[24] It has been suggested that restricting pesticide availability would curtail suicide-by-pesticides; however, it has been observed that the truly suicidal will alter their choice of method of suicide to meet their circumstances. Therefore, restricting the availability of pesticides will only have the effect of making pesticides more difficult to obtain for legitimate purposes.

While there have been repeated assertions about the potential for environmental and human problems associated with pesticides,

Map 8-2: Deaths from Unintentional Poisonings

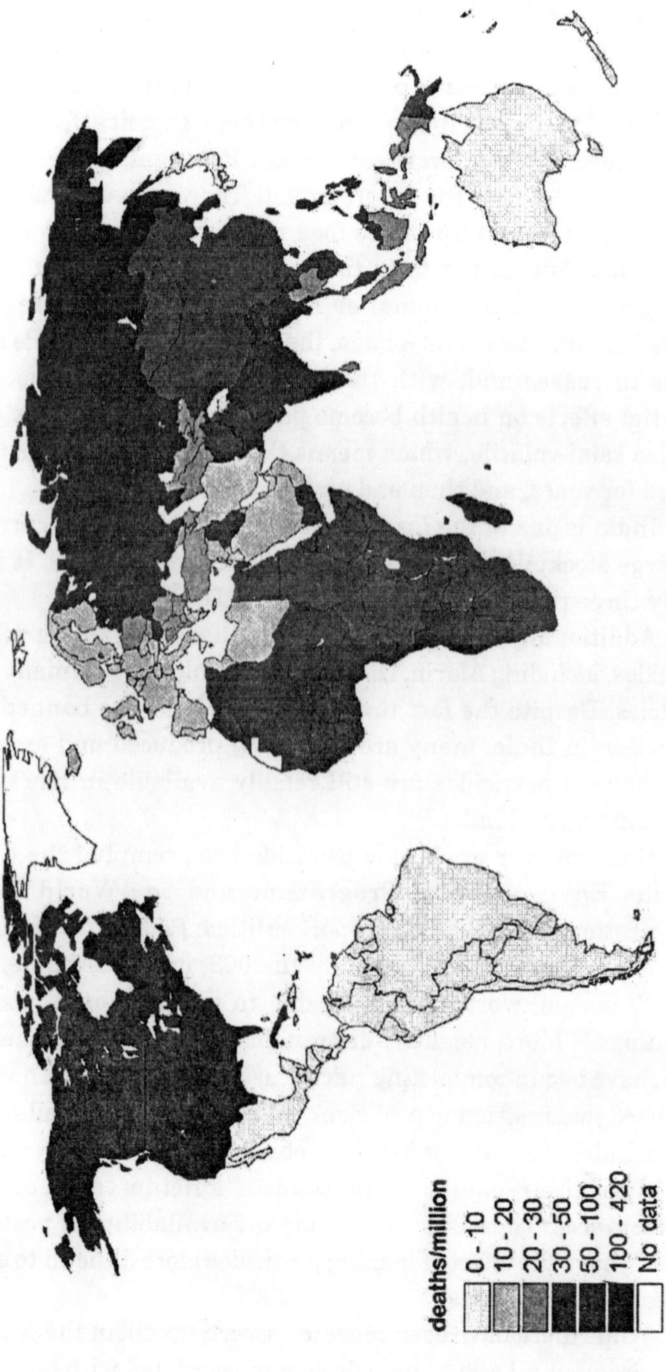

Source: Adapted and modified from (WHO, Toxic Hazards, 2008).

it was not until the "Coke" and "Pepsi" scandals in late 2003 that the issues of POPs and pesticide use were brought to the public forum.[25] It had been alleged for some time that pesticides had polluted the water sources used by beverage producers.

Coke® and Pepsi®

The Centre for Science and Environment (CSE), an Indian NGO, issued a report based its analyses of more than 50 Coke® and Pepsi® samples from around the country. Among more than a dozen alarming findings, the follow were among the worst:

(1) A cocktail of three to six pesticides was found in all samples.

(2) The average amount of pesticide residues found in all samples was 11.86 ppb, which is 23 times higher than the BIS standards for total pesticides in soft drinks (0.6 ppb).[26]

For years the CSE has issued warnings of potentially serious dangers to human beings and animals from the indiscriminate use of pesticides in agriculture and vector control. CSE was already aware of the assertion that at least a third of all known pesticide poisonings, including suicides, were reported in India, annually.

It was not until the revelation by CSE that samples of Coke® and Pepsi® had been tested in its laboratories, and had shown the presence of the commonly-used pesticides far in excess of permissible limits, that both the government and the people were stirred to action.

For some, there were signs that the charges of pesticides and other contaminants in Coke® and Pepsi® leveled by the CSE may not be as easily dismissed as had been done in the past. The controversy provoked the government's Bureau of Indian Standards (BIS) to announce that it would raise the standards for drinking water and water used in the food processing industry, bringing them in line with those set by the European Union, effective sometime in 2004.

Nearly three years later, the CSE reported that more recent samples of Coca-Cola® and Pepsi® products show even greater levels of pesticides than its 2003 study had.

CSE Director Sunita Narain told journalists in Delhi that samples from 12 states showed that Pepsi products contained 30 times more pesticides than found in 2003.[27]

Representatives for Coke® and Pepsi® rejected this claim. In December 2003 Coca-Cola and Pepsico took CSE to court over their original report and findings but ultimately they refused to litigate. Earlier, in August, the Supreme Court had refused to hear the soft drink manufacturers' petitions against CSE's report. Further, the GoI confirmed that pesticide residues existed in the soft drinks.[28]

So, how did these pollutants end up in Coke® and Pepsi® bottles? Pesticides are often washed off and become part of agricultural runoff, and ultimately end up in local rivers, lakes or tanks.Or, they may percolate through the soil to lower strata, and, eventually, into the ground water supply or aquifers. The sources of "potable" water used by these large bottling companies come from rivers and groundwater sources that have been subjected to years of poisoning by agriculturalists, often, many miles away.

It has been said that up to 90 percent of the pesticides applied to crops and croplands never reach their intended targets.[29] Instead, they end up in humans beings, who are at the top of the food chain (and to lesser degrees in the animal life below). Therefore, there is more than an ample amount of pesticide residue left after spraying a crop or the soil to make its way into the food chain, with the potential for causing harm. For every kg of pesticide sold, 900 grams make their way into the ecosystem, potentially causing biological harm to every living thing.

In 2006, blood samples were taken from a number of villagers in Punjab.[30] Two things were certain after analyzing these samples. First, every sample showed signs of HCH, also known as BHC. Second, other pesticides showed up in varying levels in every sample. The highest concentrations of pesticides in the samples were for those that have been in use the longest. This is logical, but what of the second and third generations of pesticides that have come into the market, or are about to come on the market? What will their short- and long-term legacies be?

Although the samples were taken from among villages in predominately cotton-producing areas in Punjab, areas long known for their heavy use of pesticides, it is probably safe to say that, since pesticide use has been fairly widespread throughout all of India for over four decades, everyone living in rural areas has been exposed and has accumulated sizeable amounts of pesticide residue in their tissues. Science is uncertain about the long-term effects of pesticides in humans. Science does not seem to know what levels of pesticides are tolerable and what levels trigger health problems.

Various governments and world health organizations have either banned or deemed it necessary to warn its citizens that pesticides pose a significant threat to human health. Most are still available, either on the black market or from the local seed store, or cooperative. Needless to say, much more research must be undertaken to set tolerable exposure levels, accumulation levels, and links to diseases. Without this kind of information, cultivators are dabbling with disaster, perhaps for themselves, or perhaps for future generations.Pesticides may well insure and protect the crops that cultivators sow now, but the long-term effects of those pesticides live long after the harvest has been consumed, both by humans and other animals, as well as poisoning the soil.

The public and scientific literature is replete with stories and studies having to do with health problems associated with the tertiary life cycle of pesticides. It is unfortunate that under certain circumstances there may be no alternative to their use. It is unfortunate that for a necessary short-term gain, a long-term legacy is bequeathed to generations to come. Such is the situation with pesticides in India. There may simply have been no legitimate alternative to pesticide use to insure sufficient food supplies but the price to be paid by future generations may well outweigh the satisfaction of a full stomach today.

Declining Biodiversity

One of the primary outcomes of the Green Revolution has been a very strong trend toward what is called mono-cropping or monoculture. Both terms represent the same idea — the planting of only a single crop. This has been the signature approach to agriculture in virtually all commercialized agricultures. Although monoculture often results in soil erosion or soil degradation, its most profound effect is on biodiversity.

Many different species are disappearing from the planet, being replaced by crops that are genetically uniform and have large yields. India once cultivated over 30,000 different varieties of rice, but today over 75% of production comes from fewer than 10 varieties.[31]

The FAO has warned that the large scale loss of plant genetic diversity, which contributes to the erosion of agricultural biodiversity: The spread of modern commercial agriculture and the introduction of new varieties of crops are the main causes of the loss of genetic diversity.[32]

Why Should we be Concerned with Biodiversity?

Our concern for biodiversity has both a philosophical and a pragmatic basis. Philosophically, biodiversity is worth protecting regardless of its value to humans, because it is intrinsically valuable. All species have the inherent right to survive. Humans are a part of the tapestry of Nature but we have the capacity to protect or destroy it. Practically, in the process of destroying Nature, we will put ourselves at risk. Therefore, we have a philosophical and a practical basis for ensuring the biodiversity of the planet.

Raup has suggested that, *the flora and fauna that form today's biodiversity are but a microscopic remnant of all the life forms that have inhabited the Earth over the last 3.8 billion years and may represent just 0.1% of all the species that have ever lived. Thus, 99.9% of all the life that has existed on Earth is now extinct.*[33]

As the only species capable of destroying the planet, we have an obligation to try to protect every surviving species that occupies it. We are left with a fraction of all the life forms that have ever occupied the planet. Virtually every species that is now going extinct is doing so because of human activity and not because of any other natural process. The maintenance of Earth's biodiversity is essentially maintaining life on Earth, as we know it. Its maintenance, its conservation is a prerequisite for sustainable development and, for this reason, it constitutes one of the greatest challenges of our time.[34]

The Green Revolution's Impact on Biodiversity

The inception of the Green Revolution was the beginning of one of the greatest environmental disasters in human history. It has quietly and systematically been an attack on agricultural biodiversity. In the process of its implementation, Mankind has lost literally thousands of plant species, all within the span of 60 years.

This loss of genetic diversity results from the cumulative effect of:

(1) the replacement of local crop varieties, which have developed over centuries or millennia, and have been adapted to a variety of local micro-ecological niches, by improved seed varieties; and

(2) the improved seed varieties, in general, that come from a very limited genetic base.

Most of the current HYV wheats can trace their genealogy back to Japanese Norin or Gaines Wheat, developed by Dr. Orville Vogel.[35] The same is essentially true for HYVs of rice and many other crops, like maize, etc. In many areas, improved seeds have replaced local varieties completely, and they have become the sole seed source for large areas, thus, eliminating the diversity of native crops and agricultural systems.

Narrow genetic genealogies pose the potential for catastrophic consequences in the event of unanticipated or new blights or diseases. In a monoculture situation, a new blight or disease could potentially wipe out an entire crop on a regional basis, for what effects one plant is likely to affect all the rest. Where there is genetic diversity, some plants may be wiped out but others will survive. Thus, diversity ensures survivability.

For example, during 1977-78, a rust epidemic struck Pakistan's hybrid wheats. Total wheat production dropped by 9 percent for that year, a production decline of slightly more than 700,000 tons.[36] Obviously, this was a limited outbreak but had it expanded further, it could have devastated Pakistan's long-standing wheat surplus production program.

Although many of the improved seed varieties have been developed to resist insect infestations, diseases, and environmental stress, these same qualities make them vulnerable to the unanticipated. Further, many of these seed varieties were developed elsewhere and introduced to similar but not identical environments. As a consequence, many of the new varieties are more vulnerable to local pests and diseases, for which they were not bred.[37]

At least in part, this helps to explain why it has been necessary to continue the hybridization process. In fact, in India alone, more than 640 new varieties of rice have been developed since 1965 to combat regional pest complexes and ecological niches, with even more currently in development.[38] While the development of these new varieties has been in response to the varied nature of the Indian environment and potentially improves production and yields, it has a definite downside. They need to be replaced regularly. Although the new seeds do not entail cultivator retraining to use them, they must continually repurchase and replace them. Unlike local seed varieties that had been cultivated, oftentimes for centuries, and a portion of one season's crop could be used for seed the next season, the new seeds require replacement each year. The older, local varieties then, were more economical and durable. They had evolved within a particular setting and, over time, they typically had built up resistance to local pests and diseases. Such is not the case with the new improved varieties.

Shiva succinctly observed the potential for improved seed when she wrote:

. . . *the destruction of diversity and the creation of uniformity simultaneously involves the destruction of stability and the creation of vulnerability.*[39]

Furthermore, the local varieties may possess traits that agronomists could use to improve existing crops. If these local varieties are permitted to disappear completely, there is no back-up or reserve to reestablish a tenable agricultural base, in the event of a catastrophic loss of even some of the new hybrids. For example, some of the local varieties may be resistant to drought or flooding. These traits could be harvested by plant breeders and incorporated into a new generation of crop varieties. If they disappear, however, those potentially valuable traits would be lost to science. This loss of plant diversity could result in the loss of potentially useful genetic material for future green and gene revolutions.

Wisely, agronomists have begun harvesting and storing 'archaic' seed varieties in seed banks. However, their efforts were begun well after thousands of varieties had been already lost to mankind. Those that have been lost simply can never be recovered. Seed banks also are not without their problems. As with most of man's creations, storage facilities and their contents can be lost to fire, natural disasters, power failures, or unintentional disposal.In which case, seeds that had been so arduously collected, cataloged, and stored could be destroyed or lost.Further, research has already shown that when local seed varieties have been reintroduced to their native environments, they frequently do no perform as well as they once had. Over time their native environments will have changed and the seeds will have not kept pace or continued to evolve with it. The stored seed then becomes just another variety and is only useful for genetic harvesting.

Although there are numerous seed banks around the world (FAO estimates their number to be approximately 1,400), three stand out – the International Plant Genetic Resource Institute, the Food and Agricultural Organization of the United Nations, and the U. S. Government.[40] Although the storage of collected and processed seeds are species specific, in general, seeds are dried to a moisture content below 7%, sealed in a moisture proof containers, and stored at a temperature of -18 degrees Celsius. The success of the preservation technique depends on constant monitoring and the regeneration and/or recollection when conditions fall below an acceptable level.

Also part of seed-banking is documentation. Proper documentation is necessary for the cataloging and storage of the collected seed. Without proper documentation, the collections are not very useful to researchers and plant improvement programs. The minimal information required for the seed collections to become useful are: taxonomic identification and status, the location and nature of the population from which the sample was taken, details of the collection procedure, and information on intermediate storage conditions prior to the seeds' deposit in the seed bank.

In addition to threats posed by damage or destruction, the collections face several other challenges. Certain wild species are not readily preserved in seed banks using current methodologies and techniques.Therefore, the conservation of these species becomes a difficult task. The absence of comprehensive data and the inability to quickly and easily access information often results in the duplication of conservation efforts or uneven conservation among species. Information problems also results in the failure to preserve samples, when it is believed similar samples have already been preserved, when in fact, they have not. Although data collection and information transfers and technologies are governed by the Convention of Biological Diversity, these conventions need to be standardized between participating seed banks worldwide. A universally integrated system and database is essential to conservation and preservation efforts, if for no other reason than knowing what and where samples are being stored.Therefore, a platform and compatible database system is crucial.

One recent development in the seed bank saga is the creation of what has become known as the 'Doomsday Seed Vault' in the Arctic. The Bill and Melinda Gates Foundation and several other organizations have invested millions of dollars in the construction of the vault, officially named the Svalbard Global Seed Vault, which was built on the island of Spitsbergen in the Svalbard Island group.[41] The Doomsday Seed Vault opened its doors on February 26, 2008, accepting its first shipment of seeds.[42] It is estimated that there are currently 6 million plant accessions scattered around the world in various seed banks. The new Doomsday Seed Vault is expected to have a 2 to 6 million plant capacity.[43]

The list of sponsors of the Svalbard Global Seed Vault – in addition to the Gates Foundation — include the Rockefeller Foundation, Monsanto Corporation, and Syngenta, among others, reading like a who's who of global GMO corporations. Why would these global GMO corporations fund such a venture? What is to be gained? The answer lies in the function of the Vault.

Plant breeders and researchers will be the major users of the bank's inventory. Today, the largest plant breeders are Monsanto, DuPont, Syngenta and Dow Chemical, each in its own right a major player in global GMO. Since 2007 Monsanto has held the world patent rights, together with the United States Government, for the plant trait referred to as the 'Terminator' or Genetic Use Restriction Technology (GURT).GURT is a genetic technology that causes commercial seed to become self-sterilizing after one harvest. Although Monsanto owns the patent rights to this technology, it will surely share it, through licensing agreements, with other GMOs, such as DuPont/Pioneer Hi-Bred, one of the world's largest owners of patented genetically-modified plant seeds and related agrichemicals.

It is not until one looks at all interconnections between the Rockefeller Foundation and most of the leading GMOs that support for the Vault really begins to make sense. The Rockefeller Foundation was instrumental in the Green Revolution, with its participation in the CIMMYT and IRRI. Further, it spearheaded the introduction of Borlaug's plant-breeding successes to India and Pakistan, and the introduction of the Western agricultural/agri-business paradigm, with its emphasis on fertilizers, pesticides, and herbicides.

CGIAR, another participant in the Vault project, was set up in 1972 by the Rockefeller Foundation and Ford Foundation to spread their Green Revolution agribusiness model. CGIAR's expressed purpose is to coordinate and disseminate agricultural research, and as such, it tends to serve as a camouflaged representative of its sponsors – the leading GMOs.

The diversity stored in seed gene banks around the world represents the basic raw material for plant breeding and for a great deal of basic biological research. Consolidation of 2 million or more plant seed samples in one place, and especially those classified as 'distinct species,' would represent a plant breeder's paradise. Annually, hundreds of thousands of samples from the world's seed banks are released for biological and genetic research. For this reason, it is in the best interests of these large GMOs to sponsor the Vault. It simply concentrates and streamlines individual and collective plant breeding research efforts. It will also concentrate a large share of the world's plant variety under the control of its governing board, with ability to control the availability of plant species, even in the event of an agricultural/environmental catastrophe. It places the sponsors of the project and its governing board in an incredible position of power and control.

References

1. (BC Museum, 2008).
2. (Lickacz, J., and D. Penny, 2001).
3. Tilth is the state of aggregation of a soil especially in relation to its suitability for crop growth . It also represents the degree of fineness of soil particles in the topmost soil layer.
4. (Lickacz, J., and D. Penny, 2001).
5. (Postel, Sandra, December 1989), p. 8. Postel suggests that yields have been reduced on 20 million hectares and an additional 7 million hectares have had to be abandoned.
6. (Reuters, 2000).

7. (CGIAR, 2008), mostly in the coastal areas in what is known as the Sundarbans; although salt-laden river water coming out of India also contaminates the banks of the rivers as they run through Bangladesh.
8. (Karunakaran, 2004).
9. (Brown, Lester R., 1988), p. 21.
10. As quoted by (Fitzgerald-Moore, P. and B. J. Parai, 1997?), p. 6, from (Howard, Alfred, 1949), p. 183, and (Shiva, 1991), p. 103.
11. As quoted by (Fitzgerald-Moore, P. and B. J. Parai, 1997?), fromC. G. Clarke from M. K. Gandhi, p. 83, and (Shiva, 1991), p. 103.
12. (Nidhi, Batta, ca. 2006).
13. See, (RFPD, 2007),original source for RFPD is WorldWatch. See also, (Yadev, et. al., 2000c) and (Mahapatra, Richard, 1999).
14. (USAID, 2007) suggests that, *"the rate at which groundwater is extracted in India is more than twice the rate of recharge, with some water tables now falling by one to three meters per year. As a result, India could lose 25% or more of its current crop production during the next 25 years due to unsustainable aquifer usage rates."* See also, (Majeed, 4 April 2005). Dr. Majeed is the Head of the Water Programme, IUCN Pakistan. He states: *"Many areas / sub-basins show the rate of groundwater table decline from 1 to 3 meters per year,"* page 1 of his Pilot Demonstration Activity Request Form.
15. (Brown, Lester R., 2008).
16. See, (StatPub.com, 2004).
17. (FAI/ICAR, 1974).
18. (Schultz, Theodore W., 1964), p. 3.
19. <www.indiastat.com> is an excellent source for information on a variety of subjects relating to India and her various economic sectors.
20. Mexico and China are the other two manufacturers of DDT.
21. (Sanghi, 2001), p. 66.
22. (WHO, Public Health Impact of Pesticides Used in Agriculture, 1990). See also, (WHO, Toxic Hazards, 2008).
23. (WHO, The world health report 2003 – shaping the future, 2003).
24. See for example, (Alex, R., J. Prasad, A. Kuruvilla and K. S. Jacob, 2007), (Bertolote, José M., et. al., 2006), (Front Line, 2005), (Sengupta, 2006), (WHO, Pesticides are a leading suicide method, 2006), and (Gunnell, David and Michael Eddleston, 2003).

25. The internet has numerous references to the Coke and Pepsi scandal and what was done as a consequence. Search for Coke or Pepsi, India.
26. See, (Banerjee, 2006); (Mathur, H. G., H. C. Agarwal, Sapna Johnson, and Mirmali Saikia, March 2005), village blood sample report; and (Mathur, H. G., Sapna Johnson, and Avinash Kumar, August 5, 2003), the latter source is to the CSE's actual 2003 report, which is available as a PDF download at: <http://www.cseindia.org/misc/cola-indepth/cola2006/pdf/labreport2003.pdf>.
27. (Kannan, 2008). The 2006 CSE follow up report will be available as a PDF download in the near future. Check the CSE on-line homepage at: < http://www.cseindia.org/>. See also, (Balaji, 2008).
28. (CSE Press Releases, 2003a), (CSE Press Releases, 2003b), and (CSE Press Releases, 2003c).
29. (Royal B. C. Museum, 2006). Data on fertilizer sales show a large regional variation in the use of nutrients. NPK use varies from less than 60 kg/ha in Assam, Orissa, and Madhya Pradesh (mostly rain fed areas) to more than 140 kg/ha in Punjab, Andhra Pradesh, and Haryana (irrigated land). A report on the cost of cultivation of principal crops in 2000 notes a heavy use of pesticides in rice cultivation in Punjab and Andhra Pradesh but very little in other states. Mechanization of agricultural operations is prevalent in Punjab and Haryana and is gaining ground in Andhra Pradesh, western Uttar Pradesh, and West Bengal, but is almost absent in other states.
30. (Mathur, H. G., H. C. Agarwal, Sapna Johnson, and Mirmali Saikia, March 2005).
31. (BC Museum, 2008), section 3.3.6.
32. (FAO, 1996).
33. (Raup, 1991).
34. *Ibid.*
35. For a brief history of the Rockefeller Foundation's Mexican wheat breeding program and its accomplishments, See, (Stakman, W. C., Richard Bradfield, and Paul C. Mangelsdorf, 1967), (Borlaug, Norman, 1965), and (Wortman, Sterling, 1969).
36. (PARC, 2007), Slide 1.
37. (Mehra, Shakuntla, 1981).
38. (IRRI, J. L. McLean, 2002), p. 91.

39. (Shiva, 1991), p. 81.
40. (Engdahl, Doomsday Seed Vault in the Arctic, 2007b).
41. Among the other investors in the global seed vault are: the Rockefeller Foundation, Monsanto Corporation, Syngenta Foundation and the Government of Norway. See, (Engdahl, Doomsday Seed Vault in the Arctic, 2007b).
42. (NPR, 2008).
43. *Ibid.* At present, it is estimated that, within the 1,300 to 1,400 individual seed banks around the world, there may be as many as 6.5 millon individual plant samples.

9

The Green Revolution – Socio-Economic Consequences – The Indian Experience

Box 9-1: India Comparative Data

HDI/Rank/Year: 0.619/129/2005
Per Capita GDP: 3,452 USD
Population: 1,148 million (July 2008 est.)

Labor Force in:			
	Agriculture:	60%	(17.6%)*
	Industry:	12%	(29.4%)*
	Services:	28%	(52.9%)*

* Percent of GDP

Population Below the Poverty Line: 25.0%
Population Density: 386.1 people/sq.km.
Land Area: 2,973,190 sq km.
Arable Land: 1,451,808.7 sq. km.
Arable Land Per Person: 0.126 Ha/person
Irrigated Area: 558,080 sq km (2003)
Irrigated Area as % of Arable Land: 38.4%

Introduction

While the Green Revolution was a resounding success, at least in terms of achieving the ultimate goal of foodgrain self-sufficiency, that goal was not achieved without consequences. Imbalances that had already existed in India where the Green Revolution was successful, were exaggerated by the process. These imbalances were largely regional and socio-economic in character.

Part of the reason for these imbalances was the direct consequence of the Government's decisions to concentrate its resources in those areas that, at least conceptually, had the greatest likelihood of producing the largest quantities of useable foodgrains. Part of the imbalance was a function of the specific high yielding grain varieties that were made available to the government and the cultivators. Finally, the imbalances were the result of the availability of both input and institutional and infrastructural resources.

The Ford Foundation and its Intensive Agricultural Districts Programme (IADP, 1960-1970) had been formulated with the sole purpose of:

. . . *respond[ing] to the food crisis with maximum speed, [and] the IADP strategy was to concentrate money, expert staff and agricultural inputs in a few well-endowed agricultural districts. Production was the goal: equity was not a major consideration.*[1]

The foundation was also committed to providing funding for the program's administration personnel, fertilizers, pesticides, transport and storage facilities, seed treatment and soil testing. It was also to be responsible for conducting agronomic research on problems identified in the field, the development of information and education programs, and program evaluation.

The GoI, recognized that the districts selected for the IADP experiment were already comparatively 'prosperous and agriculturally progressive.' This raised philosophical and political concerns regarding India's ability to maintain its commitment to social democracy. It was believed that the IADP violated the Government's goal of social equality by promoting and perpetuating elitism. As a consequence, additional districts were added to the program to give the appearance that it was being implemented on a cross-sectional sample of Indian districts. These "includ[ed] some [districts that were] by no means particularly suited to rapid intensification of cultivation."[2]

Very quickly, the IADP opened the eyes of Government planners — Indian agriculture was desperately in need of revitalization. Without significant changes, the specter of famine was not just a fear but an inevitability. The Government had been focusing its early Five-Year plans and attention on the need for industrialization, genuinely believing that the newly independent nation, to be truly legitimate in the eyes of the world community, must assert itself as an industrial power. The IADP helped refocus the GoI's attention on the more immediate and important problems of agriculture. Beginning with the Third Five-Year Plan, agriculture and its development became the nation's mantra. In addition, the IADP demonstrated that the country's diversity — diversity in terms of its people, climates, and soils — required programs that were specific and responsive to particular regions, rather than maintaining the 'one program fits all' approach, which is typical of centralized development bureaucracies.

The IADP also demonstrated that agricultural development could not be accomplished by using 'either/or' approaches to problems. For more than a decade, a debate had been waged over the relative importance of increased agricultural research versus the provision of extension programs. The IADP had been ostensibly an extension program, but it demonstrated that extension was ineffective in the absence of supportive, problem-solving research. For agricultural development to be successful, extension and research had to move forward hand-in-hand. One without the other only created developmental roadblocks.

In the beginning, the IADP was hampered by the absence of suitable seed varieties. Local seed varieties were simply not compatible with the goals of the IADP. By the mid-60's, however, Borlaug's improved wheat varieties became available, and together the new seeds and the IADP ushered in India's Green Revolution.

Despite the Government's best efforts, the pattern of agricultural development in India had been cast, if not in the form of official programs and policies, then in the form of tacit support for the most agriculturally productive and responsive regions throughout the nation. This pattern is still visible today. Development assistance has favored areas where reliable irrigation is present or where such irrigation could be brought on line. Rain-fed agricultural areas were relegated to the position of agricultural step-children, officially or tacitly. There is no doubt that rain-fed agriculture is now receiving greater research attention but this may be because the well-irrigated areas are coming to the limits of their capacity under current technology. There simply is nowhere to go in the absence of new agricultural technology. Rain-fed areas have been little exploited and represent the 'next most likely areas where agricultural production can be increased.'

Some of the most desperate areas are characterized by lack of rain or, at the other extreme, too much water. Some of India's potentially most productive soils fall victim to uncontrollable flooding, especially in eastern India – Bihar, Jharkhand, Orissa, and parts of West Bengal and eastern Uttar Pradesh. One need only look at a map of poverty to see that the most poverty stricken areas are those that are chronically dry or subject to uncontrolled flooding. Compare Maps 9-1 and 9-2.

Socio-Economic Consequences

Vandana Shiva puts forward the argument that the Green Revolution's transformation of India's agriculture, from subsistence to commercial:

> *. . . changed the structure of social and political relationships, from those based on mutual (though asymmetric) obligations – within the village to relations of each cultivator directly with banks, seed and fertilizer agencies, food procurement agencies, and electricity and irrigation organizations. Further, since all the externally supplied inputs were scarce, it set up conflict and competition over scare resources, between classes, and between regions . . . this generated on the one hand, an erosion of cultural norms and practices and on the other hand, it sowed the seeds of violence and conflict.*[3]

There can be no denying that the Green Revolution set up conflicts; however, in the long run, the violence and conflicts prophesized by Shiva were never fully realized. Admittedly, tensions between landowners and the landless increased. Tensions between large and small cultivators increased. These tensions never resulted in either major political conflict or broad-based violence. These tensions still remain and have remained since the inception of the Green Revolution, some 60 years ago. Most of these tensions are natural, in light of unavoidable regional and individual responses and opportunities presented by the Green Revolution. Simply put, some people prospered, while others suffered. From the very beginning, Borlaug never assumed that there would not be inequities in either the implementation or consequences of the Green Revolution. In this respect, he was pragmatic. Plants are just plants. They do not know that they are supposed to produce more for the small, poor cultivator than the large, rich cultivator.[4] Inequities continue to prevail but Borlaug's goal of reducing hunger was at least partially realized.

Map9-1: Human Poverty Index, India, 2000

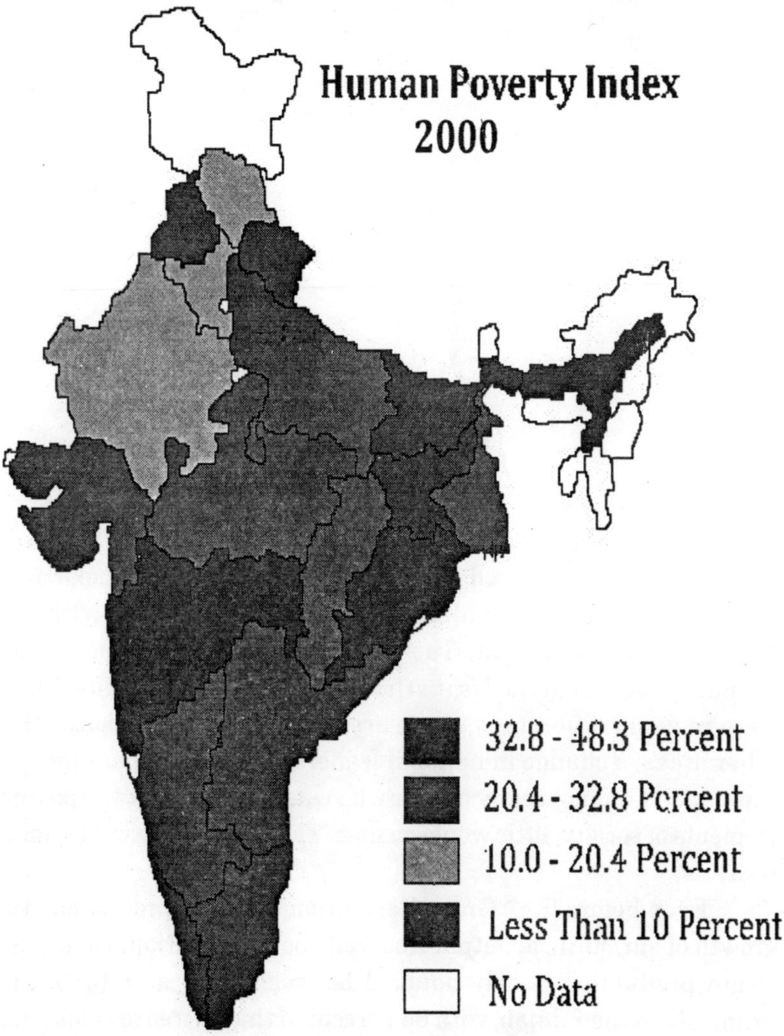

Map 9-2: Primary Environmental Hazards

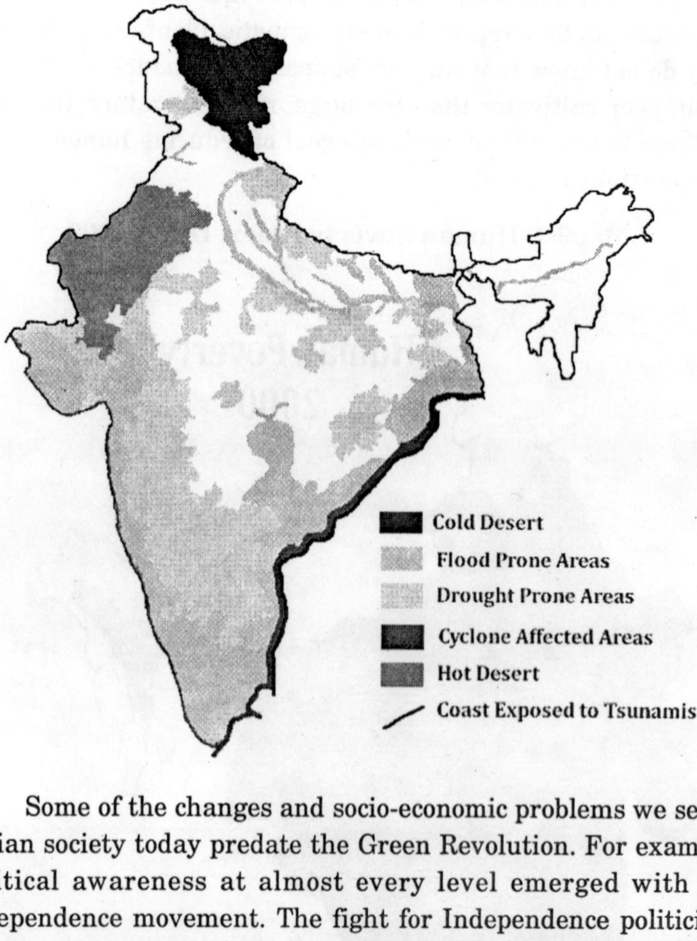

Some of the changes and socio-economic problems we see in Indian society today predate the Green Revolution. For example, political awareness at almost every level emerged with the Independence movement. The fight for Independence politicized Indian society, from the *kisans* (farmers) to the political elite. There were regional differences. Some areas were highly politicized. For other areas, a change in national leadership simply meant more of the same. It did not really matter who was in power. For the poorest elements of society, little would change. They were and would remain poor.

Even before the " Green Revolution" in grain production, the growth of agricultural output was well above the national average.[5] Grain production nearly doubled between 1965 and 1970, due primarily to the Punjab, with 66 percent of that increase came from the trio of northern states – Punjab, Haryana, and UP. This development increased disparities between Punjab and other regions of India and gave Punjabi farmers, who were primarily Sikhs, a heightened sense of self-importance. The successes of these states has remained unmatched regionally and nationally.

Income Disparities

The Case of Bihar

Although there are those who argue that there is no clear cut evidence to support it, it has been suggested that the Green Revolution either exacerbated income disparities or served to level the playing field. In general, it would be safe to say that there were significant regional differences.[6] Differences at the local and subregional level, however, may not have been as dramatic. One need only compare Punjab and Bihar to see a glaring example of regionally different responses to the Green Revolution. Punjab aggressively adopted the Green Revolution paradigm and wrested every bit of benefit from it, while Bihar's former political and agricultural preeminence simply evaporated.

Comparatively, Bihar has consistently, irrespective of the index used, occupied the lowest rung of the development ladder, year after year, while Punjab has stood near the top of that ladder.

Table 9-1: A Comparison of HDIs and Composite Development Indices for Bihar and Punjab

State	*HDI 1981*	*HDI 1991*	*HDI 2001*	*Composite Development Index 2000*
Bihar	0.237 (15)	0.308 (15)	0.367 (15)	91.31 (13)
Punjab	0.411 (2)	0.475 (2)	0.537 (2)	179.92 (1)

Source: HDIs — (Planning Commission, 2002); and Composite Development Index — Centre for Monitoring Indian Economy, October 2000.
Note: Figures in parentheses represent state ranking out of 15 major states.

Bihar has become the focus of much attention, largely because of its apparent devolution, becoming one of the most destitute states in India. The World Bank recently devoted an entire Bank Report to the problems of Bihar.[7] The World Bank list of causes of poverty in Bihar is not new; and there is no doubt that these causes are all worthy subjects and should be examined, studied, and addressed. The list is interesting but there are no earthshaking revelations or insights. There are no "Why didn't we think of that before?!" topics. It is the same list year after year, with additions that result from refinement, not new insights.

While there is little debate about Bihar's poverty, there is much debate concerning the causes of that poverty. Almost everyone acknowledges that Bihar's poverty is complex and stems from a number of interrelated problems:

- Complex social stratification.
- Insufficient and unmaintained infrastructure.
- Lack of investment strategies and incentives.
- Low rates of productivity, especially in agriculture.
- Poor urban-rural differentiation and linkages.
- Weak governance.[8]

Despite or in spite of these problems, it is agriculture that propels the state, albeit slowly, and sometimes in reverse. Agriculture is still the foundation of Bihar's economy, employing roughly 80 percent of the state's workforce, but generating only 40 percent of its GDP. Much of the agricultural production is subsistence due to productivity levels that are well below the national averages. See Table 9-2. As a consequence, there is so little or no surplus, which means that most cultivators are unable to participate in local or regional cash markets and, therefore, they have little or no cash income.

There is not a single crop or crop type that is not well below the national average or potential yields as ascertained on demonstration plots. The cultivators are truly subsistence cultivators.

Low yields, coupled with a subsistence mindset, contributes to Bihar's poverty. The percentage of India's population living below the poverty line (BPL) is approximately 27.5 percent, but for Bihar the figure is 43.2 percent, and as such, Bihar's poor represent the largest concentration of poor in India. Furthermore, Bihar has the highest rate for landless agricultural laborers in India, nearly double the national average – Bihar, 48.2 percent, All-India – 26.5 percent.[10] See Figure 9-3.

Table 9-2: Yield Gaps for Selected Crops in Bihar (kg/ha), 2009

Crop	State Average Yield	Potential Yield**	Yield Gap Average	All-India Yields
Rice	1,218	3,026	-1,818	1,940
Wheat	1,816	3,052	-1,236	2,703
Maize	1,844	4,056	-2,212	1,810
Gram	1,017	1,380	-363	792
Arhar	1,379	1,830	-451	727
Rape, Mustard	1,360	1,850	-190	1,002
Jute	1,409	2,010	-601	1,823
Sugarcane	48,856	62,780	-13,924	70,578
Potatoes	9,060	23,500	-14,440	18,161
Mango*	1,000	1,660	-660	-
Lichee*	1,000	1,850	-850	-
Banana	5,000	8,000	-3,000	-

Source: After (Yadav, C.P., B.S. Gupta, and S. Kumar, 2000)

* Yield per tree

** Yield achieved on national demonstration plots. Yield gap computed from these figures.

The only state approaching Bihar's burden of landless agricultural laborers is Andhra Pradesh, with 39.6 percent. These are imposing figures, especially when it comes to creating programs to reduce poverty. When nearly 40 percent of the population has no assets and very little real or barter income, it is difficult for development programming to begin to assist them.

Why So Many Landless Laborers?

Rural poverty, at least in India, is largely a function of access to land. As the percentage of landless agricultural wage-earners increases, so does rural poverty. The number of landless laborers has grown steadily over the last fifty-plus years throughout India. See Map 9-3. Although Bihar's agricultural laborer rate is unusually high, even for India, one has to ask why are there so many landless laborers, almost everywhere?

While Bihar's incidence of landless laborers is statistically very high, other states also exhibit high landless rates — Andhra Pradesh (39.6%), Orissa (35%), West Bengal (25%), Uttar Pradesh (24.8%) Gujarat (24.3%), among others.

The Process of Dispossession

With or without the government's notice, the character of Indian agriculture has changed rapidly in the last 35-40 years. It started out as, at best, a subsistence agricultural system, and has evolved into a market-driven, surplus-producing machine. For the new class of commercial farmers that emerged with the Green Revolution, things have turned out admirably. Many have grown from just being large- to middle-sized landholders or landlords into prosperous agriculturalists. The benefits of the Green Revolution have not, however, been equally beneficial for all agricultural classes, including the smaller landholders, tenants, and the landless laborers. Old-style land reforms, while advocating rural justice and equity, have failed these classes. Each has become increasingly impoverished as their counterparts have prospered. The prosperity of the new class of farmers is not necessarily the cause of these classes' growing impoverishment.

Even though Punjab is perceived as the standout example of agricultural development in India, and the single largest beneficiary

Map 9-3: Agricultural Laborers as Percent of Total Population by State, 2001

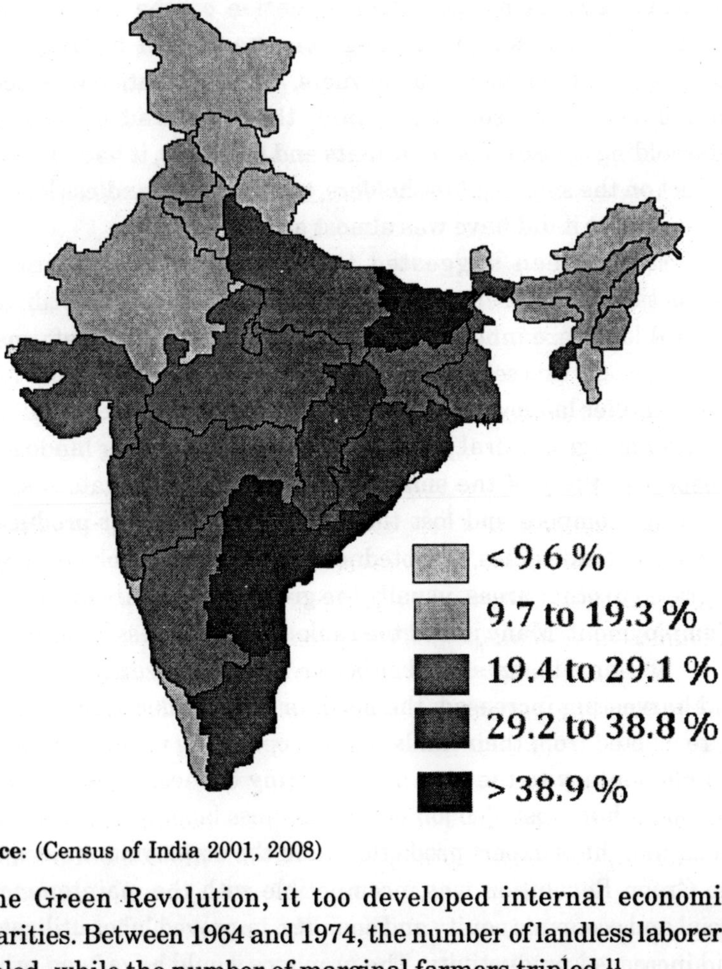

Source: (Census of India 2001, 2008)

of the Green Revolution, it too developed internal economic disparities. Between 1964 and 1974, the number of landless laborers doubled, while the number of marginal farmers tripled.[11]

The cause of this impoverishment lies in the fact that they have been and continue to be marginal cultivators, either due to the size of their landholdings and fragmentation, their lack of investment capital, poor managerial skills, and lack of education, lack of socio-economic-political linkages, or some combination of these factors. If one takes a purely philosophical look at these classes, one could define their plight as just another example of *karma*, simply their fate. They were born poor and that is the way they will stay. Philosophically, this may be an acceptable explanation, but it is not very satisfying from a humanistic point of view

The lesser agricultural classes require attention. In the past, agrarian reforms focused their attention on the elimination of intermediaries, setting ceilings on the size of holdings, and transforming tenants into landowners. All this attention was focused on the top of the social pyramid, the large and middle-sized landholding classes. For all intents and purposes, it had little or no impact on the smallest landholders, tenants, and landless laborers. What impact it did have was almost always negative.

It has been suggested that increases in agricultural production, social and economic equality and improved utilization of rural labor are inherently incompatible.[12] Agrarian reforms set out to prevent this self-fulfilling prophecy. They did not help. Many of the smaller landowners, tenants, and landless laborers continued to suffer as agricultural production rose and the larger landowners prospered. Many of the smaller, sub-marginal cultivators simply could not compete and lost their lands due to under-production, increasing land values, indebtedness, and, finally, insolvency. Some migrated to other areas, usually the growing urban areas, in search of employment. Many joined the ranks of the landless laborer class.

Marginal tenants fared no better. As mechanization in planting and harvesting increased, the need for tenants declined, and they were evicted from their lands. Larger operating units proved to be complementary to the new inputs. Many of these former tenants migrated, but most also joined the landless laborer class. It would seem, in light of expert predictions and the employment data, that the Green Revolution was incompatible with the maintenance of social and economic equity and equality, improved labor utilization, and increased productivity. The prophecy would have been proven incorrect had the Green Revolution not been so responsive to larger field cultivation and had been powered by human cultivation activities, instead of mechanization. If human labor had been the focus of the Green Revolution, the increased numbers of people who became part of the landless labor class might not have suffered as they have. Many would have prospered along with their employers. However, this is not what happened. Instead, the agricultural labor pool increased. As competition for a limited number of jobs increased, agricultural wages were driven down and rural poverty among this class of agriculturalists increased.

As a result of their abject poverty, there are few who speak for them, except in philosophical terms. They have little or no formal representation in government. They are difficult to organize and therefore they have no continuous political presence. During the pre-Independence, nationalist movement, collectively and individually, the political leaders marshaled the rural poor on more than one occasion, only to forget them once a particular political objective had been achieved vis-à-vis the British colonialists. At one time, the *Kisan Sabha* "spoke" for this group, but as with many political organizations, it became an end in itself. It grew and became an institution, not the true voice of the peasantry. A grassroots movement must be undertaken to organize the political power that rests in the hands of more than 100 million potential voters, but not just for a single issue or political objective. It must be an ongoing political endeavor that will truly speak for this poorest segment of Indian society. No one, no matter how benevolent, can speak for these people. They must find their own political voice. Outsiders can only *assume* what is best or right for them. It would be far better if they were able to speak for themselves, from a basis of personal knowledge, not from reading government compiled, statistical reports. Only members of this group can legitimately say what is needed in the form of legislative reforms to provide these underprivileged groups with much needed protection.

Over the period 1951 to 2001, the number of landless laborers has increased markedly and, at the same time, the number of cultivators has declined, almost in direct proportion to one another. In Figure 9-1. Clearly, this is the result of the marginal cultivators loss of land and their becoming landless laborers. Any cultivator who owns the least bit of land will classify himself as a cultivator, even if he earns the bulk of his livelihood serving as an agricultural laborer. It is a matter of pride.

The 1961 Census data seems to be anomalous. The increase in the number of cultivators in 1961 is most likely the result of landless tenants and sharecropper reclassification during the peak of the land reforms period in most of the states in India. Many tenants and sharecroppers received legally protected status through

Figure 9-1: Change in Percentage of Agricultural Laborers and Cultivators to Total Rural Population, 1951 - 2001[13]

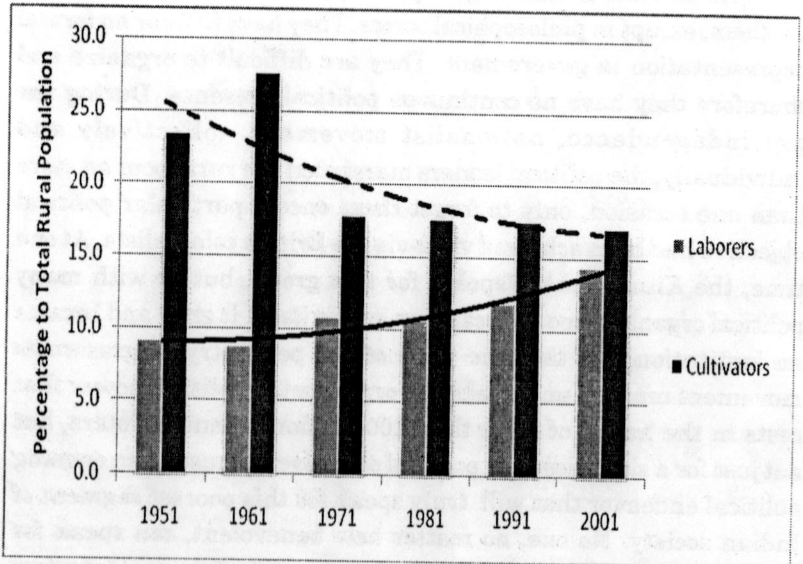

Source: From (IFFCO, 2004), Table 2.2, Population and Agricultural Workers, p. 6.

the implementation of land reforms in many states. The recognition of rights in the land resulted in their reclassification as cultivators, as opposed landless tenants and sharecroppers. The removal of the 1961 data tends to improve the slope of the trend lines and the correlation between the increase in the number of laborers and the decline in the number of cultivators.

These increased number of landless laborers has, for decades, represented two problems for the Government of India. First, although not yet tapped, they represent a potentially large block of voters that, if they could be organized and coalesced into a self-identifying political entity, could become a significant political base. Since they are such a fragmented group, they have remained comparatively passive. Political activism could change them from being passive observers of state and national politics into a formidable political entity.

Secondly, they represent one of the largest groups that comprise the undernourished population of India. Equally beleaguered are the millions of marginal cultivators that have not yet made the bureaucratic transition from being classified as a cultivator to laborer. Many of them too suffer from an inability to pay for the food they require.

The Green Revolution is directly responsible for the rapid growth of this group of India's poor. Further, in the absence of work opportunities in the major cities, in manufacturing or industry, and lacking the educational skills to perform most jobs in the rapidly rising services sector, most of these landless poor continue to live in rural areas, taking work as it becomes available. Thus they are, at best, under-employed and more frequently unemployed.

A number of interrelated processes serve to increase the number of rural poor. First, marginal cultivators lose their land as a result of indebtedness that results from periodic crop failures. Crop failures are usually associated with floods or droughts, or both, often in the same year. Second, traditional inheritance practices result in the decreasing size of cultivators' landholdings and increasing fragmentation, which, over time, results in the development of uneconomic holdings. Finally, many of these marginal cultivators are unable to acquire modern agricultural technologies or inputs, which contributes to low yields and increases their economic vulnerability.

Land Fragmentation and Farm Households with Multiple Employment

Due to rapid population growth since Independence, increased pressure has been placed on the land resources of the state. These pressures come in the form of population density and pressure placed on the land to produce more and more food to feed the people. For more than 50 years, Bihar's population decadal growth rate, between the censuses, has not been below 21 percent, and during the last decade (1991-2001) it was at an all-time high – 27.11 percent.[14] In Bihar, population density has increased from 324 to 880 people per square km between 1971 and 2001.[15] In 2001, of the major states of India, only West Bengal had a higher population density – 904 people per square km. The population density figure is all the more important, since Bihar is the least urbanized state in the Union, with an urbanization rate of only 10.5 percent, against a national average of 27.8 percent. Thus, poverty in Bihar is largely a rural problem.

With each successive generation, traditional Indian inheritance laws require that the land of the head of the family be divided among the surviving sons. Each time, the family's properties become smaller and increasingly fragmented. Eventually, these small parcels of land become uneconomic, and are not capable of supporting the typical Indian family. Increasingly, smaller landholders find themselves balancing between minimal, self-sustaining agricultural production and insolvency. In this situation, many are forced to augment their meager subsistence with other, part-time employment, becoming part of what Kuhnen has termed "farm households with multiple employment."[16] Thus begins a gradual, downward economic spiral. Furthermore, the young of those families fortunate enough to be able to attend school, develop high expectations but they have only limited economic opportunities available to them.

These households attempt to combine the cultivation of their small holdings with outside labor, usually as agricultural laborers on the lands of larger landowners. There are problems inherent in this multiple employment arrangement, however. Even small landholdings require daily attention, and this attention is usually provided *after* working all day for an employer. Also, agricultural laborers are faced with the reality that their employment is frequently only seasonal or occasional.

Eventually, the part-time agricultural laborer becomes a full-time agricultural laborer. Indebtedness to moneylenders – usually other larger landowners – almost always results in the loss of the family lands, and the small landowner becomes a landless agricultural laborer. By the time most small landholders are forced to seek outside agricultural employment, the distinction between being an agricultural laborer and a landless agricultural laborer becomes a moot point.

Population density figures serve as a proxy for the rate at which landowners become landless agricultural laborers and fragmentation of the land. The greater the population density, the greater the likelihood that farmers will become laborers.The high density figures for Bihar and the high rate of agricultural laborers tends to confirm this process and relationship. High density figures, then, also portend increased indebtedness and poverty. See Table 9-3.

Table 9-3: Percent Agricultural Laborers, Population Density, and HDI by State, 2001

State Rank	State	*Agricultural Laborers as %*	*Population Density per sq. km.*	*HDI 2001*
1	Himachal Pradesh	3.1	109	
2	Arunachal Pradesh	3.9	13	
3	Nagaland	4.0	120	
4	Mizoram	5.9	42	
5	Sikkim	6.1	76	
6	Uttaranchal	8.3	159	
7	Rajasthan	10.6	165	0.424
8	Manipur	11.3	107	
9	Assam	13.5	340	0.386
10	Haryana	15.2	478	0.509
11	Kerala	16.1	819	0.638
12	Punjab	16.4	484	0.537
13	Meghalaya	18.1	103	
14	Tripura	24.0	305	
15	Gujarat	24.5	258	0.479
16	West Bengal	24.9	903	0.472
17	Uttar Pradesh	25.1	690	0.388
18	Karnataka	26.4	276	0.478
19	Maharashtra	26.8	315	0.523
20	Jharkhand	28.3	338	
21	Madhya Pradesh	28.7	196	0.394
22	Tamil Nadu	31.2	480	0.531
23	Chhattisgarh	31.9	154	
24	Orissa	35.0	236	0.404
25	Andhra Pradesh	39.6	277	0.416
26	Bihar	48.2	880	0.367
	India	32.8	325	0.472

Source: Census of India, 2001 and (Central Statistical Organization, 2001) Figures in green cells are lowest figures. Figures in gold cells are highest figures. Figures in yellow are the highest figure for Bihar.

Landlordism

In the case of Bihar, there has been a very long tradition of landlordism, and one finds one of its most egregious forms –

Zamindari. Prior to the British takeover of Bihar all land was owned by the ruling head of state. In the 18th Century, this was the Mughal emperor. The emperor employed tax collectors, called *zamindars*, to collect taxes from the peasants. The *Zamindari* system was derived from the *bhuiyan* land tenure system of the pre-Mughal era, and was adapted by the Mughals, becoming a key economic and political institution. *Zamindars* possessed proprietary rights in the collection of rents but not in the land. *Zamindars* remained simple tax collectors until the Permanent Settlement of 1793, when the British changed the *zamindars* from revenue-managers into landlords with proprietary rights in the land and with only one obligation — pay the government a fixed amount of revenue without alteration in perpetuity.

Zamindari property, like any other property, could be freely transferred or mortgaged, and the *zamindari* right was inheritable. Once the *zamindars* were given title to their lands, the large *zamindars* began dividing their estates into numerous blocs and leased them to *ijaradars*. The *zamindars'* actions created a hierarchy of intermediaries. Most *zamindars*, particularly those of the eastern Bengal districts, created permanent intermediate tenures, which further isolated the *zamindars* from their *raiyats* – the actual holders of the land and from whom the taxes were collected. In-between the *zamindars* and *raiyats* were several degrees of interest, one layered upon the other, and all of which drew their rental income from the same plot of land and from the same *raiyat*. In the beginning, there were uncultivated lands and , overburdened *raiyats* responded to excessive taxation by simply deserting their lands and finding new land to cultivate.

The *Zamindari* system remained in place until Independence in 1947. Thereafter, attempts were made to disenfranchise them and establish progressive direct tax relationships with the *raiyats* through the enactment of land reforms. Bihar was the first state to legislate and implement a broad range of land reforms. These reforms, however, were more for reasons of political economy than as a genuine attempt to remove the *zamindars* or reorganize Bihar's agriculture or rural society. Simply put, land reforms failed in Bihar because the politicians and bureaucrats who were to implement them all came from the *zamindari* class and thus ensured that such reforms were never really implemented. The enforcement of these land reforms would mean passing power, property, and status from one group to another by legislative action. In the politically, socially, and economically hidebound context of Bihar, the elimination of the *zamindars* would mean the complete overhaul of Bihari society. That was not a real option.

For the politicians and the *zamindars*, it was much more prudent to give the illusion that something substantive was being done, than actually doing it. Once all legal avenues had been exhausted, the *zamindars* resorted to subterfuge to retain ownership of their lands and the power that such ownership provided. In the end, only the very largest *zamindars* felt the pinch of Bihar's land reforms – those with revenues in excess of Rs. 500,000.[17] The remainder 'resumed' the cultivation of their lands under the guise of *bakast* (self-tilled).

The largest *zamindars* were easy targets for the government. Among the largest *zamindaris* in Bihar were those of the Bettiah, Hathuwa, Dumrao, Ramgarh families and the Maharaja of Darbhanga.[18] These *zamindars* had created efficient revenue collecting organizations and were only interested in revenue collection, not the direct management of the land. Thus, they could not justifiably or legally claim *bakast*. The smaller *zamindars*, however, were involved in the direct management of their lands and could justifiably claim them as self-tilled. As a consequence, the *zamindari* tradition remained intact and the system of multiple tenancies remained a salient feature of Bihari agriculture.

The largest and most parasitic levels in the *zamindari* system were eliminated but that did not eliminate *zamindars*. They simply transformed themselves by changing their titles. They no longer called themselves *zamindars*. That became a pejorative term. Instead, they would be known as landowners or landholders. Many of the smaller *zamindars* actually became actively involved in the management of their holdings, while the larger *zamindars* remained absentee landlords, with layer upon layer of intermediate land tenancies.

In almost every village, a group of petty *zamindars / maliks* or *khurdia maliks* emerged, growing in power over time. As a group, they became notorious for their tyranny towards the *raiyats*, and

Box 9-2: The Maharaja of Darbhanga: More than a Zamindar[21]

The following is a slightly edited response to a question posed to Mr. Tejakar Jha after reading a paper dealing with socio-economic divergence between landlord (zamindari) and non landlord areas.

The Maharaja of Darbhanga was in a class by himself, just as his holdings were. He felt that tenant and landless laborers must be made equal partners in production, along with the zamindars. He felt that both classes should care for one another. Further, he felt that the government should suspend revenue payments so that the zamindars could waive rents in times of calamity. In turn, the zamindars should develop irrigation systems and the government should care for the transport system.

The Maharaja had a number of sugar, jute, cotton and paper mills in the region. All were supported by the agricultural produce of the region and gave a market to the farmers and employment to landless laborers in the region.

He fought to save the zamindari, not for the sake of money but based on that principle that a government could not selectively takeover private property. He won his case in the Supreme Court of India. After the promulgation of the nation's new Constitution, he pressed his case in the courts. Again, the Government was looking at defeat. Prime Minister Nehru personally came to Patna and appealed to the Maharaja to give up his zamindari, for the sake of democracy. The Maharaja gave up his zamindari in 1950 without taking a single penny as compensation.

Ninety (90) percent of the Maharaja's income came from his industrial holdings, which ranged from automobile dealerships to aviation, to agro-industries, to publications. He owned 18 industrial units and had major shares in scores of other industrial units. He owned a share in the Villiers trading firm.

He argued that industry should always play second fiddle and agriculture should be given due important in free India, because 75 percent of the population is dependent upon it.

The people of Mithila were, until 1965, three years after the Maharaja's death, in good economic condition. The farmers had enough money and great purchasing power. Slowly the government took over all the industrial units run by the Darbhanga Raj. Within a decade, all of these units were closed due to mismanagement. The economy of the region went down. The people became impoverished.

How could we say that the economy (industrial and agrarian) developed only in the region and era where there was no zamindari.

especially the agricultural laborers and sharecroppers. These *zamindar/maliks* remained in control after *zamindari* abolition. Many of them were of recognized castes, and controlled the land.[19]

As population increased after Independence, competition for the land increased exponentially, and inflamed the political, economic, and social tensions that already existed between them, their castes, and the growing number of sharecroppers and agricultural laborers, who belonged overwhelmingly to the scheduled castes. As a consequence, the competition for land contributed to inter-caste rivalries and conflict.[20]

In the end, land reforms did little for the actual tillers of the soil, the *raiyats*. Sharecropping and other forms of tenancy remained rampant, except that access to land was becoming much more competitive and rents continued to rise. Unlike earlier times, when disgruntled tenants could simply desert their lands in protest, that option was no longer tenable. There was no new land to cultivate. If a tenant abandoned his land, he found himself unemployed.The unemployed tenant's only options were to find another landlord or seek non-agricultural employment elsewhere. Since most agricultural labors tend to be illiterate, there is little opportunity for non-agricultural employment, even in the cities, where unemployment rates are already high.

The Green Revolution Arrives

When the Green Revolution was implemented in Bihar, a number of things occurred. The smallest landholders and tenants found it difficult to invest in the package of improved practices. Further, the tenants had no incentive to invest because any increase in production would inevitably accrue to the landlord. Landlords, for their part, did not invest in the improved practices on behalf of their tenants. They would, however, invest in them on the lands they cultivated or supervised directly. Here they would receive direct benefit from their investments.

Unable to invest in the production-increasing technologies, the smallest landholders and tenants succumb to indebtedness, and their lands are lost to moneylenders and larger landholders. The small parcels of defaulting tenants and sharecroppers were consolidated by the larger landowners into larger and larger parcels that were increasingly amendable to the Green Revolution technologies.Thus, the Green Revolution accelerated the increase in the number of landless laborers and the consolidation of land in the hands of larger landowners. Due to the increased value of the land, tenancies were granted only to those who had the ability to invest in yield-increasing technologies, which were, normally, other smaller but successful cultivators.

Thus, the rich got richer, and the poor, inevitably, got poorer. For many of the smallest cultivators, the new technologies were typically too expensive to adopt, unless they either had a patron or were able to obtain some form of agricultural credit. The smaller farmers also had to make decisions on how to apply their limited resources and this usually meant that they would not realize the full potential of the new technologies. The larger farmers had the luxury of being able, through either cash-on-hand or credit, to purchase the full complement of inputs and, therefore, realized the full potential of their investments.[22]

It has been reported that, in Punjab, the number of small landholders were unable to make the capital investments required by the new agricultural technologies. Between 1970 and 1981, it is estimated that the total number of operational holdings fell by as much as 25 percent.[23] The Green Revolution seems to have resulted in a shift in the distribution of operational holdings, and placed more and more land in the hands of the larger farmers.[24]

It has been suggested that, in some instances, landlords attempted to keep tenants' production low. Landlords, while unwilling to make investments in the land themselves, will discourage such investments by their tenants as well. Increased production will accrue to both the landlord and the tenant but the additional income to the tenant could result in a loosening of control on the part of the landlord. By keeping production below a level that would permit the tenant to escape his perpetual indebtedness to the landlord, the landlord could maintain control. Bhaduri observed that some landlords resisted tenants' efforts to drill tubewells, even though it would have resulted in additional revenue to the landlord through either sharecropping or rent payments. The increased income would have permitted the tenant to eliminate his debt to the landlord, in which case the tenant's position vis-à-vis the landlord would be modified, making the tenant more independent.[25]

Within the context of Bihar and West Bengal, Bhaduri suggest that in former *zamindari* areas, the local power structure is essentially semi-feudal in nature. He bases his characterization on four factors:

(1) The existence of a large-scale non-legalized sharecropping system.
(2) The tenants are perpetually in debt to their landlords.
(3) The 'ruling class,' the large landowners, operate as both landlord and moneylender to the small tenants.
(4) The small tenants do not have free access to rural markets and are frequently forced into involuntary exchanges.[26]

For the rural elite to maintain their power and control, they must keep the tenants in a state of constant debt.These landlords, as moneylenders, recognize that the return on their money is much higher if given out on loan at usurious interest rates, than as a return based on agricultural investment. Their success is dependent upon the fact that the extremely low wage paid to laborers or the high rents received from tenants, precludes sufficient surplus income for even daily consumptive purposes. Therefore, they must and do remain in a state of perpetual indebtedness. These tenants cannot escape from this exploitative relationship since to escape means that the incurred debt and interest must be liquidated first, and they do not have the resources to obtain this release. As a consequence, the tenants become bound to their landlords, as if they were serfs.

In the final analysis, the large and medium-sized landholders or landlords have gotten richer, and the small landholders, tenants, and landless have gotten significantly poorer. Many of the smaller cultivators, in fact, unable to compete for limited and increasingly expensive agricultural resources, have lost their only means of production and have been forced to either migrate in search of work or have become local, landless laborers.

In the absence of alternative employment, either in the industrial or service sectors, as the number of agricultural laborers increases, wage rates are simply lowered. Thus, the poorest segment of the agricultural community sinks deeper and deeper. For many, to live at the poverty line would be a relief.

The Malaise that is Bihar

When you visit Bihar, even the capital, Patna, you are left with an uneasy feeling.The press and academics write about Bihar's lack of development and how sad it is. Reading the reports and seeing photographs are depressing. Visiting Bihar and seeing the conditions there is even worse. Some of the criticism leveled at the state just represents opportunism and regional or political electioneering. The unfortunate thing is that most of the widespread stereotypes about Bihar are, in the main, true.

At one time, Bihar was the shining star of India. Its political activism was legendary and preceded much of the rest of the country. The people, from the lowest *kisans* (farmers) to the *babus* were politically aware. Many of the earliest agrarian movements began or had their roots in Bihar. Major political reform movements, like that of J. Prakash Narayan in the 1970s, began in Bihar, only to unravel later. Nonetheless, the movement left its imprint on Indian politics. Its government was one to be emulated. Its agricultural productivity was legendary. It was considered to be one of the major granaries of India. All that has changed.

Today, poverty is visible everywhere. There is little opportunity for upward mobility. Bihar's educational system is virtually non-existent and, as a consequence, Bihar has the lowest literacy rate of any state in India – 47.5 percent.[27] As Rakesh Anit commented:

All this is coupled with an unresponsive and corrupt civil administration. For nearly a half-century, Bihar has been consistent in one respect: poor ranking on almost all major social and economic indices. Education remains, simply put, a dead loss. With the great schools and colleges of the past having lost all strength and credibility, anyone who can afford it sends their charges to Delhi, Calcutta or elsewhere, as long as it is outside of Bihar. With young Bihari men and women clearing the country's most prestigious entry-level civil service exams year after year, it is obvious that the problems of Bihar lie not with its people.

The rotten state of Bihar's roads provides a window into the state's abysmal physical infrastructure.The lack of productive employment pushes unorganised labour to the metropolises in western India, Delhi and Calcutta, while organised labour within the state is used as cannon-fodder by the various political parties. The professional class in Patna is skeletal, with the best and the brightest having evacuated. A heavily compromised bureaucracy and judiciary are used to uphold the status quo. Faced with such a wall of inadequacy in governmental institutions, the people have decided to tune out and live their lives as best they can – in the manner of their ancestors, who similarly did not expect help from the state. [28]

The people of Bihar have simply given up.They have resigned themselves to life, seeing no way out. It is not that their land is not as fertile as the land in Punjab or Haryana.It is not because the modern agricultural inputs are unavailable. They are. It may well be that they can no longer conceive of a life of prosperity. Being unable to visual an alternative to their current situation, they are unable to achieve it.

Until November 2000, when Bihar was bifurcated into the states of Bihar and Jharkhand, the Chota Nagpur region was the center of the Bihar's only industrial base, a base that for decades has been on the 'verge of takeoff.' But it is a takeoff that has never materialized for lack of capital investment and inadequate infrastructure. With the bifurcation, Bihar was left with virtually no industrial sector. It had become part of Jharkhand.

Bihar's agriculture suffers from virtually no mechanization, small fragmented landholdings, high rates of agricultural tenancy, low productivity, and abysmally low *per capita* yield rates for almost every crop and crop type.[29] Efforts to rectify agriculture's problems of tenancy and uneconomic landholdings have been attempted with no long-term effects. Unofficial and underground land tenancies and sharecropping are rampant, harkening back to Bihar's 'semi-feudal' *zamindari* period.

Society in Bihar is predominantly rural but it is far from unified or homogeneous. Due to competition between and within castes for land control, there has been an unprecedented increase in casteism, especially in recent years. As a consequence, casteism is tearing at the very fabric of rural Bihar. In many areas, rural society has been the subject of large-scale social reform. This has not happened in much of Bihar. Caste in Bihar, maybe more so than in other regions of India, has become the essential political component. Most of the leaders of the leading political groups and parties are also the leaders of their castes. Since caste tends to be one of the primary components of modern Bihar, a break between the castes also means a break in Bihari society. It is this break, the politicization of caste, that has immobilized Bihar's politics and government, and this immobility prevents or constrains social and economic development. A further consequence of this extreme casteism is the loss of what might be termed a 'Bihari identity.' There is nothing to hold the Biharis together for the common good.

The present state of Bihar has historically been unique but that rich history has not grown or been transformed into modern day progress or institutions. Part of Bihar's failure to thrive and its growing casteism can be traced to a certain, for lack of a better term, 'Bihari recalcitrance' beginning in the mid-19th century. After the Mutiny of 1857, which involved a large number of Biharis, the British clamped down on Bihar in retaliation. In response, the Biharis turned against almost everything Western, and as a consequence, they did not follow the same path to social, economic, or political modernization as did many other parts of India. Western ideas, at the grass roots, were eschewed.

Bihar is often referred to as India's heartland. It is also the heart of Indian Hinduism and the Hindi language.The use of Hindi grew in opposition to English. Whereas English was the language of modernization, Hindi harkened to the past and traditionalism. Bihari society looked to the past, rather than the future, for inspiration. In the past, the physical environment of Bihar, with its interlaced rivers and streams, made travel difficult and protected the people from outside influences. Society took solace in that isolation, and it became its focus.

Landlordism, both past and present, was built on tradition. Likewise, despite Government's best attempts to spur social and economic development, the influences of land and social traditionalism precluded or slowed every move toward modernity. Rural Bihar remained and remains tied to the past, socially, economically, and historically.

The development of radical casteism in Bihar has had the effect of robbing Bihar of its identity. Consequently, there is no sense of Bihari nationalism. In northern India, there are, as Ashok Jha points out, two forms of nationalism – Indian and caste nationalism.[30] Someone from Rajasthan, in all likelihood, would describe himself as an India, a Rajasthani, and then his caste.Someone from Bihar would describe himself as an Indian and of a certain caste.The fact that he is a Bihari is deemed comparatively unimportant. Caste affiliation is deemed much more relevant than state citizenship. Thus, Bihar has no sub-national identity. In the absence of this kind of identity, there is no one to speak for Bihar. There are numerous caste spokesmen but few spokesmen for Bihar. As a result, Bihar seems to have no voice in national affairs. Without a voice, it is easily ignored.

Bihar was separated from Jharkhand in 2000. There were protestations from politicians but they were not accompanied by large-scale public demonstrations. Now, Tarakant Jha, a spokesman for Mithila is pressing for the creation of yet another state.[31] Again, if it were not for periodic newspaper and on-line reporting, no one would even know about the proposal to cut Bihar in half again.There is no uproar, only blog comments supporting the move. The current petition to create a State of Mithila is not the first. In 1947, the Maharaja of Darbhanga, as a member of the constituent assembly of India, proposed an amendment to the Constitution that would have created the State of Mithila.[32]

If it were suggested that Punjab, Kerala, or West Bengal be split into one or more smaller states, there would be an intrastate and national uproar. When Bihar was bifurcated, the only real debates were held privately between politicians and between those who would benefit from the division. There were no objections. There were no demonstrations. No one cares much about what happens in Bihar, not even the Biharis. Their silence speaks volumes. Bringing up caste differences, however, causes demonstrations and conflict. It simply demonstrates what is important to the Biharis. Equality, social justice, and progress are simply secondary. There is no wonder why things have unraveled for the state.

Conclusions

The Green Revolution has been blamed for a multitude of socio-economic problems – increases in poverty, income disparities, increases in unemployment, the reorganization of agriculture, fracturing of traditional family structures, and political sectarian conflict and violence. There is no doubt that the Green Revolution played a part in each of these areas but the cause? No. The seeds for each of these problem areas was sown well before the first improved seed was ever produced. Instead, the Green Revolution served as a catalyst. It simply accelerated processes that were already latent in Indian society. The same can be said of almost every society into which the Green Revolution was inserted.

Like most changes that result in improved production, whether in industry, manufacturing, or services, some people always seem to receive a disproportionate share of the benefits of the improvements. Call it entrepreneurship, opportunism, or capitalism, there are almost always winners and losers. The same is true of the Green Revolution. Some of the agriculturalists appear to have benefitted much more than others. Upon examination, in general those that benefitted most were those who were prepared to take advantage of the new technologies as they became available. They had more disposable income, more land, more access to credit, and better access to government services.The Green Revolution did not make the poor, poor. They were already poor or marginally poor. The Green Revolution simply accentuated these divisions.

By its very nature, the Green Revolution is based on a Western agricultural paradigm – investments in non-replicable inputs, irrigation, mechanization, and the production of surpluses. It is and was, after all, simply a scaled down version of Western commercial agriculture, adapted to the needs of developing countries. It arrived at a time when more food was desperately needed to avert large scale food deprivation and starvation. It was expected to increase production. It did.

People, in general, tend to anthropomorphize processes, somehow expecting them to have free will and a sense of ethnics.The Green Revolution was 'supposed' to both improve food production and solve social inequalities and promote social justice. That is simply asking too much of a plant or a planting system. Even Norman Borlaug understood that there were going to be inequities.

The Green Revolution was never envisioned as a tool of social engineering, at least by its developers. It was simply a tool for the increased production of much needed foodstuffs. It did what it was designed to do, and no more. If politicians and social philosophers saw the Green Revolution as a potential tool for curing social ills, they were being exceptionally naïve, giving a simple agricultural process the ability to change the way people think. Had it been imbued with that ability, it probably would have lived up to that expectation as well. However, it never had that ability.

Further, the politicians that sought and relied on the Green Revolution to solve both immediate and long-term food needs should be more than satisfied. If they wanted it to serve as a tool to promote social democracy, one must ask why would they concentrate their limited resources in specific regions, rather than spreading them among all those in need? The answer to this question is that the long-term ability to feed everyone was deemed, at least for reasons of political economy, more important than worrying about nuisances of political doctrine. It was deemed more important to concentrate scare resources where they would result in the greatest good. It may not be socially democratic but it *was* pragmatic. Once everyone was fed, the politicians could get back to their concerns about advancing their philosophy of social democracy.

However, once the decision had been made to concentrate resources in areas that promised the greatest return on investment, a fiscal and regional pattern resulted, and this pattern is still clearly visible today – socially and economically. Even though all the improved agricultural inputs are readily available, and seed varieties have been developed for a broad range of India's climates and ecologies, the original adoption pattern is evident.

The pattern of adoption today remains largely unchanged from the first years of the Green Revolution. Why? It is not the components of the Green Revolution. They have remained, essentially, the same from the beginning, with the exception that now there are many more seeds and seed varieties that have been tailored to much more specific environments and ecologies. They are plentiful and widely available. It is not the technologies. It is the people.

Admittedly,some cultivators simply cannot afford the improved inputs, even as their prices come down. If they cannot afford them now, they would not have been able to afford them in the past. These poor cultivators are not the problem. The problem lies with those who have the ability to adopt the new technologies but do not. In the past, it was always an issue of availability and associated cost. Currently, the purchasable inputs are readily available, and their costs are at an all-time low.

The percentage of area under improved seed is a reasonable index to assess adoption. Overall, Indian cultivators have an improved seeds adoption rate of 59 percent. The figures vary widely from state to state. For example, in Punjab and Gujarat, the percentage of area under improved seeds is 84 percent, essentially a saturation level. In states like Nagaland and Sikkim, the adoption rate is only 3 and 4 percent, respectively.[33] See Table 9-4.

In all likelihood, the adoption rate for improved seeds will never get much above 90 percent, since there are a number of food and commercial crops for which there just are not any improved varieties yet. Within this list of 'unimproved crops' one might find mustard, peppers, other vegetables, and jute. For example, if jute were grown on 95 percent of the land for commercial purposes, it would not show up in our list. In the case of Nagaland and Sikkim, we know that this is not the situation. In Nagaland, tea is an important cash crop.

The data for Nagaland and Sikkim, it must be admitted, are probably not good counter points to Punjab's and Gujarat's adoption rate figures; although they do demonstrate: 1) the variability in improved seed adoption, 2) differences in primary crop types, 3) the need for more improved seeds for certain micro-niches, and 4) alternate forms of agriculture. For example, in Nagaland, approximately 93 percent of the population depends on shifting cultivation, known as *jhuming*, which generally precludes the use of most paddy-type rices.[34] Some of the practitioners of *jhuming* do, in fact, prepare the land for the cultivation of paddy but unlike those who practice permanent terrace cultivation, yields are substantially lower.[35] Improved seed varieties are seldom used under *jhuming* but are a recognized part of terrace cultivation. *jhuming* cultivators rely primarily on *desi* (local) rice varieties.

If we look at the distribution of rates against the median value of 49.5, and the frequency of scores, 10 of the 24 major states post adoption rates in excess of 60 percent. These adoption rates, however, may be slightly misleading. The NSSO discovered that as much as 43 percent of the area classified as being sown in improved seeds were actually home grown HYVs. In many cases, the farmers only bought certified improved seeds periodically, preferring to use the seeds grown out of them for several cropping seasons.[36] With

Table 9-4: Percentage of Area Under Improved Seeds by State

State	*Adoption as Percent*
Andhra Pradesh	65
Arunachal Pradesh	24
Assam	43
Bihar	49
Gujarat	84
Haryana	48
Himachal Pradesh	32
Jammu & Kashmir	66
Karnataka	65
Kerala	37
Madhya Pradesh	40
Maharashtra	39
Manipur	61
Meghalaya	57
Mizoram	26
Nagaland	3
Orissa	40
Punjab	84
Rajasthan	68
Sikkim	4
Tamil Nadu	68
Tripura	63
Uttar Pradesh	52
West Bengal	72
India	59

Average = 49.6%
Median = 50.5%

Frequency	
> 90%	0
80-89%	2
70-70%	1
60-69%	7
50-59%	2
40-49%	3
30-39%	5
20-29%	2
10-19%	0
< 10%	2

Source: Adapted from (NSSO, 1999), Table T15, p. 31.

each replanting or reuse, yields diminished until it became apparent to the cultivators that their seed stock needed to be replaced. As a consequence of this traditional attitude toward seed propagation, yields decline, and figures focusing on area under improved seeds become inflated. In reality, if adoption rates were adjusted for 'home grown improved seeds,' the actual area under improved seed could probably be decreased by at least 40 percent. Although data on where this practice is most predominant were not provided, it is assumed that it occurs in the less prosperous, less commercial regions of the country as a money-saving strategy.

It is well documented that the cultivators of Punjab, Haryana, and Gujarat have become habituated to the purchase of certified seeds for planting purposes. To do otherwise would be wasteful of the other inputs they must purchase. New seed serves to maintain productivity and increases income, both important considerations for the commercial agriculturalist. Figures for Punjab, Haryana, and Gujarat are probably fairly accurate. It is curious that so many states fall in the 60 – 69 percent category and there are so few states with higher adoption rates, and those that are above 60 – 69 percent are generally recognized as the most agriculturally commercialized states in India, including West Bengal.

The socio-economic consequences of the Green Revolution in India has been, with only minor exceptions, mirrored wherever it has been implemented. Its most obvious negative characteristic is that it almost always increases the differences – the gap – between marginal and larger cultivators, in terms of productivity and income. It is not that the larger cultivators are necessarily better farmers but that they have the resources to take advantage of the opportunities that the Green Revolution provided. It may also be that the larger cultivators simply possess keener entrepreneurial skills. These skills, undoubtedly, often result from the availability of larger landholders to avail themselves of educational opportunities for their children, who in turn, become the next generation of family cultivators and build on their academic knowledge, not just from hard work in the fields. Stated another way, success breeds success.

Some small-scale cultivators, however, have also realized successes but their number is limited due to insufficient social and economic resources. In most cases, the smallest, least successful cultivators devolve into either landless agricultural laborers or join the ranks of under- and unemployed manual laborers in the urban areas. Even in the cities, due to economic and educational disadvantages, most workers who migrate to the city in search of employment, seldom, if ever, thrive. At the heart of the matter is the fact that entrepreneurial skills are difficult to develop in the midst of abject poverty.

References

1 (Staples, 1992), p. 16.

2 *Ibid.*, p. 17. Even some of the original districts chosen were recognized as not necessarily well suited for intensification experimentation.

3 (Shiva, 1991), p. 171.

4 (College of Food, Agricultural and Natural Resource Sciences, Date Unknown).

5 See. (Sanyal, Biswapriya, 1982), *passim.*

6 For example, (Freebairn, 1995), *passim.*

7 (The World Bank, 2005a)

8 (The World Bank, 2005a), p. 1.

9 Adapted from (Yadav, C.P., B.S. Gupta, and S. Kumar, 2000), p. 116. These later data compare quite well with data obtained during the author's original fieldwork in Darbhanga, and show an overall decline in productivity between the fieldwork years and the present.

10 Based on custom map produced by author, (Census of India 2001, 2008), using Census of India GIS data mapping services.

11 See, (Sanyal, Biswapriya, 1982), p. 83; and (Hannum, 1990), p. 160.

12 Dandekar and Rath, (1971); and Frank J. Moore (1955), pp. 124-128.

13 Although the trendlines appear to be similar, a Pearson's correlation analysis was performed on the raw data. A correlation coefficient of 0.8548 resulted.

14 (Anonomyous, 2002), Table 3, p. 13.

15 *Ibid..*, Table 5, p. 15.

16 (Kuhnen, Frithjof, 1990), p. 2.

17 Rajendra Prasad, the first president of India, made the distinction between those zamindars with revenues over Rs. 5 lakhs and with revenues under Rs.5 lakhs.

18 The Darbhanga Raj was the largest and richest zamindari in all India. The Raj encompassed approximately 2,400 square miles in Bihar and Bengal, which included 4,497 villages. The administration of the Raj employed approximately 7,000 permanent employees. Source: Tejakar Jha, personal communication. Jha is a relative of the last Maharini of Darbhanga. He maintains a website for the

Maharajadhiraja Kameshwar Singh Kalyani Foundation. See, <www.kalyanifoundation.org>.

19 Among these castes were the Yadavas, Koeris, Kurmis along with Bhumihar Brahmins, and Rajputs.

20 (Jha, Unknown).

21 The material and opinions regarding the Maharaja of Darbhanga are those of Tejakar Jha, from a personal communication, December 20, 2007. See note 15, above.

22 See, (Bhalla, G. S., and G. K. Chadha, 1982); and (Sanyal, Biswapriya, 1982).

23 (Gill, S.S., 1988), p. 2168.

24 (Bhalla, G. S., 1972), *passim*.

25 (Bhaduri, Amit, 1973), *passim*

26 *Ibid.*

27 (Census of India, 2001), Provisional figures. Kerala has the highest literacy rate, at 90.9 percent.

28 (Ankit, Rakesh, 2005).

29 (Yadav, C.P., B.S. Gupta, and S. Kumar, 2000).

30 (Jha A. K., 2006).

31 (Acoustic Nerve, 2007). See also, (Lall, 2007?); and (Maithili Parishad, 2004).

32 Information provided by Tejakar Jha, an immediate descendent of the maharini, in a personal communication, 9 September, 2007.

33 (NSSO, 1999), Table T15, p. 31.

34 (Langkau, Maike, Eva Schlecht, and Andreas Buerkert, October 9-11, 2007), p. 1.

35 (NIC, 2003).

36 (NSSO, 1999), p. 28.

10

Issues and Challenges for the Future

Introduction

Over the last decade the incidence of hunger and poverty has been reduced in South Asia. In large measure these improvements have come about as a result of changes in income levels in every sector of the economies of the nations in the region. According to the FAO's 2008 *State of Food and Agriculture in Asia and the Pacific Region*, the region as a whole is on track to achieve the Millennium Development Goal (MDG) of halving the prevalence of extreme poverty by 2015.[1] Nevertheless, more than 650 million people, half of the world's extreme poor, live in the region. The other half live in Sub-Saharan Africa.

The value of all agricultural output (all food and non-food crops and livestock commodities) has almost trebled since 1961, representing an average increase of 2.3 percent per year, well ahead of global population growth, which currently hovers around 1.7 percent per year. See Figure10-1. Although much of this growth has originated in the developed countries of the world, and although a production gap continues to exist between the developed and developing countries, it has been narrowing since the mid-1980s.

Global agricultural value added *per capita* has grown at an average rate of 0.4 percent per year in real terms since 1961, but not all regions have followed the same trend.[2] Latin America, the

Figure 10-1: Total and Per Capita Agricultural Production, 1961-2005

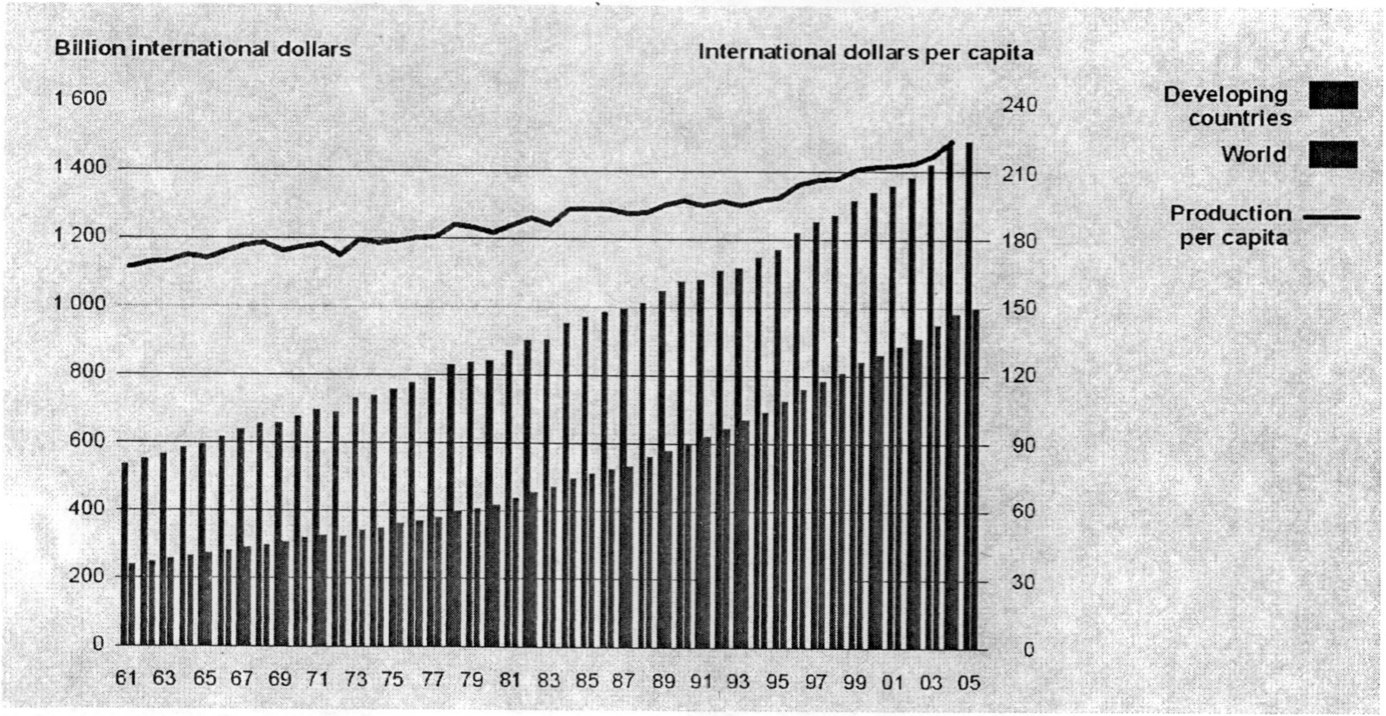

Source: (FAO, 2008), p. 120.

Caribbean, and South Asia have seen meager increases, while the East Asia and the Pacific regions have more than doubled agricultural value added over the last four decades. Sub-Saharan Africa is the only region in which *per capita* agricultural value added has not seen a sustained increase, and has, in fact, displayed an overall declining trend and considerable variation between the countries of the region. See Figure 10-2.

Figure 10-2: Annual Percent Change in Average Growth Rate In Per Capita Agricultural Value Added, By Region

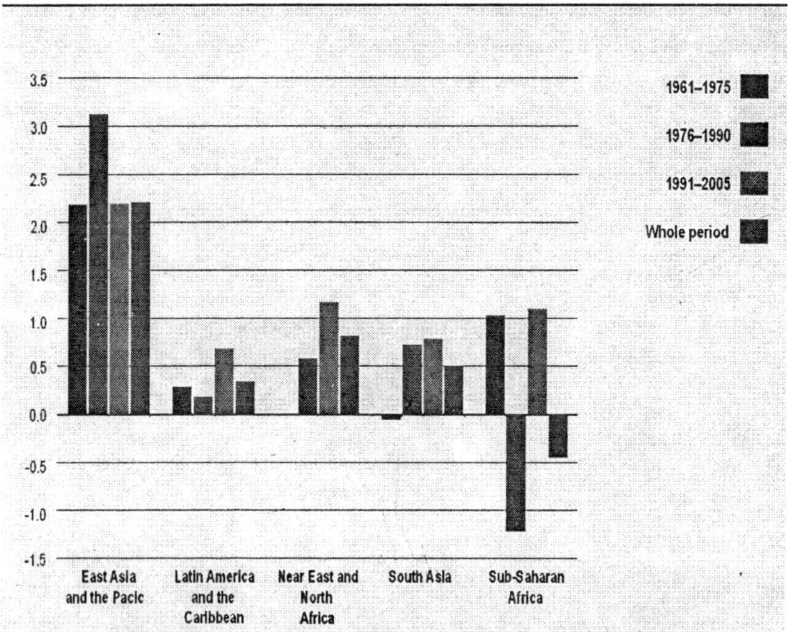

Note: Agricultural value added includes fish and forestry products. No data are available for the Near East and North Africa until 1974. Data for Sub-Saharan Africa are available from 1967and for Latin America and the Caribbean from 1965.

Source: (FAO, 2008), p. 121.

Changes in Agricultural Production and Consumption

The composition of agricultural production has changed considerably over the last four decades. The global output of cereals, oil crops, sugar, vegetables, eggs and meat has increased more rapidly than population growth rates, while the production of pulses and roots and tubers has declined relative to total population growth.[3]

Typically, urbanization is associated with higher incomes and improved transportation. Together, these dramatically alter food consumption patterns, in accordance with Engel's Law. Engel stated that the share of food in current expenditure declines as income rises, and expenditures on cereals declines, including the quantity consumed. More specifically,

. . . je aermer eine Familie ist, einen desto groesseren Antheil von der Gesamtausgabe muss zur Beschaffung der Nahrung aufgewendet werden . . . .[4]

As a consequence, growth in the dairy sector is expected to accelerate, mainly because of increased demand in both developed and developing countries. Sugar production has begun to accelerate already. Total meat production in developing countries has increased more than fivefold between 1970 and 2005. See Figure 10-3. Although

Figure 10-3: Beef, Pork, Poultry, and Mutton and Lamb Production, 1961-2006

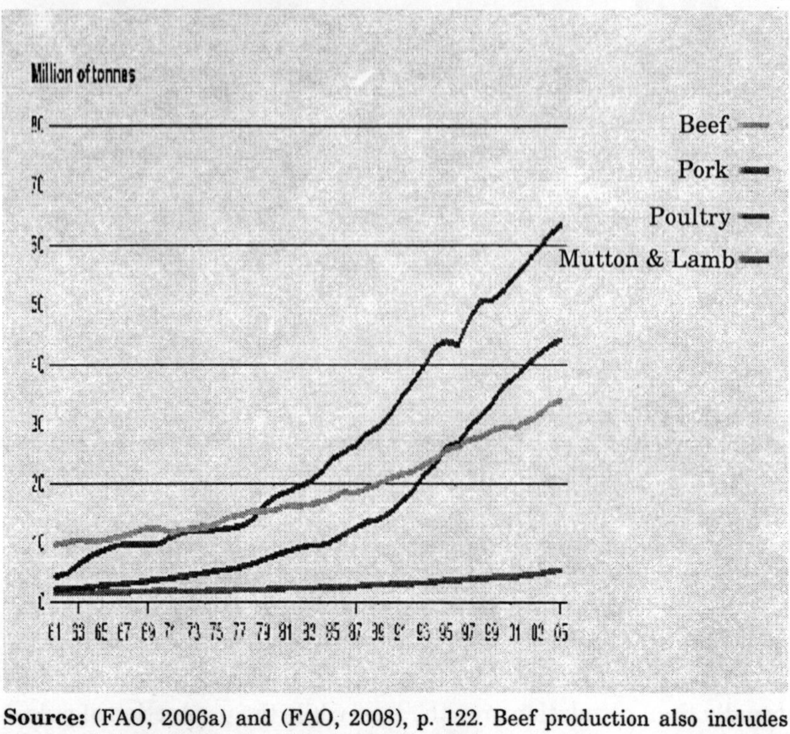

Source: (FAO, 2006a) and (FAO, 2008), p. 122. Beef production also includes meat and by-products from domesticated buffalo.

the pace of growth is slowing somewhat, global demand for meat is expected to increase by more than 50 percent by 2030.[5]

Satisfying the world's demand for meat and animal products has a substantial impact on the world's water, land and biodiversity resources and contributes significantly to climate change. Directly and indirectly, through grazing and through feedcrop production, the livestock sector occupies about 30 percent of the ice-free terrestrial surface on the planet. In many situations, livestock is a major source of land based pollution, emitting nutrients and organic matter, pathogens and drug residues into rivers, lakes and coastal waters.[6] Animals and their wastes emit gases, some of which contribute to climate change, especially methane. Land-use changes caused by demand for feedgrain and grazing land also result in greenhouse gases.[7] In fact, the FAO states categorically:

. . . the livestock sector generates more greenhouse gas emissions as measured in CO_2 equivalent – 18 percent – than transport. It is also a major source of land and water degradation. Says Henning Steinfeld, Chief of FAO's Livestock Information and Policy Branch and senior author of the report: "Livestock are one of the most significant contributors to today's most serious environmental problems. Urgent action is required to remedy the situation." Livestock shape entire landscapes and their demands on land for pasture and feedcrop production modify and reduce natural habitats.[8]

Meeting the world demand for animal food products is one of the major challenges facing world agriculture today. Until recently, a large proportion of livestock in developing countries was not raised for food, but for providing draught power and manure and as capital assets that were only disposed of in times of emergency. Livestock were an integral part of agricultural systems. This pattern is changing rapidly. Almost all growth in livestock production is now occurring within the context of industrial systems, where animals no longer are raised to supply animal power or manure.[9] The rearing of livestock is now predominantly for the purposes of food production.

Especially in South Asia, due to cultural and religion-sanctioned avoidances with regard to the consumption of pork and beef, the most rapid increases in meat consumption are in the area of poultry, which has also stimulated the production of maize as a feedgrain. This growth has been especially evident in Pakistan and even more so in Bangladesh.

Agricultural Diversification

In much of South Asia, wheat, rice, and maize represent the three primary foodgrains. Cotton and sugarcane are typically the chief cash crops. Figure 10-4, depicts yields per hectare for the primary foodgrains and cash crops in South Asia. With the exception of maize production in Bangladesh and sugarcane production in India, world yields for the primary foodgrains and all but one of the cash crops exceed those of all nations of South Asia.[11] Obviously, there is room for improvement in the area of production.

In Pakistan, outside Punjab Province and parts of Sindh, cultivators are rapidly leaving purely subsistence agricultural traditions behind. Especially in Punjab, there has been a long-time commercial tradition in agriculture, initially fostered by the British through the canal colony system. Throughout Pakistan the movement away from subsistence agricultural pursuits will inevitably mean a movement toward a more diversified, market-oriented production system. In Nepal and Bangladesh, subsistence cultivation is more the rule than the exception.

Initially diversification implied the addition of other crops and other enterprises in the production mix. As the level of commercialization increases, mixed farming systems will give way to specialized production units that are designed to respond rapidly to market price and quality signals. In many respects, this has already happened in Indian East Punjab with the Jat Sikh wheat-rice cultivators there. In fact, it was both the recalcitrance and flexibility of the Sikh farmers that precipitated India's so-called '2006 Wheat Crisis,' which probably could not have been avoided in light of the GoI's unofficial, agricultural diversification agenda.

Pakistan's need to diversify its agricultural sector is based on the same circumstances observed in India. As a result of the over-exploitation – the use of chemical fertilizers, and irrigation – the naturally rich soils of Punjab have begun showing signs of fatigue in the form of declines in the soil's organic content, significantly depleted micronutrients, increased soil salinity, and, in some places, signs of agricultural stagnation and even decline.[12]

Figure 10-4 : Yields per mt/hectare – World Records, Averages, India, Bangladesh, Pakistan, and Nepal for Wheat, Rice, Maize, and Cotton ('0,000 kg/ha)[10]

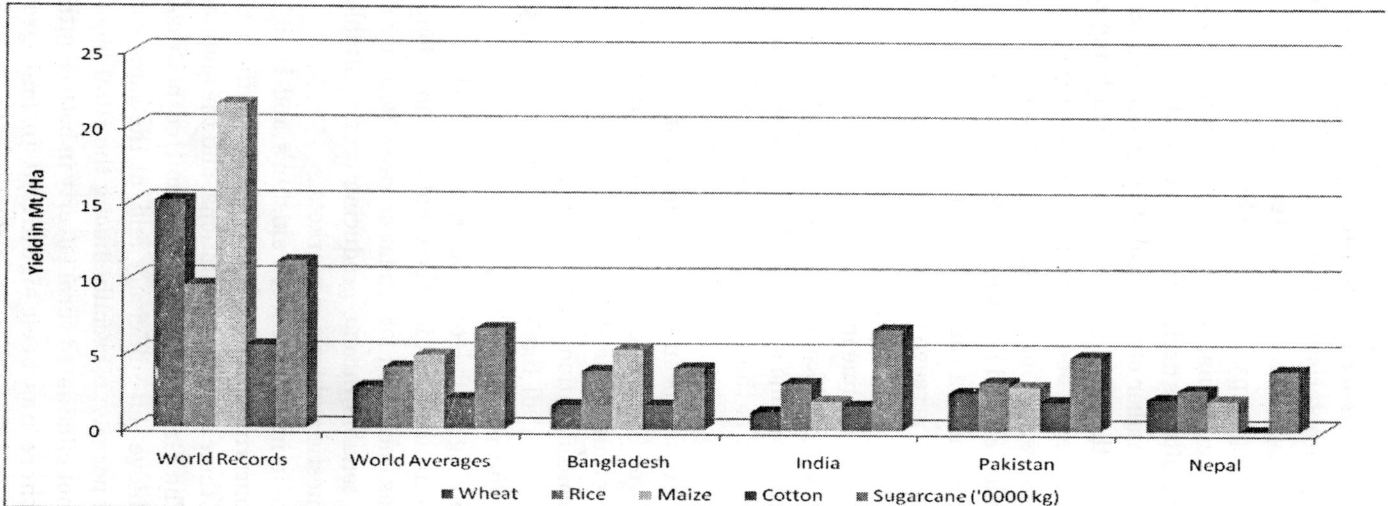

Sources: World Records: *Wheat* - (FWiSpace, 2007); *Rice* (FAO, Record Rice Yields in Egypt, 2006c) and (Bernama.com, 2007); *Maize* - (Duvick, D. N. and K. G. Cassman, 1999), p. 1622; *Cotton* - (Israeli Embassy, 1998); *Sugarcane* - (Hussain, May 2005), p. 32. World Averages and country figures: (FAO, Selected Indicators of Food and Agricultural Development in the Asia-Pacific Region,1996-2006, October 2007), **Table**: **13**, p. 48; **16**, p. 51; **19**, p. 54; **72**, p. 121; and **77**, p. 129.

The Rice-Wheat Consortium for the Indo-Gangetic Plains

In an uncharacteristic move, Pakistan, India, Nepal, and Bangladesh, along with a number of international research centers, NGOs, and farmer groups, formed The Rice-Wheat Consortium for the Indo-Gangetic Plains, in 1994. The group's charge was to investigate agriculture's decline in much of South Asia. This group has developed a number of potential strategies intended to revive agriculture in South Asia.[13] Some of the solutions being considered include: Zero-tillage, bed planting, the integration of input management for water, nutrients and all chemical inputs, like fertilizers, pesticides, and herbicides. Also part of the Consortium's package of solutions is a commitment to crop diversification and the reduction of the acreage devoted to wheat and rice.

Part of the Consortium's desire for crop diversification is to reverse the current decline in agricultural production but it is also believed that crop diversification will have a positive impact on overall nutritional and economic security. While it has been agreed that crop diversification is the key to the implementation of both the agronomic and socio-economic revitalization of the region's agriculture, there has been little consensus on how this might be achieved. At issue is the question of whether targeting wheat and rice would potentially jeopardize economic or food security, or both. Additionally, consideration must be given to cultural and national food preferences. In all likelihood, it is not practical to think in terms of replacing one or the other but rather cutting back on both, while maintaining sufficient production of both to meet grain preference requirements. It is hoped that the 'abandoned' acreage – land that was once used for wheat or rice – will be converted to commercially tenable income-producing crops suitable for local needs and domestic and foreign markets.

Since their independence, Pakistan's and India's primary agricultural concern has been the production of sufficient quantities of food to feed their growing populations, and the emphasis was on foodgrains. The Green Revolution permitted both countries to ultimately achieve self-sufficiency and, at the same time, reduce long-standing poverty, especially among the rural populations. It has reduced, not eliminated rural poverty in both countries. At the same time, there has been significant income growth, diet diversification and declines in *per capita* cereal consumption.

World Trade Organization

In 2001 a Ministerial meeting was held by the World Trade Organization in Doha, Sri Lanka. At this meeting a number of breakthroughs in multinational trade negotiations, resulted in the so-called Doha Development Agenda (DDA). There were sharp differences between the developed and developing nations on a number key issues. The most daunting of these involved agriculture. At issue were concerns regarding market access, domestic supports for agriculture, and export subsidies. The final resolution of these issues for the nations of South Asia would have a direct impact on rural development, food security, and the broad issue of poverty alleviation. India and Pakistan, as part of the G-22, were instrumental in negotiations having to do with the reformulation and reduction of tariff structures. The reduction of protective tariffs in South Asia would have a dramatic impact on overall economic activity but especially in terms of agricultural export subsidies.

As an outcome of the DDA, South Asia has witnessed sweeping reforms after years of restrictive economic policies and tight regulations. Collectively, these nations have reduced tariffs, removed trade barriers, dismantled restrictions on domestic and foreign private investment and reformed their financial systems. Average tariff rates have declined by as much as 80 percent.[14] This has had the effect of opening the trade doors of South Asia to an unrelenting onslaught from almost every nation. The opportunities for present and future trade are almost bewildering and will force the reexamination of almost every facet of the lives of the people of South Asia.

The modification of heretofore protective trade barriers is expected to have an especially profound impact on the farm systems in all South Asia. It is believed that South Asian agriculture will begin to evolve rapidly, as technologies, institutions and markets change in response to the further integration of these developing economies into the global economy. Where domestic plans were unable to move the nations of South Asia closer to the goals set by government, the globalization of the world economy seems to have had just that effect.

As the South Asian economies evolve and respond to globalization, it is assumed that agriculture in each nation will move out of subsistence food crop production to a more diversified, market-oriented production system. Initially diversification implies the addition of other crops and other enterprises at the farm household level. As the level of commercialization increases, mixed farming systems are expected to give way to specialized production units that are designed to respond rapidly to market price and quality signals. Diversification in the agricultural sector entails specialization.

The opportunities for diversification will be spurred by an anticipated rapid growth in international demands for fruits, vegetables, dairy products, fats, and oils. In addition, within the subcontinent itself, domestic demands for similar products will serve as a stimulus for economic growth, urbanization, and changing food consumption patterns.The response to these opportunities will largely depend on new technologies becoming available to farmers as well as changes in rural infrastructure, markets and incentive systems. In fact, a FAO/World Bank study suggests that agricultural intensification and diversification are the two most important sources of poverty reduction for small farmers in South Asia.[15] It is anticipated that most farmers of the subcontinent, over the next thirty years, will become semi-commercial in orientation with a progressive increase in the share of output marketed.

Another way of describing agricultural diversification is commercialization. One of the first signs of a shift toward agricultural commercialization is the increased use of artificial or chemical fertilizers. Steady increases in the use of fertilizers demonstrates the cultivators' desire to produce surpluses that can be marketed, thus bringing them under the umbrella of the cash market economy. This, in turn, leads to greater involvement in the cash economy of the region and the nation, and ultimately involves them in the global, agricultural economy, as well as a growing consumption of items that cannot be bartered for, or inputs that must be purchased with cash or credit.

Even before the reduction of agricultural tariff protection, many cultivators in Pakistan and India had already begun to recognize the changes in local and national consumption patterns and had begun to move to satisfy those new demands. If one compares agricultural growth rates for cereals versus livestock, fruits, and

Table 10-5: Changes in Irrigated Area, Fertilizer Consumption and Selected Crops During the Period 1996-2006

Country	*Irrigated Area*	*Fertilizer*	*Cereals*	*Maize*	*Fruits*	*Vegetables*	*Cotton*	*Sugarcane*
India	2.8	4.0	0.9	3.2	1.2	4.2	3.9	0.0
Pakistan	0.8	4.9	2.6	7.1	2.8	2.5	2.7	(0.1)
Bangladesh	0.5	3.9	4.7	63.0	3.0	5.2	(4.5)	(1.1)
Nepal	2.8	(13.2)	1.8	2.7	3.8	5.3	0.0	4.6

Source: (FAO, Selected Indicators of Food and Agricultural Development in the Asia-Pacific Region, 1996-2006, October 2007)

vegetables, one sees a movement toward the higher value livestock, livestock products, fruits, and vegetables. Dorjee, working in 2002-03, noted significant changes in the growth rates during the period 1979-1999 for a number of agricultural inputs and products and livestock, based on FAO Selected Indicators.[16] More current data (1996-2006), however, is not as pronounced but a similar pattern continues to exist – minor increases in irrigated area, increases in fertilizer consumption, low growth rates in cereals (rice, wheat, etc.), significant increases in maize production, increases in fruits, and significant increases in vegetable production. Surprisingly, increases in the traditional cash crops – cotton and sugarcane – showed only minor changes or, as in the case of Pakistan and Bangladesh, losses. The most startling observations were:

- Almost insignificant increases in irrigated area.
- An astounding 63 percent increase in maize production for Bangladesh.
- Significant increases in vegetable production.

Based on the numbers in Figure 10-5, one can infer that increases in fruit and vegetable production came either at the expense of cotton and sugarcane acreage, from cereal acreage, or all three. In the case of Bangladesh, increases in cereal, maize, and vegetable production came at the expense of cotton and sugarcane, in that order. Pakistan's increase in maize production seems to have been at the expense of sugarcane.

Livestock production has increased throughout South Asia over the last decade. Poultry production expanded very rapidly. Milk production rose most rapidly in Pakistan. Bangladesh and India had growth rates well above population growth rates thus enabling an increase in the *per capita* supply of milk. Meat production increased rapidly in Bangladesh. Increases in poultry production was significant in Pakistan, Bangladesh, and India.

Agricultural Integration and Diversification

It took five years for the real effects of the DDA to be felt and implemented but the lifting of restrictive, protectionist trade barriers to agricultural products has opened the world to cultivators of all sizes. Further, the trend toward production-to-retailers has also served to integrate once isolated cultivators and producers into an increasingly cash-oriented agricultural market. Essentially, this is the path that *e-Choupal* is pioneering.

The net effect of this integration is increased income, the reduction of poverty, a movement away from subsistence agriculture, and the reduction or elimination of predatory middlemen. The demise of the agricultural middleman should result in increased income to the tillers of the soil.

The diversification of agriculture in South Asia appears to be under way. The governments, believing that the globalization of the world agricultural market is the key to their economic success, have begun to dismantle the mechanical obstacles to free trade. However, there remain a number of nagging questions, the most important of which are:

- Is the current demand for South Asian fruits, vegetables, dairy products, fats, and oils by developing nations sustainable?
- Will requisite technologies, infrastructures, markets, and incentives emerge?
- Is the continued export demand sufficiently large enough to have a broad impact on the traditional agricultural systems that havedeveloped over hundreds of years and have only been slightly modified by the Green Revolution technologies?
- Cereal self-sufficiency has been the *raison d'être* for the agricultural policies of the region but if the envisioned export demand for agricultural products should fail, can domestic demand for the same products sustain long-term production?
- Assuming that the diversification of South Asian agriculture will require investments in physical and human capital, are there sufficient resources available to accomplish these ends?

2008 World Food Crisis

Beginning in the latter half of 2007, the world was witness to a significant rise in food prices. This increase seemed to accelerate during the first half of 2008, and continues in 2009. These increases have had an impact on developing nations but also in most developed nations. This 'crisis' has been blamed, largely on escalating petroleum prices. A secondary cause has been the diversion of certain grains (primarily maize) and sugarcane to the production of biofuels – ethanol and bio-diesel. Of the two, the diversion of maize production to biofuel production has undoubtedly had the greatest impact on current world food prices. Although this diversion is primarily a phenomenon in developed nations, especially the U.S., it has had a worldwide impact.

Traditionally, the U.S. and Canada have been the leading producers of the maize that found its way into the world grain market. Now, this supply is being curtailed. Again, it not the lack of production that is causing the problem, it is where and how it is being used. It is being used domestically and for non-food purposes; and even though only 20 percent of the total maize output in the U.S. is finding its way into biofuels production, it is sufficiently large enough to produce a ripple effect throughout the world.

The stimulus for the production of biofuels is largely in response to two simultaneous problems. First, is the rising cost of petroleum. Second, is the belief that biofuels will ameliorate petroleum dependency and, at the same time have a positive impact on the emission of greenhouse gases, with the result that Global Warming can at least be slowed.

While the reasoning behind the conversion of maize into biofuels is laudable, it is severely flawed. The production of maize for the purposes of biofuels production requires energy, energy in the form of petroleum for tractors, harvesters, fertilizers, and pesticides. The advocates of 'peak oil' have explored this phenomenon.[17] The conversion of maize into ethanol also requires energy, in the form of electricity or the burning of fossil fuels. The distribution of ethanol requires the use of tanker trucks and the use of petroleum. Finally, even if all the maize production in the U.S. were, or could be converted efficiently into ethanol, there simply is not enough maize to make enough ethanol to significantly reduce existing demands for petroleum products in the U.S. One estimate of ethanol production states:

. . . if all corn, wheat, rice and soya was used it would only cover around 4% of all of America's energy needs.[18]

When one looks at the economics of ethanol production, there is one inescapable conclusion: ethanol removes large quantities of potential foodgrain from the foodgrain market, which could be used for human consumption; and the cost-benefit of ethanol production is dubious. If we accept the estimates, it takes *more* energy to produce one gallon of ethanol than it makes, and we cannot produce sufficient amounts to have a genuine impact on petroleum consumption.

Energy analysts said ethanol reduces some oil use. But there have been conflicting studies about whether more energy is used to grow corn and produce ethanol than it provides as a fuel. Electricity — typically produced from natural gas or coal — is needed to operate ethanol plants, for instance, and farm equipment uses petroleum products.

Tad W. Patzek, a professor of geo-engineering at the University of California at Berkeley, said ethanol production uses far more energy than making gasoline and releases more greenhouse gases, which have been linked to global warming. He co-authored a study last year that said ***corn ethanol requires 29 percent more energy to make than it produces*** *Energy analysts said ethanol reduces some oil use. But there have been conflicting studies about whether more energy is used to grow corn and produce ethanol than it provides as a fuel. Electricity — typically produced from natural gas or coal — is needed to operate ethanol plants, for instance, and farm equipment uses petroleum products* **[Emphasis added]**.[19]

The conversion of foodgrains into ethanol does not make economic sense, because it takes food out of the mouths of people, and puts alcohol in vehicles' gas tanks. Why, then, is it being pursued so earnestly? The answer is twofold. First, the U.S. and other leading maize producers simply produce much more than can be sold and world prices are pushed down, undermining farmers' profitability. Ethanol production absorbs the surplus production, removes the grain from the world market, and prices increase. Along with increasing prices, farmers' profitability increases. In addition, huge government subsidies make its production possible, not market forces.

Second, on paper, the use of biofuels appears to have the advantage of reducing foreign oil dependency. At the same time, biofuels are supposed to help reduce the emission of CO_2 and other noxious gasses that result from burning petroleum-based fuels, and this will help in the fight against Global Warming. By this time, everyone should be standing and cheering. Just by converting foodgrains into biofuels, we are reducing our need for oil and saving the environment. Hurrah. But, what about the hungry people that those foodgrains could have fed? Something seems amiss here.

The real question: Is the conversion of maize into ethanol the best use of the grain, or will its conversion have sufficiently meaningful consequences for Mankind and the Earth to justify its conversion? Unfortunately, the answer to both questions is – No.

Constraints on Diversification

Risk Avoidance

Cultivators, in the process of deciding to change their current production patterns – to diversify their production — must make what might be perceived as an educated 'leap of faith.' It is readily accepted that humans are reluctant to make changes in their lives, a process commonly referred to as social inertia, unless they perceive the reward for such change to be substantially greater than the perceived associated costs. In the case of cultivators, contemplating a change from wheat or rice cultivation to, say, vegetables, they consciously and subconsciously calculate the risks associated with the alternatives available to them. The most important consideration involves the economic risk to the cultivator's household. If the economic risk can be shared by or transferred to other parties the willingness to make the decision to change is much easier. In much more simple terms, cultivators need some kind of safety net to insure their economic survival during the process of changeover. In the absence of such safety nets, for example, ready access to credit, cultivators are much less likely to entertain the idea of diversification. Therefore, if the governments do indeed wish cultivators to diversify, they must be willing to underwrite the cultivators' willingness to change.

Government assistance could be provided in a number of ways, each of which should provide minimal financial protection for as long as the transition takes. For example, in the case of no-till cultivation, the third year in the transition process is oftentimes the most difficult. Thus, in such a situation, the government, through guaranteed loans or crop insurance programs, should be prepared to step in and assist the cultivator. This type of long-term investment could provide major dividends for both the cultivator and the government.

Issues of Land

Land security, either in the form of landholdings or assured tenancy, is a prerequisite if cultivators are to make the decision to diversify and make the capital investments necessary. Cultivators' willingness to invest in the land will be dependent upon the belief that their investments and the resultant returns on those investments cannot be wrenched away from them at the whim of government or the tenant's landowner.

There are three areas that normally require substantial capital and human investments. First, in the case of no-till cultivation, one of the most expensive land investments is in the area of field leveling, which is necessary for both rain-fed and irrigated lands, and contouring on sloping lands. These processes are capital and human intensive. The result of such investments, however, is the more efficient distribution of available water and more uniform subsoil moisture retention.

Second, investments in irrigation networks and systems represent substantial financial outlays. Pumpsets, tubewells, distribution canals and gateways are expensive to implement, maintain, and operate.

Finally, depending on the location of the cultivator's fields, erosion control may be as important as irrigation. Farmer's choice of erosion control strategy depends on population pressure on the land, on market access, and on the appropriate erosion control techniques available. Several writers suggest that farmer interest in erosion control measures is directly related to land values and market access and is conditional on suitable technologies being made available to them.[20]

Security stemming from acknowledged land rights improves cultivators' willingness to make capital investments in their land or the land they cultivate as tenants. These same rights enhance the likelihood that the cultivator, as owner or tenant, will be able to recover the investment he has made in the land. Furthermore, secure claim or title to the land often means that the land can be used as collateral for obtaining additional investment capital, either for land improvements or inputs.

Labor Constraints

Diversification does not necessarily mean an increase in long-term labor requirements but, at least in the beginning, the preparation of the land, especially if it involves conversion from one crop-type to another (for example, rice to vegetables) may require additional labor inputs. Likewise, the development of leveled fields, irrigation canals, head works, etc., may require additional labor. If no-till cultivation is elected, long-term labor requirements may be reduced but, again, only after the initial preparation of the fields. If the crops selected are high-maintenance varieties, diversification may require additional labor inputs in the long-term or periodically, during planting, weeding, and harvesting.

At least initially, diversification may require additional labor inputs in the form of increased supervision. This time investment will typically decline as familiarity with the reworked land and the new crop variety or varieties increases.

Agricultural Research

For the diversification and commercialization of agriculture to be successful, it requires governments to rethink their long-term development strategies. In the past, almost all the agronomic research conducted under the aegis of the government was geared to one of two overlapping strategies – agricultural self-sufficiency and the package of practices that would make self-sufficiency a reality. Little attention was directed to problems that had been prophesized by some observers; for example, soil degradation, soil salinity, erosion, flooding, water logging, desertification, surface and groundwater contamination and pollution, and water depletion. As these problems manifested themselves, agronomists worked feverishly to correct them. Some were amenable to remediation and mitigation. Others, when they were finally recognized, had progressed to the point that little could be done to remediate them. The choice facing cultivators in some areas are simple: abandon their lands or die.

If there is to be a Second Green Revolution, and if it is based on agricultural diversification and commercialization, agronomic research must be reformulated. This is particularly true now that policies based on the idea of agricultural self-sufficiency are becoming obsolete, since that goal has been theoretically achieved and now the emphasis is to achieve agricultural growth through market responsiveness or is powered by economic pressures and sustainability.

Agricultural self-sufficiency, as the driving force behind agriculture, is now giving way to the idea of agricultural self-reliance. Policies based on the concept of self-reliance reflect the government's willingness to permit its food security to be based on its ability to obtain food through market forces, i.e., the government is willing to import a portion of the food needs of the country in exchange for other agricultural products or the export of other resources or products. At the same time, governments must shift their thinking away from the need to produce food surpluses and look to improving *per capita* income, which will enhance individual participation in the broadening cash-based marketplace and further insulate the people from the possibilities of famine.

Diversification – The Future?

To some extent, there always have been attempts at diversification and the commercialization of agriculture with every generation. There are always agricultural entrepreneurs. Now, however, with the relaxation of tariff barriers to the import and export of agricultural produce and inputs, increased incomes, higher rates of urbanization, and accompanying changes in food consumption, many of the governments of South Asia are attempting to foster and accelerate their country's participation in the growing global market for their crops and agricultural products. Even when cultivators either did not or would not see that increased participation in world market was in the national best interest, the government took the lead and forced them to become involved. Recognizing that world trade could provide development opportunities for their agricultural sectors, that were not being realized through domestic markets, the governments of South Asia, individually and collectively, have worked to push their agricultural sectors to become active participants. Such was the case of the artificially induced Wheat Crisis of 2006 in India.

The governments, by and large, have had to push their subsistence cultivators toward more specialized and commercialized crop production. For some of the successful cultivators, such as the Punjabi wheat-rice farmers of India and the large landholders of Pakistan, who have thrived on government price supports since the advent of the Green Revolution, their governments are pressuring them to become involved in the process of crop diversification and commercialization. The government's moves have resulted in mixed results.

Land Reforms

Land reforms in each of the countries of South Asia have been largely ineffective, except for the removal of the most egregiously large landholders. The long-term effects of land consolidation and fragmentation have had little or no real long-term consequences. Where they were initially successful, time and inheritance rights have resulted in the re-fragmentation of holdings. Research has shown, however, that the time, effort, and political maneuverings of politicians may have been more for the purposes of political economy than to see a genuine redistribution of land rights and the improvement of security in the land. Also, despite the general failure of land reform legislation, the Green Revolution was a success, where it was fully implemented. In other words, the belief that land reforms were a prerequisite to the successful implementation of the Green Revolution was patently wrong.

The fact that current land reforms have had little or no real effect on the rural socio-economic order does not mean that there is no need for reforms. Only, now, the reforms that are required must reflect a real desire to promote rural change, not to serve as a political tool or diversion. The new round of reforms must target the impediments to the continuation of the Green Revolution – some reflecting changes in agrarian structures, and others addressing institutional problems.

If one examines the pattern of the Green Revolution, the first, most noticeable characteristic of the successful areas is the size of farms. Almost invariably, the Green Revolution has been most successful in areas where large to medium-sized landholdings existed, particularly in India's northwest – Punjab and Haryana. Here, as a function of the post-Partition resettlement and land ceiling enactments, larger landholdings were permissible.

Secondly, the success of the Green Revolution may be a reflection of the large landowners' ability to obtain the requisite inputs, i.e., they had the capital necessary to invest in them. Small landholders, usually do not have sufficient capital reserves to invest, or are frequently unable to secure the necessary credit to purchase the inputs. It is not necessary to determine the cause and effect relationship between landholding size and available capital. It is enough to recognize that this relationship simply exists. In addition to having the means to pay for the inputs, most of these farmers were resourceful when it came to obtaining access to the needed inputs, either through social, political, or economic linkages. Again, small cultivators frequently do not possess nor have access to such linkages.

It should be noted, however, that not all "large landholders" were necessarily predisposed to invest in the modern inputs. Some of the larger landholders preferred to rely on time-honored tenancy arrangements. Their share of the harvest, either as rent paid in kind or in cash, produced a comfortable existence or lifestyle, without the need to invest in new, expensive inputs, no matter how much additional production might result. In time, however, even these large landholders recognized the benefit of the new inputs, with the result that they terminated many tenant and sharecropper agreements and resumed control over their lands. The end result for these laggards was a substantial increase in income.

The groups hardest hit by the Green Revolution, have been the sub-marginal cultivators, the tenants, and the landless agricultural laborers. As the most marginal cultivators lost their lands and tenants and sharecroppers were evicted from the land, the agricultural labor pool increased. As competition for a limited number of jobs increased, agricultural wages were driven down and rural poverty among this class of agriculturalists increased.

Green Revolution and Future Reforms

The Green Revolution took off in areas most suited to the implementation of the various modern technologies. The question is now, how will the Green Revolution be spread to more "marginal" areas? Even within the heartlands of the Green Revolution, there are still areas for improvement, but outside these areas there is an even greater need for both micro- and macro-institutional changes.

1) Transport. In those areas that have not been the beneficiaries of the Green Revolution, marketing is usually accomplished by hauling small quantities of grain or other produce to the nearest market place or *mandi*. After the sale of the commodity, the cultivator obtains whatever supplies he may require and hauls the spoils of the day back to his home.

One of the hallmarks of an agriculturally developed area is the existence of highly developed market orientations and commercial trucking. Truck transports carried inputs from supply houses to the villages and returned laden with marketable agricultural products. Therefore, to stimulate the rapid distribution of both inputs and produce, supports should be provided for the establishment of commercial trucking companies. The ideal solution would be to provide such incentives as deemed necessary for cooperative trucking associations to become tenable, serving a prescribed number of participating villages. In time, as the demand for transport services increase, individual, for hire, trucking companies would begin to take over where the cooperative trucking system left off.

2) Post Harvest Storage. One of the problems quickly faced by the IADP coordinators was what to do with the post harvest product. Annually, large quantities of wheat and rice are lost to pests and spoilage, due to a lack of adequate pest-free and weather-proof storage facilities. Even with *e-Choupal*, it is necessary to provide for short-term, protected storage. As produce centralization requirements increase, so do the needs for improved storage. The days of storing grains in sacks in a back room or under an awning are rapidly disappearing since such storage practices result in the unjustified loss of hard won product. Every grain of wheat or rice that is consumed by vermin or lost to spoilage, is one less grain for consumption or marketing. This realization becomes all the more important as the cultivator makes the transition from cultivator to farmer.

The need for secure storage of foodgrains has been well documented, but its use in village settings has been slow to develop.

In India about 30 to 40 per cent of the grain produced in the country is handled by the Government and private agencies, while the remaining 60 to 70 per cent is retained by village farmers for household use and consumption. The storage and warehousing facilities built by the FCI and CWC were located, mostly, in or near urban centres. Storage at the village level was neglected until village co-operatives initiated the building of improved storage facilities with the financial support of the National Co-operative Development Corporation (NCDC). Though the total storage facilities thus provided by the co-operatives is very meager . . . . The loss of food grains stored in FCI and CWC godowns is less than 1 per cent, but in the village storage systems it can be as high as 5 per cent as a national average. Wimberly . . . placed storage losses at 5 to 10 per cent. Undoubtedly there is a high loss each year that is still to be controlled.[21]

Ancillary to the problem of storage is the problem of drying grains before storage. This is not much of a problem with wheat, but post-harvest drying of rice is crucial. Currently, most cultivators are compelled to dispose of their paddy harvest soon after it is removed from the field and threshed. By immediately marketing their produce, they transfer the problems of drying to the rice traders, rice millers or rice milling cooperatives. The downside to this pattern is that all the rice is harvested and marketed at one time. Being forced to sell puts the cultivator at a disadvantage, which translates to lower prices. Were the cultivator able to dry his paddy and store it for later sale, he would receive a better price, for dry paddy demands a higher price, and storage allows for the cultivator to wait for positive changes in rice prices. The ability to store rice is analogous for wheat. If the cultivator can wait to market his produce, beyond the height of the harvest period, prices almost invariably improve. With rice, drying becomes very important, and drying is necessary for long-term storage. For wheat, drying is not necessary, but waiting for market changes demands storage.

3) Tenant and Labor Protection. With or without the government's notice, the character of Indian agriculture has changed rapidly, especially in the last 35-40 years. It started out as, at best, a subsistence agricultural system, and has evolved into a market-driven, surplus-producing machine. For the new class of commercial farmers that emerged with the Green Revolution, things have turned out wonderfully. Many have grown from just being large- to middle-sized landholders or landlords into prosperous agriculturalists. The benefits of the Green Revolution have not, however, been equally beneficial for all agricultural classes, including the smaller landholders, tenants, and the landless laborers. Old-style land reforms, while advocating rural justice, and equity, have failed these classes. Each has become increasingly impoverished as their counterparts have prospered. The prosperity of the new class of farmers is not necessarily the cause of these classes' growing impoverishment.

The cause of their continued impoverishment lies in the fact that they have been and continue to be marginal cultivators, either due to the size of their landholdings and fragmentation, their lack of investment capital, poor managerial skills, and lack of education, lack of socio-economic-political linkages, or some combination of these factors. If one takes a purely philosophical look at these classes, one could define their plight as just another example of *karma*, simply their fate. They were born poor and that is the way they will stay. Philosophically, this may be an acceptable explanation, but it is not very satisfying from a humanistic point of view. Nor would such an explanation satisfy the founders of modern India. The poor in a poor nation require attention, if not outright protection.

For this reason, and if for no other, the lesser agricultural classes now require attention. In the past, agrarian reforms focused their attention on the elimination of intermediaries, setting ceilings on the size of holdings, and transforming tenants into landowners. All this attention was focused on the top of the social pyramid, the large and middle-sized landholding classes. For all intents and purposes, it had little or no impact on the smallest landholders, tenants, and landless laborers. What impact it did have was almost always negative. Also, it has been suggested that increases in agricultural production, social and economic equality and improved utilization of rural labor are inherently incompatible.[22]

Agrarian reforms set out to prevent this self-fulfilling prophecy. They did not help. Many of the smaller landowners, tenants, and landless laborers continued to suffer as agricultural production rose and the larger landowners prospered. Many of the smaller, sub-marginal cultivators simply could not compete and lost their lands due to under-production, increasing land values, indebtedness, and, finally, insolvency. Some migrated to other areas, usually the growing urban areas, in search of employment. Many joined the ranks of the landless laborer class. Marginal tenants faired no better. As mechanization in planting and harvesting increased, the need for tenants declined, and they were evicted from their lands. Larger operating units proved to be complementary to the new inputs. Many of these former tenants migrated, but most also joined the landless laborer class. It would seem, in light of expert predictions and the employment data that the Green Revolution was incompatible with the maintenance of social and economic equity and equality, improved labor utilization, and increased productivity.The experts had been correct, in spite of the government's package of agrarian reforms, which had been designed to combat these consequences.

The prophecy would have been proven incorrect had the Green Revolution not been so responsive to larger field cultivation and had been powered by human cultivation activities, instead of mechanization. If human labor had been the focus of the Green Revolution, the increased numbers of people who became part of the landless labor class might not have suffered as they have. Many would have prospered along with their employers. However, this is not what happened.

4) Labor Substitution. Kuhnen however still believes that the three goals of increased production, social and economic equality, and the absorption of surplus labor are not incompatible. He states:

> *. . . under Asian conditions, higher production, more employment and more social and economic equality are complementary goals. Higher production, whether achieved with modern technology or within traditional agriculture, requires the application of more labour and can be reached in the long run only if the necessary social and economic equality provides incentives and the possibility for more effort on the part of the producers.*[23]

Obviously, Kuhnen's thesis does not fit known facts in India. In other Asian countries his thesis may well apply, but not so in India under current socio-economic conditions. It is generally accepted that the intensification of labor will increase productivity; however, within the Indian setting, this is not what happened. This may have been due to the fact that many of the modern inputs – HYVs (especially wheat), chemical fertilizers, and chemical pesticides - that became the foundation of the Green Revolution in India were developed under the auspices of Western agricultural advisors .

Each had been developed within the context of large-scale agricultural environments, using machines in lieu of manual labor. Therefore, the experts brought, along with the improved inputs, the cultural baggage of mechanization. It was this predisposition toward large-scale farming and mechanization that planted itself in many of the areas where the Green Revolution first got its start in India. The pattern had been set.

Kuhnen's thesis, however, is not without merit. He is perfectly correct in saying that the application of additional labor would enhance social and economic equality, but it also presupposes that the pattern already set and accepted in India can be altered. It is difficult to conceive that an already successful methodology – one based on certain modern inputs and mechanization in lieu of manual labor - would be amenable to change. There is an old saying: if it's not broken, don't try to fix it.

Substituting labor for mechanization would, however, have some definite benefits. Foremost, agricultural labor requirements would increase, as would rural incomes, especially for the landless laborers. Second, the substitution of human labor for equipment would reduce the need for high-tech machinery. This change, too, could have a negative, trickle-down effect in the machine manufacturing segment of the industrial sector. To change the existing Green Revolution paradigm, at this stage, would be tempting fate, so to speak. Would the long-term effects outweigh the short-term consequences?

If, however, Kuhnen's labor-for-machine substitution thesis were applied in areas where the current pattern of the Green Revolution had not yet been set, both approaches could coexist, with benefits accruing from both methodologies. The most difficult aspect of this change in direction would be the willingness of experts, cultivators, and the government to experiment with a different mindset or approach. While the thesis has merit, it is difficult to alter the direction of the Green Revolution in a proven and accepted form. The current pattern of the Green Revolution has momentum on its side.

Nevertheless, it would be interesting to see if the alternation in the mix of inputs, including labor-for-machine substitutions, is workable. Would production increase as suggested if mechanization was replaced by labor? Could smaller landholdings, under the new mix of inputs, be as productive as or more productive than under the current regimen? Would there be a real improvement in social justice and socio-economic equity and equality among the landless laborer class? What would be the impact on the remaining tenants and smallest cultivators? If it were to prove to be a valid alternative, there is no reason to postpone its implementation, for there may be no down side.

Almost always, under a capitalistic system, some segments of a society prosper while others do not. Within the Indian framework, all should prosper. However, it is readily recognized that not everyone has prospered as a result of the Green Revolution. The large-scale farmers and the government have benefited. The farmers have become prosperous; the government has fulfilled its commitment to feed its citizens and be free of foodgrain imports. Some will argue that the government's commitment was fulfilled much more rapidly than anyone thought possible. Others will say it took far too long, that a considerable price was paid by the ordinary citizenry.

We are not here to debate the correctness of socialism or capitalism; both have their proponents and detractors. What we do need to address is whether or not additional reforms need to be put in place to protect those for whom the Green Revolution has granted little or no relief from a state of perpetual poverty – the rural poor. This group is largely composed of marginal and sub-marginal cultivators, unprotected tenants, and landless laborers. It can be argued that all these groups have realized little benefit as a result of the Green Revolution. A case can also be made that these groups have actually suffered as a result of the Green Revolution. By almost any measure, these groups have become increasingly poorer over the last few decades. For them, the Green Revolution has only made their plight worse.

What can or should be done for these groups? As a result of their abject poverty, there are few who speak for them, except in philosophical terms. They have little or no formal representation in government. They are difficult to organize and therefore have no continuous political presence. During the pre-Independence, nationalist movement, collectively and individually, the political leaders marshaled the rural poor on more than one occasion, only to forget them once a particular political objective had been achieved vis-à-vis the British colonialists. At one time, the Kisan Sabha "spoke" for this group, but as with many political organizations, it became an end in itself. It grew and became an institution, not the true voice of the peasantry. A grassroots movement must be undertaken to organize the political power that rests in the hands of more than 100 million potential voters, but not just for a single issue or political objective. It must be an ongoing political endeavor that will truly speak for this poorest segment of Indian society. No one, no matter how benevolent, can speak for these people. They must find their own political voice. Outsiders can only *assume* what is best or right for them. It would be far better if they were able to speak for themselves, from a basis of personal knowledge, not from reading government compiled, statistical reports. Only members of this group can legitimately say what is needed in the form of legislative reforms to provide these underprivileged groups with much needed protection.

Although not a part of the "official mix" of inputs for the Green Revolution is the increased used of mechanization. Part of mechanization in Indian agriculture is undoubtedly a consequence of the adoption of the Western farming paradigm, even though the historical basis for that paradigm has virtually no similar historical or economic basis in India. In the West, labor was siphoned from the land and incorporated into the rapidly growing industrial sector, forcing farmers to work their farms with fewer and fewer labor resources. Machinery was a substitute of inadequate labor supplies. This problem does not exist in India.

It would seem that the larger Indian farmers, and to some degree, all successful farmers, are fearful of the lowest classes of agriculturalists somehow organizing themselves. To protect themselves against this "perceived" eventuality, many successful farmers have elected to invest in farm machinery, even though the Green Revolution does not necessarily require mechanization to be successful. This shift to mechanized farming leads to what some writers call the "industrialization of farming."[24] In India, this flies in the face of what every farmer sees day in and day out – under- and unemployed agricultural laborers. Instead of mechanization, farmers should be utilizing the labor resources readily available to them, right in their own villages. In the long run, the purchase of machinery is much more costly than the application of available human labor.

5) Sustainability. With each passing year, the data from areas where the Green Revolution has been established suggest that the current pattern of the revolution is not sustainable. There is no shortage of seeds, fertilizers, pesticides, or irrigation water, but it may not be sustainable for ecological and environmental reasons. Initially, yields-per-acre grew impressively. Then, after a few years, yields started to decline. This pattern was first observed by the IRRI in the Philippines, but it is now a fact of life in Indian agriculture. This decline, it would seem, is the result of long-term soil degradation. Early on in Punjab it was recognized that the new inputs, individually and collectively, were removing the micronutrients from the soil at an alarming rate, especially zinc. It was an easy matter to replenish the zinc. Now other micro-nutrients are being depleted for reasons that are still poorly understood by soil scientists.

Where yields are not declining, the rate of increase is already starting to slow or level off. In time, unless some "magic bullet" is found to correct this change in yield, a decline will surely follow.

It is not just the scientists who have observed these changes in yields. The cultivators and farmers, themselves, have recognized the phenomenon. In an article in *Business Week*, as reported by Rosert, *et. al.*, in Punjab:

Dyal Singh knows that the soil on his 3.3 hectare [8 acre] farm in Punjab is becoming less fertile. So far, it hasn't hurt his harvest of wheat and corn. 'There will be a great problem after 5 or 10 years,' says the 63-year-old Sikh farmer. Years of using high-yield seeds that require heavy irrigation and chemical fertilizers have taken their toll on much of India's farmland. So far, 6 percent of agricultural land has been rendered useless.[25]

Without addressing the problems of soil degradation, both by the use of fertilizers and pesticides, leaching, caused by irrigation, and water contamination, it may prove difficult to sustain or maintain current levels of agricultural production. Without solving the problems in areas where the Green Revolution has already been established, or providing prophylactics for areas where the Green

Revolution will be planted next, the Green Revolution may well be unable to sustain either current or future production levels. Without increasing productivity, agriculture will not be able to keep pace with population growth, even though it is slowing. At some point, as things stand now, population will increase until there is no foodgrain surplus, and, eventually, a foodgrain deficiency will become a reality, again. If there are already an estimated 340 million hungry people in India, how long will it take for hunger to turn to starvation if current yield rates decline, as all indications are that they will? In the absence of some, yet unknown solution to these ecological and environmental problems, the future does not look all that promising. We have time, but not a lot, to come up with much needed solutions. We cannot wait and see. We need to take action now.

What Should Government's Role Be

In a heavily regulated economy such as India's or Pakistan's, or most governments in developing nations, it is understandably tempting to blame the government or the center for every economic problem. Rather than take an inventory of each government's successes and failures, it would seem more productive to ask: What should government's role be within the context of rural and agricultural development

First, the most appropriate role of any government is to become the enabler of smoothly functioning markets. Toward this end, institutional (infrastructures) and regulatory reforms are needed to empower private sector activities and promote market efficiency. In the past, government regulation was deemed necessary to promote and protect nascent, cash-based market involvement. Now, it is time to begin the process of deregulation, permitting the market to grow and become more responsive. In general, government's involvement in market activities has only resulted in inefficiencies, due to the tendencies of most bureaucracies to debate, rehash, and prolong actual decision-making, and often causing more harm than good once action has been initiated.

Secondly, governments must recognize the role that the private sector plays in the distribution or goods and services. In turn, governments must move away from micro-managing every sector of the nation's economy. This is particularly true of the agricultural sector. At one time, there was, indeed, a need to micro-manage, a time when subsistence cultivation was the primary activity of almost every cultivator. Cultivators needed to be shown that there were, in fact, alternatives. Now, however, even the smallest cultivators are beginning to focus on the potentialities of commercialized agricultural production and their need to be involved in non-barter market arrangements.

Recognizing the efficacy of the private sector, as it pertains to agricultural production, will also require that governments need to rethink their investments and public expenditures, and, especially, their investment strategies. Globalization of the world economy through WTO reforms holds the potential for much wider participation at agriculture's grassroots, at the individual cultivator/farmer level. Government must encourage and nurture the global involvement of the smallest producer.

Where the private sector does not permit or provide for the smallest agriculturalist's participation, the government must act to encourage and protect the most vulnerable farmers, making sure that they have access to competitive credit and agricultural inputs. Government has a legitimate role to play, especially in terms of poverty alleviation and small farmer development. These are areas that, at least initially, private sector activities have proven to be much less effective. These are the areas that government must address. The most vulnerable must be protected, until they realize that they can protect themselves.

Thirdly, the government must take the lead in the area of agricultural research and extension. It is particularly important to address the agricultural and environmental realities before farmers of all sizes. What is required for a well financed, large landholder will be quite different from what is needed by the smallest cultivators, those that we have come to refer to as householders with multiple employment. Some of these smallest cultivators will, eventually, succumb to the economic realities of operating landholdings that have diminished with every generation, and are becoming increasingly marginal in their ability to produce even subsistence quantities of produce.

Fourth, in light of the problems evidenced as a direct result of the Green Revolution, the government must assume the role of protector of the environment. History has shown that individual farmers are incapable or unwilling to address or envision the consequences of their individual actions. Within this context, government must coordinate natural resource management programs with regard to agriculture. Of particular importance is water resource infrastructure improvement, making public irrigation systems more efficient, by reducing water losses due to seepage or water theft, where so regulated. There is need for bureaucratic streamlining of water resource agencies and canal and watershed management. Of particular concern is water table and aquifer monitoring and control. Unbridled tubewell drilling must be monitored, licensed, and controlled, with the government becoming able and willing to implement and enforce water-use regulations.

Finally, wherever possible, government must become self-policing in terms of withdrawing from involvement in those areas where private sector market forces provide a much more efficient and responsive mechanism to problem resolution. Every effort must be made to realistically evaluate the need for institutional and regulatory control. Government involvement in the regulation of economies and society have proven to be inefficient. Whenever and wherever possible, government must step aside when private sector activities perform the regulatory function more efficiently and at a much lower cost.

Government will always play a deciding role in the areas of education, the dissemination of information and the development of new knowledge and technology, as well as poverty alleviation, small farmer development, environmental protection, and quality control, both of goods and agricultural produce. Likewise, government will, of necessity, remain the policing authority for both national and international quality assurance and compliance.

If the governments restructure themselves, providing the leadership necessary for the efficient functioning of private sector activities, and withdraws needless bureaucratic obstacles to market forces, in many areas the cost of government can be reduced. Of particular importance is the reduction of redundancies that are an inherent part of almost any bureaucracy.

Conclusions

The Green Revolution fulfilled the plans and needs of the Indian government. It changed Indian agriculture from a subsistence undertaking to a highly productive commercial venture. From Independence, it took India nearly fifty years for the agricultural sector to catch up to the rapidly growing population's minimum foodgrain needs and, finally, to surpass it. In fact, this change actually took less than thirty years, from the advent of the Green Revolution. Now India enjoys food surpluses and is actively engaged in commercial, market-oriented and international foodgrain trading. This was a remarkable achievement and should be applauded.

In a comparative sense, the grain silos of the government are overflowing with surplus foodgrain production. From that standpoint, the Green Revolution was a dream come true. Many thought that it would never happen – the population was growing much too quickly for the cultivators to catch up. It is said that a third of India's population is poverty stricken.[26] While the government is stockpiling millions of tons of foodgrain, many of the poorest in Indian society are finding it increasingly difficult to obtain the food they require at reasonable prices. The Green Revolution has reduced or eliminated the need for the government to import foodgrains, but it has not eliminated hunger or suffering, especially among the poor.[27]

This achievement was not accomplished without casualties. The politicians have had to compromise their political and philosophical beliefs, all in the name of progress and the achievement of a single goal – feeding the nation's population and becoming self-sufficient in terms of foodgrain. Others, however, have truly suffered. For the least successful, marginal cultivators, the tenants, and the landless laborers, their standard of living, as a consequence of the Green Revolution, has declined. On the other end of the economic scale are the large to medium-sized landholders. They have prospered by almost every measure. Their prosperity, however, must be measured against their achievement – foodgrain surpluses for their country. Their willingness to take risks has paid off handsomely. They should not be rebuked for their successes. They should be praised. They accomplished exactly what their government asked them to do – feed the nation.

An unanticipated outcome of the Green Revolution is that there is no evidence that suggests that the formulation, legislation, and implementation of agrarian or land reforms was a necessary prerequisite for success. Years of debate, preparation, passage of legislation, and attempts to implement and enforce reforms seem to have been unnecessary. For the purposes of political-economy, however, they did serve an important purpose. Without the rural peasantry behind them, to legitimize the self-appointed nationalist leadership, independence may have taken much longer to achieve.

Reforms did remove the parasitic *zamindars* and other intermediaries, but little was achieved in the areas of tenancy and land consolidation. Slight achievements were realized in terms of rural social justice, equality, and equity. Each of these areas of reform was thought to be necessary for the improvement of agricultural productivity. History played a gigantic trick on all the players in the agricultural development process. Nothing more than making improved technologies available to farmers able to use them was necessary. With or without government intervention, had the modern inputs been made available to most cultivators, they would have adopted them.

There is no doubt that government assisted in the elimination of many bottlenecks in the development process but, by and large, it was the character of the cultivator that made the difference. Obviously, without governmental intervention, the process would have taken much longer, but the end result would still have been the same, for the Indian cultivator is as rational as any farmer anywhere. All that was necessary was being exposed to the new inputs and making them available. The Indian cultivator embraced the Green Revolution, and the rest is history. Now all that we have to worry about is the future.

Prior to the Green Revolution, for both the British and the Indian governments, increases in agricultural production were almost always the result of increasing cultivable land. Under traditional agricultural methods, neither regime was able to do anything but expand into potentially arable land areas, usually as a function of the application of irrigation or drainage. Neither had access to new agricultural technologies that could, under current cropping techniques, stimulate per unit area production or *per capita* productivity. There were no new crops, no high-yield hybrid varieties, no natural, non-organic fertilizers or pesticides – the core components of the Green Revolution. What other options were available? In reality, there weren't any.

In general both the British and the Indian governments were faced with the same complex of problems – the maintenance of social and political peace, a rapidly growing population, and a widening disparity between the amounts of food being grown and the amount needed to feed the populace. Under the circumstances they faced, they did what they could do, but they were severely limited in their options. The Green Revolution, as a mix of complementary farm practices and new, high-yielding crop varieties came "out of nowhere" like a proverbial knight in shining armor. It saved the day for the Indian government. Without the Green Revolution, no matter how we subsequently analyze or evaluate it, it came just when the government and planners were running out of options.

It was not, however, a panacea. There is no doubt that, in the end, it "solved" India's food crisis, but for how long? What is going to save India the next time — when the combined or individual effects of the Green Revolution's mix of non-organic fertilizers and pesticides, and high-yielding varieties, have exhausted the soils, polluted the surface waters and contaminated the sub-surface water tables? Where do they turn then?

Will not the government be back at the same place they were at Independence? Will the only method available to increase agricultural production be the expansion of cultivable land area? Land reforms for both governments were attempts at boosting agricultural production to feed their populations. For now, the pressure is off, but how long before it is felt again? Should the government not anticipate and appreciate the fact that in areas where the Green Revolution has already taken root, that productivity, by any standard, is declining? It may take much more that mitigation to repair the damaged soil and cleanse the water supplies, if indeed these problems can be mitigated. In addition to these environmental problems, there will be more hungry people, and many will already be showing signs of sickness because of the soil and water pollution.

The Indian government may postpone the inevitable crunch that will come from an increasing population and another stagnant agricultural sector. If India is self-sufficient in terms of foodgrain production, why is a third of the population still going hungry? The answer is that they cannot afford their share of that surplus. People starve at the base of silos full of stockpiled grain.

Land and other reforms must be put into place to short-circuit this pattern of feast or famine. It is the cycle that India has faced for hundreds of years. It is not a new phenomenon; it is just that it is getting more and more difficult to reach a state of equilibrium each time it happens. At some point, equilibrium may not be possible to achieve. There will be no additional lands that can be brought into production, there will be no Second or Third Green Revolution, and the number of hungry mouths to feed will just keep increasing.

Land reforms are still needed, but equally important is the need for such social, economic, and political reforms as will restructure Indian society. The society must be made more resilient and flexible for the next round of agricultural problems (many of which will be caused by and because of the First Green Revolution). Instead of just food problems, there will be the complications caused by associated environmental problems, and the government's failure to repair a damaged, under- or unemployed rural population. If the government cannot find workable solutions to these problems, there will be social and political unrest, but more importantly, Mother Nature will ultimately solve some of the problems in ways India's population will find most unpleasant.

References

1. (FAO, 2008), p. 1.
2. (The World Bank, 2006b), p.120.
3. (FAO, 2006e).
4. See, (Engel, 1877). Reference for the original source is frequently given as Ernst Engel, 2. edition, 1896b, s.28-29. Engel self-published many of his own works and established several professional journals. See, (Engel, Ernst, 1857), reprinted in Appendix of (Engel, Ernst, 1895)
5. (FAO, World agriculture: towards 2030/2050, Interim Report, 2006f).
6. (FAO, 2006a), p. 4.
7. *Ibid.*

8. (FAO, Livestock a major threat to environment, 2006g).
9. (Naylor, R.; H. Steinfeld; W. Falcon; J. Galloway; V. Smil; E. Bradford; J. Alder; and H. Mooney, 2005).
10. When South Asian yields are compared to world record yields, there are some major discrepancies. It must be noted, the world record yield figures are probably more illustrative than truly useful. These records, except for maize production, are not repetitive. They represent one-time events. They may qualify for inclusion in the record books but world average yields are much more enlightening. However, the world records do illustrate what could be, or can be achieved under optimal conditions of weather, rainfall/irrigation, sunlight, and exacting soil conditions. There is considerable variability in the real world which reduces the value of world record figures for comparative purposes.
11. Attention must be drawn to at least one crop and yield figure – wheat in India. The FAO's figures indicate a yield rate of only 1.2 mt/ha. It is well known that, in Punjab, yields often exceed 2.5 and 2.6 mt/ha. However, the national average is 'pulled down' by lower yields in other parts of the country.
12. (Ladha, J. K., et. al., 2003).
13. Initially, the research organizations involved with the Rice-Wheat Consortium's efforts included: CGIAR, CIMMYT, CIP, ICRISAT, IRRI, and IWMI. Later, the primary organizational leadership of the group fell to CIMMYT.
14. (The World Bank, 2002).
15. (Dixon, John A.; Aidan P. Gulliver, with David Gibbon, 2001). Downloaded version of report but without page numbers.
16. (Dorjee, Kinlay; Sumiter Broca; and Prabhu Pingali, July 2003), pp. 7-10.
17. See fore example, (Energy Bulletin, 2008); (Mabro, September 2006); (Benen, 2005); (Porter, 2005); (Committee on Energy and Commerce, December 7, 2005); (EB/DoE, 2004); (Shenoy, 2008); and (Chefurka, 2007).
18. See for example, (Conway, Matt, 2007); (Steil, 2001), "It takes about 1.3 gallons of oil to produce one gallon of ethanol," says Pimentel; and (Rothschild, 2007).
19. (Blum, Justin, 2006).
20. See, (Pingali, 1990); and (Fujisaka, S. and D. Garrity, 1998).

21. (Ojha, T. P., 2007).
22. (Dandekar, V. M., and Nikantha Rath, 1971); and (Moore, Frank J., 1955), pp. 124-128.
23. (Kuhnen, F., 1971), p. 177.
24. See, (Rosset, Peter; Joseph Collins; and Frances Moore Lappe, 2000).
25. *Ibid.*
26. *Ibid.*
27. (Waldman, 2002). This is possibly one of the most sensitive articles seen in recent years that deals with India's food situation – poverty and starvation amid plenty. It has been included in its entirety as Appendix A.

11

Poverty, Hunger and a Second Green Revolution

Introduction

Faced with over 900 million plus hungry people in the world, and the numbers continue to grow, we hear from the uninitiated: we will grow more food through the miracle of science and technology. Among this group are Monsanto, Novartis, Dow, DuPont, and other chemical companies, which have been busy reinventing themselves as biotechnology companies. Together with the World Bank , the Gates and Rockefeller foundations, and other international agencies, these agrochemical and GMO corporations suggest that we can produce more food, and free the world of hunger and starvation, if only we let them work their magic.

The original Green Revolution was based on science and modern agricultural inputs. We have seen some of the environmental and socio-economic consequences of that science, no matter how well intentioned it might have been. Now, with the perspective of time, we have to ask ourselves: Do we need new technology and more chemicals to end poverty and hunger? Do we dare unleash the corporate, free market hounds on the world, to improve world agriculture using a new, improved, supercharged version of Borlaug's Green Revolution?

Norman Borlaug, in his wisdom, understood two very important principles. First, he understood how to make plants produce more food for mankind. Second, he knew that his Green Revolution **was not** a panacea. Furthermore, he realized that his Green Revolution

. . . has [only] won a temporary success in man's war against hunger and deprivation; it has given man breathing space. If fully implemented, the revolution can provide sufficient food for sustenance during the next three decades. But the frightening power of human reproduction must also be curbed; otherwise the success of the green revolution will be ephemeral only.[1]

Borlaug had hoped that his plants and modern inputs would give Mankind three decades to come to grips with the problems of rapid population growth. He had been pessimistic. It has now been a little over 40 years since the Green Revolution established a foothold in India and Pakistan. In that time, world population has nearly doubled and a food surplus still exists. Even so, Borlaug's heartfelt desire that human deprivation would come to an end has never been achieved, even in India where Borlaug's vision of the Green Revolution sunk its deepest roots.

At the 1996 World Food Summit, a goal was set to halve world hunger by 2015. At the time it was estimated that there were 824 million undernourished people in the world. In its 2006 report, the FAO estimated that the number of hungry in the world had increased to 854 million, and even more recent estimates suggest that the number of hungry has increased by yet another 50 to 100 million, taking the total well over 900 million.[2] Overall, it would seem that no progress has been made, and it appears that the problem has gotten significantly worse.

Today there are more hungry people in the world than ever before, and more than 80 percent of the world's poor and hungry live in Sub-Saharan Africa and India. The recent surge in the number of hungry people is the result of a combination of rising demand for agricultural products, largely a function of population growth and economic development in emerging countries; the diversion of foodgrains to the production of biofuels; and a decline in yields due to the effects of drought and floods, whose incidence is increasing as a result of climate change. The world's cereal stocks are at a 30 year low of 409 million tons.[3] These trends have been exacerbated by changes in the trading policies between many developed and developing nations. For example, India recently terminated the export of foodgrains to its longtime trading partners, like Nepal and Bangladesh. Further, foodgrain speculators have begun withholding grain as a hedge and to exploit the world foodgrains futures market.

The situation is made all the more difficult by rising prices for agricultural inputs, which is most severely felt by those in developing countries. Throughout 2008, fertilizer prices have increased at a much faster rate than food prices. Developing countries, in an effort to increase their agricultural production, have pushed both fertilizer and fertilizer raw material prices higher because of simple demand dynamics. Adding to the current scenario is the rising cost of petroleum and petroleum products.

While population grown is largely responsible for the increased demand being placed on agriculture, other factors are at work as well.

The present situation is a result of the international community's neglect of agriculture in developing countries for a long time, Dr. Diouf noted. The share of agriculture in official development assistance has declined from 17 percent in 1980 to only three percent in 2006. Investment in agricultural research in developing countries is less than 0.6 percent of their Gross Domestic Product, compared to more than five percent in the OECD-countries.

Increasing agricultural production in developing countries will only be achievable by additional public and private investment. FAO estimates incremental public investment needs at about US $24 billion every year – this includes increased resources for water management, rural roads, storage facilities, as well as research and extension, Dr Diouf said.[4]

At the same time, world development agencies point to the fact that agricultural production is at an all-time high, stating that there is as much as 17 percent more food produced than needed to feed the world's population.[5] It almost sounds as if these bureaucrats are talking out of both sides of their mouths. We have millions of people who are undernourished and there is, at the same time, a worldwide food surplus. Unfortunately, they are absolutely correct.

With an estimated 900-plus million people going to bed hungry every night, obviously there is something terribly wrong with the supply and demand equation regarding world food supplies. At least part of that equation fails to take into consideration the fact that there is something fundamentally wrong in the distribution of food and the resources with which to access it. Although there is a fundamental beauty and simplicity in the food-available-food-need equation, it does not take into consideration the fact that food is a commodity and that commodity comes at a price. It cannot be grown without cost, and the growers want to be paid for their risk-taking and effort. It cannot be shipped cost-free.

Obviously, the needy cannot afford to purchase the food they need. Hunger is, after all, a function of poverty. If the poor could afford the food they need, it would be transported from areas of plenty to areas in need. Therefore, the root cause of hunger is not lack of supply or production but one of economic ability.

The first Green Revolution was a resounding success, at least within the context of producing more food. The new seeds, the use of fertilizers, pesticides, herbicides, and more and more irrigation resulted in tens of millions of extra tonnes of foodgrain each year. While production has risen dramatically, so has the number of the hungry. So, one can justifiably ask, has the Green Revolution proven itself as a successful strategy for ending hunger? Probably not, because the Green Revolution focused on production with no overriding concern for the alleviation of the root cause of hunger – poverty. The Green Revolution did nothing to redistribute purchasing power and resources to those who were undernourished.[6] If the poor do not have the money to buy food, increased production simply will not help them.

There is no worldwide famine. Famine is a localized phenomenon – usually limited to individual nations or portions of nations. Sen has repeatedly suggested that famine is more a function of public apathy than the lack of food.[7] If there is a public will, the food will be transported to those whose crops have failed and are in need. In the final analysis, we have large numbers of people who are hungry because of worldwide apathy, not because of lack of supply. Borlaug was right when he called them the 'forgotten world.'[8] In large measure, the people of Sub-Saharan Africa and India have been forgotten, or at least ignored. How else can one explain the fact that the vast majority of the poor and hungry live in these two world regions?

If official agricultural development assistance has declined from 17 to only 3 percent, as Jacques Diouf has suggested, does that not constitute tacit neglect, or is it simply an oversight?[9] Alternatively, have official development agencies and organizations resigned themselves to the inevitable, and at the same time feeling the need to justify their continued existence? Without their mantra – We can help solve your problems – and an audience that continues to believe, these agencies and aid organizations would have no purpose, except to collect and distribute, or waste absolutely huge sums of money. So, which is it?

This assessment may be simplistic and cynical but if the old adage – Actions speak louder than words – is true, how do we explain the decline in development assistance for agriculture? One explanation, as unpleasant as it may seem, is that the development agencies have begun transferring the job of assisting developing countries achieve agricultural self-sufficiency to for-profit multinationals, like Monsanto, Novartis, DuPont, Pioneer Hi-Bred (a DuPont company), Dow AgroSciences, etc. Already the World Bank and USAID have become steadfast advocates of a second Green Revolution through biotechnology. The beauty of achieving agricultural development through the agency of these multinationals lies in the fact that:

(1) The multinationals have reinvented themselves as biotechnology companies at no expense to the agencies or governments.
(2) The multinationals, by their very nature, will make the recipients of their services and products pay for those goods and services.
(3) Development agencies of donor countries will have little or no long-term outlays or commitments to agricultural development in developing nations, which means more monies for other more promising projects.

Further, any concern for political food security is first and foremost an individual nation's concern. Some advocates of food security have stepped out from under the umbrella of political correctness and have been willing to place the blame for national food insecurity squarely where it belongs.

> . . . *a human rights approach to food security places immediate and inclusive obligations on governments to create capacity for their people to feed themselves. Ideally the right to food should take its place in national laws or constitutions, with guarantees of non-discriminatory and non-political strategies. Many of the world's food security problems stem from the absence of an overriding goal to honour the right to food. A set of world trade rules might look very different if governed by such an objective rather than the focus on absolute volumes of trade.*
>
> *Countries in Africa and South Asia are also to blame for their prolonged lack of investment in rural economies which account for about 75% of world hunger. For example, African governments have yet to meet their 2003 Maputo Declaration commitment which called for 10% of national budgets to be dedicated to agriculture by 2008. Rural economies have therefore failed to grow. Poor farmers, often holding uncertain land tenure and lacking capital, plant for a mix of subsistence and surplus for market, a model chronically vulnerable to fluctuating prices or unfavourable weather. The majority of developing countries have food deficits, a serious problem for those lacking foreign currency to purchase expensive imports.*[10]

The concept of food security implies that it does not matter where a nation's or an individual's food comes from – from domestic production, imports, or trade. What is important is that the food supply fulfills the nation's and individual's needs and is reliable. This approach to feeding people fits perfectly within the conceptual framework of the globalization of the world economy. It does not, however, concern itself with domestic cultivation, large or small farmers, their right to an assured livelihood, or their potential for agricultural production. There is no 'right to farm,' no protection. Everything is governed by fair trade practices. Whether cultivators cease to exist is basically unimportant, as long as the population can reliably feed itself.

An alternative approach to food security is the principle of 'food sovereignty.' Food sovereignty places a priority for food security on the individual with the imperative that government's priority is to assist cultivators. Food sovereignty shifts the focus of food to land ownership and control, as well as providing for agricultural sustainability through a system of governmental subsidies for inputs, produce, and credit. Through these subsidies, cultivators are guaranteed the ability to survive and produce. Food is domestically produced and consumed. Food sovereignty presupposes that there can be no solution to hunger that does not have small farmers at its center.

Not surprisingly, the world's major food and development agencies subscribe to the concept of food security, and not food sovereignty. The two schools of thought find themselves floundering in light of the recent rapid increases in food and input prices. Beginning, at first as a slight increase in prices, in early 2007, prices 'took off' early in 2008 and continue to climb in 2009.[11] The FAO composite Food Price Index increased from 155 to 213 between July 2007 and July 2008, an increase of 37.8 percent. During the same period, the Cereals Price Index (CPI) increased 63.4 percent. However, the CPI had increased 92 percent between April 2007 and April 208. After reaching a high of 278 in February and April, the CPI began to decline slightly but is still well above a year ago. See Table 11-1, below.

In April 2008, it was estimated that the poorest households were spending 60 to 100 percent of their household incomes on food, without any mechanism to cope with these rising food costs.[12] In the absence of an ability to increase incomes, the only strategy left to them is to reduce their food consumption. The World Food Programme says that, at least 100 million will be added to those already below the hunger threshold, which, unlike FAO's estimate of 50 million new hungry, will push the number of hungry over the billion mark.[13]

Faced with numbers of this type, the people of the developing world, and especially those of Sub-Saharan Africa and South Asia, have little time to develop suitable food-production strategies to ward off the growing threat of starvation through famine. The situation for the food dependent trading partners of India may well be more critical than for India itself. Although many of India's people are already undernourished, there are at least sufficient stockpiles to insure that the vast majority of them do not starve completely. The situation for India's food deficient trading partners, those dependent upon India's food surpluses, are likely to suffer significantly, now that India has terminated foodgrain exports.[14]

Table 11-1: FAO Food Price Index, August 2008

FAO Food Price Index

		Food Price Index [1]	Meat [2]	Dairy [3]	Cereals [4]	Oils and Fats [5]	Sugar [6]
2000		**92**	100	106	85	72	105
2001		**94**	100	117	87	72	111
2002		**93**	96	86	95	91	88
2003		**102**	105	105	99	105	91
2004		**114**	118	130	108	117	92
2005		**117**	121	145	105	109	127
2006		**127**	115	138	123	117	190
2007		**156**	121	247	169	174	129
2007	July	**155**	120	277	157	175	131
	August	**161**	123	287	168	181	126
	September	**170**	124	290	191	190	125
	October	**174**	122	297	197	202	128
	November	**179**	126	302	199	221	130
	December	**186**	123	295	220	226	137
2008	January	**196**	126	281	235	250	154
	February	**215**	128	278	278	273	173
	March	**218**	132	276	277	285	169
	April	**215**	132	266	278	276	161
	May	**215**	141	265	270	280	155
	June	**219**	144	263	273	292	156
	July	**213**	144	265	256	274	183

[1] **Food Price Index:** Consists of the average of 6 commodity group price indices mentioned above weighted with the average export shares of each of the groups for 1998-2000: in total 55 commodity quotations considered by FAO Commodity Specialists as representing the international prices of the food commodities noted are included in the overall index.

[2] **Meat Price Index:** Consists of 3 poultry meat product quotations (the average weighted by assumed fixed trade weights), 4 bovine meat product quotations (average weighted by assumed fixed trade weights), 3 pig meat product quotations (average weighted by assumed fixed trade weights), 1 ovine meat product quotation (average weighted by assumed fixed trade weights): the four meat group average prices are weighted by world average export trade shares for 1998-2000.

[3] **Dairy Price Index:** Consists of butter, SMP, WMP, cheese, casein price quotations; the average is weighted by world average export trade shares for 1998-2000.

[4] **Cereals Price Index:** This index is compiled using the grains and rice price indices weighted by their average trade share for 1998-2000. The grains Price Index consists of International Grains Council (IGC) wheat price index, itself average of 9 different wheat price quotations, and 1 maize export quotation; after expressing the maize price into its index form and converting the base of the IGC index to 1998-2000. The Rice Price Index consists of three components containing average prices of 16 rice quotations: the components are Indica, Japonica and Aromatic rice varieties and the weights for combining the three components are assumed (fixed) trade shares of the three varieties.

[5] **Oils and Fats Price Index:** Consists of an average of 11 different oils (including animal and fish oils) weighted with average export trade shares of each oil product for 1998-2000.

[6] **Sugar Price Index:** Index form of the International Sugar Agreement prices with 1998-2000 as base.

Source: (FAO, 2008c)

With incomes already stretched to their limits, the future does not bode well for many of the people who are already below the poverty line. Unless the current food crisis eases, much larger numbers of people will succumb to starvation, all for want of sufficient income to purchase the food they need but cannot produce.

The benefits of the Green Revolution, envisioned by Borlaug in the mid-1960's, have apparently come and gone. He had hoped to give the world a little breathing room before mass starvation reemerged as a result of uncontrolled population growth. Borlaug's breathing room seems to be over.

Is it Really Over? Has the Fat Lady Sung?

There is a growing body of evidence that:

(1) The first Green Revolution is over, having reached its zenith some time in the mid-1980s or early 1990s.

(2) Green Revolution-style farming is not ecologically or environmentally sustainable.

(3) It failed to improve rural equity, social justice, or incomes for the poor, and may well have worsened the plight of the smaller landholders, agricultural laborers, and the landless laborers.

(4) It was most successful in areas that shared a unique set of social, environmental and economic attributes.

The Green Revolution: Its Timeframe

It is fairly well recognized that the Green Revolution, as we know it, obtained its final form almost simultaneously with its introduction to India and Pakistan in the mid-1960s. When it ended is a bit less clear.

Since the introduction of the first improved wheats from Mexico, Indian, Pakistani, and Bangladeshi agronomists have created numerous new types to better suit the various ecological needs of farmers in most of South Asia. Initially, much of the plant breeding for wheat was for irrigated areas. Later, more attention was directed to the development of wheats for rainfed areas. Unlike rice, however, wheat seems to have been much more adaptable to South Asia's varied wheat ecologies, and far fewer varieties were deemed necessary.

On the other hand, plant breeders found it necessary to release more than 600 improved rice varieties, in an effort to tailor rice to South Asia's varied ecological micro-niches. Rice, more so than wheat, is much more sensitive to variations in its environment. Some of the considerations for good rice yields include soil acidity, soil salinity, alkalinity, low soil fertility, micronutrient deficiencies, flooding and submergence, and drought. In addition, varieties were needed that could resist a number of insect infestations, blights, blasts, and other diseases endemic to South Asia.

Also, unlike wheat, most of the earliest rice varieties were almost all irrigated rice types developed by the IRRI, but in South Asia most of the rice is grown under rainfed conditions. Therefore, production is strongly tied to the distribution of rainfall.[15] The government's initial efforts were directed towards sponsoring ill-adapted varieties. This approach met with limited success. It was apparent that rainfed varieties were desperately needed.

Where possible the irrigated varieties were introduced. Only later were rainfed and upland varieties developed and made available. With their development, rice cultivation expanded rapidly.

Work on producing high yielding varieties of other important cereals, such as sorghums, millets, oilseeds, and barley, had to wait until the three primary cereal crops were well established and producing well. Likewise, little attention was given to the yield or production of pulses or legume crops, which constitute an important part of cereal-consuming populations' diets.

By 1984-85, the first successful improved varieties for these coarser, dryland, rainfed crops were becoming available but they did not have the same impact on the cultivators farming practices or production that wheat or maize had had. In part, less attention was given to these coarse grains for the simple reason that they were dryland, and primarily rainfed crops. For the agronomists, there was a certain pride and prestige attached to working with Borlaug's creation.

Work on the coarser grains was deemed less prestigious, despite their economic and dietary importance. Also, the coarser grains received much less research support and funding. Everyone was focused on the miracle wheats and rices. It is with the introduction of improved varieties of the coarser grains that one can say that the first Green Revolution had come to an end.

There is no doubt that the introduction of new plant varieties continued but, by and large, almost all subsequent variety introductions have been simply micro-adjustments made to existing crop types. No new 'miracle' crops have been developed in almost 20 years. The new varieties have been modified to resist new insect infestations, blights, diseases, and grow in a broader range of rainfed areas, in areas that flood frequently, or where drought conditions occur, or where photosensitivity is a factor in yield. The first Green Revolution ended by the mid-1980s.

The Green Revolution's Sustainability

As we have already seen, the Green Revolution has taken its toll on every environment into which it was implemented. Soils were degraded, either by the removal of organic matter, the removal of micro-nutrients, compaction, erosion, salinity, waterlogging, or simple overuse. The use of chemical fertilizers, pesticides, and herbicides have contaminated both surface and groundwater supplies; and irrigation has depleted surface and groundwater.

The technologies and techniques involved in the Green Revolution have caused extensive damage to the environment, some of which may never be mitigated or rectified. The addition of more and more inputs are required to maintain given levels of output. It is becoming obvious that Green Revolution agriculture is growing increasingly inefficient and more expensive. As the cost of the inputs escalate, it is clear that input costs are rising faster than either returns on investments or crop prices.

In India, Bangladesh, and Pakistan the Green Revolution technologies are no longer tenable and, therefore, unsustainable. The technologies of the Green Revolution have degraded the environment and are no longer giving back in the form of crop production.

Rural Equity, Social justice, and Incomes

The advocates of the Green Revolution believed, or at least hoped, that it would serve to improve rural equity, social justice, and incomes. From all indications, the Green Revolution, although it performed its function of improving agricultural production, did nothing to correct rural inequities and probably exacerbated them.

With or without the government's notice, the character of agriculture has changed rapidly. It started out in most areas as a subsistence agricultural system, and has evolved into a market-driven, surplus-producing machine in parts of South Asia. For the new class of commercial farmers that emerged with the Green Revolution, things have turned out admirably. Many have grown from just being large- to middle-sized landholders into prosperous agriculturalists. The benefits of the Green Revolution have not, however, been equally beneficial for all agricultural classes, including the smaller landholders, tenants, and the landless laborers. Old-style land reforms, while advocating rural justice, and equity, have failed these classes. Each has become increasingly impoverished as their counterparts have prospered. The prosperity of the new class of farmers is not necessarily the cause of these classes' growing impoverishment.

The cause of their continued impoverishment lies in the fact that they have been and continue to be marginal cultivators, either due to the size of their landholdings and fragmentation, their lack of investment capital, poor managerial skills, and lack of education, lack of socio-economic-political linkages, or some combination of these factors. If one takes a purely philosophical look at these classes, one could define their plight as just another example of *karma*, simply their fate. They were born poor and that is the way they will stay. Philosophically, this may be an acceptable explanation, but it is not very satisfying from a humanistic point of view.

For this reason, and if for no other, the lesser agricultural classes now require attention. In the past, agrarian reforms focused their attention on the elimination of intermediaries, setting ceilings on the size of holdings, and transforming tenants into landowners. All this attention was focused on the top of the social pyramid, the large and middle-sized landholding classes. For all intents and purposes, it had little or no impact on the smallest landholders, tenants, and landless laborers. What impact it did have was almost always negative.

Where was the Green Revolution Successful?

The Green Revolution was most successful in areas where one finds:

- a fairly homogenous farming population that is culturally and psychologically prepared for change and progress
- the existence of, or a system for, obtaining rural capital, i.e., credit
- the existence of available irrigation water, either canals or groundwater
- the implementation of land reforms in advance to ensure that the benefits of the new technology will be widely distributed.

Unfortunately, there are few places where this set of preconditions obtain. Within India, many of these 'ingredients' were available only in Punjab and parts of a few surrounding states. In Punjab, a ceiling on land ownership had been enacted soon after Independence, along with the consolidation of landholdings. The Punjabi society was comparatively egalitarian and culturally homogenous. As a result of the influx of the West Punjabi Canal Colonists, Punjabi society was culturally and psychologically prepared for change and progress. There was a well-developed network of rural credit societies and cooperatives. Finally, there was an as yet untapped groundwater supply and an established canal irrigation system. Together, these factors created an almost ideal environment for growing the new improved wheats introduced by Borlaug and his CIMMYT team.

Almost everywhere else in South Asia, one or more of these vital ingredients was missing, either social or technical. In Pakistan it was the government that had failed to keep pace with the new technologies. In Nepal, the people were not prepared for progress, nor had land reforms been implemented or irrigation systems set in place, or public or private credit structures organized. In Bangladesh, although the population was comparatively homogenous, years of subjugation by the West Pakistanis, had eroded their sense of entrepreneurship, irrigation systems were limited (although river water was readily available), credit was based on moneylenders, the land had not benefited from the implementation of land reforms, and a large gap existed between the rich and poor. Each of the nations of South Asia had its problems. Pakistan, in the end, was able to resolve its political resistance to change, at least to the degree that the Green Revolution can be claimed to have been a success. Not so in Nepal and Bangladesh, and in many parts of India.

If one defines the Green Revolution based on its successful implementation within the context of South Asia, the definition might read:

The Green Revolution is the transfer of modern agricultural technology, limited largely to irrigated, well capitalized areas, where it is not expected to fulfill the social needs of the nation.[18]

Borlaug did not envision the Green Revolution as a cure all for the social and economic ills of society. He was interested in feeding people. This the Green Revolution did for more than 40 years. It was not a universal success and it did little or nothing to address social ills or the incomes of the already poor. In fact, there is no evidence to suggest that it did anything other than make the rich richer and widen the gap between the rich and poor. Land from the poor, marginal cultivators accrued to the larger landlords and moneylenders. Income from increased productivity, likewise, went to the landowners in proportion to the size of their holdings. For the agricultural laborer and landless laborer, things simply went from bad to worse. For these disenfranchised souls, there is no relief.

A Second Green Revolution?

Borlaug's version of the Green Revolution did exactly was it was intended to do – it increased world food production — and until recently, it was able to accomplish that purpose. It was never conceived as, or intended to be a tool for social engineering by its originators, although many hoped that it would have just that effect. In the end, it did have socioeconomic consequences but not those hoped for. In fact, it tended to exacerbate rural social and economic animosities and divisions. The poor became poorer. The powerful became more powerful. We cannot blame the Green Revolution for these problems. They were already a part of the rural landscape well before the first hybrid seed was even conceived.

The Green Revolution was a technological breakthrough in agronomy. It consisted of a package of practices and improved seeds that, when applied according to established guidelines, increased agricultural yields, both in terms of total production and on a *per capita* basis. It was not political and had no agenda. People imbued it with political and social attributes and power. Technologies are

Box 11-1: Technology

It cannot be denied that mankind has a penchant for at least attempting to turn every new technology into a weapon. Most innovators of new technology, unless they are given the charge of developing a new weapon, are simply endeavoring to solve a problem. It is doubtful that the Wright brothers could have envisioned that their Wright Flyer, when flown at Kitty Hawk in 1903, would evolve into the B-2 bomber or the F-22 Raptor 'air supremacy' aircraft. Likewise, Alfred Nobel, in all likelihood, could not have imagined that his dynamite would become the staple of the world's armies. He was simply trying to make an unstable explosive, nitro glycerin, safer to use for the good of mankind. Unfortunately, not everything can be as accidental and benign as a sticky note.

neither inherently 'good' or 'bad.' It is all in how they are utilized. See Box 11-1.

The scientists of the CIMMYT, and later at the IRRI, did not look 'down the road' and try to anticipate what the impact of their life's work would have. They may have anticipated the good but not the bad. Success at the time was being defined as production increases that would stave off potential malnutrition. Millions of lives were at risk from hunger and starvation and results were needed fast. An increase in food production had to be the top Green Revolution priority. Concerns regarding the environment were not a priority.[19] The conventional wisdom at the time was that the environment was either insignificant or, at least, capable of being easily redressed at a future date, once the main task of feeding millions of hungry people had been accomplished.[20] In this regard, the agronomists were wrong.

Likewise, they did not consider the social or economic dislocations their seeds would cause. They were simply attempting to make their plants more productive in the name of humanity.

The Rockefeller Foundation, Part I

There are those, for whatever reason, look for conspiracies in everything. Among those is F. William Engdahl, the author of *Seeds of Destruction*. His researches have uncovered a series of linkages that are, if not conspiratorial, at least interesting and enlightening. The Rockefeller Foundation might well be credited with, if not creating the so-called 'gene revolution' in agriculture, at least underwriting it. The Rockefeller Foundation joined forces with the Mexican government, and in 1944 the Cooperative Wheat Research and Production Program, the CIMMYT, was created under the directorship of Norman Borlaug. The program's charge involved research in genetics, plant breeding, plant pathology, entomology, agronomy, soil science, and cereal technology. Within twenty years it had developed a high-yielding short-strawed, disease-resistant wheat, which became the cornerstone of the Green Revolution.

In 1960, the Rockefeller Foundation, together with the Ford Foundation and the Philippine government, organized the International Rice Research Institute in Los Baños, the Philippines. Some of the varieties that served as the starting point for future rice research are alleged to have been supplied by M.S. Swaminathan, the famed Indian agronomist.

From the early 1960s, Dr M.S Swaminathan, the Indian father of the Green Revolution, was alleged to have been the front man for the Rockefeller Foundation in India. The Indira Gandhi Krishi Vidyalaya (IGKV) had collection of 20,000 indigenous varieties of rice seeds available at the institute. These seeds were painstakingly collected by the Indian rice researcher Dr. Richaria who documented facts about each seed variety in minute detail from the farmers. Dr. Claude Alvarez reported that in the early 1960s, Swaminathan "stole" the gene bank of rice, evolved over decades by Dr Richaria, and passed it over to the Americans. India had 120,000 varieties of rice seeds; today, no more than 50 are known to be available, although more varieties may be stored in un-catalogued seed vaults somewhere.[21]

By 1971, the Rockefeller Foundation's IRRI, along with its Mexico-based CIMMYT and the International Institute of Tropical Agriculture (IITA) combined to form the global Consultative Group on International Agriculture Research (CGIAR). CGIAR was shaped through a series of private conferences held at the Rockefeller Foundation's conference center in Bellagio, Italy. One of the foundation's primary goals was to promote the genetic engineering of plants, a goal that became known simply as 'The Project.'

CGIAR drew in the United Nations' Food and Agriculture Organization, the UN Development Programme and the World Bank. Through carefully-planned political and financial maneuvering, the Rockefeller Foundation by the beginning of the 1970's was in a position to shape global agriculture policy and research.

Through generous study grants, CGIAR saw to it that leading Third World agricultural scientists and agronomists were brought to the US to study the concepts of modern agribusiness production and to carry the Western agricultural philosophy and concepts back to their homelands. In so doing, the Rockefeller Foundation had tacitly created a network of influence for US agribusiness.

The Green Revolution was, and is, essentially the transplantation of Western agricultural techniques and philosophy to Third World countries. At least initially, it involved the use of mostly expensive and western produced fertilizers, pesticides, and herbicides, paid for with loans from such organizations as the World Bank or through the USAID. Large-scale irrigation projects were required. These too were funded by the World Bank.

Once the Green Revolution was implemented, governments began developing domestic fertilizer, pesticide, and herbicide producing facilities but were still reliant on many foreign raw materials. The facilities, again, were funded by foreign investments and, oftentimes, operated under guidance from foreign manufacturers. Nevertheless, the foreign agro-input suppliers' profit shares gradually declined. Even in the area of seed development, the task fell to domestic government agencies and organization. Slowly but surely, foreign participation was reduced, and with it foreign profits.

Terminator Technology

It is not entirely clear whether the biological entropy characteristic of the earliest improved seeds was an accidental or 'engineered' characteristic of the CIMMYT hybrids. If it was accidental, it was fortuitous. It forced farmers to repurchase their seeds, if not every year, at least within two to three years, or watch yields plummet with each successive planting. If it was a planned for characteristic, again, it was fortuitous. With domestic production replacing foreign production of seeds, or foreign control of seed production, the Western agribusiness interests were being compromised. They were being squeezed out at every turn.

If biological entropy was accidental, the characteristic was not lost on the multinational seed breeders. If it was intentional, it still did not give breeders absolute control over their seeds. It normally took two or three years before cultivators were forced to repurchase their seed stocks. If the trait could be refined and controlled by the originating seed breeders, they would control the seed market indefinitely. It was only a matter of mastering the genetic technology involved in later seed development and the creation of GMOs – genetically modified organisms. In 1994, Delta and Pine Land Company (D&PLC) announced the development of genetic technology that would render second generation seeds sterile. On March 3, 1998, the USDA and D&PLC announced that they had jointly obtained US patent 5,723,765 for the Terminator technology, also known as Genetic Use Restriction Technologies or GURT.[22] Soon thereafter, Monsanto announced its intent to purchase D&PLC. For the next six years, the fate of Terminator was battled internationally and domestically in the U.S. Finally, on August 15, 2006, Monsanto announced that it would purchase D&PLC.[23] The transaction was finalized in 2007.

Now that GURT has been perfected, and international obstacles to its utilization have been overcome, Monsanto and the other allied agricultural multinationals have maneuvered themselves into a position to essentially control the future of agricultural development, under the assumption that GMOs are the only solution to the stagnation that currently affects the Green Revolution. If these multinationals have their way, the next Green Revolution will be a genetic revolution.

The noose around the world's agricultural neck may have gotten tighter with the development of yet another variant of GURT, known as 'T-GURT,' which stands for genetic trait control. This technology would make plant growth or the activation of certain genes contingent on whether or not the seed or plant is exposed to certain chemicals. Technology is now being refined and tested that would produce crops that would fail to germinate or not grow properly if they are not regularly exposed to the company's proprietary chemicals. At present, Novartis, AstraZeneca, Monsanto, Pioneer Hi-Bred, Rhone Poulenc, and DuPont are actively pursuing this line of research.[24]

Effectively, GURT and T-GURT technologies would require that farmers pay every year to have functioning seeds. Farmers would, in effect, be leasing the seed, which is exactly the relationship the large multinationals want vis-à-vis the end users of their products. The seed providers counter that the farmers are not being compelled to use their seeds. The use of their seeds is entirely an individual choice, based on perceived benefits over local or other brand name seeds. Of the options, the post germination application of T-GURT technology seems most insidious. Once the seed has been purchased and treated to permit germination, the demand for repeated application of proprietary chemicals to maintain continued growth seems like a form of extortion – pay for repeated treatments or plants die. If the farmer is unable to secure the require chemical in a timely fashion, or the vendor is unable to spray the crop on time, or the vendor is out of the product, or it cannot be gotten to the farmer in time, he loses his entire crop. There are simply too many unseen or unanticipated variables that could have an impact on repeated chemical applications. If the vendor of the repeat chemicals could be held accountable in the event of schedule or supply problems, some of the onus and risks associated with repeat applications might be reduced or eliminated.

The Rockefeller Foundation, Part II

Engdahl has taken the time to try and 'connect the dots' between the Rockefeller Foundation and its involvement with international aid agencies, public and private, and most of the agricultural multinationals. The Rockefeller Foundation's long-time involvement in genetic manipulation and engineering is alarming to Engdahl. He attributes a sinister subtext or motive to each and every one of its actions. There is no denying that the Rockefeller Foundation's involvement in worldwide agricultural development, if looked at from the point of view of a devoted conspiracy seeker, makes for exciting reading. He may be tilting at windmills, but, nevertheless, we have to ask ourselves, what if he is right?

It is hard to imagine that the Rockefeller Foundation has been carrying on a systematic genetics quest for more almost six generations, with all the changes in leadership that any large organization, like the Rockefeller Foundation has experienced.[25] Engdahl seems to believe not only that it could but that it has. Enghdahl recently wrote:

. . . the Green Revolution was a brilliant Rockefeller family scheme to develop a globalized agribusiness which they then could monopolize just as they had done in the world oil industry beginning a half century before. . . .

[For] decades the same interests including the Rockefeller Foundation which backed the initial Green Revolution, have worked to promote a second 'Gene Revolution' as Rockefeller Foundation President Gordon Conway termed it several years ago, the spread of industrial agriculture and commercial inputs including GMO patented seeds. [26]

There is absolutely no denying that that the Rockefeller family has or had extended its influence into almost every sphere of American big business; and it would make sense if, as a consummate corporate family, it sought to promote those businesses, even through its foundation. If Engdahl and others are right, the Rockefeller Foundation would be one of the most diabolical organizations since the fabled Priory of Sion.[27]

Conspiracies aside, if the leading development agencies and organizations and multinational corporations have their way, the second Green Revolution will be based on biotechnologies, with every card in the corporate deck stacked in the multinational corporations' favor. The seeds will not reproduce once planted. Proprietary chemicals will be required to either germinate the seeds or continue normal growth of the plants and yields.Cultivators will, essentially become renters of seeds, not owners.

Assuming that GMOs do not pose a threat to either the environment, other plant species, or humans, and they perform as well as advertised, what is there to lose by their adoption? First and foremost, there is the threat to worldwide biodiversity. Innumerable local plant varieties will disappear if GMOs replace traditional varieties. Thousands of crop varieties disappeared after the last round of high yielding seed varieties during the Green Revolution. The proposed biotech revolution should complete the job of eliminating those varieties that the Green Revolution did not eliminate.

We probably should not worry about the loss of these traditional varieties, however. Bill Gates, Monsanto, Syngenta Foundation, the Government of Norway and the Rockefeller Foundation will be holding most of them, along with nearly 5 million other distinct plant varieties in the Doomsday Seed Vault in Svalbard on Spitsbergen for safekeeping. Each of these benefactors only has the world's best interests at heart. Engdahl might suggest otherwise.

Numerous NGOs have fought against the GMOs and the implementation of biotech technologies. Surprisingly, those fights have been most successful in Sub-Saharan Africa, and for a while, in South Asia. Even so, biotechnologies are slowly gaining a foothold virtually everywhere. Once the World Trade Organization ruled against national import bans in the European Union, EU opposition

Map 11-1: Countries that have Adopted Biotech Crops 2007

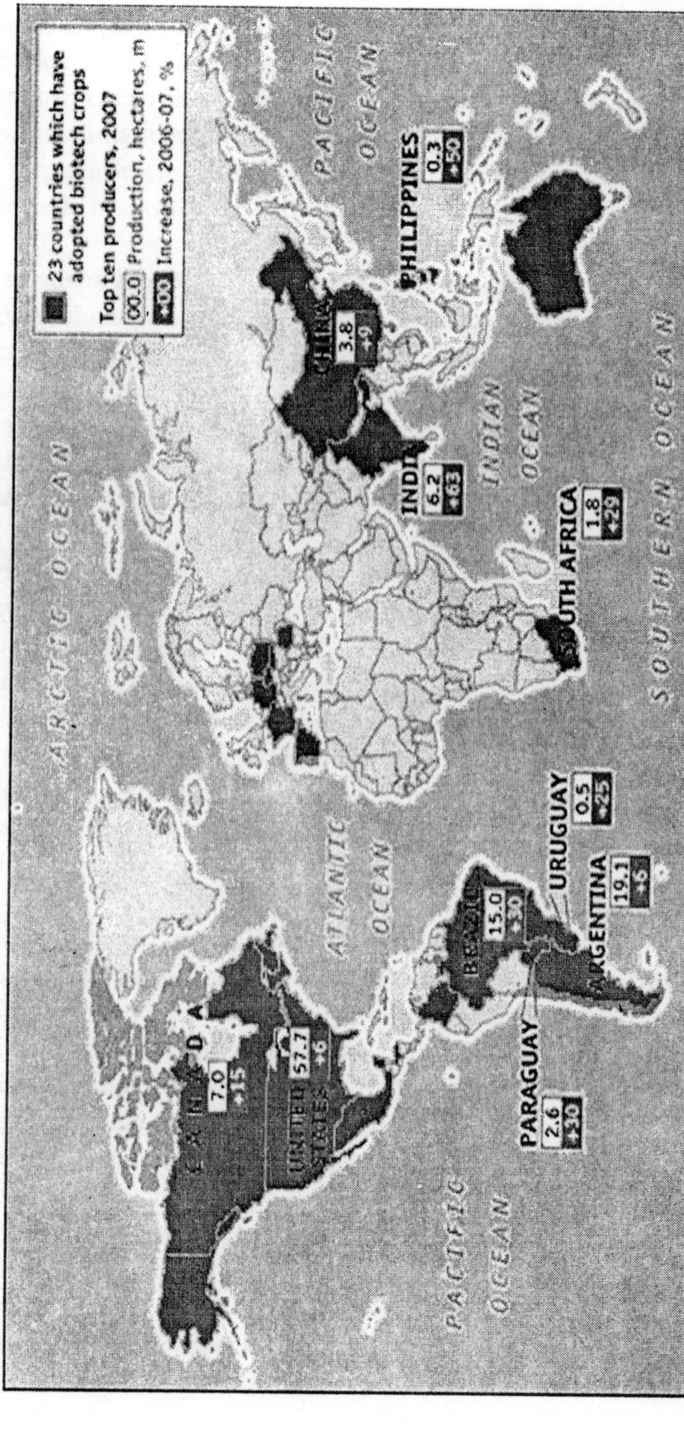

Source: (Economist.com, 2008).

to GM products began to crumble, amidst objections from a wide range of public interest groups, observers around the world recognized that official opposition to GM products would eventually wither away.[28] Part of the beginning of the retreat of the EU regarding GMO food stems from the fact that many politicians and observers are wearied by the protracted debate, recognizing the inevitable – GMOs are here to stay and have become a fact of life, even if it takes a while for the politicians and regulators to come around.[29] They are already all around us. The muscle and might of the multinational corporations, once focused on an objective, is difficult to oppose for most politicians. This may be the multinationals' strategy – simply wear the opposition down. Through 2007, 23 countries have accepted the import or use of GMO crops, and many more countries are poised to accept specific GMOs, even if they are not prepared to open their doors and gleefully embrace everything the multinationals have to offer. See Figure 11-1.

What will A Second Green Revolution Look Like?

The experience of the first Green Revolution has taught us some very important and valuable lessons. The first Green Revolution was, at least superficially, a public service undertaking. The developers of the improved, hybrid seed varieties genuinely hoped to save the world's starving and undernourished. At least in terms of pure agricultural production, these agronomists can rest assured that they fulfilled their goal. In reality, the number of undernourished people simply continued to increase, not for lack of production but because the people could not afford the food that was made available to them.

The next Green Revolution is faced with a number of pre-existing problems. The fundamental facts are that cultivable land is not limitless. Increased production cannot be based on expansion into currently untilled land. Improved crops may be able to take advantage of potentially new lands but the environmental limit of agriculture will be reached, and probably very quickly. Civilization and population have already pressed agriculture into marginal lands, at least marginal within the context of current technology. Improved technology and breeding possibilities also have their limitations. For example, applying increasing amounts of fertilizer does not result in commensurate increases in yield after a certain point. There is a genetic limit built into every seed-soil combination.

In spite of the Green Revolution, people do not get enough to eat because drought, disease, worn-out soils, pests that have become resistant to pesticides and weeds that have grown resistant to herbicides are hampering food production. Further, the crops that were so tirelessly and tediously crossbred were those that were large-volume commodity crops, not crops grown solely by small-scale, subsistence farmers. They are commercial crops, pure and simple. Why is this important? More than two-thirds of the world's cultivators grow the food they eat. They ***are*** subsistence farmers. If we are to feed the world, we need to put crops in the hands of these cultivators that will permit them to feed themselves, first. If subsistence cultivators should produce a marketable surplus that would be a bonus. First and foremost, they must feed themselves. The larger, commercial producers can and will take care of the remaining one-third of the world's population. Wheat, rice and maize are their commercial crops.

The Green Revolution failed the smaller farmers, not because they could not master the mix of inputs that the package of inputs required but because inputs required significant upfront investments. As prerequisites, cultivators needed seed, chemical fertilizers and pesticides, irrigation systems, machinery, and fuel. Basically these were beyond the capacity of the average small-scale subsistence cultivator. As a consequence, try as he might to share in the bounty of the Green Revolution, his only success was to fall deeper and deeper into debt, oftentimes resulting in the loss of his land to the larger landowners. The Green Revolution was not designed with the small subsistence cultivator in mind. It was designed by Western educated agronomists based on a particular agricultural paradigm that worked, but only within the context of comparatively large landholdings with adequate investment capital. Neither of these conditions prevailed in the areas where the benefits of the Green Revolution were most needed – Asia and Sub-Saharan Africa. One of the first prerequisites for the Second Green Revolution must be a system that is not capital intensive and is not tailored to large-scale production settings.

The Green Revolution was, no matter where it was introduced, a complicated balancing act for cultivators, requiring a level of knowledge or sophistication that was beyond the ability of many illiterate cultivators. Failing to comprehend the consequences of applying too much fertilizer, not watering sufficiently, breathing in pesticide dust, or even consuming treated seed, cultivators polluted the environment, made themselves ill, and even caused their own deaths. The inability to read prevented many farmers from learning how to properly use and store the inputs they were able to purchase and posed environmental and health risks. Therefore, a second prerequisite of the next Green Revolution is that it must be easily adopted by largely illiterate farmers using the knowledge base that every subsistence cultivator already possesses – that storehouse we call Best Practices or Indigenous Knowledge.

Finally, it must be sustainable within the context of rural Africa and South Asia, for these areas are the areas most in need of increased agricultural production. This is where the largest concentration of the poor and starving are to be found. The first Green Revolution started there. The next Green Revolution needs to start there as well.

As outlined, the requirements for the next Green Revolution are much different than those that might have been detailed had the progenitors of the original Green Revolution even thought about writing down exactly what they wanted to achieve, how best to achieve it, and anticipate the consequences of their program. Every one of the agronomists that pushed and plead for the Green Revolution were capable of extrapolating the outcomes of their actions. Unfortunately, they had one overriding concern – simply feeding people. It was a laudable goal but it came at a price in terms of people and the environment in the developing nations. We cannot make similar mistakes the second time around.

The next Green Revolution must come to grips with the issues of:

(1) Harsh growing conditions
(2) Disease
(3) Worn-out soils
(4) Pests
(5) Weeds

(6) Meeting the needs of the world's subsistence cultivators
(7) Low cost
(8) Sustainability.

The large multinationals and the advocates of an agriculture based on biotechnology say they can solve or at least deal with all these problem areas. Can they deliver? Probably not but they would have us believe they can. There is no doubt that the latest generation of genetically enhanced seeds will be a much needed improvement over those in use today. Seed manipulation can probably meet the first five, maybe six issues noted above. Can they make their system low cost and have it remain sustainable? In all likelihood – No.

The next Green Revolution in all will be driven by the large multinational, for-profit corporations. Their focus will not be on the public good. They come armed with biologically modified crops that produce food but not re-plantable seeds. These crops will be tailored to the environment within which they are to be planted. They will be pest resistant, disease resistant, drought resistant, they will be able to tolerate longer periods of submergence, they will be less photosensitive, they will be more heat and cold resistant. They will be fertilizer responsive. They will be activated and perpetuated by proprietary chemicals. They will be resistant to herbicides, so cultivators can eliminate weeds by indiscriminately spraying their crops with *Roundup®* and not having to worry about killing their crop at the same time.[30] They will produce either more calories or protein than current plant varieties, and given time, they may even be able to make plants 'taste like chicken.'

The original Green Revolution promised to end hunger with its improved seeds. The Second Green Revolution promises more of the same. If the first Green Revolution did not succeed, why should we believe that a more high-tech version will fare any better? Is this new Green Revolution going to be only an improved version of the first? Is it just repackaging?

The new GMOs may well satisfy subsistence cultivators' needs in regard to crop types and their fit in ecological micro-niches. It will only be a matter of defining what is needed and selecting plant traits that will fulfill the need.

In addition to fertilizers, an entirely new category of agrochemicals will be released into the environment. Are we to naively believe that, unlike their predecessors, they will have no negative impacts on the physical environment? They will not pollute the air, surface water, or groundwater? They will not be toxic to wildlife, domestic animals, or humans?

The earlier Green Revolution demanded significant upfront investments to acquire inputs. Will the next generation Green Revolution cost any less? In all likelihood, it will cost more. All the inputs required will be the same, except for the addition of another layer of chemicals. Instead of lowering cultivator costs and reducing the need and burden of rural credit structures, the new technology will make credit even more essential.

The next Green Revolution must also be sustainable. By sustainable we mean:

- Net long-term agricultural income must exceed the costs of production and meet the family unit's overall economic needs.
- Either restore, or at least not degrade the soil.
- It will not result in any off-site environmental damage or contamination.
- It will succeed within the context of current or easily transferable knowledge.
- It will improve, or at least not widen the socio-economic gap between classes.

If the seeds are incapable of reproducing themselves, if the agrochemicals necessary to germination and continued plant growth are not recyclable, how can a system based on non-renewable inputs be deemed sustainable? If, by sustainable we mean, as long as cultivators can pay for the inputs being offered to them, the multinationals will continue to produce them, then it will be sustainable. Unfortunately, everything about the proposed Green Revolution revolves around the ability of cultivators to purchase and repurchase non-renewable inputs. There is nothing sustainable about it. Cultivators will, if not literally, at least figuratively become the serfs of the multinationals. Once the cultivators purchase that first sack of genetically modified rice, wheat, maize, barley, or whatever, they have lost almost all their subsequent options. They are locked into an agricultural system that is controlled by a CEO in a large office, in a large corporate office building, somewhere, in all likelihood, in the U.S. Never in human history will so few have so much power over so many.

Henry Kissinger is credited with having said:

If you control the oil you control nations; if you control food, you control the people.

In light of biotechnology, this statement now needs to be revised and amended:

If you control the oil you control the country; if you control food, you control the population; and if you control the seeds, you control the world.

Unless

Most of the nations of Sub-Saharan Africa have, at least so far, resisted pressure from the agrochemical and agribusiness giants to adopt the biotech philosophy, despite the best efforts of the international aid and development communities. Their failure to jump on board the biotech bandwagon, in all likelihood, stems more from mis- and disinformation concerning the environmental and biological hazards of GMOs than either good or sound science. Green groups repetitively attacked draft EU laws on labeling organic produce saying it threatened to allow genetically modified (GMO) content to creep into what should be completely biotech-free farming.[31] Over the last few years, the biotech companies have responded to the scare tactics of the green groups but due to public skepticism regarding GM, scientists in general, and salesmen from the multinationals, in particular, the green groups' message lingers in the minds of the public and government officials.

This is not to say that the unanticipated cannot happen; however, the debate over GMOs has been on-going for nearly ten years, and in that time, the biotech companies have had the opportunity to verify and confirm their data. They have also had the time to address potential public concerns and fears. It may well be that GM ***is*** the only way to produce the food that the world needs. We have refined the old Green Revolution technologies to the point that there are few new avenues to pursue. Bold new approaches are now needed.

The primary flaw in the biotech approach to agriculture is not it the science behind it. The flaw stems from the misconception that by boosting food production it will alleviate hunger. The previous Green Revolution increased production, and yet widespread hunger did not disappear. Yes, more food is needed, but we cannot alleviate hunger unless the current social, political, cultural, and economic rules that currently govern human behavior are changed. Together, these rules determine who will benefit from almost any new technology. Almost always, there will be winners and losers. It is not the technology that causes the benefits to accrue to one group or one person over another. Benefits accrue to those in whom tradition and social rank dictate. It is not based on some cosmic scale of fairness.

Historically, the poor pay more and get less for their efforts. The poor seldom receive discounts, while their rich counterparts demand and get them. Without clout, the poor get very few breaks in life. The small farmers have no leverage. The large farmers can withhold their harvest from the market, waiting for prices to improve, while the small farmer must sell immediately to repay loans. The poor have no bargaining power. Water, in the form of irrigation, was an instrumental part of the Green Revolution. The large farmers could afford pumpsets, tubewells, sluices, and irrigation channels to get water to their crops. Many of the smaller farmers could afford none of these facilities. As a consequence, their yields were less than their more affluent neighbors. Credit availability is always easier for the well-to-do. They are able to obtain the credit they require from established credit sources, like cooperatives and banks. They seldom rely on moneylender, while the small cultivator seems always in debt to the local moneylender at usurious rates. The small farmer seldom benefits from government subsidies. These accrue to the larger farmers. At every turn, the social, economic, and political deck is stacked against the small cultivator. That is how it has always been, and unless changes are made in the 'delivery system,' that is how it will remain.

The new Green Revolution, as proposed and prophesized by the large agro-business multinationals will fare no better than the earlier Green Revolution *unless* arrangements are made to subsidize the start-up costs associated with the new biotechnologies. The vast majority of subsistence farmers, the small landholders, are not and will not be in a position to adopt the inputs that the GM seeds will necessitate. They simply will not have the capital necessary to invest in the seeds, the chemicals, fertilizers, and irrigation that will be necessary. Subsidies for these non-renewable inputs will have to come from government or from the agri-input suppliers themselves, at least in the beginning. Once the cultivators have been assured that the package of biotech practices are as productive as the suppliers say, the cultivators should have sufficient investible income to fund their own future investment needs. Once the multinationals have hooked their customers, and proven the efficacy of their products, the customer-supplier relationship will be cemented. Failure on the part of the government or the suppliers to subsidize the transition from the old agricultural technology to the new will only result in a catastrophic collapse for everyone.

If the small farmers are assisted through the capital intensive start-up period and the crops perform as advertised, agricultural self-sufficiency, at first beginning with the individual cultivator, will be realized, and will grow to village, state, and national self-sufficiency. It is the small farmer that requires the boost of assistance. The larger cultivators already have the sources of capital to make the changeover. Such an investment in the small cultivators would make good financial sense, whether coming from the input suppliers or the government. The successful small farmers will be in a position to make their own investments in the future. Such investments will further instill and insure customer loyalty. A one-time investment could easily become a business relationship for life and fulfill the goal of reducing hunger through increased production. If the small farmers cannot make the initial investment in the new technologies, there will be no business relationship and no increased productivity.

If the biotech approach to self-sufficiency in food is to work, the small cultivators must be able to invest and produce. If their self-sufficiency is established, they will have the income to purchase the food they cannot or do not produce and they, along with the large landowners and cultivators, will benefit, each according to their ability. No one will be left behind.

The gap between the rich and poor will never disappear completely. There will always be the Haves and the Have Nots but, as the rich prosper, it need not be at the expense of the less prosperous. It may not result in the absolute economic leveling that some social philosophers would like, but it would be a move in the right direction. Everyone would potentially have at least enough to eat because they are no longer so poor that they cannot grow what they require or purchase it. If the next Green Revolution could provide the mechanism for the achievement of that simple goal, absolutely no one could complain or find fault with biotechnology or the multinational biotech corporations.

References

1. From Borlaug's Nobel Lecture, December 11, 1970. (Borlaug, Norman, 1970).

2. (FAO, 2006b), p. 8. (FAO, 2008b).

3. (FAO, 2008a).

4. *Ibid.*

5. (FAO, 2002), p. 9.

6. (The World Bank, 1986a), p. 4; or (The World Bank, 1986b), p. 8, Box 1.1.

7. (Sen, 1990). Sen commented: ". . . but the threatening famines have been stopped by public action before they could become major killers."

8. (Borlaug, Norman, 1970).

9. Diouf is FAO Director-General, Rome. The decline occurred between 1980 to 2006.

10. (OneWorld.Net, 2008).

11. See (Shah, 2008) for an excellent discussion of the Food Crisis of 2008. See also, (McMullen, 2008).

12. (OneWorld.Net, 2008),

13. (CBC News and the Associated Press, 2008).

14. (Matangi Maskay, Nephil and Rojan Bajracharya, 2008).

15. Roughly 55 percent of the area under rice in India is rainfed (IRRI, J. L.McLean, 2002), p. 92.

16. Dandekar and Rath, (1971); and Frank J. Moore (1955), pp. 124-128

17. Kuhnen (1971), p. 177.

18. After (Critchfield, 1971).

19. (Wu, Felicia and William P. Butz, 2004).

20. (Conway, 1997).

21. Statements pertaining to Dr. M.S Swaminathan were attributed to Claude Alvarez, in an article in *The Illustrated Weekly of India*, March 23-April 5, 1986, referencing: www.GMWatch.org, and http://www.globalresearch.ca/. *The Illustrated Weekly of India* article by Alvarez is reproduced at: (MaSa, 2007).

22. (History Commons, 2008).

23. *Ibid.*

24. *Ibid.*

25. (Kohler, 2007), pp. 51-58.

26. (Engdahl, 2007b).

27. See (Anderson, Luke and Christina Cobb, 2001).

28. (Smith, 2008). See also, (International Herald Tribune, 2006).

29. (Reuters, 2008), (Smith, 2008).

30. (SourceWatch, 2008).

31. See for example, see (Reuters, 2005); (Pearce, 2003); (Woodworth, 2008); (KINDERLERER, 2001); (Bonny, 2003); (Prakash, 2005); (Smith, 2008); and (International Herald Tribune, 2006).

12

Water

Introduction

While humans can survive with no food for weeks, without water we perish within a few days. It is the one component of every agricultural system that is indispensible. Cultivators can grow their crops without fertilizers, pesticides, herbicides, and without improved seed varieties, but no plant will grow without a source of moisture. Water, even before the first plant was ever domesticated and cultivated, was a vital part of human existence and, as such, it has become embedded in and is a part of our cultural history.[1] There can be no culture, no civilization, no future without water.

Until recently, in terms of human existence, there was little competition for freshwater and very few environmental concerns regarding its use. Agriculture was always able to capture sufficient water to feed the population. As a result of rapid population growth in the last 100 years, a competition for existing freshwater resources has begun to emerge. Competing with agriculture are human needs for drinking water, sanitation, and industry. As the need to produce and process more food for the world's growing population increases, agriculture will need to claim a larger portion of the world's finite water resources, especially in the form of irrigation water. In gentler times, such a demand would have gone virtually by unnoticed. Water was there for the taking, despite the fact that only 1/100th of 1 percent of the world's water is readily available for human use.[2] This fact is further complicated by the fact that this miniscule amount of water is unevenly distributed around the planet.

Today agriculture is obliged to assert its claim on water within a complex framework of differing social, political, economic, and environmental objectives, as articulated by society. As a consequence, agriculture must now negotiate with these other competing human socio-economic sectors for a share of the world's freshwater supply.

Drinking water intake typically varies between 2 and 3 liters per person per day (L/person/d). In addition, there are domestic water requirements for personal and household hygiene and related requirements, which represent 30 to 300 L/person/d, varying according to standard of living and quality of water supply. Producing food requires much more water — from 2,000 to 5,000 L/person/d, depending on diet and climate differences and the efficiency of local food production systems. Most of the water used to produce food or other crops comes from rain that is stored in the soil, where it is captured by crop roots. Irrigation, practiced in places and during times where rainwater is insufficient to meet minimum crop water needs, provides a guaranteed supply of water and protects against droughts and dry spells, which seem to be on the rise.

Globally, rainfall provides about 90 percent of the water used by crops. Irrigation claims 70 percent of all the freshwater that we take from rivers, lakes, and groundwater. Agriculture is by far the largest consumer of water. It requires one thousand times more than we use to drink and one hundred times more than we use to meet basic personal needs.

For many people around the world, water is the primary cause of food insecurity, because it is the key ingredient in <u>*every*</u> agricultural system, from subsistence cultivation to large-scale commercial farming, from rainfed no-till to irrigated paddy fields. Water is also essential to industry, and manufacturing, and for drinking and sanitation.The pattern of water consumption around the world, in general, reflects the overall level of economic development. See Figure 12-1. In fact, water problems – flood or drought – are more than twice as important as conflicts, refugees,

Figure 12-1: Water Usage by World Regions

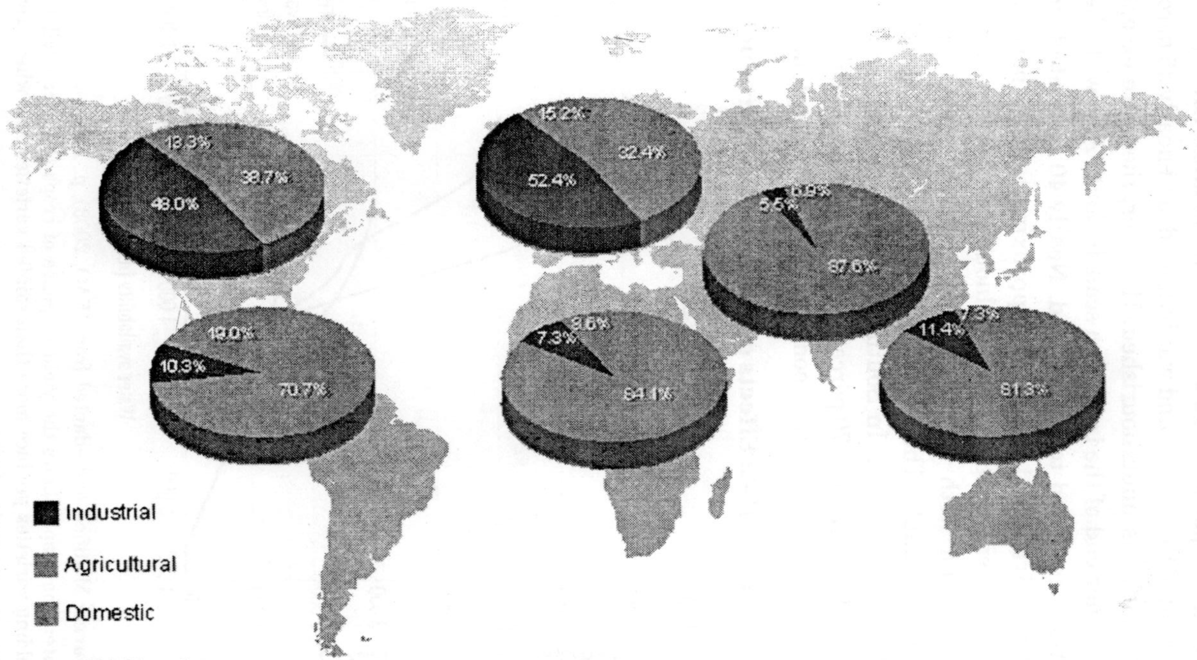

Source: (FAO), p.1.

or economic dislocations, when we look for causes of food emergencies around the world.[3]

As a general rule, people who have access to water are much less likely to suffer the effects of undernourishment. For example, during the period 1998-2000 in Sub-Saharan Africa, less than 5 percent of the arable land was irrigated, and nearly 35 percent of its population is undernourished. However, there are exceptions. At the other end of the irrigation scale is South Asia with the highest ratio of irrigated to arable land. Nearly 40 percent of the arable land is irrigated, and still approximately 25 percent of the subcontinent's population is malnourished.[4] If lack of irrigation is associated with undernourishment, the case for Africa is understandable. The situation in South Asia, on the other hand, seems inconsistent. In South Asia, other factors are a work. For example, more than 70 percent of annual rainfall comes during the three months of the monsoon (roughly June to September); most of

Figure 12-2: Effects of Water on Crop Production[7]

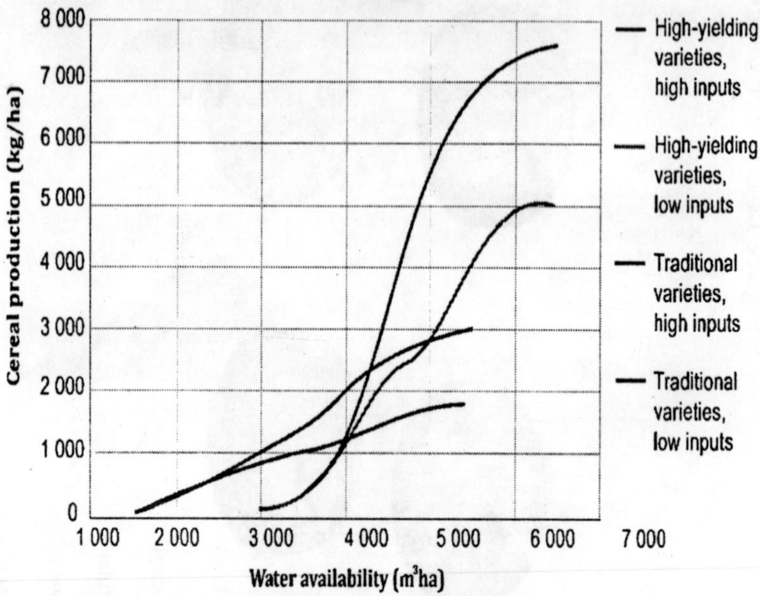

Source: Modified and adapted from (FAO, 2003), p. 19.

Note: The graph shows the yield response of crops to water availability. High yielding varieties produce more than rainfed varieties only when provided with adequate amounts of water

it drains from the land as run-off and out to sea, via the rivers, often causing death and destruction along the way. Therefore, farmers who lack irrigation must contend with water scarcity through most of the year; and those with irrigation must contend with rivers and canals that often go dry due to natural water loss and increasing use by other cultivators, as well as municipal and industrial withdrawals.

The importance of irrigation cannot be understated. Irrigation can increase yields of most crops by 100 to 400 percent, with or without the introduction of improved or genetically enhanced seed varieties and modern inputs.[5] See Figure 12-2. This increase in production, as a result of irrigation, is fundamental to providing sufficient food for growing populations. Of the world's 1.5 billion hectares of cropland, only 18 percent is irrigated.[6] The intensification of agriculture, through Green Revolution technologies, has made it possible to limit the expansion of agricultural land to a few percentage points as the population has more than doubled.

The options for increasing the amount of land dedicated to agriculture at the expense of natural forests and savannahs are limited, because land has to be both suitable and available for conversion to agriculture. The food needs of a growing population have been largely served through increased land productivity, meaning harvesting a larger quantity of crops from the existing agricultural land surface. Irrigation lifts the constraint on crop productivity that stems from insufficient and unreliable rainfall. During the second half of the 20th century, irrigation development became a component of the strategy to feed a doubling world population, with a corresponding increase in the quantity of water utilized for this purpose. Map 12-1 shows the location and extent of irrigation in the world in 2006 and the relative importance of irrigation in national agriculture, a distribution that strongly correlates with climatic conditions.

It becomes imperative for the nations of the world, and especially those in developing regions, to invest in and exploit every possible, ecologically sound opportunity to expand irrigation. In SSA, 39 million hectares are amendable to irrigation. Of this amount only 5 million are irrigated, or slightly less than 13 percent. In South Asia, an estimated 142 million hectares could be irrigated.

Map 12-1: Area Under Irrigation As Percentage Of Cultivated Land

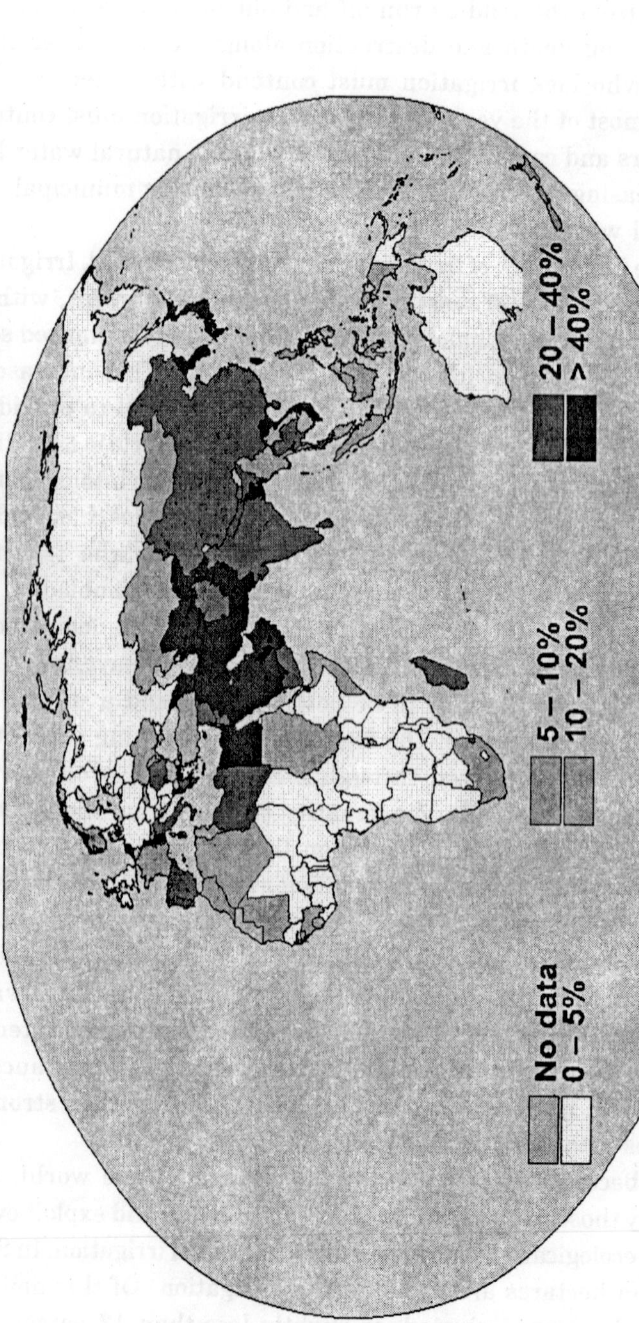

Source: FAOSTAT, 2008)

Of this amount, only 79 million hectares are currently exploited, approximately 56 percent.[8] In both areas there are still opportunities to extend irrigation, more so in SSA than in South Asia.

Although there are lands into which irrigation could be extended, concerns for the environment have begun to work at cross-purposes. Increasingly, environmentalist are pressuring agriculturalists to terminate agricultural practices that can damage the environment, especially as concerns water depletion, polluting water systems, and contribute to soil infertility, contamination, and erosion. Irrigation must be managed carefully to avoid environmental damage, which is already extensive. Overuse of water in one place can potentially mean deprivation in another.

Map 12-2: Renewable Water Exploitation Rates, 2000

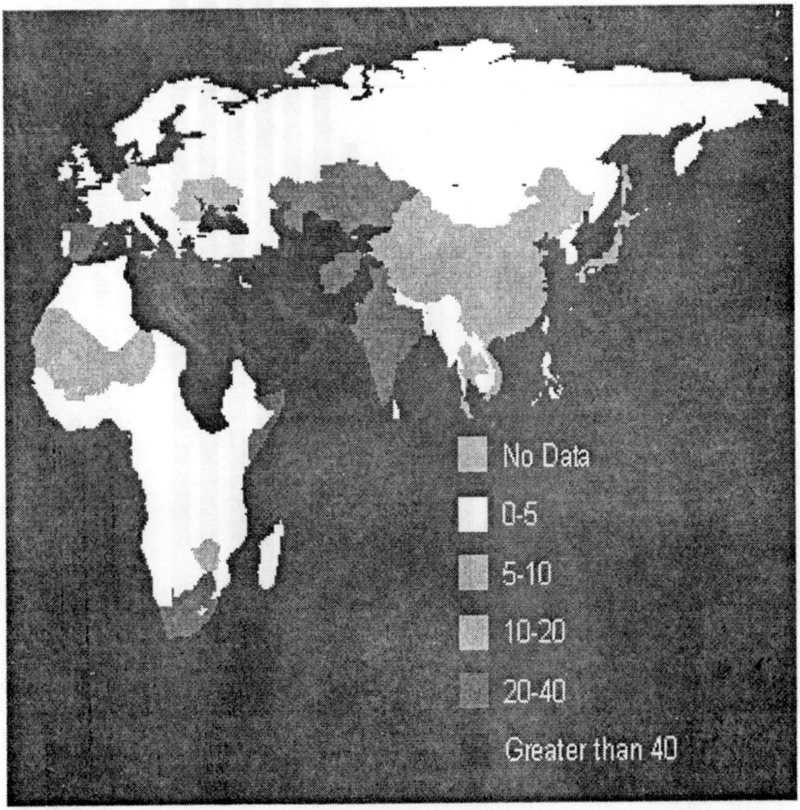

Source: Original data from (AQUASTAT, 2008),
Note: Agricultural water withdrawals as a percentage of total renewable water resources

Figure 12-3: Top 20 Countries Who are Agriculture Dependent by Percentage

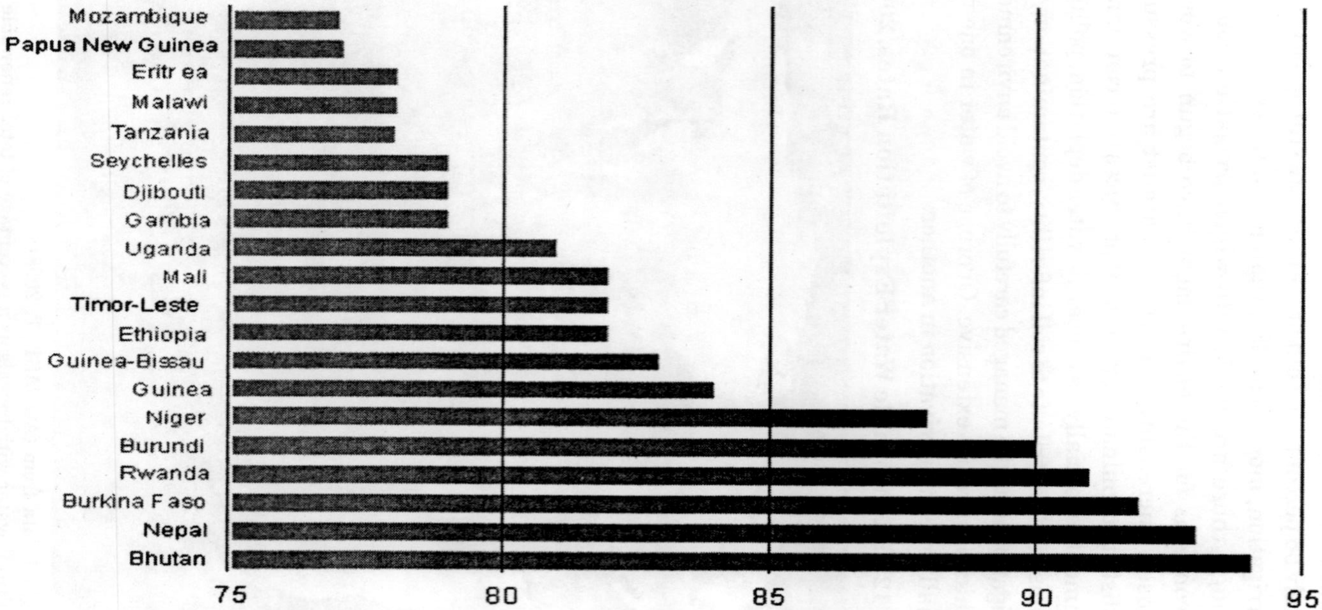

*People depending on the agricultural sector as percentage of the total economically active population

Source: Modified and adapted from (FAO), p. 14.

Note: The countries in Red are representatives of Africa. Those in Dark Blue are from South Asia, and those in Black are from Oceania.

One area of immediate concern is the current rate of exploitation of renewable water resources. Map 12-2 depicts water exploitation rates across Europe, Asia and Africa. Areas in which the exploitation rate is in excess of 40 percent, are of particular concern to environmentalist but also should be of concern to agriculturalists, because over-exploitation means depletion over time. At the other end of the scale is under-exploitation, as most of Africa. Neither extreme is acceptable, especially in light of the current levels of malnourishment in the world.

Of the top 20 nations who depend on agriculture for employment of the bulk of the nation's people, all but four are from SSA, two are from South Asia, and two are from Oceania. Of the top 20, the vast majority are among the most water and irrigation challenged countries of Africa and the world. Rural and overall economic development have by-passed most of the nations of SSA, and they remain dependent on their agricultural sector for the bulk of their national wealth and well-being.

Water for Agricultural Production

With changes in human food consumption, moving from diets largely dependent upon the three primary cereals – wheat, rice, and maize – to meat and dairy products, there is also a change in the demand and need for water. Both plants and animals consume water and return it to the environment – plants in the form of moisture through evapotranspiration, and animals in the form of digestive wastes and meat or milk products.

Wheat requires approximately 1,000 liters of water to produce 1 kilogram of grain and chaff. Other plant varieties have varying water requirements. Paddy may require twice the volume of water as wheat to produce the same quantity of grain. The production of meat and dairy, however, requires from 6 and 20 times more water to produce an equivalent amount of food. Animals need much more water than grain to produce the same amount of food. Ending malnutrition and feeding even more mouths will take still more water. The world will have to change its current and future consumption patterns if it is to have any realistic hope of feeding itself. The current trend is away from grains and toward more meat consumption, which means more water consumption.

Some specific values for the water equivalents required for the production of selected food products are provided in Table 12-1.

Table 12-1: Water Equivalents for Food Production Equivalent

Product	*Unit of Production*	*Equivalent Water in Cubic Meters per Unit*
Cattle	head	4000
Sheep and goats	head	500
Fresh beef	kg	15
Fresh lamb	kg	10
Fresh poultry	kg	6
Cereals	kg	1.5
Citrus fruits	kg	1
Palm oil	kg	2
Pulses, roots and tubers	kg	1

Source: (FAO, 1997).

Rainfed Agriculture

Unirrigated agriculture accounts for some 60 percent of production in developing countries.[9] The potential to improve unirrigated yields is restricted where rainfall is subject to large seasonal variations. With a high risk of yield reductions or complete loss of crop from dry spells and droughts, farmers are reluctant to invest in inputs such as plant nutrients, high-yielding seeds and pest management. For resource-poor farmers in semi-arid regions, the overriding requirement is to harvest sufficient foodstuffs to ensure nutrition of the household between harvests. This objective may be reached with robust, drought-resistant varieties associated with low yields. Genetic engineering has not yet delivered on its high-yield drought-resistant varieties, although current indications are that these GM-drought resistant crops will be available soon.[10] To date, most crop plants that are drought resistant also have shown a tendency to be low yielding.

Irrigated Agriculture

Unlike rainfed forms of agriculture, irrigated agriculture is dependent upon human involvement to make it possible for plants to take up the water they require to thrive. Irrigation is most beneficial in areas that are either semi-arid, and the plants obtain a portion of the water they need from rainfall, or arid lands, where the plants are totally dependent on irrigation for their survival. As such, irrigation is a powerful management tool against the vagaries of rainfall and makes it economically attractive to grow high-yielding seed varieties and to apply other modern inputs, thereby boosting yields. Figure 12-2, above, illustrates the typical yield response of a cereal crop to water availability and the relationship between irrigation, crop variety and inputs. Irrigation is crucial to the world's food supplies. In 1998, irrigated land made up about one-fifth of the total arable area in developing countries but produced two-fifths of all crops and close to three-fifths of cereal production.[11]

Most of the irrigation infrastructure has been developed in arid and semi-arid lands. Refer to Map 12-1. The low proportion of irrigated land in Sub-Saharan Africa is the result of the underdevelopment of irrigation infrastructure, in general. Therefore, the potential and need for irrigation development is highest in Sub-Saharan Africa. It has reached its highest levels of development in the Middle East, from Egypt to Pakistan, Vietnam, the Koreas, Bangladesh, and the Philippines.

Part of the reason for the delay in the expansion of irrigation facilities into areas that are currently underdeveloped is that the most attractive and economically easiest lands to develop have already been developed. Secondly, prices for agricultural commodities have not risen sufficiently to encourage government investment in lands exhibiting second class potential and requiring much more investment to achieve returns equal to those realized earlier.

Most of the expansion of irrigated land will be achieved by converting land currently in use as rainfed lands or land that has rainfed production potential but has not yet been put in use. Irrigation will turn these marginal lands into much more productive land. With or without the expansion of irrigation in Africa, a considerable increase in agricultural production can be achieved by simply expanding cultivation into unused arable land. In many cases, expansion into unused arable land, combined with irrigation, will increase yields and production significantly. The growth in wheat and rice production in developing countries will increasingly come from gains in yield, while expansion of irrigation on harvestable land will undoubtedly be a major source of growth in the production of maize.

The Case of Groundwater

The use of groundwater, water from water tables or aquifers, has a number of advantages over canal irrigation but also a number of inherent weaknesses. Among the most important advantages:

- In most cases, it is available independent of rivers, lakes, and irrigation canals
- It is available for use, when needed
- It is not seasonal in availability, like rainfall or riverine-sourced canal systems.

On the negative side, groundwater, although deemed a renewable resource, requires a long time for recharge. If too large a demand is made on the aquifer, the water level can drop; and depending on the nature and rate of recharge, it may never be replenished.

Within this context, there are two types of aquifers – those that are, comparatively speaking, quick to recharge (generations) and those that may never recharge (generally referred to as 'fossil aquifers'). These fossil aquifers are sometimes referred to as glacial reserves, and when water is extracted from them, it is called water mining.

In almost all cases, demand exceeds the recharge rate. Over very few years, the water table can decline rapidly and beyond normal pumping depths, as has happened in parts of Pakistan's and India's Punjab. When the water table recedes it oftentimes places the smaller cultivators at a disadvantage. Many lack the financial ability to either extend their wells or obtain improved pumpsets, but the larger farmers may not find the additional investment prohibitive. As a consequence, the land of the smaller cultivators may be put out of production.

Further, the lowering of the water table and its failure to recharge, can result in what is known as geological subsidence. One of the most well documented cases of subsidence involves the San Joaquin Valley in California. See Illustration 12-1. Similar but less dramatic examples of subsidence have been witnessed in India's Punjab.[12]

Groundwater is also susceptible to contamination from fertilizers, pesticides, and herbicide and industrial chemicals and liquid wastes. While it may have little effect on the use of the water for irrigation purposes, it can make the water unpotable for humans and livestock. This problem is particularly acute in the case of POPs, or persistent organic pollutants, which can cause long-term health problems for people and livestock.

Illustration 12-1: Subsidence in the San Joaquin Valley, Southwest of Mendota, California

Signs on pole show approximate elevation of land surface in 1925, 1955, and 1977

Source: *Zeizmic, from Wikipedia,* Subsidence, September 5, 2008.

In many jurisdictions, groundwater is deemed a public resource.[13] As such, the state has legal rights to the use of the resource, just as most surface water and other resources are deemed 'property of the state,' and as such, their use is subject to government control, and the state can demand payment for the use of the resource. Use permits are frequently issued for groundwater extraction. Unlike other types of use permits, however, groundwater use permit fees cannot be used to remediate the depletion of the resource.

Once the resource has receded beyond a certain point, it is up to nature when the aquifer will be recharged, if ever.

Therefore, government involvement in the use of groundwater resources is essential for the efficient and fair use and distribution of groundwater. Especially important is government monitoring of groundwater levels. Then, government must be able and willing to step in and enforce the equitable use of the resource, as well as implementing such use and maintenance strategies that will insure that the resource sill not be prematurely depleted by indiscriminate use or abuse. In developing countries, and especially in nations dominated by arid and semi-arid climatic regimens, the management of groundwater is a delicate balancing act. The government must control the use of the resource and, at the same time, not interfere with much needed agricultural production. In many cases, this balance is practically an impossibility, as either the resource becomes depleted or there is no food. In many cases, there seems to be no middle way. If the water's use is restricted, production falls. If production continues, the water resource is depleted. In these kinds of situations, governments have not proven to be the best arbiters, but neither have agriculturalists. Each group has its own agenda, and they are oftentimes at odds with one another.

Water Concerns

Water resources suffer from problems of availability, variability, and a potential for depletion. In most cases, these resources are renewable, except for some groundwater. They do, however, exist within clear limits which are set by precipitation. Under normal conditions, rainfall recharges most lakes, rivers, and the oceans. Precipitation is notoriously unreliable and variable, posing a problem for mankind. Many decisions made by the agriculturalist are dependent upon the timely availability of moisture for the soil, the seeds, and the plants. If it is not available, the soils dry, the seeds do not germinate, and the crops wither in the fields. In all of these scenarios, people suffer.

Irrigation, in general, when properly applied and managed, insures that the moisture for the soil, the seeds, and the plants is readily available and in a timely manner. However, even irrigation is dependent upon rainfall. Now, both the availability and use of water are changing on a worldwide scale. This change in availability and use have brought about increased concerns for world's water resources. The primary causes for concern are for:

- water scarcity
- water quality
- water-related disasters.

Water Scarcity

Water is a recyclable resource. It falls on the earth as rainfall and is returned to the atmosphere through the evapotranspiration of plants or evaporation from lakes, rivers, and the oceans. Humans obtain the water they need by diverting runoff for their various needs. Despite a withdrawal of only 8 percent of total annual renewable freshwater resources, it has been estimated that 26 percent of annual evapotranspiration and 54 percent of accessible runoff is appropriated by humans.[14] As population continues to grow, agricultural requirements for water, as well as industrial, manufacturing, and water for drinking and sanitation continues to increase. All these competing needs, until fairly recently, have been operating in a sustainable equilibrium. Today, however, demand is beginning to exceed availability from all sources.

It has been estimated that today more than 2 billion people are affected by water shortages in over forty countries — 1.1 billion do not have sufficient drinking water and 2.4 billion have no provision for sanitation.[15] Further, current predictions are that by 2050 at least one in four people is likely to live in a country affected by chronic or recurring shortages of freshwater.[16]

Water scarcity can come as subtly as the recession of water tables, or in the wholesale abandonment of agricultural lands.

Map 12-3: Anticipated Water Scarcity, 2025

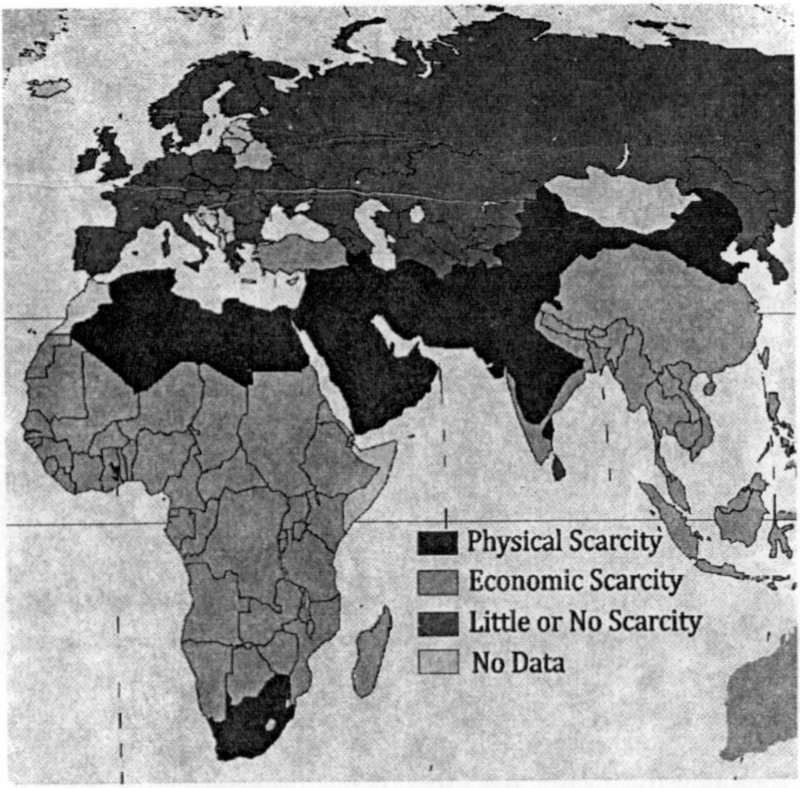

Source: After, adapted and modified from (Seckler, 1998) and (Dow, Kirstin; Edward R. Carr; Annelieka Douma;Gouyi Han; and Karl Hallding, 2005)

Groundwater over-pumping and aquifer depletion now plague many of the world's most important food-producing regions, including the north plain of China, the Punjab in Pakistan and India, portions of Southeast Asia, large areas of north Africa and the Middle East, and much of the western United States.[17] A falling water table is initially a mild warning that there is no further capacity with which to develop future groundwater. It also indicates that at least a portion of the world's current food supply is increasingly dependent on an unsustainable water resource. Therefore, one cannot count on groundwater as a reliable part of the world's long-term solution to world agriculture production.

For example Saudi Arabia, in 1994, produced nearly 5 million tons of wheat, using nonrenewable fossil groundwater. Soon thereafter, the government reduced the water subsidies that had propped up its domestic wheat production. Once the water subsidies had been eliminated, the country's wheat farmers were no longer able to finance their continued cultivation of wheat. Wheat production plummeted 62%, falling to 1.9 million tons in 1996.[18]

Financial ability, whether through savings or government subsidies, can prolong uneconomic activities but once the cost of production, or the cost of any one or more inputs exceeds the value of the output, inevitably, either production methods will be changed or production will be stopped. This is what happened in Saudi Arabia. It can occur anywhere that water scarcity increases the cost of production beyond the break-even point.

As Global Warming has an impact on the world's rainfall regime and patterns, and as variability and reliability increase, currently productive, marginal rainfed agricultural areas will contract first. Irrigation will be expanded until groundwater and canal sources of water are depleted or

severely limited. Then, irrigated land will contract, and with it the ability to feed the world's population. Changes in water supplies and growing scarcity will, of necessity, result in the inevitable reduction of the world's food supply.

Effects of Global Warming

The availability of water is complicated by Global Warming. For instance, Global Warming was heralded initially by almost imperceptible changes when the monsoons in South Asia arrived and retreated. In most cases, rainfall appears to be lessened. More recently, this phenomenon seems to have become more pronounced and widespread. In other areas, the rains seem to be more forceful and intense. As mean temperatures rise, the rates of evaporation and evapotranspiration increase, pulling water from lakes, rivers and oceans, and plants. In some areas of Africa, the rains have lessened and temperatures have risen, which has served to increase the vulnerability of the land to desertification.[19] See Map 12-4, below. Those areas most vulnerable to desertification are those immediately adjacent to deserts, since they are already in a tenuous equilibrium, and the vulnerability lessens as one moves farther and farther away from the desert front, toward areas of higher rainfall. Such is the case in Africa, as well as Pakistan and much of Northwestern India.[20] Desertification can be accelerated by man, largely through deforestation, either for obtaining wood for commercial or domestic needs or for the expansion of agriculture.

Map 12-4: Desertification Vulnerability

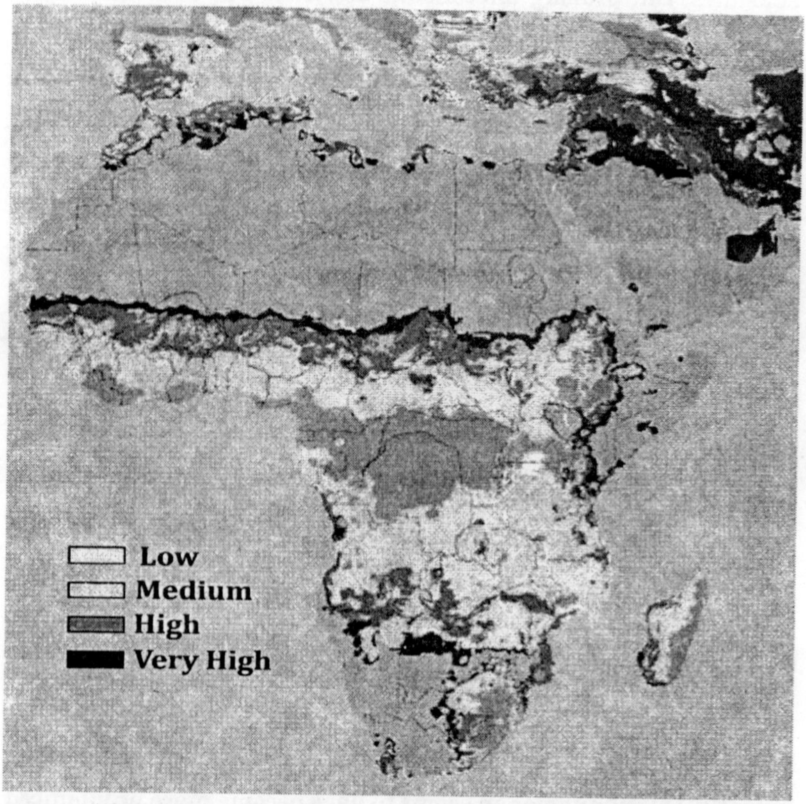

Source: (Reich, P. F.; S.T. Numbem; R.A. Almaraz; and H. Eswaran, 2008)
Note: Areas in gray are already desert. Areas in Dark Green are humid.

Water Quality

Every year millions of gallons of water are made unavailable to human needs – either for consumption, sanitation, agriculture, or industrial use – through pollution. Whenever we speak of water pollution, immediately our thoughts turn to oil tanker spills, industrial effluents being discharged into our rivers and oceans, waste water contamination, or garbage being dumped into the oceans. We give little thought to the effects of natural run-off, where pesticides, herbicides and other agricultural and domestic chemicals are carried away and into our lakes, rivers, and oceans or leaches through the soil and into groundwater supplies. Just as cattle, poultry and other livestock pollute the air with the methane they produce, they also contribute to water pollution through their biological wastes, which is carried away by run-off.

In some cases, the effects of water pollution are cumulative. For example, residues from agricultural and industrial chemicals can build-up in lakes, rivers, and groundwater. These pollutants include but are not limited to that group of chemicals known simply as POPs – persistent organic pollutants – and dioxin. Dioxins is a blanket term for a family of chemical compounds that are formed through combustion, chlorine bleaching and manufacturing processes. Dioxins are highly carcinogenic and toxic compounds, and although they do occur naturally, most are created by human activity.

Although science has yet to make a definitive statement as to the effects or consequences of POPs on people and other living creatures, it is assumed that they generally cause a variety of health problems, including cancer.[21] In the case of dioxins, however, they are recognized as definite carcinogens. It has been estimated that half of the population of the developing world is exposed to polluted sources of water that increase disease and death rates. [22]

The situation is especially difficult in developing countries where inadequate infrastructures exist for the treatment of municipal, industrial and agricultural wastes. A report by India's Centre for Science and Environment claims that:

> *India's rivers, especially the smaller ones, have all turned into toxic streams. And even the big ones like the Ganga are far from pure. The assault on India's rivers – from population growth, agricultural modernization, urbanization and industrialization – is enormous and growing by the day.... Most Indian cities get a large part of their drinking water from rivers. This entire life stands threatened.*[23]

A similar pattern exists in almost every developing nation that is attempting to effect rapid industrialization. Environmental protection, although becoming more important, still takes a back seat to the hoped for benefits of industrialization and overall economic development. Pollution, like poverty and hunger, are problems of the present, and if not addressed, it will simply get worse, and remediation may well outweigh the immediate benefits in terms of clean-up expenses, which will be paid for with future funds and future human health issues.

Water quality also is a limiting factor with regard to agricultural production. If polluted river, canal, land, tank, or groundwater is used for irrigation, those pollutants return to the food consumed, and they concentrate in our bodies. They further contaminate the land, and in some cases, become airborne. Pollution is not simply a localized, point source problem. Either through natural or human processes, pollution, once it is trapped in the environment, tends to expand beyond the original point of origin. Whether aided by water flow, air currents, or the transport of human products, pollution expands over ever increasing areas, and its influence, therefore, increases.

Water-related Disasters

As was seen with Bangladesh, water-related disasters can have a profound effect on overall development, but particularly on rural development; and these water-related disasters are increasing in both their frequency and severity. In their report, the International Conference on Freshwater wrote:

> *The world is experiencing a dramatic increase of suffering from the effects of disasters, ranging from extreme droughts to huge floods, caused by the poor management of water and land and possibly by climate change. Human society and particularly the poor are becoming more vulnerable to such disasters*[24]

Based on the EM-DAT: The OFDA/CRED International Disaster Database, more than 7,480 major and minor water-related disasters have occurred in the world between 1900 and 2005. Of these, floods accounted for half of the total disasters, water-borne and vector disease outbreaks accounted for 28 percent and drought accounted for 11 percent of the total disasters. Thirty-five percent of these disasters occurred in Asia, 29 percent in Africa, 20 percent

Figure 12-4: Distributions of Natural Disasters by Origin, 1900 – 2005

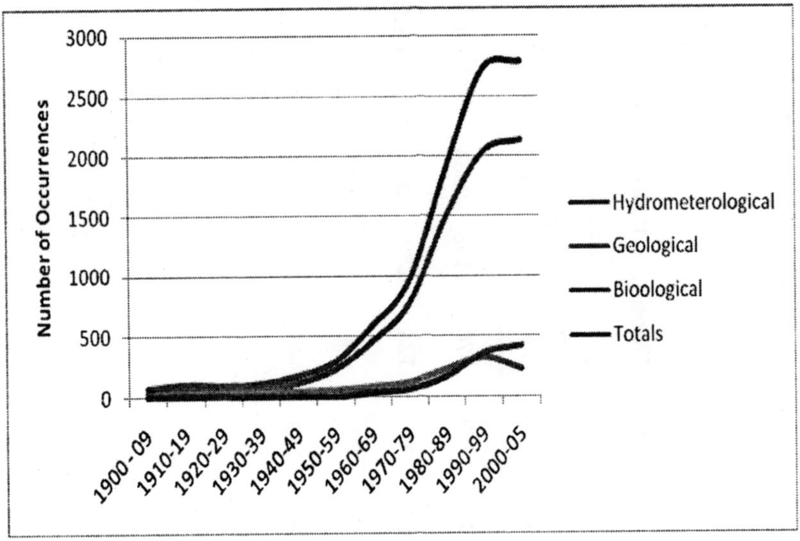

Source: (Em-Dat: Emergency Events Database, 2008)

in the Americas, 13 percent in Europe and the rest in Oceania.[25] See Figure 12- 4 and Table 12-2.These factors are restricting the potential for improving socio-economic development and in many cases causing a decline in real terms. The impacts from just one single disaster have, in some cases, lowered the Gross National Product (GNP) in poor economies by as much as 10 percent; and losses from water disasters are currently equivalent to 20 percent of new investments in water.[26] One need only look at the damage and deaths caused by the December 2004 earthquake-triggered tsunami that hit Indonesia, Sri Lanka, India, and Thailand; the tropical cyclone that hit Myanmar in May 2008; Cyclone Sidr which devastated the southwestern coast of Bangladesh in November 2007; August 2008 Kosi floods in Bihar, which have been called the worst floods in 50 years, or droughts in Australia, Southeast Asia, India, and Africa.[27]

Based on EM-Dat Emergency Events Database statistics and every day news reports, it is difficult to avoid the conclusion that hydrometerological disasters have increased, almost doubling every decade since 1930-39, until recently. The 2,135 events in 2000-05

Table12-2: Number of Recorded Worldwide Disasters by Decades, 1900-2005

Disaster Type	*1900 - 09*	*1910- 19*	*1920- 29*	*1930- 39*	*1940- 49*	*1950- 59*	*1960- 69*	*1970- 79*	*1980- 89*	*1990- 99*	*2000- 05*	*Total*
Hydrometerological	28	72	56	72	120	232	463	776	1498	2034	2135	7486
Geological	40	28	33	37	52	60	88	124	232	325	233	1252
Biological	5	7	10	3	4	2	37	64	170	361	420	1083
Totals	73	107	99	112	176	294	588	964	1900	2720	2788	9821

Source: (Em-Dat: Emergency Events Database, 2008)

are a far cry from the 28 such events in 1900-1909. See Table 12-2. If things are getting worse, is Global Warming at work?

Then consider the geological and biological events. Geological events have increased 582 percent from 1900 to 2005. No Global Warming at work here. Biological disasters have increased even more than either hydrometerological or geological disasters, increasing by 8,400 percent. Hydrometerological disasters have increased by only 7,624 percent. By any measure, things have gotten worse, but why? In approximately 100 years, the Earth seems to be rebelling against Man. This may be an anthropomorphic view of natural processes but what are we left with?

loods and Droughts

Floods, droughts, and famines, all water-related disasters, account for approximately 63 percent of all natural disasters between 1990 and 2001, with 64 percent of them occurring in Asia and Africa.[28] Floods and famines account for 57 percent of all deaths caused by natural disasters – floods (15%) and famines (42%). Between 1973 and 1997, approximately 66 million people suffered the consequences of floods. Forty-four percent of all floods occurred in Asia, taking over 228,000 lives during the decade 1987-97. Droughts, on the other hand, claimed 280,000 lives between 1991 and 2000.[29] Between them, floods and droughts are credited with having taken the lives of nearly 600,000 people during the decade ending in 2000, with the vast majority of them being in Asia.

Floods receive widespread media coverage, while famine is much less newsworthy. Flooding is much easier to sensationalize than pictures of starving people. Floods are exciting, moving things. Starvation is a much slower process. Flooding, however, by comparison, kills far fewer people than famine. Floods account for only 15 percent of human deaths, while famine kills nearly 42 percent of all those killed by natural disasters.

Based on the analysis of disaster data over the last 100 years, by CRED, using EM-Dat data, it is fair to say that floods and droughts show the fastest rate of increase. See Figure 12-5, below.

The polynomial time trend analyses of disaster data depicted above are based on best R^2 fit. The R^2 for Floods was 0.9394, for Droughts, 0.7331, for Windstorms, 0.9025, and for Geological

Figure 12-5: Worldwide Polynomial Time Trends for the Four Major Types of Natural Disasters: 1900 - 2003

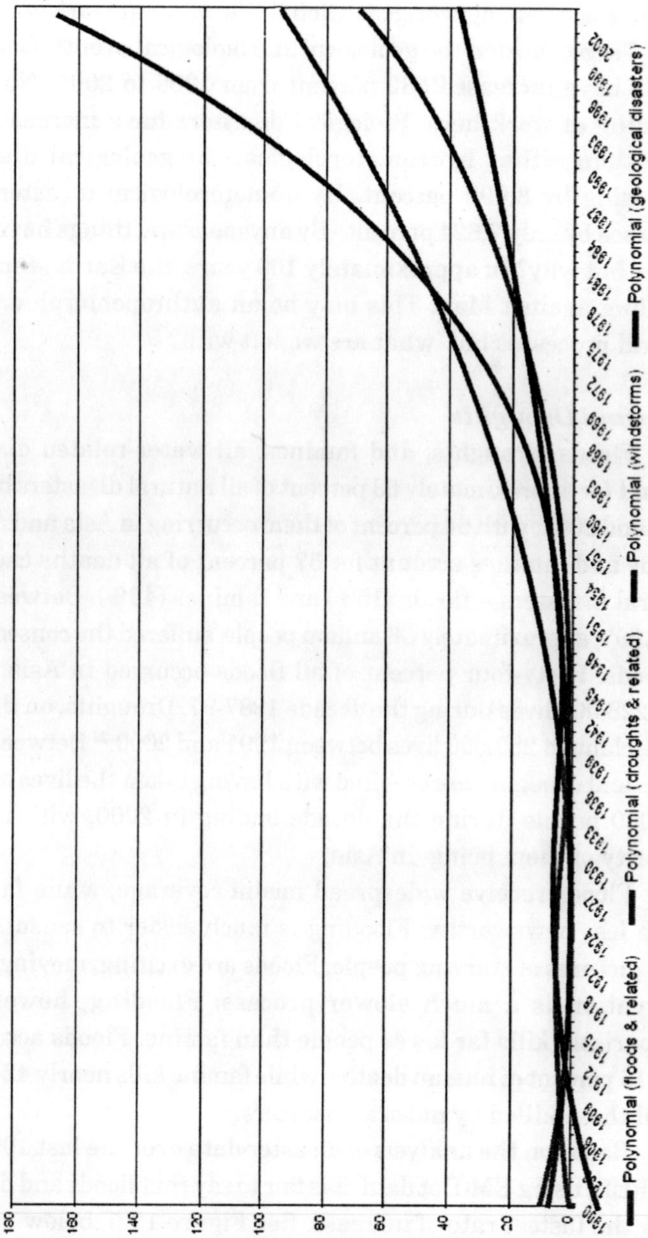

Source: (Guha-Sapir, Hargitt, & Hoyois, 2004), p. 24.

disasters, 0.8121. All are very high coefficients of determination. A perfect fit would have been unity or 1.

Droughts

Droughts are, when compared to other natural disasters, the most deadly. The media are poised to report on the effects of typhoons, cyclones, hurricanes, tsunamis, and earthquakes. Cameras and reporters are at the ready to film the victims – the survivors and the dead – during rescue operations. Once relief begins to pour in, the story fades from the TV screens and from newsprint. Droughts, and the associated famines, are much less glamorous but no less deadly. It is by far the most widespread and far-reaching natural disaster known to man.

More than 462 million persons were affected by drought (including deaths and homelessness) in South Asia alone during 2000-2004.[30] It is estimated that between 1974 and 2003, slightly more than 2 million people perished due to natural disasters and of these deaths, 75 percent occurred in Asia.[31] These figures may seem exaggerated but, in all likelihood, they are underestimated. For example, droughts reportedly killed 500,367 people in Ethiopia over the last three decades. But some estimate that the number of people who died from the great Ethiopian drought of 1984-1985 may have numbered somewhere between 600,000 and 1 million.[32]

Of the ten most devastating natural disasters, with the highest number of people killed, three of the top ten (in fact three of the top five) disasters are droughts – the 1984 Ethiopian and Sudan Drought, killing an estimated 450,000; the 1974-75 Sahelian Drought, killing an estimated 325,000; and the 1985 Mozambique Drought, killing 100,000.

The Ethiopian, Sudan, and Sahelian droughts are particularly notable, not just because of the number of people that died, but because their deaths were reported as 'deaths due to drought.' Most often, the cause of death is given as infectious diseases but rarely because of malnutrition or 'drought.' These figures are in all likelihood underestimations of the real mortality rate. These numbers of drought deaths are all the more shocking because there were, in fact, probably many, many more.

Death figures for floods and droughts are meant to be shocking. However, figures for the numbers of people affected by floods and drought are even more sobering. Table 12-3, below, summarizes the top 10 disasters with the highest number of affected over the last century. Note that , although the data cover a period of 100 years, all of the top 10 disasters have occurred in the last two decades. In light of recent tragedies, like the Indonesian earthquake and tsunami and the Myanmar cyclone of 2008, the top 10 list may change when data is updated.

Table 12-3: Top 10 Disasters with Highest Numbers Affected: 1974-2003

Rank	*Disaster Type*	*Year*	*Country*	*Number of People Affected Millions*
1	Drought	1987	India	300
2	Drought	2002	India	300
3	Flood	1988	China	223
4	Flood	1991	China	206
5	Drought	1979	India	190
6	Flood	1996	China	150
7	Flood	1993	India	128
8	Flood	1995	China	114.4
9	Flood	1999	China	100
10	Flood	1989	China	100

Source: (Guha-Sapir, Hargitt, & Hoyois, 2004), p. 29.

Asia and Africa bear a disproportionate burden of losses due to disasters. Over the last thirty years, approximately 88 percent of the total people reported killed and 96 percent of the people reported affected lived in Asia and Africa. Of the total number of people killed by natural disasters worldwide over the last decade, more than 75 percent were in Asia. This figure rises above 98 percent for droughts and famines.[33]

Floods and droughts are both a function of water. Both are destructive in their own ways. Floods can cause extensive damage to infrastructure and crops. Their impact on agriculture depends in part on the timing in relation to the cycle of the crops in the region. The area affected by floods can be immense, depending on topographical features. Floods can develop slowly and be predictable or can occur suddenly, such as is the case with flash floods or those resulting from levee breaches. Most of the mortality linked to floods is caused by flash floods, although many die as a result of subsequent water-borne and sanitation diseases. Floods may kill fewer people than they affect, but the damage they cause is pervasive and long term.

Droughts and famines do not result in infrastructure or shelter damage but they cause heavy crop and livestock losses. They cover wide areas of land and often affect several neighboring regions or countries simultaneously. Famines are much more complex and can be caused by crop failures, food shortage or lack of access to food, droughts, disasters such as floods and armed conflicts or political instability. Famines can also lead to mass migration, which can create crowded conditions with poor sanitation and lead to outbreaks of diseases.

Except for flash floods and floods caused by levee breaches, floods are often predictable. Likewise, droughts are frequently predictable, or at least anticipatable, usually developing over several years. This makes it possible to respond to droughts as they occur. Flood responses usually take the form of rescue and relief efforts. In either case, they take lives and
disrupt the normal flow of human and economic activities. They rob people of their livelihoods and often take their lives.

Water, Poverty, and Hunger

People who are water poor are frequently poor in almost every other area of their lives. Poor families find it difficult to accumulate any surpluses – financial or food — which means that it is hard to maintain consumption when their incomes are interrupted or their crops fail, or on a day-to-day basis, for that matter. Further, the poor are generally disenfranchised in other ways. They have limited legal and political rights, environmental health and protection, occupational health and safety, crime prevention and protection from exploitation and discrimination. Many rural poor suffer from limited rights to land, water and other natural resources. While the richer farmers are able to exploit groundwater resources, using pumpsets and tubewells, the small poor cultivators are financially prohibited from sharing in this resource. This fact alone places the small cultivator at a disadvantage. The implementation of national food policies (through subsidies, taxes, tariffs, food aid, etc.) can distort markets and marginalize the rural poor even more, and international trade liberalization programs intended to protect or raise the poor frequently are counter productive for them.

The rural poor lack paved roads making access to markets and health services difficult. Water plays a very big role in transportation. In some areas, waterways, large and small, provide essential transport corridors. Wherever there are floods, many key roads and bridges are often washed away in the rainy season. The rural poor are often at the end of irrigation systems, or are pushed out onto marginal lands totally dependent on erratic and unreliable rainfall. There is a lack of flood protection infrastructure. All of these problems create an ideal environment for disease transmission, vulnerability to loss of housing and possessions and, overall, a low quality of life. For many of the rural poor, the heart of their problems is access to water; water in the form of rainfall, water for irrigation, or water for drinking and sanitation purposes. Often the poor suffer from debilitating diseases which limit their ability to work their fields, all for the lack of adequate sanitation. The poor find themselves locked into a cycle of poverty, what Sachs and others call a poverty trap, from which there are very few opportunities to escape. Government routinely provide programs for rural uplift, sanitation, water development, improvement of agricultural practices, basic infrastructure, etc., only to fail to implement or fund them. Or, if funded, the programs do not make it to the remote poor in rural areas.

Africa and South Asia are special cases. They have the largest concentration of rural poor and undernourished. If they were not unique, they would be as poor or as undernourished as the poor elsewhere but they are not. They would not be classified as some of the most water scarce areas in the world. They would not be the home to some of the most persistent forms of malaria or have the highest rates of AIDS/HIV in the world. They would not be subject to more environmental disasters than much of the rest of the world – floods, famines, windstorms, cyclones, droughts, etc. But, they are.

James Clavell in his novels uses the word *joss* as a Chinese term for a kind of cosmic luck, much like *karma*. It would seem that Africa and South Asia have more than their fair share of bad *joss*. Why is this?

Africa is subject to famine, beset by disease and mostly isolated from contemporary international trade. Bad governance and rapid population growth add to the problems. Its very narrow range of exports, restricted to agricultural commodities, some mineral resources – all of which are subject to the price vagaries of international markets – further restricts economic development. Africa is similar to Asia forty years ago.

In Asia, however, high-yield staple crops, introduced during the Asian Green Revolution, enabled food production to grow rapidly as the continent's vast plains were well suited to irrigation. Agricultural income grew rapidly, and production diversified. Surplus labour migrated to the cities, leading to rapid urbanization and industrialization.

However, Africa does not have the same sort of irrigation potential as Asia. Malaria and the growing AIDs crisis have added to its burdens. Unlike Asia, which hosts coastal cities with good access to ports and sea routes, most Africans live inland, too far from ports to enable growth from industrial exports. Road, rail and inland water transport infrastructure are poor.[34]

Millennium Development Goals – Goal 1

The Millennium Development Goals (MDGs) grew out of agreements and resolutions of world conferences organized by the United Nations in the 1990s. The MDGs, initially, were known as the International Development Goals (IDGs), formulated and based on Development Assistance Committee's *Shaping the 21st century: The Contribution of Development Co-cperation*, published in May 1996.[35]

MDGs included the latest development issues such as debt relief, partnership and economic growth through trade and investment, etc. In September 2000, the Millennium Summit adopted the United Nations Millennium Declaration, which established 8 goals to be achieved by 2015. Goal 1 was: Eradicate Extreme Hunger and Poverty. This goal was further subdivided into:

Figure 12-6: Progress Toward Halving World Poverty, 1990 - 2002

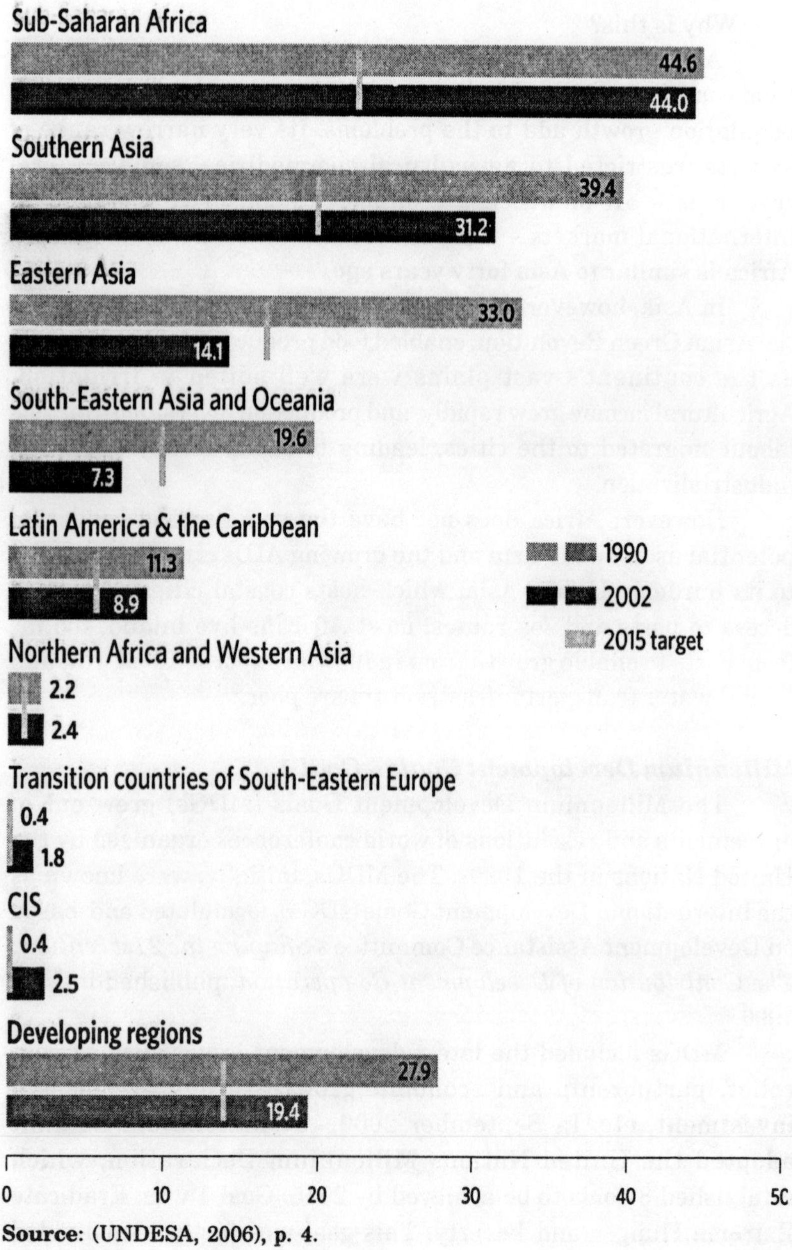

Source: (UNDESA, 2006), p. 4.

Source: Based on (FAO, 2003), p. 29.

Figure 12-7: Progress Towards the Millennium Development Goal for the Undernourished[38]

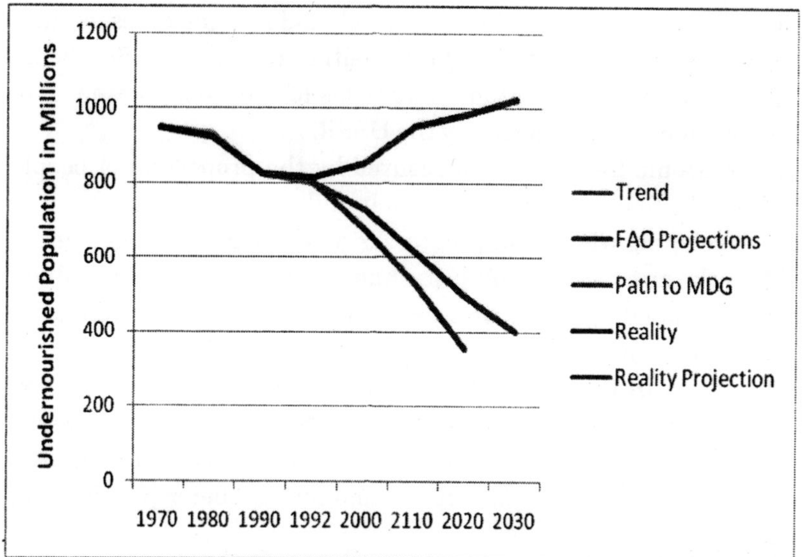

It has now been over eight years since the MGDs were formulated and programs were laid in place to assist the world's nations toward the achievement of the development goals. In 1990 there were an estimated 1.2 billion people – approximately 28 percent of the world's population – that were living in poverty. By 2002, the world's poor had decreased to 19 percent, with East Asia leading the way to poverty alleviation.[36] In South Asia, the poverty level declined by nearly 8.5 percent. In Sub-Saharan Africa, while the poverty rate declined nominally, from 44.6 to 44.0 percent, their numbers, however, increased by 140 million.[37] Many Sub-Saharan countries are now showing potential for long-term growth that could raise standards of living; however, these glimmers of hope have been observed before. See Figure 12-6.

Figure 12-7, shows the trends toward meeting Goal 1. Based on available data at the time, the trend line toward meeting the goal and the reality trend line were nearly identical, as they should be. They were historically verifiable data. It is after the development of the MGDs in 1996 and their implementation in the form of programming in 2000 that the FAO Projections, the Path toward

MDG, Reality, and the Reality Projection trend lines diverge, and significantly, If the trend lines are even close to reality, the goal of halving world poverty by 2015 is at best wishful thinking. Obviously, there has been progress, especially in East and Southeast Asia. Elsewhere, progress has been nominal, and in some cases, certain regions have lost ground – the transition countries of Southeast Europe and the CIS nations (Countries of the Commonwealth of Independent States), formerly the USSR.

Chronic hunger – as measured by the proportion of people lacking the food needed to meet their daily needs – has declined in the developing world. But progress is nowhere near fast enough to reduce the number of people going hungry. An estimated 824 million people in the developing world were affected by chronic hunger in 2003; and indications are that that number has increased by 50 to 100 million in the period 2007-08, alone, due to the recent 'Food Crisis.' The worst-affected regions – Sub-Saharan Africa and South Asia – have made progress but their advances have not kept pace with those made in the early 1990s, and the number of people going hungry is increasing.

Despite increases in food production, people keep falling prey to the poverty line defined as income is less than $1 a day. If we assume that water is the primary ingredient in the agricultural mix, and Global Warming is causing catastrophic changes in the world's precipitation patterns, especially increasing its variability and reliability, the prospects for meeting the first millennium goal of halving world poverty by 2015 is little more than wishful thinking. It is what the statesmen, philosophers, and international development agencies 'would like to see' happen. To be very candid, it appears to be an absolutely impossible task. Almost everything we know about people and natural and manmade environmental change militates against success. There is no 'silver bullet' that will create the water we need, or get it to where we need it most desperately. Without water, deserts cannot bloom, no matter how much we want them to, and we lose acre after acre to desertification each day. We are losing ground, literally, and in terms of our ability to feed ourselves at even a minimal level. If a solution is not found, Ehrlich's and the Meadows' doomsday predictions of the late 1960's and early 1970s could be at long last just over the horizon.[39] Had it not been for the Green Revolution, with all its inherent problems, these doomsayers' predictions might have actually occurred much earlier.

Borlaug envisioned his work as providing Mankind with thirty years to come to grips with rampant population growth. His efforts gave us an extra decade, and we still have not dealt with it. Now, our problem is complicated by climate change, environmental degradation, increasing poverty and hunger, and no real, practical solutions. Soon, we will have to face the hard fact that there ***are*** limits to growth when we live within a finite world.

References

1. See the seminal work (Sauer, Carl O., 1952), and a more recent elaboration of that work (Gupta, Anil K., 2004). In all likelihood, the first cereal to be domesticated was wheat, somewhere in the Middle East during the Holocene, 10,000 to 7,000 BCE.
2. Water is a finite resource: there are an estimated 1,400 million cubic kilometers on earth and circulating through the hydrological cycle. Nearly all of this is salt water and most of the rest is frozen or under ground.
3. *Ibid*. See the graphic showing Causes of Food Emergencies in Developing Countries in (FAO), p. 3.
4. *Ibid*., pp. 3-4.
5. *Ibid*., p. 8.
6. (UNESCO, 2006), p. 250.
7. The original of this graph appeared in: (Smith, M.; Fereres, E.; and A. Kassam, 3-5 December 2001).
8. (FAO, 2003), p. 8.
9. (FAO, 2003), p. 18
10. See, for example, (Farm Press Editorial Staff, 2008); (GMO Safety, 2008); (Stancich, 2008); (Staff Writers, 2006); and (Li Ching, Lim and Jonathan Matthews, 2004).
11. *Ibid.*
12. Written in Punjabi and published by the Sikh Students Federation, *Jal Bin Sakh Kumlavati* (Without Water, Offshoots Wither), documents a variety of water and water-related problems occurring

in Indian Punjab. The Punjabi version of this document can be downloaded in PDF at <http://www.sikhstudentsfederation.com/link7/Punjab-Water-Crisis.pdf >.

13. (Burke, Jacob J. and Moench, Marcus H., 2000).
14. (Shiklomanov, 1997).
15. (WHO/UNICEF, 2000) and (UNESCO, 2003), p. 10.
16. (Gardner-Outlaw, 1997).
17. (Postel, Sandra L., 1996).
18. The example is based on (Postel, Sandra L., 1998) and data from (USDA, 1997).
19. (Reich, P. F.; S.T. Numbem; R.A. Almaraz; and H. Eswaran, 2008).
20. See, for example, (Daily Times, 2004); (Hassan, 2007); (Faye, Bernard; and Palmated Esenov (eds), 19-21 April 2004); (Dregne, 1986; Dregne,Harold E., 1983; Anantha Rama, K.; A. Tsunekawab; D. K. Sahac; and T. Miyazaki, 1999); (SAARC); (Ortega, September 14, 2007); (Reilly, 2007); and (UNESCO, 2004).
21. See (Sanghi, Rashmi, 2001) for an excellent discussion of POPs.
22. (UNESCO, 2003), p. 11.
23. (CSE, 1999), p. 58. As this book is being written, the sixth in the CSE's reports on the environment is being prepared for publication.
24. (FME, 3-7 December, 2001).
25. (UNESCO, 2003), p. 272.
26. *Ibid.*
27. See, for example, (Timmons, Heather; and Hari Kumar, 2008); (Tun, 2008); (ADB, 2006); (BBC, 2006); (FAO Newsroom, 2007); (Simons, 2007); (Ahmed, 2004); and (Associated Press, 2005).
28. (UNESCO, 2008).
29. *Ibid.*
30. (UNESCAP, March 3, 2005), p. 4.
31. (Guha-Sapir, Hargitt, & Hoyois, 2004), p. 14.
32. *Ibid.*
33. (Guha-Sapir, Hargitt, & Hoyois, 2004), p. 29.
34. After (Sunday Times/Sachs, 2005a) and (Sachs, 2005b).
35. (DAC, May 1996).
36. (UNDESA, 2006), p.4.
37. *Ibid.*
38. At the 1996 World Food Summit, the Millennium Development Goal of halving the number of the world's hungry by 2015 was adopted.

The estimated number of undernourished was estimated to be a conservative 800 million in 1990-92.

39. See, (Ehrlich, 1968); and (Meadows, Donella H., et. al., 1972).

13

Summing Up

Introduction

Although our focus has been on hunger, poverty, and the Green Revolution, other themes have arisen.Each country in Sub-Saharan Africa and South Asia is unique, historically, culturally, and environmentally. Each has responded somewhat differently to the opportunities and problems association with the Green Revolution. Here we will look at some of these themes.

South Asia

India

India's success and problems are legion. Probably, no country has borne more scrutiny when it comes to the Green Revolution. On the positive side, India has served as the prototype for the Green Revolution.Although it can truly be said that the Green Revolution began in Mexicó in the late 1950s, it was not until Borlaug and the CIMMYT introduced their improved wheat varieties to India that the Green Revolution was initiated beyond a doubt. Along with all the success came problems, and for many of these problems, solutions. These problems were administrative, political, social, economic, and environmental. Some of these problems were, or could not be resolved.

The technologies involved in the Green Revolution reflected a Western mindset or Western agricultural paradigm that carried with it certain assumptions, beliefs, and strategies. In general, the adaptation of this mindset to the Indian context was not completely successful. Cultures and traditions collided. In part, the collision was the consequence of differences in how people perceive what agriculture is, not what it does. In many Western societies, it simply feeds people as efficiently as possible. It is a commercial undertaking. At one time it was a large part of people's way of life but now, it is just a business. It is a game of strategy. Those who play well, prosper. Those who play not so well, fail.

In India, before the Green Revolution, agriculture was as much a way of life as it was a way to feed people. In general, there was so little surplus that cultivation for profit was largely unthinkable. Likewise, attachments to the land, in addition to its productive attributes, had historical, social, political, hereditary, as well as economic importance. Certain groups in India were more culturally prone to the assimilation of the Green Revolution's underlying tenets. Others, while wishing to take advantage of the Green Revolution's production-increasing aspects, had more difficulty with the wholesale adoption of its underlying principles.

The package of practices advocated by Borlaug and the CIMMYT worked best in those areas that were most environmentally similar to central and northern Mexico, hot and dry – Punjab, Haryana, parts of Uttar Pradesh, and Gujarat. Here wheat production flourished as the inputs, especially water, became available. The process of adoption was limited by geography as well as the government's decision to concentrate its limited agricultural resources. For over a decade, the Government gave the states of the Northwest preferential access to these resources. Here the Green Revolution was most indelibly rooted. Other areas were less socially, economically, and environmentally prepared to adopt the improved wheats and the associated package of practices. This pattern of early adoption has remained largely intact. The Indian Northwest stands apart from the rest of India. Nowhere else was the Green Revolution so well implemented nor as productive.

Although India has introduced literally hundreds of improved rice varieties, as an adaptation to its varied rain patterns and ecologies, these varieties have not had an impact as profound as that of wheat in the Northwest. In large measure, the adoption of improved rice varieties has only contributed to a higher standard of living for most subsistence cultivators. Nowhere is its cultivation as extensively commercialized as in Punjab, now the leading rice producer in India – a state that until fairly recently only cultivated a little high quality rice as a *kharif* cash crop alternative.

It would be a misnomer to even imply that the Green Revolution was adopted only in India's Northwest. Today, nearly 60 percent of all cultivated land is planted in one improved seed variety or another, but the adoption of pesticides and herbicides has lagged behind seed. Fertilizer use is now almost universally accepted. Even so, yields do not approach the seeds' genetic potential.

Food, Famine, and Sen

Today, India's domestic foodgrain production exceeds domestic requirements, at least on paper. In reality, millions remain malnourished – the single largest concentration of malnourished people in the world, and India was, until recently, a net food exporter. This situation, however, is not necessarily the fault of the Green Revolution but, rather, the inability of nearly 360 million people to purchase the food they need.

One of the true ironies of the Green Revolution is that it was designed to improve people's lives by increasing the amount of food that could be made available to them. This the Green Revolution did, but at the same time increasing numbers of people became increasingly destitute. Globally, food was in abundance but people continued to starve. They were not starving for lack of food. They were starving because of their inability to procure it – poverty-induced starvation.

Amartya Sen's critics may find fault with his deductive methodology or his interpretation of fact, but of all his findings, one seems to be axiomatic. Even during times of famine, it is not the absolute lack of food that is the problem. It is peoples' inability to access it that results in deprivation and starvation. Poverty is the root cause of hunger.

Changing View of the Green Revolution

Initially, the Green Revolution in India was a success.Today it is a 'qualified' success. It has been downgraded, not because it failed to produce the food India needed so desperately but because those amazing increases in production have begun to slow and even stagnate. Population growth, however, has not stagnated and will soon catch up to production, which will make the plight of the poor and already hungry even worse.

With the world's best agricultural technology at its disposal, why is India's agriculture stagnating? The problems that developed along with the implementation of the Green Revolution, or because of it, have been discussed elsewhere. Here we will only categorically summarize them.

India and Pakistan shared the benefits of the Green Revolution almost simultaneously. However, due to Pakistan's internal, institutional barriers, it did not have the same immediate impact on Pakistan's agricultural sector. Once these barriers were recognized and addressed, soon thereafter, Pakistan achieved food security.

India, on the other hand, can be said to have been the Green Revolution's first Asian test bed; and Punjab, Haryana, and western Uttar Pradesh were its first beneficiaries. It is here that the problem-side of the Green Revolution first emerged and has been most intensely felt. It is these same kinds of problems that are likely to develop as the Green Revolution unfolds in other states, areas, and regions of the world but have not due to lack of time. Or, alternatively, based on the problems experienced in India and Pakistan, and their recognition, it is hoped that similar problems can or were avoided elsewhere.

The primary problems resulting from the implementation of the Green Revolution include, but are not necessarily limited to:

- The degradation of once fertile soils
- The depletion and contamination of groundwater supplies
- Inadequate irrigation infrastructure
- Inadequate credit structures
- The dispossession of small and marginal cultivating landholders.

Degradation of Soils

The Green Revolution technologies have taken their toll on the soils of India. Once fertile soils have been mined of their nutrients, and chemical fertilizers have been used in an attempt to feed and sustain crops. These soils are, today, little more than sterile mediums into which plants sink their roots for support. Once drawing on organic nutrients, they now draw in chemicals. Water applied to them simply percolates to deeper horizons, taking unused components of applied fertilizers, pesticides, and herbicides with them, where they accumulate and contaminate the water tables farther below. Where the soils have been compacted, plow pans are formed. Where the contaminated water stands, waterlogging or saline soils result. Map 13-1, demonstrates just now degraded the soils of India have become.

Map 13-1: India – Human Induced Soil Degradation

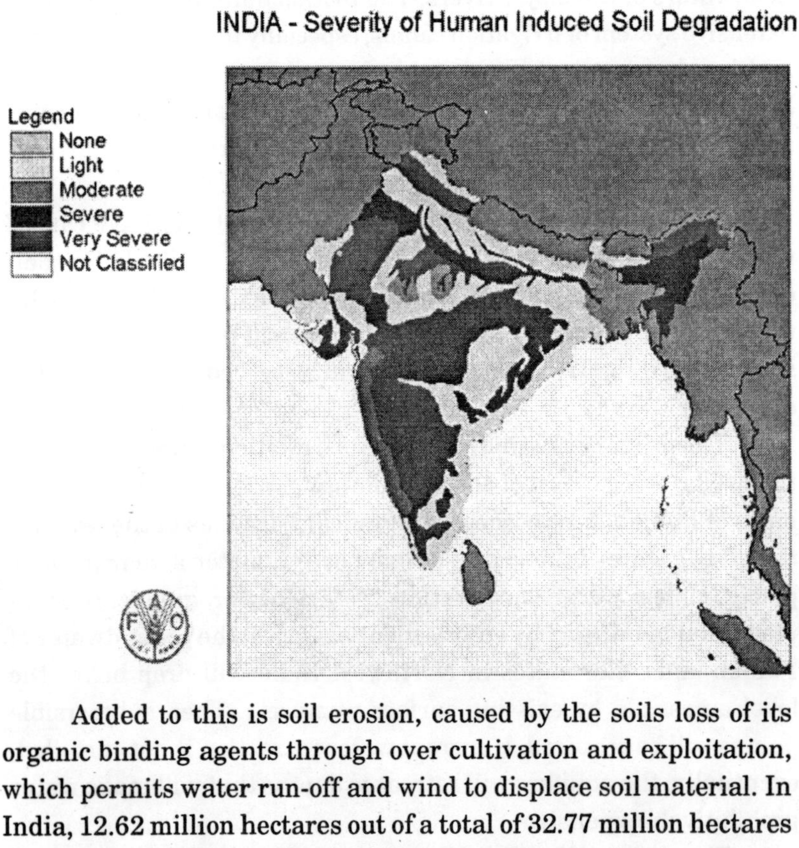

Added to this is soil erosion, caused by the soils loss of its organic binding agents through over cultivation and exploitation, which permits water run-off and wind to displace soil material. In India, 12.62 million hectares out of a total of 32.77 million hectares of agricultural land is affected by severe water erosion.[1]

Desertification, although not technically soil erosion, does normally lead to erosion, as the land is desiccated and is no longer able to sustain trees, brush, and grasses that would otherwise stabilize the soil. Increasing rainfall variability, the frequency of drought or near drought conditions are increasing. Now, in Gujarat, East Rajasthan, parts of western Uttar Pradesh, Punjab, and Haryana – the primary wheat growing areas of Northwestern India – the probability of drought conditions has increased to once in three years. Desertification under these conditions becomes a real possibility and may be, in some cases, irreversible.

Depletion and Contamination of Groundwater

Canal systems are dependent upon runoff captured by the headwaters of the major rivers. The British built and connected an extensive system of irrigation canals, especially in India's northwest, and in what is now Indian and Pakistani Punjab. Subsequent to Independence, the Indian Government improved and extended canal systems all over the country, especially in Gujarat and Rajasthan, boosting agricultural production in those states.

Now, however, overuse and rainfall variability have caused many of the downstream users to find no water available for their crops. In the absence of water containment facilities, the rivers dry up during the dry season, and the farmers must resort to alternative sources of irrigation water in the rain-starved portions of the country.

The primary alternative source of irrigation water has become tubewells, using diesel or electric pumpsets. Within the last decade, parts of Punjab have witnessed significant declines in the levels of the state's water tables, dropping by over a meter a year in some places. Unless water conservation or efficiency programs are set in place, and monitored by enforcement agencies, the groundwater of Punjab and other states in Northwest India will drop below the level accessible by existing surface pumpsets. Then submersible pumps will be required. If current water extraction is not curtailed, eventually, the aquifers will retreat to depths that will make water prohibitively expensive.

The misuse of fertilizers, pesticides, and herbicides has resulted in the contamination of surface and groundwater reserves, making them dangerous for consumptive purposes, as well as potentially jeopardizing even their use for the purpose of irrigation. The contamination stems from human misuse of toxic and potentially carcinogenic agricultural and industrial chemicals. Once contaminated, there is little or nothing that can be done to remove these chemicals and toxins from the water supplies. Some water sources may be unusable forever, without sophisticated filtration. Others may be rehabilitated through natural processes. Human intervention, in all likelihood, will have no remedial effect for the aquifers.

Inadequate Irrigation Infrastructure

It has been seen that, in almost every country of South Asia, there are opportunities for the expansion of irrigation. The only limiting factors:

- the availability of government funds to construct large-scale systems,
- declining supplies of riverine water, due to climatic changes, and
- the depletion of groundwater resources.

Already, governments are hesitant to support the construction of large-scale irrigation projects because of the fear that their investments will not result in satisfactory returns and due to the increasing difficulty of obtaining requisite approvals for such projects from a very well organized and vocal environmental minority.

Inadequate Credit Structures

From the very beginning, financial ability proved to be the primary obstacle to the adoption of the package of inputs that were part of the Green Revolution. In many respects, even today, for small cultivators, access to credit is still beyond their means. Many live on the brink of insolvency. Without access to credit, they will generally lose their only real asset, the family lands. Then they will join the ranks of those migrating to the urban areas in search of employment, or remaining within familiar surroundings and becoming landless agricultural laborers, which contributes to driving day wages down, until they are no longer high enough to support even the poorest of their numbers.

The Dispossession of Small and Marginal Cultivating Landholders

The number of agricultural laborers has increased simultaneously with the decline in the number of cultivators. See Figure 13-1. Marginal cultivators, in general, lose their lands to local moneylenders, who are frequently also larger landlords or landowners. Some of these disposed, former landowners, become tenants, share croppers, or, more likely, landless laborers.

Figure 13-1 – Change in Percent Landless in Rural Areas, All-India, 1951 - 2001

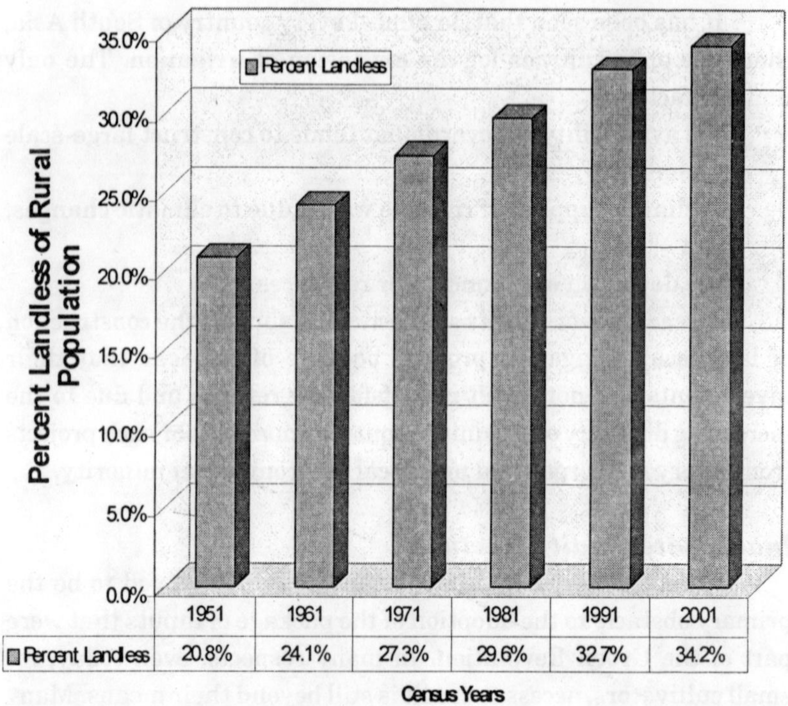

Source: Census of India, 1951-2001

In the absence of alternative forms of employment outside agriculture, the largely illiterate landless become trapped in rural areas and become increasingly under- and unemployed. Further, what work they are able to obtain is normally seasonal at best. This combination of factors contributes to their increased destitution and they become dependent on state support.

NREGS

Recently, a controversial rural program, known as the National Rural Employment Guarantee Scheme (NREGS) was initiated to assist this growing group of people. Although it is a step in the right direction, the rural unemployment problem far exceeds the resources available to deal with it. Furthermore, like many such programs, it is subject to corruption and misuse.[2]

The NREGS was launched in 200 districts in 14 states in 2006. It promised 100 days of wage labor to one adult member of every rural household that volunteered for unskilled work. Recently, in Hardoi, U.P., an administrative audit was undertaken to determine why the program was, apparently, not working, and because of numerous complaints from the district that had been lodged with both the state and central governments.

The investigating panel discovered some very disturbing problems. The administrators and village chiefs, who had been given the responsibility for administering the program, were found to be misusing their powers. They were forging muster rolls, disqualifying job seekers, and embezzling program funds. It was determined that caste and class differences had undermined the effectiveness of the program. Traditionally, the landowning upper castes had controlled much of rural society through their occupation of the offices of village headmen, revenue collectors, and priests. The landless poor were, generally, from the lowest castes, other religious minorities, and those outside the caste system, the Dalits. It was determined that the Thakurs and Brahmins, who had traditionally dominated most of the positions of power in the villages, were still doing so.

The NREGS makes it mandatory that a job card be issued to every family. However, many of the poorest families were not issued their cards until just before the investigative team had arrived. Records showed that villagers, who had been issued cards, were never given work. Others, who had no cards, were given work. Those that had received the work were often paid less than the minimum amount they were entitled to – 60 Rs. per day – the program administrators kept the difference. Unlike other areas where the NREGS had been implemented – Andhra Pradesh, Rajasthan, and Uttar Pradesh — not a single woman had received work, few had received a work card, and none had received any work or payments under the program.

Some women were prevented from taking part in the NREGS program; because their husbands felt it would dishonor them or their family. Family honor was more important than feeding their family. Women in the lowest castes did not seem to face the same caste/social bias.

Following the audit, the guilty village officers and program administrators were disciplined, especially the BDOs. The villagers were promised greater oversight by officials from outside the district. In response, the local officials and administrators drafted a memorandum to the Rural Development Commissioner, indicating that they would no longer participate in the NREGS program in their areas.

If the state and central governments call the local officials' bluff, and replace them with dedicated, impartial administrators, the NREGS program could promote rural social reform, as well as begin to alleviate some of the rural poverty.[3] Or, it could become just another mismanaged government-sponsored program, reinforcing the rural elites' power and enriching them further. The Hardoi case could be an exception, but it could also be an indication of how the program is implemented and administered. Again, this could be an example of just another one-method-fits-all type program. Tailoring government-sponsored programs at the district or block levels may well be the only way such programs can be effectively implemented. Admittedly, tailoring such programs to the smallest administrative units represents a significant departure from normal program implementation strategies, and will entail significantly higher program costs, due to the increased number of development officers needed for its equitable implementation.

The Green Revolution is Not to Blame

The Green Revolution did not cause the increase in the number of landless laborers or malnourished. It simply was a set of techniques that, when implemented, resulted in increased agricultural production and *per capita* productivity, both of which were the goals of the Indian government. It fulfilled the needs of the people and government planners but aggravated already existing social and economic problems. Borlaug has repeatedly said that his agricultural system was not political, the seeds and other inputs were designed to do but one thing, produce more food. This they did.

Built into the Green Revolution, as implemented in India, is the assumption that, if applied as presented, it would increase agricultural production. As formulated by the farm boy from Iowa, who subscribed to and accepted the values inherent in the American Midwestern way of life, it did exactly what it was designed to do. It was, first and foremost, an American system of agriculture, which presupposed:

· Large landholdings
· Readily available inputs
· A limited and declining supply of human labor
· Readily available information through extension programs
· Commercial, non-subsistence farming.

Since these conditions prevailed in arid, northern Mexico, when Borlaug initiated his wheat cross-breeding efforts at the CIMMYT, it proved successful. It had never been tried in an area characterized by exceedingly small landholdings, scarce inputs, or where a large pool of human labor existed, like India.

The Punjabi experience demonstrates the efficacy of the system. It was never intended to be a tool for social engineering, social leveling, the improvement of social justice or equity. That is what the decision-makers at the highest levels wished for, knowing full well that its basic principles were anathema to these social and economic ideals. However, that is the nature of political economy – say and do what you must to remain in power.

Politicians and bureaucrats may seem mercenary but in reality, they are only being practical. They prioritize their problems, estimate their resources, and implement a plan that best addresses the problem.[4] No solution is foolproof, nor will one solution solve every aspect of the problem. Such is the case with the Green Revolution. It resolved, at least temporarily, India's need for increased foodgrain production, which was necessary to eliminate the possibility of large-scale famine and uncontrollable political unrest.

Also, the Green Revolution was first and foremost, a capitalistic system set within the context of an avowed social democracy. Although not mutually exclusive, they often work at cross purposes. Almost inevitably, under capitalism, there are winners and there are losers. In India, the Green Revolution demonstrated this.The larger, better financed cultivators prospered. The smaller, under financed cultivators suffered and, because of their disadvantages, were forced off their lands, to join the ranks of the landless agricultural laborers, becoming increasingly destitute in the process. Food production increased, only more and more people became unable to benefit from that increased production. Food surpluses existed, only to see more and more people starve due to their growing poverty.

The Green Revolution in India was a prototype. India became a planner's handbook for what to do, what not to do, and highlighted some of the potential problems that could emerge during the rural development process.The difficulty however, is that India must now deal with the environmental and social consequences of the Green Revolution's implementation, which may be as daunting as the problems it was used to solve, for there are now social, political, economic, and environmental problems that had not been anticipated. There is an old adage: As you solve one problem, you create more. This is exactly what has happened in India with its adoption of the Green Revolution.

Pakistan

Pakistan could easily have become the ultimate test bed for the Green Revolution. It has achieved high levels of Green Revolution variety adoption. It has out-performed India and Bangladesh in the Green Revolution. Only China, among major countries, has out-performed Pakistan.[5]

With the exception of water availability, due to the overriding aridity of Pakistan's climate, other aspects of Pakistan made it the perfect setting for the Green Revolution. Landholdings were comparatively large.The agricultural labor pool was small and shrinking. Mechanization represented no obstacle. The people were psychologically predisposed to commercial agricultural pursuits due to the canal colony experience under the British. Once the government realized it was obstructing the Green Revolution's progress, it took remedial action, especially in the areas of inputs availability, subsidies, and marketing.

In the beginning, Pakistan's Punjab was the beneficiary of the British, large-scale irrigation system, and this permitted the Pakistanis to adopt the Green Revolution rapidly. In fact, within only 3 years, West Pakistan became self-sufficient with regard to foodgrain, especially wheat, while East Pakistan floundered agriculturally, economically and politically.

Under the belief that the size of landholdings was skewed in favor of a few large landholders and upon advice from foreign agricultural and development advisors, the Government of Pakistan has repeatedly attempted to implement land reforms intended to redistribute landholdings more equitably among cultivators. Each time these initiatives have been defeated. In 2005, the Government of Pakistan passed a resolution that effectively prohibits government intervention in landholding size, thereby eliminating the possibility of land ceilings or any other restrictions on the size of landholdings.[6]

Nevertheless, planners and social and economic equalitarians would still like to see the largest landholders' lands broken up and redistributed for the sake of rural equity and social justice. Table 13-1 summarizes landholdings by size. The largest number of farms, roughly 42 percent, fall in the under 2 hectare category, but area-wise they constitute only 16 percent of the cultivable area. Farms above 5 hectares account for 14 percent of the farms but represent 56 percent of the farmed area. Equally important is where these landholdings are. From the beginning, the largest landholdings were located in Punjab Province. Of the 367,895 largest landholdings, 53 percent are found in Punjab Province, where the Canal Colonies were first established. In light of the adherence to traditional inheritance laws, the fact that so many large landholdings are still in existence is amazing. The remaining large landholdings are scattered throughout the much more arid and irrigation deprived provinces, like Sindh and Baluchistan, and their existence is more a function of necessity, especially within the context of livestock management. The lands in Punjab, on the other hand, are much better watered and, therefore, agriculturally much more productive. It is these farms that the advocates of land ceilings and redistribution would like to see broken up, even if such actions would, in all likelihood, result in lower *per capita* production.

Table 13-1: Landholding Sizes in Pakistan, 2005

Size of Farm (Hectares)	*Farms Number*	*%*	*Farms Area Hectares*	*%*	*Avg. size of Farm Area (Hectares)*
Under 0.5	1290098	19	362544	2	0.3
0.5 to under 1.0	1099330	17	821245	4	1.0
1.0 to under 2.0	1425370	22	1981277	10	2.5
2.0 to under 3.0	966411	15	2256772	11	5.0
3.0 to under 5.0	890755	13	3442507	17	7.5
5.0 to under 10.0	580200	9	3891228	19	12.5
10.0 to under 20.0	260791	4	3324310	16	25.0
20.0 to under 40.0	77773	1	1955330	10	50.0
40.0 to under 60.0	15277	<1	689070	3	100.0
60.0 and above	14054	<1	1682491	8	150.0

Source: (Ministry of Food, Agriculture & Livestock, 2005), Table 65.

Pakistan is also well ahead of most of the countries in South Asia with regard to the implementation of Corporate Agricultural Farming (CAF) programs.The government has actively pursued business relations with foreign partners and sought participation in the development of supermarket-type grocery retailers, where field-to-market relations are envisioned. Such a move would, effectively, disenfranchise the hierarchy of middlemen that currently exists between the producers and the end-users of agricultural produce.This would release the funds currently skimmed off by the intermediaries and, hopefully, would result in higher prices paid to the actual producers.

Although talked about in India, CAF has not been pursued as earnestly as it has been in Pakistan. There, due to the nature of the nation's landholdings, CAF represents a potentially and comparatively easy transition. It will not be until these types of networks and structures are put into place that the problem areas will become apparent. Often what seems simple and easy to implement results in problems that no one could have realistically anticipated and they often come from the most unexpected sources. We will have to wait and see what develops and how these problems are addressed.

Environmentally, many of the same problems faced in India are equally important in Pakistan. Even though Pakistan inherited an elaborate canal irrigation system, by its very nature, it was limiting. Pumpsets and tubewells were obviously the most efficient ways of expanding irrigatable land. Just as elsewhere, the tubewells have drawn down the aquifers, permitting groundwater contamination and potentially threatening the very existence of irrigation-based agriculture in some areas. For this reason, no-till agriculture has grown in importance, lowering the demand on the aquifers and, possibly, permitting their recharge. If groundwater use patterns continue unabated, inevitably land will be lost to production for the simple lack of water – a problem already recognized by the agricultural and economic development agencies.

Unlike India, Pakistan has had a tradition of having insufficient agricultural laborers to work the land. In lieu of human laborers, mechanization, in the form of tractors, has been substituted for increasingly expensive human labor. The only limitation faced by the Pakistani farmers is the institutional availability of the equipment needed. Therefore, every effort is being made by the government to induce investors and producing partners to increase domestic machinery production – a strategy that appears to be working.

As in the beginning, governance and political instability continues to play a role in Pakistan's agricultural and socio-economic development. Internal political divisiveness has effectively brought many programs and program development to a virtual standstill. Added to the opposition of the ruling military regime, and its support of the American's war against the Taliban in Afghanistan, has been the internal discord between a variety of political parties and alliances over a broad range of issues.[7] Paraphrasing one recent political writer's comment: Politics is holding the Pakistan economy hostage.[8] In addition to the political wrangling between the political parties, is the September 6th 2008 election of Asif Ali Zardari as the country's 11th elected president since 1956. Within the tumult that is current Pakistani politics, it is difficult to formulate, let alone implement, development programs or sustain the economic social structure necessary for continued development and the resolution of the country's environmental problems.

The recent manifestation of political unrest, stemming from the political insurrection activities of the ultra-conservative, Islamic factions, spearheaded by the Taliban, has served to further undermine the elected government. This insurgency is particularly entrenched in the Swat Valley, where armed bands have confronted, defeated, and executed numerous Pakistan miltary personnel, sent there to enforce law and order

In the absence of internal political stability, fiscal stability has suffered, with the real possibility that Pakistan could find itself losing its favorable fiscal rating because of the possibility that it will be unable to meet its current debt service payments, amounting to nearly US $ 350 million weekly. Current foreign exchange reserves have fallen to a recent all-time low. Some officials suspect that Pakistan has only 3 months worth of reserves for the payment of imports. Thereafter, it is anyone's guess; although, the most likely stop-gap strategy will be dependence on international credit, especially coming from the World Bank.

With people jockeying for position within the new government, there is little time to attend to the business of state, let alone be concerned with the plight of the rural population, or the political effects of an inflation rate that is near 22 percent, pushing the poor farther and farther from being able to buy food. Unless the politics of Pakistan become settled, there is little hope that Pakistan's drive toward the MDG of halving poverty will be met.

Bangladesh

Bangladesh is a unique case. Of all the nations of South Asia, it is the most noticeably challenged by environmental problems, most of which are not of human origin. Nowhere else are so many environmental hazards and natural disasters visited on so many people so frequently. Year in and year out, Bangladesh must contend with floods (riverine and flash, and tidal surges), windstorms, cyclones, torrential rainfall, tornadoes, arsenic contamination of groundwater, earthquakes, mudslides, erosion, and droughts.

With all the storm and monsoon rainfall, drought would not seem to be a serious threat. However, droughts can and frequently do follow on the heels of the monsoons. Droughts disrupt the agricultural economy of the country, resulting in hunger, instability, and insecurity. The northwestern part of the country is particularly vulnerable to drought conditions.

Erosion is associated with almost every flood and tidal surge. Even when the floods are gentle, large quantities of soil are swept out into the Bay of Bengal, building the Sunderbans and the submarine delta of the main rivers as they enter the Bay of Bengal.

The individual natural disasters are devastating, but repetitive damage results from the combined onslaught of the various types of natural disasters that besiege Bangladesh. The country is literally under siege by nature, causing physical damage to the land and property, as well as posing a serious threat to agricultural and overall economic development.

Climate Change

In a country dominated by the vagaries of nature, any change in climate must be examined closely, for it could portend either the reduction or increase of natural disasters, especially wind related disasters, of which Bangladesh has suffered 137 such events in the last 100 years, second only to the famine of 1943 in terms of lives taken.[9]

Current thinking suggests that Bangladesh will become warmer and wetter as a result of current trends in climate change. Higher precipitation may increase the area and depth of flooding, which will require additional measures for protection and adaptation. Other probable impacts may include disruption of the monsoon rhythm, prolonged drought, and increased frequency of cyclones. The most serious consequence of climate change for Bangladesh will be a rise in sea level along the Bay of Bengal coast, causing submergence of 10 to 20 per cent of the land (including the Sundarbans), as well as saline intrusion in the rivers. Although climate change is a long-term process, the implications for Bangladesh could easily be described as potentially catastrophic.

Erosion

The lands of Bangladesh are inherently fertile alluvial soils that are frequently replenished by silt deposits from multiple riverine flood events each year. Under normal circumstances, this would mean that nature would seem to be compensating for the devastation she exacts throughout the year. However, she compensates for the gift of silt with erosion.

Erosion is a regular and recurring phenomenon. Erosion of land surfaces, riverbanks, and coastal areas is already causing serious problems for the country. An increase in rainfall in summer will, in all likelihood, increase the surface erosion. Land erosion will intensify through current deforestation and other land use changes. Especially destructive is riverbank erosion, which removes large quantities of fertile soil and land area from agricultural production and is frequently associated with rivers changing their courses, causing economic and transport dislocations.

Of equal importance is coastal erosion. Coastal erosion is particularly destructive due to the lack of elevation along the coast of the Bay of Bengal. The coastal lowlands are especially at risk due to high monsoon winds, wave action, strong currents, strong tidal action, and storm surges.[10] In the likelihood of increased wind-related storms and activity, due to Global Warming, Bangladesh's coastal areas are likely to be increasingly battered and damaged.

Climate Change and Agriculture

Agricultural yields are especially responsive to changes in climate, be they increases or decreases in temperature, rainfall, or direct sunlight. How climate change will have an impact on Bangladesh is uncertain, but if predictions are correct, there will be more rainfall and rising temperatures. How these will affect crop yields in Bangladesh will be a function of the extent of change in temperature and moisture availability, which, in all likelihood, will be unevenly distributed over the country due to physiographic variations.

Rice, in particular, is sensitive to sunlight, temperature, and moisture availability. For the best yields, each rice variety has limits, and unless the environment remains stable and within the variety's specific tolerance range, its yields will typically suffer. Change in the environment may mean simply the substitution of one variety with another existing variety; or it could mean that entirely new varieties will be needed to cope with the specific changes in the cultivator's area.

Table 13-2: Types of Disasters and their Impacts in Specific Disaster Prone Areas, Bangladesh

Disaster Type	*Areas Affected*	*Impact*
Flood	Floodplains of the Brahmaputra-Jumna, Ganges and the Meghna Rivers	Loss or Agricultural production., disruption of communication and livelihood system, injury, damage and destruction of immobile infrastructure, disruption to essential services, national economic loss, evacuation, and loss of human lives and biodiversity, displacement and suffering of human population
Cyclone and Storm Surge	Coastal areas and off-shore islands	Loss or Agricultural production., disruption of communication and livelihood system, damage and destruction of immobile infrastructure, injury, national economic loss, evacuation, and loss of biodiversity and human lives, displacement and suffering of human population, temporary shelter
Tornado	Scattered areas of the country	Loss of human life and biodiversity, injury, damage and destruction of property, damage to cash crops, disruption in lifestyle, damage to essential services, national economic loss and loss of livelihood

(Contd.)

(Contd. Table 13.2)

Disaster Type	*Areas Affected*	*Impact*
Drought	Almost all areas, especially the Northwest region of the country	Loss of agricultural production, stress on national economy and disruption of properties
Flash Flood	Naor Basins of the North-east region and South-eastern hilly areas.	Damage to standing crops, disruption of lifestyle, evacuation and destruction of properties
Erosion	Banks of major rivers and streams	Loss of land, displacement of human population and livestock, disruption of production, evacuation and loss of property
Landslides & Mudslides	Chittagong and Chittagong Hills Tracts	Loss of land, displacement of human population and livestock, evacuation, damage of property and loss of life.
Earthquakes	Northern and central parts of the country	Damage and destruction of property, loss of life and change in geomorphology

Source: Adapted from: (UNEP-RRC.AP, 2001) [Online version].

Along these lines, Walker and Steffan suggest that climate change will be most beneficial to developed countries, since these countries are largely located in areas of temperate climate.[11] Any changes in the climates of tropical and sub-tropical areas will, undoubtedly, be disadvantageous, since increased temperatures, in particular, would make them more vulnerable to negative impacts on crops, soils, insects, weeds, and diseases. Further, Global Warming will increase sea levels, which will result in the inundation of much of Bangladesh's coastal croplands, if not permanently, then, at least temporarily. This will result in the loss of potentially cultivable land due to increased salinity.[12]

Also, as the sea levels rise, there is a very good possibility of salt water intrusion into the groundwater aquifers of Bangladesh. When freshwater is extracted from groundwater aquifers, and salt water is present, the salt water will almost inevitably seek to fill the deficit. A similar problem exists in many areas but is especially serious in areas like Florida in the United States, where population growth, associated with periodic drought conditions, is making increased demands on the state's aquifers and contributing to salt water intrusion.[13] Likewise, in Bangladesh, during the winter, water flowing into the rivers from the surrounding mountains and hills and from the rivers of India, is reduced substantially. Thus the natural recharge rates of the aquifers is reduced. It is during these times that the Bangladesh aquifers are most vulnerable to salt water intrusion, especially along the coast.

Climate Change and Biodiversity

Increased temperatures and changes in the moisture regime of Bangladesh will also have an impact on the country's existing biodiversity. Many plants, crops, and ecologies are dependent upon specific temperature and water availabilities, as well as water quality. Increased temperature will force some species of plants to retreat to those areas that best meet their normal habitat, which will mean that they will move to higher elevations, with a similar pattern of migration for the plants that once inhabited the area. The plants will retreat to areas that match their old habitant, until there is nowhere for them to go. In the end, some plants will find no satisfactory habitat and they will disappear. The Sundarbans, a strip of higher ground immediately behind the mangrove swamps along the coast of Bangladesh, might be completely inundated by a one-meter rise in sea level. The area may shrink, and there is the real possibility that many plant and animal species in the area will become extinct, a process that could move wave-like through the country, and right up the hill and mountain slopes.

The Future for Bangladesh

Bangladesh is one of the most impoverished countries in the world, and decidedly so within the context of South Asia. Agriculture remains the strength and weakness of the country. Agriculture represents the key to the nation's long-term survival and growth, as well as the source of and solution to its all-pervasive poverty. However, unlike any country of South Asia, Bangladesh is beset by an environment that is becoming increasingly hostile.

There have been sectoral changes in the country. In 1975 agriculture was responsible for more than 60 percent of the GDP; it now represents just over 21percent.[14] Much of the agricultural sector's contributory share of the national economy has been replaced by major gains in the industrial/manufacturing sectors but especially in the services sector, which now represents more than 52.5 percent of Bangladesh's GDP.[15] Part of the transition from agriculture to manufacturing and services has come at a cost. By comparison to India, Pakistan, and Nepal, Bangladesh is small. As a consequence, the expansion of these sectors has tended to eat away at cultivable land, through urbanization, homesteads, and infrastructure. In fact, the cultivated area has declined by approximately 1 percent per year since 1985-86 and the average farm size has fallen from 2.26 to 1.69 acres.

These changes in Bangladesh's economy have not been without an impact on its poverty. In 1981-82, the percentage of people living below the poverty line was 71 percent. By 2004, that percentage had dropped to 40.9 percent, with greatest improvement having been made in the rural areas, with a drop of 32.9 points, compared with the urban decline of 24.4 points. Although:

This might have happened due to more influx of urban slum population because of landlessness, land erosion and other social deprivations. [16]

In Bangladesh each year landholding size and area under cultivation decline, and population numbers increase, even at an annual growth rate under 2 percent. In this scenario, at some time in the near future, population will exceed the production capacity of the land. Current agricultural technology is being pushed to its limits. Only two alternatives are open to the people of Bangladesh – substantially increase the shift of population into the none agricultural sectors, with rapid increases in personal income, allowing the people to purchase their food from both domestic and imported sources; or increase production through further agricultural intensification. Of these two options, the second is probably the least realistic in light of currently available agricultural technology.

Future production must come from less land using sustainable quantities of inputs. This combination of problems can only be resolved through increases in agricultural research. This research, in addition to dealing with the simple agronomic balance between available land and the need for increased production must also deal with an environment that is growing increasingly unfriendly. It must deal with the current level of natural hazards and, assuming the Global Warming phenomenon will have a significant effect on the country, deal with an ever more hostile environment. These challenges can only be resolved through agricultural research.

While it is a simple, logical statement, the Government of Bangladesh, due to seemingly other high priority problems, has failed to make requisite investments in agricultural research. While government expenditures in agriculture have increased, albeit slowly, that portion of the expenditures for agricultural research has actually declined, just when it is needed most. Agricultural research and development investments have declined from 3.9 percent during the period 1976–81, to 2.9 percent in the period 2001–04.[17] Considering what is at stake, this is unacceptable. Further, agricultural research and development are notorious for the interval between initial investment and useable results. Investments made 10 years ago, in many cases, have only recently begun to be implemented in cultivators' fields. Bangladesh, in all likelihood, does not have the luxury of time. The need for tenable solutions for the food-population problem will be upon Bangladesh much more quickly than it knows.

Nepal

Most outsiders have an idyllic image of Nepal that includes picturesque mountain landscapes, deep green valleys with rivers running through them, crystal clear air, and quaint, peaceful people. The predominant Western view of Nepal is one of a place of retreat from the hustle and bustle of modern urban life. No one thinks about insurgents roaming the hills and mountains, killing people, kidnapping innocent civilians and ransoming them, or placing improvised explosive devices (IEDs) along roadways, or bombing and burning buildings. Ironically, all these images are true.

Insurgency in Nepal can be traced back nearly 5 decades. It is not a recent political phenomenon. It was not until the Communist Party, Maoists, the CPN(M) declared a 'people's war' in February 13, 1996, however, that Nepal's peace and tranquility was completely shattered. The CPN(M) was the most radical of the left wing political parties in Nepal, and it was dedicated to a social and economic order as advocated by Mao during the so-called Cultural Revolution.[18] Until November of 2001, the CPN(M) engaged in periodic talks with the standing government of Nepal, then they launched a nationwide offensive. Since then, the level of violence has escalated, leaving as many as 8,000 Nepalis dead, most of them killed in little more than a year.[19]

As a consequence of the political instability and increasing violence in the country, many Nepalese have sought unofficial asylum abroad. Those relatives that do not possess either useful skills or training, remain behind. These relatives, however, have not been forgotten. Relatives living abroad regularly send remittances home to ease the hardship of their trapped, less fortunate relatives. It is estimated that more than 25 percent of Nepal's gross national product may come from such remittances.[20]

Currently, the largest source of foreign exchange is tourism. The primary source of income is the land, where nearly 80 percent of the workforce is employed, with little or no opportunity for transition to the manufacturing or services sectors, and there are few opportunities outside agriculture. In addition, social and historical factors have concentrated the nation's resources and power in the hands of less than a 1/3rd of the nation's population. This minority effectively controls all positions of power and influence.[21]

Part of their domination stems from their caste and a command of the national language of Nepal. Only the top two castes – the Brahmins and Chhetris – are tutored and fluent in Nepali. The speakers of other languages and the other castes are much less fluent, a language that is required for government participation. Thus, nearly 2/3rds of the nation is effectively disenfranchised from government service. This has led to charges of unfair advantage.

Given such socio-economic division, it would be expected that politics would play a significant role in mediating contending demands. For the country is a functioning parliamentary democracy. Here again, there is more than meets the eye. A democracy only since 1990, Nepal suffers from the, by now, all-too-familiar problems of the genre "emerging democracy": corruption, inefficiency, and lack of focus. Compounded by a lack of state integration, the political system has been able to foster little save a lack of legitimacy.[22]

Against this backdrop of social and economic inequality and political disenfranchisement, the CPN(M) demanded the creation of a people's republic based on Maoist principles. In effect, this meant the end to the Nepalese monarchy and the creation of a national constitution. Economically, there was to be an end to capitalist exploitation; socially, an end to caste, ethnic, religious, and linguistic exploitation. Since the Nepalese monarchy was unwilling to negotiate itself out of existence, the CPN(M) initiated its peoples' war to force the issue. Although the CPN(M) has repeatedly advocated a political solution to the impasse between itself and the government, it has repeatedly retreated to the use of violence to achieve its goals.

The primary strategy followed by the Maoists is to use terrorism to create a spatial and political vacuum that the Maoists then fill. Using this strategy, the CPN(M) has expanded its sphere of social, economic, and political influence, mostly in the hills of Nepal. The hills provide the CPN(M) physical and military security, because of its difficult terrain and isolation.

The local government offices and officials were often the initial targets for the insurgents, destroying all government property and records, and burning the buildings to the ground and killing all government officials. The Nepalese police and security forces were not up to the task of fending off the insurgents, and the government effectively retreated to defensible positions, the larger towns and the capital. Using these tactics time and again, the Maoists have effectively contained the government in the larger settlements, leaving rural Nepal undefended.

By 2003, of slightly more than 1,400 of Nepal's approximately 3,900 Village Development Committees (VDCs), had fallen to the Maoists and the VDC workers, both elected and government employed, had been either killed or had fled.[23] In addition, the insurgents cut roadways, bridges, dams and hydropower facilities, aqueducts, telephone towers and electric lines, airport control towers and more than 400 post office were systematically destroyed.[24]

As a result of the government's desire to secure peace, it expanded the RNA, increased the number of Armed Police Force personnel, and established what became known as 'Unified' units, equivalent to SWAT teams. These increases served to balance out the efforts of the Maoists to achieve political dominion through violence. By 2005, the organized frontal violence of the CPN(M) had been all but stopped.[25] Disorganized acts of terrorism and violence, however, continue throughout the country.

Finally, in early 2005, in the absence of the government's ability to secure a peaceful resolution to the communist insurgency, direct Royal rule was announced. This action resulted in the establishment of an alliance between the various opposition parties, all of whom opposed royal rule. Ultimately, the military stood aside and the monarchy was effectively pushed aside. Following a number of interim arrangements, a Comprehensive Peace Agreement was signed in November 2006. This agreement effectively brought the Maoists into the system and ended the old order. In January of the following year, an Interim Constitution was approved, and the Maoists formally entered the parliamentary government soon thereafter.

Even though formally a part of the government, the Maoists have made it clear that a parliamentary democracy is unsatisfactory and that it will not achieve the kinds of change that they deem necessary. They remain committed to the eradication of all vestiges of the old order and replacing it with their vision of a Maoist state, which would include state involvement in all aspects of Nepalese social, economic, and political life.

The Maoists' vision include social justice and equity in the distribution of all resources. Marks points out that,

. . . there is little understanding of just why resources are scarce (i.e., as already mentioned, a population that has exceeded the carrying capacity of the land) or why there is inequity (there is, essentially, no economy) has not been given a great deal of thought. If one is to judge by what has occurred thus far in the Maoist-controlled areas, redistribution is the immediate priority: seizing from those who have in order to give to those who have not – though the implementation generally classifies as 'have-nots' the same Maoist cadre who are carrying out the redistribution. The truly poor remain just that.[26]

The Maoists have effectively fomented a form of anarchy throughout the country, through continued violent attacks on people and their own government facilities, now that they are part of the establishment. The consequence is that there is little central control anywhere in the country, thus little advancement socially, economically, or politically. In a sense, under the communists, Nepal is organizationally little different from what it was before it was integrated almost two hundred years ago. It has devolved into a series of fiefdoms governed by a loosely organized and disorganized Communist ideology.

Under these circumstances, it is entirely understandable why Nepal remains one of the least developed, least progressive nations in the world. The people remain chained to the land in the absence of anywhere else to go. Economic development is almost at a standstill, yet foreigners – nearly a quarter of a million annually – flock to picturesque Nepal to experience the charm the country seems to offer. Most are absolutely oblivious to the social, economic, and political undercurrents that are at work all around them. The travel brochures provide them with all they need to know before booking their treks, kayaking expeditions, mountain climbing, or shopping for Nepalese handicrafts. Behind the glossy travel brochures lies a truth that most tourists will never know or would little understand.

Sub-Saharan Africa

There is no polite way to say this: the people of Sub-Saharan Africa are hungry and the world development agencies and organizations have been helping them remain that way. The donor countries of the West have been helping the wrong way. Millions of tons of food are shipped to 'the people of Africa' every year. Some of it actually gets to the people most in need. Much of it, however, simply disappears, only to resurface in the black market, where free food becomes food for sale. The donor nations, undoubtedly more out of a sense of guilt, find it easier to ship surplus food from the abundance of the West than actually helping the African people feed themselves. Famine relief assuages Western guilt. It does little more than keep starving people alive today to starve another day. Can anyone honestly believe that, in the long run, this is a solution?

An old Chinese proverb reads:

Give a man a fish and you feed him for a day. Teach a man to fish and you feed him for a lifetime (Author unknown).

We have all heard this proverb but we fail to consider its ramifications within the context of a starving Africa. We continue to ship the African people 'fish' rather than giving them the tools necessary to 'fish' for themselves. The multinational agribusiness corporations are willing to sell them the tools to fish but will never give them away. For the multinationals, food is business and business means profits. Who better to exploit than those who need food and do not have it. Promise them whatever you must but make sure they buy your products. Now, the Chinese proverb might read:

Give a man a fish; you have fed him for today. Teach a man to fish; and you can sell him fishing equipment.

This is a cynical and pejorative view of how development agencies and organizations, and multinational corporations operate but the truly unfortunate thing is that it is accurate.

For the better part of 60 years, since the nations of Sub-Saharan Africa began obtaining their independence in the late 1950s, the West has appeared helpless to address Africa's economic problems, or possibly more accurately, disinterested. In either case, Africa is the poorest region of the world, even exceeding East Asia or South Asia. Although South Asia is the home to nearly half of the world's poor and hungry, the people of Africa are poorer and hungrier.

Currently, there are two distinct groups advising the world's development agencies. On the one hand is Jeffrey Sachs of Columbia University, formerly an economics professor at Harvard University and the Director of the United Nations Millennium Project. He is the outspoken advocate of the pro-foreign aid group. It is his contention that, by massively boosting foreign aid to the countries of Sub-Saharan Africa, the people will be in a position to save, invest, and grow domestically. They will be able to extricate themselves from what he and others term the African Poverty Trap.

In the other corner is William Easterly of NYU, formerly an economist with the World Bank. Easterly contends that, despite the hundreds of billions of dollars already provided to the countries of Africa, little seems to have been achieved. He suggests that, if the people of Africa were, indeed, caught in some kind of poverty trap, surely they could have bought their way out with the money already provided. Economic development in Africa will depend — as it has elsewhere and throughout the history of the modern world — on the success of private-sector entrepreneurs, social entrepreneurs, and African political reformers. It will *not* depend on the activities of patronizing, bureaucratic, unaccountable and poorly informed outsiders.[27]

Many Westerners, as they sit wide-eyed before their television sets, watching images of starving African children, casualties of genocide, child soldiers, AIDS patients and famine deaths, are routinely invited to "Save Africa," "Save the Child," or contribute to such organizations as "Nothing but Nets." Rock stars and other celebrities want every world government to set aside an amount equal to 0.7 percent of the nation's GDP to be used for foreign aid to Africa, as well as the cancellation of outstanding African debt.[28] Or, concerts, like "Live Aid" are organized to raise money for famine relief.

Focusing on African tragedies, while laudable, diverts attention away from the real problems and solutions for Africa. There are those in Africa who are changing their lives and the lives of the people around them. They do so against tremendous odds, admittedly, but they do it nonetheless. When all is said and done, development everywhere is homegrown. While G-8 ministers and rock stars fuss about a few billion dollars here or there for African governments, the citizens of India and China (where foreign aid is a microscopic share of income) were busy increasing their own incomes by $715 billion in 2005.[29] In fact, in 2006, the number of Indian billionaires increased to 23, ten of whom were created in just one year. While African economies struggled, stagnated, and failed, the Indian and Chinese economies grew, with China in the lead and India following with an average growth rate of 8 percent per annum.[30]

Edward Miguel sums up the situation:

China and India . . . were at African per capita income levels in the 1970s. It is striking how high foreign aid to Africa currently is in per capita terms: overseas development assistance is a full order of magnitude higher in Africa than in China or India, as it was during the critical 1980-2000 period when those Asian countries moved forward economically and Africa declined. There is no doubt that foreign aid is not necessary for economic development.[31]

Further, much of the aid sent to Africa simply disappears before it can have the desired effect on the nations' economies. Corruption usurps or misdirects aid payments almost as a matter of course. However, aid payments continue without any reservation. Aid agents know this is the normal way of doing business in many African countries but that does not stop them from asking for still more funds. In effect, the aid agents and agencies are as much a part of the problem as the recipients.

Violence and Tribalism

Violence, whether fostered by political differences or tribal animosities, seems to exist just below the surface in almost every African society. Sometimes it exposes itself, especially during times of political turmoil, and presidential elections, as witnessed recently in Zimbabwe and in Kenya. If the domestic violence of one country was limited to that country, all would be well. However, it often spills over into adjacent countries, in the form of refugees attempting to avoid involvement or outright persecution. It can also cause economic dislocations between neighboring countries. For example, in January 2008, demonstrations in Kenya resulted in the disruption of oil shipments to Uganda.

Although violence seems to be an ongoing problem throughout Africa, it must be admitted that some long-standing disputes have finally been, at least temporarily, resolved. The conflicts in Liberia, Sierra Leone, and Sudan have been settled; and the war in Angola seems to be on its way back to the peace table, again. As conflicts in one country seem to be coming to an end, animosities in other nations are festering, waiting for the right igniter to bring it to the surface. Since political and ethnic violence are some of the most important contributors to sustained poverty and social dislocations, the decline in violence in Africa is applaudable. The unfortunate aspect of both political and ethnic violence is that they are never forgotten. They may simmer and smolder, only to be resurrected again when 'the time is right.' It is only a matter of time, in most cases.

India is ethnically and linguistically fractured but an Indian identity holds the country together. Africa does not possess a pan-African identity. It is too tribalized and factionalized to achieve such an identity. Even individual countries have difficulty establishing a national identity that the people can rally around. In large measure, the failure of individual governments to achieve national consensus may well stem from the European scramble to establish colonies in Africa early in the 20th Century, carving out and delimiting colonies in a capricious manner. Groups that had been antagonistic toward one another for hundreds of years were arbitrarily thrown together and forced to coexist – people of different cultural and linguistic origins.These animosities did not simply disappear under colonial domination, and they have not been resolved as a function of independence.

Not all conflicts have been racially or ethnically charged, but within the ranks of each of the major combatants, various tribal groups find an opportunity to exact retribution for real or perceived slights and abuses from the past. Some of these wars were the result of genuine political or ideological differences that were not amenable to resolution through negotiation until well into the conflict. The most deadly of these civil wars was the Second Sudanese Civil War, which is estimated to have caused the death of 1.9 million civilians plus combatants.[32]

Causes of Africa's Problems

Sachs and others have repeatedly suggested that geography, disease, demography, population distributions, and inadequate infrastructures, especially transportation networks, are largely responsible for Africa's current state. In Africa, almost every possible explanation can find a sympathetic ear, largely because each has, to a limited degree, a certain amount of truth to it.

The social and political problems facing Africa are, at best, daunting. When one combines these problems with its environmental challenges, there is no wonder that little has been achieved toward the amelioration of African poverty and hunger. Despite attempts, the Green Revolution failed to take root in Africa. The South Asian version of the Green Revolution was simply not adaptable to much of Africa. In large measure this was because the cereals upon which it was based were not essential parts of most African diets, and there were no improved varieties for the foods that were.

Eighty to 90 percent of African families depend on subsistence agriculture. They grow and eat their own food.[33]

For these cultivators, little has been done to improve the agricultural infrastructures necessary for the emergence of a surplus-producing agriculture. Access to the improved inputs, as they existed, was hampered by the dispersed character of the population, few towns and cities, few centralized market places, and the existence of only a rudimentary transportation network. It is no wonder that cultivators focused on self-preservation. There was little opportunity to get any existing surpluses to markets. This spatial and economic isolation contributed to the evolution of micro-adapted agriculture and the development of localized survival strategies.

Agriculture – The Root Problem

Further, in the absence of other economic alternatives in rural areas, agriculture becomes the only avenue for social and economic development. Expectations are high that agriculture will provide the base for national economic growth and lift millions out of poverty. Along with other factors such as markets, prices, inputs and security of land tenure, water's importance cannot be underestimate as part of the mix needed to meet these individual and national aspirations.

Water

Water has always been a problem in Africa. In some areas, there is adequate rainfall for agriculture but large areas of Africa are subject to prolonged periods of drought, or dry seasons. Little attention has been devoted to the development of irrigation. Now, with the advent of increased rainfall variability, the result of climatic changes caused by Global Warming, and in the absence of a well developed irrigation system, cultivable land will be reduced.

Around the world, irrigation has proven to be one of the greatest production-improving technologies available. Traditionally, irrigation has been evaluated solely on its ability to improve national and regional economies. Now, its importance also must be gauged on its ability to improve livelihoods on a much smaller scale – households and their well-being, for it is at this lowest level that starvation begins.

Also, water, in light of climate change and its consequences for agriculture, must be considered, especially if the Millennium Development Goals are to be achieved, or even approximated within the context of Africa. Water is essential to agriculture and the achievement of halving the number of poor.

Currently, less than 1/3rd of Africa's potentially irrigatable land is under irrigation. Therefore, here is ample opportunity for its expansion. Meeting the MDGs for Africa will necessitate a doubling of the area currently under irrigation and, therefore, irrigation must be a part of Africa's overall development agenda. Unfortunately, the reality is that the governments of Africa have numerous other priorities that are deemed more important than making large-scale investments in irrigation systems or providing subsidies for groundwater based, small-scale irrigation systems. As a consequence, irrigation advocates are suggesting a twofold approach to Africa's irrigation problems. Extract whatever development resources that exist for traditional irrigation systems, but barring the availability of such funding, attempt to modernize and increase agricultural production on rainfed lands.

The problem with devoting limited resources to rainfed agriculture is that water scarcity is becoming a serious problem, and it will only get worse. It is estimated that most of the countries of Africa will be vulnerable to water scarcity or under stress by 2025. See Map 13-2. Symptoms of economic water scarcity include inadequate infrastructure development, so that people have trouble getting enough water for agricultural and domestic purposes; high

Map 13-2: Current Water Scarcity

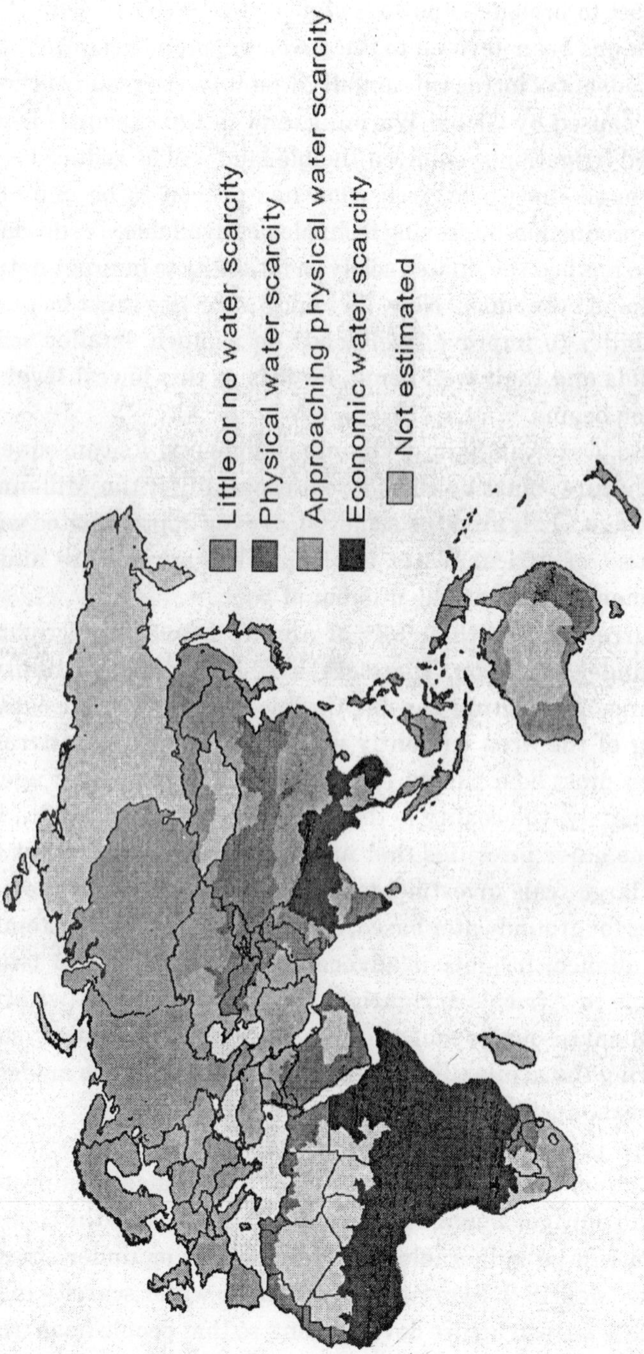

Source: Adapted and modified from (Molden, David (ed), 2007), p.63.

vulnerability to seasonal water fluctuations, including floods and long- and short-term drought; and inequitable distribution of water even though infrastructure exists. Much of Sub-Saharan Africa experiences economic water scarcity, and there are many pockets across the globe where water resources are inequitably distributed. Further, recognizing the value of irrigation to productivity, most new irrigation has been installed on already productive rainfed agricultural lands, rather than applied to new agricultural lands. This raises agricultural production but has not resulted in the expansion of agriculture into potentially productive new lands. There is a certain unnecessary repetition built into this scenario. An effort must be made to implement new irrigation on new lands, not in already productive land, to achieve maximum benefit.

Although the expansion of irrigation in Sub-Saharan Africa is poorly developed, during the 1960s and 1970s, irrigation infrastructure was commissioned as part of settlement programs in some countries but, in general, very little has been done to expand irrigation, and even less has been done to develop sources of water. Almost all African irrigation is surface irrigation, with its inherent shortcomings – water loss through seepage and evaporation. If irrigation is to be extended, cheaper systems must be developed, systems that minimize the loss of scarce water through non-productive soil losses and evaporation.

More importantly, in the mid-1980s, based on poor performance of the newer irrigation systems, the very agencies that had pushed for increased irrigation capacity performed a turnabout, reducing funding for all types of irrigation. Among these was the World Bank.[34] Lending for irrigation did not pick up until the late 1990s, and even by 2002-05, lending for irrigation was still only half of what it had been in the late 1970s and early 1980s. At its peak, funding for irrigation amounted to more than a billion USD per year.[35]

The decline in public investment in irrigation and foreign funding in Africa has been caused by a sharp drop in cereal prices in the 1980s. Second, there was growing recognition of the poor performance of irrigation systems. Third, there was a rise in irrigation construction costs. Falling grain prices and rising construction costs reduced benefit-cost ratios, and this discouraged policy-maker's willingness to make further investments. Finally, there was a growing environmental lobby that opposed large dams, due to the environmental degradation and social dislocations that sometimes resulted. Reflecting these environmental concerns, the World Commission on Dams (WCD) was created in 1997. It reviewed the experience with large dams and established a policy-making framework for the evaluation of new large-scale dam projects.[36] As a consequence, few new dam projects have been funded in most non-Communist countries since the creation of the WCD.

Only recently have countries allied with and dependent upon Western sources of funding or lending and institutional lenders begun to reconsider the construction of major irrigation works. Among the leaders in this renewed interest in large-scale irrigation is the World Bank. The new approach to the construction of irrigation infrastructure is pragmatic and each project needs to meet a predetermined set of criteria. Above all, the World Bank is advocating a position of partnering with recipient nations, rather than simply project funding. Thus, Western environmental sensitivities and concerns become more easily enforceable.[37]

Following the World Bank's lead, other lending organization and aid agencies are becoming involved in irrigation projects once again. A twin strategy has emerged. On the one hand are large-scale projects, like the Indian project that will link several rivers, providing water for water-scarce areas from water-abundant areas. The second strategy is to fund very small-scale irrigation investments at the individual end-user level. These projects will almost invariably involve funding for individual tubewells and pumpsets. Unlike the larger-scale projects, which will be dependent upon formal environmental assessments, the small-scale investments will not require similar environmental statements of impacts. Therefore, the potential for environmental problems, while not having the same environmental consequence as a project proposing to interlink rivers and changing the distribution of large quantities of water, both from the rivers and into previously unirrigated lands, could be significant. We have already seen that rampant use of tubewells and pumpsets can cause the depletion of groundwater resources and even cause subsidence. These potentials must be addressed wherever individual tubewell and pumpset investments are being considered. How vulnerable are the water resources being proposed for exploitation?

The demand for increased irrigation capacity is prompted by the need to produce more food, but any evaluation of where irrigation investments are to be made also depends on what crops will be grown, as well as anticipated changes in diets and standards of living changes, which will have future consequence for cropping patterns. It is difficult to say exactly what the future cropping patterns will be, but, as we have seen in the case of Pakistan, and elsewhere in the world, improved standards of living tend to be accompanied by declining demands for cereals and increases in other crops and allied agricultural sectors, like oilseeds, meat and dairy. These factors need to be addressed when making investments for future irrigation and cropping.

Food Habits

In Sub-Saharan Africa roots and tubers are by far the most important component of the average African's diet, and are expected to remain so for some time to come. In all regions except Sub-Saharan Africa there has been a significant increase in the consumption of vegetable oils over the last three decades. Meat consumption increased in all regions except Sub-Saharan Africa. These facts need to be considered in making any kind of investment in African agriculture. One must ask, as the African standard of living improves, will current consumption patterns continue to prevail, or will they begin to shift toward the consumption of more calorie-rich vegetable oils, meat, and dairy products, as seen in other regions of the world? Answers to these types of question need to be answered in order to make informed investment decisions at all levels.

Likewise, if dietary changes do occur, what impact will they have on water consumption? In general, improved standards of living result in greater demands for water -- water for agriculture, for drinking purposes, for sanitation, and for industrial purposes. These changes need to be anticipated and addressed beforehand.

The problem in Africa is that now the people are hungry. It is well and good to be environmentally cautious, but that caution is currently a luxury of the West, which can afford to be cautious. Few Westerners are starving. The question before us, and the people of Africa is one of: How do the people of Africa begin to feed themselves NOW?

Solution Priorities

The solutions are not simple, nor are they cheap, and they will not happen overnight. Food production is a time-consuming process, and increasing production seems like it is measured in decades. The people of Africa do not have decades. They need implementable solutions now. What can be done?

First, although rife with the potential for environmental degradation, the first priority is to increase the acreage under irrigation, and because of the dispersed nature of the African people, this will have to be achieved through tubewells and pumpsets. National governments, working with donor nations will need to provide such subsidies as will permit the small African landholder to obtain tubewells and pumpsets, and require realistic, long-term payback periods. This investment alone, could increase agricultural production by 100 to 400 percent, using existing crop and seed types.

Second, transportation infrastructures and markets will need to be improved, if cultivators are to become involved in the regional and national cash economy. Improved transportation is necessary to get the cultivators' surpluses to markets, and the markets are necessary for the fair and equitable sale of surplus produce. As part of market reform, the governments will need to implement fair and equitable minimum price supports program for essential foods, providing the cultivators with a reasonable profit, one that will encourage them to want to produce more.

Third, the governments must be willing to subsidize improved agricultural inputs. At first, this could be limited to fertilizers, then expanding the availability of such inputs to pesticides and herbicides. As *per capita* productivity increases, subsidies can be gradually decreased, until market forces can effectively regulate the inputs.

Fourth, as subsidies for inputs come on line, extension services must be made available to the cultivators, for without information, the likelihood of misuse of the inputs increases, especially for pesticides and herbicides. The farmers must become familiar with their inputs and the best way to maximize them.

Finally, while the first four components of this strategy are being set in motion, agricultural research and development organizations must be created to either develop crops for Africa's many ecological niches or assist in the development of GM crop types.

This five step approach builds on each prior step in a progressive manner. Water will increase production, and this increased production will serve to improve family livelihoods and well-being. Once the family unit is cared for, surpluses can be marketed, involving the people in the national cash economy, which will stimulate other sectors through the increased demand for goods and services. Improved inputs will further increase production, resulting in more surpluses and more market involvement. Each step in the sequence results in greater production, larger surpluses, and market involvement.

The introduction of improved seed varieties or GM crops becomes important once the people have become familiar and comfortable with the services of extension personnel, for the use of the HYVs or GM crops will require much more knowledge on the part of the cultivator. The question that needs to be asked is whether or not GM crops are needed. If national research and development facilities are created, it may be possible to avoid the introduction of GM crop types, which, depending upon one's view of the potential dangers of such crops with regard to biodiversity and genetic spill-over issues, would need to be addressed at the individual cultivator and national levels. However, these decisions must be made based on clear and unequivocal information, tempered with common sense. Neither vested interests nor the misinformation from either side of the GM debate should sway the decision-making process. Accurate and factual information and data are all that is needed. Everyone can be made to understand the basic principles involved in GM technologies, and this information needs to be circulated for everyone involved to be able to make an informed decision.

There is no magic to the five steps outlined above. None of them will be easy to achieve. Africa has been down for so long, in some ways the people have become their own worst enemy. Defeatism seems to have become a way of life. This is simply a function of trying to survive. If one has nothing to look forward to, it is easy to become self-defeated. It is time to help the African people help themselves. We already know that massive foreign aid does not automatically result in development. Development starts

Appendix

Selected Comparative Data – India, Pakistan, Bangladesh, Nepal and Selected Countries of Sub-Saharan Africa and the World

Country	*HRI Rank 2005*	*HRI*	*GDP Per Capita*	*%Population Below Poverty Line*	*Population ('000s)*
Gabon	119	0.667	6,954.00	-	1,485.83
Namibia	125	0.650	7,586.00	23.9	2,088.67
India	129	0.619	3,452.00	25.0	1,147,995.90
Ghana	135	0.553	2,480.00	28.5	23,382.85
Pakistan	136	0.551	2,370.00	24.0	167,762.04
Bangladesh	140	0.547	2,053.00	45.0	153,546.90
Nepal	142	3.534	1,550.00	30.9	29,519.11
Sudan	147	0.526	2,083.00	40.0	40,218.46
Zimbabwe	151	0.513	2,038.00	68.0	12,382.92
Senegal	156	0.499	1,792.00	54.0	12,853.36
Nigeria	158	0.470	1,128.00	70.0	138,283.24
Tanzania	159	0.467	744.00	36.0	40,213.16
Congo	168	0.411	714.00	-	66,514.51
Chad	170	0.388	1,427.00	80.0	10,111.34
Mozambique	172	0.384	1,242.00	70.0	21,284.70
Mali	173	0.380	1,033.00	36.1	12,324.03
Burkina Faso	176	0.370	1,213.00	46.4	15,264.74
Somalia	-		600.00	-	9,558.67
Iceland	1	0.968	36,510.00	-	304.37
United States	12	0.951	41,800.00	12	303,824.65
World		0.473	9,643.00		6,667,563.00

(Contd.)

(Contd. Appendix)

Country	Population Density	Population Growth Rate	National Land Area (Sq. Km.)	Arable Land (Sq. Km)	Arable Land as % of National Area
Gabon	5.8	1.954	257,667.0	3,1 17.8	1.21
Namibia	2.5	0.947	825,418.0	8,171.6	0.99
India	386.1	1.578	2,973,190.0	1,451,808.7	48.83
Ghana	101.3	1 .928	230,940.0	40,506.9	17.54
Pakistan	215.4	1.805	778,720.0	190,319.2	24.44
Bangladesh	1,146.6	2.002	133,910.0	74,172.8	55.39
Nepal	206.2	2.095	143,181.0	23,009.2	16.07
Sudan	16.9	2.134	2,376,000.0	161,092.8	6.78
Zimbabwe	32.0	0.568	386,670.0	31,861.6	8.24
Senegal	66.9	2.580	192,000.0	24,019.2	12.51
Nigeria	151.8	2.382	910,768.0	300,735.6	33.02
Tanzania	45.4	2,072	886,037.0	37,479.4	4.23
Congo	29.3	3.236	2,267,600.0	64,853.4	2.86
Chad	8.0	2.195	1,259,200.0	35,257.6	2.80
Mozambique	27.1	1.792	784,090.0	42,576.1	5.43
Mali	9.9	2.725	1,240,000.0	46,624.0	3.76
Burkina Faso	55.8	3.109	273,800.0	48,353.1	17.66
Somalia	151.2	2.824	627,337.0	10,288.3	1.64
Iceland	3.0	0.783	100,250.0	70.2	0.07
United States	33.2	0.833	9,161,923.0	1,650,062.3	18.01
World	44.5	1.159	149,940,000.0	19,957,014.0	13.31

(Contd.)

(Contd. Appendix)

Country	Arable Land Per Person (Hectares)	Irrigated Land (Sq. Km.)	Irrigated Land as % of Arable Land	% of Laborforce in Agriculture	Industry	Services
Gabon	0.210	70.0	2.25	60.0	15.0	25.0
Namibia	0.391	80.0	0.98	10.8	33.4	55.8
India	0.126	558,080.0	38.44	60.0	12.0	28.0
Ghana	0.173	310.0	0.77	37.3	25.3	37.5
Pakistan	0.113	182,300.0	95.79	42.0	20.0	38.0
Bangladesh	0.048	47,250.0	63.70	63.0	11.0	26.0
Nepal	0.078	11,700.0	50.85	76.0	6.0	18.0
Sudan	0.401	18,630.0	11.56	80.0	7.0	13.0
Zimbabwe	0.257	1,740.0	5.46	66.0	10.0	24.0
Senegal	0.187	1,200.0	5.00	77.5	22.5	
Nigeria	0.217	2,820.0	0.94	70.0	10.0	20.0
Tanzania	0.093	1,840.0	4.91	80.0	20.0	
Congo	0.098	110.0	0.17	0	0	0
Chad	0.349	300.0	0.85	80.0	20.0	
Mozambique	0.200	1,180.0	2.77	81.0	6.0	13.0
Mali	0.378	2,360.0	5.06	80.0	20.0	
Burkina Faso	0.317	250.0	0.52	90.0	10.0	
Somalia	0.108	2,000.0	19.44	71.0	29.0	25.0
Iceland	0.023	-	-	5.1	23.0	71.8
United States	0.543	223,850.0	13.57	0.9	20.5	78.5
World	0.299	2,770,980.0	13.88	40.2	20.5	39.3

Sources: (UNDP, *HDR* 2007/2008), Table 1, pp. 229-231; and (CIA, *World Factbook*, 2008), on-line version. Some figures computed.

Notes: Column 2 — HRI ranking based on 177 countries. Column 4 – GDP *per capita* in USD.

Column 10 – Land area excluding bodies of water. Columns 15-17 – Based on occupation.

Figures from *CIA World Factbook*, as available 28 June 2008. On-line figures are updated periodically and may, therefore, change.

\- No data available or unranked.

as an attitude, an attitude that things can get better. The African people have lived under such deplorable conditions for so long that they have forgotten what better is.

Sub-Saharan Africa's problems are daunting but they are not insurmountable nor unsolvable. Their solution will require imagination and determination, and possibly one other ingredient that seems to have been missing within the context of much of Africa — entrepreneurship at every level, from the cultivator in the field to the head of state. At every level, entrepreneurs need to be encouraged to find solutions that work, and these individuals need to be recognized and rewarded for their efforts. Development is always home grown. It is time to cultivate the people as well as crops.

References

1. (UNEP, 2000).
2. (Bhatty, 2006).
3. *Ibid.*, See for example, (Rediff Money Desk, 2005); (Mohanty, 2006); and India eNews.com, "Gujarat blamed for failure of employment scheme,"12/21/2006.
4. As envisioned by two of its earliest proponents, Ilchman and Uphoff, political economy is "the analysis of the consequences of political choices that statesmen and other persons make involving the polity's scarce resources" (Ilchman, Warren F. and Norman Thomas Uphoff, 1971), p. 26.
5. (Evenson, 2005).
6. (Rashid, 2004); (Rizvi, 2002); (Pakissan.com, 2002); (Business Recorder, 2005); and (Shahzad, 2003), as examples.
7. Included in this list of parties and alliances are: Mutihida Qaumi Movement (MQM), the National Awami Party, Alliance For Restoration of Democracy (ARD), the National Workers Party, Communist Mazdoor Kissan Party (Communist Workers Peasant Party), The Muslim League of ex Prime Minister Nawaz Sharif, the religious fundamentalist (largely supporters of Osama bin Laden and the Taliban), the Labour Party of Pakistan (LPP), and the Pakistan Peoples Party (PPP), among others.
8. (Fazl-e-Haider, Syed, 2008).

9. From 1904 to 2004, wind related storms have taken over 610,000 lives. The only famine took an estimated 1.9 million lives. See, http://www.sdnbd.org/sdi/issues/floods_drainage/2004/data/disaster%20from%201904%20to%202004.htm, for summary of natural disasters in Bangladesh from 1904 to 2004. Based on EM-Dat, database.
10. See, (Ali, A., 11 October 2000), as referenced in (UNEP-RRC.AP, 2001), p. 102.
11. (Walker, Brian; and Will Steffan, 1997).
12. (Huq, Saleemul. (ed), 1999).
13. (South Florida Sun Sentinel, 2007).
14. See, (BBS, 2006), See the Table entitled: Some selected macro-economic indicators
15. *Ibid.*
16. (Hoque, A. Y. M. Ekramul, et. al., 2004), p. 2, Table 1.
17. (Ahmed, Raisuddin and Zahurui Karim, 2006), p. 143.
18. See (Karki, Arun and David Seddon, 2003) for a sympathetic synopsis of the view from the left. Cited by (Marks, Thomas A., 2004), p. 27.
19. (Marks, Thomas A., 2004) plus references and discussion of casualty numbers, pp. 27-28. See, the United Nations Office for the Coordination of Human Affairs (OCHA) for both regular Situation Reports and library report lists regarding Nepal's insurgencies at: http://ochaonline.un.org/Default.aspx?alias=ochaonline.un.org/nepal.
20. Nepal has a GDP of approximately USD 5.5 billion and a national budget of USD 1.1 billion. Annual remittances have risen to as much as 1.6 billion USD in 2007. See (Ratha, Dilip and Zhimei Xu, 2008).
21. Of special importance in this Hindu dominated country are the Brahmins and Chhetris castes.
22. (Marks, Thomas A., 2004), p. 4.
23. VDCs are the basic political and development presence in the GoN's administrative structure.
24. (Marks, Thomas A., 2004), p. 13.
25. (Marks, Thomas A., 2008).
26. *Ibid.*
27. (Easterly, William, 2006).

28. (Make Poverty History, 2006). Of these charities and political action groups, only Nothing but Nets at least is targeting a specific problem. Nothing but Nets wants to supply mosquito nets in an effort to prevent or at least reduce the incidence of malaria.
29. (Easterly, William, 2006).
30. (Elliot, Michael, *et. al.*, 2006), 10 Ways India is Changing the World, p. 27.
31. (Miguel, Edward, 2008), p. 10.
32. (U.S. Committee for Refugees, 2001). See also, (al'Salaam & deWaal, December 6, 2006).
33. (UNWater and FAO, 2007), p. 13.
34. (Donkor, S., 2003). See also, (Hilmy Sally, December 2003), p. 22.
35. (Rosegrant, Mark W., and M. Svendsen, 1993).
36. (WCD, 2000).
37. See, (The World Bank, 2004) and (The World Bank, 2006).

Works Cited

It is the purpose of this Works Cited section to provide the reader with access to most of the materials used to document the themes followed in each of the chapters. This list is far from exhaustive. Had it been a bibliography of works cited, works consulted, or works available, it would be several times longer. One need only consult the web, make a query, and page after page of related entries will appear. As it is, the Work Cited is over 600 entries long.

Many of the entries are web sites. Every effort was made to avoid those sites with an agenda, for example, blogs, politically motivated sites, etc., such as Greenpeace. The sites of major organizations, like the UNEP and FAO, have been used extensively. Likewise, every effort has been made to obtain copies of the documents cited herein, many of which are available as PDF files and are free to download. This is especially true of most development agencies and organizations. Some private organizations, however, are somewhat more parochial, wishing to profit from their various reports and publications, or at least recover some of the costs associated with them.

Often, data or quotes of others have been attributed by reference. While it may be academically permissible to do so, every effort has been made to track down the original information or quote source, to verify each for content and context. It will be admitted, sometimes original sources can be elusive but with persistence, the original sources normally can be found. It must be confessed, some reference librarians will come to cringe when they lay eyes on you, after a while. Reference librarians can be, on the other hand, some of the most resourceful and helpful people a researcher can ever want to meet.

Abel, Martin E. (1971). *Differential Rates of Growth in Rural Incomes Resulting from Specific Government Policies Lie the New Agricultural Strategy, Staff Paper 71-8.* Department of Agricultural and Applied Economics, University of Minnesota.

Acharya, Sanjaya. (2004). Measuring and Analyzing Poverty (With A Particular Reference To The Case Of Nepal). *The European Journal of Comparative Economics , 1* (2), 195-215.

Acoustic Nerve. (2007, June 30). *Maithili Speaking People Demand Separate State.* Retrieved August 21, 2007, from http://www.nerve.in/bihar/news:252350071138

ADB. (2006, March 03). *Indonesia: Tsunami Summary.* Retrieved September 01, 2008, from Asian Development Bank: http://www.adb.org/media/Articles/2005/6618_tsunami_impact_Indonesia/default.asp?RegistrationID=guest

Ahmad, Sultan. (2006, September 04). *Initiatives for the Second Green Revolution.* Retrieved June 19, 2008, from Dawn the Internet Edition: http://www.dawn.com/2006/09/04/ebr3.htm

Ahmed, R., S. Haggblade, and T. E. Chowdhury (eds). (2000). *Out of the Shadow of Famine: Evolving Food Market and Food Policy in Bangladesh.* Baltimore: Johns Hopkins University Press.

Ahmed, Raisuddin and Zahurui Karim. (2006). Chapter 6 - Bangladesh: Uncertain Prospects. In P. G. Pardy (Ed.), *Agricultural R&D In The Developing World: Too Little, Too Late?* (pp. 129-154). Washington, D.C.: International Food Policy Research Institute.

Ahmed, Z. (2004, July 22). *Drought Fuels India Farmer Fears.* Retrieved September 01, 2008, from BBC News - UK version - International version: http://news.bbc.co.uk/1/hi/world/south_asia/3916559.stm

Alam, S. (2003). Environmentally Induced Migration from Bangladesh to India. *Strategic Analysis , 27* (3), 422-438.

Albertini, Rudolph von, and Albert Wirz. (1982). *European Colonial Rule; 1880-1914: The Impact of the West on India, South East Asia and Africa.* Greenwood Publishing Group.

Alex, R., J. Prasad, A. Kuruvilla and K. S. Jacob. (2007). Self-Poisoning With Pesticides In India. *The British Journal of Psychiatry, 190*, pp. 274-275.

Ali, A. (11 October 2000). Vulnerability of Bangladesh to Climate Change and Sea Level Rise. *International Day for Disaster Reduction Seminar*. Dhaka.

Ali, I. (March 1994). *Sikh Settlers in the Western Punjab During British Rule*. Lahore University. Lahore: Centre for Management and Economic Research.

Ali, I. (1988). *The Punjab Under Imperialism, 1885-1947*. Princeton: Princeton University Press.

Ali, T. M. (Ed.). (1999). *Civil Wars in Africa : Roots and Resolution*. Montreal: McGill Queen's University Press.

AllExperts. (2008, July 22). *E-choupal*. Retrieved July 22, 2008, from E-choupal Encyclopedia: http://en.allexperts.com/e/e/e/e-choupal.htm

al'Salaam, T., & deWaal, A. (December 6, 2006). *The Sudanese Conflict: Civil War or Genocide?* Cambridge: Harvard Extension School.

AMCOST. (November 2006). *Cairo Declaration*. Cairo: Extraordinary Conference of the African Ministerial Council on Science and Technology, EXT/AU/EXP/ST/13 (II), Rev.1.

Anantha Rama, K.; A. Tsunekawab; D. K. Sahac; and T. Miyazaki. (1999). Subdivision And Fragmentation Of Land Holdings And Their Implication In Desertification In The Thar Desert, India. *Journal of Arid Environments*, *41* (4), 463-477.

Anderson, Luke and Christina Cobb. (2001, August). From the Green Revolution to the Gene Revolution. *The Canadian Friend*, *97* (3), pp. 10-11.

Ankit, Rakesh. (2005, November-December). *Analysis, Modern Zamindari*. Retrieved March 15, 2007, from Himal Southasian: http://www.himalmag.com/2005/november/analysis_8.html

Annamalai, Kuttayan and Sachin Rao. (August 2003). *What Works: ITC's E-Choupal and Profitable Rural Transformation, What Works Case Study*. Ann Arbor: University of Michigan Business School.

Anonomyous. (2002). *Population and Envrionment in India*. Unknown.

Anstey, V. P. (1977). *The Economic Development of India*. London: Orient Longman, Green.

Anupindi, R. (2002-03). *Going Direct to the Farmer: ITC's e-Choupal Initiative*. Retrieved July 21, 2008, from Michigan Business

School Document: http://mba.tuck.dartmouth.edu/digital/Programs/CorporateEvents/SupplyChainThoughtLeaders/session6.pdf

Anwar, J. (2004, January 23). *Arsenic and Uranium in Fertilizer.* Retrieved August 23, 2008, from SOS-Arsnic.Net: http://www.sos-arsenic.net/english/tsp.html,

AQUASTAT. (2008). *Irrigation Water Use Per Country In The Year 2000.* Retrieved August 29, 2008, from AQUASTAT: FAO's Information System on Water and Agriculture: http://www.fao.org/nr/water/aquastat/water_use/irrwatuse.htm

Asia Africa Intelligence Wire. (2003, September 30). *Punjab Tractors Ltd.* Retrieved June 23, 2008, from Access My Library: http://www.accessmylibrary.com/coms2/summary_0286-24405936_ITM?email=wolverine31@r ogers.com& library= Bradford % 20West%20Gwillimbury%20Public%20Library

Asia Pulse News. (2001, December 26). *India Sets World Record For Maize Yield.* Retrieved July 14, 2008, from Access My Library: http://www.accessmylibrary.com/coms2/summary_0286-27251756_ITM

Associated Press. (2007, August 30). *Arsenic in Drinking Water Seen as Threat.* Retrieved December 21, 2007, from <www.newsvine.com/_news/2007/08/30/931411-arsenic-in-drinking-water-seen-as-threat>.

Associated Press. (2005, March 14). *SE Asia Sounds Alarm Over Worst Drought in Decades* . Retrieved September 01, 2008, from The Standard - China's Business Newspaper: http://www.thestandard.com.hk/stdn/std/World/GC14Wd04.html

Ateng, B. (1996). *Chapter 7, Part II: Comparative Advantage And Crop Diversification In Bangladesh.* Retrieved June 14, 2008, from The World Bank, Bangladesh Agriculture in the 21st Century: http://wbln0018.worldbank.org/lo%20web%20sites/bangladesh%20Web.nsf/0/370f3af793c 7c4154625 6711001bb 7c1?OpenDocument

Atta-Krah, K., et. al. (October 2004). *Regional Consultation on Genetic Engineering / GMOs for Development in Eastern and Southern Africa.* IDRA and IPGRI.

Attaran, Amir and Jeffrey Sachs. (2001, January 6). Defining And Refining International Donor Support For Combating. *Lancet*, *357*, pp. 57-61.

AU/NEPAD. (August 2005). *Africa's Science and Technology Consolidated Plan of Action.* African Union and New Partnership for Africa's Development.

AU/NEPAD. (July 2006). *Freedom to Innovate: Biotechnology in Africa's Development. Draft Report of the High Level African Panel on Modern Biotechnology.* African Union and New Partnership for Africa's Development.

Avery, D. T. (August 2002). *World Food Summit Endorses Biotechnology.* Centre for Global Food Issues.

Bahada, Khan, Muhammad Jama, and Hamdullah Azim. (2004). *Effect Of Weeds On Cane Yield And Content Of Sugar Cane.* Retrieved August 19, 2008, from Weed Science Society of Pakistan: http://www.wssp.org.pk/10127.htm

Balaji, C. (2008, August 05). *Five Years Ago On Aug 5, Toxic Pesticides And Insecticides Were Reported In Coca-Cola And Pepsi Co Soft Drinks.* Retrieved August 10, 2008, from Newshead.com - World News Forecast: http://www.newsahead.com/preview/2008/08/05/india-5-august-2008-five-years-ago-toxins-found-in-coke-pepsi/index.php

Banerjee, Abhijit and Lakshmi Iyer. (2005). History, Institutions and Economic Performance: The Legacy of Colonial Land Tenure Systems in India. *American Economic Review , 95* (4), 1190-1213.

Banerjee, S. (2006, August 02). *Soft Drinks Still Unsafe....* Retrieved August 10, 2008, from CSE Issue in Depth: http://www.cseindia.org/misc/cola-indepth/cola2006/cola_press2006.htm

Bangladesh News. (2008, July 12). *Submergence Tolerant Variety To Boost Rice Output.* Retrieved August 03, 2008, from BangladeshNews.Com.db: http://www.bangladeshnews.com.bd/2008/07/12/submergence-tolerant-variety-to-boost-rice-output/

Bastola, T. S. (February 15, 2005). *One Hundred Years of Census Taking in Nepal: The 2011 Census.* Central Bureau of Statistics, Nepal.

Batta, N. (2007, 07). *Judicious Use of Water Resources.* Retrieved from <http://dswcpunjab.gov.in/contents/data_folder/Nidhi_Batta_Paper.htm>.

Bayly, C. A. (1987). *Indian Society and the Making of the British Empire.* Cambridge: Cambridge Univesity Press.

BBC. (2006, November 16). *Bangladesh Cyclone Kills Hundreds* Retrieved September 01, 2008, from BBC News, UK version, International version: http://news.bbc.co.uk/1/hi/world/south_asia/7097678.stm

BBS. (1996). *Agricultural Census.* Dakha: Bangladesh Bureau of Statistics.

BBS. (2006). *Statistics Bangladesh 2006.* Dakha: Bangladesh Bureau of Statistics.

BC Museum. (2008). *3. Agricultural Land-use.* Retrieved August 11, 2008, from Living Landscapes: http://www.livinglandscapes.bc.ca/thomp-ok/env-changes/land/ch3.html

Beck, D.L.; J.L. Miller; and M.P. Hagny. (1999). Successful No-Till On The Central and Northern Great Plains of the United States. *Proceedings of the 7th National Congress of AAPRESID, 18-20 August.* Mar del Plata, Argentina: AAPRESID.

Benen, S. (2005, June 03). *Peak Oil Wrap-up.* Retrieved August 24, 2008, from Washington Monthly - Political Animal: http://www.washingtonmonthly.com/archives/individual/2005_06/006421.php

Bernama.com. (2007, June 27). *Hybrid Rice Strain Fetches US $500,000.* Retrieved July 15, 2008, from Bernama.com: http://www.bernama.com.my/bernama/v3/news_world.php?id=342345

Bertolote, José M., et. al. (2006, Aprio). Suicide, Suicide Attempts And Pesticides: A Major Hidden Public Health Problem. *Bulletin of the World Health Organization (BLT)*, *84* (4), pp. 257-336.

Bhaduri, Amit. (1973). A Study in Agricultural Backwarness Under Semi-feudalism. *Economic Journal*, *83* (329), 120-137.

Bhalla, G. S. (1972). *Changing Structure of Agriculture in Haryana: A Study of the Impact of the Green Revolution.* Chandigarh: Punjab University Press.

Bhalla, G. S., and G. K. Chadha. (1982, May 15). Green Revolution and the Small Peasant: A Study of Income Distribution in Punjab Agricutlure - I. *Economic and Political Weekly* 17 (20).

Bhatty, K. (2006, December 15). *Development-India: Job Guarantee Plan Upsets Rural Pecking Order.* Retrieved January 23, 2007, from IPS: http://ipsnews.net/news.asp?idnews=35859

Bihar, National Informatics Centre. (2006). *The Changing Face of Urban Bihar*. PDF on-line document. Retrieved June 15, 2008, from: http://urban.bih.nic.in/Docs/Changing-Face-of-Urban-Bihar-in-English.pdf

Binayak Sen and David Hulme. (May 2004). Chronic Poverty in Bangladesh: Tales of Ascent, Descent, Marginality and Persistence,The State of the Poorest 2004/2005. In Binayak Sen and David Hulme (Ed.), *Chronic Poverty in Bangladesh*. Manchester: Bangladesh Institute of Development Studies (BIDS), Chronic Poverty Research Centre (CPRC), and Institute for Development Policy and Management (IDPM), University of Manchester.

Biswas, K. (2003, June 22). *Damned if You Do . . .* Retrieved July 05, 2008, from Boloji.com - Environment: http://www.boloji.com/environment/19b.htm

Black, R. (2007, August 30). *World Facing Arsenic Timebomb*. Retrieved August 23, 2008, from BBC News, On-line Eddition, International News: http://news.bbc.co.uk/2/hi/science/nature/6968574.stm

Blum, Justin. (2006, February 18). *Fuel for Growth*. Retrieved July 21, 2008, from Washingtonpost.com: http://www.washingtonpost.com/wp-dyn/content/article/2006/02/17/AR2006021702109.html

Bokor, R. (Spring 2004). *Resistance to Genetic Engineering in Africa*. Retrieved 06 10, 2008, from Synthesis/Regeneration: A Magazine of Green Social Thought — On-line: http://www.greens.org/s-r/34/34-06.html

Bonny, S. (2003, April 15). *Why Are Most Europeans Opposed To GMOs? Factors Explaining Rejection In France And Europe*. Retrieved August 26, 2008, from Electronic Journal of Biotecnology: http://www.ejbiotechnology.info/content/vol6/issue1/full/4/

Borlaug, Norman. (1970, December 11). *Nobel Lecture: The Green Revolution, Peace, and Humanity*. Retrieved August 23, 2008, from Nobelprize.org: http://nobelprize.org/nobel_prizes/peace/laureates/1970/borlaug-lecture.html

Borlaug, Norman. (1965). Wheat, Rust, and People. *Phytopathology*, *55*, 1088-1098.

Boserup, E. (1965). *The Conditions of Agricultural Growth and the Economics of Agrarian Change under Population Pressure*. Chiocago: Aldine.

Boven, Karin; and Jun Morohashi. (eds). (2002). *Best Practices Using Indigenous Knowledge*. The Hague and Paris: NUFFIC and UNESCO/MOST.

Brar, D. K. (n.d.). *Green Revolution and Punjab Ecology: A Temporal-Spatial View*. Retrieved April 28, 2008, from Punjabilok — Agriculture: http://www.punjabilok.com/agriculture/green_revolution_pun_ecology.htm

Brown, K. (. (2005). *Encyclopedia of Language and Linguistics* (2nd ed.). Oxford: Elsevier.

Brown, L. R. (2006, June 15). *World Grain Stocks Fall to 57 Days of Consumption: Grain Prices Starting to Rise*. Retrieved April 26, 2008, from Earth Policy Institute - Eco-Economy Indicators: http://www.earth-policy.org/Indicators/Grain/2006.htm

Brown, Lester R. (2008, June 04). *Falling Water Tables, Falling Harvests* . Retrieved August 09, 2008, from Earth Policy Institute, Book Bytes: http://www.earth-policy.org/Books/Seg/PB3ch04_ss2.htm

Brown, Lester R. (1988). *The Changing World Food Prospect: The Nineties and Beyond, Worldwatch Report No. 85*. Worldwatch Institute.

BTRC. (2008, May). *PSTN Phone Subscribers in Bangladesh*. Retrieved July 14, 2008, from Bangladesh Telecommunications Regulatory Commisson: http://www.btrc.gov.bd/newsandevents/pstn_phone_subscribers/pstn_phone_subscribers_may_2008.php

Burke, Jacob J. and Moench, Marcus H. (2000). *Groundwater and Society, Resources, Tensions and Opportunities:Themes in Groundwater Management for the 21st Century*. New York: Institute for Social and Environmental Transition and UN. Department of Economic and Social Affairs.

Business Line. (2004, January 11). *Punjab Tractor Hold*. Retrieved June 23, 2008, from Sify News: http://sify.com/news/politics/fullstory.php?id=13357432

Business Recorder. (2005, Jaunary 15). *Government Takes U-Turn On Land Reforms Policy - A Recorder Report*. Retrieved May 15, 2008, from Business Recorder: http://brecorder.com/index.php?id=146325&currPageNo=20&query=malik&search=1&term=2004- 10-01|2006-12-31&supDate=

Business Recorder. (2007, Bebruary 19). *News Channel: Increase In Agriculture Yield Vital For Food Security: Study* . Retrieved August 19, 2008, from Pakissan.Com: http://www.pakissan.com/english/news/newsDetail.php?newsid=13086

Calvert, H. (1922). *The Wealth And Welfare Of The Punjab: Being Some Studies In Punjab Rural Economics.* Lahore: Civil and Military Gazette Press.

Carter, Richard and Kamini N. Mendis. (2002). Evolutionary and Historical Aspects of the Burden of Malaria. *Clinical Microbiology Review* , *15*, pp. 564-594.

Cassen, R. H. (1976). *India: Population, Economy, Society.* New York: Holmes & Meier.

CBC News and the Associated Press. (2008, April 22). *'Silent Tsunami' Of Hunger Threatens World: WFP.* Retrieved August 23, 2008, from CBCnews.ca: http://www.cbc.ca/world/story/2008/04/22/un-world-food.html

CBD. (Decembeer 7, 2006). *Compilation of Views and Proposed Operational Texts on Liability and Redress in the Context of the Cartagena Protocol.* Convention on Biological Diversity.

CBS. (2004). *Nepal Living Standards Survey 2003 / 04.* Kathamandu: Central Bureau of Statistics, National Planning Commission, Government of Nepal.

Census of India 2001. (2008, August 12). *Census of India Maps.* Retrieved August 12, 2008, from Census of India Maps - GIS: http://www.censusindiamaps.net/IndiaCensus/Map.htm

Census of India, 2. (2001). *Census of India, 2001, Provisonal Data.* Office of the Registrar General, Government of India.

Central Statistical Organization. (2001). *Statistical Abstract of India, 1971-2001.* New Delhi: Ministry of Statistics and Programme Implementation, Government of India.

CGIAR. (2008, May). *Seasoned for Salt.* Retrieved August 09, 2008, from CGIAR News: http://www.cgiar.org/enews/may2008/story_10.html

Chakraborty, A. K.; Saha, K. C. (1987). Arsenic Dermatosis From Tubewell Water In West Bengal. *Indian Journal of Medical Research* , *85*, pp. 326-334.

Chatterjee, I. A. (Ed.). (2006). *Slavery and South Asian History.* Bloomington: Indiana University Press.

Cheema, G. S. (2001). *Democracy, Governance and Development: A Conceptual Framework [On-line PDF document].* Retrieved 05 16, 2008, from http://unpan1.un.org/intradoc/groups/public/documents/un/unpan005781.pdf

Chefurka, P. (2007, May 13). *Peak Oil, Carrying Capacity and Overshoot: Population, the Elephant in the Room.* Retrieved May 15, 2008, from 321 Energy: http://www.321energy.com/editorials/chefurka/chefurka051207.html

Chowdhury, N., Morris, M., & Meisner, C. (May 26, 1994). *Comparative Advantage of Wheat in Bangladesh: Technological, Economic and Policy Issues.* IFPRI/CIMMYT.

Chowdhury, U. K., et. al. (2000). Groundwater Arsenic Contamination In Bangladesh And West Bengal, India. *Environmental Health Perspectives , 108*, pp. 393-397.

CIA. (2008). *The 2008 World Factbook: Country Profiles.* Washingtron, D.C.: Central Intelligence Agency (CIA).

College of Food, Agricultural and Natural Resource Sciences, University of Minnesota. (Date Unknown). *Political Aspects of the Green Revolution:.* Retrieved June 19, 2007, from Norman Borlaug Through the Years: http://www.cfans.umn.edu/printview/Political_Aspects_of_the_Green_Revolution.html

Committee on Energy and Commerce. (December 7, 2005). *Hearing Before The Subcommittee On Energy And Air Quality, Serial 109-41.* Washington, D.C.: U.S. Government Printing Office.

Conway Gordon, Lele U, Peacock J, and Piñeiro M. (1994). *Sustainable Agriculture For A Food-Secure World.* Washington, D.C.: Consultative Group on International Agricultural Research (CGIAR).

Conway, G. (1997). *The Doubly Green Revolution: Food for All in the 21st Century.* New York: Penguin Books.

Conway, Matt. (2007, August 7). *Ethanol Fuel - The Controversy Behind It.* Retrieved July 21, 2008, from AboutMyPlanet: http://www.aboutmyplanet.com/alternative-energy/ethanol-fuel/

Cosgrove, B. andF. R. Rijsberman. (2000). *World Water Vision: Making Water Everybody's Business.* London: World Water Council, Earthscan Publications Ltd.

Critchfield, R. (1971, May 02). *It's a Revolution All Right.* Retrieved June 28, 2008, from APF Newsletter of Richard Crithfield: http://www.aliciapatterson.org/APF001970/Critchfield/Critchfield16/Critchfield16.html

Crutchfield, J. (2008, July 11). *India Cotton: Record Crop Remains Forecast for 2008 / 09.* Retrieved July 14, 2008, from World Agricultural Production - July 2008;USDA FAS International Production Assessment Branch reflects official USDA estimates released in the World Agricultural Supply and Demand Estimates (WASDE-460) : http://www.thecattlesite.com/articles/1550/world-agricultural-production-july-2008

CSE Press Releases. (2003c, August 21). *Government Confirms Pesticides in Soft Drinks.* Retrieved August 11, 2008, from CSE Press Releases: http://www.cseindia.org/AboutUs/press_releases/press_20030821.htm

CSE Press Releases. (2003a, December 16). *Pepsico Backs Out in Court.* Retrieved August 10, 2008, from CSE Press Releases: http://www.cseindia.org/AboutUs/press_releases/press_20031216.htm

CSE Press Releases. (2003b, August 13). *Suopreme Court Refuses to Entertian Coke Petition.* Retrieved August 10, 2008, from CSE Press Releases: http://www.cseindia.org/AboutUs/press_releases/press_20030813.htm

CSE. (1999). *The Citizen's Fifth Report.* Delhi: Centre for Science and Environment.

Cunningham, J. D. (1853). *History of the Sikhs, From Origin of the Nation to the Battles of the Sutlej.* (2. Edition, Ed.) London: John Murray [On-line digital copy of original].

DAC. (May 1996). *Shaping the 21st Century: The Contribution of Development Co-operation.* Organization for Economic Co-Operation and Development (OECD), Development Assistance Committee(DAC).

Daga, Anshuman. (2002, March 06). *India's "Poor-Friendly" Simputer Set For May Launch.* Retrieved May 15, 2007, from Ciol.com - A Reuter's Online Artacle: http://www.ncoretech.com/products/ia/simputer/newsroom/news/pdf/ciol6mar2002.pdf

Dahal, N. (2005, August). *Perceptions of Climate Change in the Himalayas.* Retrieved June 30, 2008, from Tiempo Climate Change Bulletin: www.tiempocyberclimate.org/newswatch/

Dahlberg, K. A. (1979). *Beyond the Green Revolution: The Ecology and Politics of Agricultural Development.* New York: Plenum Press.

Daily Times. (2004, September 1). *UNDP Provides $ 0.56m Against Desertification.* Retrieved August 30, 2008, from Daily Times: http://www.dailytimes.com.pk/default.asp?page=story_1-9-2004_pg7_41

Dandekar, V. M., and Nikantha Rath. (1971, January). Poverty in India, I & II. *Economic and Political Weekly*, *6* (1 & 2), pp. I - 25-49 and II - 106-146.

Darling, M. L. (1931). *The Punjab Peasant in Prosperity and Debt.* (3. Edition, Ed.) London: Oxford University.

Derpsch, R. (1999). Expansión mundial de la SD y avances tecnológicos. *In Proceedings of the 7th National Congress of AAPRESID, 18-20 August.* Mar del Plata, Argentina: AAPRESID.

Dey, A. (2005, November 4). *The Indian Economy Blog.* Retrieved April 28, 2008, from 1.3.5 Hunger in India — Basic Questions, Miscellaneous: http://indianeconomy.org/2005/11/04/hunger-in-india/

Dilley, Maxx; et. al. (2005). *Natural Disaster Hotspots: A Global Risk Analysis.* Washington, D.C.: The World Bank.

Directorate of Economics & Statistics. (2005). *Year-wise Irrigation Statistics, 2003-04.* New Delhi: Government of India, Directorate of Economics & Statistics.

Dixon, J and A. Gulliver. (2001). *Farming Systems and Poverty: Improving Farmers' Livelihoods in a Changing World.* Rome and Washington, D.C.: FAO and World Bank.

Dixon, John A.; Aidan P. Gulliver, with David Gibbon. (2001). *Farming Systems and Poverty – Improving Farmer's Livelihoods in a Changing World.* Rome and New York: Food and Agriculture Organization of the United Nations and The World Bank.

Dogra, B. (1984). *Empty Stomachs and Packed Godowns: Aspects of the Food System in India.* New Delhi: Bharat Dogra .

Donkor, S. M. K. (2003). Development Challenges of Water Resource Management in Africa. *African Water Journal - Pilot Edition*, *1*, 1-19.

Dorjee, Kinlay; Sumiter Broca; and Prabhu Pingali. (July 2003). *Diversification in South Asian Agriculture: Trends and Constraints, ESA Working Paper No. 03-15.* Rome: Agricultural and Development Economics Division,The Food and Agriculture Organization of the United Nations.

Doro, Marion E. and Newell Maynard Stultz . (1970). *Governing in Black Africa* . Ann Arbor: University of Michigan Press.

Dow, Kirstin; Edward R. Carr; Annelieka Douma;Gouyi Han; and Karl Hallding. (2005). *Linking Water Scarcity to Population Movements From Global Models to Local Expieriences* . Stockholm: Stockholm Environmental Institute, Poverty and Vulnerability Programme.

Dregne, H. E. (1986). Desertification of Arid Lands. In F. A. El-Baz (Ed.), *Physics of Desertification* (pp. 4-34). Dordrecht, The Netherlands, The Netherlands: Martinus, Nijhoff.

Dregne,Harold E. (1983). *Desertification of Arid Lands.* New York: Taylor & Francis.

Duvick, D. N. and K. G. Cassman. (1999). Post–Green Revolution Trends in Yield Potential of Temperate Maize in the North-Central United States. *Crop Science* , *39* (November-December), 1622–1630.

East, W. G. (1965). *The Geography Behind History.* New York: The Norton Library - W.W. Norton and Company, Inc.

Easterbrook, G. (1997, January). *Forgotten Benefactor of Humanity.* Retrieved August 19, 2008, from The Atlantic Online: http://www.theatlantic.com/issues/97jan/borlaug/borlaug.htm

Easterly, William. (2006, February 16). *The West Can't Save Africa.* Retrieved September 09, 2008, from Washingtonpost.com: http://www.washingtonpost.com/wp-dyn/content/article/2006/02/12/AR2006021201150.html

EB/DoE. (2004, December 16). *US Dept Of Energy Office Supports Peak Oil Theory.* Retrieved August 27, 2008, from Energy Bulletin: http://www.energybulletin.net/node/3664

Economist.com. (2008, February 21). *The Next Green Revolution.* Retrieved August 23, 2008, from Economist.com-Business-Agricutlure: http://www.hexima.com.au/pdf_files/articles/Green_Revolution-Economist.pdf

Ehrlich, P. R. (1968). *The Population Bomb.* New York: Ballantine Books.

Ekboir, J. (2002). *CIMMYT World Wheat Overview and Outlook 2000-2001: Developing No-till Packages for Small-Scale Farmers.* Mexico, D.F.: CIMMYT.

Ekboir, J.M., K. Boa, A.A. Dankyi. (2001). *Impact of No-till Technologies in Ghana, Working Paper*. Mexico, D.F.: CIMMYT, Economics Program. Elliot, Michael, et. al. (2006, 07 03). India Awakens: India Inc. (M. Elliot, Ed.) *Time*, pp. 22-32.

Elliot, Michael, et. al. (2006, 07 03). India Awakens: India Inc. (M. Elliot, Ed.) *Time*, pp. 22-32.

eLiteral. (2006). *Payment Gateway India (TRANSECUTE)*. Retrieved September 16, 2007, from eLiteral: http://services.eliteral.com/payment-gateway-india/

Em-Dat: Emergency Events Database. (2008). *Em-Dat Database: Trends and Relationships Period 1900-2007*. Retrieved July 06, 2008, from Natural Disasters, The OFDA/CRED International Disaster Database – www.emdat.be, Université Catholique de Louvain, Brussels (Belgium).: http://www.emdat.be/Database/Trends/trends.html

Encore Software. (2008, January 27). *Simputer*. Retrieved July 22, 2008, from Encore Software: http://www.ncoretech.com/products/ia/simputer/index.html

Energy Bulletin. (2008, July 17). *Peak Oil Primer and Links*. Retrieved August 16, 2008, from Energy Bulletin: http://www.energybulletin.net/primer

Engdahl, F. W. (2007b, December 04). *Doomsday Seed Vault in the Arctic*. Retrieved August 11, 2008, from Global Research.ca — Centre for Research on Globalization: http://www.globalresearch.ca/index.php?context=va&aid=7529

Engdahl, F. W. (2007a). *Seeds of Destruction: The Hidden Agenda of Genetic Manipulation*. Montreal: Global Research.

Engel, Ernst. (1857, 2. edition, 1896, s.28-29)). *Die Productions und Consumptions-verhaltnisse des Königsreiche Sachsen*.

Engel, Ernst. (1895). Die Lebenskosten Belgischer Arbeiter-Familien Fruher and jetzt. *International Statistical Institute Bulletin, 9*, 1-74.

Engel, Ernst. (1857). Die Productions- und Consumptionsverhaeltnisse des Koenigsreichs Sachsen. *Zeitschrift des Statistischen Bureaus des Koniglich Sachsischen Ministeriums des Inneren* (8 & 9).

Engineer, M. H. (February 22, 2008). *Adjusting the Human Development Index for Morbidity*. http://web.uvic.ca/~menginee/mypapers/HDIwithMortality.pdf.

Ernest L. Molua, E. L. (March 2002). *The Future of Agriculture in Sub-Saharan Africa: Challenges and Agenda for Action.* On-line PDF.

Evenson, R. E. (2005). The Green Revolution and the Gene Revolution in Pakistan: Policy Implications. *The Pakistan Development Review , 44* (4, Part I).

FAI. (1972). *Rice.* New Delhi: Fertilizer Association of India.

FAI/ICAR. (1974). *Soils of India.* Delhi: Fertilizer Association of India and Indian Council of Agricultural Research.

FAO. (2008a, July 2). *About 50 million more hungry people in 2007.* Retrieved August 4, 2008, from FAONewsroom: http://www.fao.org/newsroom/en/news/2008/1000866/index.html

FAO. (2008b, July 3). *About 50 Million More Hungry People In 2007 Due To High Food Prices.* Retrieved August 24, 2008, from Hunger Notes: http://www.worldhunger.org/articles/08/global/no_hungry.htm

FAO. (2003). *Agriculture, Food and Water.* Food and Agriculture Organization of the United Nations and the UN Water Assessment Programme.

FAO. (2002). *FAOSTAT Data Base.* Rome: Food and Agricultural Organisation.

FAO. (2006e). *FAOSTAT Statistical Database.* Rome: Food and Agriculture Organization of the United Nations.

FAO. (September 2005). *Food Security and Agricultural Development in Sub-Saharan Africa.* New York: Food and Agriculture Organization.

FAO. (2006g, November 29). *Livestock A Major Threat To Environment.* Retrieved July 21, 2008, from FAONewroom: http://www.fao.org/newsroom/en/news/2006/1000448/index.html

FAO. (2006a). *Livestock's Long Shadow: Environmental Issues and Options.* Rome: Food and Agriculture Organizaton of the United Nations.

FAO Newsroom. (2007, June 13). *Lesotho Faces Deep Food Crisis After One of Its Worst Droughts In 30 Years.* Retrieved September 01, 2008, from FAONewsRoom: http://www.fao.org/newsroom/en/news/2007/1000597/index.html

FAO. (1996, April 26). *Press Release 96/9 — State of the World's Plant Genetic Resources.* Retrieved August 11, 2008, from State of the World's Plant Genetic Resources: http://www.fao.org/WAICENT/OIS/PRESS_NE/PRESSENG/H8F.HTM

FAO. (2006c, September 05). *Record Rice Yields in Egypt.* Retrieved July 14, 2008, from FAONewsroom: http://www.fao.org/newsroom/en/news/2006/1000387/index.html

FAO. (2002). *Reducing Poverty and Hunger, the Critical Role of Financing for Food, Agriculture, and Rural Development.* New York: World Food Program & Food and Agriculture Organization of the United Nations.

FAO. (October 2007). *Selected Indicators of Food and Agricultural Development in the Asia-Pacific Region,1996-2006.* Bangkok: Food and Agriculture Organization of the United Nations(FAO), Regional Office for Asia and the Pacific.

FAO. (2006b). *State of Food Insecurity in the World.* Rome: Food and Agriculture Organization of the United.

FAO. (2006d). *State of Food Insecurity in the World.* Rome: Food and Agriculture Organization of the United Nations.

FAO. (2007). *The State of Food and Agricultue.* Rome: Food and Agriculture Organization of the United Nations.

FAO. (2008). *The Statc of Food and Agriculture in Asia and the Pacific Region, 2008.* Bangkok: Food and Agricultural Organization of the United Nations, Regional Office for Asia and the Pacific.

FAO. *Water at a Glance: The Relationship Between Water, Agriculture, Food Security And Poverty.* New York: Food and Agricultdure Organization of the United Nations, FAO Water.

FAO. (1997). *Water Resources of the Near East Region: A Review.* Rome: Food and Agriculture Organzation of the United Nation.

FAO. (n.d.). *Women: Users, Preservers And Managers Of Agro-Biodiversity.* Retrieved 05 04, 2008, from FAO: Focus: http://www.fao.org/focus/e/women/Biodiv-e.htm

FAO. (2002). *World Agriculture: Towards 2015/2030. Summary Report.* Rome: Food and Agriculture Organization of the United Nations (FAO).

FAO. (2006f). *World agriculture: towards 2030/2050, Interim Report.* Rome: Food and Agriculture Organization of the United Nations.

FAO. (2008c, August). *World Food Situation: High Food Prices.* Retrieved August 24, 2008, from Food Price Indices, August 2008: http://www.fao.org/worldfoodsituation/FoodPricesIndex/en/

FAO/AGL. (2005, December 12). *India — Severity of Human Induced Soil Degradation.* Retrieved September 06, 2008, from Land and WaterDevelopment Division — National Soil Degradation Maps: http://www.fao.org/landandwater/agll/glasod/glasodmaps.jsp?country=IND&search=Display+map+%21

Farm Press Editorial Staff. (2008, July 29). *Researchers Predict Increase of Drought-Resistant Crops Within 10 Years.* Retrieved September 17, 2008, from Western Farm Press: http://westernfarmpress.com/news/drought-crops-0728/

Fatah, S. (2008, March 24). *Suicide Rate Growing As Debt Cripples India's Farms.* Retrieved July 21, 2008, from The Star.Com: http://www.thestar.com/News/World/article/350058

Faurès, Jean-Marc and Guido Santini (eds). (2008). *Water and the Rural Poor: Interventions for Improving Livelihoods In Sub-Saharan Africa.* Rome: Food and Agirculture Organizaton of the United Nations.

Faye, Bernard; and Palmated Esenov (eds). (19-21 April 2004). *Proceedings of the NATO Advanced Research Workshop on Desertification, Combat and Food Safety. Series 1: Life and Behavioural Sciences, Vol. 362.* Ashgabad: ISO Press and NATO.

Fazl-e-Haider, Syed. (2008, August 28). *Politics Hold Pakistan Economy Hostage.* Retrieved September 05, 2008, from On-Line Asia Times: http://www.atimes.com/atimes/South_Asia/JH28Df02.html

Federal Research Division. (November 2005). *Country Profile: Nepal.* Washington, D.C.: Library of Congress.

Fitgerald-Moore, P. and B. J. Parai. (After 1996). The Green Revolution. *Lectures on Techology.* Calgary, Alberta, Canada: On-line PDF file.

FME. (3-7 December, 2001). *Official Outcomes of the International Conference on Freshwater.* Bonn: Federal Ministry of the Environment (FME).

Freebairn, D. K. (1995). Did the Green Revolution Concentrate Incomes?: A Quantitative Study of Research Reports. *World Development*, *23* (No. 2), 265-279.

Front Line. (2005, July 26). *Seeds of Suicide: India's Desparate Farmers.* Retrieved August 11, 2008, from Frontline World - Rough Cut: http://www.pbs.org/frontlineworld/rough/2005/07/seeds_of_suicid.html

Frontline World. (2005, July 26). *Rough Cut: Seeds of Suicide, India's Desparate Farmers.* Retrieved July 14, 2008, from http://www.pbs.org/frontlineworld/rough/2005/07/seeds_of_suicid.html

Fujisaka, S. and D. Garrity. (1998). Developing Sustainable Food Crop Farming Systems For The Sloping Acid Uplands: A Farmer Participatory Approach. *Proceedings of the Fourth Southeast Asian Universities Agroecosystem Network Research Symposium* (pp. 1982-1993). Khon Kaen, Thailand: International Rice Research Institute.

FWiSpace. (2007, November 1). *World record wheat yield exposes UK growing constraints* . Retrieved July 14, 2008, from Over the Hedge - Arable Barometer farmers' diary: http://www.fwi.co.uk/community/blogs/arablebarometer/archive/2007/11/01/world-record-wheat-yield-exposes-growing-constraints.aspx

Gallup, John Luke and Jeffrey D. Sachs. (2001). The Economic Burden of Malaria. *American Journal of Medical Hygiene* , *64* (1 & 2 S.), 85-96.

Gann, Lewis H., and Peter Duignan. (1967). *The Burden of Empire: A Reappraisal of Western Colonialism South of the Sahara.* Hoover Institute.

Ganzel, B. (2007). *Farming in the 1950s and 60s: India and Pakistan.* Retrieved June 19, 2008, from Wessels Living History Farm: http://www.liv inghistoryfarm.org/farmiginthe50s/crops_16.html

Gardner-Outlaw, T. a. (1997). *Sustaining Water, Easing Scarcity: A Second Update.* Washington, D.C.: Population Action International, Population and Environment Program.

Geyer, H. S. (2006). *Global Regionalizaton: Core Peripheral Trends.* Cheltenham, UK : Edward Elgard Publishing.

Ghimire, R. (2008, June). Environmental Concern In Nepalese Agriculture. *The Journal of Agriculture and Environment* , *9*, pp. 41-45.

Gill, G. J. (2002). *Food Security in Nepal, Working Paper 231.* Overseas Development Institute.

Gill, K. S. (1972). *Wheat Market Behavior in Punjab and Haryana.* Ludhiana: Punjab Agricultural University, Departent of Economics and Sociology.

Gill, S.S. (1988, October 15). Contradictions of the Punjab Model of Growth and Search for an Alternative. *Economic and Political Weekly*.

Gizewski, Peter and Thomas Homer-Dixon. (April 1996). *Environmenntal Scarcity and Violent Conflict: The Case of Pakistan.* Washington, D. C.: American Association for the Advancement of Science and The University of Toronto.

GlobalSecurity.Org. (2008). *Insurgency in Nepal.* Retrieved September 08, 2008, from Seer Sight Intelligence: http://www.globalsecurity.org/military/world/war/nepal_insurgency.htm

GMO Safety. (2008, August 12). *Drought-tolerant Wheat: "Promising Results".* Retrieved September 17, 2008, from GMO Safety - Field Trials in Australia: http://www.gmo-safety.eu/en/news/654.docu.html

Gohil, J. (2004, January 18). *e-Choupal.* Retrieved May 23, 2007, from The Desi Flavour: http://jgohil.typepad.com/desiflavor/2004/01/echoupal.html

GoI (Raj). (1904). *Chenab Colony Gazetteer.* Government of India.

GoI (Raj). (1915). *Chenab Colony Settlement Report.* Government of India.

Golden Rice Humanitarian Board. (2008). *History of the Golden Rice Programme: The Road to the Farm is Bumpy.* Retrieved September 27, 2008, from Goldenrice.org: http://www.goldenrice.org/Content1-Who/who2_history.html

Golden Rice Humanitarian Board. (2007). *The Importance of Micronutrients.* Retrieved September 27, 2008, from Golden Rice - Golden Rice.org: http://www.goldenrice.org/Content3-Why/why1_vad.html

GoP. (n.d.). *Chapter-1 Introduction — PDF File.* Retrieved June 12, 2008, from www.pakistan.gov.pk/divisions/environment-division/media/Chapter_1_napchp.pdf -

GoP. (2006). *Economic Survey of Pakistan, 2005-06.* An Accountancy Publicaton. Government of Pakistan (GoP).

GoP. (May 2003). *Pakistan Agricultural Census, 2000.* Islamabad: Agricultural Census Orgaizaiton,Statistics Division.

GoP. (1995). *Pakistan Economic Survey, 1994-95.* Government of Pakistan (GoP).

Gotsch, C. H. (1982). Tractor Mechnization and Rural Development in Pakistan. In K. Ali, *The Political Economy of Rural Development.* Lahore: Vanguard Publicatons.

Government of Bihar. (1973). *Bihar Famine Report, 1966-67.* Patna: Secretariat Press.

Government of India (GoI). (1949). *First Five-Year Plan.* New Delhi: Planning Commission.

GRAIN. (September 2006). *Another Silver Bullet for Africa.* Against the Grain. Retrieved as PDF file from: *www.grain.org/articles_files/atg-7-en.pdf*

Guha-Sapir, P. D. (2004). *Thirty Years of Natural Disasters1974-2003: The Numbers.* Louvain-la-Neuve, Belgium: Centre for Research on the Epidemiology of Disasters and Presses universitaires de Louvain.

Gunnell, David and Michael Eddleston. (2003). Suicide By Intentional Ingestion Of Pesticides: A Continuing Tragedy In Developing Countries. *International Journal of Epidemiology*, 32, pp. 902-909.

Gupta, Anil K. (2004). Origin Of Agriculture And Domestication Of Plants And Animals Linked To Early Holocene Climate Amelioration. *Current Science*, *87* (1), 54-59.

Haggblade, S. (April 2004). *Building on Successes in African Agriculture.* International Food Policy Research Institute.

Hannum, Hurst. (1990). *Autonomy, Sovereignty, and Self-Determination: The Accommodation of Conflicting Rights.* Philadelphia: University of Pennsylvania Press.

Hårsmar, Mats., (ed). (2007). *Agricultural Development in Sub-Saharan Africa.* Stockholm: Expert Group On Devleopment Issues, Ministry of Foreign Affairs.

Hassan, B. (2007, Februray 12). *Wheat Yield And Food Security.* Retrieved aUGUST 31, 2008, from Dawn - The Internet Edition: http://www.dawn.com/2007/02/12/ebr6.htm

Hawking, S. (2001). *The Universe in a Nutshell.* New York: Bantam Books.

Hay, S. I., et. al. (2004). The Global Distribution and Population at Risk Of Malaria: Past, Present And Future. *The Lancet Infectious Diseases*, *4* (6), pp. 327-336.

Headrick, D. R. (1988). *The Tentacles of Progress: Technology Transfer in the Age of Imperialism: 1850-1940.* New York: Oxford University Press.

Heim, Krisiti and Sandi Doughton. (2006, September 13). Gates, Rockefeller Charities Take Aim At African Hunger. *The Seattle Times* . Seattle: The Seattle Times - Local News.

Hill, Ryan and Yemi Katarere. (Unknown). Colonialism and Inequity in Zimbabwe. In *Conserving the Peace: Resources, Livelihoods and Security* (pp. 247-271).

Hilmy Sally, A. I. (December 2003). Agricultural Land and Water Management for Poverty Reduction and Economic Growth in Sub-Saharan Africa: Setting the Research Agenda. *African Water Journal - Pilot Edition , 1 (Pilot)*, 20-29.

Hine, J.L. and S.D. Ellis. (2001). *Agricultural Marketing and Access to Transport Services.* TRL Limited.

History Commons. (2008, August). *Context of December 19, 1999: Monsanto Announces Merger with Pharmacia & Upjohn Inc; Drops Bid for Delta & Pine Land.* Retrieved August 25, 2008, from History Commons: http://www.historycommons.org/context.jsp?item=gm-101&scale=2#gm-101

Hobsbawm, Eric. J. and Terence O. Ranger. (1983). *The Invention of Tradition.* New York: Cambridge Univesity Press.

Holt-Gimenez, Miguel A, Altieri, and Peter Rosset. (October 2006). *Food First Policy Brief No. 12: Ten Reasons Why the Rockefeller and the Bill and Melinda Gates Foundations' Alliance for Another Green Revolution Will not Solve the Problems of Poverty and Hunger in Sub-Saharan Africa.* Oakland: Food First/Institute for Food and Development Policy.

Hoque, A. Y. M. Ekramul, et. al. (2004). *Statistics for Monitoring Attainment of MDGs in Bangladesh.* Dakha: Bangladesh Bureau of Statistics.

Hossain, M., Janaiah, A., & Husain, M. (2003, June 21). Hybrid Rice in Bangladesh Farm-Level Performance. *Economic and Political Weekly* , pp. 2517-2522.

Hossain, Mahabb, et. al. (October 2003). *Rice Research, Technolgoical Progress, and Impacts on the Poor: The Bangladesh Case (Summary Report).* Washington, D.C.: International Food Policy Research Institute.

Howard, Alfred. (1949). *Food Shortage and Agricutlure.* Ahmedabad: Navjivan Publishing House.

Howard, S. (2001, March 12). Retrieved July 11, 2008, from Causes, Effects And Responses To Flooding:The UK And Bangladesh : http://www.hewett.norfolk.sch.uk/curric/NEWGEOG/floods/floodreport.htm

Huq, Saleemul. (ed). (1999). *Vulnerability and Adaptation to Climate Change for Bangladesh.* Boston: Kluwer Academic Publishers.

Hussain, I. (2008, August). *Pakistan: Water Logging, Salinity Eat into Farmers' Yields.* Retrieved August 19, 2008, from Asia Water Wire -Water Currents: http://www.asiawaterwire.net/node/64

Hussain, I. (May 2005). *Pro-poor Intervention Strategies in Irrigated Agriculture in Asia: Issues, Lessons, Options and Guidelines Bangladesh, China, India, Indonesia, Pakistan and Vietnam. Project Final Synthesis Report.* Colombo, Sri Lanka: International Water Management Institute (IWMI).

IAC. (2004). *Realizing the Promise and Potential of African Agriculture: Executive Summary.* InterAcademy Council.

IDRC-CRDI. (2008, 05 10). *Facts and Figures on Food and Biodiversity.* Retrieved 05 04, 2008, from Seed that Give: www.idrc.ca/en/ev-31631-201-1-DO_TOPIC.html - 2008-05-10 - Cached

IDRC-CRDI. (2008, 05 09). *The International Research Development Centre.* Retrieved 05 10, 2008, from IRDC: www.idrc.ca/en/ev-104217-201-1-DO_TOPIC.html - 2008-05-09 - Cached

IEG. (June 2007). *Development Actions and Rising Incidence of Disaster, Evaluation Brief 4.* Washington, D.C.: World Bank, Independent Evaluation Group (IEG).

IFAD. (2006). *Annual Report 2006.* Winnipeg: International Fund for Agricultural Development.

IFAD. (2002). *Assessment of Rural Poverty in Asia and the Pacific.* Rome: International Fund for Agricultural Development.

IFAD. (2001). *Rural Poverty Report 2001: The Challenge of Ending Rural Poverty.* Oxford: International Fund for Agricultural Development (IFAD).

IFFCO. (2004). *Agricultural Statistics at a Glance.* New Delhi: Indian Farmers Fertiliser Co-operative Limited (IFFCO).

IFPRI. (2004). *Ending Hunger in Africa:Prospects for the Small Farmer.* Washington, D.C.: International Food Policy Research Institute.

IISD. (Wednesday, February 7, 2007). Biosafety Policy Brief. *African Regional Coverage Project*, *5* (1).

Ilchman, Warren F. and Norman Thomas Uphoff. (1971). *The Political Economy of Change.* Los Angeles, London: University of California Press.

IMF. (May 2007). *Nepal: Poverty Reduction Strategy Paper Progress Report, IMF Country Report No. 07/176.* Washington, D.C.: Internatonal Monetary Fund.

Indira, A.; M. R. Bhagavan; and I. Virgin. (2005). *Agricultural Biodiversity and Biosafety in India: Expectations, Outcomes and Lessons.* Bangalore and Stockholm: Centre for Budget and Policy Studies and Stockholm Environment Institute.

International Herald Tribune. (2006, February 07). *WTO Rules EU Import Ban Illegal.* Retrieved August 25, 2008, from International Herald Tribune, Business: http://www.iht.com/articles/2006/02/07/business/gmo.php

IRRI. (1996). *Recording and Using Indigenous Knowledge: A Manual.* International Rice Research Institute, Phillipines.

IRRI, J. L. McLean. (2002). *Rice Almanac: Rice Around the World,* (Third ed.). International Rice Research Institute.

ISAAA. (January 2008). *Enhancing Partnerships for Agricultural Development.* Nairobi: International Service for the Acquisition of Agri-Biotech Applications.

Islam, M. Aminul; and M. Fazlul Bari. (2006). *Embankments.* Retrieved July 14, 20078, from Banglapedia: http://banglapedia.org/HT/E_0049.HTM

Islam, M. M. (1997). *Irrigation, Agriculture, and the Raj: Punjab, 1887-1847.* New Delhi: Manohar Publishers.

Islam, N. (ca. 1990). *Flood Control in Bangladesh: Which Way Now?* Retrieved July 7, 2008, from Bangladesh Environment Network: http://www.ben-center.org/flood/flood_essay_ NazrulIslam.htm

Israeli Embassy, U. (1998, May). *Israeli Agriculture: Coping with Growth.* Retrieved July 14, 2008, from Israeli Embassy, U.K.: http://www.israel-embassy.org.uk/web/pages/copegrow.htm

ITC - e-Choupal. (2006, December 08). *The Big Picture.* Retrieved December 08, 2006, from e-Choupal: http://www.itcportal.com/sets/echoupal_frameset.htm

IWMI. (No Date). *The Socio-Ecology of Groundwater in India.* Retrieved August 04, 2008, from IWMI Recent Research: http://www.lk.iwmi.org/home/socio-ecology_groundwater.htm

Iyob, R. (1997). *The Eritrean Struggle for Independence.* . Cambridge: Cambridge University Press.

Jaffrelot, Christophe (ed). (2004). *History of Pakistan and Its Origin.* Antheum South Asian Studies Series.

Jalilian, Hossein and John Weiss. (November 2004). Infrastructure, Growth And Poverty: Some Cross Country Evidence. *Paper prepared for ADB Institute Annual conference on 'Infrastructure and. PDF publicaton*, p. 24. Asian Development Bank Institute.

Jalota, S. K., et. al. (2007). Simulated Crop Yields Response to Irrigation Water and Economic Analysis: Increasing Irrigated Water Use Efficiency in the Indian Punjab. *Journal of Agronomy*, *99*, 1073-1084.

Jha, A. K. (2006, November 06). *Why Bihar Failed to Develop.* Retrieved May 15, 2007, from American Chronicle: http://www.americanchronicle.com/articles/42328

Jha, H. (Unknown). *Caste War in Central Bihar.* Retrieved August 1, 2007, from The Bihar Times, A Passage to Bihar: http://www.bihartimes.com/castwar.html

JICA. (March 2003a). *Country Profile Study on Poverty: Bangladesh.* Japan International Cooperation Agency.

JICA. (March 2003b). *Country Profile Study on Poverty: Nepal.* Japan International Cooperation Agency.

Johnson, E. A. (1970). *The Organization of Space in Developing Countries.* Cambridge, Massachusetts: Harvard University Press.

Jolly, A. (2008, July 22). *Punjab to Initiate Pilot Project on Olive Cultivation over 300 Hectares.* Retrieved August 03, 2008, from The India Post: http://www.theindiapost.com/?p=3483

Jones, E. L.; and S. L. Woolf (eds). (1969). *Agrarian Change and Economic Development: The Historical Problems.* Methuen: London.

Kannan, S. (2008, August 2). *Pepsi and Coke \Under Fire Again.* Retrieved August 10, 2008, from BBC News, U K Version: http://news.bbc.co.uk/2/hi/south_asia/5239758.stm

Kanoute, A. C. (November 2004). Green Genetic Engineering in the light of Environment Protection Health and Poverty Alleviation. *Conference for Biosciences and their Challenges in International Law* . Bonn.

Kapur, Shilpi and Sukkoo Kim. (2006). *British Colonial Institutions and Economic Development in India.* St. Louis: Washington University and NBER.

Karim, R. (September 1992). *Studies on Maize in Bangladesh.* IFPRI, Bangladesh Food Policy Project.

Karki, Arun and David Seddon. (2003). The People's War in Historical Context. In A. Karki, & D. Seddon (Eds.), *The People's War in Nepal: Left Perspectives* (pp. 3-48). Delhi: Adroit Publishers.

Karunakaran, N. (2004, September 10). *Living with Floods.* Retrieved August 20, 2007, from Counter Currents: http://www.countercurrents.org/en-naren_100904.htm

Katsaris, A. (2005, October 1). *Decolonization.* Retrieved April 28, 2008, from Wikipedia: http://en.wikipedia.org/wiki/Image:Colonization_1945.pngvv

Katsaris, A. (2008, April 22). *Image:ColonialAfrica.png.* Retrieved September 01, 2007, from Wikipedia: Colonisation of Africa: http://en.wikipedia.org/wiki/Image:ColonialAfrica.png

Kendie, D. (2005). *The Five Dimensions of the Eritrean Conflict 1941-2004.* Signature Book Printing, Inc.

Khalequzzaman, M. (2004, July 26). *Flood Mitigation Through Best Management Practices.* Retrieved July 09, 2008, from The Daily Star, Vol. 5, No. 60: http://www.thedailystar.net/2004/07/26/d407261501112.htm

Khalequzzaman, Md., Fazlay S. Faruque, and Amal K. Mitra. (2005, August 14). Assessment of Arsenic Contamination of Groundwater and Health Problems in Bangladesh. *International Journal of Environmental Research and Public Health , 2* (2), pp. 204-213.

Khandker, Shahidur R.; Zaid Bakht; and Gayatri B. Koolwal. (April 2006). *The Poverty Impact of Rural Roads: Evidence from Bangladesh, World Bank Policy Research Working Paper 3875.* Washington, D.C.: The World Bank.

Kijima, Yoko; and Peter Lanjouw. (September 2003). *Poverty in India During the 1990s: A Regional Perspective, Working Paper No. 3141.* Washington, D.C.: The World Bank.

Kinderlerer, J. (2001). *Genetically Modified Organisms: A European Scientist's View.* New York: Kinderlerer.

Kiszewski, Anthony, et. al. (2004). A Global Index Representing the Stability of Malaria Transmission. *American Journal of Tropical Medicine and Hygiene*, *70* (5), 486-498.

Kitio, V. (2008, 06 07). *The End of Famine in Africa.* Retrieved 06 07, 2008, from PDF on-line document: http://www.africa-ata.org/african_famine.pdf

Kohler, S. (2007). The Green Revolution: Rockefeller Foundation, Case 20. In J. L. Fleishman, J. S. Kohler, & S. Schindler, *Casebook for the Foundation : A Great American Secret* (p. 354). New York: Public Affairs.

Koirala, G.P. and Thapa, G.B. (1997). *Food Security Challenges: Where Does Nepal Stand?, Research Report Series 36.* Katmandu: Winrock International Institute for Agricultural Development.

Kothari, A. (2007). *Traditional Knowledge and Sustainable Development.* Winnipeg: International Institute for Sustainable Development (ISSD).

Krishan, G. (2004, Spring). Demography of the Punjab, 1849-1947. *Journal of Punjab Studies*, *11* (1), pp. 77-89.

Krishna, Vijesh V., N.G. Byju , and S. Tamizheniyan. (2007, May 25). *Integrated Pest Management In Indian Agriculture: A Developing Economy Perspective.* Retrieved June 13, 2007, from University of Minnesota, Radcliffe's IPM World Textbook: http://ipmworld.umn.edu/chapters/Krishna.htm

Krishnakumar, R. (1999, September-October). *Flood Management: The Kosi Untamed.* Retrieved April 30, 2007, from Frontline, Volume 20, No. 16: http://www.hindu.com/fline/fl1620/16200650.htm

Kuhnen, F. (1971). *Agricultural Supply, Marketing and Processingin Asia and their Relation to Other Institutions and Services Supporting the Agricultural Producer.* Berlin: German Foundation for Developing Countries.

Kuhnen, F. (1990): What is Agriculture: Need for a New Paradigm. *Journal of Rural Deveopment*, *13*, 1-8.

Kumar, S. S. (2005, October). *Award for e-Choupal.* Retrieved May 13, 2007, from DEVELOPMENT GATEWAY AWARD 2005: http:/ /www.i4donline.net/oct05/dgaward.pdf

Ladha, J. K., et. al. (2003). How Extensive are Yield Declines in Long-term Rice-Wheat Experiments in Asia? *Field Crop Research , 81,* 159-180.

Lahmeyer, J. J. (2002, February 02). *Population Statistics.* Retrieved 05 02, 2008, from Congo [Kinshasa]: http:// www.populstat.info/Africa/congokic.htm

Lahmeyer, J. J. (2003, December 09). *Population Statistics.* Retrieved 05 02, 2008, from South Africa: http://www.populstat.info/ Africa/safricac.htm

Lahmeyer, J. J. (2003, July 23). *Population Statistics.* Retrieved 05 02, 2008, from Sudan: http://www.populstat.info/Africa/ sudanc.htm

Lahmeyer, J. J. (2003, July 27). *Population Statistics.* Retrieved 05 02, 2008, from Zimbabwe: http://www.populstat.info/ Africa/zimbabwc.htm

Lahmeyer, J. J. (2003, July 19). *Population Statistics.* Retrieved 5 2, 2008, from Pakistan: http://www.populstat.info/Asia/ pakistac.htm

Lahmeyer, J. J. (2003, July 23). *Population Statistics.* Retrieved 05 02, 2008, from Sudan: http://www.populstat.info/Africa/ sudanc.htm

Lahmeyer, J. J. (2004, December 3). *Population Statistics.* Retrieved May 2, 2008, from Bangladesh: http://www.populstat.info/ Asia/bangladc.htm

Lahneyer, J. J. (2003, May 18). *Population Statistics.* Retrieved 95 02, 2008, from Mali: http://www.populstat.info/Africa/ malic.htm

Lall, R. R. (2007?). *A Petition for Separate Mithila State (In Hindi).* Retrieved August 14, 2008, from Knowing How to Know: http://www.petitiononline.com/MITHILA/petition.html

Langkau, Maike, Eva Schlecht, and Andreas Buerkert. (October 9-11, 2007). Abstract of: Assessing Agricultural Sustainability and Food Security in Nagaland (N.E.-India). *"Utilisation of diversity in land use systems: Sustainable and organic approaches to meet human needs.* Tropentag.

Lear, S. (2005, December 6). *Specialist: For Wheat Yield Gains, Try To Be More Understanding.* Retrieved July 15, 2008, from Purdue University News: http://www.purdue.edu/UNS/html3month/2005/051206.Conley.wheat.html

Leddy, G. (2002). *Unknown*. Berkeley, California.

Li Ching, Lim and Jonathan Matthews. (2004). *GM Crops Have Failed.* Retrieved September 17, 2008, from ISIS - The Institute of Science in Society: http://www.mindfully.org/GE/GE3/GM-Crops-Have-Failed.htm; See also, http://www.i-sis.org

Lickacz, J., and D. Penny. (2001, May 30). *Soil Organic Matter.* Retrieved August 08, 2008, from Alberta Agriculture and Rural Development (AARD): http://www1.agric.gov.ab.ca/$department/deptdocs.nsf/all/agdex890?opendocument

Limao, N. and A.J. Venables. (1999). *Infrastructure, Geographical Disadvantage and Transport Costs.* London: Mimeo. Department of Economics London School of Economics.

Limbu, R. (1995, May 8). *Enmvironment, Inter Press Services (IPS), Down the Kosi - High Dreams and Real Fears.* Retrieved July 12, 2008, from Panos South Asia: http://www.panossouthasia.org/Left_read.asp?leftStoryId=66&leftSectionId=3

Lipton, Michael; and Richard Longhurst. (1985). *Modern Varieties, International Agricultural Research, and the Poor, Study Paper No. 2.* Washington, D.C.: Consultative Group on International Agricultural Research (CGIAR) and the World Bank.

Lobe, Kenton. (February 2007). *A Green Revolution for Africa: Hope for Hungry Farmers?* Winnipeg: Canadian Foodgrains Bank Working Paper.

Logan, Tracey. (2001, September 24). *India's Simple Computer For The Poor.* Retrieved January 30, 2007, from BBC News/Scicence and Technology: http://news.bbc.co.uk/1/hi/sci/tech/1560771.stm

Long, Jessica. (2007, August 12). *WTO Kills Farmers: India Free Market Reforms Trigger Farmers' Suicides.* Retrieved August 04, 2008, from Global Research.ca: http://www.globalresearch.ca/index.php?context=va&aid=6522

M IT. (2002). *Search For Cleaner Water Causes Major Problems With Arsenic In Bangladesh Public Water Supply, Vol. 16, No. 2.* Retrieved August 21, 2008, from Civil and Envronmental Engineering at MIT: http://web.mit.edu/civenv/html/people/alumni_newsletters/winter_02/art5.htm

Mabro, R. (September 2006). *The Peak Oil Theory*. Oxford Institute for Energy Studies.

Magrath, John (ed). (October 2006). *Africa - Up in Smoke 2*. International Institute for Environment and Development.

Mahapatra, Richard. (1999, October 15). *Parched Punjab*. Retrieved July 23, 2007, from Punjabilok: http://www. punjabilok. com/misc/environment/parched_pun.htm

Maithili Parishad. (2004, December 12). *Patna Book Fair: A Voice for Mithila State*. Retrieved August 14, 2008, from Antarrashatriya Maithili Parishad: http://www.geocities.com/ maithili_parishad/meetings/bookfair.html

Majeed, A. (4 April 2005). *Pilot Demonstration Activity for Cooperation Fund for the Water Sector*. Quetta: Abdul Majeed, Head Water Programme, IUCN Pakistan.

Make Poverty History. (2006). *I'm Going To Be The Biggest Pain In His Ass*. Retrieved September 09, 2008, from Make Poverty History: http://archive.makepovertyhistory.ca/e/bono.html?q=e/ bono.html

Malaysia Today. (2005, 06 07). *Malaysia Today*. Retrieved 05 14, 2008, from Nigeria's corruption totals $400 billion : http:// www.malaysia-today.net/Blog-e/2005/06/nigerias-corruption-totals-400-billion.htm

Mammo, T. (1999). *The Paradox of Africa's Poverty: The Role of Indigenous Knowledge, Traditional Practices and Local Institutions-The Case of Ethiopia*. Trenton, New Jersey: Red Sea Press.

MAP. (2008, 06 06). *Data - Downloads - Map - Global P. f. Limits - Landscape*. Retrieved 2008, from Malaria Atlas Project: http://www.map.ox.ac.uk/MAP_PfLimits-landscape.png

MapsofIndia.com. (2006). *Irrigated Area Map - India*. Retrieved September 11, 2008, from Compare Infobase Ltd. 2006, Map XL: http://mapxl.com/indiamaps/irrigated-area.html

Marks, Thomas A. (2004). *Insurgency in Nepal*. Carlisle, PA: Strategic Studies Insistute.

Marks, Thomas A. (2008, April). *The Maoists in Nepal Strategies of Subversion and Subterfuge*. Retrieved September 08, 2008, from Faultlines: Volume 19: http://www.satp.org/satporgtp/ publication/faultlines/volume19/Article2.htm

MaSa. (2007, April 30). *The Great Gene Robbery by Claude Alvarez.* Retrieved August 25, 2008, from Swami's Capers: http://swamiscapers.blogspot.com/2007/04/great-gene-robbery-by-claude-alvares.html

Matangi Maskay, Nephil and Rojan Bajracharya. (2008, June). Rising Food Prices in South Asia: Cyclical or Permanent? *Trade Insight, 4* (2), pp. 20-21.

Mathur, H. G., H. C. Agarwal, Sapna Johnson, and Mirmali Saikia. (March 2005). *Analysis of Pesticide Residues in Blood Samples from Villages of Punjab.* New Delhi: Investigations Centre for Science and Environment.

Mathur, H. G., Sapna Johnson, and Avinash Kumar. (August 5, 2003). *Analysis of Pesticide Residues in Soft Drinks.* New Delhi: Centre for Science and Environment and Pollution Monitoring Laboratory.

Matthews, L. L. (2004). *GM Crops Have Failed* . Retrieved September 17, 2008, from ISIS - The Institute of Science in Society : http://www.mindfully.org/GE/GE3/GM-Crops-Have-Failed.htm; See also, http://www.i-sis.org

Mayuga, J. L. (2007, August 27). Scientists Target Release Of Golden Rice By 2011 To Fight Global Malnutrition. *BusinessMirror (The Philippines)* .

Mazumder, R. K. (2003). *The Indian Army and the Making of Punjab.* Delhi: Permanent Black, Distributed by Orient Longman.

Mbeki, M. (2005). *Perpetuation Poverty in Sub-Saharan Africa.* London: Internation Policy Press.

McFall, J. J. (1991). Populaton: A Lively Introduction. *Population Bulletin , 46* (2), 1-43.

McMullen, A. (2008, January 07). *Forget Oil, The New Global Crisis Is Food.* Retrieved August 27, 2008, from Financial Post - Home: http://www.financialpost.com/story.html?id=213343

Meadows, Donella H., et. al. (1972). *The Limits to Growth.* New York: Signet Books from the New American Library.

Meek, J. (2002, 08 22). *London Review of Books Letters Page.* Retrieved 06 11, 2008, from Everyone has a Voice: http://www.lrb.co.uk/v24/n13/print/meek01_.html

Mehra, Shakuntla. (1981). *Instability in Indian Agriculture in the Context of the New Technology.* New York: International Food Policy Research Institute (IFPRI).

Meisner, Craig; Michael Morris; and Nuimuddin Chowdhury. (1996). *Soil Nutrient Limitations of Intensive Rice-Wheat Cropping Patterns of South Asia.* Retrieved July 13, 2008, from CIMMYT and CIGAR. Dhaka: http://www.css.cornell.edu/faculty/hobbs/File%20posters/Meisner98.pdf

Mellinger, A. D., J. D. Sachs, and J. L. Gallup. (1999). *Climate, Water Navigability, and EconomicDevelopment, Working Paper No. 24.* Cambridge: Center for Internatonal Development at Harvard University (CID).

Miguel, Edward. (2008, May-June). Is it Africa's Turn? Progress in the World's Poorest Region. *Boston Review - New Democracy Forum* , pp. 7-12.

Mike C. (2007, July 31). *Maize / Corn Production by Country, Yield mt / ha.* Retrieved July 14, 2008, from Swivel Preview: http://www.swivel.com/graphs/show/21468299

Ministry of Food, Agriculture & Livestock. (2005). *Agricultural Statistics of Pakistan, 2004 - 2005.* Islamabad: Government of Pakistan.

Mishra, D. K. (2005, July-August). *The Flood That Was, The Flood to Come.* Retrieved August 19, 2007, from Himal South Asian: http://www.himalmag.com/2005/july/analysis_5.html

Mishra, G. (2005, December 20). *Why Suicides by Farmers?* Retrieved July 15, 2008, from Z Net: http://www.zmag.org/znet/viewArticle/4785

MOAC. (2007). *Statistical Information on Nepalese Agriculture.* Kathmandu: AgriBusiness Promotion and Statistics Division Statistical (ABPSD), Ministry of Agriculture and Cooperatives (MOAC), Government of Nepal.

Moazam, M. (1982). The Pattern of Adoption of Green Revcolution Technology and its Effects on Landholdings in the Punjab. In K. Ali, *Pakistan: The Political Economy of Rural Development.* Karachi: Vanguard Publications.

Modi, Vijay. (December 2005). *Improving Electricity Services in Rural India, CGSD Working Paper No. 30.* New York: Center on Globalization and Sustainable Development, The Earth Institute at Columbia University.

Mohanty, S. (2006). *Common Minimum Programme and the Social Sector Investments.* New Delhi: Centre for Budget & Governance Accountability.

Molden, David (ed). (2007). *Water For Food, Water For Life : A Comprehensive Assessment of Water Management in Agriculture.* Sterling, VA: Earthscan; International Water Management Institute; Comprehensive Assessment of Water Management in Agriculture (Program).

Molua, Ernest L. and Mummy W. Rajab. (March 2002). The Future of Agriculture in Sub-Saharan Africa: Challenges and Agenda for Action. *A paper presented at the African Researchers' Association Seminar On "Strategies for Improving the Quality of Life in Africa.* Clemson University.

Moore, Frank J. (1955). *Land Tenure Legislation in Uttar Pradesh.* Berkeley: South Asia Studies, Institute of East Asiatic Studies, University of California.

MoP. (2005). *Discussion Paper on Rural Electrification Policies (Pursuant to Sections 4 & 5 of the Electricity Act 2003).* New Delhi: Ministry of Power, Government of India.

Morris, B. L., et. al. (2003). *Groundwater and its Susceptibility to Degradation: . . . Early Warning and Assessment Report, Series RS o3-3.* Nairobi: United Nations Environent Programme.

Moussa, Sami Zaki. (March 2002). *Technology Transfer for Agriculture Growth in Africa, Economic Research Paper No. 72.* Abidjan, Côte d'Ivoire: African Development Bank.

Murray, C. J. L., and A. D. Lopez. (1997). Mortality By Cause For Eight Regions of The World: Global Burden Of Disease Study. *Lancet , 349,* pp. 1269-1276.

Nakashima, D. (2000). What Relationship Between Scientific And Traditional Systems of Knowledge? In A. M. Cetto (Ed.), *Science for the Twenty-First Century: A New Commitment* (pp. 432-444). Paris: UNESCO.

Navdanya. (2004, July 15). *India's Agrarian Suicides.* Retrieved July 14, 2008, from Navdanya: http://www.navdanya.org/news/04july15.htm

Naylor, R.; H. Steinfeld; W. Falcon; J. Galloway; V. Smil; E. Bradford; J. Alder; and H. Mooney. (2005). Losing the Llinks Between Livestock and Land. *Science , 310,* 1621-1622.

Nelson, M.; R. Dudal; H. Gregersen; N. Jodha; D. Nyamai; J. Groenewol; F. Torres; and A. Kassam. (1997). *Report of the Study on CGIAR Research Priorities for Marginal Lands.* Rome:

Consultative group on international agricultural research, Technical Advisory Committee Secretariat, Food and Agriculture Organisation.

Nelson, S. A. (2006, March 26). *Natural Disasters — River Systems and Causes of Flooding.* Retrieved July 08, 2008, from Earth & Environmental Science - EENS 204: http://www.tulane.edu/~sanelson/geol204/riversystems.htm

Netaid.org. (1999-2007). *Poverty Myth #15.* Retrieved 05 01, 2008, from FACT: Availability Of Food Is Not The Primary Cause Of Hunger.: http://www.netaid.org/global_poverty/poverty-myths/poverty-myth-15.html

Neumann, G. (2007, 02 07). *Corruption FAQ.* Retrieved 05 14, 2008, from Transparency International: http://www.transparency.org/news_room/faq/corruption_faq

Newman, B. (January 2007). *A Bitter Harvest: Farmer Suicide and the Unforeseen Social,Environmental and Economic Impacts of the Green Revolution in Punjab, India.* Oakland, CA: Institute for Food and Development Policy.

NIC, Z. D. (2003). *Agriculture in Zunheboto.* Retrieved August 15, 2008, from National Informatics Centre, Zunheboto District: http://zunheboto.nic.in/files/agri.htm

Nijhawan, I. P. (1975). Socio-Political Institutions, Cultural Values, and Attitudes: The Impact on Indian Economic Development. In J. S. Uppal (Ed.), *India's Economic Problems: An Analytical Approach* (pp. 23-42). New Delhi: Tata-MccGraw-Hill.

NPR. (2008, February 26). *'Doomsday' Seed Vault Opens.* Retrieved August 11, 2008, from NPR World: http://www.npr.org/templates/story/story.php?storyId=38254288

NSSO. (June 2005). *Report 499(59/33/2): Access to Modern Technology for Farming.* Ministry of Statistics and Programme Implementation. New Delhi: National Sample Survey Organizaiton, Government of India.

NSSO. (1999). *Report 451(54/31/3): Cultivation Practices in India.* Government of India, Department of Statistics and Programme Implementation. New Delhi: Natonal Sample Survey Organization, Government of India.

Nwokeabia, H. (January 2006). *Linking Agricultural Innovations to Knowledge Sharing in Africa* . World Bank, IK Notes.

OCHA. (December 2007). *Drought in Africa: 1980 - 2001.* OCHA Regional Office for Central and East Africa.

Ogwang, T. a. (2001). *The Choice of Principle Variables for Computing Human Development Indicators.* University of Regina, Department of Economics, Discussion Paper # 97.

Ojha, T. P. (2007, January 27). *Improved Post-Harvest Technology to Maximize Yield and Mimimize Quantitative and Qualitiative Losses.* Retrieved May 21, 2007, from Grain Storage and Preservation: http://www.unu.edu/unupress/unupbooks/80478e/80478E0d.htm#Grain%20storage%20and%20preservation

Olson, James Stuart; and Robert Shadle. (1991). *Historical Dictionary of European Imperialism.* New York: Greenwood Publishing Group.

OneWorld.Net. (2008, mAY). *Food Security Guide:Millennium Development Goals and Hunger.* Retrieved August 24, 2008, from OneWorld.Net: http://uk.oneworld.net/guides/food?gclid=CP3tj-WOp5UCFR-uQAodFS4mkw#The%20Right%20to%20Food

Organski, A. F. (1968 (Digitized version May 2007)). *World Politics* . New York : Knopf, University of California (Digitized).

Ortega, L. (September 14, 2007). *B3 Desertification.* Bern: Federal Department of Foreign Affairs, Swiss Agency for Development and Cooperation – SDC, Thematic Resources, Division NRU.

Oxfam Canada. (2008, 05 08). *World Hunger Facts 2008: Food for Thought: Food Facts.* Retrieved 05 08, 2008, from Hungry for Change: http://act.oxfam.ca/hungryforchange/inded.htm

Pakissan.com. (2002). *Feudalism Prevails As CAF Approved By Federal Cabinet.* Retrieved Aeptember 05, 2008, from News Channel : http://www.pakissan.com/english/news/2002/june/cabinet.aprroves.caf.shtml

Pandher, S. (2006, 07 06). *Crop Rotation Alone Cannot Cause Fall In Water Level.* Retrieved from The Hindu: http://www.thehindu.com/2006/08/05/stories/2006080514150300.htm

Panos South Asia. (2007). *Environment.* Retrieved July 12, 2008, from Panos South Asia: http://www.panossouthasia.org/Left_read.asp?leftStoryId=3&leftSectionId=3

Parayil, G. (1992). The Green Revolution in India: A Case Study of Technological Change. *Technology and Culture* , *33* (No. 4), pp. 737-756.

PARC. (2007). *Wheat Production Trends in Pakistan - PPT Presentation.* Islamabad: Pakistan Agriculdtural Research Council (PARC).

PatnaDaily.com. (2007, February 3). *Security at Bihar-Nepal Border Tight; Government Issues Travel Advisory.* Retrieved July 3, 2008, from PatnaDaily.Com: http://www.patnadaily.com/news2007/feb/020307/security_tight_at_bihar_nepal_border.html

Paudyal, Kamal R., et. al. (2001). *Maize in Nepal:Production Systems, Constraints, and Priorities for Research.* Kathmandu: NARC (Nepal Agricultural Research Council) and CIMMYT (International Maize and Wheat Improvement Center).

Pearce, F. (2003, September 10). *GMO Import Ban Caught In Crossfire.* Retrieved August 26, 2008, from NewScientist: http://www.newscientist.com/article.ns?id=dn4147

Pelum Association and Practical Action . (2005). *The Crisis in African Agriculture.* Practical Action/Pelum Association.

Pingali, P. L. (1990). Institutional and Environmental Constraints to Agricultural Intensification. In G. McNicoli, and M. Cain (Eds.), *Rural Development and Population* (pp. 243-260). New York: Oxford University Press and the Population Council Inc.,.

Pinstrup-Anderson, P., and Schioler, E. (2001a). *Seeds of Contention.* Baltimore: Johns Hopkins University Press.

Pinstrup-Anderson, P., and Schioler, E. (October 2001b). *Seeds of Contention.* Washington, D.C.: Internatonal Food Policy Research Institute.

Planning Commission. (2002). *National Human Development Report 2001.* New Delhi: Government of India.

Population Association of Pakistan. (No Date). *Population of Pakistan.* Retrieved July 31, 2008, from Population Association of Pakistan: http://www.pap.org.pk/statistics/population.htm

Porter, A. (2005, June 10). *'Peak Oil' Enters Mainstream Debate* . Retrieved August 21, 2008, from BBC News, Business, UK Home Version : http://news.bbc.co.uk/1/hi/business/4077802.stm

Postel, Sandra L. (1996). *Dividing the Waters: Food Security, Ecosystem Health, and the New Politics of Scarcity.* Washington, D.C.: WorldWatch Institute.

Postel, Sandra L. (December 1989). *Water for Agriculture: Facing the Limits, Worldwatch Paper 93.* Worldwatch Institute.

Postel, Sandra L. (1998). Water for Food Production: Will There Be Enough in 2025? *BioScience*, *48* (8), 629-637.

Potrykus, I. (2000, October 23). *The Golden Rice "Tale"*. Retrieved September 28, 2008, from AgBioView: http://www.biotech-info.net/GR_tale.html

Prakash, C. (2005, Decembewr 29). *Groups Attack Proposed EU Law on GMOs*. Retrieved aUGUST 26, 2008, from GMO Food for Thought: http://www.gmofoodforthought.com/2005/12/groups_attack_proposed_eu_law.html

Prasad, E. (2003). *Bihar's Flood Survival Mechanism*. Natural and Social Resource Management.

PRB. (August 2007). *2007 World Population: Data Sheet*. Washington, D.C.: Population Reference Bureau.

Press Room. (2001, November 01). *Ccavenue Welcomes Citibank To Its Network* . Retrieved December 15, 2006, from Avenues e-Business: http://www.avenuesasia.com/1_nov_2001.htm

Priest, S. H. (2001). *A Grain of Truth: the Media, the Public,and Biotechnology*. Lanham, MD : Rowman & Littlefield Publishers .

Quadir, I. Z. (2000, February). *Connecting Bangladeshi Villages*. Retrieved July 13, 2008, from http://www. telecommons.com/villagephone/quadir.html

Rahman, M. M. (2004). *The Report of the National Coordinator*. National Maize Coordinator. Retrieved August 14, 2008, from: *www.rwc.cgiar.org/RSCRTCC/2004/Sessions/9/**Coordinator%**20Rpt%20(RW)-Bangladesh.pdf*

Rai, P. S. (2004). *Punjab's Water Dispute*. Retrieved from Witness84: http://wwwwitness84/cp,/water/

Rajab, E. L. (2002). The Future of Agriculture in Sub-Saharan Africa: Challenges and Agenda for Action. Clemson University: African Researchers' Association Seminar On "Strategies for Improving the Quality of Life in Africa.

Rajivlochan, M. (2006). *Suicides: Facts and Possible Policy Interventions*. Pune: Yashwantrao Chavan Academyof Development Administration.

Ramamurthi, Bhaskar. (2002, March 14). *Connecting All Villages in India*. Retrieved July 21, 2008, from n-Logue: http://in3.org/articles/IIT.htm

Ramonet, I. (1998, November). *The Politics of Hunger* . Retrieved August 1, 2008, from Le Monde Diplomatique: http://mondediplo.com/1998/11/01leader

Rao, C. H. H.; S. K. Ray; and K. Subbarao. (1988). *Unstable Agriculture And Droughts: Implications For Policy, No. 47.* Delhi: Institute for Economic Growth, Studies in Economic Development and Planning.

Rashid, A. (2004, July 31). *Comment: Poverty and Land Reform.* Retrieved August 05, 2008, from Daily Times: http://www.dailytimes.com.pk/default.asp?page=story_31-7-2004_pg3_2

Ratha, Dilip and Zhimei Xu. (2008). *Migration and Remittances Factbook, 2008.* The World Bank, Development Prospects Group.

Raup, D. M. (1991). *Extinction: Bad Genes Or Bad Luck?* New York: W.W. Norton and Co.

Ravallion, M. (2000). *On The Urbanisation of Poverty (Mimeo).* Washington, D.C.: The World Bank.

Rediff Money Desk. (2005, August 22). *All About India's Rural Job Guarantee Scheme.* Retrieved December 21, 2006, from Rediff.Com - Business: http://www.rediff.com/money/2005/aug/22spec1.htm

Regmi, Bimal R. and A. Adhikari. (2007). *Human Development Report 2007 / 2008:Country Case Study – Nepal.* Kaski, Nepal: UNDP and Local Initiatives for Biodiversity, Research and Development (LI-BIRD).

Reich, P. F.; S.T. Numbem; R.A. Almaraz; and H. Eswaran. (2008). *Land Resource Stresses and Desertification in Africa.* Retrieved August 30, 2008, from USDA - Natural Resources Conservation Center: http://soils.usda.gov/use/worldsoils/papers/desertification-africa.html

Reilly, W. M. (2007, June 28). *The Challenge Of Desertification.* Retrieved August 31, 2008, from Terra Daily - Climate Science: http://www.terradaily.com/reports/The_ Challenge_ Of_ Desertification_ 999.html

ReliefWeb. (2008, July). *South Asia Regional Maps, Regional and Country Maps.* Retrieved July 03, 2008, from ReliefWeb Map Centre: South Asia: http://www.reliefweb.int/mapc/asi_sth/index.html

Reuters. (2008, Hune 1). *EU Experts Set To Debate Three New GMO Applications.* Retrieved August 25, 2008, from Checkbiotech: http://greenbio.checkbiotech.org/news/2007-04-18/EU_experts_set_to_debate_three_new_GMO_applications/

Reuters. (2000, November 10). *FACTBOX - The How, Where And Cost Of Salinity* . Retrieved August 09, 2008, from Forests.Org: http://forests.org/archive/spacific/thhowwhe.htm

Reuters. (2005, December 22). *Green Groups Fear Gmos Creeping Into EU Organic Law.* Retrieved August 26, 2008, from http://www.futura-sciences.com/newsrss-green-groups-fear-gmos-creeping-into-eu-organic-law_108808_0.php

Reynolds, M.P.; Pietragalla, J.; Braun, H-J. (eds). (2008). *Internatonal Symposium on Wheat Yield Potential: Challenges to International Wheat Breeding.* Mexico, D.F.: CIMMYT (International Maize and Wheat Improvement Center).

RFPD. (2007). *Water, Water Everywhere . . . . ?* Retrieved July 11, 2007, from Water, Rotarian Fellowsip for Population and Development: http://www.rifpd.org/Overview/Predicaments/Environment/Water/water.html

Rizet C. and J. Hine. (1993). A Comparison of the Costs and Productivity of Road Freight Transport in Africa and Pakistan. *Transport Reviews , 13* (No. 2), 151-165.

Rizvi, S. A. (2002, July 08-14). *Corporate Agriculture Farming.* Retrieved September 05, 2008, from Pakistan Economist: http://www.pakistaneconomist.com/issue2002/issue27/f&m3.htm

Rodney, W. (1973). *How Europe Underdeveloped Africa* (From transcript of 6th edition). London and Dar-Es-Salaam: Bogle-L'Ouverture Publications, and Tanzanian Publishing House.

Rohtak, A. K. (2002, December). *Dream Bihar.* Retrieved February 12, 2007, from Hardnews: http://www.hardnewsmedia.com/portal/2005/12/235

Roke. (2006, March 22). *Image: Africa Independence Dates.PNG.* Retrieved August 7, 2008, from Wikipedia: http://en.wikipedia.org/wiki/Image:Africa_independence_dates.PNG

Ronald Laboratory. (2006). *Submergence Tolerance* . Retrieved August 03, 2008, from Ronald Laboratory: http://indica.ucdavis.edu/research/research-project-overviews/submergence_tolerance

Rorabacher, J. A. (2008). Gerrymandering, Poverty and Flooding: A Perennial Story of Bihar. *Economic and Political Weekly, 43*(7), 45-53.

Rosegrant, Mark W., and M. Svendsen. (1993). Asian Food Production in the 1990s: Irrigation Investment and Management Policy. *Food Policy , 18* (1), 13-32.

Rosset, P. (2000, March/April). *Lessons from the Green Revolution.* Retrieved from Food First: http://www.foodfirst.org/media/opeds/2000/4-greenrev.html.

Rosset, P. M. (2006). *Food is Different: Why We Must get the WTO Out of Agriculture.* Fernwood Publishing.

Rosset, Peter; Joseph Collins; and Frances Moore Lappe. (2000, March/April). *Lessons from the Green Revolution.* Retrieved September 15, 2007, from Tikkun Magazine: http://nature.berkeley.edu/srr/Alliance/lessons_ from_the_ Green_ revolution.htm

Rotarian Fellowship for Population and Development. (2007, September). *Water, water everywhere . . . ?* Retrieved September 2007, from Water: <http://www.rifpd.org/Overview/Predicaments/Environment/Water/water.html

Rothschild, G.H.L. (1998). Advances in Hybrid Rice Technology: Introduction: IRRI's Role and Vision for Hybrid Rice. In S. E. S.S. Virmani (Ed.), *Advances in Hybrid Rice Technology: Proceedings of the 3rd International Symposium on Hybrid Rice* (p. 443). Los Banos, Philippines: International Rice Research Institute.

Rothschild, S. (2007, August 12). *Corn-Fed Ethanol Production Fuels Controversy.* Retrieved July 21, 2008, from RedOrbit: http://www.redorbit.com/news/science/1031370/cornfed_ ethanol_ production_fuels_controversy/index.html

Royal B. C. Museum. (2006). *Living Landscapes.* Retrieved May 15, 2007, from Agricultural Inputs Market Trends & Potentials in India: http://www.livinglandscapes.bc.ca/thomp-ok/env-changes/land/ch3.html

RUPE. (2006b, December). *Wheat Imports — A Tool for Reshaping India's Agriculture — How the Wheat Crisis of 2006 Was Created, Section III.* Retrieved December 15, 2007, from Aspects of India's Economy, No. 42: http://www.rupe-india.org/42/wheat.html.

RUPE. (2006a, December). *Wheat Imports – A Tool for Reshaping India's Agriculture — Section II. How the Wheat Crisis of 2006 Was Created.* Retrieved August 14, 2007, from Aspects of India's Economy, No. 42: http://www.rupe-india.org/42/crisis.html

Rural Poverty Portal. (2008, January 01). *Rural Poverty in Africa.* Retrieved August 05, 2008, from Rural Poverty Portal: http://www.ruralpovertyportal.org/english/regions/africa/index.htm

Russell, Steven. (2004a). The Economic Burden of Illness for Households in Developing Countries: A Review of Studies Focusing on Malaria, Tuberculosis, and Human Immunodefficiency Virus/ Acquired Immunodefficiency Syndrome. *The American Journal of Tropical Medicine and Hygiene, 71* (2nd Supplement), 147-155.

SAARC. (n.d.). *Current Trends in South Asia.* Retrieved August 31, 2009, from SAARC Coastal Zone Management Centre: http://www.sczmc.org/pages/17

Sachs, J. D. (2005b). *The End of Poverty: Economic Possibilities for Our Time.* New York: Penguin Books.

Sachs, Jeffrey D., et. al. (March 22, 2004 Version). *Ending Africa's Poverty Trap.* Millenium Project, Working Paper, PDF.

Sachs, Jeffrey D., et. al. (April 29, 2004 Version). *Ending Africa's Poverty Trap.* New York: Draft Report.

Sachs, Jeffrey D., et. al. (April 29, 2004 Version). *Ending Africa's Poverty Trap.* Millenium Project, Working Paper, PDF.

Safiuddin, Md., and Md. Masud Karim. (November 2001). *Groundwater Arsenic Contamination in Bangladesh: Causes, Effects and Remediation.* Chittagong: Proceedings of the 1st IEB international conference and 7th annual paper meet, Institution of Engineers.

Saha, Bimal Kumar. (2001). Changing Pattern of Agrarian Structure in Bangladesh: 1984-1996. In A. Abdullah (Ed.), *Bangladesh Economy 2000 Selected Issues* (pp. 73-85.). Dakha: Bangladesh Institute of Development Studies.

Sainath, P. (2007, April 07). *Farm Suicides in India, The Result of Profit Driven "Free Market" Reforms*. Retrieved August 04, 2008, from Global Research.ca: http://globalresearch.ca/index.php?context=va&aid=5296

Sandhu, G.R. (1993). *Sustainable Agriculture: A Pakistan National Conservation Strategy Sector Paper.* Karachi: IUCN-World Conservation Union.

Sanghi, Rashmi. (2001, July). Living in a Chemical Environment — Persistent Organic Pollutants. *Resonance* , 64-73.

Sanyal, Biswapriya. (1982, Fall). How Revolutionary was India's Green Revolution? *South Asia Bulletin*.

Sarkar, R. K., J. N. Reddy, S. G. Sharma and Abdelbagi M. Ismail. (2006, October). Physiological Basis Of Submergence Tolerance In Rice And Implications For Crop Improvement. *Current Science* , pp. 899-906.

Sauer, Carl O. (1952). *Agricultural Origins and Dispersals.* New York: American Geographical Society.

SAWTEE. (2008). *Trade Insight.* (K. Adhikari, Ed.) *4* (2).

Sayre, K. (1998). *Ensuring the Use of Sustainable Crop Management Strategies by Small Wheat Farmers in the 21st Century, Wheat Special Report No. 48.* Mexico, D.F.: CIMMYT.

Schultz, T. (1964 and 1971). *Transforming Traditional Agriculture.* New Haven: Yale University Press.

Schultz, Theodore W. (1964). *Transforming Traditional Agriculure.* New Haven: Yale University Press.

Schwartzberg, Joseph E. (ed). (1978). *A Historical Atlas of South Asia.* Chicago and London: University of Chicato Press.

SDNP Bangladesh. (2004). *Floods 2004.* Retrieved July 5, 2008, from Sustainable Development Networking Programme (SDNP) Bangladesh: http://www.sdnbd.org/sdi/issues/floods_drainage/2004/index.htm

Seckler, e. a. (1998). *World Water Demand and Supply, 1990 to 2025: Scenarios and Issues, Report # 19.* Colombo : International Water Management Institute Research.

Sehgal, R. (2005, May). *Is It Diversify or Perish For Farmers In The Punjab.* Retrieved May 23, 2007, from InfoChange News & Features: http://www.infochangeindia.org/features276.jsp

Sen, A. (1999). Democracy as a Universal Value. *Journal of Democracy , 10* (3), pp. 3-17.

Sen, A. (1990, 08 02). *Public Action to Remedy Hunger.* Retrieved 05 14, 2008, from The Hunger Project: http://www.thp.org/reports/sen/sen890.htm

Sen, A. (1999 [World Press Freedom Day], 05 03). *What's the Point of Press Freedom?* Retrieved from Microsoft online file: www.wan-press.org/IMG/doc/int-en_sen.doc

Sen, A. (1997, July 14). Human Rights and Asian Values: What Lee Kuan Yew and Le Peng Don't Understand About Asia. *The New Republic*. ***217(2-3)*** 1-9, Retrieved as PDF from: http://www.hmb.utoronto.ca/HMB303H/weekly_supp/week-02/Sen_Asian_Values.pdf

Sengupta, S. (2006, September 19). *On India's Farms, a Plague of Suicide* . Retrieved July 12, 2008, from New York Times: http://www.nytimes.com/2006/09/19/world/asia/19india.html

Shah, A. (2008, 03 04). *Causes of Poverty*. Retrieved May 03, 2008, from Global Issues: http://www.globalissues.org/TradeRelated/Poverty.asp

Shah, A. (2008, August 10). *Global Food Crisis 2008*. Retrieved August 27, 2008, from Global Issues: http://www.globalissues.org/article/758/global-food-crisis-2008

Shahzad, I. (2003, May 26). *Confused Priorities On Agriculture*. Retrieved September 05, 2008, from Dawn. the Internet Edition: http://www.dawn.com/2003/05/26/ebr5.htm

Shankari, U. (2007). *Hungry Corps and Seeds of Bondage*. Retrieved August 25, 2008, from ubpages: http://hubpages.com/hub/Hungry-Corps-and-Seeds-of-Bondage

Sharma, Dinesh C. (2004, March 24). *Linux-Based Handheld Debuts In India*. Retrieved July 23, 2007, from CNet.com: http://news.cnet.com/Linux-based-handheld-...-India/2100-1041_3-5181303.html

Sharma, R. K. (1992). *Technical Change, Income Distribution, and Rural Poverty*. Delhi: Shipra Publishers.

Shenoy, B. V. (2008, April 21). *Peak Oil Theory: The Indian Response*. Retrieved August 27, 2008, from Deccan Herald: http://www.deccanherald.com/content/Apr212008/editpage 200804 2063770.asp

Shergill, H. S. (2005). Wheat and Paddy Cultivation and the Question of Optimal Cropping Pattern for Punjab. *Journal of Punjab Studies*, *12* (2), 239-250.

Shiklomanov, I. A. (Ed.). (1997). *Comprehensive Assessment of the Freshwater Resources of the World*. Geneva: World Meteorological Organization.

Shiva, V. (1991, March-April). The Green Revolution in Punjab. *The Ecologist, 21* (2).

Shiva, V. (1992). *The Violence of the Green Revoloution: Third World Agriculture, Ecology and Politics.* New Jersey: Zed Books, Ltd.

Shrestha, A. C. (1999). Maximum Temperature Trends in the Himalaya and its Vicinity: An Analysis Based on Temperature Records from Nepal for the Period 1971 – 94. *Journal of Climate , 12*, pp. 2775-2789.

Sidhu, H. S. (27 July 2002). Crisis in Agrarian Economy in Punjab — Some Urgent Steps. *Economic and Political Weekly , 37* (30).

Simms, A. a. (July 2005). *Africa - Up in Smoke?* IIED.

Simons, P. (2007, April 20). *The Big Dry is Worst Drought in 1,000 Years.* Retrieved September 01, 2008, from TimesOnline: http://www.timesonline.co.uk/tol/news/world/article1680174.ece

Singh, M. (2001). Reflection on Colonial Legacy and Dependency in Indian Vocational Education and Training (VET): A Societal and Cultural Perspective. *Journal of Work.*

Singh, N. K. (2003). *Encyclopedia of Bangladesh.* Arnol Publications Pvt. Ltd.

Singh, P. (1997). *Political Economy of the Punjab: An Insider's Account.* New Delhi: MD Publicatons.

Singh, P. (2008, August 19). *Punjab is Gripped by a Severe Water Crisis (Shortage of Water Leads to Disaster).* Retrieved September 05, 2008, from Punjab — The Land of Five Rivers: http://www.mygoth.com/blog/panjab_blog/index.php?showentry=663

Sinha, K. (2006 , September 25). *UN Report Slams India For Farmer Suicides.* Retrieved July 15, 2008, from The Times of India - India: http://timesofindia.indiatimes.com/articleshow/2021582.cms

Smith, A. (1937). *The Wealth of Nations* (Modern Library Edition). New York: The Modern Library.

Smith, J. (2008, June 10). *EU To Propose More Flexible GMO Food Imports.* Retrieved August 25, 2008, from Checkbiotech: http://greenbio.checkbiotech.org/news/2008-06-10/EU_to_propose_more_flexible_GMO_food_imports/

Smith, M.; Fereres, E.; and A. Kassam. (3-5 December 2001). Crop Water Productivity Under Deficient Water Supply. *Expert Meeting on Crop Water Productivity Under Defi cient Water Supply.* Rome.

Snow, R. W., et. al. (2005). The Global Distribution of Clinical Episodes of Plasmodium Falciparum Malaria. *Nature* , *434* (10 March), pp. 214-217.

SourceWatch. (2008, June 05). *Monsanto and the Roundup Ready Controversy.* Retrieved August 27, 2008, from SourceWatch: http://www.sourcewatch.org/index.php? title= Monsanto_ and_the _Roundup_Ready_Controversy

South Florida Sun Sentinel. (2007, July 06). *Salt Water Intrusion Threatens To Taint Coastal Wells In South Florida* . Retrieved September 06, 2008, from Tallahassee.Com: http:// tallahassee.com/legacy/special/blogs/2007/07/salt-water-intrusion-threatens-to-taint.html

Spencer, D. (September 2001). *Will They Survive? Prospects for Small farmers in sub-Saharan Africa.* Bonn: International Conference Organised by the International Food Policy Research Institute (IFPRI).

Staff Writers. (2006, September 30). *Gene Switch Makes Crops Drought-Resistant When Needed.* Retrieved September 17, 2008, from Terra Daily - Farm News: http://www.terradaily.com/reports/ Gene_Switch_Makes_Crops_Drought_Resistant_When_Needed_999.html

Stakman, W. C., Richard Bradfield, and Paul C. Mangelsdorf. (1967). *Campaigns Against Hunger.* Cambridge: Harvard University Press.

Stancich, R. (2008, February 14). *GM Food Special Report: Crops That Survive Climate Change.* Retrieved September 17, 2008, from Climate Change Corp - Technology: http://www. climate changecorp. com/content.asp?ContentID=5157

Staples, E. S. (1992). *Forty Years: A Learning Curve: The Ford Foundation Programs in India,1952-1992.* New Delhi: The Ford Foundation.

States Bureau. (2008, July 23). *Punjab Gears Up To Cultivate Olives.* Retrieved August 1, 2008, from The Financial Express: http:/ /www.financialexpress.com/news/Punjab-gears-up-to-cultivate-olives/339041/

StatPub.com. (2004, January 30). *India Fertilizer Output Exceeds Target.* Retrieved June 14, 2007, from StatPub.com: http:/ /www.statpub.com/open/77806.html

Steil, M. (2001, March 01). *The Ethanol Equation.* Retrieved July 21, 2008, from Minnesota Public Radio: http://news.minnesota.publicradio.org/features/2005/03/21_steilm_ethanolenergy/

Stronach, B. (2006, June 6). Solution For Africa's Food Crisis. *Toronto Star.*

Sunday Times/Sachs. (2005a, June 17). *Myth Vs. Fact: Is Africa The Lost Continent?* Retrieved September 03, 2008, from Straight Up - Jan Herman, The Arts Journal, June 2005 Archives: http://www.artsjournal.com/herman/2005/06/

Super Admin. (2006, September 06). *Bangladesh and its Agriculture Sector.* Retrieved September 19, 2008, from ReportBD.Com - Reports, Assignment, Case Study: http://www.reportbd.com/articles/25/9/Bangladesh-and-its-Agriculture-Sector/Page9.html

Swedish fusilier. (2008, April 22). *Image:ColonialAfrica.png.* Retrieved September 11, 2008, from Wikipedia : http://www.google.ca/imgres?imgurl=http://www.solarnavigator.net/geography/geography_images/africa_ colonial_geography.png&imgrefurl=http://www. solarnavigator.net/geography/africa.htm&h=571&w=509&sz= 10&tbnid =QAsrd Ry93 nAJ::&tbnh =134&tbnw=119&prev=/images%3F

Talbot, I. A. (1991). British Rule in Punjab, 1849-1947: Characteristics and Consequences. *The Journal of Imperial and Commonwealth History*, *19* (2), 203-222.

Talbot, I. A. (1996). *Khizr Tiwana, The Punjab Unionist Party and the Partition of India.* Surrey: Routledge.

Talbot, I. A. (2004, Spring). The Punjab Under Colonialism: Order and Transformation in British India. *Journal of Punjab Studies*, *14* (1), pp. 3-10.

Tannahill, R. (1988). *Food in History.* New York: Three Rivers Press, Crown Publishing Group.

Tatla, Darshan Singh. (1995). Sikh Free and Military Migration During the Colonial Period. In R. Cohen (ed), *The Cambridge Survey of World Migration* (pp. 69-73). Cambridge: Cambridge University Press.

Tavares, N. (2005, October 1). *Image:Colonization 1945.png.* Retrieved May 15, 2008, from Wikipedia: http://en.wikipedia.org/wiki/Image:Colonization_1945.png

ThaindianNews.Com. (2008, July 23). *Punjab to Push for Olive Cultivation with Israeli Help*. Retrieved August 03, 2008, from Thaindian News: http://www.thaindian.com/newsportal/business/punjab-to-push-for-olive-cultivation-with-israeli-help_10075043.html

The Global Fund. (2005). *JIV/AIDS, Tuberculosis and Malaria:The Status and Impact of the Three Diseases*. The Global Fund.

The Hunger Site. (2008, May 06). *International Hunger Facts*. Retrieved May 06, 2008, from The Hunger Site: About Hunger: http://www.thehungersite.com/clickToGive/about thecause. faces?siteID=1&link=ctg ths abutthecause from home maincolumn

The World Bank. (June 30,1995). *Bangladesh: Agricultural Growth with Diversification: Prospects and Issues. Background Papers*. New York: The World Bank.

The World Bank. (2008c). *Bangladesh: Priorities for Agricutlure and Rural Development, Background*. Retrieved June 15, 2008, from Agriculture in South Asia: http://web.worldbank.org/WBSITE/EXTERNAL/COUNTRIES/SOUTHASIAEXT/EXTSAREGTOPAGRI/0,,contentMDK:20273763~ menuPK:548213~ pagePK:34004173 ~pi PK:34003707~theSitePK:452766,00.html

The World Bank. (1997, June). *Bangladesh: Rice Is Life* . Retrieved September 19, 2008, from CGIAR Newsletter: http://www.worldbank.org/html/cgiar/newsletter/june97/9bang.html

The World Bank. (2005a). *Bihar: Towards a Development Strategy*. Washington, D.C.: The World Bank.

The World Bank. (2000). *Can Africa Claim the 21st Century*. Washington, D.C.: The World Bank.

The World Bank. (2008d). *India: Priorities for Agriculture and Rural Development, Background*. Retrieved 2008, from Agriculture in South Asia: http://web.worldbank.org/WBSITE/EXTERNAL/COUNTRIES/SOUTHASIAEXT/EXTSAREGTOPAGRI/0,,content MDK:20273764 ~menu PK:548214~page PK:34004173~ piPK:34 003 707~theSitePK:452766,00.html

The World Bank. (2004). *Local Pathways to Global Development*. New York: Knowledge and Learning Group, World Bank.

The World Bank. (2008b). *Nepal: Priorities for Agriculture and Rural Development, Background*. Retrieved July 03, 2008, from

Agriculture in South Asia: http://web.worldbank.org/WBSITE/EXTERNAL/COUNTRIES/SOUTHASIAEXT/EXTSAREGTOPAGRI/0,,content MDK:20273771 ~menu PK:548215 ~page PK:34004173 ~piPK:34003707~theSitePK:452766,00.html

The World Bank. (June 26, 2006). *Nepal: Reslience Amidst Conflict: An Assessment of Poverty in Nepal 1995-96 and 2003-04,Report No. 34834-NP.* Washington, D.C.: The World Bank, Department of International Development (DFID), and Asian Development Bank (ADB).

The World Bank. (2008a). *Pakistan: Priorities for Agriculture and Rural Development, Background.* Retrieved 2008, from Agriculture in South Asia: http://web.worldbank.org/WBSITE/EXTERNAL/COUNTRIES/SOUTHASIAEXT/EXTSAREGTOPAGRI/0,,conten tMDK:20273773 ~menu PK:548216 ~pagePK: 34004173~piPK:34003707~theSitePK:452766,00.html

The World Bank. (2008, April 29). *Poor and Hungry Cannot Afford to Wait, World Bank President Says.* Retrieved June 15, 2008, from News and Broadcast: http://web.worldbank.org/WBSITE/EXTERNAL/NEWS/0,,content MDK:21749 013~page PK:642570 43~piPK:437376~theSitePK:4607,00.html

The World Bank. (1986a). *Poverty and Hunger Issues and Options for Food Security in Developing Countries, A World Bank Policy Study.* Washington, D.C.: The World Bank.

The World Bank. (2006a). *Reengaging in Agricultural Water Management: Challenges and Options.* Washington, D.C.: The World Bank.

The World Bank. (2002). *Regional Brief: South Asia.* Washington, D.C.: The World Bank.

The World Bank. (May 9, 2003). *The CGIAR at 31: An Independent Meta-Evaluation of the Consultative Group on International Agricultural Research.* New York?: Operations Evaluation Department, The World Bank.

The World Bank. (2004). *Water Resources Sector Strategy: Strategic Directions for World Bank Engagement.* Washington, D.C.: The World Bank.

The World Bank. (2007). *World Bank Assistance to Agricultural in Sub-Saharan Africa: An IEG Review.* Washington, D.C.: The World Bank.

The World Bank. (2006b). *World Development Indicators Database.* Retrieved September 12, 2008, from WDI Online: http://publications.worldbank.org/WDI/

The World Bank. (1986b). *World Development Report 1986.* New York (Oxford University Press) for: The World Bank.

The World Bank. (2005b). *World Development Report 2006.* Washington, D.C.: The World Bank.

Thomas, J. (2007, July 10). *Arsenic Filter for Water Offers Hope to Millions.* Retrieved August 23, 2008, from America.gov: http://www.america.gov/st/washfile-english/2007/July/200707101534051CJsamohT0.6979181.html

Thomas, William L. (ed). (1956). *Man's Role in Changing the Face of the Earth: An International Symposium.* Chicago: Publishd for the Wenner-Gren Foundation for Anthropological Research and the National Science Foundation by the Univeristy of Chicago Press.

Tikva, P. (2002, June 24). *VSAT News - Gilat Dominating Indian VSAT Market.* Retrieved September 15, 2007, from Space Daily: http://www.spacedaily.com/news/vsat-02i.html

Time. (2006, July 03). India, Inc. *Time Magazine, Canadian Edition , 168* (1), pp. 22-35.

Timmons, Heather; and Hari Kumar. (2008, August 29). *Millions Are Displaced by Floods in India* . Retrieved August 31, 2008, from New York Times - Asia Pacific: http://www.nytimes.com/2008/08/30/world/asia/30india.html?

Tiwari, M. with Ojha, G., Upadhyay, S., Maharjan, K.H. and Huddleston, B. (2002). *Profiles of Vulnerable Groups in Nepal.* Rome: U.N. Food and Agriculture Organization.

Tiwari, R. (2007, September 25). *Growing Olives In The Desert With Some Help From Israel.* Retrieved August 03, 2008, from The Indian Express: http://www.indianexpress.com/story/220851.html

Todaro, M. P. (1977). *Economics for a Developing World: An Introduction to Principles, Problems and Policies for Development.* London: Longman Group.

Torero, Maximo and Shyamal Chowdhury. (April 2004). Infrastructure for Africa: Overcoming Barriers to Development. *A Paper prepared for the 2020 Africa Conference, Kampala, Uganda .*

Tun, A. H. (2008, May 07). *Burma Cyclone Death Toll May Top 100,000: U.S. Diplomat.* Retrieved August 31, 2008, from

National Post: http://www.nationalpost.com/news/story. html?id=499011

U. S. Library of Congress. (No Date). *Country Profiles.* Retrieved July 31, 2008, from Population: http://www.country-studies.com/

U.S. Committee for Refugees. (2001, April). *Sudan.* Retrieved September 09, 2008, from News and Resources: http://web.archive.org/web/20041210024759/http://www.refugees.org/news/crisis/sudan.htm

U.S. Library of Congress. (No Year). *Country Studies - Nepal.* Retrieved July 31, 2008, from Population: http://countrystudies.us/nepal/28.htm

UN Nepal Information Platform. (2008, July 08). *Thematic Maps.* Retrieved August 20, 2008, from UN Nepal Information Platform: http://www.un.org.np/maps/mapsublist.php?type=2

UN Population Division. (2008, July 06). *World Urbanization Prospects:The 2007 Revision Population Database.* Retrieved July 06, 2008, from Department of Economic and Social Affairs: http://esa.un.org/unup/p2k0data.asp

UNAIDS. (September 2000). *Summary Booklet of Best Practices.* Geneva: Joint United Nations Programme on HIV/AIDS (UNAIDS).

UNCTAD. (2008). *Cotton.* Retrieved August 19, 2008, from Info Comm: http://r0.unctad.org/infocomm/anglais/cotton/Crop.htm#rendements

UNDESA. (2006). *The Milennium Development Goals Report 2006.* New York: United Nations Department of Economic and Social Affairs (DESA).

UNDP. (2008, September). *Goal 1: Eradicate Extreme Poverty And Hunger.* Retrieved September 03, 2008, from Millennium Development Goals: http://www.undp.org/mdg/goal1.shtml

UNDP. (2007a). *Human Development Index (HDI) Trends (2005).* Retrieved May 03, 2008, from Human Development Reports: http://hdr.undp.org/external/flash/hdi_map/

UNDP. (2007b). *Human Development Report 2007 / 2008.* New York: United Nations Development Programme.

UNDP. (2007b). *Human Development Report 2007 / 2008.* New York: United Natons Development Programme (UNDP).

UNDP. (2007c, November). *Human Development Report 2007/2008.* Retrieved May 15, 2008, from Human Development Reports: http://hdr.undp.org/en/reports/global/hdr2007-2008/

UNEP. (2000). *Land.* Retrieved September 07, 2008, from Asia-Pacific Outlook - Chapter 1, Emerging Issues: http://www.rrcap.unep.org/apeo/Chp1b-Land.html

UNEP-RRC.AP. (2001). *State of the Environment - Bangladesh 2001.* Bangkok: Unated Nations Envrioment Programme Regional Resource Centre for Asia and Pacific.

UNESCAP. (March 3, 2005). *Achieving Environmentally Sustainable Economic Growth, E/ESCAP/SO/MCED(05)/7.* Seoul: UN Economic and Social Commission.

UNESCAP. (2008, March 27). *Bangladesh: Briefing for the Launch in Dhaka, 27 March 2008.* Retrieved September 19, 2008, from http://intranet.unescap.org/survey2008/notes/bangladesh.pdf

UNESCAP. (24-29 March, 2005). Mced 2005, Achieving Environmentally Sustainable Economic Growth:. Seoul: United Nations Economic and Social Commission for Asia and the Pacific (ESCAP).

UNESCO. (2004, January 14). *Facts and Figures: Desertification and Drought*. Retrieved August 31, 2008, from The United Nations Convention to Combat Desertification (UNCCD): http://www.wateryear2003.org/en/ev.php-URL_ ID= 5137& URL_ DO= DO_TOPIC&URL_SECTION=201.html

UNESCO. (2008). *Global Education Database - UNESCO.* Retrieved September 28, 2008, from USAID Office of Education: http://qesdb.usaid.gov/cgi-bin/broker.exe? _program =gedprogs. ged_country_une.sas&_service=default

UNESCO. (2003). *Water for People Water for Life: The United Nations World Water Development Report.* Barcelona: United Nations Educational, Scientific and Cultural Organization (UNESCO) and World Water Assessment Programme.

UNESCO. (2006). *Water: A Shared Responsibility — The United Nations World Water Development Report 2.* Paris: United Nations Educational, Scientific and Cultural Organization (UNESCO).

UNESCO. (2008). *World Water Management Programme.* Retrieved September 01, 2008, from The Water Portal: http://www.unesco.org/water/wwap/facts_figures/managing_risks.shtml

UNFCCC. (2004). *The First Ten Years*. Bonn: United Nations Framework Convention on Climate Change.

UNHCR. (2007). *Statistical Yearbook 2006*. New York: United Nations High Commission on Refugees.

UNWater and FAO. (2007). *Coping with Water Scarcity: Challenge of the Twenty-first Century*. New York: United Nations Water and Food and Agriculture Organization.

UNWFP. (2008). *Food security in Bangladesh*. Retrieved July 06, 2008, from World Food Programme in Bangladesh: http://www.wfp.org/bangladesh/?NodeID=25

USAID. (2007, January 23). *Groundwater Management*. Retrieved September 15, 2008, from USAID Envrionment: http://www.usaid.gov/our_work/environment/water/groundwater_mgmt.html

USAID. (March 2002). *Guidelines FY 2002 Program for Biosafety Systems*. Office of Agriculture and Food Security, Bureau for Economic Growth Agriculture and Trade.

USAID. (July 3004). *USAID Agricultural Strategy: Linking Producers to Markets*. Washington, D.C.: U.S. Agency for International Development.

USDA. (June 2007). *Food Securty Assessment, 2006*. Washington, D.C.: United States Department of Agriculture, Economic Research Service.

USDA. (1997). *Production, Supply, and Distribution (electronic database)*. Retrieved from U.S. Department of Agriculture: http://mann77.mannlib.cornell.edu/data-sets/international/93002/

Venkatasubramanian, K. (2001, 05 03). *Whither agro-development in Punjab* . Retrieved 05 24, 2008, from The Hindu Business Line-The Internet Edition: http://www.blonnet.com/2001/05/03/stories/040303kv.htm

Waldman, A. (2002, December 02). *Poor in India Starve as Surplus Wheat Rots* . Retrieved May 15, 2007, from The New York Times - World: http://query.nytimes.com/gst/fullpage.html?res=9D0CE0 D91E38F931A35751C1A9649C8B63

Walker, Brian; and Will Steffan. (1997). *An Overview of the Implications of Global Change for Natural and Managed Terrestrial Ecosystems*. Conservation Ecology.

Watkins, Kevin, et. al. (2007). *Human Development Report 2007/2008 — Fighting Climate Change: Human Solidarity in a Divided World*. New York: United Nations Development Programme (UNDP).

WCD. (2000). *Dams and Development: A New Framework for Decision-Making*. London: Earthscan, World Commission on Dams.

Weisman, Doris, Lioba Schoninger, and Iris Weingartner. (October 2006). *The Challenge of Hunger: Global Hunger Index: Facts, determinants, and trends*. Bonn: Deutsche Welthungerhilfe and International Food Policy Research Institute.

WHO. (2006, September 06). *Pesticides Are A Leading Suicide Method*. Retrieved August 11, 2008, from World Health Organizaton: http://www.who.int/mediacentre/news/notes/2006/np24/en/index.html

WHO. (1990). *Public Health Impact of Pesticides Used in Agriculture*. New York: World Health Organization.

WHO. (2003). *The World Health Report 2003 – Shaping the Future*. Geneva: World Health Organization.

WHO. (2008). *Toxic Hazards*. Retrieved August 11, 2008, from The Health and Environment Linkages Initiative (HELI): http://www.who.int/heli/risks/toxics/chemicals/en/index.html

WHO. (2005). *World Malaria Report 2005*. Geneva: World Health Organization and UNICEF.

WHO/UNICEF. (2000). *Global Water Supply and Sanitation Assessment*. Geneva: World Health Organization/United Nations Children's Fund.

Wiesmann, Doris, et. al. (October 2007). *The Challenge of Hunger 2007. Global Hunger Index: Facts, determinants, and trends*. Bonn: Deutsche Welthungerhilfe, International Food Policy Research Instiutute, and Concern Worldwide.

Willcocks, W. (1984). *Ancient System of Iirrigation in Bengal and its Application to Modern Problems* (Reprinted Edition ed.). Delhi: B.R. Publishing Corp.

Wolf, Edward C. (1986). *Beyond the Green Revolution: New Approaches for Third World Agriculture, Worldwatch Paper 73*. Worldwatch Institute.

Woodworth, C. (2008). *GMOs: Corporate Agribusiness Plays Russian Roulette With Our Food* . Retrieved August 26, 2008, from

Healthy Choice Directory: http://www.naturalchoice.net/articles/gmos.htm

Wortman, Sterling. (1969). The Technological Basis for Intensive Agriculture. *Agricultural Developmet—Proceedings of a Conference.* New York: Rockefeller Foundation.

Wright, A. (2004). *The Death of Ramon Gonzalez.* Austin : University of Texas Press.

Wu, Felicia and William P. Butz. (2004). *The Future Of Genetically Modified Crops: Lessons From The Green Revolution.* Santa Monica, CA: Science and Technology Policy Institute (Rand Corporation).

Yadav, C.P., B.S. Gupta, and S. Kumar. (2000). Export Potential of Agricultue. In J. Prasad (Ed.), *Export Potential of Indian Agriculture: Bihar—Perspective and Issues* (pp. 113-122). New Delhi: Mittal Publications.

Yadav, R. L., B. S. Dwivedi, and P.S. Pandey. (2000b). *Rice-wheat Cropping System: Assessment.*

Yadav, R. L., B.S. Dwivedi and P. S. Pandey. (2000c, February (1). Wheat-rice Cropping System: Sustainability under Green Manuring and Chemical Fertilizer Inputs. *Field Crops Research, 65* (1), pp. 15-30.

Yadev, et. al. (2000c). *Cropping in India II: Irrigated Systems 4, Slide 10 and 11.* Retrieved August 15, 2007, from PowerPoint Presentation

Zaidi, S. A. (1999). *Issues in Pakistan's Economy.* Karachi: Oxford University Presss.

Zymelman, M. (1990). *Science, Education, and Development in Sub-Saharan Africa.* Washington, D. C.: The World Bank.

The author has compiled a CD with most of these documents preserved on it. If you, as an interested reader, would like to have these files sent to you via e-mail, simply write and arrangements will be made to get the files to you. Feel free to e-mail me at: hungerinsouthasia@rogers.com

Index

C

R

S

U

V